Studies in Church History

22

MONKS, HERMITS AND THE ASCETIC TRADITION

MONKS, HERMITS AND THE ASCETIC TRADITION

PAPERS READ AT
THE 1984 SUMMER MEETING AND
THE 1985 WINTER MEETING OF
THE ECCLESIASTICAL HISTORY SOCIETY

EDITED BY

W. J. SHEILS

PUBLISHED FOR
THE ECCLESIASTICAL HISTORY SOCIETY

BY

BASIL BLACKWELL

1985

© Ecclesiastical History Society 1985

British Library Cataloguing in Publication Data

Ecclesiastical History Society, *Summer Meeting (1984)*
   Monks, hermits and the ascetic tradition: papers
   read at the 1984 Summer Meeting and the 1985 Winter
   Meeting of the Ecclesiastical History Society.—
   (Studies in Church History; 22)
   1. Asceticism—History
   I. Title   II. Ecclesiastical History Society,
   Winter Meeting (1985)   III. Sheils, W. J.
   IV. Series
   248.4′7′09   BV5021

ISBN 0–631–14351–3

Printed in Great Britain by
T.J. Press Ltd, Padstow

PREFACE

'Monks, Hermits and the Ascetic Tradition' provided the theme for the summer conference of the Society held in 1984 at Southampton University and for the subsequent winter meeting held in King's College, London. The Society is grateful to both institutions for their hospitality which, on occasion, represented a marked contrast to the ideals and life-styles under discussion in the academic sessions. The choice of theme, drawing our attention to the role of asceticism in Christian history, was made by Professor Henry Chadwick whose presidential address provided both a wide ranging and stimulating introduction to the conference as well as to this volume. The papers published here represent a selection of those delivered in response to Professor Chadwick's theme.

Once again the Society would like to express its gratitude to the British Academy for financial assistance with the cost of publication.

W. J. Sheils

CONTENTS

Contents

Contents

LIST OF CONTRIBUTORS

HENRY CHADWICK (*President*)
Regius Professor Emeritus of Divinity and Fellow of
Magdalene College, Cambridge

SISTER ANN FRANCES CSMV
St Mary's Convent, Wantage

BERNARD ASPINWALL
Lecturer in Modern History, Glasgow University

L.W. BARNARD
formerly Senior Lecturer in Theology, University of Leeds

DOMINIC AIDAN BELLENGER
Monk of Downside Abbey

PETER BILLER
Lecturer in History, University of York

CLYDE BINFIELD
Reader in History, University of Sheffield

ERNEST O. BLAKE
Reader in History, Southampton University

BRENDA M. BOLTON
Lecturer in History, Westfield College, University of London

CHRISTOPHER N.L. BROOKE
Dixie Professor of Ecclesiastical History and Fellow of
Gonville and Caius College, Cambridge

VIRGINIA DAVIS
Research student, Trinity College, Dublin

DAVID J. HALL
Under Librarian, The University Library, Cambridge

List of Contributors

SUSAN HARDMAN
Lecturer in Ecclesiastical History, University of Durham

the late JANE HERBERT
formerly Lecturer in History, Strawberry Hill College,
Twickenham

PEREGRINE HORDEN
Fellow, All Souls College, Oxford

DAVID J. KEEP
Senior Lecturer in Religious Studies, Rolle College, Exmouth

CHRISTOPHER KITCHING
Assistant Secretary, Royal Commission on Historical
Manuscripts

RENE M. KOLLAR
Assistant Professor of History, St Vincent College and
Seminary, La Trobe, Pennsylvania

JOHN ANTHONY McGUCKIN
Lecturer in Dogmatics, La Sainte Union College,
Southampton

BRIAN PATRICK McGUIRE
Lektor, The Medieval Centre, Copenhagen University,
Denmark

JOHN McMANNERS
Fellow of All Souls College, Oxford

COLIN MORRIS
Professor of Medieval History, Southampton University

DONALD M. NICOL
Koraes Professor of Modern Greek and Byzantine History,
Language and Literature, King's College, University of
London

List of Contributors

COLIN PHIPPS
   Research student, King's College, University of London

JULIA M. H. SMITH
   Lecturer in History, University of Manchester

MICHAEL E. WILLIAMS
   Head of Studies in Theology, Trinity and All Saints College,
   Leeds

A.D. WRIGHT
   Lecturer in History, Leeds University

GEORGE YULE
   Professor of Church History, University of Aberdeen

THE ASCETIC IDEAL IN THE
HISTORY OF THE CHURCH

by HENRY CHADWICK

ASCETICISM is in no way specifically Christian. It runs
from the Pythagoreans to Pachomius, from Sufi mystic-
ism and Buddhist withdrawal to Greenham Common and
the protesters of modern western society. But within the Christian
tradition asceticism has played so substantial a role, at times beset by
controversy, that it seems right for an Ecclesiastical History Society
to concentrate on the phenomenon and its consequences. The
ascetic life is no doubt understood only from within by those who
are or have been monks and nuns; and that is the case with a
relatively small proportion of our Society's members, who are
usually the object of an affectionate but silent envy in those of us
who have to work away in university arts faculties harassed by cuts
and committees in an unsympathetic world, where government
policy seems like piecemeal demolition by explosive and where a
rotten botanist seems to be more valued than a first-rate historian.
Admittedly, in the second half of the 20th century the cloister has
been having its problems too. But it is a matter for reflection that,
in the case of contemplative orders, there is no evidence in the
decline of vocations.

The ascetic ideal has found its institutional expression in monasticism. Theologians are especially interested in the ideology and
spirituality which have impelled men and women to startling acts
of renunciation; and historians seem especially concerned to map
the social and economic consequences. We ask, for example, how it
came about that those who had abandoned all their possessions
came, as communities, to receive rich endowments and to be a
power in the land; or how the prudence and strong work-ethic of
monks brought them a commercial success to which they were by
prime intention indifferent, and so provoked the envy of worldly
laymen whose main goal was making money but who were less
canny and less industrious. The question is of course familiar to

I

historians of the Cistercians. The issue is found as early as the first of all such communities founded by Pachomius in the loop of the Nile near Dendera in the time of Constantine the Great. Pachomius solved major problems of employment and security for wretched peasants, and his large monastic houses, with their strict accounting system and quasi-military organisation, were an economic success. This precipitated a painful though temporary split over the question whether the communities existed for essentially religious reasons to which agriculture and trade were subsidiary, or whether it was proper for the monks to take on even more labour and to enlarge their horizons and investment as they grew in economic strength.[1]

The driving force of asceticism is, after all, a renunciation of success in this world. And this is not specifically or distinctively Christian. The ascetic ideal looks different in various religious frameworks. In one, methods of meditative prayer are followed by individuals who thereby aspire to realise the divine element latent in the soul of man. In another there exists an organised institution to help the adept to achieve total liberation from the transient world and its suffering, providing a prop to enable the individual to reach this state of undisturbed bliss by training the soul's inherent powers. In a third type, the individual is not usually found in a hermitage but made a member of a community where by reading, by prayer, and by sharing in the sacraments, he may be brought under the control of divine grace and be touched by a redeeming holiness. One associates the first type with Hinduism, the second with Buddhism, and the third with Christianity. Each type presupposes a different understanding of the nature and destiny of man, and also a different conception of the nature and significance of mystical experience. And that observation may admonish us to be

---

[1] The early lives of Pachomius, in Greek, Coptic, and (later) Arabic, record acute conflict between Pachomius' second successor Horsiesi, supported by Apollonius the abbot of Monchosis, and Theodore, before whose protest against the subordination of religion to commerce Horsiesi retired from the parent house at Pbau, leaving Theodore to succeed as 'general' of the Pachomian houses.

The earliest Greek Life is edited by F. Halkin (1932); the Coptic translated into French by L.T. Lefort (1943); the Arabic into French by E. Amélineau (1889). I attempt a survey in 'Pachomios and the idea of sanctity', in *The Byzantine Saint*, ed S. Hackel (1981), reprinted in the Variorum volume, *History and Thought of the Early Church* (1982).

alert to the possibility of underlying variations within the Christian tradition which is our special concern as ecclesiastical historians.

Although the title of my discourse is wide to the point of absurdity, I hope to give it some ingredient of particularity and concreteness by inviting attention to the thoughts on our subject found in St Augustine. My hope is that the particular will serve to illustrate the general, which is in itself an Augustinian way of proceeding: he composed his *Confessions* as a personal autobiography which would also illustrate the story of Everyman. But there are additional reasons for the choice. Augustine brings to the fore, by the circumstances and motivation of his conversion, the conviction that authentic, serious Christianity is and must be ascetic, and that there is something second-class and compromising about forms of it which do not take literally some of the harder sayings of the gospels. That is a controversial proposition; but it was a self-evident axiom not only to Augustine but to most of his western contemporaries. For example, of the proconsul Apringius (executed in 413 on a charge of supporting a rebellion) Augustine reports that he used to say how he would have wished to become a monk if only he had not married before his baptism.[2] His unbaptised friend Verecundus, who lent him and his friends the villa at Cassiciacum, used to say that his marriage to his Christian wife deterred him from becoming a Christian because he would have wished to become a monk.[3] If one has occupied a high social position in the world, one would wish to stay in the top class if one joined the Church.

Very rightly our principal accounts of early western monasticism give the highlights to Jerome, Cassian, Gregory, and Benedict, and often have to take one a little quickly past Augustine. But the debate about Augustinian concepts of salvation helps to make sense of subsequent western thinking about the monastic ideal. The insistence on free and unmerited grace as the foundation of Christian hope does not lead Augustine to draw the inference that there is no moral and spiritual ladder up to God which Christians are called, in union with the mediator, to ascend. Augustine's opposition to the Pelagian proposition that under the gospel saints can be unflawed by sin, in no way qualifies his vision of the

[2] Aug. *Ep.* 151, 8.
[3] Aug. *Conf.* iv, 3, 5.

3

Christian pilgrimage as a response to the true love of God of which righteousness is the substance.

John Cassian and the ascetic men of southern Gaul in the fifth century, especially the British divine Faustus, bishop of Riez, occupied a position which not only seventeenth-century Jansenists would think semi-Pelagian. And since then many books have contrived to give the impression that the monastic ideal must somehow presuppose a semi-Pelagian doctrine of grace. If one looks to Gregory of Nyssa and the Greek East, it is certainly the case that the quest for spiritual perfection is linked to a doctrine of the cooperation of the human will with divine grace; and that is one of the attractions of Greek ascetical theology to western humanists to whom Augustine and Luther are not immediately congenial. Is the full-blooded Augustinianism of Luther and Calvin at the root of the Protestant rejection of monasticism as an institution? Luther and Calvin understood justification *sola fide sola gratia* to mean that we may get to heaven exclusively on the ground of the imputation to us sinners of the righteousness of Christ, and used language which reduced to zero the role of the human will in making any kind of offering to God or in making efforts to strive after goodness. They talked as if moral virtue is, to the justified, virtually effortless, a 'necessary' outflow in which specific acts of will and intention had no part to play. Were these Reformers dotting *i*s and crossing *t*s which Augustine had untidily left unattended? That is, is there some inherent conflict between ultra-Augustinian doctrines of grace and the quest for perfection through disciplined exercises, forgoing even the good and innocent, training the soul to be fit for the presence of God?

Reformation hostility to monasticism is no doubt a product of late medieval disillusion and lay resentment. It is remarkable how slowly Luther moved from criticism of the disappointing actuality to a rejection of the institutional structure as such.[4] In the Wartburg

---

[4] B. Lohse, *Mönchtum und Reformation: Luthers Auseinandersetzung mit dem Mönchsideal des Mittelalters*, Forsch. z. Kirchen- u. Dogmengeschichte 12 (Göttingen 1963). In the 17th century the Anglican Archbishop John Bramhall remarked 'I do not see why monasteries might not agree well enough with reformed devotion': *Works*, p. 65, from *A Just Vindication* (ed Dublin 1677). In modern German Lutheranism the Berneuchen group has played an important part in restoring ascetic life lived under rule in community. The 19th-century Anglican revival has been chronicled by A.M. Allchin, *The Silent Rebellion*.

in November 1521 Luther finally came to write his 'Judgment on monastic vows' (WA 8, 577ff.) where he shows himself to be restating a critique already voiced by John Wyclif: In holy scripture vows are not prescribed. The distinction between counsels and precepts is artificial; for all Christ's counsels are in effect precepts (580, 20ff.). The saying Matt. 19,12 allows celibacy to be a proper private and personal choice, but does not suggest that it is a rule to be imposed on an entire category of disciples. (Luther does not sense the inconsistency of these two last propositions). Evangelical poverty is to use one's resources for the common good. Luther is found to agree with Clement of Alexandria that it is an inner attitude of mind rather than an external act (587, 3ff.). Moreover, a vow is a permanent commitment which seems to Luther incompatible with the freedom of faith (591, 5ff.). By a vow the counsel is changed into a precept, gospel becomes law. Monastic vows are incompatible with proper love of one's neighbour, with duty to one's parents, and with service to one's fellow-men. And situations do not remain static: can vows be really thought valid irrespective of any changes in personal circumstances which may occur? Luther is surprisingly unsympathetic to the evident fact that vows, whether in matrimony or in a monastery, are promises with so strong a sense of obligation that they help individuals to remain true to their calling.

It is very unnecessary here to offer evidence of the unpopularity of monks and especially friars in the later middle ages. One of Dr Anne Hudson's recently published *English Wycliffite Sermons* (i p. 286) draws a contrast between the first monks who were like the poor saints of the apostolic church at Jerusalem and the situation now when monks are 'turned into lords of this world, most idle in God's travail'. One picks up Coulton's *Five Centuries of Religion* for a classic liberal-protestant and rationalist critique of medieval religion in general and monasticism in particular. But then one discovers in Dom David Knowles' great *History* an even more formidable indictment, the anger of a devout Benedictine scholar at the human failures in pursuit of a great ideal. David Knowles had exhaustingly high standards. Yet the question of the highest interest is not whether abuses and scandals occurred, for it is certain that they did; nor whether those who had renounced the world had become so rich that envious secular persons thought they had too much. The root question concerns the validity of the ascetic ideal, and whether its pursuit is inherently superior to an active Christian life in a vocation lived out in the secular world. One recalls that at the end of the second century Clement of Alexandria, who must rank as a founding father of Greek ascetical theology and was deeply sympathetic to the celibate ideal, also remarked that the married man has unique opportunities for character-training in the innumerable irritations of family life.[5]

The vehement rejection of monasticism by the Reformation is almost moderate in comparison with that of the Enlightenment. And in its more religious aspects is not the Enlightenment a forcible reassertion of ultra-Pelagian doctrines of unimpaired human dignity, rationality and freedom? If one wants to find the strongest indictment of monasticism, one would go not to Melanchthon but to Voltaire or to Gibbon's 37th chapter, where the twenty pages on the early monks constitute one of the most strident specimens of sustained invective and cold hatred to be found in English prose. The ascetics, says Gibbon, understood man as a criminal, God as an arbitrary tyrant. To gain eternal happiness they tortured themselves with misery. To enforce this on their own rebellious minds, they inculcated submission and credulity in such a way as to make themselves the slaves and tools of ecclesiastical tyrants, like Cyril of Alexandria in the 5th century. Echoing the pagan historian Eunapius, Gibbon speaks of the monks as 'swarming' like insects (language which might lead one to have exaggerated notions of the number of monks in late antiquity, though it is true enough that they were or could be influential; and when they organised a sit-in, there was nothing to be done but yield.)[6] So Gibbon saw the monks as defying all we understand by civilisation and culture. Every sensation offensive to man was thought acceptable to God; pleasure and guilt are synonymous. Monkery means for Gibbon superstition, fanaticism, degeneracy. Reason being set aside, monks could not allow gentle and humane feelings to moderate their judgments. In a terrible and gross sentence Gibbon writes that

---

[5] Clem. Alex. *Stromateis* vii, 70. Clement's place in the history of ascetical theology is the subject of a fat monograph by W. Völker, *Der wahre Gnostiker nach Clemens Alexandrinus*, TU 57 (1952).

[6] For an early monastic sit in see Cyril of Scythopolis, *Vita Sabae* 56, p. 151 Schwartz. It was effective.

6

'a cruel, unfeeling temper has distinguished the monks of every age and country.' Gibbon is most reluctant to acknowledge the agrarian and educational achievements of the monasteries. 'If it be possible to measure the interval between the philosophic writings of Cicero and the sacred legend of Theodoret, between the character of Cato and that of Simeon (Stylites), we may appreciate the memorable revolution which was accomplished in the Roman empire within a period of 500 years.'

We see Gibbon refusing to distinguish between abuses of or lapses from the ideal and the ideal itself. He thinks that to exalt humility and the negation of human dignity and achievement must inevitably produce degeneracy. That is to assert that a corrupt monasticism is what Christianity is sure to entail, the moment its teachings are taken seriously. All that Gibbon objects to in Christianity finds its most striking manifestations in monastic institutions and practices. Granted it may have produced by accident some unintended good, yet all that good could have been better achieved by more sensible and direct means.

Take away the rhetoric, subtract Gibbon's refusal to distinguish between the ideal and the actual, the goal and the abuses, and one will still have to concede that there remains a question to answer. For the underlying axiom of Gibbon's objection is that the ascetic ideal makes people so otherworldly as to be of no use in this world: monks do not increase the wealth of nations or build empires.

Augustine would have been unmoved by the observation. He once remarks that the validity of the ascetic life depends on recognition that the true aim of life now is not to be comfortable or held in honour, but to attain salvation in the life to come.[7] Withdrawal from society is of the essence, he writes to his friend Nebridius; for freedom from self-concern and anxiety is discovered only as each individual worships God in the secret places of the mind.[8] This letter was written when Augustine was still young and inclined to echo all he had learnt by reading Plotinus and Porphyry. The mature Augustine observes that the massive multitude pressing for entry to the Church has brought huge congregations but little change in their moral behaviour. So he sees the Church allegorically portrayed in St Peter's ship taking in such a vast catch

---

[7] *Sermo* 46, 10.
[8] *Ep.* 10, 2–3.

of fish that it begins to sink.[9] The ascetic movement is for him a protest against blurring the distinction between the Church and the world.

Augustine found his feelings mixed as he contemplated the social pressure to join the Church. He regretted that the influential aristocratic landowners were slow to become Christians and to carry their dependants with them,[10] but he also feared and regretted the hypocrisies produced by conformism.[11] He once mentions that 'some highly placed persons pretend to support the Church, but in private express cold hatred.'[12] In Augustine's lifetime the Church was capturing Roman society, and it could prejudice one's career if one were known to be explicitly hostile to Christianity, though many aristocrats long remained quietly and elegantly sceptical.[13]

---

[9] *Tr. in ev. Joh.* 122, 7.

[10] *En. in Ps.* 54, 13 'Plerumque dicunt homines: Nemo remaneret paganus si ille (sc. nobilis) esset christianus. Plerumque dicunt homines: Et ille si fieret christianus, quis remaneret paganus?' (The text continues that the ark is going round Jericho's walls which will soon fall.) *Conf.* viii, 4, 9 'plus autem superbos (hostis) tenet nomine nobilitatis et de his plures nomine auctoritatis.' *En. in Ps.* 30, II, iii, 7: 'Tam pauci non christiani remanserunt ut eis magis obiciatur quia christiani non sunt quam ipsi audeant aliquibus obicere quia christiani sunt.'

[11] *Ep.* 93, 17. Augustine feared the government pressure on the Donatists to end the schism would produce hypocritical Catholics, which after 411 was in part the case (*Gesta cum Emerito* 2 – some reconciled, some doubting, others remain at heart Donatist but conform outwardly – written in 418; cf. *c.Gaudentium* i, 24, 27 written in 420 of the situation ten years previously). *De Baptismo* iv, 10, 14 offers the timeless comment that converts to Catholicism from Donatism were more zealous for unity than members of old Catholic families. This text, of 400–401, belongs to the years before government pressure became strong.

[12] *Ep.* 136, 3 (412) from Marcellinus to Augustine, mentions that the principal landowner round Hippo had ironically praised Augustine and declared himself quite unconvinced of the truth of Christianity. On the hatred of silently resentful pagans see *De Civ. Dei* vi praef. Christian processions at high festivals were a special cause of irritation (*En. in Ps.* 32, II, ii, 9). Pagans had ceased to go to the temples but paganism remained dominant in their hearts: *En. in Ps.* 98, 2 'Magis remanserunt idola in cordibus paganorum quam in locis templorum.' *S. Denis* 18, 7 p. 97, 26 ed Morin (Misc. Agost. I) 'Quod destitit in templis ipsorum remansit in ore ipsorum.' *Sermo* 62, preached at Carthage in 399 after the edicts closing temples, show that pagan senators were putting social pressure on Christian clients. *En. in Ps.* 62, 20 'Nemo audet modo publice loqui contra Christum: iam omnes timent Christum.' *Ibid* 119, 4 'Tanta auctoritas Christi est ut reprehendere iam Christum nec paganus audeat.'

[13] *En. in Ps.* 103, iv, 4 'Multi pusilli saeculi nondum crediderunt, multi primates saeculi nondum crediderunt.... Oderunt ecclesiam, premuntur Christi nomine; non saeviunt quia non permittuntur.' (Their anger is at the closure of the temples and prohibition of sacrifices.)

The social pressure to conform was enhanced as the Church succeeded in identifying its cause with that of the empire. Well-known texts of Optatus and others treat Christianity and *Romanitas* as almost interchangeable terms,[14] and Augustine's much cooler view of the Roman empire provoked some resentment and criticism from people who thought a Catholic bishop should be supportive of the government.[15] Augustine's long struggle with his conscience about the coercion and civic disincentives applied to the schismatic Donatists ended with him coming to terms with an element of hypocrisy,[16] and this was assisted by the fact that he was already painfully conscious of the mixed motives with which some converts were being drawn to join the Church.[17] People came to baptism hoping it would be the door to success in a secular career, or that God would grant them good health and prosperity.[18] Moreover, the bishop of a substantial city was in process of becoming a *patronus*, a man of influence who would get one out of trouble with the taxmen or the magistrates.[19] Augustine regretfully noted how converts continued to guide their life by astrologers' almanacs, charms, and amulets.[20] The men were slow to appreciate that as Christians they could sleep with their wives but not also with their slave-girls, as virtually every pagan paterfamilias took for

---

[14] *Optatus* iii, 3 p. 74, 3 Ziwsa (CSEL 26): 'non enim respublica est in ecclesia sed ecclesia in republica, id est in imperio Romano, quod Libanum appellat Christus in canticis canticorum.' (*Cant.* 4, 8). 'Veni de Libano, id est de imperio Romano, ubi et sacerdotia sancta sunt et pudicitia et virginitas quae in barbaris gentibus non sunt.' For the emperor Theodosius II in 431 Christianity is 'religio Romana' (*Acta Conc. Oecum.* I i, 1, p. 112, 31).

[15] *Sermo* 105, 12, preached at Carthage 410–11. Among many studies of Augustine's view of Rome and the empire see especially F.G. Maier, *Augustin und das antike Rom*, Tübinger Beiträge zur Altertumswissenschaft 39 (1955).

[16] *Sermo* 80, 8 sadly concedes that 'perhaps we cannot convert the mass of men to live good lives'. *Sermo* 7, 9 explains the Greek *hypocrisis* means *simulatio*: used of those who 'nomine Christiano malunt hominibus placere quam Deo.'

[17] e.g. *Cat. Rud.* 9.

[18] *Ep.* 98 to Boniface bishop of Cataquas in Numidia; *ep.* 140, 29 to Honoratus 'on the grace of the New Testament', of 411. Honoratus may be the Manichee friend to whom in 391 Augustine dedicated *De utilitate credendi*; but the name was common and one cannot be sure. See A. Mandouze, *Prosopographie chrétienne du Bas-empire* I (Paris 1982) p. 564 s.v. Honoratus 4.

[19] H. Chadwick, *The Role of the Christian Bishop in Ancient Society*, Colloquy 35 of the Center for Hermeneutical Studies, Berkeley, 25 February 1979 (1980).

[20] *Cat. Rud.* 11; *Tr. in ev. Joh.* 6, 17 etc. (such references are numerous in Augustine).

granted.[21] The world had come into the Church with the success of the Christian mission, and worldly clergy gained popularity by being known to be easygoing on matters of discipline.[22] Even Augustine's beloved and venerated mother Monnica is described by him as 'still living in the suburbs of Babylon'.[23]

By contrast, in the last book of the *Confessions*, the dedicated ascetics who live in continence are 'the living soul of the faithful' (*anima viva fidelium*).[24] In *Confessions* xiii Augustine is engaged in demonstrating that both in creation and in redemption God pursues the same pattern, allowing that which he has created to turn from him, but then turning all things back towards himself. And so the first chapter of Genesis turns out to be an elaborate allegorical statement of the being of the Church as the vehicle of redemption and holiness. Here the ascetics are the missionaries of the Church, great 'fires burning with holiness and glory'.[25] They live in community, daily chanting hymns of prayer and praise sung antiphonally,[26] and daily reading holy scripture.[27] They work with their hands, and 'the best monasteries' have fixed hours for all these activities.[28] The monks share all possessions and call nothing their

---

[21] *Sermo* 9, 4–5 and 11; esp. *Sermo* 224, 3; *S. Guelf.* 18, 2 p. 500, 13 (ed Morin).

[22] *Ep.* 21; *sermo* 46 and 137, 13–14.

[23] *Conf.* ii, 3, 8.

[24] *Ibid* xiii, 34, 49.

[25] *Ibid* xiii, 19, 24–25.

[26] *Ibid* ix, 9, 15; *En. in Ps.* 46, 1.

[27] *Ibid* 99, 12: '(in monasterio) magni viri, sancti, quotidie in hymnis, in orationibus, in laudibus Dei, inde vivunt, cum lectione illis res est; laborant manibus suis, inde se transigunt; non avare aliquid petunt; quidquid eis infertur a piis fratribus cum sufficientia et cum caritate utuntur; nemo sibi usurpat aliquid quod alter non habeat; omnes se diligunt, omnes invicem se sustinent.' (The text continues that some monks do not rise to these heights.)

For the classic studies of Augustine's monastic ideals and organisation, a general reference must suffice: L. Verheijen, *La Règle de saint Augustin* (Paris 1967); A. Zumkeller, *Das Mönchtum des heiligen Augustinus*, (2 rev ed Würzburg 1968) = Cassiciacum 11. See also Verheijen, *Nouvelle approche de la règle de Saint Augustin*, = Spiritualité orientale et vie monastique 5 (Abbaye de Bellefontaine 1980), and his lecture, *St Augustine's monasticism in the light of Acts 4, 32–35* (Villanova University Press 1979). There is good matter in articles by R. Lorenz, *ZKG* 77 (1966), 1–61; A. Wucheren-Huldenfeld, *Zeits. f. kath. Theol.* 82 (1960), 182–211.

A modern English translation of the Rule in both masculine and feminine versions is done by Raymond Canning with introduction and commentary by T.J. van Bavel (London 1984).

[28] *De opere monachorum* 37.

own.[29] They seek to memorise holy scripture by heart,[30] an activity which Augustine thought also useful to the head since it facilitated the exegete's endeavours to explain obscure texts by similar texts which are plain.[31]

Augustine's monastery at Hippo attracted lay Christians from other North African dioceses, especially if at home they had fallen foul of their local clergy. Augustine was debarred by canon law from accepting clergy from another diocese without express leave of the other diocesan; but there was no rule against providing a refuge for unhappy laity.[32]

Most of the North Africa monks came from a wide cross-section of society, with a majority being emancipated slaves, peasants, artisans.[33] In Augustine's world, free wage earners lived a more precarious and hungry life than many slaves.[34] The monastery offered little by way of physical comfort, but it afforded shelter and security such as many outside did not possess. The food would be frugal (normally meat was only for guests), but at least one did not starve and wine was allowed.[35] Yet among the African monks there were occasional senators,[36] and especially in the nunnery we hear of class tensions. Rich ladies resented giving all their money to the convent they joined, where their arrival provided a standard of communal living to which out in the world the poor sisters could never dream of aspiring.[37]

[29] *En. in Ps.* 99, 12, above n 27.
[30] *De opere monachorum* 20.
[31] *De doctrina christiana* ii, 9, 14.
[32] *Ep.* 64, 3.
[33] *De opere mon.* 22, 25.
[34] *Sermo* 159, 5. Adam Smith (*The Wealth of Nations* I, viii, 41) remarked that the cost to the master of slave labour is greater than that of employing free labour on the basis of a day-wage. It seems clear that in North Africa only a minority of the labour force consisted of slaves. But wealthy traders raided African villages to supply Italy, kidnapping the children of Roman citizens or buying those of destitute parents. *Ep.* 10* Divjak (*CSEL* 88) reveals the difficulties when a sufficiently paid colonus working on a Hippo church estate sold his wife *per meram avaritiam*.
[35] *De moribus* i, 33, 72; Possidius, *Vita Augustini* 22, written soon after Augustine's death, gives an eye-witness account of meals at Augustine's table. The portrait of Augustine as a man given by Possidius is perhaps the more impressive and vivid because Augustine's theology passed entirely over the head of his biographer.
[36] *De opere mon.* 25 and 33.
[37] *Ep.* 211. Augustine (*De civ. Dei* v, 6) mentions that the twin sister of a Count was a consecrated virgin. The acceptance of the ascetic ideal by aristocratic Roman ladies is well attested in the correspondence of Jerome.

Augustine wanted his monastic communities for men and women to be a model of reconciliation, cooperation and mutual aid. His hope of creating a kind of foretaste of heaven, living the angelic life of harmonious praise and sanctity, was often rudely shattered. 'We find by experience that ascetics can become avaricious.'[38] Virgins had to have it explained to them that physical virginity merely in itself got one nowhere.[39] Not all the nuns always dressed modestly, and some among them were given to gossip, litigiousness, and excessive fondness of the bottle.[40]

Among the schismatic Donatists there were also ascetics, though they did not call them *monachi* or group them in houses called *monasteria*.[41] The ascetics of the Donatist church appear, at least in Augustine's unfriendly portrait, as bands of wandering ascetics, of both sexes, who lived a nomadic life moving from province to province in North Africa, *Circumcelliones* specialising in terrifying attacks on either pagan festivals or catholic churches. At pagan feasts they were known for their unstoppable charge on the band and its musical instruments.[42]

Augustine disapproved of Catholic ascetics of no fixed abode, wanderers in the Mediterranean world, '*nusquam fixi, nusquam stantes, nusquam sedentes*'. They lived, he says, by mendicancy or by hawking relics of doubtful credit.[43] Augustine also disliked their long hair, worn in imitation of Samson and the Nazirites; they ignored St Paul's warning that to a man long hair is a disgrace.[44] Evidently Augustine expected his communities to keep their hair

---

[38] *De bono viduitatis* 26 (written in 413).

[39] *En. in Ps.* 90, ii, 9 '... corrupta corde quid servat in corpore? Adeo mulier catholica praecedit virginem haereticam.' (The Donatists had their *sanctimoniales*: *En. in Ps.* 44, 31; *c. ep. Parmen.* ii, 9, 19). Cf. *En. in Ps.* 99, 13 'Invenis sanctimoniales indisciplinatas ... Multae non stant in domibus suis, circumeunt domos alienas, curiose agentes, loquentes quae non oportet, superbae, linguatae, ebriosae; etsi virgines sunt, quid prodest integra caro, mente corrupta? Melius est humile coniugium quam superba virginitas.'

[40] *En. in Ps.* 75, 16 'Quid si enim sit corpore integra et mente corrupta? ... Quid si nullus tetigerit corpus, sed si forte ebriosa sit, superba sit, litigiosa sit, linguosa sit?'. *De bono conjugali* 29–30.

[41] *En. in Ps.* 132, 3. The title Circumcelliones was given to these ascetics by the Catholics, because they specially venerated the shrines (*cellae*) of their martyrs. They called themselves *Agonistici*, the militant tendency.

[42] *Ep.* 185, 12; *Sermo* 62, 17; *c.Gaudentium* i, 28, 32; 38, 51.

[43] *De opere monachorum* 36.

[44] *Ibid* 39 and 41.

short. But we have no text to mention a tonsure in his writings. The long-haired monks who lived on charity answered the appeal to St Paul by the argument that, on the apostle's own confession in Philippians iii, he failed to attain perfection, and they liked to suggest that this was connected with the sad fact that Paul worked with his own hands.[45] They were above all that.

Two such wandering monks appear in one of Augustine's letters (262) as cause of a considerable headache for the bishop. They had succeeded in persuading a devout married lady to hand over virtually all the family wealth and to dress herself in widow's weeds. Her husband returned from travels to find a provocative situation, and contracted a relationship with another woman, which Augustine then had to censure as adulterous.

If in Augustine's monastery there was a novitiate, we do not hear about it. But it is certain that solemn vows were taken—a *professio* was made. A lapse by a professed nun (*professa sanctimonialis*) caused him pastoral problems on one occasion.[46] The theme of the nun as the bride of Christ is powerfully orchestrated in the tract on Virginity which Augustine wrote for a nunnery, probably that at Hippo. The sisters are told they should consider only how to please God by interior beauty. In the passion of the heart they are naked to God's eyes only.[47] And the model for their vow is in the Blessed Mary herself, whose words to Gabriel 'I know not a man' show that she must previously have taken a vow.[48]

When vows were broken and the monk or nun left the house to rejoin the saeculum, Augustine was sure this could never be pleasing to God. He specifically places in parallel the vow of the ascetic with the vow made in a marriage contract which is legally binding.[49] But some monks and nuns were subjected to pressure by their families.[50] A young nun who had risked parental displeasure by entering a convent would continue to be pressed by her ambitious mother to come out and marry some eminently suitable

---

[45] *Tr. in ev. Joh.* 122, 3.
[46] *Ep.* 9* Divjak (*CSEL* 88, 43, 15). Cf. *Sermo* 355. Augustine sometimes uses *propositum* in this sense.
[47] *Sermo* 161, 12.
[48] *De sancta virginitate* 4.
[49] *De bono viduitatis* 14.
[50] *S. Denis* 20, 12, p. 123 (ed Morin).

man on her list of eligibles.[51] 'No brother residing in a monastery should ever say: I am leaving, for it is not monks alone who will get to the kingdom of heaven.' True, the others may attain heaven too; but they have made no vow and the monk has. He should not look back like Lot's wife.[52]

That in Augustine's time the vows included renunciation of property and of marriage is certain. That they included obedience in set terms is not attested. But Augustine certainly took it for granted that a monk or nun is obliged to obey the superior. 'Obedience', he once quotes, 'is the matrix of virtues and the universal virtue.'[53] The quotation is not from Cicero or Seneca; a glance at the Latin Thesaurus reveals the instructive fact that almost all the references for *oboedientia* are from Christian literature. In their ethical treatises classical writers do not discuss obedience. The remark quoted has the ring of Ambrose, who in his *Exposition of St Luke's Gospel* declares that 'obedience to the heavenly precepts is the foundation of all virtues' (*fundamentum* v. 82); and perhaps Augustine, who was familiar with this commentary, may be giving the sentiment a more colourful expression than its original author.

The Christians, who spoke much more about 'freedom' than their pre-Christian ancestors, needed to lay some stress on the morality of obedience. Moreover, they inherited the biblical notion of man's duty as the humble acknowledgement of creatureliness and finitude before the infinite Creator.

Experience quickly taught Augustine that as many human problems were created as solved by collecting members of the same sex in an insulated community protected from the outside world. 'Entrants do not know themselves. How can the superior of the monastery know their intentions? They make a promise to live a holy life, and then turn out to be evil.' So far as I can discover,

---

[51] *Sermo* 148, 2: God is angered when a professed virgin marries. *Ep.* 3* Divjak (CSEL 88, 21–25), undated, tells of a widow who vowed the virginity of her daughter when she was sick. Now recovered, she wishes her daughter to be released from the obligation and asks if, instead, she may substitute a vow of her own widowhood. Augustine's verdict is that the girl's reward in heaven will surely be greater if the vow is kept, and that the mother's duty is to encourage her to keep it.

[52] *En. in Ps.* 75, 12.

[53] *De bono conjugali* 32 (CSEL 41, 228, 6). A good survey of ancient texts is given by K.S. Frank in *RAC* x (1976) s.v. Gehorsam.

Augustine is the first person to coin the phrase 'there are crooks in every profession': *in omni professione ficti.*[54]

Monastic discipline in North Africa was not light. In a letter to Jerome Augustine expresses his ideal as 'Christian severity tempered by love'.[55] And, of course, we know from Augustine's exposition of the loving nature of paternal chastisement that benevolent discipline included flogging.[56] One of the new letters of Augustine unearthed by Johannes Divjak (ep. 20*) speaks of a monk being beaten after he had been found talking with nuns at an unfitting hour.[57] Julian of Eclanum, Augustine's junior in south Italy, and the scourge of his old age, mentions monks sleeping on rough pallets and flagellating themselves.[58] One does not know how general this discipline was. But Augustine is for restraint. His exposition of Eph. v, 29 'No man hates his own flesh' is to the effect that the purpose of mortification is to extinguish desire, not to damage physical health which is very wrong.[59] In North Italy during the 370s and 380s, as also among the contemporary Priscillianists in Spain, there were ascetics who used to go barefoot even in winter, thinking this obedience to the Gospel (Matt. x, 10).[60] Augustine did not agree with such literalism. In the *Confessions* he remarks that Alypius took up the practice.[61] But Augustine argued that Christ himself must have worn sandals or John the

---

[54] *En. in Ps.* 99, 11–13.
[55] *Ep.* 40, 7.
[56] *Ep.* 133, 2. Christ's example in cleansing the temple justified this limit of discipline. See W. Waldstein's article s.v. Geisselung in *RAC* ix (1974).
[57] *CSEL* 88, 96, 24.
[58] *c.Jul.* vi, 46 f.
[59] *De doctrina Christiana* i, 24.
[60] The anti-Priscillianist council of Saragossa (380) deplores the custom 'nudis pedibus incedere'. Filastrius of Brescia (81) followed by Aug. *Haer.* 68, opposes a heresy which held walking barefoot to be a Christian duty after the examples of Moses at the burning bush and the prophet Isaiah. John Cassian (*Inst.* i, 9) records that Egyptian monks removed their shoes for eucharistic communion. H. Chadwick, *Priscillian of Avila* (Oxford 1976) pp. 17–18.
[61] *Conf.* ix, 6, 14: Alypius went barefoot in N. Italy during the winter of 386–7 as a mortification in preparation for baptism. The pagan Eunapius records that the sophist Prohaeresius when in Gaul walked unshod in winter and wore a threadbare cloak: *Vitae Sophistarum* x, 7 p. 492 Boissonade. Ambrosiaster (commentary on 1 Cor. 12, 23) praises barefoot Christians in humble clothing. Jerome, ep. 22, 19, 6 (Moses, Joshua, and Jesus' disciples went barefoot, and the soldiers who cast lots for Jesus' clothing had no shoes 'for the Lord did not possess what he forbade to his servants.').

Baptist could not have pronounced himself unworthy to untie them.[62]

Augustine's voice was on the side of moderation. His view of fasts was that they had become excessive and should be diminished.[63] The theme that mortification is a penitential process of propitiating God for one's sins and for the indiscretions of one's youth is strikingly absent—the more so when one considers that Augustine had a number of such indiscretions to record. On the other hand, Augustine also has remarkably little to say about the monk's aspiration to reach a passionless perfection;[64] though he uses the already conventional language about the 'angelic' life to describe the celibate ideal when he is writing for his Hippo nunnery in *De sancta virginitate*.[65] The Pelagian controversy brought out in him expressions of deep reserve before the idea that moral perfection is actually attainable in this life. Indeed in the nineteenth book of the *City of God* he lays down that in this life 'our righteousness consists more in the forgiveness of sins than in the perfection of virtues'[66] – a sentence which caused much embarrassment to some hypersensitive counter-reformation critics of Luther.

In Augustine's foundations the monks and nuns wore distinctive clothing, the *habitus monachorum* or the *cilicium*,[67] and were recognisable in the street by their dress and cap as being 'servants of God'. Augustine remarks with crushing irony how people coming away from the amphitheatre will be heard expressing pity for them.[68] Many of the African monks fasted except on Saturdays and Sundays.[69]

Augustine did not share Jerome's admiration for dirt and squalor. He thought it ostentatious.[70] He once observes that one

---

[62] *Sermo* 101, 7. Similarly Gaudentius of Brescia, *sermo* 5 (*CSEL* 68, 43–48).
[63] *Ep* 36, 25.
[64] *De civ. Dei* xiv, 6 defines *apatheia* as not the absence of all feeling which would be worse than all vices, but a freedom from all irrational disorder in the mind; and that state will be realised in the next life, not in this. Heaven has room for love and joy, not for sorrow and pain.
[65] *De s. virg.* 12 and 54. Cf. K.S. Frank, *Angelikos Bios* (Münster 1964).
[66] *De civ. Dei* xix, 27 'Ipsa quoque nostra iustitia, quamvis vera sit propter verum boni finem ad quem refertur, tamen tanta est in hac vita ut potius remissione peccatorum constet quam perfectione virtutum.'
[67] *De opere mon.* 36; *ep.* 48, 4; cf. *saccellum*: *En. in Ps.* 13, 26.
[68] *En in Ps.* 147, 8.
[69] *Ep.* 36, 8.
[70] Augustine washed his face daily and judged an unwashed state to be self-advertisement: *De sermone Domini in monte* ii, 12, 41.

consequence of the Fall, by which Adam was condemned to work by the sweat of his brow, was that Eve found her partner repellently malodorous.[71] It is a little surprising, when one recalls the part played by the story of Athanasius' life of Antony in the narrative of his conversion, that hermits played a negligible role in Augustine's overview of African ascetic life. Occasionally hermits are mentioned as heroes who live alone in deserts or on islands, without benefit of the sacraments or even a Bible.[72] Antony, he recalls, had learnt the entire Bible by heart.[73] Augustine knew of the holy men of the Egyptian desert from having read Jerome's notorious 22nd letter, on which he drew for some of the information in the first book *De moribus*.[74] But even at that early stage of his career in the Church, when his fairly recent decision to pursue the ascetic life would still have been to the fore, he was inclined to sympathise with those who thought hermits wrong to ignore the service which they might render to others.[75]

In Augustine asceticism is always a means to an end, instrumental to contemplation. Both in his theology and in his experience action and contemplation were the two poles between which life had to be lived out. In this life active, in the next contemplative—the polarity is symbolised by Martha and Mary, by Peter and John, and especially by Jacob's two wives Leah and Rachel who receive an extended allegorical treatment in the *Contra Faustum*[76] as part of a refutation of the Manichee contention that the polygamy of the patriarchs disqualifies the Old Testament as a handbook of ethics. The two themes correspond to means and ends, to toil and finished achievement, to the purging away of sins now in order that we may enjoy the light of God in unclouded splendour.[77] Augustine found the duties of being a bishop painfully burdensome, and was eloquent about the *sarcina episcopi*. He once remarks that no one without direct experience of the job would ever believe what innumerable cares press upon a bishop, and he

---

[71] *En. in Ps.* 133, 2.
[72] *De vera religione* 5; *De doctrina christiana* i, 39, 43; *c.Faustum* v, 8.
[73] *De doctrina christiana* i praef. 4.
[74] See the careful demonstration of Augustine's debt by J.K. Coyle, in his commentary on *De moribus ecclesiae catholicae* (Fribourg, Switzerland 1978).
[75] *De moribus* i, 31, 65 ff., where Jerome's information is being drawn upon.
[76] *c.Faustum* xxii, 53–54.
[77] *De ordine* ii, 14, 39–43; *De consensu evangelistarum* i, 5, 8; iv, 10, 20; *De civitate Dei* viii, 4; *De Trinitate* xiii, 20, 26; *Tr. in ev. Joh.* 101, 5; 124, 5.

could not help resenting his duties as arbitrator in disputes about money and property.[78] The heavy burden brought to an early death one of his monks, Profuturus, who became bishop of Cirta, a town where there was a powerful Donatist opposition led by the ex-Catholic lawyer Petilian who became the Donatist bishop.[79] Amid such duties Augustine tells of his longing for leisure to contemplate,[80] an *otium* of body and mind which in one youthful letter he speaks of as prerequisite for mystical communion with God, indeed 'deification'.[81] But that is not to say that he would have thought it other than gross dereliction of duty to refuse ordination.[82] Surprisingly he can express sympathy with bishops who left the hubbub of their episcopal duties.[83] The North African churches were desperately short of clergy of sufficient, or indeed of almost any quality. Church councils deplored the *indigentia clericorum*,[84] and the quality of what was available may be estimated by Augustine's sombre remark that there were few churches where there were no ex-clergy who had had to be degraded.[85] One of the Divjak letters (22*) says how hard it is to find suitable and willing candidates for ordination in towns. The imperial laws about *munera* meant poverty for clergy, and not all were like Francis of Assisi. So a reluctance to accept holy orders was common, and that no doubt

---

[78] See Maurice Jourjon, 'Sarcina: un mot cher a l'évêque d'Hippone', in *Recherches de science religieuse* 43 (1955) pp. 258–62. Characteristic texts are *Ep.* 85, 2; 149, 34; 242, 1. Augustine's problem arose from the social duties accidental to his spiritual office, and especially arbitrations between quarrelling members of his flock. 'No one without experience of the job would ever guess what duties fall on us bishops' (*De opere monachorum* 37).

[79] *Ep.* 71, 2. Profuturus' career in Mandouze, *Prosopographie* s.v. On Petilian's forced ordination: *c.litt. Petiliani* ii, 104, 239.

[80] *De civ. Dei* xix, 19; *S. Frangip.* ii, 4 p. 193 (ed Morin).

[81] *Ep.* 10, 2.

[82] *Qu. Heptat.* iv, 54 'None has the right to refuse the sacraments of ordination.' *De vera religione* 51 (a law of providence that none is helped by higher powers to grasp grace unless he is willing to help inferiors); cf. *Conf.* x, 4, 6: 'hi sunt servi tui, fratres mei, quos filios tuos esse voluisti dominos meos, quibus iussisti ut serviam si volo tecum de te vivere.'

[83] *c.Cresconium* ii, 11, 13. The text is clearly intended to defend the honour of a Catholic bishop, such as Maximianus of Bagai who, having suffered fearful violence from the Donatist majority at his town, left Bagai. Augustine himself threatened to resign over the Fussala affair if the Pope reinstated the delinquent Antoninus; *ep.* 209, 10.

[84] See the Hippo Breviary, 37 *Concilia Africae* ed Munier, p. 43, 212; Council of Carthage, 16 June 401, p. 194, 421.

[85] *c.litt. Petiliani* iii, 32, 36.

helps to explain why in most cases ordination was the consequence of some physical coercion by the congregation, as in the case of Augustine himself.[86] Augustine felt that too many Christians were like the idle man in the parable who hid his solitary talent in the ground and put it to no use.[87] The new monasteries could train men in a frugal life, and become nurseries of bishops,[88] who would go out to gather their presbyters round them in a clergy-house, eating and praying regularly together. At Hippo Augustine was to find his city clergy disinclined to accept so austere a way of life.[89]

One weakness in Augustine's ascetical theology lay in his attitude to sex and marriage. He would, of course, have nothing to do with the Manichee estimate of sexuality as an inherent evil. The generally acknowledged superiority of the unmarried state could not imply that marriage itself was not a good gift of the Creator.[90] Nevertheless, he also thought, and in the Pelagian controversy came to say with a mounting crescendo, that in human nature as it now is the sexual impulse is the supreme symptom or expression of the irrational, the uncontrollable, the obsessive condition of the human psyche in its fallen condition. The physiology of the impulse was at war with will and reason. Within marriage itself, therefore, he thought conjugal relations ought, so far as possible, to be restricted to procreation, and viewed as a sad necessity—to be done *cum dolore*.[91] He found it natural to follow the exegesis of the Parable of the Sower according to which 30-fold is the reward for

---

[86] *Sermo* 355, 2; Possidius, *Vita Aug.* 4. Cf. *ep.* 173, 2, and *De adult. conjug.* ii, 22 (*CSEL* 41, 409, 15) 'violentia populorum'. Above n. 79 on Petilian among the Donatists.

[87] *De fide et operibus* 32; *sermo* 339, 4. Cf. *Tr. in ev. Joh.* 57, 2 (the scarcity of preachers is because Christian love is now so cold, and leisured students shrink from toil).

[88] *Ep.* 48 to the monastery at Capraria.

[89] *Sermo* 355. A good study by M. Zacherl, 'Die vita communis als Lebensform des Klerus in der Zeit zwischen Augustinus und Karl dem Grossen', *Zeit. f. kath. Theol.* 92 (1970) pp. 385–424.

[90] *Sermo* 96, 10 opposes the rejection of this acknowledgement. In *Retract.* ii, 22 Augustine claims that *De bono conjugali* (401), the argument of which is that marriage is good but celibacy better, was directed against the heresy of Jovinian (against whom Jerome had written two books before 395). Jovinian regarded it as Manichee to assert the moral superiority of celibacy as such. Though not mentioned in *De bono conjugali*, Jovinian appears elsewhere in Augustine: esp. *De haeres.* 82; *De Nuptiis et Concup.* ii, 5, 16; 23, 38; *c.duas epp. Pelag.* i, 2, 4, classifies Julian of Eclanum with Jovinian because of his contention that Augustine's estimate of sexuality is Manichee. The real target was Jerome.

[91] *Sermo* 51, 25.

faithfully married believers, 60-fold for chaste widows, 100-fold for virgins.[92] One could be content with the inferior grade and still hope for some modest reward hereafter. But those aspiring for the highest prize would remain unmarried. On this it is enough to observe that if married Christians are placed in an inherently inferior spiritual category and the unmarried in an inherently superior one, it can have demoralising consequences for both categories.[93]

Augustine may have had his problems with the residents of his foundations, but we do not hear of those extremes of asceticism which fascinated Gibbon and Voltaire. Africa had no pillar saints, no spectacular hero-figures of the kind one reads about in John Moschus' *Spiritual Meadow*, no Himalayan climbers of the ascetic life competing with one another. Augustine saw the monastic movement as a protest against the infiltration into the churches of the secular loves of power, honour, wealth; a defiance of materialist values and disordered sexuality. Monks were there to show the Church that discipline is actually possible, and that the simplicities of the sermon on the mount can be acted out. The monks evidently did more for education and the transmission of culture than Gibbon and the Enlightenment wished to concede. They trained many bishops and missionaries. The monasteries were a microcosm of that dual role which the Church has often had to play, combining a battle school for the soldiers of Christ with a field hospital for those who cannot cope with the world's conflicts and storms, nor indeed with their own.

In Augustine's eyes the greatest service that monks can render to the Church is in prayer and in sacrificial example.[94] As historians we are not really in any position to offer an evaluation of the function and utility of intercessory prayer and contemplation. They are imponderable by man, and we shall not expect to read sympathetic accounts of monks from those who can see no useful purpose served by worship and prayer and frugality. Yet even those who think every activity ought to have some utilitarian

[92] *De bono conjugali* 46. Augustine regards this exegesis as possible, not necessarily the only possible.
[93] *Contra Faustum* v, 9 speaks of married Christians in the world as mercenary auxiliaries in Christ's army. Cf. Origen, *Hom. in Num.* 26, 10.
[94] *De moribus* i, 31, 66; *ep.* 130, 20.

justification and make a contribution to the enhancement of material wealth may still acknowledge the enviable detachment of the monks, their freedom from pursuit of the world's hollow crowns, their deliverance from the need to tell white lies and to be smoothly diplomatic.[95]

Augustine, then, wanted asceticism, but anticipated Cassian and Benedict in wanting it to be moderate, to have a human face, above all to be lived in a community where members would seek to 'bear one another's burdens'. (The Pauline text functions as a kind of motto for his Rule.) He did not want his communities to be self-centred or remote from the ordinary congregations. Moreover, high culture was in his bloodstream. His ascetic renunciation at conversion in 386 so little carried the immediate implication that he was turning his back on everything, that the Cassiciacum dialogues seemed to the author of the *Confessions* thirteen years later to breathe a too worldly and literary culture;[96] and after 386–7 one of his first projects for publication was a series of handbooks to the seven liberal arts. The pedagogue remained powerful in him to the end. He did not think his very unbookish flock at Hippo should have a feeling of inferiority if they did not always use the correct forms of words as desiderated by professional teachers of grammar.[97] But he could not suppress the wish to teach them 'correct' usage, and he himself could hardly write a letter without an echo of Cicero or Virgil. He could even get a sentence from Sallust into a sermon (*S.* 81, 9). *De Doctrina Christiana*, begun in 396, but not completed (with the provision of a preface) until thirty years later, became a manifesto on the character of Christian culture, which needs educated people to interpret scripture correctly. Admittedly, because this culture is designed to serve the one end of biblical exegesis in commentary or pulpit, Augustine could make only the most peripheral place for technology, and thereby influenced many centuries of western thinking after him. Nevertheless, the work made Cassiodorus' *Institutio* possible.

---

[95] It is no doubt to be seen as an aspect and expression of Augustine's ascetic ideal that he is hostile to mendacity, above all in the cause of religion.

[96] *Conf.* ix, 4, 7 'ibi quid egerim in litteris iam quidem servientibus tibi, sed adhuc superbiae scholam tamquam in pausatione anhelantibus testantur libri disputati cum praesentibus et cum ipso me solo coram te'.

[97] *En. in Ps.* 36, 3, 6; 138, 20 (*ossum* vulgarly used for *os*).

Likewise, the man who insisted on community of goods in the monastery, was ready to defend the right of private property outside it,[98] admittedly with the crucial qualification that the juridical right is subject to an overriding moral imperative. The possessor of wealth has an obligation to use it for the common good, not for selfish ends.[99] To this extent Augustine might be said to have adumbrated a doctrine of vocation for laity working in the saeculum which is not exclusively oriented towards the institutions created by the Church. He did not think a high-ranking bureaucrat was right to remain a catechumen and to defer baptism until he had laid down his office.[100] Perhaps Augustine oscillated. Can a Christian properly engage in innocent employments in human society with a wholly untroubled conscience? Augustine contributed something to the notion that perhaps in the conscience there ought to be a cloud, if no larger than a man's hand, and that the really serious work of dedicated servants of God was done within the framework of monasteries. Therefore the movement he did so much to foster and to moderate would eventually come to incur the critical questionings of a Wyclif or a Luther, themselves an expression of a widespread lay envy of monastic power.

From the moment of his conversion in the summer of 386 Augustine's ideal was monastic. Although he submitted to the call to serve as presbyter and then as bishop, his ideal for the life of the 'secular' clergy (to use an anachronistic term) remained deeply ascetic; he took it for granted that his clergy, even if married, would no longer live with their wives, and that celibacy was part of the priestly calling.[101] It never occurred to him that his doctrine of grace might one day be supposed to be in tension with his ascetic aspirations. But then Augustine never understood his doctrine of predestination and grace to imply a denial of free will or a mitigation of the demand for striving after holiness of life.[102] His strong insistence on justification as an act of God which is not for

---

[98] *Tr. in ev. Joh.* 6, 25; *ep.* 93, 20.

[99] *Ibid* 153, 26; esp. *Sermo* 50, 14; *De Trin.* xii, 9, 14.

[100] *De civ. Dei* xix, 6.

[101] The principal texts which presuppose that celibacy is the duty of bishops and presbyters as well as of monks are *Conf.* vi, 3, 3; x, 30, 41; *Adult. Conj.* ii, 20, 22 (*CSEL* 41, 409, 12); *S. Guelf.* 32, 1, p. 569 (ed Morin).

[102] The treatise *De spiritu et littera* of 412 denies the sufficiency of the human will for doing the will of God, but concedes that the assent of the will is necessary.

our imitation in no sense qualified his stress on sanctification by the imitation of Christ.[103] The absoluteness of human dependence on divine grace for salvation at every stage did not touch his recognition that if marriage is good and virginity better, then one must make a distinction between precept and counsel.[104] Augustine certainly expected many to follow that counsel in respect of marriage. Paradoxically the Pelagian appeal to Christ's words to the rich young ruler ('Sell...') as enforcing the total renunciation of wealth he saw to be more difficult: the Lord's words were a *consilium perfectionis*, not a requirement.[105] But he goes on to add that he had himself taken a vow of poverty and had sold his property.[106] More than once he observed that 'to have more than you need is to keep what belongs to another'.[107] While he believed none could enter heaven without justifying grace as a baptised believer, he also held that in both heaven and hell there are variations of reward.[108] Venial sins (among which he included conjugal relations in marriage without intention to procreate)[109] did not bar the just's entry to heaven but qualified the degree of bliss.

To conclude, Augustine's asceticism with a human face is not without its power and glory. He would certainly have thought Luther gravely mistaken on the subject of monastic vows. Paradoxically, he would have thought Gibbon and Voltaire right in seeing authentic Christianity as otherworldly. But then he would have come back at them with the formidable retort that their world view presupposed that human life belongs entirely to the saeculum, and that its primary values will then be located in power, honour, wealth, and sex. Augustine thought this no road to *beata vita*.

Magdalene College
Cambridge

---

103 *De peccatorum meritis*, i, 18.
104 *Conf.* xiii, 19, 25; *De s. virg.* 14; *De Bono conjug.* 30; *De Adult. Conjug.* i, 14, 15.
105 *Ep.* 157, 33.
106 *Ibid* 157, 39.
107 *En. in Ps.* 147, 12; *sermo* 206, 2.
108 *De spiritu et littera* 48, and elsewhere.
109 *c.Faust.* 22, 46; *De Nupt. et Concup.* i, 14, 16 f.

CHRISTIAN ASCETICISM AND THE EARLY SCHOOL OF ALEXANDRIA

by J. A. McGUCKIN

T HIS paper offers three considerations: a) the Jewish ascetical tradition in the life of Jesus and the primitive Gospel tradition; b) the Alexandrian system offered by Clement and Origen, which through developing monasticism did so much to set the tone of ascetical doctrine throughout the ancient Christian world; and c) what relation, if any, survived between Jesus and his great Alexandrian disciples in this matter, after the lapse of a century and a half. It is thus a study in continuity and discontinuity.

Prayer, Fasting and Almsgiving in Judaism

Late Judaism is familiar with prayer, fasting and almsgiving as the chief expressions of asceticism. They are three methods of having one's sins forgiven by God.[1] Among them, fasting is the supreme representative of 'Tapeinosis' or humbling oneself before the Lord. The Torah prescribed one day of fasting on Yom Kippur, a national day of lament and repentance.[2] By the time of Zechariah a day of lament and fasting in the fourth, fifth, seventh, and tenth months was instituted to mark the destruction of the temple.[3] The Book of Esther commends a fast at the time of Purim.[4] By the rabbinic era the four days of lamentation were rarely mentioned but the fast on the fifth month[5] had survived and was also marking the anniversary of the destruction of the second temple, an event which according to rabbinic lore, happened on the same date as that of the first. At this time the Megillat Ta'anit (Roll of Fasts) listed twenty four days of observance, but almost all were voluntary. In the time of Jesus the Pharisees were noted for their zeal in practising

---

[1] cf. Apoc. Eliae 22 seq 'It forgives sins, heals diseases, drives out spirits, and has power even to the throne of God.'
[2] Lev. 16. 29f; 23, 27 seq; Num. 29. 7.
[3] Zech. 7. 3, 5; 8. 19.
[4] Esther 9. 3.
[5] 9th Ab.

voluntary fasts on Tuesdays and Thursdays.[6] The Essenes and the Baptist sect equally had a notable ascetic tradition. At this period fasting had come to be almost the distinctive badge of the Jewish tribe for onlooking gentiles.[7]

Fasting was an aspect of mourning the dead.[8] As a spiritual symbol, then, it became a way of lamenting the feeling of the absence of God to Israel—a feeling that became critical in times of national or personal distress. At such times the Jew would fast[9] so that the sight of his mournful self-humbling would evoke the pity of Yahweh.[10] This is why stress was placed on the need for externally observable signs of distress when fasting.[11]

Judaic fasting, then, had an intimate relation to prayer, as the sure method of having one's prayer heard, or as the manner of making clear what was a particularly important prayer.[12] In the Midrash Aba Gorjon it says: 'He who puts on sackcloth and fasts, let him not lay it off until what he prays for takes place'.[13] Fasting was itself a prayer of repentance to call on God's mercy, and was fittingly practised, therefore, by the ascetic figure of John the Baptist[14] who preached both prayer and repentance.[15] This is the dominant note in Jewish ascetical tradition. The notion of cultic or ecstatic fasting is minor in comparison.[16] Even the prophetic denunciations of external fasting without internal renewal[17] do not

[6] Didache 8. 1; Lk. 18. 12.

[7] Tacitus Hist. 5. 4. 'Longam olim famem crebris adhuc jejuniis fatentur.' Suetonius, Aug. Caes: 76. 3. 'ne Judaeus quidem tam diligenter sabbatis jejunium servat quam ego hodie servavi.'

[8] cf. 1 Kings 21. 7; Joel 2. 13; Is. 58. 5; Est. 4. 3; Neh. 9. 1; Jonah 3. 5; Dan. 9. 3; 1 Sam. 31. 13; 2 Sam. 1. 12.

[9] Jud. 20. 26; Jer. 36. 6, 9; 2 Chr. 20, 3 seq.

[10] 2 Sam. 12. 16; 1 Kings 21. 27; Ps. 35. 12; Ps. 69. 10.

[11] Eg. dirt, sackcloth and ashes, and unkempt hair. Mt. 6. 16.

[12] 1 Macc. 3. 47; 2 Macc. 13. 12; Bar. 1. 5; Judith 4. 9f; Tb. 12. 8; Josephus, Ant. 19. 349; Lk. 2. 37; Test. Jos. 4. 8; 10. 1; Test. Ben. 1. 4; One also fasted to confirm a vow cf. 1 Sam. 14. 24; Num. 30. 14; Mk. 14. 25; Acts 23. 12.

[13] Ibid 6a. cf. TDNT, ed Kittel. 4. 930–31.

[14] Mk. 1. 6; Mt. 11. 8, 18.

[15] Lk. 11. 1; Mt. 3. 2.

[16] cf. Ex. 34. 28; Dt. 9. 9; Dan. 9. 3; 10. 24f; 10. 12. The idea survives in later apocalypticism: 4 Ezra 5. 13, 19; 6. 31, 5 etc; Apoc. Bar. (Syr) 9. 2; 12. 5; 20. 5 etc; Apoc. Abr. 9. 7; Asc. Is. 2. 7–11. The notion of cultic fasting (Baptismal and Eucharistic) survives into contemporary Christianity in Catholic and Orthodox practice.

[17] Jer. 14. 12; Is. 58. 1; Zech. 7. 5; 8. 16–19; Joel 2. 13.

dim or check the Jewish enthusiasm for fasting as a religious exercise though they do make an impression on the Alexandrian Fathers.

The practice of almsgiving in later Jewish tradition was equally associated with prayer.[18] The Book of Tobit was particularly concerned with commending the practice of almsgiving as a righteousness that led to the forgiveness of sins.[19] Luke, the evangelist, had a very high regard for the practice himself. He described it as ascending to the throne of God[20] in the manner of praise and good works. The Synoptic tradition added its own voice by apparently requiring that almsgiving should be done secretly and from a right intention.[21]

Jesus and Asceticism

At first sight the Jewish notion of asceticism as prayerful fasts and almsgiving would appear to run on as a presupposition in the doctrine of Jesus, which only adds the prophetic requirements of interiority and secrecy in both acts to restore the original point of 'Tapeinosis',[22] in the best rabbinical manner.[23] And yet, on closer examination, there are problems with this analysis. The two logia of Jesus in Luke that require his disciples to give alms[24] are making this precise point only because of some redactive dexterity on the part of the evangelist. At Lk. 11: 41 he has no Markan source and from the Matthean parallel[25] it is clear that Luke has personally inserted the injunction to give alms. Similarly Lk. 12: 33 has the hallmarks of being the evangelist's typical adaptation of Jesus' radical requests for the renunciation of goods,[26] in his evangelistic interest to redirect the primitive eschatology of the Jesus movement in an ecclesial and ascetical direction. It is the same with the idea

---

[18] cf. Sirach. 7. 10, 14–15.
[19] Tb. 12. 8–10; 14. 4, 11.
[20] Acts 10. 4.
[21] Mt. 6. 1–4; Mk. 12. 43–44.
[22] cf. Ps. 35. 13; Ps. 69. 10.
[23] As in the parable at Lk. 18. 12.
[24] Lk. 11. 41: 'But give for alms those things within and lo, all things are clean for you.' Lk. 12. 33: 'Sell your possessions and give alms, and get purses that do not wear out.'
[25] Mt. 23. 25 seq.
[26] As at Mk. 10. 21, or Lk. 14. 33.

that fasting is required of the disciple as a regular activity. The command to fast is laid to Jesus, but the whole terms of the discourse in which it appears in Mt. 6: 2–8 emerges on closer study to be a Halakah on Sirach 7: 10, 14–15, a book we perhaps associate more with Syrian Christianity of the Sophic strain[27] than with the historical Jesus. A literary analysis of Matthew's First Didactic Discourse of Jesus[28] shows that the stylised format of the sayings comes from the pen of Matthew. It is a literary form not a verbal one. The evangelist is here collecting, systematising and regulating the Jesus Logia for doctrinal purposes. The evangelist has already announced as the keynote of all his editorial work the theological principle of a strict continuity between the praxis of the old covenant and that of the new. This dogmatic premiss is set out at the beginning and again at the end of that First Discourse[29] in terms that are so evidently anti-Pauline that they must post-date Jesus by at least a generation. If the general theological context is thus rendered somewhat dubious, and the immediate literary format (when you perform X do not do Y, rather do Z) is to be laid at the door of the Jewish evangelist, then the original Jesus logion about fasting begins to look as if it were the simple injunction: 'Do not fast like the hypocrites.' In this form it can be interpreted as a call to end the practice as easily as a call to reform it. It depends on our presuppositions of how 'orthodox' was Jesus, and the views of Matthew on that point might differ from ours.

This question mark over Jesus' attitude to fasting is found again in the Markan logion on why the disciples of John and the Pharisees fasted, but not the disciples of Jesus.[30] Mark's theological point in the passage is to argue a radical break, in Jesus, with the old tradition. This evangelist frequently uses such evidence to argue for the rights of a Hellenistic Church in the Pauline manner, but there are parallel texts, such as Jesus' rejection of the tradition of the elders,[31] which suggest that the attitude, if not the ecclesiology, might have been that of Jesus himself. The logion of Mt. 11: 18[32]

[27] Matthew's Church of Antioch is a likely contender here.
[28] Mt. 5–7.
[29] cf. Mt. 5. 17–19; 7. 13–23.
[30] Mk. 2. 18–20.
[31] Mk. 7. 5–9.
[32] 'John came neither eating nor drinking ... the Son of Man came eating and

implies some ambivalence in Christ's attitude to fasting. In Mk. 2: 18f the practice of fasting is allowed only as a memorial of the Passion of Jesus. The phrase: 'they will fast then on that day' possibly being used by Mark to allude to the liturgical fast of Good Friday, celebrated in the Roman Church. If we remove the prophetic or proleptic element from the section, and also remove the Christocentric interpretation that attributes the Bridegroom title to Jesus himself (implying that the Church is the Bride) we can arrive back at a tentative reconstruction of the original logion in which Jesus refers to Yahweh as the Bridegroom of Israel (a fairly mainstream symbol of covenant fidelity and covenant restoration) and which now bears a quite different message to the effect that the disciples cannot fast because the ministry of Jesus has removed all need for lamenting the absence of Yahweh from his people. The Kingdom of God has come with the signs of Jesus; the point of fasting no longer holds valid. This might illustrate for us the purpose of using the wedding feast as a symbol of the Kingdom in some of the parables,[33] and also Jesus' practice of eating publicly with sinners.[34] Is this rite of festivity his peculiar prophetic sign (like the broken pots of Jeremiah) that encapsulated his message? In his case – a celebration of his faith in the nearness of God, his hope in the ultimate fruitfulness of his ministry, and perhaps a wry highlighting of the paradox of how few ordinary Israelites were prepared to come to his feast on his terms.

The only other logion about fasting belongs really to a different order.[35] Mk. 9: 29 belongs properly to the genre of exorcism directives. Of course there were many Jewish exorcists, even in Palestine, so the saying could be dated to Jesus himself. But in the main, the cryptic text is so heavily Hellenised[36] that it raises problems of date and location. In any case it belongs more to the

---

drinking and they say 'lo! a glutton and a drunkard, a friend of tax collectors and sinners'.

[33] cf. Mt. 22. 1 seq; 25. 1 seq.

[34] Mk. 2. 15–17.

[35] Mk. 9. 29. Mt. 4. 2–4 is similarly not a statement about fasting but a literary evocation of the theme of Israel in the wilderness.

[36] cf. parallels in Plutarch, *Isis* + *Osiris* 26; Apuleius, *Met.* 2. 24; Clement, *Protreptikos* 2. 21. 2. In the magical papyri, fasting strengthens one's power of magic to cast out spirits: Preisendanz, p. 235; also Cat. Cod. Astrologorum Graec. 3. 53. 13. Texts given in *TDNT* 4, p. 927.

peculiar and restricted practice of cultic fasting, and not to the mainstream Jewish ascetical attitude.[37]

From this summarily argued review I am obviously tending to the conclusion that Jesus was not an ascetic figure, and was not so for dogmatic reasons to do with the vividness of his own sense of the closeness of Yahweh's providential power for Israel. It may be ironical that perhaps the one clear exception to the general rule, when Jesus does begin to fast, is to hasten by vow the realisation of his hope for this Kingdom, on the eve of his betrayal.[38] If we still wish to consider Jesus' asceticism I think we need to look elsewhere – at the concept of his prophetic endurance and single-minded devotion to the demands of his apocalyptic mission.

Clement: The path to Apatheia

If we turn now to Alexandria in the last decade of the second century we find a quite different picture. Clement offers us a very practical and very urbane system of Christian ascesis. Perhaps to call it a system is to overemphasise its scope, for throughout his work Clement never regarded ascesis as a proper subject for dogmatics, or as an issue that should be treated *per se*. It was for him merely a method of achieving something else. His *Paedagogus 2–3* represented a practical manual of etiquette and moral directives. The whole conception was modelled on the Stoic manuals of discipline and in its course he employed long excerpts from Musonius, the teacher of Epictetus. The work was a blend of late Stoicism, Neo-Platonism, and the Logos doctrine of the Apologists which inspired his central premiss that in morals man must follow nature, that is reason.[39] This Christian eclecticism gave a moderate and humane cast to his work. He said: 'There is nothing too vehement or too intense about the pedagogy of the Logos, but it is moderate and held in a just and right balance.'[40] Ascesis, or

---

[37] Mk. 9. 29 is arguably a reminiscence from a group of early Christian exorcists who assembled such stories based on Jesus (loosely). The apocalyptic idiom of exorcism is significantly different from the common practice of magical exorcism in both Judaism and Hellenism of the mid First century.

[38] Mk. 14. 25.

[39] 'Everything contrary to right reason is sin.' Paed. 1. 13. 1. A[nte] N[icene] C[hristian] L[ibrary] 4 (1868) p. 184.

[40] Paed. 1. 12. 98. 3. ANCL 4 p. 182.

gymnastic exercise, was like a toning up of spiritual faculties useful for all grades of Christian but particularly relevant to the less experienced. The keynote of such preparation was *Euteleia* (frugality) a word, as he explained, that has the extremely practical connotations of a good bargain, getting one's money's worth from a deal: 'Frugality is the highest degree of wealth, as good as a limitless income, expended on what is necessary, and to the extent that it is necessary.'[41] And again, 'Those who bear frugality with chaste gravity have good provision for the journey to heaven.'[42] Frugality was central to his thought in so far as it was an exercise in self-simplification – simplifying the conditions of man's exterior life and thus beginning to simplify the multiform fragmentation of his psychological desires. The process was designed to bring our inner complexity down into a resolution and a coherent direction; a quiescence designed to restore hegemony to the soul in man's composite anthropology.

Clement was no dualist and rejected the view that asceticism was a punishment of degenerate flesh. In the *Stromateis* he noted that the body may be inferior to the soul, but it is certainly not bad, merely requiring a rational and respectful guardianship: 'The soul of the wise man, the gnostic, which sojourns in the body, conducts itself towards the body gravely and respectfully, with no inordinate desires, ready to leave its abode if the time of departure should beckon.'[43] The correct method of restoring spiritual hegemony was by the moderation of our natural desires, their right ordering not by their suppression. This is why, in his celebrated exegesis on the Rich Young Man[44] he interpreted Jesus' demands for renunciation as in reality meaning liberation from cupidity, and the right employment of one's resources in charity, since only by use (a faculty of will) does one enter the realm of the moral. This process of frugal ascesis was a sensitisation of the Christian in Clement's view: 'In the end gnosis is granted only to those fit and chosen for it, on account of the very great preparation and prior training necessary to hear what is being said to us, to compose our lives, and to advance wisely to a point beyond the righteousness of the

---

[41] Paed. 3. 8. *ANCL* 4 p. 304.
[42] Paed. 3. 7. *ANCL* 4 p. 302.
[43] Stromateis 4. 26. *ANCL* 12 (1869) p. 216.
[44] Quis Dives Salvetur.

Law.'[45] There is here a three-fold division of ascesis: a training in frugality to sensitise the soul to the Word of God, a subsequent growth in simplicity (which is a mimesis of the simplicity of God's being) and finally a transcendence of the old order (Law) to a realisation of a profound union with God (Gnosis). This is why ascetical exercises in Alexandrian thought were never penitential in character, but instructive. The body is never punished, but in certain areas deprived of immoderate needs and brought back to an ordered system. His thoughts on the ascesis of sleep clearly demonstrate this: 'Sleep is not for indulgence but for reconstitution after labour. We must therefore sleep so as to be easily wakened... We ought to rise several times at night to bless God ... like the angels who are called 'The Watchers'.'[46] For Clement all things in the created order were good, except sin which was irrational and chaotic, and hence not part of creation proper. Morality, therefore, and by implication asceticism, could never deny materiality, but rather should strive to order it correctly[47] by detachments rather than renunciations. This accounts for Clement's genuine defence of the value of marriage and sexuality, even though his sexual ethic would appear extremely rigorous to a modern reader,[48] as for example enjoining continence on the couple from the time of conception to parturition since procreation is the only logical justification of the sexual faculty.[49]

As the whole purpose of this ascetical training was to restore the hegemony of the spirit in man, it is not surprising that Clement rarely spoke of asceticism without allegorising it beyond its immediate import. He invariably described the fasting mentioned in Scripture, for example, as referring to moral behaviour not abstinence from food;[50] 'Fastings signify abstinence from all kinds of evil.'[51] Asceticism, for him, was ideally fulfilled in the observance of the evangelical commands, the code of moral perfection. He said: 'According to Law the gnostic fasts by abstaining from

[45] Str. 7. 10. *ANCL* 12 p. 446.
[46] Paed. 2. 9. *ANCL* 4 pp. 240–1.
[47] Str. 4. 13. *ANCL* 12 p. 182.
[48] cf. Str. 6. 12. *ANCL* 12 pp. 361–2.
[49] Str. 7. 12. *ANCL* 12 p. 457.
[50] Following the prophetic tradition outlined in Is. 58. 4. cf. Tertullian, *De Jejunio* 2; Barnabas 3. 1; Justin Dial. 15. 1 seq; Diognetus 4. 1.
[51] Str. 6. 12. *ANCL* 12 p. 363. Also Paed. 3. 12. *ANCL* 4 p. 335.

bad deeds, and according to Gospel perfection he fasts by abstaining from evil thoughts.'[52] He similarly interpreted the saying on
eunuchs as requiring the Christian to cut off all inordinate desires.[53]
His thought here is reminiscent of Philo who used the analogy of
God only holding converse with the virginal soul that remains
aloof from the *Pathemata* of the sensory world.[54]

In this spiritualising, allegorical approach he was admittedly
speaking mostly about the gnostic stages of advanced spirituality,
but at times he barely concealed his low opinion of some of the
ascetics who inhabited the Alexandrian Church at that time: 'There
are certain things practised in a vulgar manner by some people such
as control over pleasures, either out of regard for the promise, or
out of fear of God. Well such self-restraint is the first step of gnosis
and an approach to something better ... but the perfect man "bears
all things and endures all things"[55] solely from love.'[56] For him, the
ascetic could only be the man who knew to what end his effort was
directed: 'It is not he who merely controls his passions who is called
the continent man, but he who has also achieved the mastery over
good things, and has acquired the perfections of gnosis from which
he produces the fruits of virtuous acts.'[57]

The direction of all this effort (though not itself the goal) was
Apatheia, which we can perhaps best define as an approximation to
moral aseity. In practice it is seen in stability and tranquillity of
soul.[58] It is the doctrine of *apatheia*, fed from many sources but
thoroughly Christianised in his hands, which was perhaps the most
distinctive aspect of Clement's ascetical doctrine. This state of
passionlessness, however, was merely the guiding light that brought
man to a higher goal, the final stage in the process of advance-
ments. *Apatheia* was not senselessness, it rather heightened our
capacity for *agapé* and brought the soul, finally to that union with
God for which it longed. His subjection of the notion of *apatheia* to

[52] Str. 7. 12. *ANCL* 12 p. 461. Cf. Str. 4. 21. *ANCL* 12 p. 199.
[53] Str. 3. 7. 59: 'To emasculate oneself from all passions.' *Ibid* 3. 15. 99: 'Those who
emasculate themselves from all sin.'
[54] Philo. Spec. Leg. 2. 30.
[55] I Cor. 13. 7.
[56] cf. i Jn. 4. 18–19; Str. 7. 12 *ANCL* 12 p. 457.
[57] Str. 7. 12. *ANCL* 12 p. 457.
[58] Str. 6. 9. *ANCL* 12 pp. 344 seq.

that of *agapé*[59] is one of the Clement's most notable contributions to Christian philosophic theology.

In this way he described the moral life as the mimesis of God in Christ, which led to man's deification: 'Let us listen to the Logos and assume the impress of our Saviour's truly salvific life. Meditating on the heavenly mode of life in which we have been deified, let us anoint ourselves with the immortal and perennial bloom of joy.'[60] He laid stress on frugality and inner peace as the core of this process precisely because they were simplifying factors that assimilated the complex condition of man to the simple *apatheia* that is properly the character of God alone. For Clement this ascetic experience of simplification and renewed direction in one's Christian life was the central aspect of the experience of theosis in this life.[61] In response to the experience we begin to live the very life of God on earth—that is to live by justice and mercy.[62] The only motive left in the heart of the pure gnostic was 'to spend his life after the image and likeness of the Lord.'[63] When a gnostic had reached this state and was divinised by his contemplation of God he was no longer said to possess the knowledge of God, but to be a living knower of God.[64] At this juncture, asceticism, having fulfilled its purpose, gave way to a constant communion of prayer, anticipating even on earth the time when: 'having passed through all purification ... they are now pure in heart, close to the Lord, restored to everlasting contemplation and called by the name of gods.'[65]

Origen:[66] *The ascent to divine love*

Origen's thought on asceticism shows much affinity with that of Clement, especially when the latter was at his most eloquent on the subject of mystical union. There are no direct points of literary dependence, however. Origen had perhaps less of his predecessor's spirit of rational moderation but there emerges in his thought the

[59] Str. 4. 18 (after 1 Cor. 13) *ANCL* 12 pp. 190 seq.
[60] Paed. 1. 12. *ANCL* 4 pp. 181–3.
[61] cf. Str. 4. 22. *ANCL* 12 pp. 202–7; Str. 6. 9. *ANCL* 12 pp. 344–9.
[62] Str. 2. 19. *ANCL* 12 p. 57.
[63] Str. 4. 22. *ANCL* 12 p. 203.
[64] Str. 4. 6. *ANCL* 12 p. 157.
[65] Str. 7. 10. *ANCL* 12 p. 447.
[66] c. 185–253.

figure of a kind and sympathetic man. He was also more overtly coloured than Clement by Neo-Platonic influences, which showed themselves in his greater interest in describing the mystical union with God. Origen also, surprisingly, was more prepared than Clement to offer an asceticism without the qualification of constant allegorisation, as a salutary exercise for all Christians of whatever stage of growth.

We can remark from the outset that in Origen's system the body was not the cause of sin, but rather sin that was the cause of bodies.[67] It was in the realm of spirit that fragmentation and disorder came into our condition, and our present life in the body will therefore find its liberation only in consequence of a primary realignment of our spirits on the Logos. The whole of material creation was prepared by God precisely as a training ground for the restoration of our souls. As with Clement, then, the dominant note in Origen's ascesis was the ascent to spiritual wisdom through mastery of our disordered bodily desires, so that man's soul was enabled to assume hegemony over his life and accelerate its return to spiritual union with the Logos. For Origen this was the only true motive and unique reason for Christian asceticism.[68] The whole of this process of restoration was the universal Apokatastasis of the Logos in which he restored the divine image in his creation. It was this greater breadth of metaphysical vision[69] that Origen brought to his work that marked him off from Clement as having a clearer soteriological inspiration in his thought. The soteriological principle of the restoration of the image, so primary in the thought of Athanasius and the later Fathers, was first articulated fully in its ascetical implications by Origen.

He saw the power that temptation had to seduce man as rooted in the vagaries of his fallen state. Man was not a stable being, far less stable indeed than when in his state of psychic pre-existence (and even then fallen from grace). The soul was called back by the incarnation of the Logos to resume its hegemony. By this struggle it atoned for its earlier and more recent sin and was able to ascend

---

[67] cf. C. Blanc. 'L'attitude d'Origène à l'égard du corps et de la chair.' *Stud. Pat.* 17 (1982) p. 843.

[68] cf. Con. Cels. 5. 49. *ANCL* 23 (1872) p. 320. Also in Lev. 10. 2. For a general analysis see E.T. Bettencourt, *Doctrina Ascetica Origenis* (Rome 1945).

[69] From pre-existent fall to ultimate Apokatastasis.

with Christ once more in the spiritual orders. Ascesis was not just a way of manifesting repentance to the Logos, but a very reconstitution to ontological stability in the life of the Logos and his own order of being. In the *De Principiis* 2.2. Origen noted that man's imbalanced ontology sent him into a deteriorating spiral of sensual decline. It was the function of ascesis to put a brake on this decline, and then to reverse it. That reversal could be accelerated according to one's growing maturity and spiritual strength. As he said: 'We ought to know that the mortification of the works of flesh is achieved through patience; not suddenly, but little by little. For beginners they must let them die down, then when they begin to make more fervent progress and their spirits are filled to greater capacity, they not only let them die down but begin to root them out. Then, when they reach perfection there is no longer found in them any trace of sin, either in thought or word or deed.'[70] Such was his exegesis of the Pauline concept of the crucifixion of the ungodly passions.[71] The end of ascetical endeavour was reached when dominion over our passions was complete. He taught that this goal would be achieved by all those who strove for it by grace, and urged them to have enduring patience.[72] For only when this hegemony was achieved was the soul liberated into its original destiny. It was reawakened to its former psychic faculties and found the ultimate reason for its being in loving union with the Logos: 'After devoting themselves to God and preserving themselves free from all contagion of evil spirits, after being purified by lengthy abstinence and imbued with holy and religious training, holy and immaculate souls are thus enabled to participate in the divinity and earn the grace of prophecy and other divine gifts.'[73] In the Prologue to his *Commentary on Canticles* he expressed the thought several times: 'The soul is moved by heavenly love and longing when, having clearly beheld the beauty and fairness of the Logos it falls deeply in love with his loveliness and receives from the Word himself a certain barb and wound of love.'[74]

[70] In Romanos. 6. 14; *PG* 14. 1102B.
[71] *Ibid.* 6. 1.
[72] *Ibid.* 6. 9.
[73] De Princ. 33. 3. See also Prologue to Canticles, in *Ancient Christian Writers*, 26 (1957) p. 44.
[74] On the arrow of love cf. Lxx Is. 49. 2. F. Field, 'Origenis Hexaplorum quae supersunt.' 2 (Oxford 1875) p. 414, n 15.

Origen had a definite hierarchy of ascetical orders of achievement. First in line were the Apostles. Ranking after them came
martyrs,[75] virgins of both sexes, and then the ascetics. He commended the role of the ascetic in the Church far more than
Clement, and defined them as those who denied their bodies to
make a living sacrifice to their Lord.[76] This is why he gave great
prominence in his ascetical thought to the virtue of chastity. He
commended the practice of vows of celibacy[77] and in his *Hom. In
Jeremiam* he noted that: 'there are some who practise[78] virginity and
continence and others who practise monogamy simply because
they think that anyone who remarries is damned.'[79] He corrected
this as a false notion but there is no doubt where his sympathies lay,
for he went on to describe this as an example of a 'happy error'
leading people to do the right thing.[80] He himself taught that the
monogamous, the widows, and the celibates formed the Church of
Christ who were destined to be crowned in glory. Those who
married twice were not of the Church proper but of the class of
those who 'called upon the name of the Lord'. They would be
saved, but they would not be crowned by Christ.[81] This dominant
emphasis on chastity was a reflection of his great soteriological
principle that the soul should look to the love of its beloved
only—that is the Logos, the Bridegroom of all souls from pre-
existent times.

While Origen did not dismiss the physical aspect of fasting, then,
he did condemn the practice if it was meant as a lamentation for the
Passion of Christ. He regarded this as a Judaising error of Alexandrian women, and pointed out that they had forgotten that the
death of Christ was a victory that should rather be celebrated.[82] It
was a notable concern of his at several junctures to distance
Christian practices from those of the Synagogue—very much
before the eyes of the local Christians. He labelled Jewish
asceticism as 'superstition', and when mentioning the Christian

---

[75] cf. Exhortation to Martyrdom 1. 3.
[76] In Romanos 9. 1.
[77] In Numeros 24. 2.
[78] Askousi.
[79] In Jer. 20. 4.
[80] His exegesis on: 'You have deceived the Lord.'
[81] cf. H. Crouzel. *Virginité et Mariage selon Origène* (Paris 1963) pp. 152–60.
[82] In Jer. 2. 13. (*SCR*, 238 pp. 48–9).

practices of Lenten Fasts and Wednesday and Friday fasting, it is clear that the motive that was nearest his heart for this particular practice was its role in the preservation of chastity ...[83] a spiritualistic interpretation of the eunuch saying that, unlike Clement, he came to only later in life.

Conclusions

The eschatological springs that fed Jesus' ministry in a real way resisted systematisation. The vividness of his sense of the nearness of God preempted his observance of rituals of lament. We could conclude that we have no systematic doctrine of ascesis from Jesus himself, beyond the witness of his own life and his heroic endurance for the sake of his ministry—an endurance that was tested by a martyr's death. The immediacy of his apocalyptic experience and the manner in which early Christian tradition was formulated left no systematic doctrine either on prayer, fasting or alms—things that to the Jewish mentality were the basic core of an ascetical programme. The fact that we find specific instructions on all three things in the Gospel tradition before the eighties of the First century is a testimony to the desire of Jesus' early disciples to affirm religious practices that seemed necessary for a coherent ecclesiology in what was emerging as a historically enduring movement.

The Alexandrian Fathers, with their precise ascetical plans show more continuity with the insight of Jesus, it could be argued, than with the praxis of the early Jewish communities. The Alexandrians were both concerned to mark a radical division between the motives for Jewish fasting and Christian asceticism, and to do so on dogmatic grounds. Both the Jewish inspirations for fasting, that is a) the evocation of God's pity and b) the lament for the absence of God/ destruction of the Temple/ death of Christ – were dogmatically abandoned by Clement and Origen in favour of the doctrine of the Incarnation – the God who dwells in our midst, in our very heart, who is no longer absent, and who has decisively won the victory of our reconciliation. In licensing asceticism and being largely responsible for articulating the meaning of asceticism for generations of Christians to follow, they set it off on a wholly new course of spiritual ascent – an ascent aimed at Hesychia, or peaceful communion with God.

[83] In Matthaeum 15. 4.

Christian Asceticism and Alexandria

The Alexandrian synthesis is, of course, no longer apocalyptic in anything like the same way as Jesus. We may wonder what relation exists any longer between the two, over the chasm of a century and a half, a different intellectual idiom, and a different language. But the Alexandrian striving after communion with God by refusing to take present reality as the sole criterion of truth was, in a certain sense, an echo of the apocalyptic insight of Jesus. The patristic asceticism was a kathartic celebration of life, a sensitisation to higher psychic levels, and in its own way was faithful to the memory of one who came 'eating and drinking' to try and excite his contemporaries with the heady new wine of God's dawning reign of Justice. There is a continuity here that abides through all the discontinuities.

La Sainte Union College,
Southampton

THE DEATH OF ASCETICS: SICKNESS AND MONASTICISM IN THE EARLY BYZANTINE MIDDLE EAST

by PEREGRINE HORDEN

HOW should an ascetic die? Aaron the presbyter knew how. He had always led an exemplary life. Born in Armenia, probably during the first quarter of the sixth century, he entered a Monophysite Syrian monastery in early youth. He there distinguished himself for his humility, his unremitting labour in the monastery's vineyard and guest-house, and his abundant zeal for the ascetic life. Frequently he would stand up all night. Only in old age did he consent to the luxury of a rug-covered plank as his bed.

Old age brought new trials however. Aaron's health deteriorated – to the evident alarm of John of Ephesus. John was an admirer, close friend and colleague of some thirty years' standing; he naturally included a brief account of the presbyter's career in his *Lives of the Eastern Saints*.[1] 'Once,' John writes of Aaron, 'he fell under a serious disease of gangrene in his loins;'

> and he bore this affliction with great discretion, until his loin was eaten up and mutilated and had vanished down to its root, and his disease began to enter his inner organs. But seeing that he was afflicted by a harsh malady and was cruelly rent in private, we besought him to tell what his illness was. But he for his part, until his wound had worsened severely, held fast – constant in prayer and filling his mouth with praise and thanksgiving to God.[2]

To pray and to endure: that, we might suppose, was the only decent course for a monk of Aaron's ascetic calibre during what seemed likely to prove his final illness. Asceticism is martyrdom

---

[1] c38, ed and trans E.W. Brooks *PO* 18 pp. 641–5. Aaron died in 560: see p. 644. John wrote the *Lives* in the late 560s: see *PO* 17 p. VII.

[2] *PO* 18 pp. 643–4 (trans Harvey: see n7 below).

continued by other means, an enslavement of the flesh that liberates the spirit. Like fasting and celibacy, like perching on a column or squatting manacled in a cage, the ravages of disease are simply one more extremity that will assist the holy man's soul on its path towards the ascetic ideal.[3] Treatment of a physical ailment is unnecessary; indeed it is spiritually damaging. Aaron might have endorsed the unambiguous response John of Ephesus attributes to Thomas, another Armenian ascetic, who was urged to let poultices be applied to the worsening sores on his feet:

> Then, when these feet are anointed with drugs, and are rubbed by many persons and cleansed with great care, someone would perhaps come and say, 'They have enough, now let them pay for the outward show with which they have been magnified, lest they be requited for it in hell.'[4]

Yet Aaron was in no position to adopt such a rigorist stance; and the matter was eventually taken out of his hands. John's account of his illness continues thus:

> Finally, when he could no longer pass water he was forced and so persuaded to reveal and make known his disease. Then the whole of his loin was found eaten away and consumed, so that the physicians contrived to make a tube of lead and placed it for the passing of his water, while also applying bandages and drugs to him. And so the ulcer was healed. Furthermore, Aaron lived eighteen years after the crisis of this test, praising God, and having that lead tube in place for the necessity of passing water.[5]

This striking passage has usually been noted as evidence of the history of surgery and of general Byzantine attitudes to medicine.[6] Only now is it beginning to attract the serious attention it warrants.

---

[3] Cf. among a vast literature P. Nagel, *Die Motivierung der Askese in der alten Kirche und der Ursprung des Mönchtums*, *TU* 95 (1966); [Arthur] Vööbus [*History of Asceticism in the Syrian Orient* 2 vols to date, *CSCO sub* 14, 17 (1958, 1960)].

[4] c21, *PO* 17 p. 292.

[5] *PO* 18 p. 644 (trans Harvey).

[6] H.J. Magoulias, 'The Lives of the Saints as Sources of Data for the History of Byzantine Medicine in the Sixth and Seventh Centuries', *BZ* 57 (1964) pp. 127–50 at p. 143; Peregrine Horden, 'Saints and Doctors in the Early Byzantine Empire: the Case of Theodore of Sykeon', *SCH* 19 (1982) pp. 1–13 at p. 10.

The Death of Ascetics

Susan Ashbrook Harvey argues that John's *Life* of Aaron is a document of much greater – although more local – significance than medical historians have supposed.[7] She contends that it points to 'an expedient alliance' between physicians and ascetics characteristic of the Monophysites in a time of troubles marked by warfare, plague, natural disaster and Chalcedonian persecution.[8] Aaron's operation was thus a pragmatic departure from the ascetic norm – prompted by circumstance and justified by success.

It is from the perspective of Dr Harvey's paper, and of the evidence she presents in it, that I wish to look once more at Aaron's touching history. I suggest that its diagnostic potential is not limited to Monophysite saints in John of Ephesus; that it perhaps divulges more about the way the ascetic life could be led in the early Byzantine empire than Dr Harvey allows.

If that suggestion has any force however, it is clearly not because the passage in question accords even with what we find elsewhere in John's hagiography. Thomas the Armenian after all conforms to expectation in equating submission to medical care with vainglory: a respect for the flesh which would entirely frustrate the ascetic's spiritual ambition. Nor does the resolution of Aaron's suffering accord with what we usually find in hagiographical works from the same tradition as the *Lives of the Eastern Saints* but dealing with other places, periods and ascetic styles. These works, too, apparently confirm our general presuppositions.

Benjamin, an octogenarian monk of Nitria in the fourth century and an unfailing healer, obviously accepted no remedy for the dropsy which bloated him so repulsively. 'Pray,' he said according to Palladius, 'that the inner man may not contract dropsy. My

[7] Susan Ashbrook Harvey, 'Physicians and Ascetics in John of Ephesus: an Expedient Alliance', forthcoming. I am most grateful to Dr Harvey for allowing me to see and profit from this paper, originally read to the Symposium on Byzantine Medicine at Dumbarton Oaks in 1983, in advance of its publication in the proceedings (in *DOP*). I am also indebted throughout to [H.] Chadwick ['John Moschus and his Friend Sophronius the Sophist', *JTS* 24 (1974)] pp. 41–74. Professor Hall, Jonathan Katz, Professor Wallace-Hadrill and Judith Wilson have kindly advised me on particular points.

[8] See also S. Ashbrook, 'Asceticism in Adversity: an Early Byzantine Experience', *Byzantine and Modern Greek Studies* 6 (1980) pp. 1–11; [S. Ashbrook] Harvey, 'The Politicisation of the Byzantine Saint' [*The Byzantine Saint* ed Sergei Hackel, Studies Supplementary to Sobornost 5 (1981)] pp. 37–43, and *Asceticism and Society in the Sixth Century Byzantine East* (forthcoming).

body did not help me when in good health, nor has it caused me harm when sick.' He lived only another eight months in immobile agony but continued as a healer of others right up to the end.[9] Attributing Benjamin's words to another ascetic in his *Spiritual Meadow* John Moschus even has him pray that his illness last a good while.[10] This was to ensure his salvation, not to prolong his life. In a passage which bears some resemblance to John's *Life* of Aaron, Moschus also reports the attitude to sickness of Barnabas, an anchorite who pierced his foot on a thorn when going down to drink from the Jordan. Barnabas refused to consult a doctor. His foot became so gangrenous that he had to give up his hermit's life and move to a lavra. The more the outer man suffered, he told visitors, the more the inner one flourished.[11]

'For this is the great asceticism: to control oneself in illness and to sing hymns of thanksgiving to God.'[12] Aaron's kind saw illness as deeply salutary, an advantageous opportunity for renewed self-discipline. To be in continuous good health for three years gave rise to anxiety.[13] Cure should come, if at all, from God rather than from physicians. Theodore of Sykeon, for example, was cured of two illnesses first through the intercession of Cosmas and Damian and later with the help of the Virgin, who in a vision offered him tablets and left him with the time-honoured advice to keep taking them.[14]

Less miraculous cures were to be avoided by holy men. God discerns the state of an ascetic's soul whereas physicians do not. And that distinction is crucial: illness is salutary in its aetiology as well as in its effects. The body is an index of sin. An affliction of the loins such as Aaron's would thus have been taken as a symptom of lust. Even with castration becoming relatively infrequent among ascetics there remained disease to cool the promiscuous. In Palladius's account of Heron the lapsed ascetic loses his genitals through

---

[9] Palladius [*Historia Lausiaca* ed G.J.M. Bartelink (Verona 1974)] c12. Cf. c55.

[10] Moschus [*Pratum spirituale*, PG 87. 3 coll 2851–3112] c8.

[11] Moschus c10. Cf. *Apophthegmata Patrum* [alphabetical collection, PG 65 coll 72–440] Daniel 4, trans [Benedicta] Ward [SLG, *The Sayings of the Desert Fathers* (London and Oxford 1975)] p. 52.

[12] *Apophthegmata Patrum* Syncletica 8, trans Ward p. 232.

[13] Moschus, ed Th. Nissen, *BZ* 38 (1938) p. 358, c5.

[14] *Vita Theodori* [*Syceotae* ed and trans A-J. Festugière, *sub hag* 48, 2 vols (Brussels 1970)] cc39, 77.

a severe ulceration consequent upon high living and unbridled desire. He is restored to health as a eunuch.[15]

The collective insistence of these texts seems plain. The monk should be indifferent to all physical suffering – whether he is a virtuoso of mortification like the elder Simeon, or a less celebrated solitary like Zoilus the reader, who lived in a verminous cell, did his own cooking and laundry, and earned a little money by calligraphy.[16] Illness is to be interpreted: it is always of the utmost spiritual significance. To seek to avoid the death of the body may be to risk the death of the soul. My body kills me, I kill it[17] – such is general ascetic philosophy.

It is in this light that the oddity of Aaron's cure has to be regarded. John's account is striking for two reasons. First it contains no interpretation of disease. No moral failing on Aaron's part is held responsible for either the gangrene or the retention of urine. He is not said to have been possessed, which is the hagiographer's usual alternative to sin as an explanation of disease. And no diminution of his ascetic worth and exemplary standing is implied in the operation's aftermath. His body did not die; yet neither did his soul. The illness was a test – but one which Aaron can hardly be said to have failed or shirked. For no pain is more excruciating than that of acute urinary retention: gangrene of the loins (necrosis, as doctors would now describe it) is mild in comparison. Aaron stoutly endured the lesser pain; no one can be expected to tolerate the greater.

John's account is striking, secondly, in that no supernatural intercession is reported to have brought Aaron's suffering to a close. God did not miraculously relieve his pain or spare him further torture by taking his life. Physicians were summoned instead, and summoned as a matter of course. They must have arrived quickly: the pain of retention comes suddenly, giving no advance warning, and is not to be borne for more than a few hours. Yet John does not even mention the physicians' arrival on the scene, let alone justify it. He clearly knew whom he could depend

[15] Palladius c26. Cf. Moschus c14. On castration see *The Sentences of Sextus* ed Henry Chadwick (Cambridge 1959) pp. 109–12; Vööbus vol 1 pp. 257–8.

[16] *La Vie et les miracles de Saint Syméon Stylite l'ancien* ed M. Chaîne (Cairo 1948) p. 18 (the Coptic *Life*); Moschus c171.

[17] Palladius c2.2.

upon and did not expect his readers to find anything untoward in that dependence. Aaron's problem was solved with bandages, drugs and a leaden tube. No eulogy of the physicians is forthcoming even though they performed the operation so well that the gangrene did not return – as well it might before the age of Lister – and the catheter continued to function.

How do we explain this seeming departure from the norm of ascetic conduct? Dr Harvey rightly suggests that it is John's behaviour as much as Aaron's which needs explaining. The way Aaron suffered in secret until the last possible moment could have been written up approvingly by Moschus or Palladius. 'Constant in prayer and filling his mouth with praise and thanksgiving to God,' he obviously knew the spiritual benefits that accrue from bodily infirmity. It was John, we may infer, who at last made him reveal the origin of a pain to which no amount of self-control was equal.

Dr Harvey has also emphasized that John wrote his *Lives* to honour ascetics who were for the most part devoted to practical philanthropy among stricken Monophysite communities. They had no time for accidie or sexual desire; and theirs was a world in which there was no miraculous escape from the hardships at hand.[18] If a moral is to be found in John's story it is the importance of Aaron's continuing ministry.

The problem here is that Aaron is by no means among the greatest of the philanthropists whom John presents to us.[19] It is hard on the presbyter to suppose his virtue to be merely a lack of opportunity. And John would surely not have thought Aaron's philanthropy was worth the price of his soul if that had been in question. Moreover if John's response to the sickness of ascetics was pragmatic, as Dr Harvey believes, it is still not clear why pragmatism should in a medieval context prompt a trust in physicians, rather than in God, and a lack of concern with the spiritual meaning of illness. Nor is it clear why dire circumstances should have been conducive to pragmatism of this sort. The hardships which form the sombre background to the *Lives of the Eastern Saints* are not so very much worse than those we glimpse in the *Spiritual Meadow*, a Chalcedonian work in which charity is just

[18] Harvey, 'The Politicisation of the Byzantine Saint', p. 40.
[19] *PO* 17 cc3, 12, 15; 18 cc34, 35.

as much a sign of sanctity as it is with John and whose author does not apparently share John's attitude to illness.[20]

At this point John's Monophysitism might be brought into play. Dr Harvey proposes that John's belief in the unity of the human and the divine in Christ would have had particular implications for his view of how God was present and active in creation. We do not yet know much about the effects of a particular Christology on everyday concerns in this period. But the work that has been done, say on the Christology of Severus of Antioch or Philoxenus of Mabbug, is far from indicating that their thought was conducive to that 'demythologizing' of disease of which John seems to have been capable.[21] And nothing strictly comparable to it can be found in the writings of other Monophysites such as John Rufus.[22]

A different approach is perhaps called for: one that gives less weight to the local conditions in which John wrote. For there is enough evidence that the type of cure Aaron enjoyed, though rare in hagiographical terms, is not unique. In Moschus for instance, an ascetic is advised by doctors to eat meat and, despite the horror of the rigorists, is defended for acting rightly.[23] In Theodoret one ascetic suffering from severe colic apparently resorts to medicine first and prayer afterwards.[24] And it is Theodoret himself who persuades another ascetic to accept minor alleviation of his distress during his first illness and a purgative during his second – a purgative he drinks only after hearing an emotive plea (such as we do not find in John) that he should stay alive and thus prolong his ministry.[25] There are also a number of apophthegmata which show that a sick ascetic might well receive quasi-medical assistance from his brothers. As long as he did so in the right spirit his behaviour remained exemplary.[26]

The departure from the norm which John's narrative of Aaron represents is therefore not without parallel. How then – to return to

[20] Cf. Chadwick pp. 61–3, 72–4.
[21] Cf. Roberta C. Chesnut, *Three Monophysite Christologies* (Oxford 1976) pp. 47–50, 70–75; André de Halleux, *Philoxène de Mabbog* (Louvain 1963) pt 3.
[22] *Plerophories* ed and trans F. Nau, *PO* 8 pp. 50–1, 65–7.
[23] Moschus c65.
[24] Theodoret (of Cyrus, *Historia Religiosa* ed and trans Pierre Canivet and Alice Leroy-Molinghen, 2 vols *SCR* 234, 257 (1977, 1979)] c22. 4.
[25] Theodoret c21. 8, 11. Cf. c2. 18.
[26] *Apophthegmata patrum* Aio, Arsenius 36, Theodore of Pherme 26, trans Ward pp. 16–17, 37, 77–8.

the principal question – do we set about explaining it? It is well to be precise about what requires an explanation here and what does not. The setting of Aaron's operation is Constantinople and we should not be surprised to find that highly skilled surgeons were available.[27] We should not be surprised, either, to find churchmen turning to doctors willingly and as a matter of course. John bishop of Hephaistu, for example, needed an excuse to go to the city to see the empress. What could have been more natural than for him to plead an appointment with his doctors when seeking permission from the patriarch? John of Ephesus at least reports the ruse without betraying disapproval or amazement.[28] We have been misled by the hagiographical topos, most frequent in the miracle books of urban shrines, by which doctors are condemned for their exorbitant fees and their patients are castigated for trusting them too much. The Church was far from rejecting their services. Holy men like Theodore happily passed on some of their clients to local doctors. Other saints, such as Sampson, had trained as physicians themselves and put their training to good use in the numerous ecclesiastically-controlled hospitals.[29]

This essentially favourable attitude to medicine was echoed in monasteries as well, and explanation can begin with them. By the standards of those singled out in John, Theodoret, Moschus or Palladius most Byzantine monks were not of course ascetic. Their resort to secular as distinct from spiritual medicine, whether in their monastery's own infirmary or privately with healers roundabout, was not thought incompatible with the minimal asceticism

---

[27] The technique of installing a catheter had been described in pseudo-Galen, *Introductio seu medicus, Claudii Galeni Opera Omnia* ed C.G. Kühn (Leipzig 1821–33, repr Hildesheim 1965) c19, vol 14 pp. 787–8. On medical schools see now N.G. Wilson *Scholars of Byzantium* (London 1983). Aaron died in 560 (cf. n1 above). John says that he lived for eighteen years after his operation, and eighteen sounds more precise than John's usual round figure of thirty (cf. *PO* 17 p. 291; 18 p. 626). The operation can therefore be dated to the early 540s, when we know John to have been generally in Constantinople. See *PO* 18 p. 643 and [Ernest] Honigmann, *Evêques et évêchés Monophysites d'Asie antérieure au VIe siècle, CSCO sub* 2 (1951) p. 208.

[28] *PO* 18 p. 536. On John of Hephaistu see Honigmann p. 165. Cf. Theodoret *Letters* 114, 115, ed Yvan Azéma *SCR* 40, 98, 111 (1964, 1965, 1982).

[29] *Vita Theodori* cc145–6. Mt Athos MS Philotheou 8 fol 198ᵛ.

that monastic seclusion implies.[30] A vast range of ascetic regimes was practised. Monks seeking to achieve the highest standard of asceticism would, as for example enjoined in one of the Macarian homilies,[31] have had nothing to do with doctors. The rest set their sights a little lower; and these were the ones unlikely to receive detailed hagiographical notice, especially in Syria where asceticism could be witnessed at its most horrifyingly inventive.

Aaron was conceivably one of the relatively few lesser lights in the ascetic firmament whose boundless courage, yet also whose eventual willingness to submit to treatment when in unbearable pain, has been recorded for posterity's edification. A pointer to the existence of others can perhaps be derived from the frequent instances in the hagiography where a bishop – John of Ephesus or Theodoret for example – is reported to have urged an ascetic to moderate his austerity. That the monk did so hardly proved that he was a poor ascetic or no ascetic at all: it rather showed that he was a sensible one. For what transpired between bishop and monk was hardly a clash between rival conceptions of monasticism – moderate Greek and rigorist Syrian for example.[32] It was a modest contribution to a less partisan debate about the nature and purpose of the ascetic life which cannot so easily be related to cultural geography. There were many reasons why ascetics should make minor adjustments to their self-imposed regime: to avoid a hubris bred of competition, to fulfil a pastoral obligation, or simply to survive.

That of Syrian fanatics apart, the ascetic way of life can be characterized under three headings. Each of them has some bearing

---

[30] Cf. *Barsanuphe et Jean de Gaza: Correspondance* trans Lucien Regnault *et al* (Solesmes 1972) cc225, 327, 508; Theodore of Petra, *Vita Theodosii Coenobiarchae* trans A-J. Festugière, *Les moines d'Orient* vol 3.3 (Paris 1963) c16; Palladius c7; *Syriac and Arabic Documents Regarding Legislation Relative to Syrian Asceticism* ed Vööbus (Stockholm 1960) pp. 16, 30, 175; Basil, *Regulae Fusius Tractatae* c55, *PG* 31 coll 1043–52; Diadochus of Photice, *Capita Gnostica* ed Edouard des Places *SCR* 5 (1955) c53.

[31] *Die 50 Geistlichen Homilien des Makarios* ed Hermann Dörries, Erich Klostermann and Matthias Kroeger, *Patristische Texte und Studien* 4 (Berlin 1964) c48. 3–6. Cf. Makarios/Symeon, *Reden und Briefe: Die Sammlung I des Vaticanus Graecus 694 (B)* ed H. Berthold, *GCS* (Berlin 1973) Logos 55. 3, vol 2 p. 168. I owe these references, and the final one in n30 above, to the kindness of Dr Chadwick. For a general, comparativist perspective see Vööbus vol 2 cc8, 9.

[32] *Pace* Vööbus. Cf. *Lives of the Eastern Saints*, *PO* 17 p. 181, 18 p. 627; Theodoret c21. 6.

on how we are to understand John's account of Aaron. First, if the ascetic should not strive officiously to keep alive then neither should he kill himself.[33] The evidence of John's *Lives*, if no other, shows that his attitude was not confined to 'Greek' monasticism. It had its 'Syrian' counterpart. Secondly the holy man was often the best judge of the state of his own soul and his physical condition. He generally foresaw his death. He knew which illness he might seek to ameliorate, which one should be endured because it was a sign of moral failure or a test of nerve, and which should be faced in the confidence that his work was done and his end was approaching.[34] Thirdly whatever the hagiographers say – and it could have suited their purpose to magnify the seriousness of holy men's ailments – the pathology of asceticism may not all the time have been as grave as it appeared. Endurance of sickness was not necessarily a supreme test.

It is time we ceased marvelling aimlessly at the physical stamina and frequent longevity of the great Byzantine ascetics. A more worthwhile perspective on their seeming immunity to degradation and disease is to be had from a comparison with recent Hindu ascetics whose mortifications frequently exceeded theirs and whose pathology can be studied with some closeness. I do not suggest that being a stylite was merely a way of working off surplus flab. But I do urge that we scrutinize the anthropology of asceticism – from which we may well learn that once an ascetic has absolutely conquered his body the illnesses he contracts are often comparatively minor and readily endured.[35]

Aaron's was of course no minor complaint: the generalization attempts to explain the habitual response rather than the particular challenge. Nor does it take us far enough. A favourable monastic and episcopal attitude to physicians; a flexibility of ascetic practice for the sake of survival; an ascetic's capacity to distinguish among illnesses and modulate his behaviour even more finely; the possibility that consummate ascetic technique enhanced rather than diminished health – these still do not necessarily make doctors welcome.

---

[33] Palladius c19; Vööbus vol 2 p. 293, with vol 1 pp. 154–5 on ascetic suicide.

[34] Cf. Theodoret c2. 18; *Historia Monachorum in Aegypto* ed A-J. Festugière *sub hag* 34 (Brussels 1961) bk 10 c17; *Vita Theodori* c39.

[35] John Campbell Oman, *The Mystics, Ascetics and Saints of India* (London 1903) remains a valuable ethnography. Joachim Friedrich Sprockhoff, *Saṃnyāsa: Quellenstudien zur Askese im Hinduismus* vol 1 (Wiesbaden 1976) is more a literary study.

There remain three ways in which their presence could have become spiritually palatable. The first was through the ascetic's achievement of a requisite perfection in accepting their attentions. If an ascetic can unsex himself to the extent that he remains indifferent to naked women (as some obviously could) he can learn the equivalent attitude to physicians.[36] Secondly, and alternatively, perhaps disease is not always 'psychosomatic' – the consequence of a particular sin, or of possession, or as a divine punishment or test. Even for a holy man it can have a more straightforwardly physical aetiology. There is evidence of such a view in Byzantine imperial legislation implicitly attributing ill health to poverty, in the literature of *Erotapokriseis* (or questions and answers) and in some of the hagiography.[37] John of Ephesus makes clear what is elsewhere presented obscurely. He saw, and perhaps Aaron was persuaded to see, that on this occasion gangrenous loins and retention of urine betokened nothing spiritual and that a remedy was close at hand.

Thirdly however, God's presence at the operation and His guidance of the scalpel is quietly implied in John's apparently factual description. To trust in physicians, and to hold that a naturalistic explanation can be given of some, but only some, diseases, is not to despair of supernatural aid. Byzantine surgery should be rated highly, but not too highly. John did not make that mistake. An operation on an ascetic was for him no ordinary operation. Compare his account of Aaron's cure with his description in the *Ecclesiastical History* of the moribund Justin II preparing for the removal of stones lodged in his bladder:

> When ... physicians came to cut them away, they requested him, after the usual cowardly manner of physicians, to take the lancet in his hand and give it to them; and he ... said, 'Fear not:

[36] Moschus cc3, 36, 194.

[37] Cf. pseudo-Justin (? Theodoret) *Quaestiones ad orthodoxos* c55, PG 6 col 1297; pseudo-Anastasius Sinaita, *Quaestiones* c94, PG 89 col 732. On *Erotapokriseis* see Gilbert Dagron, 'Le saint, le savant, l'astrologue: étude de thèmes hagiographiques à travers quelques recueils de "Questions et réponses" des Ve–VIIe siècles', *Hagiographie, Cultures et Sociétés IVe–XIIe siècles* (Paris 1981) pp. 143–55; *Theognosti Thesaurus* ed Joseph A. Munitiz CC Series Graeca 5 (1979) pp. CIX–CXXIII. See also Evelyne Patlagean, *Pauvreté économique et pauvreté sociale à Byzance 4e–7e siècles* (Paris 1977) pp. 101, 104–5 for the legislation and the hagiography. Passages such as the Greek *Vita prima* of Pachomius, ed F. Halkin *sub hag* 19 (1932) c52 might also be considered in this context.

even if I die, no harm shall come to you.' A deep incision was then made in both his groins, and the whole operation so barbarously performed that he was put to extreme torture.[38]

Aaron was spared such agony. His physicians were presumably not Chalcedonian bunglers. Yet that he survived the ordeal and lived another eighteen years can indeed, in modern eyes, be accounted a miracle.

All Souls College
Oxford

[38] Pt 3 bk 3 c6, ed E. W. Brooks *CSCO* 105–6 (1935–6) trans P. Payne Smith (Oxford 1860) p. 177.

CELTIC ASCETICISM AND CAROLINGIAN AUTHORITY IN EARLY MEDIEVAL BRITTANY

by JULIA M. H. SMITH

IN the earlier Middle Ages, Brittany enjoyed a mixed reputation as a region in which to lead a life of ascetic discipline and dedication to God. The (eleventh-century?) Life of Mewan describes Samson and his disciples leaving Britain for a life of spiritual exile. They headed for Brittany because, according to the hagiographer, the region was not only a 'desert' where life would be harsher than elsewhere, but also because the ferocity of its inhabitants made it crueller.[1] Others were not so sure whether this was an advantage. Abelard's tribulations as abbot of Saint-Gildas-de-Rhuys are well known: though himself originating from *Bretagne gallo*, he complained that the Bretons of *Bretagne bretonnante* were a barbarian, lawless race, and that the monks of Saint-Gildas were dissolute and uncontrollable.[2] Abelard's comments echo a long tradition of French, or Frankish, castigation of the Bretons, stretching back at least to the ninth century.[3] This criticism often expresses more than hostility to a *gens* whose language made them incomprehensible and hence ridiculous: amongst the tensions it reflects are problems of Christian discipline and ecclesiastical authority which the Frankish church was unable fully to resolve.[4] In exploring behind the Bretons' bad reputation, it is worthwhile investigating both the ascetic practices of early medieval Brittany and the reactions to those practices of the Frankish church. In so doing, I hope to elucidate my juxtaposition of 'Celtic asceticism'

[1] *Vita S. Mevenni*, ed B. Plaine, *An Bol* 3 (1884) cap iii p. 144.
[2] *Historia Calamitatum*, ed J. Monfrin (4 ed Paris 1978) pp. 98–9.
[3] For example, *Ermold le Noir, Poème sur Louis le Pieux et Epîtres au Roi Pepin*, ed E. Faral (Paris 1932) lines 1296–9 pp. 100–2; *Raoul Glaber, Les Cinq Livres de ses Histoires (900–1044)*, ed M. Prou (Paris, 1886) II.3 p. 30; *Guillaume de Poitiers, Histoire de Guillaume le Conquérant*, ed R. Foréville (Paris 1952) I.44 pp. 108–10.
[4] These problems are discussed in the context of the secular church hierarchy in J.M.H. Smith, 'The "Archbishopric" of Dol and the ecclesiastical politics of ninth-century Brittany', *SCH* 18 (1982) pp. 59–70.

and 'Carolingian authority' by showing how Breton ascetic traditions were modified under the impact of Carolingian political
circumstances.

Migrations from Britain to Armorica in the late- and post-
Roman period resulted in the establishment within Gaul of Breton-
speaking communities, with their own distinctive forms of social
and political organisation.[5] Their religious practices also set them
apart from the Gallo-Frankish church, and in this ascetic customs
were no exception. Some time between 509 and 521 three Gallic
bishops, Licinius of Tours, Melanius of Rennes and Eustochius of
Angers, wrote a letter to two Breton priests, expressing concern
that they were indulging in heretical behaviour of a kind never
before encountered in Gaul. The Bretons, Lovocat and Catihern,
were accused of travelling around from hut to hut taking a portable
altar and saying mass wherever they went and of being assisted in
this by *conhospitae*, women who helped serve at the altar and who
shared their lodgings, but were not necessarily their close blood
relations.[6] Syneisactism, the custom of ascetic men and women
living chastely together, was widespread in early Christian circles
and was perpetuated in the early Irish and British churches. In
Ireland this was of practical value in providing assistance to
evangelising clergy and support for women converts. It might also
be a form of ascetic rigour, whereby the Irish saint submitted
himself to temptation by sharing his bed with one or even two
virgines subintroductae in order to make his struggle against the flesh
all the greater, and all the more forcibly to demonstrate his
chastity.[7] This form of ascetic association is but one, striking,
example of the considerable number of similarities between the
monasticism of Celtic regions and the early Christian east; the letter

---

[5] For recent surveys, see L. Fleuriot, *Les Origines de la Bretagne* (Paris 1980); W.
Davies, 'Priests and rural communities in east Brittany in the ninth century',
Etudes Celtiques 20 (1983) pp. 177–97; M. Planiol, *Histoire des Institutions de la
Bretagne* (5 vols Mayenne 1981–4 (but written in the 1890s)) vols 1, 2.

[6] Printed by L. Duchesne, 'Lovocat et Catihern', *Revue de Bretagne et de Vendée* 57
(1885) pp. 5–21; also by P. Labriolle, *Les Sources de l'Histoire du Montanisme*
(Fribourg/Paris 1913) pp. 227–30.

[7] H. Leclercq, 'Mariage spirituel', *DACL* 10 cols 1881–8; R.E. Reynolds, '*Virgines
subintroductae* in Celtic Christianity', *HTR* 61 (1968) pp. 547–66, with references
to earlier discussions. Reynold's study of Celtic syneisactism extends to Robert of
Arbrissel, but Robert is not so much characteristically 'Celtic' as characteristic of

to Lovocat and Catihern indicates that such features were present in the early Breton as well as in the Irish church.

But as for Licinius, Melanius and Eustochius, their letter translated these unfamiliar ascetic pursuits into a disciplinary problem. They threatened Lovocat and Catihern with canonical sanctions, and regarded their behaviour as a threat to the unity of the church. This reaction was similar to that of those Gallic bishops who had to deal with Wulfilaic, an aspiring stylite near Trier. Gregory of Tours reported their firm instructions to him to get down off his column.[8] Gallo-Frankish bishops were not generally inclined to accept such ascetic eccentricities as marks of true holiness.[9] They preferred to impose their authority to constrain ascetic rigours within what were considered appropriate limits.

Knowing where to draw the line might be difficult, as another incident which sheds light on early Breton ascetic traditions will show. A Breton pilgrim named Winnoc stopped off in Tours during Gregory's episcopate. Impressed by his great abstinence and spirituality, Gregory ordained him priest and prevailed upon him to remain in Tours. Winnoc's ascetic discipline included the gesture of raising a cup of wine and instead of drinking, merely touching the cup with his lips. This is another example of deliberate exposure to temptation as a form of heightened asceticism. But in this case, Gregory had misjudged his man, for Winnoc succumbed to drink and, having run amok whilst inebriated, had to be chained away in a cell.[10]

The case history of Lovocat and Catihern together with that of Winnoc provide the only contemporary evidence for the ascetic traditions of the early Breton church. But they are both examples

---

his age, when experiments with syneisactism were again common. See Grundmann, p. 36 and n 46; G. Constable, 'Aelred of Rievaulx and the nun of Watton: an episode in the early history of the Gilbertine order', *Medieval Women*, ed D. Baker *SCH Subsidia* 1 (1978) pp. 205–26 at pp. 219–20. Sharing a bed as an explicit test of chastity recurs in some heretical circles: Salimbene thus describes Segarelli, *Chronica* a 1248, *MGH SS* 32 p. 257. I am grateful to Peter Biller for this reference.

[8] *Lib[ri] Hist[oriarum Decem]* VIII.15, *MGH SRM* 1 (2 ed) pp. 381–3.

[9] See the comments on Wulfilaic of P. Brown, 'Eastern and western Christendom in late antiquity: a parting of the ways', *SCH* 13 (1976) pp. 1–24 at p. 16, and of [P. Magdalino, 'The] Byzantine holy man [in the twelfth century]', *The Byzantine Saint*, ed S. Hackel (London 1981) pp. 51–66 at p. 60.

[10] *Lib Hist* V.21, VIII.34, *MGH SRM* 1 (2 ed) pp. 229, 403–4.

seen through the eyes of disapproving Gallic bishops. In order to view early Breton religious communities in a Breton perspective, it is necessary to turn to hagiographical traditions. Yet here the perspective is generally far from contemporary. The only Life which may well be earlier than the late ninth century is the *vita prima* of Samson of Dol. Its date of composition is still hotly disputed, though it is plausible, perhaps indeed probable, that it is of seventh-century origin.[11] Whatever its date, this Life is much more informative about the early stages of Samson's career in the British Isles than it is about his activities after migration to Brittany and the foundation there of the monastery of Dol. It offers a lively description of Samson's progression up the *scala spiritualis* from his early days in the relatively lenient atmosphere of Illtud's monastery at Llantwit to the solitude of a cave on the banks of the Severn from which he emerged to be consecrated bishop, together with an account of his monastic foundations and spiritual observances.[12] It has been widely plundered as a source for early Welsh history:[13] but by the same token it cannot help directly in understanding Breton circumstances. Yet it is important in that it held up to the community at Dol a picture of ascetic spirituality centring around prayer, trance-like meditation on scripture, fasting and manual labour, which was confirmed by Samson's many miracles.[14] It presents a tradition in which there was no hard and fast distinction between eremitic and coenobitic forms of monastic life, and which

---

[11] The most recent survey of the dispute is [J-C.] Poulin, 'Hagiographie et politique. [La première vie de saint Samson de Dol]', *Francia* 5 (1977) pp. 1–26.

[12] *De die in diem quasi per scalam spiritualem ascendens altius atque altius.* [R. Fawtier, *La Vie de Saint*] *Samson.* [*Essai de Critique Hagiographique, BEHE* 197] (Paris 1912) I.13 p. 113. Samson's career in Britain and Ireland is the subject of I.1–51; events in Brittany and Francia are relegated to I.52–61.

[13] For example, most recently by W. Davies, *Wales in the Early Middle Ages* (Leicester 1982) pp. 151–3.

[14] Well summarised at I.21: 'admirabilem atque eremiticam immo et caelestem vitam infatigabiliter ducens, non diebus, non noctibus, ab orationibus et a colloquiis Dei cessabat, totum diem operibus manuum et orationibus ducens, totam vero noctem in mysticis Sanctarum Scriptuarum intelligentiis, lucernam sui mansioni portans ut ad legendum intentus, aut aliquid scriberet, aut de spiritualibus theoricis meditaretur.' (*Samson*, p. 121). The parallels between the portrayal of Samson in the *vita prima* and Sulpicius Severus's portrait of Martin have been stressed by Poulin, 'Hagiographie et politique', but he goes too far in seeing Samson as 'un "alter ego" de Martin'.

left much room for personal judgement alongside the discipline of a monastic rule.[15]

In addition to the *vita prima* of Samson, there is a fairly substantial corpus of Lives written in the later ninth century. These concern saints who were all monks and sometimes also bishops, and who commonly moved freely, as Samson did, between Wales, Ireland, Cornwall, Brittany and beyond. Leaving aside for one moment the contemporary evidence from Redon, all the remaining hagiographical traditions relate to saints purported to have lived in about the sixth century. They are, therefore, direct evidence only for what ninth-century communities knew, or liked to hear, about their founding fathers.[16] The Lives provide a literary image of ascetic traditions, refracted by the usual conventions of hagiographical writing. An example is the Life of Paul Aurelian, traditionally accepted as the founder of the bishopric which bears his name, Saint-Pol-de-Léon. This was written in 884 by Wrmonoc, for use in the cathedral on the saint's feast day.[17] In literary terms it is one of the most polished and sophisticated Breton Latin texts of Carolingian date, but in other respects it is a tissue of traditions about Paul, many of which are common to other Breton and Welsh *vitae*.[18] It is concerned with sanctity before asceticism, and thus we are shown much more clearly the miracles and rigours

---

[15] Characterised in the account of Samson's rule of the island monastery founded by Piro, where Samson was appointed abbot in succession to Piro, who had died by falling down a well whilst drunk: 'Obediente illo non voluntarie fratres suos secundum rectam regulam suaviter instituebat, atque hoc loco, non plus anno et dimidio primatum tenens, heremitam se plus quam caenobitam monachum fratres iudicabant' (*Samson*, I.36 p. 133).

[16] For general discussions of these works, see P. Riché, 'Les Hagiographes bretons et la renaissance carolingienne', *Bulletin du Comité des Travaux Historiques et Scientifiques* (1966) pp. 651–9; F. Kerlouégan, 'Les vies des saints bretons les plus anciennes dans leurs rapports avec les îles britanniques', *Insular Latin Studies* ed M. Herren (Toronto 1981) pp. 195–213. The many eleventh-century or later Lives of Breton saints are not considered here; for summary discussions, see F. Duine, *Mémento des Sources Hagiographiques de l'Histoire de Bretagne* (Rennes 1918).

[17] [C. Cuissard,] 'Vie de Saint Paul [de Léon en Bretagne]', *Revue Celtique* 5 (1881–2) pp. 413–60 at pp. 417–8. Wrmonoc claims to be reworking an earlier account. Some credence is given to this by his use of spellings of Breton names that were archaic by the late ninth century. K.H. Jackson, *Language and History in Early Britain* (Edinburgh 1953) pp. 41–2.

[18] The dismissive remark of L. Bieler is apt: 'We notice the almost complete absence not only of genuine historical information, but even of original legendary tradition'. 'The Celtic hagiographer', *TU* 80 (1962) pp. 243–65 at p. 258.

of mortification which are the external and observable facets of Paul's life, and are left largely to assume a life of inner spirituality. To approach such a work in search of 'historical' information is unrewarding, but as an image of the saint compounded of various hagiographical stereotypes, it has its uses. Thus Wrmonoc asserts the priority of contemplative to active life in phrases plagiarised from Cassian.[19] He draws on the traditional vocabulary of retreat from the distractions of worldly society towards solitude, but fails to create from this any picture of spiritual advance.[20] Each of Paul's moves to a *locus secretior* is not in practice accompanied by any real withdrawal further from human society, or by increased ascetic discipline, and the theme has thus become a handy topos.[21] The miracles which Wrmonoc ascribes to Paul are the stock in trade of any Breton hagiographer, albeit on a large and dramatic scale.[22] In conventional fashion, Paul is depicted as reluctant to receive episcopal consecration, and it is only after this has been achieved by sleight of hand that he turns to teaching and evangelising.[23] Although Paul started his ascetic life in Wales in Illtud's monastery, and ended it in the monastery he founded on the island of Batz, near Saint-Pol, most of the time the lifestyle which Paul and his companions pursue is one which blurs any distinction between solitary and coenobitic monasticism: his followers are free to seek out their own secluded dwelling sites, yet declare that they obey Paul in everything.[24] We are left with a picture of what Poulin has described as '*sainteté imaginée*', which reveals how the community of Saint-Pol remembered its founder, but with little idea of how far this may have corresponded with Paul's '*sainteté vécue*'.[25]

---

[19] 'Vie de Saint Paul', cap vi p. 249; see F. Kerlouégan, 'Les Citations d'auteurs latins chrétiens dans les vies des saints bretons carolingiennes', *Etudes Celtiques* 19 (1982) pp. 215–57 at pp. 237–8.

[20] A useful study of this vocabulary is J. Leclercq, '*Eremus* et *eremita*: pour l'histoire du vocabulaire de la vie solitaire', *COCR* 25 (1963) pp. 8–30.

[21] 'Vie de Saint Paul', caps vii, xi, xviii pp. 430–1, 436–7, 449.

[22] For example, 'Vie de Saint Paul', caps xiv (three springs with healing properties gush out), xv (dealings with wild animals include stroking a wild sow suckling her litter), xviii (copes with a serpent at least one hundred and twenty feet long) pp. 440–2, 442–3, 446–9.

[23] 'Vie de Saint Paul', cap xix pp. 449–52.

[24] 'Vie de Saint Paul', cap xiii pp. 439–40.

[25] The expressions are derived from J-C. Poulin, *L'Idéal de Sainteté dans l'Aquitaine Carolingienne d'après les Sources Hagiographiques* (Quebec 1975); see the important

Early Breton Asceticism

Within the medley of stereotyped miracles and mortifications that makes up the Life of Paul Aurelian and other ninth-century Lives, certain themes suggest the influence of Irish ascetic and hagiographical traditions. Paul, for example, left his native land to set out abroad, tossed by the tide wherever God might take him.[26] The Life of Malo includes what is probably the earliest extant version of the *Navigatio Brendani*.[27] Winwaloe had a vision of Patrick, whose example he hoped to follow, and he also recited the entire psalter daily in the fashion specified in several Irish monastic rules associated with the culdees, that is, fifty psalms at a time, whilst standing in cold water or with arms outstretched in a cruciform or whilst genuflecting.[28] Inasmuch as these ninth-century Breton hagiographers see their heroes within a wider ascetic tradition, it is to the authority of the desert fathers to which they look. Wrmonoc refers to the example of the *eximius pater* Antony, as the first teacher of a life of solitary rigour,[29] whilst Wrdisten in his Life of Winwaloe likens the life of manual labour of the monks of Landévennec to that of the Egyptian monks.[30]

The image of ascetic life to be derived from the late ninth-century accounts of early Breton saints is, then, one which looks beyond Welsh and Breton horizons to Irish and eastern traditions for further inspiration. Above all, it is an image characterised by diversity and flexibility of ascetic regimes. But what relation, if any, did this picture bear to actual ninth-century practices? By

---

review article of W. Pohlkamp, 'Hagiographische Texte als Zeugnisse einer "histoire de la sainteté"', *Frühmittelalterliche Studien* 11 (1977) pp. 229–40, and also J. Leclercq 'Le Monachisme du haut moyen âge (VIIIe–Xe siècles)', *Théologie de la Vie Monastique* Collection Théologie 49 (Paris 1961) pp. 437–445.

[26] 'Vie de Saint Paul', cap ix pp. 432–3. On Irish traditions of spiritual pilgrimage, A. Angenendt, 'Die irische Peregrinatio und ihre Auswirkungen auf dem Kontinent vor dem Jahre 800', *Die Iren und Europa im früheren Mittelalter*, ed H. Löwe (Stuttgart 1982) I pp. 52–79.

[27] It figures in both ninth-century versions of the Life, the earlier anonymous version and its revision by Bili. J.F. Kenney, *The Sources for the Early History of Ireland vol 1: Ecclesiastical* (New York 1929) pp. 406–12, 417–8.

[28] *Vita [S.] Winwaloei [primi abbatis Landevenecensis*, ed C. de Smedt,] *An Bol* 7 (1888), I.19, II.9, 14 pp. 205–6, 225, 227. On the recitation of the psalter in culdee rules, L. Gougaud, *Christianity in the Celtic Lands* (London 1932) pp. 90–50; K.W. Hughes, *The Church in Early Irish Society* (London 1966) pp. 178, 180, 186–7.

[29] 'Vie de Saint Paul', cap vi p. 429.

[30] *Vita Winwaloei*, II.12 p. 226.

resuming a Frankish perspective, a discrepancy between the perception and the reality becomes evident.

The long-standing Frankish mistrust of individual forms of ascetic zeal reached its culmination in the monastic regulations of Louis the Pious. Inspired by the reforming endeavours of Benedict of Aniane, Louis's legislation of 816–817 regulated the monastic life of all communities within his empire, and made the Benedictine Rule the sole permissible form of monastic observance.[31] In supporting a monastic rule that laid especial stress upon obedience, Louis and his circle of close advisers turned monastic harmony and uniformity into a means towards fulfilling their ideal of imperial unity.[32] By sending out *missi* and issuing diplomas to individual communities, the emperor specified in detail the legal status and religious observances of monasteries throughout the Frankish lands. Louis's legislation did not intend to allow individual holiness to challenge imperial authority.[33]

As part of Louis's empire, Brittany was not exempt, and diplomas to regulate Breton communities and impose Benedictine uniformity on them were issued.[34] The impact of this legislation is best demonstrated in the Life of Winwaloe written between 857 and 884 by Wrdisten, abbot of the monastery founded by Winwaloe at Landévennec. Although the work is primarily concerned with the life and miracles of the saint, two passages reveal clearly that the monks of Landévennec were deeply affected by Louis's reforms. First, there is a long speech addressed to the young saint as he leaves

---

[31] [Ed J. Semmler,] C[orpus] C[onsuetudinum] M[onasticarum vol] 1 [ed K. Hallinger] (Siegburg 1963) pp. 451–81. On the significance of this legislation, J. Semmler, 'Die Beschlüsse des Aachener Konzils im Jahre 816', ZKG 74 (1963) pp. 15–82; 'Reichsidee und kirchliche Gesetzgebung', ZKG 71 (1960) pp. 37–65; P. Schmitz, 'L'Influence de Saint Benoît d'Aniane sur l'ordre de Saint Benoît', SSSpoleto 4 (1957) pp. 401–15.

[32] Carolingian commentaries on the Benedictine Rule lay great stress on obedience: M.A. Schroll, Benedictine Monasticism as reflected in the Warnefrid-Hildemar Commentaries on the Rule (New York 1941) p. 182. See also T.F.X. Noble, 'The monastic ideal as a model for empire: the case of Louis the Pious', RB 86 (1976) pp. 235–250.

[33] Compare Magdalino's comments on the reign of Manuel Komnenos 'Byzantine holy man'.

[34] I examined Louis's Breton diplomas in more detail in 'Breton monasteries and the reforms of Louis the Pious', a paper presented to the Seventh International Congress of Celtic Studies, Oxford 1983, forthcoming.

his teacher Budoc, to set out to found his own monastery. Budoc cautions Winwaloe against accepting innovations in monastic custom not firmly rooted in scripture or the fathers, and against listening to the false advice of wandering, scrounging hypocrites.[35] Its strongly worded tone suggests that the question of whence a monastery derived its customs was one of importance at Landévennec. In a later passage, Wrdisten inserted into his description of the ascetic regime allegedly instituted by Winwaloe the full text of a diploma of Louis the Pious of 818.[36] This ordered the monks to abandon their traditional, Irish tonsure and *conversatio*, and for the sake of uniformity and unity with the *universalis ecclesia* to adopt the Rule of Saint Benedict. In likening the monastery's observances up until 818 to the practices of the Egyptian monks, Wrdisten commented that these rigorous traditions were gladly abandoned by some of the weaker monks, who had found the scant clothing ration allowed to them sadly inadequate; and indeed, the provisions of the capitulary of Aachen of 816 are considerably more generous in this respect.[37] The impact of Carolingian reform upon Landévennec was, then, a relaxation of ascetic discipline; but the implication of Budoc's speech is that it also affected the link between the monks and the memory of Winwaloe. After 818, the community no longer derived its way of life and hence its sense of corporate identity from ascetic traditions associated with its founder, but simply from an imperial fiat. Carolingian authority had replaced reverence for Winwaloe as a source of monastic regulation.

Some of the best evidence for the way in which Carolingian, Benedictine observances were propagated in Brittany comes from Redon. This monastery was founded in 832, and managed to establish close links with both Louis the Pious and Nominoe, his representative in Brittany. An account of its early history occupies the first section of the *Gesta Sanctorum Rotonensium*, a work written about forty years after the monastery's foundation.[38] This describes

---

[35] *Vita Winwaloei*, I.21 p. 209.

[36] *Vita Winwaloei*, II.13 p. 227.

[37] *Vita Winwaloei*, II.12 p. 226; Compare *La Règle de Saint Benoît*, 6 vols ed A. de Vogüé and J. Neufville, cap 55 vol 2 *SCR* 182 (1972) p. 618; *Synodi primi Aquisgranensis decreta authentica* clauses 19–20, *CCM* 1 pp. 461–2.

[38] F. Lot, 'Les *Gesta Sanctorum Rotonensium*' in his *Mélanges d'Histoire Bretonne* (Paris 1907) pp. 1–13.

how the newly formed community was instructed in the Benedictine Rule by Gerfred, a Frankish hermit living in Brittany.[39] Gerfred was remembered at his own monastery, Saint-Maur-de-Glanfeuil, for his twenty years as a hermit, and for his great abstinence.[40] The continuation of an eremitic strand within the ordered monasticism of the ninth century tends to be overshadowed by the scale of Benedict of Aniane's coenobitic endeavours, but the example of Gerfred is a reminder that Louis's reforms did indeed leave room for some individuals to progress within the Benedictine tradition from a community to a solitary life.[41] Gerfred's outstanding asceticism and his appreciation of the wide scope and purpose of Benedictine monasticism must have well fitted him to act as adviser to the new Breton community.

From Redon, Benedictine practices were gradually disseminated in other ways. For example, a monk from Léhon came to Redon to learn how to live according to the Rule.[42] And as Redon grew, it acquired control of nearby small communities, described in charters as *monasteriola*.[43] Their size and organisation are quite obscure, but once in Redon's control they disappear from the record, and I suspect they may have been tiny cells, hardly more than hermitages, whose members were quietly absorbed into the regular Benedictine life at Redon.

Beyond Landévennec and Redon, the impact of Carolingian authority on Breton ascetic traditions is much harder to document. Shreds of evidence afford room only for tentative speculation about changes elsewhere. One work which includes suggestive remarks is the Life of Guenael. A disciple of Winwaloe and portrayed as a

---

[39] *Gesta [Sanctorum Rotonensium* ed J. Mabillon, *ASOSB* 4 pt 2] I.3 pp. 194–5.

[40] Odo of Glanfeuil, *Historia Translationis S. Mauri, MGH SS* 15 pt 1 p. 470.

[41] Redon provides a further example: Fidweten, a Breton companion of Gerfred in the woods of central Brittany, reached Redon after Gerfred had left and appears to have been a 'hermit in residence' there. *Gesta* II.5 pp. 207–8. See also the comments on hermits within Benedictine monasticism of G. Constable, 'Eremitical forms of monastic life', *Istituzioni Monastichi e Istituzioni canonicali in Occidente, Miscellenea del Centro di Studi Medioevali,* 9 (1980) pp. 239–64 and J. Leclercq, 'Pierre le Vénérable et l'érémitisme clunisien', *Petrus Venerabilis,* ed G. Constable and J. Kritzeck *SA* 40 (1956) pp. 99–120 especially pp. 99–112. Leclercq's list of hermits in the Carolingian period is far from exhaustive.

[42] *Gesta* III.3 pp. 216–7.

[43] *Cartulaire de l'Abbaye de Redon en Bretagne,* ed A. de Courson (Paris 1863) nos xi, xcvii, appendix iv, xl + xlv pp. 11–12, 73–4, 354, 369, 371–2. There are other *monasteriola* which escaped take-over by Redon.

practitioner of characteristically Celtic ascetic rigours, Guenael was buried in the monastery he founded on the island of Groix.[44] The *vita* notes that laymen and women were for a long time prohibited access to the saint's tomb, and that only after Nominoe had had a new monastery built could people of both sexes visit the shrine.[45] Was Nominoe acting here as an exponent of Carolingian norms? It was he who as Louis the Pious's governor in Brittany presided over the foundation of Redon, and at Redon, the access of women as well as men to its relic collection is well attested.[46]

If such a change in the relations between laymen and women and their local monastic saint may indeed be attributable to Carolingian influence, it is some indication of how great the impact of Frankish authority on Breton monastic traditions may perhaps have been. Whilst Breton hagiography of the ninth century looked back to early traditions of spiritual pilgrimage, harsh ascetic rigour and secluded solitude, the ninth-century communities in which those writers lived were organised along different principles.[47] Whether or not Louis's efforts to integrate the Breton monasteries into his *Reichskirche* ever fully succeeded, the attempt at least left an indelible impact upon Breton ascetic traditions.

University of Manchester

---

[44] *Vita Guenaili*, cap 2 *ASB Nov.* vol 1 p. 677.

[45] *Vita Guenaili* cap. 3 p. 678. This chapter, an account of the *translatio* of Guenael's relics, cannot have been written earlier than their removal to Paris and Corbeil in the 960s, but the theme of the exclusion of women from the *claustra monachorum* is common. See 'Miracles de Saint Magloire', ed A. de La Borderie, cap iv, *Mémoires de la Société Archéologique et Historique des Côtes-du-Nord* 2nd ser 5 (1891) p. 235; and Wrdisten reports that Winwaloe's prohibition against women entering the monastic enclosure at Landévennec was still in force at the time he was writing the Life. *Vita Winwaloei*, II.5 p. 220.

[46] *Gesta* II.9 p. 211.

[47] In this context it is to be recalled that Wrmonoc was a pupil of Wrdisten, and that he wrote his Life of Paul Aurelian as a monk at Landévennec during Wrdisten's abbacy. Preface to the 'Vie de Saint Paul', pp. 417–8.

ROMUALD – MODEL HERMIT: EREMITICAL THEORY IN SAINT PETER DAMIAN'S *VITA BEATI ROMUALDI*, CHAPTERS 16–27

by COLIN PHIPPS

S AINT Peter Damian stands among the most important exponents of the revitalised eremitism which played so prominent a role in the religious reforms of eleventh-century Italy. Afterwards cardinal-bishop of Ostia, papal legate and doctor of the church, he was from 1043 prior of the eremitical community of Fonte Avellana, which he had first entered in 1036/7 and for whose constitutions he was so largely responsible that he can be counted virtually as its refounder.[1] Fonte Avellana, however, owed its origins, probably in the 990s, to Saint Romuald of Ravenna. The community derived the general tenor of its spirituality from his, and it is clear that the image of the saint which Damian was able to build up impressed him deeply. The *Life* of the saint, which he wrote not later than 1042,[2] was the first major work in what was to grow into his considerable *corpus*, and far exceeds in length any of his later hagiographical products. His image of Romuald became his own model. In the process, the image seems to have become imbued for its part with the colouration of Damian's own concerns. The whole *Life* took on a shape and a structure determined not by Damian's hard knowledge of the man but by his schematisation, his programme, of Romuald's spiritual growth. The *Life* is the vehicle of a kind of argument.

The nature of this argument is unusual. Most early medieval saints' Lives consist largely of stories of miracles intended to

---

[1] The most important modern biography of Damian is J. Leclercq, *Saint Pierre Damien: ermite et homme de l'église* (Rome 1960). This includes a valuable assessment of the nature and usefulness of Damian's biography of Romuald, pp. 22–36. On Fonte Avellana, there is a good entry by G.M. Cacciamani, *DGHE*.

[2] A summary of the research behind the dating of the work is available in [J.] Howe, ['The Awesome Hermit: The Symbolic Significance of the Hermit as a Possible Research Perspective' in *Numen* vol 30, fasc 1 (1983) n 3 pp. 115–16.

demonstrate the power exercised by the saints at their shrines; this constitutes an argument in only a very limited sense. Damian was aware that expectations of this kind attached to hagiography and deliberately resisted them. In his prologue he claimed to be writing partly for the multitude of faithful who flocked to Romuald's tomb and witnessed miracles there because, he said, he feared that the saint's far-flung fame, spread only by word of mouth, would otherwise fade with time; but, he continued, Saint John the Baptist himself is not recorded as the agent of any miracles and he would not record many of Romuald's but rather concentrate on the order of his *conversatio*, his life in orientation to God, 'which pertains to edification in every way.'[3] As Romuald's shrine was not at Fonte Avellana but at Val di Castro, Damian had no special interest and may not have had very great knowledge of his miracles in any case.

In addition to this concern for the multitude, Damian claimed to have been moved by 'the pleas of many brethren.'[4] These brethren presumably included those of Fonte Avellana and at some points the record of *conversatio* takes on something of the function of a *Rule*, recording ascetic or devotional practices which are known from other sources to have become the customs of that very community. But Damian was at another monastery at the time of writing (San Vincenzo *ad Petram Pertusam*) and analysis of the narrative clearly indicates that he had gathered reminiscences of Romuald from other houses (for example, Sant'Apollinare in Classe, by Ravenna, where Romuald had first entered religion and where he had later been for a short period abbot[5]); this would suggest that the brethren he expected to be interested in the *Life* were not all eremitical. Taken with the multitude of faithful, these addressees add up to a virtually limitless audience, inside and outside the monasteries and hermitages, both for the present and

[3] See *Petri Damiani Vita Beati Romualdi* ed G. Tabacco (Fonti per la storia d'Italia 94; Rome 1957) prol pp. 10–11. [This edition will be hereafter cited as *Vita Romualdi*.] Tabacco's note to this, n 5, p. 10, suggests that he believes Damian does in any case relate many miracles, a point he makes also in his preface, p. lv. Virtually none of these, however, are shrine miracles and most of them have allegorical or other symbolic significance relative to the stages in Romuald's spiritual growth at which they are recounted.

[4] *Ibid* p. 10.

[5] The story of the vision of Saint Apollinaris himself at Sant' Apollinare, proving his relics were there, is an example. *Ibid* cap 2 p. 18.

with an eye on posterity. The greater part of the work, in harmony with this, is concerned not with the hermit's *conversatio* in the narrower sense of ascetic and devotional practices but in the broader sense of his functions as such an ascetic, in relation to non-eremitical members of the Christian community who did not live in the same way (both coenobitic and secular) and even to pagans. The argument of the *Life*, that is to say, is primarily a theory of eremitism, an argument as to why men should wish to associate themselves with Romuald, of how such as he serve God more effectively – as Damian believed – than all others. There is no other work in his *corpus* which exactly compares.

The context of this argument was the tension between eremitism and coenobitism in the contemporary religious reform movement.[6] The monasteries as they actually existed did not satisfy men like Damian. They did not measure up to the glories of ancient Egypt or Syria, to which Saint Benedict himself had referred the hearers of his *Rule*.[7] It was not necessary to overthrow the Benedictine coenobitic tradition but to reform and add to it, to restore the eremitical element and aim which Damian believed – most probably incorrectly – Benedict himself had wished to promote but for which he had not legislated. Thus Fonte Avellana, and perhaps more importantly Camaldoli, developed an eremitism, on the pattern of the ancient *laura*, conformable in many respects to the *Rule* and largely governed under it.[8] It is perhaps not surprising that the majority of the extant manuscripts of the *Life* of Romuald are descended from lost exemplars traceable to communities of what grew into the Camaldolese congregation, some incorporating interpolations of the Camaldolese *Constitutions*. The *Life* assisted in

---

[6] A detailed consideration of this issue in relation to Damian, with extensive references to other secondary works, was made by O. Capitani, 'San Pier Damiani e l'istituto eremitico' *SSSpoleto* (1965) pp. 122–63. The place of eremitism in relation to coenobitism in Damian's later thought is considered by G. Miccoli, 'Théologie de la vie monastique chez Saint Pierre Damien (1007–1072)' in *Théologie de la vie monastique: Études sur la tradition patristique* (Théologie: Études publiées sous la direction de la Faculté de Théologie S.J. de Lyon-Fourvière vol 49: Paris 1961) pp. 459–83.

[7] For the Vulgate text Damian probably knew, slightly different from the more ancient texts most recently edited: [P.] Delatte, [*The Rule of St. Benedict* (London 1921)] cap 73 pp. 492–5.

[8] See especially G. Tabacco, 'Romualdo di Ravenna e gli inizi dell'eremetismo Camaldolese' in *SSSpoleto* (1965) pp. 73–121.

the propagation of this form of ascetic religion. One manuscript found its way into a Cistercian house, but it is not known when.[9]

The formal solution of the eremitic/coenobitic problem represented by these communities, however, occurred largely after Romuald's own time, and he himself figures in the origins of coenobia as well as hermitages. Very little is known about him, no work other than Damian's was produced in which his activities were more than fleetingly recorded, and he gets no more than a passing reference in works where he is not venerated.[10] His lasting influence has been in the monasteries and hermitages, largely as the model Damian made him. This means that all attempts to reconstruct Romuald's authentic life and personal spirituality are fraught with great difficulty. An outline extracted mainly from Damian's account was accepted with varying degrees of criticism in three modern biographies now about sixty or seventy years old, and chronology was attempted.[11] These studies underlie the short notes of dictionaries and books of saints and they incorporate many points which cannot be verified. More recent historians have used the work in discussions of wide-ranging and not particularly eremitical traditions: Saward, for example, on holy fools; these may have some value but tend to exaggerate or distort imagery used only in passing by Damian and to support a different (his eremitical) theme.[12] The present paper will not attempt to evaluate the actuality of Romuald's life. The author's own concern with a

---

[9] *Vita Romualdi* pp. i–xxxiii.

[10] The only significant alternative record is by Bruno of Querfurt in *Vitae quinque fratrum, MGHSS* vol 15 cols 709–38.

[11] W. Franke, *Romuald von Camaldoli und seine Reformtätigkeit zur Zeit Ottos III* (Berlin 1913); P. Ciampelli, *Vita di san Romualdo abate, fondatore dei Camaldolesi* (Ravenna 1927); A. Pagnani, *Vita di san Romualdo* (Camaldoli 1927).

[12] J. Saward, *Perfect Fools: Folly for Christ's Sake in Catholic and Orthodox Spirituality* (Oxford 1980) especially pp. 49–51: Saward considers this aspect of Romuald's spirituality with inadequate attention to its overall character and sources. D. Weinstein and R.M. Bell, *Saints and Society: The Two Worlds of Western Christendom, 1000–1700* (Chicago and London 1982) p. 85, mention the *Vita Romualdi* only in relation to sexual temptations (on the basis of one sentence in it); this would give a totally distorted impression to readers unfamiliar with the work. Howe has offered an interesting approach to the *Vita* in relation to the hermit as a socio-religious symbol, but with inadequate concern for the problems involved in dealing with such a text as a literary construct. The same weakness affects M.B. Becker, who uses dubious information from the *Vita* repeatedly in *Medieval Italy: Constraints and Creativity* (Bloomington 1981).

particular kind of asceticism and the relationships it sustained is sufficiently central to our concerns.

His statement of eremitical theory is spread virtually through the entire work of seventy-two chapters and is the unifying principle around which the otherwise ramshackle and disjointed narrative coheres. The core of the argument, however, where it most directly concerns the relationship of monks and hermits and the role of asceticism in this relationship, is to be found in twelve chapters, sixteen to twenty-seven. The argument is expressed in various ways: through the example of the saint, through events which link in to conventional Scriptural or hagiographical imagery with established significations, and through almost explicit statements of principle. Two quotations may mark the points between which the argument moves. The first is an almost explicit statement of what eremitism is not:

> [Romuald] pondered this within himself, that henceforth, for the remainder of his life, he would content himself with his own salvation and lay aside entirely the care for others. Upon this reflection a great terror invaded his mind that if he should resolutely persist in this that he had mentally conceived, he might have no doubt that he would perish, rendering himself damnable in divine judgement.[13]

The second is a model of how eremitism should be:

> at length ... when many brethren had been gathered and settled in single cells, he kept the rigour of the eremitical life with such fervour both in himself and in others that all whom the renown of their life was able to reach held it to be wondrous.[14]

Thus the true response of the hermit saint is not to live for himself alone. He is a *virtuoso* whose fervour must draw into his own holiness lesser brethren also. Between these two quotations, Damian considers why this burden of souls is not appropriately expressed in coenobitic abbacy. The argument thus falls into three sections: denying selfish isolationism, rejecting coenobitism and identifying true eremitism.

---

[13] *Vita Romualdi* cap. 18 pp. 43–4.
[14] *Ibid* cap 26 p. 55.

The first section, where it is shown that the model hermit is not selfish, is a series of six chapters (sixteen to twenty-one) of which the most important are the first three. These are built upon a complex of Scriptural and hagiographical texts including a section of Saint Athanasius's *Life of Saint Antony*. In the first two of these chapters, Romuald is, like Antony, tempted by demons, in the course of which he is physically beaten.[15] At the end of this traditional temptation the story takes on a heightened significance; the devil begins to attack Romuald in his very eremitism:

> When the devil saw ... that he could not prevail against the attendant of God in himself, he converted to cunning plots, and wheresoever the sainted man went, he aroused the hearts of his disciples in malice against him. For whereas it had been impossible for Romuald to be held back from the vehemence of his own fiery fervour, at least the devil might restrain him from care for others' salvation, and whereas it did not even begin to be possible for him to be overcome himself by the enemy, perhaps he would not deny victory on behalf of others.[16]

The argument has thus moved from the tradition of Saint Antony to that of Saint Benedict; this burden of souls is after the order of that enjoined on abbots in the *Rule*.[17]

Developing this, Damian relates in the third of these chapters[18] a story in which the attack of the demons is indeed taken over by unruly monks; the brethren of Bagno, a monastery Romuald has himself built and near which he continues to dwell in seclusion, involving himself remotely in the conduct of the community. After a disagreement, partly over his opposition to their (unspecified) wicked habits, he is beaten up and physically expelled. It is at this point that he is tempted to the above-cited central sin of concern only for his own salvation. His success against such temptation is contrasted with the highly figurative punishments suffered by the monks. An especially heavy snowfall causes their monastery to collapse upon them in the night, and they are injured in various

---

[15] *Ibid* cap 16–17 pp. 40–1. In the Evagrian translation, *Vita [Beati] Antonii [Abbatis]* cap 7–8, *PL* 73 cols 131–2.
[16] *Vita Romualdi* cap 17 p. 41.
[17] Delatte cap 2 pp. 35–55.
[18] *Vita Romualdi* cap 18 pp. 42–5.

ways. The injury which Damian saves for last and upon which he comments explicitly, is a partial blinding:

> From one a very eye was plucked out; and rightly did he endure the division of bodily light who, divided against his neighbour, had let slip one – even though he retained the other – of the lights of twofold charity.[19]

The lights of two-fold charity are love of God and love of the neighbour, the two aspects of the Golden Rule.[20] The monk who is divided against his neighbour has presumably retained the love of God. Damian thus counters further the common, and ancient,[21] belief that a hermit will withdraw in his love of God to the neglect of his neighbour while the coenobium is the preserve of the 'social virtues'. The demon-inspired brethren of Bagno – only the first (and worst) of coenobium after coenobium, 'wheresoever the sainted man went',[22] to be roused in malice against him – have celebrated their victory over Romuald by preparing a banquet to replete themselves in wordly voluptitude. This is related in terms of a parody of the heavenly banquet with Christ which is the true goal of religious. They have rejected Romuald and his teaching because they still love the world, from which he has definitely withdrawn and wishes to withdraw them. Monks represent the demons in his life not because Damian believed them all to be evil – none of his writings would support such an interpretation – but because he believed that coenobia are by their very nature closer to the world than the desert places. The coenobite has therefore made, by comparison, only an incomplete conversion, his *conversatio* is not totally oriented to God and it threatens corruption of the hermit's whose is. As God is Himself the source of love, it follows that it is not possible for coenobites to be more loving than a good

---

[19] *Ibid.*

[20] See Matthew 22: 37–40.

[21] This was expressed most straightforwardly in the fourth century by Saint Basil of Caeserea. See C.H. Lawrence, *Medieval Monasticism: Forms of Religious Life in Western Europe in the Middle Ages* (London and New York 1984) pp. 18–9. Saint Benedict was more deferential to hermits while pointing out only the dangers of their life and offering no positive encouragement for anyone to adopt it. See Delatte cap I pp. 27–30 (Delatte's own comments on this are contentious but not eccentric).

[22] See n 16 above.

hermit, and in the tension of their relationship it will be the hermit who shows his love by risking his own purity to continue to care for theirs and the coenobite who is angered by the call to a *conversatio* beyond his own.[23]

Romuald's success against the temptation to selfish isolation thus results in a significant addition to the mortificatory value of his asceticism. Already in chapter sixteen he has dwelt briefly in a swamp habitation before he has been tempted by the demons. In the extremely short chapter nineteen, following in the order of the narrative directly after his expulsion from Bagno, St. Apollinaris appears to him and instructs him to return to Sant'Apollinare where he has suffered an earlier conspiracy. Romuald obeys at once, and that is the end of the story. In the equally short chapter immediately following he is back, alone, in a swamp habitation, of which the air is so corrupt and the stench so great that when he leaves it he is terribly swollen and his hair has fallen out. His appearance is not at all that which he bore when he enclosed himself there. His very flesh has gone as green as a newt. Both stench and corrupt air are traditionally associated simultaneously with demons and with death. Green flesh is that of a rotting corpse. Romuald is in a state of advanced mortification. Most notable about this is that it contrasts directly with Athanasius's record of Antony after his twenty years of battles with demons in the fort of the Outer Mountain:

> All were astounded [wrote Athanasius] both at the grace of his countenance and the dignity of his body, which had not swollen in the quietness, nor did pallor haunt his face because of his fasts and the battle with the demons; but on the contrary, the old comeliness of his members persisted as if no time had passed.[24]

---

[23] This is reminiscent of a statement of Saint Gregory the Great in relation to Saint Benedict's troubles with the murderously fractious brethren of Vicovaro: 'sicut pravis moribus semper gravis est vita bonorum'. A. de Vogüé and P. Antin, *Grégoire le Grand: Dialogues, tome 2* (SCR 260; Paris 1979) bk 2 cap 3:4 p. 142. From Benedict's departure to solitude in this same chapter (3:5–12 pp. 143–9) rather than from his own *Rule* Damian might have derived his belief in Benedict's high regard for solitude.

[24] *Vita Antonii* cap 13, col 134.

This Athanasius immediately interprets as indicative of the purity and stability of Antony's soul; as body and soul are one, he implies, purity of the soul preserves purity of the body.[25] Damian is clearly not suggesting a putrefaction of Romuald's soul. His conception of the relationship between body and soul is clearly a little different; but the philosophy of the situation is not his concern. He has already established that the true passion of the hermit is his burden of souls, his most fearsome adversaries monks. Antony has been tempted only by demons but Romuald by both. His suffering in the swamp has been juxtaposed immediately with his return to the monastery. Romuald's is implicitly a fuller mortification because it is a fuller temptation.

The same view of the coenobitic/eremitic relation underlies the second aspect of the argument, that it is not appropriate for the hermit to exercise his care for others' salvation by becoming a coenobitic abbot. Damian deals with this opposite deflection from the eremitical way in chapters twenty-two and twenty-three, where the Emperor Otto III imposes the abbacy, the *animarum regimen*, of the same Sant'Apollinare upon Romuald against his will. This takes place in the emperor's palace after the emperor has rested for a night in the hermit's cell at Pereo, to which he has gone to fetch him in person. The seeds of disaster are already apparent in the contrast of dwellings. The rest which is enjoyed in the hermit's cell is a standard image of contemplation, the foretaste of heaven.[26] The coenobitic abbacy is imposed in the worldly palace. The *animarum regimen* has a worldly aspect just because it *is regimen*. It does not conform to the powerlessness of Christ which will emerge as a theme of chapters twenty-five and twenty-six. The result of Romuald's abbatial appointment is the opposite of rest. He is lashed with murmurings and scandals (continuing the physical-beating imagery of the earlier episode) such that not only is his own perfection threatened but the practices of the monks become much worse. This *animarum regimen* from within the coenobium is no more beneficial than the care exercised for Bagno from without. This is not the answer. Romuald resigns the abbacy after a short period. He travels south to Tivoli, where he settles a rebellion of

[25] *Ibid.*
[26] This is discussed at length by J. Leclercq, *Otia monastica: Etudes sur le vocabulaire de la contemplation au moyen age* (SA 51, Rome 1963) pp. 13–26.

the city against the emperor, reforms an anchorite (Venerius) who has sinned by leaving his initial coenobium without abbatial permission and who thereafter follows Romuald's prescription through to sanctity under his own abbot's (rather vague) supervision, and instructs the emperor and a companion of his in penitence after they have murdered an enemy to whom they had sworn safe-conduct.

The burden of souls which it is this model hermit's vocation to bear is thus largely extra-coenobitic (although he continues to involve himself in passing with various coenobia through the rest of the *Life*) and it is unofficial. Romuald has been first a coenobite, however briefly, and has gained the permission of his abbot at Sant'Apollinare for his initial withdrawal to the desert;[27] he has thus fulfilled the minimum requirements for a legitimate hermit laid down in St. Benedict's *Rule*.[28] For the rest of the *Life* no-one approves the various geographical translations he makes, no-one appoints him to the *magisterium* he exercises over hermits and coenobites (other than in the undesirable case of Sant'Apollinare) and his relationship with the regular authorities of the various monasteries he visits remains undefined. Damian shows almost no concern for the ecclesiological aspect of his appointment to authority. His authority seems to derive directly from his ascetic prowess, right from chapter six where he first emerges into a position of leadership in a small group-hermitage because his rigours are the greatest there.[29] The reason for this seems to be the assumption by Damian of a certain kind of mystical theology. When in chapter three the brethren of Sant'Apollinare have threatened themselves in their resentment of Romuald with the abyss of iniquity by conspiring against him, the embryonic saint has saved them, as well as himself, by retreating into individual prayer in the closet of his heart. The closet of the heart is constantly associated in Damian's work with the hermit's cell. The young Romuald there anticipates his later function. It is the holy individual who saves the commun-

---

[27] *Vita Romualdi* cap 4 p. 20.
[28] See Delatte as in n 21 above.
[29] 'Romualdus ... cepit de virtutibus in virtutes mirabiliter crescere et reliquos fratres sancte conversationis gressibus longius anteire, ut iam quicquid inter fratres sive de spiritualibus sive etiam de corporalibus ipse decerneret, cunctis volentibus, eius omnimodo sententia prevaleret.' *Vita Romualdi* cap 6 p. 26.

ity; the community, by contrast, has threatened the holy individual with destruction. Salvation, after all, is ultimately attained when men are 'gathered' into the virtue of Christ.[30] Damian's Romuald therefore operates throughout the *Life* by conforming himself through asceticism and prayer to life with God, bringing others to Him through assimilation into his own kind of *conversatio* in the varying manners and degrees appropriate to them and through the broadcast of his *virtus* through his ascetical teaching.[31] Many he saves will remain coenobites, but it cannot be appropriate for the hermit saint to return himself to a life in common. He must be free to exercise to the full his *uncommon virtus*. And yet he must neither isolate himself nor fail to provide for those who are called to follow him into eremitism but for whom the unappointed *magisterium* and un-pastored life of the model himself are not appropriate. For Romuald is a holy figure to be wondered at, an ideal for religious to keep before their eyes. Damian does not expect him to be fully emulated, nor does he intend to call into existence a new generation of sarabaites and gyrovagues justifying themselves by his example.[32] Obedience is always a cardinal virtue, and Romuald himself has instructed the anchorite Venerius to resubmit his *conversatio* to his abbot.[33] What is required for those who would follow Romuald most closely is a non-coenobitic, properly eremitic, but institutional answer.

The answer is provided when he forms the eremitical community of Pereo, in the same place from which the emperor removed him to the abbacy and where brethren are now settled in single cells and yet are assimilated to Romuald's own ascetic rigour such that Damian can record that he kept it 'both in himself and in others'.[34] These others he converts when making peace between the emperor and the rebellious worldly city of Tivoli. He leads them first to St. Benedict's own monastery of Monte Cassino. Damian suggests no reason as to why he did this and records nothing of what they did there, about what status they took, how long they remained or

---

[30] See especially John 17.
[31] Damian emphasises this latter aspect particularly at the end of *Vita Romualdi* cap 27 p. 61.
[32] On the definition of sarabaites and gyrovagues see Delatte cap 1 pp. 30–4.
[33] *Vita Romualdi* cap 24 p. 51.
[34] 'et in se et in aliis.' See n 14 above.

under exactly whose *regimen* they passed their time. He is satisfied to record that the converts passed through St. Benedict's house on their journey of conversion. Eremitism continues on from coeno-bitism rather than stands in opposition to it.

The manner of completion of this journey is especially instruc-tive. Romuald exchanges a fine horse given to him by a king's son, whom he had converted to monasticism, for an ass so that he might more fully imitate Christ. It has already been implied that the abbacy of Sant'Apollinare had an intrinsic association with the Ottonian royal palace and was radically dissociated from Romuald's cell at Pereo. Romuald now exchanges, in the mother house of coenobitism, a royal horse given to him by a royal coenobite for the prophesied creature Christ rode into Jerusalem to His proclamation as King of the Jews and the last days preceding His Passion on the Cross labelled with that title.[35] The full glory of Romuald as an image of this Highest King Who is the *Redemptor*, as Damian here styles Him,[36] of His own subjects, is thus revealed as he prepares to travel, his converts from the imperial household with him, to establish the model group hermitage at Pereo. It is a commonplace of monastic literature that in the monasteries there is a foretaste of the heavenly Jerusalem, eternal life with God Himself. But here Pereo is in the place of Jerusalem and Monte Cassino is the Mount of Olives, a place to be venerated but only the starting-point of the royal journey to the royal city.[37] Romuald takes his converts on to Pereo, where, as Damian emphasises, he has himself dwelt before,[38] and thus assimilating them to his own *conversatio*, establishes them in single cells following the rigorous asceticism outsiders found so wondrous.

In chapter twenty-seven, Saint Bruno of Querfurt's *conversatio* at Pereo is described as transcending that of all the other brethren by a long way. This has become possible because he is in such a single cell. He does not conform to a common standard. Through him, salvific *virtus* continues to be transmitted out to those beyond the bounds of the institution; for in the same chapter he goes forth

---

[35] See Matthew 21: 1–9 and 27: 27–37.
[36] *Vita Romualdi* cap 26 p. 55.
[37] See n 35 above.
[38] 'Cum his igitur omnibus superius nominatis Romualdus ad Pereum, ubi dudum habitaverat, rediit.' *Vita Romualdi* cap 26 p. 55.

from Pereo to convert the Slavs and is crowned with martyrdom in Prussia. At Pereo Romuald is a hermit who cares for the salvation of others. Those who are salvifically affected by the *virtus* emanating from this place are even beyond the bounds of Christendom.

Pereo is an elite community. Damian does not expect all religious to emulate it. And Romuald's *Life* is far from finished. He will go on for many chapters yet caring for the salvation of those around him in various ways. But in these chapters is the essence of Damian's eremitical argument. Only in the hermitage can the fullest ascetic and devotional relationship with Christ be developed, away from the infection of communal sin. Only by caring for the salvation of others can the hermit love his neighbour as God commanded. The solution is the group hermitage. There he may be a follower of both Antony and Benedict, a double blessing in this world.

King's College, London

A HERMIT GOES TO WAR: PETER AND THE ORIGINS OF THE FIRST CRUSADE

by E.O. BLAKE and C. MORRIS

J UST over a century ago Heinrich Hagenmeyer published his definitive book on Peter the Hermit.[1] It has shaped most subsequent discussions of Peter's career, and it must be said at once that no completely new material has come to light since then. There is, however, a problem of perpetual interest posed by the divergences among twelfth-century accounts of the origins of the First Crusade. Until the advent of modern historiography, it was accepted that the expedition was provoked by an appeal from the church of Jerusalem, brought to the west by Peter the Hermit, who had visited it as a pilgrim, had seen a vision of Christ and had been entrusted by the patriarch with a letter asking for help against the oppression of the Christians there. The crusade was on this view born in the atmosphere of pilgrimage, visions and popular preaching which continued to mark its course, and is so evident in, for example, the discovery of the Holy Lance and the visions and messages which accompanied it. Peter is in some sense the embodiment of these charismatic elements, and there is no controversy about his prominence in the history of the movement. He appears as a sensationally successful preacher, who recruited and led a large contingent which left in advance of the main armies, and was cut to pieces in Asia Minor. Thereafter, he appears in the chronicles in a variety of capacities: as a runaway, and an ambassador to the Moslems, as an adviser, as an associate with the popular element among the crusaders, and finally as a guide to the sacred sites at Jerusalem. It is, however, not with these wider aspects of his career that we wish to deal in this paper, but with his special role in the summoning of the expedition. The older view was that he was its first author. Every student of the early church is familiar with

---

[1] [H.] Hagenmeyer, *Peter [der Eremite* (Leipzig 1879)]. French version, *Le vrai et le faux sur Pierre l'Hermite* (Paris 1883).

militant monks and hermits. It was once believed that Peter, their spiritual descendant, was the most supremely successful of all the ascetic warmongers.

This version of the causes of the First Crusade had one great advantage. Whatever the uncertainties about Urban's speech at Clermont, we are sure at least of one thing: he named Jerusalem as its final objective. It is mentioned in all the surviving versions of the decrees of the council, in all three letters which Urban wrote about the crusade, in charters of departing crusaders and in three of the four early versions of Urban's speech.[2] The choice of Jerusalem as a goal can be explained very simply if there was an appeal from the church there. Modern historians have discarded this story as legendary, but at the price of losing the most obvious reason for the plan which was adopted.[3] Since they have also been inclined to discount the stories of Moslem oppression of the eastern Christians, it has become increasingly difficult to see why the crusade took place at all. Of course, it is still possible to find reasons for the choice of Jerusalem as a goal. It has been suggested that (on the evidence of a later Byzantine chronicler) the emperor Alexius craftily suggested Jerusalem because he knew that it would rouse the enthusiasm of the Latins. It is certainly true that Gregory VII had briefly mentioned Jerusalem in his project for an eastern expedition in 1074. More generally, the welding together of

[2] Robert Somerville, *The Councils of Urban II. i: Decreta Claromontensia* (Amsterdam 1972) pp. 74, 108, 124. Letters to Flanders and Bologna in H. Hagenmeyer, *Epistulae et cartae* (repr Hildesheim-New York 1973) no 2 and 3; to Vallombrosa in P. Kehr, *Italia Pontificia* III p. 89 no 8 (*Göttingen Nachrichten* 1901 p. 313). On departing crusaders, H.E.J. Cowdrey, 'Pope Urban's preaching of the First Crusade', *History* 55 (1970) pp. 177–88. Jerusalem is prominent in the acccounts of Urban's address in Guibert [of Nogent, *Gesta Dei per Francos*, *RHC Occ*, IV]; Robert [of Reims, *Historia Iherosolimitana*, *RHC Occ* III]; and Baudri [of Bourgueil, *Historia Jerosolimitana*, *RHC Occ* IV]. It is absent from the summary of the address in Fulcher of Chartres, *Historia Hierosolymitana*, ed H. Hagenmeyer (Heidelberg 1913) but Fulcher makes it clear that he regarded it as the intended objective (i.33 p. 323; i 5 p. 149; ii 16 p. 428).

[3] F. Duncalf, 'The Peasants' Crusade', *American Historical Review* 26 (1920–1) pp. 440–53, expressly states that 'the first mention of Peter's activity finds him in Berry soon after the Council of Clermont' (p. 442), and Y. Le Febvre, *Pierre l'ermite et la croisade* (Amiens 1946) dismisses the story of Peter's earlier involvement as a legend (p. 113). Peter's pilgrimage is mentioned, but given only a small place in the emergence of the crusade, in [S.] Runciman, [*A History of the Crusades* vol I (Cambridge 1951)] pp. 113–4, and [H.E.] Mayer, [*The Crusades* (Oxford 1972)] pp. 42–3.

traditions of pilgrimage and holy war would have helped to make Jerusalem the natural objective of a military campaign.[4] These suggestions certainly have some validity, but they do not readily account for Urban's choice of objective. The awkwardness of the problem is illustrated by the extremely radical solution proposed by H.E. Mayer, who has suggested that Urban did not so much as mention Jerusalem when he proclaimed the crusade.[5] As we shall see, the idea of Peter as the originator has a lot of loose ends, but when these are pulled too hard, large sections of the seamless robe of history seem to be coming away with them. It is time to take a new look. What we want to do in this paper is to examine the account of Peter given by the French crusading chroniclers, who preserve no tradition of his activity before the council of Clermont, and then, in the light of their evidence, to turn to a consideration of the alternative account, which modern historians have abandoned.

The French tradition

We have two surviving chronicles of the crusade written by eye-witnesses who accompanied it to Jerusalem: the anonymous *Gesta Francorum* and the history by Raymond of Aguilers, both completed soon after the fall of the city. However, they say very little about the origins, and for more information we have to turn to two 'second-generation' chronicles, extensive re-writes of the *Gesta Francorum* by Robert of Reims and Guibert of Nogent. Both describe the recruiting campaign conducted by Peter, whom Guibert had seen personally.[6] From these and other early accounts, only two things can be said with total confidence about Peter's career before 1095. He was born in the neighbourhood of Amiens (although the date and his family background are unknown) and he had become a hermit (but we do not know where).[7] It can, indeed, be safely concluded that he made rather a display of his eremitical calling, for almost all writers describe him as Peter the Hermit – an

---

[4] P. Charanis, 'Byzantium, the west and the origins of the First Crusade', *Byzantion* 19 (1949) pp. 17–36; E. Caspar, *Das Register Gregors VII (MGH Ep* ii) II.31, pp. 165–8; C. Erdmann, *The Origin of the Idea of Crusade* (Princeton 1977).
[5] Mayer pp. 10–12.
[6] Robert i.5, p. 731; Guibert ii.8, p. 142. Guibert's words *circumire vidimus* are naturally read as indicating that he had seen Peter.
[7] Hagenmeyer, *Peter* pp. 30–40.

unusual style, without any place- or family-name. This is a sadly thin *curriculum vitae* for a man who was to help change the course of European history, and we must see if we can find at least some plausible guesses for items to be added under 'education', 'travel' and 'previous career'.

The First Crusade was proclaimed by Pope Urban II at Clermont in November 1095. No early source tells us whether Peter was there, but it is clear that shortly afterwards he was preaching the movement in France. The description of his mission by Guibert of Nogent contains striking parallels with the so-called 'poverty and preaching' movement which was beginning to flourish in northern France, led by such men as Robert of Arbrissel and Bernard of Tiron. Peter's operations were based upon the cities: *urbes et municipia ... circumire*. This does not exclude an audience of country people who would find the towns to be natural gathering-points, but it warns us not to speak too glibly of Peter's followers as 'the Peasants' Crusade'. Guibert tells us that Peter gave liberally to the poor from contributions he received, and provided dowries for prostitutes. This accentuates the urban character of his ministry, for prostitution was an evil of the cities, and it is reminiscent of Robert of Arbrissel's ministry to the prostitutes. The adoration addressed to Peter by his followers was extreme. Guibert remarks that 'I do not remember that anyone has been so honoured'. He was held to be semi-divine, and the hairs from his mule were treated as relics. Reverence of this type is disquietingly like that enjoyed, some ten years later, by the heretic Tanchelm of Antwerp.[8] It is understandable that, as we shall see, some chroniclers were highly critical of Peter; they included Robert of Reims, whose account on the whole is a hostile one.

Several members of the eremitical movement had a background in the cathedral schools. Saint Bruno, founder of the Carthusians, had taught theology, and Robert of Arbrissel was a Paris man. We have no clear statement that Peter had been at the schools, but several writers remarked on his eloquence, quickness and intelligence, and it may be significant that Guibert commented that the

---

[8] See R.I. Moore, *The Birth of Popular Heresy* (London 1975) pp. 31, 34. Robert similarly reported that Peter 'super ipsos praesules et abbates apice religionis efferebatur', i.5, p. 731.

poor obeyed him 'like a master'.[9] It would be a mistake to suppose that intelligence and academic training always go together, but it is a reasonable assumption (not more than that) that we can add a period of formal study to Peter's *curriculum vitae*.

Guibert's description of Peter has a further remarkable feature. Although it is supposed to be an explanation of the assembling of the First Crusade, it has none of the features of a recruiting campaign, but reads like a description of a poverty-and-preaching mission. It is strange that Peter should have been giving his campaign funds to the poor, and using them as dowries for prostitutes. When Guibert mentions that Peter left his hermitage 'with what intention I do not know', and that he went around the cities 'on the pretext of preaching' he is clearly intending to be offensive, but it is an inappropriate remark to make about someone engaged in a recruiting drive, which is a very specific purpose. The passage gains in cogency if we suppose that before 1095 Guibert had seen Peter in action as a popular preacher (the monastery of Fly, where Guibert was a monk, was not far from Amiens) and that he was giving a background description of Peter's earlier preaching career.

None of this tells us how Peter came to be mixed up with the First Crusade, but it does give us some pointers. Urban II was a keen patron of the 'apostolic life' movement in its concern with preaching and poverty. As a Frenchman and former prior of Cluny, the pope would be familiar with the situation in France, and his sympathies are revealed in his friendly relations with Robert of Arbrissel early in 1096. It would not be surprising if the pope were willing to listen to a prominent poverty-and-preaching man and use him as his agent. Unfortunately, we do not know whether Peter had formal papal authority for his preaching. Under canon law, he required it as a basis for preaching in more than one diocese, but no one actually tells us that he received it.[10] As a matter of fact, Peter is the only crusading preacher of whom we know in

---

[9] Hagenmeyer, *Peter* pp. 46–8, where however he dismisses the idea of Peter's learning.

[10] Conversely, there is good reason to think that the preaching of Robert of Arbrissel was authorised by Urban II early in 1096, but no evidence that he was actually involved in preaching the crusade. Baudri, *Vita Roberti de Arbrissello* ii 14 (*PL* 162.1050 C), printed Hagenmeyer, *Peter*, pp. 370–1. However, in a passage discussed later, Albert of Aachen describes Peter as 'factus praedicator'.

France, apart from the pope himself. There appears to have been a lot of eremitical activity, for we are told that 'many hermits and recluses and monks, unwisely leaving their domiciles, set out to go on the Way', but that is not to say that they were functioning as preachers.[11]

So far we have stayed within the framework of French chronicle writing, with its assumption that Urban was the originator of the crusade and Peter one of its preachers. It does, however, display some odd features. For one thing, no French writer knew what had happened before Clermont. Guibert and Robert, as conscientious historians, attempted to fill the gap by making use of a supposed letter from the emperor Alexius to count Robert of Flanders, but they remain very vague about the circumstances. Modern historians can follow the traces back to the presence of Greek ambassadors at the council of Piacenza in the spring of 1095, but this is mentioned by only one chronicler, and was entirely unknown to the French writers.[12] There is, as we have seen, a further gap in the chain between Urban II and Peter the Hermit, of whose relationship no coherent account is given. Indeed, Guibert and Robert seem to have little idea of Peter as a crusading preacher; they know him (and, at least in Robert's case, dislike him) as an 'apostolic life' man, and have no idea how he came to be involved. What is more, Peter's whole position in the French tradition is odd. He is *sui generis*; not one of the crusading preachers, but the only one known to us, and the recruiter of a large expedition under his own command. This raises questions about his way of operating and his involvement in the project, to which no answer is forthcoming in the sources we have so far examined. But the most measurable difficulty in the accepted scheme is a matter of dating. Urban's speech at Clermont was probably made on 27 November 1095. Peter the Hermit arrived at Cologne with his followers on 12 April 1096, and they had arrived at Constantinople before the contingents of the princes had assembled in the west.[13] Even assuming that Peter started his campaign on the morrow of Clermont, that

[11] Baudri i.8, p. 17.
[12] Bernold, *Chronicon* (*MGH SS* V p. 462).
[13] See Runciman pp. 106–27 and H. Hagenmeyer, *Chronologie de la première croisade* (repr Hildesheim 1973).

still leaves only just over four months in which he toured northern France, stopping to preach in many cities; assembled and organised a large force (for it does not seem to have been a mere rabble); provisioned it to march in Lent, the worst time of the year for supplies; and completed a journey of perhaps 250 miles. It cannot be said that this is totally impossible, but it does strain one's credulity. The only way of avoiding this problem of time-tabling is to suppose that Peter had been in touch with the pope during the three months before Clermont, when Urban was in France and laying plans for the expedition; and that he was involved in preaching, or at least in planning, before the formal public announcement in the last week of November. This is the point at which we are obliged to listen to the other tradition about the origin of the First Crusade.

The tradition of Peter as the initiator of the Crusade

There are four twelfth-century versions of a story which credits Peter the Hermit with a crucial part in the launching of the crusade. They are all relatively late and must be in some manner interdependent.[14] Albert of Aachen's history must have been completed between 1119 and about the middle of the twelfth century.[15] Of William of Tyre's *Historia Rerum in Partibus Transmarinis Gestarum* the section on the First Crusade was written between 1167 and 1173.[16] A brief fragment on the beginning of the crusade which includes the story belongs to the period from 1112–18 to *c.*1130–40.[17] The *Chanson d'Antioche* written by Graindor of Douai cannot have been written before *c.*1180, but Graindor claims to be re-fashioning an older *chanson*, composed perhaps by a

---

[14] The relevant passages are printed in parallel columns in Hagenmeyer, *Peter* pp. 320–329.

[15] Between the last event recorded in it (1119) and the date of the earliest extant MS (*c.*1140–50 according to [P.] Knoch, [*Studien zu Albert von Aachen* (Stuttgart Beitraege zur Geschichte und Politik I, Stuttgart 1966)] pp. 28, 82; 1158 according to [C.] Cahen, [*La Syrie du Nord à l'Époque des Croisades* (Paris 1940)] p. 12.

[16] *RHC Occ* I bks 1–8; Knoch pp. 29–30.

[17] It survives in the only MS of the *Historia Belli Sacri*, prefixed to the latter (*RHC Occ* III p. 169 seq), which is variously dated *c.*1140 or *c.*1130–40, and it used the *Gesta Tancredi* by Radulf of Caen (*RHC Occ* III) written 1112–1118 (Cahen pp. 9–11; Knoch p. 45).

participant in the crusade.[18] To these sources must be added Anna Comnena's account of Peter in her *Alexiad*,[19] written some time after 1139, and a group of annals mainly of the second half of the twelfth century, which include an entry on Peter's preaching, first found, it seems, in annals compiled at Harsefeld near Stade known as the Rosenfeld Annals *c.*1130.[20]

Albert and William of Tyre are the most explicit about the role to be assigned to Peter. In Albert he makes a dramatic entrance at the very beginning of the history:

A priest, called Peter, once a hermit ... with all the natural power (*instinctus*) at his command first urged the constancy of this Way, in every admonition and sermon, in *Beriu* (or *Beru*, usually identified as Berry) a region of the said kingdom, having been made a preacher. In response to his assiduous admonition and summons bishops, abbots, clerics, monks, after that laymen – the highest nobility, princes of the various kingdoms, and all the common people, both chaste and unchaste, adulterers, homicides, thieves, perjurers, robbers – indeed every kind of Christian profession, even of the female sex, all, moved by penitence, gladly joined the Way. On what occasion and with what intention this hermit preached this Way and was its first initiator (*primus auctor*) the present page will show.[21]

Then, by way of a flash-back, we are told of Peter's pilgrimage to Jerusalem 'some years before the beginning of the Way'. Once there, he rebuked the Patriarch for allowing the pagans to defile the Holy Sepulchre. The Patriarch appointed Peter as his envoy to summon help, and Peter promised, for the sake of the Patriarch and the cleansing of the holy places, to go back and seek out first the

---

[18] Date and composition are the subject of debate, most recently by L.A. Sumberg, *La chanson d'Antioche: Étude historique et litteraire. Une chronique en vers français de la première croisade par le pèlerin Richard* (Paris 1968) and Suzanne Duparc-Quioc. [*La Chanson d'Antioche.* (Documents relatifs à l'histoire des croisades XI, 2 vols Paris 1977, 1978)]. For the dates see Duparc-Quioc 2 p. 252 and for a summary of the literature on the chanson *ibid* p. 19.

[19] The relevant excerpt is printed in Hagenmeyer, *Peter* p. 304 seq.

[20] *Annales Rosenveldenses, MGH SS* XVI p. 101 (Wattenbach-Holtzmann, *Deutschlands Geschichtsquellen im Mittelalter, Deutsche Kaiserzeit* I pp. 596–597).

[21] Albert 'Historia Hierosolymitana', *RHC Occ* IV bk 1 cap 2.

Pope, then all the chiefs of Christendom to inform them of the situation in Jerusalem. Albert's word for Peter's special function is *legatio*.[22] Then follows the familiar story of Peter's vision. Jesus Christ in majesty appeared to him while asleep in the Church of the Holy Sepulchre with the command to get a letter of authorisation as his envoy (*litteras legationis nostrae*) with the seal of the holy cross from the Patriarch, and then to report back home the oppressions suffered by Christ's people at the holy places and to 'rouse the hearts of the faithful to come out and purge the holy places at Jerusalem and restore the holy offices. For through dangers and divers trials the gates of Paradise shall now be opened to those who have been called and chosen.'[23] Peter, duly provided with such a letter authorising his divine *legatio*, took sail for Bari and delivered his *legatio* to the Pope at Rome, who promised to obey the 'commands and prayers of the holy man'. 'For this reason', says Albert, 'the Pope crossed the Alps'. Eventually at Clermont

> the bishops of all France and the dukes and counts and the great princes of every order and rank, after hearing the divine commission and the pope's appeal, agreed to God's request for an expedition at their own expense to the sepulchre itself ...[24]

There are two distinct elements in Albert's narrative: the first is Peter's preaching in Berry and its universal appeal; the second is his Jerusalem pilgrimage leading to Clermont and the spread of the movement. The other three accounts launch straight into the second of these – Peter's pilgrimage as the prime initiative for the crusade. The account given by William of Tyre is very close to Albert, but with differences in both detail and presentation,[25] especially in that Peter is said to have preached the crusade in France already before Clermont,

> and in (preaching) this same word he was most necessary to the Pope, who had decided to follow him across the mountains without delay for, performing the office of a forerunner, he had prepared the minds of his hearers for obedience, so that the

[22] *Ibid* bk 1 cap 3.
[23] *Ibid* cap 4.
[24] *Ibid* cap 5, followed by an earthquake portending the departure of legions from diverse kingdoms, see below p. 96.
[25] *Ibid* caps 11–16.

Pope might more easily persuade them to accept the same proposal and more easily incline the minds of all towards himself.[26]

William attributes Clermont canons directed at reforming the peace to the suggestion of Peter[27] and in his version of Urban's speech 'the present letter from Jerusalem, brought to us by hand of the venerable Peter who is present', is cited to corroborate the reports of persecutions there.[28] After the capture of Jerusalem, William adds, alone among the sources, that Peter, recognised by Christian residents as the man who had visited the city four or five years before and who had taken letters to the western princes, was accorded much honour as the one who alone, after God, was responsible for restoring the holy city to its former freedom.[29]

Closer to Albert is Graindor's *chanson*, although this sets the story into a different context and a sequence of events which is clearly fictitious. Graindor proposes to sing of the deliverance of Jerusalem and will give the 'true beginning' which modern *jongleurs* do not have.[30] This is Peter's expedition, which itself begins with his visit to pray at the Holy Sepulchre and ends in disaster at Civetot.[31] Peculiar to Graindor is that this is followed by the chronological impossibility of a second visit to the Pope with a call for vengeance, which leads to Clermont and the princes' crusade.[32]

The *Fragment* has a very terse account, which shares some features more nearly with Albert, others with William of Tyre. It adds a description of Peter's person drawn from Radulf of Caen, including the remark that Peter travelled only by donkey, never by horse or mule and refers to the *legatio* as a message sent from heaven (*coelitus delegatum*) which the Pope received gladly, content to put into operation a plan which he had already often considered in his heart.[33]

[26] *Ibid* cap 13.
[27] *Ibid* cap 14.
[28] *Ibid* cap 15, p. 42.
[29] *Ibid* bk 8 cap 23.
[30] Duparc-Quioc 1 p. 20 verse 13.
[31] *Ibid* 1 p. 21 verses 68–77.
[32] *Ibid* 1 pp. 53–54.
[33] Hagenmeyer, *Peter* pp. 320–328, under the heading *Historia Belli Sacri*. It is impossible within the limits of this paper to define the variants and agreements in these four sources more closely. They are discussed in detail by Knoch pp. 32, 45–51; Duparc-Quioc 2 pp. 100–102, 148–149; Hagenmeyer, *Peter* pp. 53–94.

If we could accept the substance common to these sources, the problems concerning the origins would simply go away. Peter's mission provides an excellent reason why a military expedition to aid Christians in the East came to be directed at the deliverance of Jerusalem, in the form of a pilgrimage, authorised by Christ, with the promise of rewards akin to indulgence. But before we can accept it, we must come to terms with the criticism of Heinrich von Sybel in the tradition of the Ranke seminars of 1837, and the formidable argument of Hagenmeyer, that these sources present a cobweb of legend woven in the four decades after the capture of Jerusalem round a nutkin of fact—that is, a pilgrimage which failed to reach Jerusalem and a record of preaching, astonishing no doubt, but begun only after the crusade had been formally launched by Urban at Clermont.[34]

Hagenmeyer dismissed the notion that Peter preached the crusade before Clermont chiefly on the basis that Albert does not say so and that William of Tyre got him wrong. He argued convincingly that Albert does not explicitly place Peter's preaching before Clermont. Albert, it is agreed, while placing the preaching in Berry first in the sequence of his *narrative*, does not clarify where it should fit in the *chronological* sequence of his flash-back from the Jerusalem pilgrimage to Clermont and the crusade. William is not accepted as an independent witness, since he was thought to have relied on Albert as his main source for the First Crusade. William, it is argued, developed his picture of Peter as Urban's forerunner entirely from a false interpretation of Albert's narrative sequence, which suggested to him, wrongly, that Peter's preaching preceded Urban's appeal.[35] The pilgrimage and vision, on the other hand, were to be accepted as stories circulating some four decades after the crusade, but as of dubious authority for reconstructing its history. William of Tyre is again discounted as dependent on Albert. The stories in Albert, the *chanson* and the *Fragment* were conjectured plausibly to be derived from a common source probably presenting the story in its simplest form as in the *Fragment*.[36] Nevertheless, the substance of this tradition was to be relegated to the status of legend because there was no hint of it in eye-witness

[34] *Ibid* pp. 80–81.
[35] *Ibid* pp. 86–94.
[36] *Ibid* pp. 52–59.

accounts of the crusade.[37] The acid test was a passage in Anna Comnena:

> A certain Kelt, Peter by name and nick-named Koukoupetros, going away to worship at the Holy Sepulchre and having suffered much at the hands of Turks and Saracens, with difficulty got back to his country. And he did not bear failing in his object, but decided to undertake the same journey again. But seeing that it was necessary not to undertake the journey to the Holy Sepulchre alone again ..., he devised a clever plan. This was to preach in all the Latin countries: 'A divine call (*or* voice) bids me to proclaim to all the counts of France that they should all leave their homes and set out to worship at the Holy Sepulchre and to endeavour with heart and mind wholeheartedly to deliver Jerusalem from the hands of the Agarenes.[38]

Hagenmeyer regarded Anna as an older and more trustworthy source than the four Latin sources. He accepted that she too put the blame for the crusade upheaval on Peter. But her crucial evidence for him was that Peter was prevented from ever reaching Jerusalem, and therefore the account of his vision there must be apocryphal and is best to be explained as a mythical accretion to Peter's reputation.[39]

What is left, then, of Peter's reputation? An abortive Jerusalem pilgrimage, inspired preaching after Clermont, an enormous but unsuccessful expeditionary force, and a relatively 'low profile' for the rest of the crusade.[40] To restore his claim to be rated as the initiator of the crusade it would be necessary to improve the standing of the four Latin sources and, if possible, to reduce the gap

---

[37] *Ibid* pp. 70–79.

[38] This translation from the Greek (Hagenmeyer, *Peter* pp. 304–305) is deliberately literal to capture the ambiguity of the original. The natural meaning here of 'failing in his object' is presumably that he did not succeed in worshipping at the Holy Sepulchre; yet his trouble with the Turks seems to have occurred only on his return journey. Cf. the translation by [E.R.A.] Sewter, *The Alexiad of Anna Comnena* (Penguin 1969)] p. 10.

[39] Hagenmeyer, *Peter* pp. 79–81. In Sybel's view the tendency behind the growth of this legend was to ascribe the chief part of the papal influence on the crusade to the ascetic ideal in the person of Peter; [Heinrich von] Sybel, [*Geschichte des ersten Kreuzzugs* (2 ed Leipzig 1881)] p. 195.

[40] See below p. 97.

between the development of the tradition and the events of the crusade to a period too short for the growth of legend. Two chinks appear in Hagenmeyer's armour. There seems to be no strong reason why William of Tyre should have been more easily deceived by Albert's narrative sequence than his more modern commentators. As for Anna, Hagenmeyer, while aware of the various considerations which colour her account, did less than justice to them and placed a disproportionate emphasis on, a relatively insignificant part of it. The hub of it is surely a story which gave Peter the credit for initiating the crusade. This story suited Anna's book because she might well have wished to avoid any suggestion that an appeal from Alexius, which she does not mention, might have provoked the crusade with its unpleasant consequences for Byzantium, and more certainly because she wished to contrast Peter's pious intentions with the princes' secret aims for conquest. Precisely what obstacles Peter met on his first pilgrimage would have little importance for her and some forty years after the event might have become blurred in her mind, and this may explain the vagueness of her phrase 'failing in his object'. Moreover, the whole tone of the story suggests that she may be deliberately trivialising the cause of the crusade to puncture the self-righteous piety of the Latin crusaders. The more substantial core of her information, which may reflect Peter's own opinion of his role, corroborates rather than contradicts the Latin tradition of a repeat Jerusalem pilgrimage and of Peter's divine commission.[41]

It is clear that the accounts of the First Crusade in Albert and William of Tyre are in some manner closely related. Since Sybel's analysis it has been accepted that William used Albert as his 'leading source'.[42] More recently Peter Knoch in a detailed examination has found this relationship better explained by the conjecture of a source, now lost, independently used and re-written by both. This would have contained an account with a special interest in Duke Godfrey's expedition and in the contingent from Lorraine and the

[41] According to Albert Bk 1 cap 15, Peter 'statura pusillus sed sermone et corde magnus' explained the pilgrimage aim of the crusade to Alexius in Constantinople. Cf. Sewter, *The Alexiad* p. 311. But that still leaves the objection that writers of crusade accounts at first hand made no comment about Peter's special commission when they mention his name.

[42] Sybel p 111, with an impressive appreciation of William's crusade history, pp. 108–142.

Lower Rhine, beginning with Peter's pilgrimage, the so-called People's Crusade and the march of Godfrey to Constantinople, and describing after that the main phases of the crusade until the capture of Jerusalem.[43] This is not the place to present a detailed investigation. The possibility that William used Albert cannot be wholly excluded, but the close correspondence in phrasing, sequence and matter, although intermittent, yet turning up again and again until the final stage of the advance on Jerusalem, strongly suggests a single source which served both William and Albert as a skeleton as well as at times the body of their narrative.[44] Such a source, written by a member of Godfrey's contingent, would make the story of Peter's pilgrimage and its influence on the crusade part of an account of comparable date and authority with the anonymous *Gesta Francorum*, Fulcher and Raymond of Aguilers.

Recent work on the *Chanson d'Antioche* has suggested a similar conclusion, if arrived at by a different route. Suzanne Duparc-Quioc faced the same question of overlapping information in Albert and Graindor.[45] She rejected the explanation that Graindor had drawn the common matter from Albert on plausible grounds and concluded with reasonable certainty that the passages in common, which include Peter's pilgrimage and vision but not his second visit to the Pope which makes chronological nonsense of Clermont, must have been part of an older chanson, attributed to Richard le Pèlerin, re-fashioned by Graindor and utilised, among other sources, by Albert.[46] This earlier writer's selection and treatment of his material, whether of heroic incident or the experiences of the poor pilgrims, reveal an intimate acquaintance with the crusade of a participant with a special interest in the Flemish contingent.[47] This thesis of another lost source is still subject to debate, but it seems reasonable to accept the more limited conclusion that Peter's pilgrimage did feature in the old *chanson* as a prelude to an account of his own expedition.

---

[43] Knoch pp. 29–63 and see Appendix below.

[44] For samples of the evidence see Appendix below.

[45] The question is central to any analysis of Graindor's *chanson* and the literature is extensive. See especially now Sumberg and the summary of literature in Duparc-Quioc 2 p. 19.

[46] See Appendix below.

[47] Especially the lords of Saint-Pol who held a fief in the Artois and apparently the ruffian *Tafurs*, Duparc-Quioc 2 pp. 229–234 and Sumberg, 'The "Tafurs" and the First Crusade', *Medieval Studies* 21 (1959) pp. 233–234.

It follows from these re-assessments that a tradition which ranks Peter as *primus auctor* or 'the true beginning' of the Jerusalem Way was current in the regions of the Lower Rhine and Flanders, not only, respectively, in the times of Albert (1119–40) and Graindor (from 1180), but at the time of the crusade itself before it could be exposed to the creation of legend. It also follows that, if William of Tyre did not use Albert, he must have derived his notion of Peter as Urban's forerunner from some other source. There is no other evidence by which Peter's preaching can be dated before 1096.[48] The sequence of Albert's narrative finds a parallel in local annals, especially those following Ekkehard's chronicle in north-west Germany, but also Sigebert of Gembloux and Bernold of Constance.[49] There is usually no entry mentioning the crusade before 1096. The annalists, like Albert, fixed the first entry on the crusade chronologically by the date of departure of Peter's expedition, but without a separate time reference for the preaching which preceded it.[50] One exception is an important entry which first occurs in the Rosenfeld Annals:

> 1096. In this year, that something was imminent for the age which had never been seen or heard before, was presaged by frequent signs from the sky, of which one shall be recorded here, so that more faith can be put in the others. One evening, according to the testimony of those who saw it, with not a cloud in the air, balls of fire, as it seemed, shone forth in different places and reconstituted themselves in another part of the sky. It was observed that this was no fire but angelic powers which, by their migration, were signifying the movement and foreshadowing the departure of people from their places, which later seized nearly all the western world. To make manifest what these signs had portended, a man named Peter emerged in the regions of *Hyspania*, who, as is said, first a recluse, thence leaving his cell (*claustris*) moved all *Provincia* with his preaching, and not only common men, but also kings, dukes and other worldly powers. To come to greater things, bishops, monks and the other orders of the church he persuaded to follow him, carrying round a *cartula*, which he

---

[48] Cf. Hagenmeyer, *Peter* pp. 108–112, 123–128.
[49] *MGH SS* VI, p. 367; *ibid* V, p. 464.
[50] E.g. Frutolf-Ekkehard; see Appendix below.

claimed to have fallen from heaven, which said that all Christendom from all parts of the world must migrate in arms to Jerusalem, drive the pagans out from there and take possession of it with its region for ever. This he used to confirm with the following testimony from the Gospel, where Jesus, preaching about the destruction of that city, concluded with the words: "And Jerusalem shall be trodden down by the gentiles, until the times of the gentiles are fulfilled."[51] As all agreed with his words, kingdoms were emptied of rulers, cities of bishops (*pastores*), villages of their inhabitants. Not only men, but boys and even a considerable number of women have undertaken this Way (*iter*).[52]

The annal found its way into a number of north German annals.[53] There are several important inferences to be drawn from it. It seems to have been lifted from somewhere fully-phrased, which dates it somewhat before *c.*1130.[54] The conception of a divine commission if one may make allowance for the different guise of a *cartula* fallen from the sky, matches other versions, especially that of Anna's divine call and the Fragment's heaven-sent message. The information on Peter's preaching in France, which corresponds with Albert, is surely authentic since the certainty of the fact that Peter preached from this text is essential for the explanation of the portent. But this is firmly dated 1096, with Peter's emergence subsequent to it.

William of Tyre therefore stands alone in making Peter's preaching in France precede Urban's arrival there and in giving him a part to play at Clermont. His testimony is not to be despised. One may wonder whether he had a local Jerusalem source of information on Peter.[55] This would explain his knowledge of Peter's host

---

[51] Luke 21, 24; but the Vulgate distinguishes between *gentes* and *nationes*: 'et Jerusalem calcabitur a gentibus: donec impleantur tempora nationum'.

[52] *MGH SS* XVI, p. 101.

[53] E.g. *Annales Stadenses, Annales Palidenses* (Poehlden), *Annales Magdeburgenses, Annalista Saxo*. See below, Appendix p. 107; also Knoch p. 51 n54.

[54] Below, Appendix p. 107.

[55] William was born about 1130, perhaps in Jerusalem, and probably spent some of his boyhood there (William of Tyre, *A History of Deeds done beyond the Sea*, trans E.W. Babcock and A.C. Krey (New York 1943) I pp. 6, 8; Knoch p. 29.

there, of Peter's reception after the city's capture, and his detailed account of preparations made in it in readiness for the siege.[56] More certainly, his words appear to have been chosen with care. Peter is given the office of forerunner as necessary to Urban and preceding him in preaching the crusade, but, of course, by the obvious allusion to John the Baptist in relation to Jesus, he is secondary in authority.[57]

In conclusion, we might hazard a guess that William's careful phrasing could be a judicious solution to an old controversy about Peter's role which went back to a year or two after the crusade. The emphasis on the *primus auctor* in Albert or his source sounds deliberately assertive, especially when set against the 1096 annal of Bernold of Constance, which speaks of the great multitude beginning the march to Jerusalem 'of which expedition the Lord Pope was the *maximus auctor*.'[58] Shades of such a controversy appear in Frutolf/Ekkehard.[59] Frutolf ended his 1096 entry on Peter with the note that 'some however used to say later that he was *hypocrita*'.[60] Ekkehard in 1105/6 erased this note, but indirectly seems to have strengthened the indictment; burning, he says, to vindicate the reputation of the crusade as divinely ordained and to refute the more simple-minded, who, scandalised by the misconduct and failure of the expeditions of Gottschalk, Volkmar, and Emicho, had interpreted the whole design as being 'vain and frivolous'. This led him into an exposition of Gospel apocalyptic on two fronts. On the one hand, the crusade is divinely ordained. The Gospel trumpet has sounded. The signs foretold in Matthew chapter 24, Luke 21,

---

[56] Bk 1 cap 11; Bk 8 cap 8; Bk 8 cap 23.

[57] '*Praecursor*' is a commonly used epithet, of course, for John the Baptist, though not in the gospels, e.g. 'praecursore enim iam functo officium praeparata via domini' (Tertullian, *Adv. Marcionem*, Opp I, 18, 7, *CCSL* I, p. 590); 'primum Baptista Johannes regnum caelorum praedicat ut praecursor Domini hoc honoretur privilegio (Jerome, *Commentaire sur S. Matthieu* I, *SCR* 242 p 88).

[58] *MGH SS* V, p. 464.

[59] This chronicle is best now consulted in the edition by F.-J. Schmale and I. Schmale-Ott, *Frutolf[s und] Ekkehard[s Chroniken und die Anonyme Kaiserchronik]* (Freiherr vom Stein Gedaechtnis Ausgabe: Ausgewaehlte Quellen zur deutschen Geschichte des Mittelalters 15, Darmstadt 1972), where the relationship between Frutolf's chronicle and the revision and continuation of it by Ekkehard has been clearly worked out and presented in the text.

[60] Frutolf under the year 1096 (*ibid* pp. 106–108). It may suggest that the name Petrus Heremita was sometimes satirised as Petrus Hypocrita. For Ekkehard's amendment see *ibid* pp. 124–126.

and Mark 13 are here,[61] and this is exemplified by a handlist of occurrences to prove it.[62] On the other hand, the same texts speak of false prophets who will arise and deceive even the chosen.[63] Not the French, who responded easily because of pestilence and famine, but common people and others from other nations, contrary to the papal edict, had been called early to the Land of Promise by certain prophets risen among them.[64] Peter is not named. The chief targets are Gottschalk, Volkmar and Emicho.[65] But according to Albert Gottschalk had gone 'on the admonition of Peter'.[66] Peter's cohorts are described slightingly as a 'laughing stock to the pagans'[67] included, it seems, among the chaff contrasted with the pure grain which is represented by Godfrey and the other princes who are the leaders of the 'true *militia* of God',[68] and the failure of the early expeditions could be easily explained, if the signs could be shown to identify his emergence among the people as that of one of the pseudo-prophets.

Is there a case for the rehabilitation of Peter the Hermit? We are left with a tradition circulating in the regions of the Lower Rhine and Flanders, and later matched in north-west Germany, which must be set on equal terms with the tradition in the French sources. It credits Peter with a divine commission for an operation which has all the characteristics of the full-blown crusade – pilgrimage in arms, deliverance of Jerusalem, indulgence – communicated by him to the Pope and to the peoples in the West. His preaching was in apocalyptic vein and had an enormous response. Although his name needed no explanation among fellow-crusaders,[69] the failure

---

[61] Under the year 1099, *ibid* p. 130, and, issued separately from the chronicle under the title 'Hierosolymita' *ibid* p. 326 seq, but only the prologue to it is here printed. For the full text see *RHC Occ* V pt I pp. 11, 16–21.

[62] Frutolf-Ekkehard pp. 132, 142–144. The opening entry in Frutolf's 1096 annal may have given Ekkehard the cue, i.e. '*Signum in sole*' which matches Luke 21, 25 '*signa in sole*'.

[63] *Ibid* p. 144.

[64] *Hierosolymita* p. 17.

[65] But, interestingly, Peter was to be cited by St Bernard, with regard to the Second Crusade, as a dire warning to people against listening to anyone who, 'amans gerere primatum inter vos', might wish to go it alone in advance of the main expedition, J. Leclercq, 'L'encyclique de Saint Bernard en faveur de la croisade', *RB* 81 (1971) pp. 282–308 esp p. 299.

[66] Albert bk 1 cap 23.

[67] *Hierosolymita* p. 21.

[68] *Ibid.*

[69] His appearances in the *Gesta Francorum* are oddly ambivalent. The name Petrus Heremita clearly needs no introduction, as when mentioned among the crusade

of his expedition left a blight on his reputation,[70] and the emphasis placed on Clermont by Fulcher, Baudri and Robert the Monk obscured the influential role remembered in the Lorraine/Flanders tradition, which was revived strenuously by Albert and William of Tyre. On any showing, the gap between event and written tradition cannot be more than twenty years or so and, in view of the re-assessment of the sources, it is likely that these reports were circulating at the time of the crusade itself.[71] They receive strong independent confirmation from Anna Comnena and the north-German evidence from the Rosenfeld Annals and these may reflect a version of Peter's contribution put about by the man himself in conversation or preaching. In the historiography of the crusade it would replace the link missing since Sybel's critical assault between the papal intention to bless a military expedition to the East and a pilgrimage to deliver Jerusalem by force, which could confidently rest on the authority of Christ's command and the promise of divine indulgence.

---

leaders (p. 2) and as envoy to Kerbogah (pp. 66–67). He is not with his troops in their fatal battle, having gone to Constantinople because he could not command their obedience (p. 4). He is brought back, with William Carpentarius, to Antioch in disgrace, but his secret withdrawal is explained as due to 'immense misery' (p. 33). He stayed in Jerusalem when the princes rode out to do battle at Ascalon (in contrast to Albert's story that he turned out by special request to join the army later with the holy Cross) but took a leading part in organizing the clergy at Jerusalem in processions, prayer and almsgiving. It looks as though the Anonymous silently avoids a possible criticism of the Hermit's poor attendance record in battle. Raymond d'Aguilers also introduces Peter without comment (pp. 44, 79). But the blame for the Civetot disaster and the consequent growth in confidence of the Turks is not the fault of Peter but of Alexius (pp. 44–45); Peter is noted as having to be forced to bow to Kerbogah (p. 79) and mentioned, without explanation, as the man put in charge of the poor, clergy and lay folk, for the distribution of their half share of the tithe (p. 111).

70 Baudri still calls him *Petrus quidam magnus heremita* (*RHC Occ* IV, p. 15). But Robert the Monk ascribes the failure of his expedition to the lack of a prudent chief (and the word *prudens* may well, as in the *Gesta Francorum* carry the sense 'proud homme', prowess) to rule it, 'just as every congregation of men which is not governed by a *bonus auctor* languishes daily if a languid head is put in charge of it' (*RHC Occ* III, p. 732). Guibert used the occasion of Peter's flight from Antioch because of the food shortage there to ridicule him in a few satirical verses on the themes of 'the star fallen from the sky' and 'practise what you preached', rebuking him for his immoderate diet and his failure to live up to the name of Hermit (*RHC Occ* IV, p. 174; Hagenmeyer, *Peter* pp. 47, 219).

71 Especially if Knoch is right in dating Albert's prologue as early as 1100–1101 and Books 1–6 (as far as the capture of Jerusalem) soon after 1102 (p. 89).

APPENDIX

Albert of Aachen and William of Tyre

The challenge by Peter Knoch to the long-established thesis of Heinrich von Sybel that William used Albert as his 'guiding source' deserves serious consideration.[1] Knoch's detailed examination has certainly confirmed that the two texts correspond closely in overall content, sequence of narrative, sentence structure, and within the overlapping matter he lists some thirty verbal echoes.[2] But in each of these respects there are also marked divergences. This complex relationship he found to be better explained by conjecturing a source common to both works. He adduced both general and particular grounds, of which only a sample can be given here. Sybel, for instance, is argued to be at his weakest in trying to explain why William stopped using Albert after his account of the capture of Jerusalem. There is no reason to assume that there was ever a recension of Albert ending in 1099 which William might have used. Yet with a complete text of Albert up to 1119 before him it is difficult to see why he should have ignored valuable information on the expedition of 1101. In particular, certain divergences in the shared material, especially dates and lists of names, are thought to imply that the authors made different use of the same source. In Albert, for instance, on 8 March Walter Sansavoir 'in the beginning of the Jerusalem Way, entered the kingdom of Hungary' – a clumsy construction which appears to apply the date to Walter's entry into Hungary, whereas to make chronological sense it must refer to the beginning of Walter's march. William in an echoing passage, writing that on 8 March Walter was 'the first to start the journey and, crossing the German kingdom, descended into Hungary', avoids the error. It is unlikely, argued Knoch, that this would be an accidental result of William's expanding of Albert's phrase or, since William would have no

[1] Knoch pp. 29–63.
[2] *Ibid* pp. 31–37.

independent knowledge of the date, of deliberate correction, while a re-styling by both of a common source would provide the simplest explanation.[3] Another example is a list of Duke Godfrey's companions in which, though in other respects identical with Albert's, William inserted four further names, which again suggests that they made selective use of the same source.[4] Oddly, one of the most telling pieces of evidence may be one quite unimportant as such, a list of booty taken after the victory at Dorylaeum. William includes 'phalanges of camels such as our men had previously not seen'. Albert has a similar list, amid other shared information, but without the relative clause.[5] It is difficult to see what could have prompted William to add this phrase, which does not occur in similar lists in the eye-witness accounts, while it is easy to accept that Albert might have omitted it from the source they shared.

The chief weight in Knoch's argument falls on the relationship between the versions of Peter's pilgrimage in Albert, William and the *Fragment*. This story he regarded as necessarily derived from a source shared by the three because of the close correspondence of content and phrasing and, on the other hand, because of variants shared by any two of the three.[6] Given the need for postulating a common source in one instance, it can be shown to provide a satisfactory explanation for the relationship between the texts overall. By this process Knoch reconstituted the contents of a lost account of the crusade which traces Peter's pilgrimage as a catalyst of the movement, the expeditions of Walter, Peter, Gottschalk and those who attacked the Jews; the march of Godfrey to Constantinople, his negotiations with Alexius and the arrival of the other princes; the capture of Nicaea; the battle of Dorylaeum followed by the march to Heraclea; the quarrel between Baldwin and Tancred in

---

[3] Albert bk 1 cap 6 'in initio viae Jherusalem intravit regnum Ungariae'; William bk 1 cap 18 'primus iter arripuit, et pertransiens Teuthonicorum regnum in Hungariam descendit'; Knoch pp 37–38, and on the different dating of Godfrey's negotiations with Alexius and of arrival at Antioch, *ibid* pp 40, 172.

[4] Albert bk 2 cap 1; William Bk 2 cap 1; Knoch pp. 39 (with other examples), p. 156, and for similarly varying lists at Nicaea and Antioch pp. 163–164, 187.

[5] Knoch pp. 60–61, as evidence of the author as a participant. William's account of Dorylaeum is compiled from several sources, the booty list being partly in common with Albert bk 2 cap 43, partly with Baudri (*RHC Occ* IV p. 36). The additional observation occurs in no extant source.

[6] Cf. Hagenmeyer, *Peter* pp. 56–58.

Cilicia and Baldwin's move to Edessa; the siege and capture of
Antioch and the countersiege and battle with Kerbogha; the march
to Jerusalem and its capture. The author is taken to be a follower of
Godfrey's contingent, on whose march, activities and followers he
is particularly well informed, and he is thought to have written the
section up to Godfrey's departure before Summer 1098, if his lack
of animosity towards Alexius can be taken as a guide.[7] This
re-affirms the existence of a 'Lotharingian chronicle' which Kugler
once thought to have identified, but which his passionate but
inadequate advocacy failed to establish.[8]

The argument for a 'Lotharingian chronicle' is not even now
conclusive, but it reaches a high degree of probability and, though
subject to some modifications, can be strengthened. One important
modification is that the close, if intermittent, correspondence
between the two texts does not extend as far as the siege of
Jerusalem. The last clear instance of it occurs in Godfrey's dispatch
of Tancred and a hundred knights to help the Christians in
Bethlehem during the advance from Ramle to Jerusalem.[9] In the
description of the siege and capture of the city the common
structure of the narrative glimpsed elsewhere does not recur, and
there are no echoes in the stories of Godfrey's election or thereafter.
Up to the siege, however, the correspondence is striking, varying
in degree from sentences which are identical word for word to long
sections bearing a kind of ghostly resemblance, including the
occasional use of the same words or, at other times, the same sense
conveyed by different vocabulary and style or, at the other
extreme, to mere overlap of content. This correspondence is
intermittent, at times broken up by different material, but the
insistence with which the full-blooded echoes recur suggests
strongly not a source selectively consulted, as when William used
information from Raymond d'Aguilers, Fulcher or Baudri, but a

---

[7] Knoch pp. 54–62.

[8] He thought to have identified the 'spirit and style' of this chronicle by a detailed
analysis of the first six books of Albert (but without consideration of a possible
common source with William). This depended heavily on subjective distinctions
between sober historical matter likely to derive from a 'chronicle' and accretions
of epic and legendary character more appropriate to *chansons*, for which only the
Chanson d'Antioche could be used as a check. B. Kugler, *Albert von Aachen*
(Stuttgart 1885) and *Analekten zur Kritik Alberts von Aachen* (Tuebingen 1888).

[9] Albert bk 5 caps 44–45; William bk 7 caps 24–25.

written source which provides the main structure of the narrative. This could be either Albert or Knoch's common source, but in no case can either possibility be totally excluded. The balance of probabilities, which favours the common source, may be illustrated by a small sample of the narrative structure, of trivial and perhaps therefore significantly revealing variants, of anecdotes told with a different emphasis, and of references by William to his source.

The story of the siege of Nicaea, for example, in both content and narrative structure differs from other accounts.[10] In Albert and William content and sequence for the arrival of the crusaders and the battle with Soliman's relief force broadly tally.[11] Some incidental facts, as the number of the enemy put at 50,000, occur at different points,[12] and there are greater differences. Albert interposes a speech by the bishop of Le Puy and that Soliman's vanguard of 10,000 were all archers and, wrongly, makes Robert of Normandy take part in the battle.[13] Both record that enemies' heads were catapulted into the city and that 1,000 heads were sent to Alexius,[14] but only William (and, interestingly, the *Chanson d'Antioche*[15]) note that captives were also sent to him. Both accounts distinguish two phases of the siege: the first, on the arrival of the crusaders when the city was not wholly invested; the second, when the investment was complete. Albert (and the *chanson*) describe the siege-order in detail listing over 50 names, placed in the first phase (*in prima obsidione*), including, wrongly, Robert of Normandy.[16] William includes a similar list, in the same order[17] but limited to the main leaders only and placing it in the second phase, which is correct for Robert of Normandy. After William's siege-order the two accounts converge in a description of the seven weeks' siege

[10] Albert bk 2 caps 21–30; William bk 2 caps 21–23, bk 3 caps 1–6.
[11] Albert bk 2 caps 21–28; William bk 2 cap 21 to bk 3 cap 4.
[12] Albert bk 2 cap 25, describing Soliman's departure from Nicaea to collect help; William bk 3 cap 3 on Soliman's return with help.
[13] All in Albert bk 2 cap 27. William mentions the same 10,000 in bk 3 cap 4.
[14] Albert bk 2 cap 28; William bk 3 cap 4.
[15] V 1684.
[16] Albert bk 2 cap 22 seq; *Chanson* v 1156 ff.
[17] In contrast with Raymond d'Aguilers (p. 43) and *Gesta Francorum* (pp. 15–16) which also list only the leaders but begin with Bohemund. Only Albert, the *Chanson* and William begin with Godfrey (which upsets the clock-wise order). William has added orientation by points of compass from Raymond.

and the deaths of Baldwin Calderun and Baldwin de Ganz,[18] including a story of the collapse of the siege engine of Hartmann and Heinrich de Ascha told in similar terms but differing in their description of the immediate circumstances of the collapse. In Albert the attackers misdirected the push and failed to negotiate the uneven ground: in William the machine succumbed to large stones hurled by the defenders.[19] For the rest of the siege William's account could be an expansion of Albert. The Nicaea section illustrates the different kinds of contact also found elsewhere between the two texts.[20] William's could be seen as adapted from Albert, if we could assume that he supplemented it with even quite trivial information of his own. He could well have removed the siege order to the second phase, as more appropriate, having learned from Raymond d'Aguilers, who draws particular attention to this, that Robert of Normandy was not yet present during the first phase. But, on the other hand, the inclusion of Robert of Normandy in Albert's list suggests more probably that William has preserved the original and correct place of the siege-order while Albert advanced it to the earlier phase not noticing that Robert did not belong.[21]

[18] Albert bk 2 cap 29; William bk 3 cap 5 in slightly less detail, but including passages identical in phrasing. The death of Guy de Porsessa is described in the same sense but different words, *ibid*.

[19] Albert bk 2 cap 30; William bk 3 cap 6.

[20] A similar structure in accounts of the expeditions of Walter Sansavoir and Peter (Albert bk 1 cap 16 seq; William bk 1 cap 23 seq) and of Godfrey (Albert bk 2 cap 1 seq; William bk 2 cap 1 seq); the battle of Dorylaeum and the great thirst (Albert bk 2 cap 38 seq; William bk 3 cap 13 seq); the excursion of Tancred and Baldwin into Cilicia (Albert bk 3 cap 5 seq; William bk 3 cap 17 seq; the Antioch siege (Albert bk 3 cap 37 seq; William bk 4 cap 13 seq) but with greater variations between divergences (eg on the fall of the city) and close overlap (eg the stories of Swein and the Tent, below); the battle with Kerbogah (Albert bk 4 cap 30 seq) including a possibly significant variant between William's correct 'per superiorem portam' (bk 6 cap 4) which cannot be directly derived from Albert: 'per portam insuperabilem' (which makes no sense, bk 4 cap 31).

[21] Perhaps misled by some phrase in his source which he rendered 'in prima obsidione' (bk 2 cap 22) and related to his earlier passage on Godrey's arrival at Nicaea 'quo ipse Dux primus obsidionem…constituit fieri' (cap 21). The question is complicated by Graindor's *chanson* which has a long siege-order largely corresponding to Albert's and in the same place, which begins with the words 'Primerains se logea Godefrois de Buillon' (v 1156). This could be the source of Albert's error, if he did use a version of the *chanson*. The siege-orders are printed for comparison in Duparc–Quioc 1 pp. 72–73 and discussed *ibid* 2 pp. 149–50. See discussion below.

Trivial variants in passages otherwise closely related may be the most telling. They are too unimportant to be deliberate amendments by William and there is no known source from which he could have supplied them, so that they are most easily explained by William preserving a detail from a common source which Albert later altered[22] or abbreviated[23] or added,[24] or by each dipping into it selectively.[25] Equally suggestive of a common source is the anecdote of the wonderful tent sent by Baldwin of Edessa to Godfrey, but diverted by the crafty Pancratius to go to Bohemund instead. In Albert's account Godfrey and Robert of Flanders urged Bohemund with pacific words to restore what he had unjustly received. Bohemund refused. On the advice of the other leaders they tried again, but provoked by Bohemund's 'grave response' decided to attack him in his camp, whereupon Bohemund handed over the tent to prevent discord arising among the people. According to William, Godfrey met Bohemund to get the tent back *violenter*. Bohemund claimed a just title to it by the gift of Pancratius, but was won over by the prayers of the leaders and, to save a tumult among people and princes, returned the tent. William then delivered a homily rebuking a man so famed for his modesty and dignity as Godfrey for seeking recovery of so mean an object with such importunity. In Albert Godfrey appears as the injured party: in William Bohemund has a just claim. It is hard to see how William could have extracted that from Albert's words, and yet he must have had something very like Albert's account of the planned attack to warrant the rebuke to Godfrey. It looks as though both depend on a basic version of the story which gave scope for developing their particular slant.[26]

A few references by William to his sources could well refer to Albert's history. Writing about the famine in Antioch he decided

---

[22] Eg Godfrey's fight with the bear (Albert bk 3 cap 4; William bk 3 cap 17).

[23] Eg the wounding of Franco and Sigemar (Albert bk 4 cap 35; William bk 6 cap 8), and the booty list mentioned above.

[24] Eg the chapter on Swein, adding the death of Florina, daughter of the Count of Burgundy (Albert bk 3 cap 54; William bk 4 cap 20).

[25] Eg the daily ration allowed to the impoverished Hartmann: 'panem unum cum portione carnis vel piscis ex suo proprio sumptu' (Albert 4 cap 54); 'ut ei de mensa ducis panis pro quotidiano stipendio, quasi magnum deputaretur' (William bk 6 cap 22).

[26] Albert bk 4 cap 9; William bk 5 cap 9.

not to protract his 'compendium' of history unduly by reporting the sufferings of individual princes, although the *veterum traditiones* do have this information. This comes at a point where Albert's account of the famine ends with Godfrey paying 15 marks silver for the vilest camel and his steward Baldric 3 marks for a goat. This could have triggered off William's remark, although it does suggest that his source had a rather longer list of such experiences.[27] Elsewhere William sarcastically rejects an identification, which occurs in Albert, of the river Orontes, commonly called Fer, with the river *Farfar Damasci*.[28] But of particular interest is a passage where both authors comment on the credibility of their sources on the appalling story of the pregnant women suffering from extremes of thirst.[29] Albert wrote: '*Comperimus etiam illic, non ex auditu solum, sed ex veridica eorum relatione qui et participes fuerunt eiusdem tribulationis*'. William comments more cryptically: '*Accidisse dicitur illa die, quod nulla alia tradit historia*'. Is it likely that William should cap Albert's insistence that he has cross-checked his sources with the dry remark that he found it in no other history? Or is it not easier to suspect that Albert and William, each in their own way, are commenting on some third manner of protestation of credibility in a common source?

The cumulative weight of probabilities deduced from the structure of the narrative, as instanced in the section on the Nicaea siege, from the relationship implied by trivial variants and close but in some ways dissimilar versions of particular incidents, and perhaps also from this last reference by William to his source, give some added force to Knoch's argument in favour of the lost 'Lotharingian chronicle'.

Albert of Aachen and the Chanson d'Antioche

Graindor's *chanson* has been shown to divide into two parts. The second part, beginning with the arrival of Corboran before Antioch (v. 6566) is thought to be based on a literal translation from Robert of Reims, while the first part, beginning with the pilgrimage and

---

[27] Albert bk 4 cap 37; William bk 6 cap 7.

[28] Albert bk 3 cap 33; William bk 4 cap 8; but this could equally well have stood in a common source.

[29] Albert bk 3 cap 2; William bk 3 cap 16.

vision of Peter the Hermit, in many places closely resembles the account by Albert of Aachen.[30] It is generally agreed that, as Graindor claimed, an older *chanson* which he re-fashioned underlies his version.[31] It would have been possible for Graindor (writing after *c.* 1180) to have drawn his material from Albert or, conversely, for Albert to have used the older *chanson*, and a decision on this question affects the degree of credibility to be given to the story of Peter's pilgrimage. The most judicious assessment is still that of Claude Cahen. He found the resemblances between Albert and Graindor were so close that they must derive from a written source, while the differences between them preclude the possibility that either copied the other. He concluded that Albert was based on fragmentary writings and oral reports, that the same sources were at the base of Graindor, but that Albert also knew an early version of the latter's *chanson*.[32]

The argument has been taken a stage further by Suzanne Duparc-Quioc. She confirms plausibly that Graindor could not have used Albert[33] and in the notes to her edition has presented a case that all the passages in common indicate borrowings by Albert from the old *chanson*. The subject is still a matter for discussion,[34] but it is possible to separate from it the section concerning Peter's pilgrimage. For this the relevant part of Graindor's *chanson* is what he calls the 'vrai commencement' which modern *jongleurs* do not have. Duparc-Quioc identifies this as comprising Peter's expedition cut to pieces at Civetot, in that it supplies the beginning of the song of the *Chétifs*, captives in the hands of the Turks. Graindor here creates a wholly fictitious sequence of events – seen as part of his re-fashioning – from Peter's return from Jerusalem and report to the Pope, who authorises Peter's own expedition, to the disaster at Civetot followed by a second visit to the Pope to raise an avenging army, which leads to Clermont and the crusade.[35] From this chronological fantasy the pilgrimage and vision are, however,

---

[30] Cahen pp. 13–14; Duparc–Quioc 1 p. 325; 2 pp. 108 seq, 148 seq and for a review of the literature 2 pp. 19–22. The corresponding passages are printed in her edition.

[31] *Ibid* 2 pp. 144–147.

[32] Cited above.

[33] Duparc–Quioc 2 p. 170.

[34] Especially note Sumberg, [*Chanson d'Antioche*].

[35] Duparc–Quioc 2 pp. 100–102, and for what follows also 2 p. 148 and 1 pp. 30–36.

distinguished as derived from the older *chanson*, partly because of the close resemblance to Albert and partly because of the introductory words used by Graindor. This distinction is disputed,[36] but can be maintained.

Graindor proposes to sing a *chanson* on the deliverance of Jerusalem (v. 11). He will give the 'true beginning' which new *jongleurs* do not have (v. 13). This deals with the expedition led by Peter who was God's avenger (v. 40) which failed. It is a true story (v. 67). Thus begins the *geste* of Peter's expedition, how he has come to the Sepulchre to pray and God appeared to him and told him to come back with vengeance, and the slain will gain Paradise (vv. 68–77). He has heard it sung in another *chanson*, unrhymed, which he will re-fashion (v. 78 f). This prologue continues to v. 266, where starts the *estoire* which he has promised and the beginning of which is Peter's expedition (v. 267). Clearly according to this text the old *chanson* contained Peter's pilgrimage and vision as a prelude to his own expedition. But it is difficult to see this old *chanson*, or this alone, as the source of Albert's version in view of the variants between them,[37] and it looks as though we may have to assume one of those writings which Cahen thought to be basic to both for a common source.[38] This enters the realm of speculation. But one might at least observe that the term 'vrai commencement' might not after all refer to Graindor's fantasy, but could render a phrase in the old *chanson*'s source similarly reflected in Albert's *primus auctor*.

The north-German tradition

The 1096 portent related to Peter's preaching in southern France appears first as an annal in the first section (to 1130) of the *Annales*

[36] Eg Sumberg pp. 364, 365.

[37] The chief differences in the *chanson* are the ports used in Italy—vv 274 (Barlet), 325 (Brandis); Peter's complaints are not, as in Albert part of his speech to the Patriarch (v 278 seq); in the *Chanson* the Patriarch defers his reply to the next morning (v 290 seq); God appears in majesty, not Jesus, as in Albert (v 299 seq); in the *Chanson* Peter pays an extra visist to the Sepulchre, mounts ass, and leaves the country under great difficulty (which corresponds to the Fragment v 321 seq). See Hagenmeyer, *Peter* p. 56 seq.

[38] Cf. also Sybel who concluded that the old *chanson* must have been made up of a number of separate songs, perhaps composed in the camp and written down, and soon circulating abroad, from which some items reached Albert (*Geschichte des ersten Kreuzzugs* pp. 84–85).

A Hermit goes to War

Rosenveldenses (a corruption of the placename Harsefeld near Stade).[39] This entry stands out in content, length and style from the other terse annals, and seems to have originated in a different context, but has been traced to no earlier source. It circulated in northern Germany in the second half of the twelfth century, copied into, for instance, the *Annales Stadenses*,[40] *Annales Palidenses*,[41] *Annalista Saxo*,[42] *Annales Magdeburgenses*[43] and Helmold's *Chronica Slavorum*.[44] It was also integrated with Ekkehard's chronicle in a manuscript of the late twelfth century.[45] Ekkehard's chronicle is a revision and continuation of the work by Frutolf of Michelsberg (Bamberg) whose last annal, for 1099, was written in 1100. Ekkehard made his first revision in 1105/6, revising the annals for 1098 and 1099, and a new recension in 1116/7, when he removed his account of the crusade to an independent appendix, called *Hierosolymita*.[46] The Rosenfeld annal must at an earlier stage have been incorporated in a Frutolf version of the chronicle, from which – imbedded in a section of Frutolf's text including the reference to Peter called *hypocrita* – it was transferred to the revised version of Ekkehard in the late-twelfth century manuscript.

Southampton University

[39] *MGH SS* XVI p. 101, only incompletely extant in a fourteenth-century MS, but reconstructed from *Annalista Saxo* and the *Magdeburg Annals*. The foundation of Harsefeld (1101) was connected with Herrand, bishop of Halberstadt 1090–1102 (Wattenbach—Holtzmann 1 pp 596–599). Cf. Knoch p. 51; Hagenmeyer, *Peter* p. 117.

[40] *MGH SS* XVI p. 317.

[41] *Ibid* p. 71.

[42] *MGH SS* VI p. 728 f.; written *c.*1144–52 (K.Jakob, *Quellenkunde der deutschen Geschichte im Mittelalter* (6 ed H. Hohenleutner 1968) 2 pp. 94–95.

[43] *MG SS* XVI pp. 178–179; begun *c.*1145 (*ibid* p. 109).

[44] *MGH SS* XXI p. 33 f.

[45] Found in an eighteenth-century Goettingen MS, said to be a copy of MS Bodl. Laud. Misc 633 and associated with the *Annales Palidenses*. It is discussed in *Hierosolymita*, *RHC Occ* V pp. xi–xii.

[46] *Frutolf—Ekkehard* pp. 4–8. 32–39.

MONK AND CANON: SOME PATTERNS IN THE RELIGIOUS LIFE OF THE TWELFTH CENTURY

by CHRISTOPHER N.L. BROOKE

IF you were a religious of the 11th or 12th centuries choosing the order in which you were to find your vocation, how did you distinguish order from order, monk from canon? How did you determine gradations of the ascetic life? If you were a founder or benefactor, planning to found a new religious house, how did you determine which order to favour? At a time when asceticism and the religious orders flourished as never before, choice must have been bewildering. There is a copious contemporary literature arguing the relative merits of this mode and that; and modern scholars have offered a remarkably wide variety of advice.[1] Some have proceeded on the assumption that there must have been a fundamental difference and have pursued it as best they might; others, disappointed in the chase, have doubted if any true difference existed. Some have seen all such differences engulfed in the deeper stream of new impulses and modes which affected every approach to the religious life in this age; others have said that to lose track of such differences is to take a very superficial view of the meaning of the rules of St Augustine and St Benedict.[2] It is very

---

[1] From the immense literature I select the following which are particularly helpful: Giles Constable's reprinted studies, *Religious Life and Thought (11th–12th centuries)* and *Cluniac Studies* (Variorum Reprints, London 1979–80) and his *Medieval Monasticism: a select bibliography* (Toronto 1976); Caroline W. Bynum, *Docere verbo et exemplo: an aspect of 12th century spirituality* (Harvard Theological Studies 31, Missoula 1979) and *Jesus as Mother: Studies in the Spirituality of the High Middle Ages* (Berkeley etc 1982) – cited as Bynum 1979 and Bynum 1982; the work of J.C. Dickinson cited at nn 7 and 41 below; and the volumes of the Atti delle Settimane internazionali di studio Mendola = Miscellanea del Centro di Studi Medioevali 3–6, Milan 1962–71: *La Vita Comune del clero nei secoli XI e XII* (3, 2 vols 1962), *L'eremitismo in Occidente nei secoli XI e XII* (4, 1965), *I laici nella 'Societas Christiana' dei secoli XI e XII* (5, 1968), *Il monachesimo e la riforma ecclesiastica (1049–1122)* (6, 1971) – cited as La Mendola 3–6.
[2] Cf. for what follows [C.] Brooke and [W.] Swaan [, *The Monastic World* (London 1974)] cap 8; the view there expressed of the Rule of St Augustine has been

easy indeed to take an entirely sceptical view; and I propose to start by stating the case for saying there was no difference visible to all in every part of Europe – that no general statement of the difference stands up to close inspection. But to rest the matter there, I am sure, would be superficial and mistaken – and so in the second part of this paper I embark on the much more hazardous path of determining where the difference lay. I shall try not to add another definition to the scrap heap, but to show by looking at a number of local situations how it might have appeared both externally to a founder and at a deeper level to an educated man with some discernment of different approaches to the ascetic life and religious spirituality. Yet the ultimate abiding impression is of the strangeness of the central fact: at a time when men were seeking their own religious vocation in numbers never before approached in medieval Europe – and patrons lavishing resources on an unparalleled variety of new religious houses – it is especially difficult for us to observe in many cases where the differences lay.

At a superficial level there is an obvious explanation of the paradox. It is often the case that the distinctions most taken for granted are the most difficult for the outsider to discern. When my wife and I once asked the way in Stockholm we were told by a friendly Swede who was as lost as we were that he would hail the next native of Stockholm who passed – 'you can tell them by their physiognomy', said he; and chose a victim with deliberate care who turned out to be an Englishman. The Florentine will tell you that the character of the folk of Prato and Siena differs in a marked degree from those of Florence, even though you may never meet anyone who precisely answers to any of his characters. The old inhabitant of a Cambridge college will tell you more in sorrow than in anger that there are certain appreciable inferiorities in the character of Oxford, and with much more precise and emphatic characterisation the traditional failings of the college next door. Here is a difference which is keenly observed and deeply felt and totally obscure to any outside observer.

In the Prologue to the Canterbury Tales Chaucer presented a well known conundrum.

---

severely criticised as too negative. For the rules themselves, see esp *Le règle de S. Benoît* edd A. de Vogüé and J. Neufville (*SCR* 181–6, Paris 1971–2); L. Verheijen, *La règle de S. Augustin* (2 vols Paris 1967).

A monk ther was, a fair for the maistrie,
An outridere, that lovede venerie,
A manly man, to been an abbot able.
Ful many a deyntee hors hadde he in stable ...
The reule of seint Maure or of seint Beneit,
By cause that it was old and somdel streit
This ilke monk leet olde thynges pace,
And heeld after the newe world the space ...
What sholde he studie and make hymselvene wood [mad],
Upon a book in cloystre alwey to poure,
Or swynken with his handes, and laboure,
As Austyn bit? Howe shal the world be served?
Lat Austyn have his swynk to hym reserved![3]

There is confusion here, say the commentators; Chaucer has made three rules out of one. The monk must have followed St Benedict's rule if he was really a monk, and there never was a rule of St Maurus; why then this reference to the rival rule of St Austin, St Augustine?

What makes Chaucer's satire so delectable and so lasting is in part at least the marvellous skill with which he creates simultaneously the illusion of an individual and the illusion of a type. The monk is both a general portrayal of a class of men – he might equally well be a Black Monk or a Black Canon – and a sharply drawn character, who might be X or Y, whom we know well. I call these two marks of his *Prologue* illusions since it seems to me likely that he intended them so. He can hardly have thought all monks and canons were mighty hunters, or all friars rascals, still less all parish priests men of the holy simplicity of his poor Parson; indeed he says as much. For some of the individual characters precise originals have been claimed, and J.M. Manly showed indeed that the host carried the name of an actual London inn-keeper of the day.[4] But even he admitted that Chaucer seems to have got his wife's name wrong – fortunately, in view of the shrewish character he gives her; and it really makes little difference whether we suppose that Chaucer used

---

[3] Chaucer, *Canterbury Tales, Prologue*, lines 165–88 ed F.N. Robinson (Oxford 12974) pp. 18–19.
[4] J.M. Manly, *Some new light on Chaucer* (London 1926) esp pp. 78–81; on the monk, p. 262.

traits from known persons of his day or not. I am myself sceptical if there was more drawing from life than was required to catch and entertain his audience; if there had been, the illusion of type would have been difficult to sustain; and I rather suppose that Professor Manly and his successors have been caught in a delicate web of Chaucer's weaving. For the monk, however, Manly contented himself with hinting that he knew who he was or might be, and it was left to Ramona Bressie and after her David Knowles, in what I regard as a rare indiscretion of that great scholar, to trace the lineaments of the monk in William Clown, abbot of Leicester, one of the notable hunting abbots of the 14th century.[5] There are indeed links, but for our purpose it is the other limb of Chaucer's satire which counts: his monk was both monk and canon; for they are all one. In most European languages today – and in virtually all before the reformation – the word monk, *monaco, Mönch, moine, monje*, can equally well mean canon or friar; and it is only in modern English, the one language in Europe devised by folk who knew not monks, that it is a solecism to call Martin Luther, the Austin Friar, a monk.

Chaucer's monk was of the late 14th century. What happens if we go back into the 12th century: was it not altogether different then? It is hard to give any precise answer to this question. But there is much to suggest that the distinction was often not so apparent as it is to us. We rarely know what passed in a patron's mind, but there are many indications that no fundamental difference was apparent. Among the most notable of 12th century patrons was King David I of Scotland, who was evidently a connoisseur: he planted, or had a hand in planting, black monks from Tiron at Kelso, Black Canons at Holyrood, Jedburgh and Cambuskenneth, White Monks at Melrose, Newbattle, Dundrennan and Kinloss, and encouraged his constable to plant White Canons at Dryburgh.[6] He doubtless knew a good deal about the different modes of life and customs of these orders and respected it; but there is no evident difference in function, or even in the siting, of the orders. He was only one of a number of patrons who favoured both Augustinians and Cistercians; and although Walter

---

[5] D. Knowles, *Religious Orders in England* 2 (Cambridge 1955) pp. 365–6.
[6] *MRHS* pp. 66, 68–9, 72, 74–7, 88–93, 101 (some doubt attaches to Dundrennan, and he was not sole founder of them all); cf. Brooke in La Mendola 6, p. 143.

Monk and Canon

Espec, founder of Kirkham and Rievaulx, did try (it seems) to convert his Austin Canons into Cistercian monks – it was a lamentable failure – it is clear that the site and function of a Cistercian house in the 1130s did not appear fundamentally different to him from that of an Augustinian in the 1120s.[7] Most telling is the story of the Premonstratensian Canons. In central Europe, so I understand, recent research has attempted to preserve some features of the conventional distinction between Cistercians and Premonstratensians to show that the monks tried to avoid and the canons, in some degree, to foster pastoral work.[8] Both had a role to play in the resettlement of German-speaking people east of the Elbe. Both represent the advance of western ideas and culture. Both were expected to engage in missionary enterprise as well as in the contemplative life. The involvement of the Cistercians in the mission is still under discussion, but it is agreed that the Morimond filiation in central Europe fitted into the landscape more rapidly and readily than their western colleagues, and never attempted isolation and self-sufficiency to the same degree.[9] In England the relation between the orders, in quite a different way, was equally remarkable. Throughout the 12th century foundations of Austin Canons were popular. The enormous proliferation of tiny houses both of canons and of monks makes statistics almost meaningless, but it seems to be broadly true that for independent foundations as opposed to cells and minor dependencies canons always led the field. But in the period 1132–1152, notoriously, the Cistercians had a marvellous success: almost all the major English and Scottish houses were founded then, and the invasion of Wales and Ireland began.[10] In 1152 the Cistercian General Chapter passed its famous decree forbidding new foundations,[11] and in 1153 St Bernard died. Viewed from the perspective of central Europe and the children of

[7] [J.C.] Dickinson[, *The Origins of the Austin Canons and their introduction into England* (London 1950)] p. 123.
[8] For current research see J. Kłoczowski, 'Polonia' in *Dizionario degli Istituti di perfezione* 7 (Rome 1983) cols 45–68, 75–7; and *idem*, 'Die Zistercienser in Klein-Polen und das Problem ihrer Tätigkeit als Missionare und Seelsorger' in *Die Zistercienser: Ordensleben zwischen Ideal und Wirklichkeit, Ergänzungsband* edd K. Elm and P. Joerissen (Cologne 1983) pp. 71–8.
[9] *Ibid.* I am much indebted for help in this passage to Jerzy Kłoczowski and Urszula Borkowska; and to discussions with my former pupil Nicholas Coulson.
[10] *MRHEW* pp. 110–28; *MRHS* pp. 72–7; *MRHI* pp. 114–44.
[11] Canivez p. 45.

Morimond, this decree was nugatory; but viewed from England and the daughters of Clairvaux in particular, the picture is quite different. There was a virtual stop for a whole generation; and after 1152 Cistercian foundations in England never again became more than a trickle.[12] The Premonstratensians, who only counted a handful of houses before the 1150s, flourished in their stead.[13] The first Premonstratensian house in England was founded at Newsham in Lincolnshire in 1143 and they spread from there to Alnwick in Northumberland and Easby under the shadow of Richmond Castle in Yorkshire in the late 1140s and early 1150s; but the great leap forward began with the foundation of Welbeck in 1153-4, and the kind of patron who had favoured the Cistercians under Stephen was founding Premonstratensian houses, in similar situations, under Henry II. Very characteristic of the great lords of this period was Ranulf of Glanville, Henry II's chief justiciar, who in 1171 founded Butley Priory for the Augustinian Canons, and in 1183 Leiston for the Premonstratensians.[14]

In exactly the same period the Gilbertine canons enjoyed their heyday.[15] This may have had more to do with the chronology of their founder, who died in the same year as Henry II, than with the movements of kings and patrons; and it is not entirely correct to class the Gilbertines as canons. They show to perfection, indeed, some of the ambiguities we are investigating. Originally founded to provide a secure institutional framework for the devout women who gathered round Gilbert at Sempringham, they rapidly grew into a double Order; and in the long run St Gilbert subjected the nuns to the rule of St Benedict and the men to the rule of St Augustine – without ever explaining to posterity precisely why he did so.[16] It was common for nuns in this period to be members of

[12] *MRHEW* pp. 112–28; for the general picture in the Order, L. Janauschek, *Originum Cisterciensium Tomus I* (Vienna 1877) pp. 131–282.

[13] *MRHEW* pp. 183–93; H.M. Colvin, *The White Canons in England* (Oxford 1951); and see next note.

[14] See R. Mortimer in *Leiston Abbey Cartulary and Butley Priory Charters*, (Suffolk Rec S, Suffolk Charters, Ipswich 1979) esp pp. 1–5; see also Mortimer in *BIHR* 54 (1981) 1–16, on Ranulf of Glanville and his family and their foundations.

[15] On the Gilbertines see Rose Graham, *S. Gilbert of Sempringham and the Gilbertines* (London 1901); R. Foreville, *Le Livre de S. Gilbert de Sempringham* (Paris 1943 – a new ed, as *The Book of St Gilbert*, by R. Foreville and G. Keir will be published in OMT); and the forthcoming general study by B. Golding.

[16] *Vita S. Gilberti* cap 17 (in *The Book of St Gilbert* forthcoming; see meanwhile *MA* 6, 2, Insertion on 'The Order of Sempringham' p. xii).

no very definite order (like the ministering Mr Chadband in *Bleak House*, who was 'attached to no particular denomination'), but to follow the rule (so far as we can penetrate into a very obscure region) of their chaplains.[17] This has recently been made abundantly clear by the work of Dr Sally Thompson. St Gilbert, like St Norbert, founder of the White Canons, was deeply influenced by Bernard of Clairvaux; and Gilbert indeed tried to arrange a merger.[18] But the Cistercians would have nothing to do with women – a stance they maintained for some considerable time until they awoke one day to find that there were nuns in their Order, a circumstance which bewildered them as much as it has confused modern historians of the order.[19] As for Norbert, he was a missionary through and through, and the full Cistercian vocation was not for him. But orders often have their revenge on their founders; and to the patrons of the late 12th century the difference between White Monks and White Canons was much less apparent. As for St Gilbert, the indications are that he thought his menfolk should perform the role of Martha, his ladies of Mary – and as to why that made Austin's rule appropriate for the men, Benet's for the women, that is a problem to which we shall return.

Another very powerful indicator of the common ground between canons and monks lies in their buildings. Modern scholars have been so much concerned to discover differences in the planning of the houses of different orders that they have sometimes lost sight of the fundamental fact that they liked to live in buildings of an extraordinary uniformity. I have studied this in a separate paper and so will resume the point briefly.[20] The characteristic monastic enclosure, with church, cloister, chapter house, dormitory, refectory and parlours grouped in a close-knit unity, was repeated with remarkably little difference in every part of western Christendom by almost every order of monks and canons. We

[17] See Sally Thompson's London PhD Thesis on 'English Nunneries: a study of the post-Conquest Foundations *c.* 1095–*c.* 1250' (1984).

[18] *Vita S Gilberti* cap 13–14, MA 6, 2, Insertion pp. xi*–xii*.

[19] It has now been admirably clarified by Sally Thompson, 'The problem of the Cistercian nuns in the twelfth and early thirteenth centuries', *Medieval Women*, ed D. Baker (*SCH Subsidia* 1 1978) pp. 227–52.

[20] In an unpublished lecture 'Cloister and College: aspects of religious life and planning in the late middle ages' delivered at Westfield College, London, in February and Emory University, Atlanta, Georgia before the Medieval Academy of America in March 1984.

cannot trace its origin in the present state of knowledge, but the structure, and the name of the cloister and some other parts, is already clear in the famous St Gall plan of the 9th century.[21] It is fully recorded in surviving buildings and excavated sites from the 11th century on, and only began to be seriously modified at the end of the Middle Ages. The reason for this modification is clear. The monastic plan represented the most complex design for a domestic building or group of buildings known in 11th and 12th century Europe: even more complex and articulated than most castles and palaces; it was more than chance that the English kings used Westminster Abbey as the major element in their greatest palace.[22] But it was always designed for communities living in common. It had to be severely modified by communities of hermits, as by the Carthusians; and much change was needed to adapt it to the living habits of the late middle ages and early modern times, when a greater diversity of smaller rooms – and ultimately, personal privacy – came to be accepted in religious houses as in major secular buildings. The monastic cloister in its heyday is a very remarkable monument both to the living habits of the central middle ages, and to the communal ritual of monastic life: the cloister is only the natural centre of a community (at least in the climate of northern Europe) whose life revolves round ritual processions conducting the inmates to rooms designed to cater for every phase of their life and every bodily function. There was sufficient of ritual and meditation in the life of secular canons for cloisters to be a normal feature of secular cathedrals in the south and an occasional feature of northern cathedrals – and it is fascinating to observe how William of Wykeham, who doubtless enjoyed his own community's cloister on the occasional spring mornings when he visited Winchester Cathedral, implanted a cloister on his academic communities in Winchester and Oxford.[23] But if we look more generally at the planning of Oxford and Cambridge colleges in the

[21] See W. Horn and E. Born, *The Plan of St Gall* (3 vols Berkeley etc 1979) esp 1 pp. 241–309 and 2 pp. 315–59 (C.M. Malone and W. Horn on the influence of the plan).
[22] See *The History of the King's Works*, ed H.M. Colvin 1 (London 1963) cap 4 pt 4 and cap 12.
[23] See G. Jackson Stops in *New College Oxford 1379–1979*, ed J. Buxton and P. Williams (Oxford 1979) pp. 155–6, 175–7; J. Harvey in *Winchester College, Sixth Centenary Essays*, ed R. Custance (Oxford 1982) cap 3, esp p. 81.

late middle ages – designed within a narrow world for a very precise function, for communities of students all engaged in the same life and the same kind of work – we must be struck by how greatly they differ compared with the monastic enclosures of the whole of Christendom of earlier days.[24]

Within the framework there were differences indeed. The Cistercians achieved a unique degree of uniformity, partly by the centralised organisation of their order, partly by their deliberate efforts in this direction; partly, no doubt, by recruiting expert masons among their early lay brothers. And their monastic complexes normally made much more provision for lay brothers than other orders. Thus lay visitors were forbidden from their churches, and the naves dedicated to the lay brothers; the western range of the claustral buildings provided refectory and dormitory for lay brothers; and in early days at least provision was made for choir monks and lay brothers not normally to meet.[25] In contrast the Premonstratensians, who shared so many of the features of the Cistercians, show the least uniformity, the most irregularity, of all the major orders of the century.[26] In part this may be due to the present state of knowledge; in part to the paucity of evidence for Premonstratensian planning; but it may well be that there was in this region a genuine difference. It cannot, however, be attributed to the fact that one order was of monks, the other of canons, for there are some Augustinian houses which show quite a close imitation of some Cistercian practices, such as the night stair from dormitory to transept.[27]

[24] See n 20; R. Willis and J.W. Clark, *The Architectural History of the University of Cambridge and of the Colleges of Cambridge and Eton* (4 vols Cambridge 1886) and the *RCHM* (England) vols on *City of Oxford* and *City of Cambridge* (1939, 1959).

[25] See (D.] Knowles and [J.K.S.] St Joseph, [*Monastic Sites from the Air* (Cambridge 1952)] esp p. xix; M. Aubert, *L'architecture cistercienne en France* (2 ed 2 vols Paris 1947) I p. 317 for lay brothers' choirs, 2 cap 4 for lay brothers' quarters; see C. Brooke, *Medieval Church and Society* (London 1971) p. 166 n – but further consideration of the evidence e.g. of the choir screen at Maulbronn (Brooke and Swaan, plate 243) makes probable that Aubert was right that lay brothers could not normally see the high altar.

[26] Knowles and St Joseph pp. xxii–xxiii, 150–83.

[27] Examples are Cartmel (J.C. Dickinson in *Trans. Cumberland and Westmorland Antiqu. and Arch. Soc.* 45 (1946) p. 57); Hexham (plan in W.T. Taylor, *Hexham Priory*, ed of 1970 at end); Bolton ([A. Hamilton] Thompson, [*History and Architectural Description of the priory of St Mary,*] Bolton[-in-Wharfedale* (Thoresby Soc 30, 1928)] p. 146).

Most of the literature distinguishing one order from another was controversial, the work of angry men defying their rivals. But there is one work which is wholly eirenical in purpose, the *Libellus de diuersis ordinibus*, revived and commented for us splendidly by Giles Constable and Bernard Smith.[28] This is the only surviving work of the 12th century which sets to work in a systematic way to analyse the differences between monks and canons, and different modes of each, with the specific purpose of showing that they all have a place in God's providence, all are justified in their callings – though not necessarily free from errors and aberrations – and all supported by biblical precedents, if properly understood. Just the thing, we should have said, to appeal to King David and his like. Yet it survives only in one manuscript, and that incomplete; there is no evidence that it strayed from the see of Liège where it was written until it was printed by the Maurists in the 18th century and until the manuscript fled to England, probably in the 19th.

Even though the author's peaceful intent is unusual in the written literature, it was not unusual in real life. Some of the most zealous of the controversialists were compelled to beat their swords into plough-shares. Even St Bernard, zealous in pursuit of everything corrupt in the traditional monasticism – as he had to be to justify the conversion of many Benedictines and Cluniacs to what he fervently believed to be a better life – was curbed and tamed by Peter the Venerable to speak lovingly and warmly of Cluny herself.[29] Among more ordinary mortals, Gilbert Foliot, the eminent English Cluniac, counted several Cistercians (including St Aelred) among his close friends, and delivered one of the frothiest of obituary notices on Bernard himself – a panegyric of his order as much as of the man – immediately after his death.[30] Yet unlike his own former abbot, Peter the Venerable, Gilbert was not always a peaceable man, and he is perhaps most widely known for the violence of his polemics against Thomas Becket. In ordinary intercourse it is likely that good relations between different orders

[28] *OMT* (1972), here cited as *Libellus*.
[29] This is reflected in Bernard's correspondence with him: *Opera S. Bernardi* edd J. Leclercq, C.H. Talbot and H.M. Rochais (Rome 1957–78) 7–8, Epp 147–9, 228, 265, 267, 364, 387–9, 521–esp 228.
[30] *Letters and Charters of Gilbert Foliot ...*, edd Adrian Morey and C.N.L. Brooke (Cambridge 1967), no 108 pp. 146–9; cf. A. Morey and C.N.L. Brooke, *Gilbert Foliot and his Letters* (Cambridge 1965) p. 77.

were as common as bad in the heyday of 12th century monasticism; doubtless the spirit was abroad so perfectly characterised between the orders of friars in the saying attributed to the Franciscan leader Albert of Pisa – that the Franciscans should dearly love the Dominicans for various good reasons, among others that they sometimes showed them what *not* to do.[31]

The author of the *Libellus* divided the religious of his world into hermits, monks and canons – placing his own order last, as he specifically points out to the monkish friend to whom the work was addressed;[32] and the monks and canons he divides into those who dwell far and those who dwell near the abodes of men, the more contemplative and the more active as we should say. He perceives indeed that there are distinctions within monks and canons more remarkable than those between them – yet this is never quite distinctly stated, for his purpose is not so much to divide and analyse as to show the common place all hold in God's purposes. Furthest from his own way of life (for he was evidently a canon regular living close to the abodes of men) were the hermits.

> Come then, whoever you are that love the solitary life, and take an example from him who was the first to be called just, and receive an increase of good works. See also whether our Jesus did anything that could be compared to this kind of life. It is written of Him in St John's Gospel: 'Jesus therefore, when he knew that they would come to take him by force and make him king, fled again into the mountain, himself alone.' Behold my Jesus withdrawing alone into the mountain, lest the hermit should doubt whether he should live alone in the mountains or the wilderness.[33]

Thus 'by withdrawing into the mountain or the desert, as is proper for hermits, he consecrated their life in Himself.'[34] And he goes on to observe from a wide range of biblical precedents that all recollected folk, not only full-time hermits, may profit from a spell of solitude. This is very characteristic. He distinguishes carefully

---

[31] Fratris Thomae ... de Eccleston, *Tractatus de adventu Fratrum Minorum in Angliam*, ed A.G. Little (edn of Manchester 1951) p. 82.
[32] *Libellus* pp. 2–3, cf. p. xv.
[33] *Ibid* pp. 10–11; cf. John 6:15.
[34] *Ibid* pp. 12–13.

the various modes of the common life – for monks far from human habitation and in towns and the hubbub of life; for canons likewise in both types of place – and yet he carefully avoids suggesting that any of these is either perfect or decadent; he finds a place for all. Even the monks distracted by the affairs of their tenants and serfs may be reckoned to do it for the sake of their serfs.[35] The outward looking are justified as well as the inward. It seems a pity that this gallant ecumenical endeavour commanded so little attention in its own day.

The perceptions of the *Libellus* present a formidable obstacle to anyone who wishes to assert that there was a fundamental and universal difference between monks and canons in the early 12th century; and I shall spare you the details of the many arguments which have been mounted on this issue. Let me just say that those scholars who have done most to illuminate and deepen our knowledge of the religious life of the 11th and 12th centuries have commonly in the process stressed the variety of experience and aspiration which can be seen within the canonical and the monastic orders. As examples from a larger gathering I cite only Charles Dereine, who especially penetrated into the roots of the more ascetic canonical foundations, Premontré among them; Jean Leclercq who has specifically argued (perhaps a little too precisely, but from a unique experience of the literature) that though one can discern a 'monastic theology' in this epoch one cannot distinguish a specifically canonical theology from it; and Giles Constable, the tendency of whose many studies is to see all the rich and complex manifestations of the religious life as ultimately part of a seamless robe.[36] A heroic attempt has been made in recent years by Professor Caroline Bynum to find a genuine thread of difference.[37] She sets aside earlier attempts, especially to see clear-cut differences of pastoral role or between the inward and outward looking viewpoints of the orders. But she finds a constant theme in the literature

---

[35] *Ibid* pp. 40–3.

[36] E.g. Charles Dereine, art 'Chanoines' in *DHGE* 12 (Paris 1953) cols 353–405; and arts in *RHE* 41 (1946) pp. 365–406, 42 (1947) pp. 352–78, 46 (1951) pp. 534–65; cf. Bynum 1982, pp. 26–7 nn; J. Leclercq in La Mendola 3, 1 pp. 117–41; G. Constable, Trevelyan Lectures forthcoming, and see above n 1 meanwhile. Bynum 1982 pp. 25–6 notes scholars who see sharper differences, most notably (and with great subtlety) Sir Richard Southern, *Western Society and the Church in the Middle Ages* (Harmondsworth 1970) pp. 241–50.

[37] Bynum 1979; Bynum 1982 cap 1.

of instruction and spiritual direction – that monks emphasise the formation of character, the duty to lead the religious life, to form their own monastic personae, while canons are repeatedly enjoined to teach by word and example. She admits that it is not wholly watertight – what can one do with a man of such universal charity as Peter of Celle, John of Salisbury's intimate friend, who addresses monks and canons alike with equal concern?[38] I do not doubt that there is a perception in Professor Bynum's work or profound interest, though I share her critics' doubts whether so slender a thread of evidence will bear quite the weight she has perforce to lay on it, and whether one can possibly know from such evidence how the generality of monks and canons viewed themselves.[39]

I wish to take quite a different approach. It has often been observed, to take a profane example, that historically the words Republican and Democrat have meant clean different things in different states and regions of the United States – that the parties are alliances of local groups and factions without any substantial common definition. Yet it would be foolish to deny that the differences have in many times and places been profound, or that the parties have existed. Not to press the analogy too far, it seems natural to suppose that in many local situations a sharper focus may have been discernible than from a global view. Thus a close look at monks and canons in areas such as Bavaria where early houses of Augustinian canons particularly flourished would doubtless be extremely instructive; as too the comparison between Cistercian and Premonstratensian endeavours in what was then eastern Germany at which we have glanced before.[40] But to give a clearer view of the variety and complexity of the local perspective I shall take my examples from Britain, and in doing so traverse ground so clearly and authoritatively covered by John Dickinson over 20 years ago.[41] I have often had the experience of checking my best

---

[38] Peter of Celle's *De disciplina claustrali* (PL 202 cols 1097–1146) is discussed in Bynum 1979 pp. 157–60; Bynum 1982 p. 37.

[39] See esp R.M. Thomson in *Speculum* 56 (1981) pp. 598–601, a very perceptive critique, though perhaps not doing full justice to the penetration and subtlety of Caroline Bynum's analyses.

[40] See esp P. Classen in La Mendola 3, 1 pp. 304–48 and references; N. Backmund, *Monasticon Praemonstratense* 1, 2 pts (2 ed 1983); above n 9.

[41] See Dickinson *passim*, and many individual studies, most recently on St Augustine's Bristol: *Essays in Bristol and Gloucestershire History*, ed P. McGrath and J. Cannon (Bristol 1976) pp. 109–126.

ideas on the canons in his book and finding them anticipated there, though I think my purpose and approach is in some ways different from his, and I occasionally differ on the details of the story.

Three of the houses from which the English canons principally sprang point the contrasts and the paradoxes of the story at the outset. St Gregory's at Canterbury was set there by Archbishop Lanfranc as a hospital, that is to say, as a welfare institution in the city – to do work inappropriate to the monks of his cathedral or of St Augustine's abbey – and we may take Eadmer's word for it that he staffed it with regular canons, even though it seems quite clear that its establishment as a full Augustinian house came later.[42] What seems to have happened is that it was converted from a hospital and social service centre (as we should interpret the phrase) into an Augustinian priory in which the hospital was a minor element; and that is a process often repeated in the 12th and 13th centuries.[43]

If we examine the grander institutions of the city of London we shall find no such evident contrast between the life and work of a great abbey or cathedral priory and a hospital and social service centre, because there was no great abbey in the city, unless one counts the not too distant Westminster. The chronicle of Holy Trinity Aldgate is in form a much later document, nor is the foundation history of St Bartholomew's contemporary; yet it is clear that both enshrine genuine contemporary traditions of the purposes and activity of their founders, Queen Matilda and Canon Rahere.[44] Matilda, as befitted the daughter of St Margaret and sister of King David I of Scotland, was much interested and involved in religious foundations, and doubtless played a considerable part in

[42] See *Cartulary of the Priory of St Gregory, Canterbury*, ed Audrey M. Woodcock (Camden Third Series 88 1956) esp pp. ix–xi.
[43] There are examples noted in *MRHEW* pp. 155–80 – Cold Norton, Conishead etc; the most remarkable case is St Bartholomew's London which was founded in 1123 as both priory and hospital, though the hospital may well have been embarked on first; but the hospital was separated from the priory later in the 12th century ([C.] Brooke and [G.] Keir, [*London 800–1216, the Shaping of a City* (London 1975)], pp. 325–8; see N. Kerling in *Guildhall Miscellany* 4, 3 (1972) pp. 137–48. See *MRHEW* p. 311 for the numerous hospitals served by canons or brothers under the rule of St Augustine without forming regular priories.
[44] Brooke and Keir pp. 314–28; chronicle of Holy Trinity Aldgate in *The Cartulary of Holy Trinity Aldgate*, ed G.A.J. Hodgett (London RecS 7 1971) pp. 223–33; *The Book of the Foundation of St Bartholomew's Church in London* ed N. Moore (*EETS* 163 1923); also modern English translation by H.H. King and W. Barnard, ed E.A. Webb (London 1923).

inspiring her husband's outbreaks of good works. The story the Aldgate chronicler tells of her brother David's horror in finding her washing the feet of lepers fits the strongly practical pastoral bent of her own foundations[45] – a house of canons in London which was evidently intended to combine pastoral responsibility of some kind with the liturgy and ritual of the religious life; and the leper hospital of St Giles in the Fields, safely beyond the limit of Holborn – even if the traveller who becomes entangled today in the swirl of streets at the foot of Tottenham Court Road, which mark the site laid out by Matilda, will search in vain for any surviving fields. Even more sharply defined is the purpose of St Bartholomew, founded by a converted courtier in the same court of King Henry I, to improve and care for an insalubrious area just outside the city walls, and allow space both for a large hospital and a community of canons.[46] It is instructive to observe in this case that the interests of the two halves rapidly diverged, so that in the second half of the 12th century it was thought expedient to separate the house of canons from the hospital, and to put an experienced lay administrator in charge of the hospital. Notoriously, it was this separation which saved St Bartholomew's hospital at the Dissolution of the Monasteries; and its survival is a reminder of Rahere's assumption that canons and welfare went hand in hand and of his successors' rapid dismantling of his plan.

Examples of Augustinian houses with their origin in hospitals, or with some evident connexion with pastoral affairs, or at least with city communities, could be multiplied without effort. Let two suffice. At Leicester successive overlords gathered all the churches of the town by a great act of power into the hands of communities of canons, first secular, within the walls, then regular, without.[47] This was the great abbey over which the mighty hunter, William Clown, later presided. However much or little he did for the churches of Leicester, it can hardly be doubted that the Norman lords had taken it for granted that the great church would perform the role of the ancient minster it replaced, and be a centre of worship and a leader in the religious life of the town. In this respect

[45] *Cartulary of Holy Trinity Aldgate* pp. 223–4; Brooke and Keir pp. 318–19.
[46] See n 44.
[47] A. Hamilton Thompson, *The Abbey of St Mary of the Meadows, Leicester* (Leicester 1949) cap 1.

the intention seems identical to that of the founder of St Andrew's priory in the next county town of Northampton, who was King David's half-brother and predecessor in the earldom.[48] In this case the original scheme is overlaid by later events, for new churches were founded and the priory lost much of its patronage; but so far as one can tell the original conception was the same – save that St Andrew's was a Cluniac priory, St Mary of the Meadows at Leicester Augustinian. It is doubtful if Simon de Saint-Liz saw the significance in this which Matilda or David might have seen; though we may take it that a Cluniac priory was less well placed in the late 12th century for defending its patronage than an Augustinian abbey.[49]

The other example is Cambridge, where we find (so far as we can penetrate an obscure area of scholarship) the precinct of a house of canons blossoming into a parish; that is to say that in the late middle ages the immediate environs of the priory by the river (as a native of Cambridge is likely to say, beside the gas works) formed the nucleus of a parish which extended over virtually the whole of the east fields of Cambridge.[50] The origin of this story, which seems to be (in the present state of knowledge) unique to Cambridge, goes something like this. The priory of St Giles was founded by the castle by the Norman sheriff Picot and his pious wife Hugolina about 1092. The late 13th century chronicle which enshrines those facts is cemented by many charters of doubtful authenticity; but on the whole I am inclined to think the story it tells more authentic than its charters – a situation, pace the shade of J.H. Round, only too familiar to students of medieval charters.[51] The site for St Giles was small and water scarce, so early in the 12th century they were moved to the more salubrious riverside of Barnwell – a description which I am bound to say reads oddly to one who has known from a child the muddy banks of the murky

[48] On the churches of Northampton see Michael Franklin, 'Minster and Parishes: Northamptonshire Studies' (Cambridge PhD Thesis 1982) cap 2, esp pp. 86–98 – cited by kind permission of Dr Franklin; and studies by M. Franklin and others in *Northamptonshire* 5, *RCHM England* (1984).

[49] See n 48.

[50] See [C.] Brooke, 'The Churches of Medieval Cambridge'[, in *History, Society and the Churches*, edd D. Beales and G. Best (Cambridge 1985)] pp. 49–76.

[51] *Liber Memorandorum ecclesie de Bernewelle*, ed J.W. Clark (Cambridge 1907) esp pp. 38–42.

Cam in that region. There they settled round a hermit's cell and ancient chapel of St Andrew.[52] The endowment of the priory of St Giles and St Andrew grew apace, based on the tithes of almost the whole of the west field which became the parish of St Giles, and of the east field, which became (perhaps after the Dissolution) the parish of St Andrew the Less.[53] The parishes of Cambridge were shaped within the city precinct, and the canons' empire among the agrarian tithes was evidently established before the parish boundaries could spread through the fields; and this had the curious consequence that the priory had parochial rights over what was in effect a large parish. The other precinct formed in the eastern fields, that of the nuns of St Radegund, likewise composed a parochial precinct, in that case not so large, but sufficient to preserve in the grounds of its successor, Jesus College, a substantial open space close to the city ditch.[54] In this story, once again, it stands to reason that tithes and pastoral responsibility were intimately linked in early days. In the 12th century, if one adds the ephemeral community of the canons of the Holy Sepulchre, then canons following Austin's rule came near to monopolising this city of many churches and few inhabitants.[55]

All this supports a familiar pattern – of canons as folk nearer to the city centres, to the ordinary lives of the community, to pastoral care, at least in origin and in principle. But even before Matilda set her hand to Aldgate one of her chaplains, named Ernisius, had gone into partnership with a knight turned hermit to found Llanthony in the bleakest and remotest corner of Gwent under the Black Mountain.[56] John Dickinson has doubted the veracity of the Llanthony chronicle and dismissed it as a 13th century compilation with much anachronism in it. This was partly due to the curious way in which it is presented in Dugdale's *Monasticon*. A closer look at the Cotton

---

[52] *Ibid* pp. 41–2.

[53] Brooke, 'The Churches of Medieval Cambridge' n 50.

[54] J.G. Sikes and Freda Jones in *VCH Cambridgeshire* 2 pp. 218–9; A. Gray, *The Priory of St Radegund, Cambridge* (Cambridge Antiquarian Soc 1898); *The Atlas of Historic Towns* 2, edd M.D. Lobel and W.H. Johns (London 1975), Cambridge (separately paginated).

[55] Brooke, 'The Churches of Medieval Cambridge' n 50; M. Gervers in *Actes du XXIIe Congrès International d'histoire de l'Art* (Budapest 1969 publ 1972) p. 363.

[56] *MA* 6, 1 pp. 129–31. The chronicle in BL MS Cotton Julius D x, fols 30ᵛ–50ᵛ and has never been printed in full: for the various extracts in print, see *HRH* p. 172.

MS. convinced me long ago – and not me alone – that it was mainly written *c.*1170 and is a more coherent document than had been supposed.[57] It is true that it makes Llanthony in some sense an offshoot of Merton Priory which was not founded till 1114, but this very likely means no more than that in due course it received canons from Merton who converted it into the familiar Augustinian pattern. The account of the foundation, and of how Ernisius and William fought off an attempt by the king and queen to make a mighty foundation out of it, seems to me essentially authentic.[58] Yet it would be very puzzling if we had no other examples of Augustinian houses founded on obviously Cistercian sites. Indeed Llanthony outbid the Cistercians before they began; it is doubtful if a site so open to Welsh raids, so remote from other ecclesiastical centres, would really have been acceptable to the Cistercians; and after a generation the canons of Llanthony gratefully accepted an alternative site on the edge of Gloucester. For a while the original home became a cell and Lanthony by Gloucester became an urban Augustinian house notable for its library and school; in the end the two were separated and the old house had a life of its own again.[59] But by then something of the original conception had been forgotten. Yet in 1103, before Cîteaux had been heard of on these shores, we may well believe that for a modest house aiming for obscurity and apostolic poverty, the traditional Benedictine mode seemed too grand, too crushing – like the endowment with which the king and queen threatened it. A number of Augustinian houses were indeed founded in sites similarly remote: such were Nostell, founded by another royal clerk from the same circle, in a similarly remote site; Lanercost, originally as exposed to Scottish raids as Llanthony was to Welsh; and Bolton, due to a move in the early 1150s from the original home near Skipton, to a site which the early canons must have known was extraordinarily similar to the Cistercian sites of Rievaulx or Fountains chosen 20 years before.[60] Doubtless the present church at Bolton deceives us as to the

---

[57] Dickinson esp pp. 111–12 and nn; see refs in n 56.

[58] See refs in n 56.

[59] *HRH* pp. 172–3; for its library see N.R. Ker, *Medieval Libraries of Great Britain* (2 ed London 1964) pp. 108–12.

[60] See *VCH Yorkshire* 3 pp. 195–9 (Bolton), 231–5 (Nostell); *VCH Cumberland* 2 p. 152 (Lanercost); Dickinson pp. 120–1 (Nostell); Thompson, *Bolton*; Sir Charles Clay in *EYC* 7 *passim*, esp no. 2 and n (Bolton).

original conception, for it is large and spacious and Gothic; the cloister is a reminder of the modesty and simplicity of the first foundation there. The canons of Bolton sought a place for apostolic poverty and simplicity as they interpreted them, remarkable in its contrast to Leicester or Barnwell or to Lanthony by Gloucester. The mantle of Austin was very large and broad; but the example of the first Llanthony, and the long years when both houses were under a single regime, is a reminder that it is not simply that some houses were large and urban, others small and rustic: the conception of early canons' houses could include all these elements together. The many impulses of the religious life of the 12th century could be combined in a fashion which constantly bewilders us. Yet at Llanthony in 1103 or Leicester in 1143 or in London or Cambridge at any time the reason why one was surrounded by Austin's men would have seemed tolerably clear. In the local situation it makes sense, even if the general condition defies every effort at definition.

What then of the flow of comment, of Professor Bynum's treatises? Let me say at once that her analysis of the treatises, her revelation of the varieties and richness of attitude they reveal, is of lasting value, even if the conclusions seem relatively slight. For what is established is that there was a tradition in the 11th and 12th centuries which emphasised the duty of canons to teach by work and example – '*docere verbo et exemplo*'. With many qualifications carefully noted she denies that this element appears in their monastic contemporaries.[61] It is an intriguing point, even if we must allow for its limited force. No-one doubts that monks sometimes preached or that most of them did so rarely. But it is impossible to believe that 11th and 12th century monks were in any doubt or ignorance of the importance of example: it is as if one should say that a schoolmaster – used all his life to emphasise to his friends and colleagues the importance of sound instruction – was totally unaware that his charges also instruct and affect one another. This would be to lay too much weight on a particular literary genre, and in substantial measure Dr Bynum is aware of it. Thus she cites among her monks Abelard and his rule for nuns (reasonably observing that he was 'more pedagogue than monk') and

---

[61] Bynum 1979 *passim*.

Aelred of Rievaulx.[62] Interpretation of Abelard's Rule has been bedevilled by doubts as to the authenticity of the correspondence in which it is embedded. I take it that controversy is dying away; and that we can more clearly see that the Rule is a painstaking answer of a not very inspired character to a series of propositions put to him by Heloise, some of them paradoxical. Her letter is manifestly based on the presupposition that example, especially the wrong sort of example, is only too powerful and effective; she quotes Ovid's *Art of Love* to prove the point.[63] And so she demanded, not just a Rule – but two documents; the first to be a catalogue of examples of holy women and the part they had played in the life of the Church. And if that prolix document is not meant by both Heloise and Abelard to illustrate the positive force of example in the life of nuns, I do not know what it is for; it is certainly not a work of history. Aelred is a more complex case; and Dr Bynum's analysis of his teaching about example is one of the most subtle and satisfying parts of the book.[64] For she shows that in his treatises he is concerned to set a limit to the value of example; for he is primarily concerned with the monk as learner, and he sees occasions for instance when it is better for a man to be separated from a pattern of life on which he too much depends. The difference here is partly that Aelred proceeds with much greater psychological subtlety than the canons. If one wants Aelred a little more crudely presented, one finds in Walter Daniel's *Life* – an enchanting and often very revealing book, but evidently less sophisticated than Aelred's own writings – the statement that, when Abbot William put the young Aelred in charge of the novices at Rievaulx, his purpose was to make them 'worthy vessels', but also 'examples of perfection to those who truly yearn to excel as patterns of goodness'.[65] We may readily accept that there were many gradations between the most inward-looking or eremitical of religious

---

[62] Bynum 1979 p. 100; cf. pp. 101–4. On changing views of the authenticity of the letters of Abelard and Heloise, see refs in J.F. Benton's article in *Renaissance and Renewal in the twelfth century*, edd R.F. Benson and G. Constable, with C.D. Lanham (Cambridge, Mass. and Oxford, 1982–3) p. 266 n 12.

[63] Ep 5, ed J.T. Muckle in *Mediaeval Studies* 17 (1955) pp. 241–53 at p. 242; for what follows Epp 6 and 7 (the Rule), ed Muckle *ibid* pp. 253–81 and ed T.P. McLaughlin in *Mediaeval Studies* 18 (1956) pp. 241–92.

[64] Bynum 1979 pp. 134–7, 188–9.

[65] Walter Daniel, *The Life of Ailred of Rievaulx* ed F.M. Powicke (NMT 1950) p. 23.

and the most outward looking, and practical; that in between one will find in the 12th century men of Aelred's subtlety and ascetic experience who are concerned with the finer problems of advance in the religious life, and caring for communities mainly contemplative. This Dr Bynum has perceived at a deep level. It is not at all the purpose of this lecture to say that there were no differences. But there were perhaps no sharp dividing lines: the religious life and religious aspirations resembled a spectrum, with many subtle shades of colour – many slight differences adding up in the end to major divisions. And these were often shifting, and all subject to the many winds which blew. The patron who wished to found a religious house or the aspirant who sought his vocation might often be inspired with a dazzling vision; but each must equally often have been confused and blinded by the profusion of indistinguishable goods laid out in the shop for his choice.

Gonville and Caius College
Cambridge

THE TRANSFORMATION OF HERMITAGES INTO AUGUSTINIAN PRIORIES IN TWELFTH-CENTURY ENGLAND

by JANE HERBERT

THE transformation of eremitic communities into Augustinian priories was a notable feature of early Augustinian growth; during the twelfth century no less than about 50 houses of the order began in this way.[1] The popularity of the eremitic way of life had increased considerably during the eleventh century[2] and, once established, a hermit often inspired others to join him, thus becoming the unwitting instigator of a religious group which needed formal organization. The Rule of St. Augustine was the constitution most frequently adopted in these circumstances.[3] This was because it provided a general framework for community life rather than a set of detailed instructions and could therefore be assimilated more easily by an established group.

A cursory glance at the documents describing examples of this change from hermitage to priory reveals a notable difference between the continental evidence and the sources available for England. The intrinsic nature of eremiticism, with its stress on withdrawal from society, precludes the possibility of any contemporary account of this development. On the continent, however, it was common practice to make some attempt at recording the deeds of the hermit involved and the early history of the house, usually in the form of a *Vita* or a *Historia Fundationis*, within a few generations of the community being established. Aureil, for example, produced an outline of its origins in the *Vita Gaucheri*, which recounts the

---

[1] [L.] Milis, 'Ermites et chanoines [reguliers au XIIe siecle]' [*Cahiers de Civilization Medievale* 22 (1979)] p. 75.

[2] For a general introduction to this subject see: *L'eremitismo in Occidente nei secoli XI e XII* Miscellanea del Centro di Studi Medioevali p. 4 (Milan 1965).

[3] Milis, 'Ermites et chanoines', 63; for the Rule itself see L. Verheijen. *La regle de Saint Augustin* 2 vols (Paris 1967).

exploits of its hermit-founder Gaucher,[4] whilst Seher, who became the first prior of Chaumouzey in 1093, wrote the *Primordia Calmosiacensia*.[5] There are only two comparable sources for the eleven English priories which developed from hermitages in the twelfth century. The early history of Nostell, which became an Augustinian house under royal patronage *c.* 1114, at the instigation of Ralph Adlave, chaplain to Henry I, is related in the *De Gestis de Actibus priorum Sancti Oswaldi Nostel*,[6] a work written at the priory between 1392 and 1428 during the abbacy of Robert of Quixley. The transformation of Deepdale hermitage into Dale priory, a venture patronised by the Grendon family between 1155 and 1158, is described in the chronicle of Thomas of Muskham,[7] a canon of the house in the mid-thirteenth century. We do have a similar account, given in the *Itinerarium Kambriae*[8] of 1188–91, for the community of Llanthony, which was set up by a knight called William at the end of the eleventh century and remodelled as an Augustinian house *c.* 1108 on the advice of St. Anselm, but this was written by an outsider, Gerald of Wales. The surviving evidence for this process in the other eight cases dating from the twelfth century[9] does little to indicate the circumstances of the change, being generally confined to passing references to the community which preceded the Augustinian house in charter material. There are extant cartularies for only three priories: Felley founded in 1152, Bushmead, established *c.* 1215 and Healaugh Park, set up *c.* 1218. The sixteenth century cartulary of Felley preserves only a mutilated version of the priory's foundation charter,[10] but, fortunately, this makes reference to 'brother Robert, the hermit,[11] to whom Felley was granted'. At both Bushmead[12] and Healaugh Park,[13] prelimin-

---

[4] '[La] Vie de Saint Gaucher [,fondateur des chanoines reguliers d'Aureil en Limousin] [ed J. Becquet, *Revue Mabillon* 54 (1964)] pp. 25–55.

[5] *MGH SS* 12 pp. 324–47.

[6] [J. Burton] *M[onasticon] E]boracense]* (York 1758) pp. 300–1.

[7] *MA* 6 (i) pp. 892–5.

[8] *Giraldi Cambrensis [Opera* 6 ed J.F. Dimock (*RS* 21 1868)] pp. 39–40.

[9] There was one other transformation of this type which took place during the thirteenth century; by 1270 the hermitage of Sprawlesmede in Somerset had become the priory of Burtle, see: *HRH* p. 139, 151; *VCH Somerset*, ii p. 139.

[10] BL Additional MS 36872, FOL 24[v].

[11] 'frat[er] Robert[us] heremit[us]'.

[12] [The] *Cartulary of Bushmead Priory* [edd G.H. Fowler and Joyce Godber (*Bedfordshire Historical Record Society* 22 1940)] p. xv.

[13] *VCH Yorkshire* 3 p. 216.

ary attempts to regularize the community preceded the adoption of the Augustinian Rule. This means that their cartularies, compiled in the fourteenth and sixteenth centuries respectively, contain a sequence of charters leading up to the formal establishment as an Augustinian house, all of which indicate the origins of the community. The first grant in favour of Bushmead, dated between 1187 and 1196, is addressed to 'St. Mary of Bushmead, William, chaplain of Colmworth, and the brothers serving God there';[14] whilst at Healaugh Park 'the land of the hermitage of Healaugh'[15] was given to a group, under the leadership of Gilbert, a monk of Marmoutier, at some time before 1161. In the cases of Calwich, Bicknacre and Poughley the grant of the old hermitage site to the new priory is mentioned in surviving royal confirmations. Calwich, established as an independent Augustinian community *c*.1130, was handed over to Kenilworth as a priory cell before 1148[16] and a charter issued by Henry II in 1163 confirmed the *haeremitorum de Calewich*[17] to Kenilworth in this dependent capacity. Bicknacre, founded in 1175, was also known as the church of St. John the Baptist of Woodham. It is therefore possible to trace the connection between hermitage and priory through a similar document of 1157, preserved in *inspeximus* form, which confirms 'the hermitage of Woodham to brother Jordan, canon and hermit, and to all his successors serving God and St. John the Baptist there'.[18] For Poughley, set up between 1160 and 1178, the link is indicated in a charter of Henry III, again included in an *inspeximus*, which confirms to the house Ralph's gift of 'the hermitage of Cleufordemere ... where the site of the ... priory now is'.[19] The evidence for the last two houses, Charley and Ulverscroft, is even more incidental in character; both appear as hermitages with three resident brethren in the *Matriculus* compiled for Hugh of Welles,

---

[14] 'deo et sancte Marie de Bisshemeade et Willielmo capellano de Colmorde et fratribus ibidem deo servientibus', *Cartulary of Bushmead Priory* No 17.
[15] 'terram heremi quod est in nemore de Helaghe' [*The*] *Chartulary* [*of the Augustinian Priory of St. John the Evangelist*] *of Healaugh*, [ed J.S. Purvis (Yorkshire Archaeological Society Record Series 92 1936)] 1 p. 9.
[16] *HRH* p. 139, 151; *VCH Warwickshire* 2 p. 237.
[17] 'heremitorum de Calewich' *MA* 6 (i) p. 224.
[18] 'heremitagium de Wodeham fratri Jordano canonico et heremitae, et omnibus successoribus eius' *ibid* p. 446.
[19] 'heremitorium de Cleufordemere ... ubi nunc situs est eiusdem prioratus' *ibid* p. 409.

bishop of Lincoln, in 1220.[20] Ulverscroft had become an Augustinian house towards the end of the twelfth century, and Charley joined the order at the beginning of the thirteenth,[21] but both houses had clearly retained so much of their former identity that the change had become blurred in contemporary minds.

Why should there be such a contrast between the scanty English evidence and the comparatively abundant narrative sources of the continent? The answer to this question lies in an important underlying difference between Augustinian houses of this type on either side of the English channel. A priory which produced a surviving narrative account of its early history as many of the continental houses did, needed considerable financial resources; it had to attract or train a man of scholarship, who had the skills of a scribe,[22] provide him with the opportunity for study and a range of writing materials,[23] besides providing adequate archival facilities in which the completed manuscript might be properly stored. It comes as no surprise to discover that of the two English houses which boast such a document, Nostell grew into one of the larger houses of the order, with twenty-six canons a complement of lay brothers and an annual income of £122 in 1291,[24] whilst Dale became a member of the wealthy, independent congregation of Arrouaise c.1180.[25] The other English priories of this type were among the smallest and poorest religious houses in the country: in 1291 Felley had five or six brethren and an annual income of £11,[26] whilst Poughley had six or seven inmates and £15 in revenue.[27]

The character of these English houses was moulded by the

[20] *Rotuli Hugonis de Welles* 1 ed W.P.W. Phillimore (Canterbury and York Society 1 1909) p. 255.

[21] BL Harleian Charter III A6, dated 1174, contains a confirmation by Alexander III of the adoption of the Rule of St. Augustine at Ulverscroft. For Chorley see *HRH*, p. 153.

[22] Augustinian canons usually wrote their own works rather than dictating them to scribes; this followed accepted monastic tradition, see M.T. Clanchy [*From Memory to Written Record* (London 1979)] p. 97.

[23] *Ibid* pp. 89–97.

[24] *Taxatio* [*Ecclesiastica Anglie et Walliae Auctoritate P. Nicholai IV circa A.D. 1291* (Record Commission 1802)] pp. 38, 46, 74, 242, 300, 305, 313, 321, 325.

[25] [H.M.] Colvin, [*The*] *White Canons* [*in England* (London 1951)] p. 174; [*The*] *Cartulary of Dale Abbey* [ed A. Saltman (Historical Manuscripts Commission, JP11, 1967) p. 4.

[26] *Taxatio* pp. 264, 310, 312, 339.

[27] *Ibid* pp. 191–2, 197.

circumstances of their foundation, which differed radically from those found on the continent. The wave of revival and reform which swept through the Western Church during the eleventh century had combined with increasing alienation from the values of the developing urban scene to promote the eremitic way of life.[28] In the majority of cases the change from hermitage to priory was dependent upon this selfsame spiritual zeal; the guiding impetus for the transformation usually came from within the community itself, and was based on a desire to safeguard religious standards in the face of increasing numbers. Chaumouzey priory[29] provides a good example of this process in action. At some time before 1074, a priest named Anthenor set up an eremitic community in the diocese of Toul which was attracting large numbers of recruits by the time of his death *c.* 1090. At that point the brethren, amongst whom the desire to work together 'for the purpose of restoring the condition of the early church' was strong, made a collective decision to become Augustinian canons. It was only after their priory had been established, albeit on an unofficial basis, that the community received secular patronage: in 1091 a certain Hadwige persuaded her husband Theodoric to grant the house a more permanent site at Chaumouzey. The *Primordia Calmosiacensia* describes her imploring her husband to make God his heir, by leaving his property to the community, as they were childless. The assertion that this patronage was motivated solely by devout piety gains credibility from the fact that it was Pibo, bishop of Toul, rather than Theodoric and Hadwige, who established the priory on a formal basis by the grant of a confirmation charter in 1093; this indicates that the couple were content to give aid in a subordinate capacity, and were not attempting to establish themselves as founders in order to gain temporal prestige and influence. We can trace a similar pattern of foundation in a multitude of other Augustinian houses, including Aureil,[30] Chancelade,[31], Herival[32] and Neumoustier.[33]

[28] L. Genicot, 'l'Eremitisme du XIe siècle dans son contexte economique et social' *Miscellanea* pp. 45–69.

[29] *MGH SS* 12 pp. 326–9; [L.H.] Cottineau, *Repertoire* [*Topo-Bibliographique des Abbayes et Prieures* 2 vols (Macon 1935)] 1 cols 747–8.

[30] 'Vie de Saint Gaucher' pp. 42–52; Cottineau, *Repertoire* 1 col 208.

[31] *GC* 2 col 1502; Cottineau *Repertoire* 1 cols 689–90.

[32] A. Calmet, *Histoire de Lorraine* 3 vols (Nancy 1748) 3 preuves cols cxi–cxiii; Cottineau, *Repertoire* 1 cols 1405–6.

[33] *GC*, 3 col 1002; Cottineau, *Repertoire* 1 col 2059.

The potency and importance of the spiritual force involved is highlighted by three special cases: Arrouaise, St. Victor and Premontré. In 1090 Hildemar, with two companions, set up a hermitage in the diocese of Cambrai which was to be formally established as the priory of Arrouaise c. 1121.[34] Similarly, in 1108, the famous scholar William of Champeaux took up the eremitic life at the old hermitage of St. Victor by the gates of Paris, and the community which gathered round him was officially established as a priory in 1114 under royal patronage;[35] and in 1119 St. Norbert of Xanten retired to the ruined chapel in the forest of Courcy near Laon which became the priory of Premontré two years later.[36] The spiritual zeal of these communities was such that, having adopted the Rule of St. Augustine, they were inspired by the austere example of Cîteaux to formulate much stricter observances than were generally followed. Each gained a widespread following and, as a result, became the founding house of an independent and influential Augustinian order. The dynamic spirituality which led the foundation of Arrouaise, St. Victor and Premontré was a heightened version of the devout piety behind the creation of mainstream Augustinian houses from hermitage communities.[37] Therefore, the impressive success it engendered helps us to see how these ordinary Augustinian priories could attract the patrons and recruits which turned them into sizeable, prosperous houses, well able to finance the recording of their early history.

We do catch glimpses of the intense spirituality of the continent in England. At Bushmead the community was regularized by Hugh son of Oliver of Beauchamp between 1187 and 1196. However, it was not until c. 1215–33, on the initiative of the zealous prior Joseph of Coppingford, that the priory adopted the Rule of St. Augustine.[38] Joseph's spiritual calibre is indicated by the fact

[34] MGH SS 15 (ii) cols 1118–21; L. Milis, L'ordre des chanoines reguliers d'Arrouaise (Bruges 1969) pp. 93–6.

[35] F. Bonnard, Histoire de l'Abbaye royale et l'ordre des chanoines reguliers de St.-Victor de Paris 2 vols (Paris 1904–8) I pp. 1–17.

[36] MGH SS 12 cols 681–3; C. Dereine, 'Les origines de Premontré' RHE 42 (1947) pp. 370–73; Colvin, White Canons pp. 1–2.

[37] J.C. Dickinson, The Origins of the Austin Canons and their Introduction into England (London 1950) p. 78.

[38] Cartulary of Bushmead p. xvi; this development was confirmed by Gregory IX in 1236 (ibid No 3).

that he seems to have been a hermit in his own right before joining
the community at Bushmead: *c.*1225–33 Simon Costentin, lord of
Coppingford, made Bushmead a gift of 'the hermitage of Coppingford with the chapel, buildings and appurtenances which Joseph the
chaplain had'.[39] Joseph appears to have had considerable impact on
the priory, for three centuries later Leland recorded that the canons
of Bushmead venerated a hermit as their founder[40] and, as Joseph
was responsible for the introduction of the Augustinian Rule into
the community, it seems more likely that this accolade was
conferred upon him rather than on the original Bushmead hermit.
Perhaps the best example of fervent spiritual motivation is to be
found in the early history of Cockersand, which was recorded by
Thomas Tonge, Norroy King of Arms on his Visitations of the
North in 1530. Tonge wrote:

> Be it noted that the monastery of Cokersand was first founded
> by Hugh Garthe, an heremyt of great perfection, and by such
> charitable almes as the said Hugh Garthe dyd gather in the
> countre he founded an Hospitall callid Cokersand, with iii
> Chanons in the said Hospitall, a master and ii brethren, and
> was callid Mr. of the Hospitall of Cokersand. Then ... it was
> changed from the Hospitall to a priory ... of White Canons.[41]

The change from hermitage to hospital took place some time
before 1184 and the final transformation into a priory had occurred
by 1190.[42] In the best continental tradition these developments
were entirely due to the spiritual charisma and personal drive of the
hermit concerned.

It is interesting to note that the spiritual force behind these
developments at Cockersand provides the only example in England
of the establishment of a priory belonging to a strict Augustinian
congregation, in this case that of Premontré, on a hermitage site.
This was because the pre-Gregorian stance on church matters
adopted by William I and largely upheld by his successors, allowed
the widespread spiritual revival of the continent only limited

[39] 'hermitagium de Copmaneford cum capella edificiis ... et rebus aliis ad illud
   pertinentibus que Joseph capellanus ibidem unquam tenuit vel habuit' *Ibid* No 238.
[40] Leland, *Collectanea* 1 p. 68.
[41] B.L. Harleian MS 1499, article 69; cf. *The Chartulary of Cockersand Abbey*, 3 (ii) ed
   W. Farrer (*Chetham Society* n.s. 57, 1905) p. 758.
[42] *HRH* pp. 184, 187; Colvin, *White Canons* pp. 138–9.

impact in this country. As a result, the growth of eremiticism had a rather different basis here. The movement emerged as an expression of English reaction to the Norman conquest and its social consequences;[43] most of the recluses in England for whom we have personal details were of Anglo-Danish or English stock.[44] They operated on the fringes of established social groups and, set apart by their aura of holiness, served the important function of arbitrator in the resolution of tensions arising within the community and the wider world as a result of the political and economic adjustments enforced by the age. Their piety, being so closely intertwined with contemporary society, was inevitably of a more practical variety than the white-hot spirituality found on the continent. This meant that when the time came to reorganize their hermitages on a more formal basis the flexibility allowed by the less rigorous demands of the mainstream Augustinian movement were a more favoured option than the strict observances of the Arrouasians, Premonstratensians and Victorines.

The moderate spiritual traditions of English hermitages had an important influence on the character and volume of the sources surviving from Augustinian houses founded on hermitage sites. As such a house had less exacting standards to live up to than a continental equivalent it had less impetus for recording its early history in order to create a touchstone for the community. The extent and generosity of the support the house could attract was also reduced and this meant that it was not so capable of financing such ventures. Although more vital documents, such as charters which defined the rights and property of a priory, were kept, their chances of survival were diminished by the lack of funding available for proper archive facilities.

The limited general appeal these priories gained from their spiritual reputation combined with the climate of strong secular control in ecclesiastical matters to allow secular patrons to play a far

---

[43] H. Mayr-Harting, 'Functions of a Twelfth-Century Recluse', *History* 60 (1975) pp. 337–8.

[44] The only notable exceptions were Benedict, monk of Auxerre, whose eremitic community in Yorkshire formed the basis of Selby abbey (*The Coucher Book of Selby* 1 ed J.T. Fowler (Yorkshire Archaeological and Topographical Association Record Series 10, 1890) pp. 6–19) and Gilbert, monk of Marmoutier who was similarly responsible for the beginnings of the Augustinian priory at Healaugh Park in the same county (see above n3)

more central role in the fortunes of these houses than had been the case in Europe. Accordingly, their character and motives were firmly imprinted on the communities they sponsored. The patrons involved were socially heterogeneous, but the meagre foundation grants received by the majority of these houses is explained by the fact that a higher incidence of names appears towards the lower end of the social scale. The crown did figure in their number by virtue of Henry I's involvement with Nostell priory.[45] About a third, however, were landowners of purely local importance: Serlo of Grendon, lord of Bradley, who founded Dale; Ralph Britto, lord of Annesley, who set up Felley; Jordan and Alice of Sancta Maria, who instituted Healaugh Park; and Ralph of Chaddleworth, who was responsible for Poughley. And an equal number were only marginally more elevated in social terms: Maurice son of Geoffrey, founder of Bicknacre, was a former sheriff of Essex[46] as well as a lord of Tilty; Hugh son of Oliver of Beauchamp, founder of Bushmead and lord of Eaton Socon was also a cadet relation of the Beauchamps of Bedford;[47] Nicholas, lord of Gresley and founder of Calwich, was also the ward of Geoffrey of Clinton,[48] treasurer and chamberlain of Henry I: and Hugh of Lacy, lord of Ewias, who played a central role in the beginnings of Llanthony Prima, was also kin to the important Yorkshire Lacys.[49]

The social gap between the crown and these other patrons seems to have been filled to some extent by two founders drawn from the foremost rank of the Anglo-Norman nobility: the two small Leicestershire houses of Ulverscroft and Charley appear to have been set up by Beaumont earls of Leicester. A charter of Alexander III, dated 1174, mentions that the site of Ulverscroft priory was the gift 'comitis Legrecestrie'; [50] the subsequent confirmation, in the same document, of a grant of thirty acres in Charnwood forest made to their priory by Ranulf of Gernon, earl of Chester, suggests that the Robert in question was Robert le Bossu, earl of Leicester 1118–68. Charter evidence also suggests that Charley was founded

[45] See below pp. 140–1.
[46] See for example *PR* 6 Hen. II pp. 9–10, or *PR* 8 Hen. II p. 68.
[47] I.J. Sanders, *English Baronies* (Oxford 1960) p. 40.
[48] *MA* 6 p. 224.
[49] W.E. Wightman, *The Lacy Family in England and Normandy 1066–1194* (Oxford 1966) p. 183 and pedigrees at end.
[50] BL, Harleian Charter III A6.

by Robert le Bossu's son and heir, Robert Blanchmains. Another of Alexander II's charters of 1174[51] confirmed the *locus Sanctae Mariae Charleia* to the Benedictine priory of Luffield, which was set up by Robert le Bossu in 1116–18;[52] whilst in 1190, the year of Robert Blanchmains' death, his widow granted the priory of Ulverscroft to the Norman house of St. Evroult,[53] which had close connections with the Beaumont family. These transactions indicate that the Beaumonts held the patronage rights enjoyed by a monastic founder and his family, and their dates point to Robert Blanchmains as that founder.

Beaumont involvement in the fortunes of Charley illustrate well the decisive nature of the role played by secular patrons in the establishment and development of these houses in England. Dale abbey is another good example.[54] Serlo of Grendon granted Depedale, including the hermitage established there by a baker from Derby, to his godmother, who was popularly known as the 'Gomme of the Dale'. She ensured that the spiritual traditions established at Depedale were maintained by encouraging her son, Richard, to become a priest in order that he might serve the oratory set up by the hermit. Then, *c.*1160, she persuaded Serlo to ask Calke priory to send a group of canons to colonize the site. Serlo granted Depedale to the brethren who came, and their community formed the nucleus of Dale priory.

The predominance of external forces in the transformation of hermitages into Augustinian houses in England, rather than the internal forces characteristic of the continent, resulted in secular rather than religious considerations coming to the fore in foundation projects. As the Gomme's son became a canon at Dale, it seems probable that her desire to secure his future was an important factor behind the foundation of the priory. The personal nature of the Gomme's intentions stands in stark contrast to the major political aims which led to Henry's sponsorship of Nostell priory. The confusion over the origins of the community is reflected in the fourteenth-century history of the priory which records that the Lacy family considered itself, and was regarded by others, as the founding patrons of Nostell, although the canons later preferred to

[51] *MA*, 4 p. 349.
[52] *HRH* pp. 55, 70; *VCH, Northants* 2 p. 95.
[53] *Cal. Doc. Fr.* No 651.
[54] *MA* 6 (ii) pp. 892–4.

concede this dignity to Henry I.[55] The beginnings of a religious community sprang up at Nostell, near Pontefract, in the early twelfth century with the encouragement of Ilbert I of Lacy and his son, Robert.[56] Political circumstances, however, meant that Lacy lost his large and compact holding of the castellery of Pontefract in 1114, as they constituted a major political threat to royal power in the north-east, and the property passed to Hugh of Laval.[57] It was usual for a new landholder to assume the patronage of the religious foundations established by his predecessor, for such communities functioned as spiritual counterparts to the secular power of their founder and by adopting them a new lord could both benefit from this state of affairs and emphasize that the replacement of his predecessor was complete. We see this at Little Dunmow, where Robert fitz Richard, the recipient of the Baynard barony confiscated in 1111, was later referred to as the *primus patronus*[58] of the community established by a cadet branch of the Baynard family.[59] This was not the case at Nostell. Henry took control of the community himself instead of allowing it to pass to Hugh of Laval with the castellery of Pontefract. The king wanted to establish a royal presence in the locality to counter Laval's power in the area and saw that Nostell, sited as it was *iuxta castellum Pontisfracti*,[60] would be an ideal instrument for the task. Henry tightened his grip over the community by reorganizing it as a full Augustinian priory *c.*1122.[61] This manoeuvre was no doubt intended to expunge the memory of Robert Lacy in order to ensure that royal command of the community's loyalty would not be challenged by Laval and the establishment could be relied upon to fall in with his intentions. In all probability, the king's task was made easier by an understandable inclination on the part of the canons to promote a successful monarch rather than a disgraced nobleman as their founder.[62]

[55] *ME* p. 300.

[56] [W.E.] Wightman, '[Henry I and the Foundation of] Nostell Priory' [*Yorkshire Archaeological Journal* 41 (1963–66)] p. 57.

[57] *Ibid* p. 59.

[58] BM Cotton Ms Cleopatra C III fo 281ʳ.

[59] *Ibid*; cf. 'The Cartulary of Little Dunmow Priory' ed R.E. Levy (unpublished M.A. thesis University of Virginia, 1971) Nos 1–2.

[60] *EYC* 3 No 1428.

[61] Wightman, 'Nostell Priory' p. 58; *EYC* 3 No 1428.

[62] Cf. Southwick priory; see, Emma Mason, 'The King, the Chamberlain and Southwick Priory' *BIHR* 53 (1980) pp. 1–10.

The cases of Dale and Nostell illustrate family concern on the one hand and political manoeuvre on the other. In the majority of cases the secular motivation involved was composite in character and included an element of both extremes. Most founders had the conventionally pious wish to provide for the spiritual welfare of themselves and their families by establishing a religious commun- ity, a desire which was closely related to the creation of a family mausoleum. In fulfilling this spiritual function a monastery gained increased impact as a tangible symbol of its founder's territorial lordship and thus helped to consolidate his family's future hold over its lands. This is quite clear in the circumstances surrounding the foundation of Poughley priory. In 1158 Richard Bassett unsuc- cessfully disputed the title held by Abingdon abbey to the Chaddle- worth manor in which Poughley was situated.[63] Ralph of Chaddle- worth was presumably the father of Robert of Chaddleworth, who is recorded as holding this manor from Abingdon in 1182,[64] so that his foundation of Poughley, c. 1160, on a site about a mile and a half from the village of Chaddleworth[65] can be seen as part of an attempt made by either a new tenant, or one who had been recently under threat, to consolidate his control over his fee by the establishment of a family mausoleum at its centre.

There were two important factors at work which helped to ensure that the wish to found a religious house in these circum- stances took form as the transformation of a hermitage into an Augustinian priory. In the first place there is the influence which a hermit wielded in the community to consider. This potent force could be of great use to a lord if it was used to his benefit: William fitz Walter, lord of Haselbury, had particular reason to be grateful to the hermit Wulfric for the devoted support he gave against Matilda, queen of Stephen, during the Anarchy.[66] By the same token, of course, this power would have been something of a liability if it were not subordinated to the lord's will, specially if, as in the cases such as Ralph of Chaddleworth, Ralph Britto of Annesley and Serlo of Grendon the hermit in question lived hard

---

[63] *Chronicon Monasterii de Abingdon* I ed J. Stevenson (*RS* 2 1858) pp. 188–9.
[64] Rymer, *Foedera* I p. 43.
[65] *VCH Berks* 4 p. 163.
[66] *Wulfric of Haselbury by John of Ford*, ed M. Bell (Somerset Record Society 47, 1932) p. 108.

by the lord's main power base. An attempt made by these lords to transform a hermitage into an Augustinian house may be seen as a bid to harness the influence of the hermit by placing it beneath the yoke of patronage. Gerald of Wales's description of the early history of Llanthony Prima refers to the generous grants made by Hugh of Lacy, lord of Ewias, to the eremitic community which stood 'in the very deep valley of Ewias'[67] against the will of the inmates;[68] it seems probable that he did this in order to be accepted in the role of 'first and foremost lord and patron',[69] which title was later conferred on him. The earls of Leicester may well have taken an interest in the outlying communities of Charley and Ulverscroft for a similar reason. The eremitic groups which developed into these priories were sited deep in the heart of Charnwood forest.[70] Their complete isolation within the Beaumont lands probably made them as threatening as a group situated near to a power centre.

Secondly, we must take note of the material and spiritual attractions that the transformation of a hermitage into an Augustinian house had for founders of predominantly local importance. Prevented by financial restrictions from providing the funds for a prestigious Cluniac or Cistercian house, they found in the Augustinian canons an order willing to accept a frugal endowment.[71] By establishing their Augustinian house on a hermitage site they were able to set up a religious house with a grant of little more than the site of an existing hermitage, which was in any case already occupied on an unofficial basis. At Bushmead, Hugh of Beauchamp gave his priory its site and the right of priority grinding at the mills of Eaton Socon and a road leading from the priory[72] to 28 acres of land which he granted to the house in a supplementary charter;[73] whilst Jordan and Alice of Sancta Maria

---

[67] 'in valle de Ewias profundissima' *Giraldi Cambrensis* p. 37.
[68] 'quoties imprimis seu domini et patroni sui Hugonis de Lacy primi et primaevi, seu aliorum fidelium largitione, tam terris quam beneficiis ecclesiasticus coepit locus hic locupletari dolentes valde' *ibid* p. 40.
[69] *Ibid.*
[70] See for example, a description of Ulverscroft priory written in 1536 which remarks of the house, 'it stands in a wildernesse in Charnewood forest' (*L and P Hen. VIII*, x p. 496).
[71] R.W. Southern, *Western Society and the Church in the Middle Ages* (Harmondsworth 1970) p. 246.
[72] *Cartulary of Bushmead* No 17.   [73] *Ibid* No 19.

handed over to their priory of Healaugh[74] the site of the house and a small area of defined woodland. Indeed, in several cases, Poughley and Felley for example, the foundation grant made to the priory consisted of the site alone. The same situation occurs amidst interesting circumstances at Bicknacre. In the financial year 1165–66 Maurice son of Geoffrey was excused a debt to the crown[75] which dated from his last period in office as sheriff of Essex during 1163–64,[76] on the condition that he founded a religious house. He turned this concession to advantage by creating an Augustinian priory from Woodham hermitage, at the low cost to himself of the site involved.[77] A small Augustinian priory in possession of so few temporal endowments would confer very limited prestige on its founder. However, the ploy of creating the house from an existing eremitic community associated it closely with a spiritual tradition which carried considerable social *cachet*. The desirability of such a connection is illustrated by the foundation of Barnwell priory in 1112: its patron Pain Peverel, sheriff of Cambridgeshire, deliberately sought out an abandoned hermitage as the site for his house.[78]

The development of hermitages into Augustinian priories took a quite different direction in England from that established on the continent. The prevailing climate of secular control which was maintained in the English church after 1066 and the influence of the conquest on the nature of eremitic ventures in this country meant that the initiative for the pace and character of this change came from secular patrons rather than from within the communities themselves. The motivation of these patrons included a measure of pious intention, but was more dependent on secular considerations arising from the patron's desire to secure the material fortunes of his family. The particular attraction of this type of foundation was that it conferred far more prestige on its founder than was warranted by the financial outlay demanded. This explains its place within the development of the Augustinian order in England as an option favoured by patrons drawn from the lower ranks of the nobility. Once the identity of those responsible for the majority of

[74] *Chartulary of Healaugh*, 7.
[75] *PR* 12 Hen II p. 123.
[76] *PR*, 10 Hen II p. 36.
[77] *MA* 6 (i) p. 446.
[78] *Liber Memorandum Ecclesie de Bernewelle*, ed J.W. Clarke (Cambridge 1907) p. 42.

these transformations in England has been established and explained the contrast with continental norms, and the financial implications of the difference, explain why there are abundant continental sources whilst those for England remain hard to come by.

MONASTIC FRIENDSHIP AND TOLERATION IN TWELFTH-CENTURY CISTERCIAN LIFE

by BRIAN PATRICK McGUIRE

RIENDSHIP is a commonplace of monastic life. What more congenial environment could be found for the formation and cultivation of friendships than the protective recesses of monastic cloisters? Here existed the time, charity and mutual concern so painfully absent in the outside world. In the cloister men could get to know each other and to experience each other in the fellowship of Christ. Under a mild and understanding abbot, they could discover, as Ailred of Rievaulx did in the twelfth century, that God is friendship.

This ideal picture existed as reality in only a few periods of monastic history in the West. Available sources indicate a very limited and elitist cult of friendship in the Anglo-Saxon and Carolingian worlds from about 750–850, as well as a much more broadly-based practice of friendship in the cloister from about 1050–1200.[1] Since the 1960s there has been in some monastic communities a greater openness and toleration of individual or particular friendships than was the case earlier in this century. But the centuries since the thirteenth have not been kind to the sweet loves of the cloister. A fifteenth-century patriarch of Venice and zealous church reformer warned against the scandals that are caused by the formation of exclusive bonds among individual monks.[2]

---

[1] For full documentation see my forthcoming book, *Friendship in the Middle Ages: The Monastic Experience* (Cistercian Publications: Kalamazoo, Michigan). I am greatly indebted for guidance in this paper to Sir Richard Southern, Peter Brown, Jean Leclercq, Chrysogonus Waddell, and to the Trappist community at New Clairvaux, California.

[2] Lawrence Giustiniani (1381–1455), *De disciplina et perfectione monasticae conversationis*, cap 10 in *Opera Omnia*, I (Venice 1751): 'Interdicenda est privata conversatio in collegiis servorum Christi, quae quamquam in nullo alio reprehensibilis sit, sine proximorum tamen scandalo fieri nequit'.

After the Reformation such friendships were practically outlawed in most communities.[3] In the East, the Rules of Saints Pachomius and Basil leave little room for the cultivation of such bonds. Pachomius worried about physical intimacy among monks, while Basil wanted to eliminate all bonds that resembled the exclusiveness of kinship in Egyptian village society.[4]

The history of monastic friendship in the East hardly exists, while in the West it has been brief. Even if monks and nuns in recent decades have again begun to investigate the possibilities of such human bonds,[5] their predecessors have generally been sceptical about the spiritual benefits such closeness might bring. Ever since John Cassian's famous sixteenth collation on friendship, there has been fear that exclusive friendships would lead to cliques and end in conspiracy against the discipline and order of monastery life.[6]

Cassian left open the possibility of individual friendships within the community, but most of his considerations centre on creating harmony in the cloister as a whole rather than in making individual friendships possible. Benedict recommended the reading of Cassian (cap 73), but said nothing in his Rule about friendship in itself. He warned, however, against the danger that one monk defend another (cap 69). His fear was the growth of cliques and conspiracies.

What comes across in the early literature of monasticism, both in East and West, is a conviction that the uniformity and peace of community life require that there be no special bonds, no particular preferences. Benedict leaves a loophole for the abbot. He is not to prefer one monk to another, except on the basis of merit (cap 2). But the Rule of Saint Benedict can hardly be looked upon as a solid foundation for the cultivation of friendships in the cloister.

Toleration – or outright encouragement – of monastic friendships as exclusive bonds within the community appears to be

---

[3] See "amitiés spirituelles", *Dictionnaire de Spiritualité* (Paris 1927) I pp. 521–29.
[4] Amand Boon, ed *Pachomiana Latina* (Bibliothèque de la Revue d'Histoire Ecclésiastique 7 Louvain 1932) esp Praecepta § 92–7. The Rules of Saint Basil can be found in *PG* 31, and relevant sections at cols 921, 936–7, 940–1, 996–1001.
[5] As seen in Sister Michael Connor, 'The First Cistercian Nuns and Renewal Today', *Cistercian Studies* 5 (1970) pp. 131–68.
[6] Michael Petschenig, ed *Iohannis Cassiani Conlationes XXIIII* (CSEL 13 Vienna 1886) p. 462. Abbreviated as *Conl*.

an exceptional and not a general phenomenon in monastic life. As Basil insisted, we are to love our fellow monks equally.[7] This negative evaluation of special loves can be explained as the result of three elements in monastic life. In the first place, by definition being a monk or a cloistered person requires breaking away from the bonds of the world. Here the two most familiar bonds are those of kinship and of friendship. Jesus himself had demanded that his followers leave everything, and even hate their families (Luke 14: 26). Any devout monk had to fasten his loyalty and loves on God and not on men. To allow the old bonds of kinship or friendship into the cloister was to invite divisions within the community. To tolerate new bonds of friendship to form there was to invite inside the secular and limiting way of life.

A second reason for the outlawing of friendship is the fear that close relationships among the monks, especially the young, will lead to homosexual love. We have remarkably little material on this matter in Western sources, while Eastern monastic literature is fairly outspoken about the danger. It is important to see the monastic fear of sex among men as only one element among several that contributes to a low evaluation of friendships. Freudian psychology has little to offer in explaining monastic life and mentalities. Monastic behaviour is by no means the simple story of repression of sexual needs. Monastic culture at best evidences a form of transsexuality, in which sexual behaviour instead of being kept back somehow disappears as a major factor in everyday life. There is no doubt, however, that some of the Eastern legislation against particular friendships is based on fear of homosexual love.

A third factor contributing to a lack of toleration for individual friendships is, as one would expect, a perennial insistence on living together in a community where all exclusive groups or cliques are outlawed. This is probably the most important factor in undermining confidence in close relationships in the cloister. How can monks practise charity towards their neighbours if they admit by their work and actions that some neighbours are more desirable than others? The easiest apparent solution is that of Saint Basil: to insist on equal loves. Even in the eighteenth century a Benedictine commentator on Cassian recommended that even though inward

---

[7] *Constitutiones Monasticae*, PG 31 col 1418.

feelings could distinguish loves, outward behaviour had to treat all members of the monastic community equally.[8]

With all these reasons for avoiding particular friendships, it might seem remarkable that there have been periods in monastic history when such bonds were allowed a place in the cloister. In the Anglo-Saxon and Carolingian period this opening can be explained on the basis of a superficial acquaintance with monastic tradition and a perhaps naive optimism about the possibilities of friendship. When Alcuin and other Carolingian abbots wrote letters of friendship, their model in describing their relationships was the letters of Jerome. In him they saw clever epigrams and not the conflict of loyalties that such friendships could create. At the same time the Carolingian evidence of friendship comes from men who, even if they are monks, also function outside of a clearly defined structure of monastic life. Alcuin is more court teacher than abbot at Tours. If we look back at his Anglo-Saxon predecessor, Boni-face, we find that he was brought up as a monk but wrote to his friends as a missionary and prelate. There is friendship here, but monasticism itself is in flux. A lack of finished structure leaves room for the presence of individual bonds of friendship among literary men.

In the period after about 1050, we find evidence of monastic friendship at a time when monasteries were taking on organisation-al structure. Reform monasticism and ordered relationships among communities still left room for the cultivation of friendships within monasteries and between monks of different monasteries. Institu-tionalization and intimate personal bonds could exist together, for example, at Saint Anselm's Bec in Normandy. An easy explanation for this new cult of friendship is that monastic life shared in the 'gay clerical culture' of which the Yale historian John Boswell has recently written.[9] In Boswell's mind, the period from about 1050–1150 witnesses substantial manifestations of homosexual

---

[8] This is Alard Gazet, whose commentary is most easily available together with the text of Cassian in *PL* 49 col 1044: 'haec, inquam, et his similia, ne cui forte scrupulum moveant, intelligenda sunt, quoad externam conversationem et fami-liaritatem, sive de exterioribus et communibus amicitiae et charitatis signis et officiis, quae omnibus fratribus aequaliter, id est, indifferenter et promiscue, exhibenda sunt'.

[9] *Christianity, Social Tolerance and Homosexuality* (Chicago and London 1980) esp cap 9, 'The Triumph of Ganymede'.

loves among clerical men, as seen in poetry, letter-writing and chronicles. Boswell is ambiguous about the extent to which central monastic figures like Anselm also shared in this culture. But his book leaves the impression that men like Anselm and Ailred of Rievaulx must be seen in the context of homosexual loves.

This is an explanation of human behaviour which I find far too one-dimensional. Ailred of Rievaulx's experiences of love in youth may be explained in terms of homosexual attachments, but his conversion to Cistercian life transformed his behaviour and attitudes. It is all too limiting to think of his work and writings in terms of a crude sublimation of his sexual impulses. *Conversio* for the medieval monk meant not just leaving the sexual enjoyments of the world for the love of God; it implies the metamorphosis of self, so that one's sexuality becomes integrated in the totality of being, is lost in it, and then re-formed in it.

The best way of looking at the monastic friendships of this period is to concentrate on the Cistercian Order, for here we find the clearest and fullest expression of such bonds. In the Cistercian experience there are three vital factors that provide a foundation for monastic friendships. These are an awareness of classical and patristic traditions of friendship; the feudal background of twelfth-century recruits; and an emphasis on personal experience as a necessary element for advancement in the monastic life. Other factors probably also contributed to the Cistercian toleration and even encouragement of such friendships, but these seem to me the dominant ones. Certainly one can speak of how Cistercians transformed their sexual yearnings into spiritual loves, but it is important to see friendship among men in the cloister in a broader historical, social, psychological and religious context than that of sexuality alone.[10]

The Cistercians built on the sources from classical and patristic fathers that concerned friendship. Ailred's devotion to Cicero's *De Amicitia* is well-known, but it must also be noticed that the main patristic source for his treatise on friendship is not Augustine but

---

[10] Here I am greatly indebted to the seminar for interpretative studies at the Division of Humanities and Social Sciences, California Institute of Technology, Pasadena, where John Benton invited me in 1982 to present a paper on dreams and visions in Cistercian literature.

Ambrose.[11] The latter's *De Officiis* has a section on the duties of friendship, and here the reservations of the desert fathers about human bonds are replaced by a late Roman confidence in the value and rewards of friendship.[12] Ambrose gave Ailred the assurance he needed that there could be a clearly Christian friendship. Just as Ambrose structured his *De Officiis* on the corresponding work by Cicero, so too Ailred could build his *De Spirituali Amicitia* on Cicero's work. Like so many of his monastic colleagues, Ailred received classical culture through the medium of the Western Fathers. Since these themselves were Romans, they made the transition from pagan to Christian culture seem all the more natural and painless.

Recent research has also revealed how the Cistercians fostered a revival of Seneca and Pseudo-Seneca in the twelfth century, and this includes the various letter collections where friendship is expressed.[13] Sister Benedicta Ward has shown in a seminal article how the Cistercian conception of the eremitic life was far from the historical reality that we find in the early Christian centuries.[14] The Cistercians picked and chose what best suited them, their community existence, and their sense of liturgy. In the matter of friendship we find a similar talent for selectivity. The utilitarian aspect of Ciceronian friendship, its Stoic ideal of tranquillity and the removal of the passions – these elements are ignored in order to celebrate the joys of friendship. But the sources are essential in providing patterns for imitation and points of departure for the life of the New Monastery and its daughters.

The Carolingians had favoured Jerome in their idealization of friendship, the Jerome of facile phrases and pithy epigrams. Behind the passionate expressions of friendship in the Cistercians we find not the letters of Jerome but the *Confessions* of Saint Augustine. For all Augustine's insistence on the limitations of human bonds as compared to the permanence and stability of the love of God, he

[11] Ailred's *De Spir[itali] Amic[ttia]* is available in a critical edition by Anselm Hoste (*cc* Continuatio Medievalis 1 1971).
[12] PL 16 col 25–194, esp bk III caps 127–31.
[13] Lecture at the Medieval Centre, Copenhagen University, November 1982, by Professor Birger Munk Olsen, on the basis of his exhaustive survey of the survival and transmission of classical texts in medieval sources.
[14] 'The Desert Myth', *One Yet Two*, ed B. Pennington (Kalamazoo 1976) pp. 183–99.

admitted in his next breath that he could not live without his friends.[15] For the Cistercians Augustine managed to sum up the yearning of the soul for total unity with God, but also the impossibility of isolating oneself from other men who sought the same totality.[16] Ailred, as is well known, patterned the first lines of his treatise on friendship not on any elegant phrases from Jerome, but on Augustine's desire to love and be loved. Ailred saw his youth in Augustine's terms. His waywardness, seeking, and eventual finding of the love that holds all other loves in place followed the Augustinian pattern. And Ailred could look to Augustine for assurance that once the change of life, *conversio*, is complete, friendship instead of being eliminated can be moved onto a higher spiritual plane. Augustine could give Ailred and other Cistercians the assurance they needed of the worth of friendship, a witness not to be found in Eastern Fathers.

A second decisive element in the Cistercian background that provides a basis for friendship is their social origins in the lower nobility and the pattern of feudal life.[17] When men became Cistercians, they did not leave their families and milieu in the same way as men who became desert hermits left their villages in fourth-century Egypt. Bernard brought his whole family into the religious life and even saw to it that his sister was cared for, even if Cistercians in their first decades normally avoided the organised care of women. But one's sister was different. After entrance into the religious life kinship bonds still mattered, and so there was corresponding room for those of friendship. The two bonds are found together in the monastic experience. When the one is severed, the other must also give way, as in the Eastern experience.[18] But Bernard could first leave his family and then as

---

[15] Contrast, for example, his Confessions IV, ch 7 and 8, after the death of his boyhood friend.

[16] In this context Possidius's biography of Augustine should be looked upon as the record not just of Augustine but of the community he formed and in which Possidius shared (like Eadmer with Anselm much later, or Walter Daniel with Ailred).

[17] Jean Leclercq, *Monks and Love in Twelfth-Century France* (Oxford 1979) pp. 8–16.

[18] I am grateful to Peter Brown for a conversation on monasticism in Late Antiquity, where he emphasized a link between kinship and friendship. Bonding provides insights also into the medieval experience. For a surprising study of friendship, see his *The Cult of the Saints* (Chicago and London 1982).

William of Saint Thierry shows so well in the *Vita Prima*, cajole, convince and compel all its members to join him at Clairvaux or become associated with other monastic foundations.

Bernard is not alone in this metamorphosis of whole feudal families into monastic ones. The arrival of Bernard with his dozens of friends at the gates of Cîteaux may be a turning point in the history of Cîteaux, but it is not a unique moment. The stories of Caesarius of Heisterbach a century later are full of evidence of knightly young men who laid their armour on the altar of Mary and became spiritual knights instead of temporal ones.[19] The Cistercians continued to be the aristocrats in the cloister that they had been outside. For them the bonds of loyalty remained essential, not just in relationships among father and daughter houses, but also in individual friendships. One of Ailred's main concerns in his treatise is how to terminate friendships.[20] Unlike Jerome he does not claim that bonds can never be broken if they are true. But as a son of feudal society he insists that there must be a rigorous and clarified procedure for severing such links. He believes that love will always continue among friends, but he concedes that it can sometimes become impossible to show love to a troublesome friend.

Feudal society, in the sense of an aristocratic group of landowners tied to each other by mutual dependence and bonds of loyalty, found its fullest monastic expression in the Cistercians. Unlike the desert fathers, they admitted how much they needed each other. In their communities, they conceded a hierarchy of human relationships in which the young as well as the old could seek each other out in forming bonds of friendship. New spiritual loyalties replaced those of family.

A third decisive element in the Cistercian toleration of monastic friendships is an emphasis in the new order on combining personal experience with monastic ideology. Here again Ailred can be our guide, taking as a point of departure for his exposition of friendship not just Ambrose and Augustine, but also his own boyhood experience of the relevance to his own life of Cicero on friendship. At a later point Ailred had discovered in Augustine the same

---

[19] *Dialogus Miraculorum* ed J. Strange (Cologne 1851) I p. 45: Dist. Prima, cap 37, 'De conversione Walewani militis, qui armatus ad ordinem venit'.

[20] *De Spir. Amic.* lib. 3, 40–44.

human needs he had felt in himself as a youth. This experiential approach to friendship, regarded as an expression of the love that every human being needs to have, may seem natural and even banal to us. But to the monk fed on the *Vitae Patrum* which equated monasticism with asceticism, the rich pastures of friendship would normally be considered a temptation away from the rocky wastes of desert life. For Basil and Pachomius it was essential to strangle the passions, to reach the *apatheia* which left room in oneself only for the indwelling of the Spirit. Thus Ailred's conviction that one could move from one form of love to another is a new departure in monastic theology and psychology.

The result of this approach is that Cistercian writers frequently tell us about themselves, their youths, conversions, and friendships. There is an autobiographical element in Cistercian writing different from that found in the reformed Benedictinism of Bec, where an Anselm showed disapproval of Eadmer's efforts at biography.[21] The Cistercians are the founders of the autobiographical *exemplum*, extrapolating from their own personal experience, needs, desires, hopes and achievements to the situation of mankind in general.[22] At least on one occasion, Bernard sought to share his own experiences with that of a friend, William of Saint Thierry, whom he invited to his sickbed so that William, also ill, could read the Scriptures and talk with him.[23] Individual experiences are integrated into the wisdom of the group, and one of the main ways of communicating such experience is through the vehicle of friendship.

Instead of trying to kill their passions, the Cistercians believed in transforming them and moulding them into their monastic experience. Bernard, for example, could allow himself to admit on the death of his brother how deeply he had loved the man.[24] He could tell his monastic audience how much he would miss his brother because Gerard had taken care of all practical matters at Clairvaux

---

[21] R. W. Southern, *The Life of Saint Anselm by Eadmer* (OMT 1972) lxxii p. 150: 'Qualiter servata sint aliter quam praeceperit ipse pater Anselmus de quo scripta sunt'.

[22] See my 'The Cistercians and the Rise of the Exemplum in early Thirteenth Century France', *Classica et Medievalia* (Copenhagen 1982).

[23] *Vita Prima* (PL 185) bk I cap 59.

[24] *Sermones Super Cantica Canticorum* 26: 3–8 in edd J. Leclercq, C. H. Talbot, H. M. Rochais, *S. Bernardi Opera* I (Rome 1957).

BRIAN PATRICK McGUIRE

as cellarer. Bernard's lament is a highly literary production, but it is also an admission of how much men in community depended on each other, as well as how Bernard continued to look at his spiritual brother as his brother in the flesh and close friend.

Bernard's lament for his brother may well be based on Ambrose's lament centuries earlier for his dead brother.[25] Once again a Cistercian could look back to one of the Western Fathers for support in expressing a personal experience. Without Bernard's words and tears it would not have been possible for Ailred to stop in the midst of writing his *Mirror of Charity* to weep for his beloved Simon, the greatest friend of his early monastic life.[26] This famous passage has to be seen in the context of the work as a whole, and not just as a fascinating insight into Ailred's psyche. Ailred wrote the *Speculum Caritatis* on the order of Bernard, who wanted it to be shown once and for all that a monk could belong to a community and at the same time cultivate the impulses of love within himself. Love and discipline could coexist, Bernard insisted, and after meeting the attractive Ailred, he apparently decided that here was the monk who summarized in his sensitivity and ability for friendship the Cistercian cult of love. So Ailred was ordered to write a treatise about love. In doing so, Ailred could reach speculative heights, but these are tempered by the evidence of his own personal life. There was no gap between high monastic theology and intense individual experience. For Ailred as well as for Bernard the two could combine in the totality of Cistercian life.

When Ailred completed his treatise on spiritual friendship late in life, he revised his earlier strictures about the immature sensual friendships of young monks.[27] He indicated that even these imperfect relationships should be tolerated in the cloister because they can grow into more spiritual bonds. Here Cistercian optimism and tolerance towards friendship reach a high point. After two decades as abbot and the formation of a second close friendship in his old age, Ailred was still loyal to the ideal of friendship. He willingly

[25] *De Excessu Fratris Sui Satyri, PL* 16, cols 1345–1414.
[26] Gerard died in 1138: B. Griesser, ed *Exordium Magnum Cisterciense* (Rome 1961) p. 153, and Bernard wrote his lament immediately afterwards. Ailred met Bernard at Clairvaux in the spring of 1142 and began his *Speculum Caritatis* on his return to England: Aelred Squire, *Aelred of Rievaulx* (Kalamazoo 1981) p. 25. The lament is in bk II, cap 34.
[27] *De Spir. Amic.* 3:85–7.

risked misinterpretation and misuse of his allowance of youthful friendships. Once again Ailred could base his theoretical optimism on what he himself had experienced in the cloister and what he had seen among his own monks. In a community of love there could be imperfect as well as more perfect loves among the monks, all of them in one way or another leading to the love of God.

Behind Bernard's and Ailred's idealization and practice of friendship undoubtedly lies the experience of the first decades at Cîteaux. One wonders if the little band of monks which stayed behind with Stephen Harding after Robert had returned to Molesmes had time and room in their lives for spiritual friendships. The very title of their code of monastic organisation, the *Carta Caritatis*, indicates that love was a major concern. But what kind of love? The love of the desert that emerges from strict discipline and is weaned away from individual human affections? Or the love of the rich valleys of Clairvaux and Rievaulx, where monastic community contains within itself the growth of particular bonds? Father Chrysogonus Waddell is at present completing a study showing that the *Carta Caritatis* is based on the language and conceptions of John Cassian's collation on friendship.[28] If this is so, then it is Cassian's collective ideal of monastic concord that was uppermost in the minds of Stephen Harding and his companions. Even so, one can reason that just as Ailred could not have written about friendship without a decisive impulse from Bernard, so too Bernard could not have entered the New Monastery at Cîteaux with his friends and kin without the understanding and acceptance of Stephen Harding that such bonds could be renewed and strengthened in the monastic life. We are only beginning to detect the outlines of Stephen Harding's personality, but a single letter brilliantly analysed by Father Waddell would seem to indicate that he valued monastic friendship highly, even if he looked upon it more in collective than in individual terms.[29] The arrival of Bernard at Cîteaux in 1112 may have given Stephen Harding the necessary impulse to transform this collective ethic of friendship into one that made room for particular friendships.

---

[28] 'Cassian and the *Carta Caritatis*', was a paper presented at the Cistercian Conference in Kalamazoo in May 1983.

[29] 'Notes towards the Exegesis of a Letter by Saint Stephen Harding', *Noble Piety and Reformed Monasticism* (Studies in Medieval Cistercian History 7 Kalamazoo 1981) pp. 10–39.

Moving back even further in time, Stephen Harding also has to be seen in terms of what came before him. He is a product of the reforming Benedictinism of the late eleventh century, the same matrix from which Anselm's letters of friendship spring. Cistercian friendships, however, are more convincing and complete than the Anselmian variety, for in the latter language flies far ahead of human experience and leads to disappointments and misunderstandings for the recipients of declarations of friendship.[30] The Cistercians managed to combine exquisite language with individually-oriented friendships. These become visible to us in the decades from about 1130 to 1170. Patristic and classical traditions of friendship were absorbed and renewed. The social background of feudalism was maintained, instead of being eliminated inside the cloister. Most of all, monks were encouraged to advance in love of God through integrating their personal impulses and experiences with the life of the community.

The period for the expression of monastic friendship is almost as short as that of the greatest expansion of the Cistercian Order. Elsewhere I have shown how friendships among monks are to a certain extent in the next period, from about 1170 to 1230, replaced by close male-female bonds.[31] The Cistercian opening to women took place not only in institutional terms but also in personal ones. This resulted from a male desire to maintain the religious and personal intensity of bonds that earlier had been exclusively male. Even if women to a certain extent do replace men, the practice of monastic friendship finally disappears from view. This can partly be explained in terms of the growing institutionalization of the Cistercian Order, where functions of government, property administration, and links with other institutions in society became more important than the cultivation of individual bonds within the monastery.[32] There is no doubt that there were still friendships in the cloister, but the fact that they disappear from view is indicative of a change of emphasis and concern in Cistercian life.

[30] See my 'Love, Friendship and Sex in the Eleventh Century: The Experience of Anselm', *Studia Theologica* 28 (1974) pp. 111–52.
[31] 'The Cistercians and the Transformation of Monastic Friendships', *Analecta Cisterciensia* 37 (1981) pp. 1–63.
[32] One of the best and earliest expressions of this change is a letter by Alexander III, in J. Leclercq, 'Epîtres d'Alexandre III sur les cisterciens', *Revue Benedictine* 64 (1934) pp. 68–82.

At the same time the Cistercians became disillusioned with women. The care of female monasteries sapped the resources of great monasteries like Villers in what today is Belgium.[33] After 1225 the monks tried to extricate themselves from new commitments to female houses. Thus institutional involvements made individual bonds less spontaneous, and the entire climate of contact on a personal level became much less favourable. From the 1240s onwards the most enlightened Cistercians seem to have concentrated on the interior reform of their order and on getting involved in the universities.[34] Scholastic learning here as elsewhere replaced monastic experience as the great source of challenge to the brightest and best men in European life.

A reflection of the Cistercian withdrawal from monastic friendship can be seen in the new Franciscan Order and its Rule. At one point the monks are encouraged to be each other's friends, but later on there is a warning against the formation of intimate friendships.[35] This might be read only as a prohibition of close friendships with men and women outside of the order, but the ambiguity of the language allows an interpretation including all particular relationships, whether inside or outside the monastery. Even though Saint Francis clearly made friends among his earliest followers and showed loyalty to them, there is an apartness in him that kept him from being the type of model for friendship that the Cistercians could so easily find in Bernard. Francis is often remembered for his friendship with Saint Clare, but here too we find hesitation. Francis tried to make sure that the two of them were not seen together in public. Clare would have to come at dead of night to him, for he feared scandal.[36]

The Franciscan ambiguity towards friendships is a point of departure for direct intolerance. Total prohibition is rare, however: usually there is only indifference to the phenomenon, a sense that

---

[33] E. W. McDonnell, *The Beguines and Beghards in Medieval Culture* (New York 1969) pp. 105–19.

[34] 'The Challenge of Scholasticism' in Louis Lekai, *The Cistercians: Ideals and Reality* (Ohio 1977) pp. 77–83.

[35] Rosalind B. Brooke, *The Coming of the Friars* (London 1975). The rule VI p. 123 'Wherever the brothers are or happen to be, they shall act as intimate friends one to another.' XI p. 125 'Nor shall they form close friendships with men or women, so that no scandal arise between brothers or on their account for any such reason.'

[36] *The Life of Saint Clare*, trans Pascal Robinson (Philadelphia 1910) p. 10.

close bonds among men or women in the religious life lead nowhere. In the *Imitation of Christ*, for example, Thomas à Kempis makes no polemic against particular friendships, but he makes it clear that the only dependable friend to have is Jesus.[37] Anyone else will be a disappointment.

This very concentrated outline of the practice and ideology of monastic friendship might make it seem as if the Cistercian experience is a parenthesis in an otherwise generally intolerant or at best indifferent attitude towards such bonds. But the Cistercian experience is important because it provided an alternative to the desert's ethic of self-denial and total separation from the monk's past experience. The Christian community of the Egyptian desert was a collection of individuals seeking salvation apart from each other, while the Cistercian community of the Western European valley was a collection of individuals finding their salvation in and through each other. The individual monk could maintain exclusive areas of his own experience and use these not as something to be cauterized or excised from his being but as a part of himself that could grow and mature in the religious life. Such individuality and intimacy can easily threaten the common harmony of a community. Cassian saw the faint possibility of such close bonds, and twelfth-century Cistercians built on Cassian's careful beginnings. The toleration of bonds of friendship in Ailred, in Bernard, and in lesser-known Cistercians is a sign of the richness and variety of twelfth-century Christian life in the West.[38] And perhaps also a reminder that human beings are not as limited in their capacities for loving each other and forming communities of love as we twentieth-century pessimists sometimes might feel.[39]

The Medieval Centre
Copenhagen University,
Denmark

[37] *De Imitatione Christi* II pp. 8–9.
[38] There are *exempla* of friendship in twelfth century miracle collections from Clairvaux, as Troyes MS Bibl. mun. 946. See my 'A lost Clairvaux Exemplum Collection found', *Anal. Cist.* (1983) pp. 27–62.
[39] For a contemporary Catholic evaluation of spiritual friendship, see Paul M. Conner, *Friendship between Consecrated Men and Women and the Growth of Charity* (Rome 1972).

VIA ASCETICA: A PAPAL QUANDARY

by BRENDA M. BOLTON

'RESCUE us O Lord Pope from barbaric power and sub-
jugation to laymen' was the cry of despair from the clerics
of Grandmont which reached Pope Innocent III about the
year 1215.[1] It indicated the growth of the appeal to Rome which
took place in the Cannon Law of the twelfth century.[2] Many other
examples of an increase in papal authority occurred at this time.
The extension of papal jurisdiction is one of two important
developments of twelfth- and thirteenth-century Christendom
with which this paper will be concerned.

This jurisdictional extension of papal authority was both a
resolution of and a reaction to the second important development,
namely the spiritual crisis or ferment of the time, known as the *vita
apostolica*.[3] This imitation of the life of the apostles was claimed, not
only by the apologists of the monastic tradition to justify their
conventional forms of cenobitic life and by the new religious
institute of canons regular but also by a whole host of contempor-

---

[1] 'Eripe nos, Domini, de potestate barbarica et a servitute laicali', Martène and
Durand, *Thesaurus* I (Paris 1717) cols 845–7.
[2] For general comments on appeals to the Curia and papal jurisdiction see G. Le
Bras, *Les institutions ecclésiastiques de la chrétienité mediévale, Histoire de l'Église* 12
(Paris 1964) 1; [R.W.] Southern, *Western Society [and the Church in the Middle Ages,]*
(Harmondsworth 1970) pp. 104–17 and in particular [C.R.] Cheney, *Innocent III
[and England,]* Päpste und Papsttum, 9 (Stuttgart 1976) pp. 97–120 and J. Hourlier,
L'Âge Classique (1140–1378): Les Religieux, Histoire du Droit et des Institutions
de l'Église en Occident, 10 (Paris 1974).
[3] E.W. McDonnell, 'The *Vita Apostolica*: Diversity or Dissent?' *CH* 24 (1955) pp.
15–31; G. Olsen, 'The Idea of the *Ecclesia Primitiva* in the Writings of the
Twelfth-Century Canonists', *Traditio* 25 (1969) pp. 61–81; [L.K.] Little, *Religious
Poverty [and the Profit Economy in Medieval Europe]* (London 1978); [C.H.]
Lawrence, *Medieval Monasticism* (London 1984) pp. 125–45; [B.M.] Bolton, *The
Medieval Reformation* (London 1983) pp. 18–32 and above all (M.-D.) Chenu,
*Nature, Man and Society [in the Twelfth Century: Essays on New Theological
Perspectives in the Latin West,]* trans J. Taylor and L.K. Little (Chicago 1968) pp.
239–46.

ary religious movements then beginning to appear.[4] Few of the religious were to remain unmoved by the example of the first Jerusalem community and from the ferment emerged a whole spectrum of different interpretations, variously emphasising simplicity, voluntary poverty, manual labour, and itinerant preaching, but all related to a christocentric piety. For many the *vita apostolica* would only be achieved through a life of strict discipline and sacrifice – to live like Christ through holy effort, based upon acts of inward or outward virtue or through self-imposed hardship and deprivation to achieve greater personal purity. This gave rise to an austere element,[5] a harsher strand of the *vita apostolica* which may perhaps be seen as a *via ascetica*. It was to be a more regular and monastic road to salvation with the many outward and visible signs of asceticism so desired by its participants.

The papacy, in seeking to exercise its increased jurisdiction in both spiritual and temporal matters, faced mounting problems because of the vast complex of religious orders which had come into being in the twelfth century.[6] The responsibility of the pope as *abbas universalis*, which meant bringing monasteries under canonical protection, became an increasingly important part of his duties.[7] When extended to new monasteries, it became a vital instrument for monastic change and reform and was embodied in the Roman chancery formula *Religiosam vitam*.[8] This extended use of such a collection of standardised formulae made it possible for a variety of

---

[4] *Ibid* pp. 202–38. For further insights into some of these movements see M.B. Becker, *Medieval Italy: Constraints and Creativity* (Indiana 1981) and [H.] Leyser, *Hermits and the New Monasticism: [A Study of Religious Communities in Western Europe 1000–1150]* (London 1984).

[5] O. Chadwick, *Western Asceticism* (Philadelphia 1958) pp. 13–31; H. Chadwick, *The Early Church*, (Harmondsworth 1967); [D.] Knowles, *From Pachomius to Ignatius: [A Study in the Constitutional History of the Religious Orders]* (Oxford 1966).

[6] [M.] Maccarrone, 'Primato Romano e Monasteri [dal Principio del Secolo XII ad Innocenzo III',] in *Istituzioni Monastiche e Istituzioni Canonicali in Occidente (1123–1215), Mendola* (Milan 1980) pp. 49–132.

[7] *Ibid* pp. 63–4. This principle, first enunciated by Gregory VII, reached its highest development with Innocent III. Apostolic protection was transformed into a papal institution, expressing the exercise of the pope's jurisdiction over the whole Church.

[8] 'Religiosam vitam eligentibus, apostolicum convenit adesse praesidium'. For a discussion of the use of this formula see M. Tangl, *Die päpstlichen Kanzleiordnungen von 1200–1500* (Innsbruck 1894) pp. 229–32.

institutions both to be confirmed and also, at the same time, to be enriched by the granting of much valued privileges. This was an innovatory concept, allowing as it did, a shift of emphasis from simple protection to much needed reform.[9] By the mid-twelfth century, a so-called 'clause of regularity' had been further developed as a condition of confirmation.[10] This not only ensured the permanence of established rules such as those of Benedict or Augustine but also applied to those institutions or observances referred to as *ordo* or *religio* and which in themselves represented a new way of life.[11] As a result of this, a profound transformation of the relationship between the papacy and the religious orders was accomplished within the framework of the protection of St. Peter.[12] Thus papal authority was able to penetrate into the cloister in spite of not always being welcome.

The problem, however, was to be particularly acute in those monasteries which were already exempt from episcopal authority and which were attached *nullo medio* to the Holy See.[13] Here, because the spiritual and temporal condition was often deplorable, the papacy was liable to be brought into disrepute by its inability to supervise them.[14] Such calls as existed for their reform and renewal, were met with resentment and sometimes even with rejection. Divergent responses were rife and indeed epitomised the whole papal dilemma of the way of the *via ascetica*. The many natural, individual human quests for the *vita apostolica* and a consequential *via ascetica*, with either a return to the way of the hermit or the founding of new strict orders could so easily lead away from the control and unity of the Church; but all were in need

[9] Maccarrone, 'Primato Romano e Monasteri' p. 74.

[10] J. Dubois, 'Les ordres religieux au xiie siècle selon la Curie romaine', *RB* 78 (1968) pp. 283–309 especially pp. 285–7.

[11] Maccarrone, 'Primato Romano e Monasteri' pp. 74–5; Chenu, *Nature, Man and Society* pp. 225–7.

[12] For a highly significant discussion of the implications of the development of the idea of *protectio Sancti Petri* see Maccarrone, 'Primato Romano e Monasteri' pp. 50–77.

[13] [G.] Schreiber, *Kurie und Kloster [im 12 Jahrhundert. Studien zur Privilegierung, Verfassung und besonders zum Eigenkirchenwesen der vorfranzicanischen Orden vornehmlich auf Grund der Papsturkunden von Paschalis II bis auf Lucius III 1099–1181,]* Kirchliche Abhandlungen 65–68, 2 vols (Stuttgart 1910) I, pp. 47–55, 207–9.

[14] [Die] Register [Innocenz' III, Bd I: 1. Pontifikatsjahr 1198/9] edd O. Hageneder and A. Haidacher (Graz-Köln 1964) 2a, p. 6. Letter of 9 January 1198 to all abbots, priors and religious of the kingdom of France.

of papal direction.[15] The popes of the period faced this dilemma in varying states of perplexity. Perhaps the least perplexed was Innocent III who, at the age of thirty-seven, as Lothair de Segni, was elected Pope in January 1198.[16] This may have been because of his ability to grasp both the significance and the number of the wide range and diversity of the views being expressed and also to insert them into an ecclesiastical structure. As the incumbent of Peter's chair at this crucial point, he was a man of exceptional vigour and purpose. He has been described as 'the most brilliantly apparent of all thirteenth century popes'.[17] His actions highlighted the competing problems of the nature and extent of papal jurisdiction and the wish to have complete freedom in the form the *via ascetica* should take.[18] He wished to use this jurisdiction to facilitate the operation of an acceptable form of asceticism within the bounds of the Church. Innocent regarded monks as 'his very special sons since it is through them that God finds the highest and worthiest of the glory due to him'.[19] He tells us that as Pope 'there had come to him the mission to maintain religion in the churches of God and to develop it'[20] and that the prosperity, maintenance of standards and reform of monasteries were particularly close to his heart. At first he attempted to work both through the older traditional Benedictine monasteries and also through the newer orders, particularly the

[15] Schreiber, *Kurie und Kloster* 1 pp. 62–3. For a series of valuable studies on the problems of eremitism see *L'Eremitismo in Occidente nei Secoli XI e XII, Mendola* 4 (Milan 1962) and Leyser, *Hermits and the New Monasticism* pp. 78–86.
[16] From the vast range of literature, the following are particularly useful. A. Luchaire, *Innocent III* 6 vols (Paris 1904–8); H. Tillmann, *Papst Innocenz' III* (Göttingen 1954), now available as *Pope Innocent III*, trans W. Sax, *Europe in the Middle Ages*, Select Studies 12 (North Holland 1980); [M.] Maccarrone, *Studi [su Innocenzo III,] Italia Sacra* 17 (Padua 1972); Cheney, *Innocent III*; [W.] Imkamp, [*Das] Kirchenbild Innocenz' III [1198–1216),]* Päpste und Papsttum, 22 (Stuttgart 1983); [S.] Sibilia, 'L'Iconografia di Innocenzo III', *Bolletino della Sezione di Anagni della Società Romana di Storia Patria* 2 (Rome 1953) pp. 65–120; G.B. Ladner, *Die Papstbildnisse des Altertums und des Mittelalters*, 2 (Vatican City 1970) pp. 53–79.
[17] [R.] Brentano, *Rome before Avignon: [A Social History of Thirteenth-Century Rome]* (London 1974) p. 148.
[18] For a brief yet stimulating account of Innocent's policies see B. Tierney, *The Crisis of Church and State* (New Jersey 1964) pp. 127–38; Cheney, *Innocent III* pp. 1–10 and Bolton, *The Medieval Reformation* pp. 97–111.
[19] 'Nos enim, vos tamquam speciales Ecclesie filios, per quos nomen Domini dignus et excellentius praedicatur', *Register* I, 2a, p. 6. Letter of 9 January 1198.
[20] *Register* I, 176, pp. 262–3.

Cistercians.[21] Indeed, he referred to the Cistercians and the Carthusians as 'the best of monks'.[22] It was not long before he was to suffer serious disillusionment in regard to the spiritual aspects of the *via ascetica* although, in more practical matters, he was able to make provision in the Fourth Lateran Council to regulate the application of the Rule of St Benedict through the institution of a triennial General Chapter for individual, autonomous Benedictine monasteries and to do the same for houses of Augustinian canons.[23]

Innocent himself had always shown a particular sensitivity to those aspects of the *vita apostolica* which stressed the increasing demand for a more ascetic, simpler and more personal spiritual life. He appreciated that for many conventional monasticism was not the only road. He was aware that the hermit ideal of withdrawal into a solitary wilderness was in many ways commendable. It could, however, be seen as too personal and private a quest and there was a danger that many individuals and groups might be tempted towards an even more extreme and exclusive form of asceticism.[24] This might even lead to a desire for mortification, an exercise in endurance with no relief and little hope, through the attempt to achieve the annihilation of the individual self. In such cases, a move towards heresy was always a possibility. But there were others, as Innocent was well aware, for whom the *via ascetica* had no attraction at all, while the approach of still more was half-hearted, to say the least. A glimpse at his life and character will enable us to understand more clearly the efforts that this pope had to make to resolve the quandary of an acceptable *via ascetica* with which he was faced.

Some evidence for his early views on the regular life, on his personal *via ascetica* and on the principles underlying his asceticism

---

[21] [U.] Berlière, 'Innocent III et [la réorganisation des] monastères bénédictins', *RB* 20–22 (1920) pp. 22–42, 145–59; P. Schmitz, *Histoire de l'Ordre de Saint Benoît* 3 (Maredsous 1948) pp. 42–55; R. Brentano, *Two Churches. England and Italy in the Thirteenth Century* (Princeton 1968) p. 259 and Maccarrone, *Studi* pp. 223–6.

[22] 'Cum inter omnes religiosos nostri temporis viros Cisterciensis et Carthusiensis ordinum fratres magna per Dei gratiam polleant honestate...', *PL* 216 (1855) col 469. Letter of 11 October 1211.

[23] *COD* (3 ed Bologna 1973) Canon 12 pp. 240–1; Maccarrone, *Studi* pp. 246–62.

[24] For a discussion of such dangers see Grundmann, pp. 70–127; B.M. Bolton, 'Poverty as Protest', *The Church in a Changing Society*, Publications of the Swedish Society of Church History, New Series, 30 (Uppsala 1978) pp. 28–32; Leyser, *Hermits and the New Monasticism* pp. 18–24.

can be drawn from a number of sources close to him. The *Gesta Innocentii tertii* presents to us the figure of the Pope and his policies through the eyes of an anonymous contemporary cleric in Rome, probably an employee of the Papal Chancery.[25] The biography, whilst written in an admiring tone, has the advantage of being backed by precise dating, although it stops suddenly at the end of 1208 or early in 1209.[26] It is valuable for the information it provides about Innocent's early career and his chosen life style which perhaps owed much to the fact that he was educated at the Benedictine monastery of S. Andrea on the Celian Hill in Rome where the shadow of its great founder, Pope Gregory I, must have been much in evidence.[27] Studies at Paris and Bologna led to a notable reputation as theologian and philosopher[28] and after he returned to Rome, probably during the pontificate of Lucius III,[29] he was ordained a sub-deacon during the brief pontificate of Gregory VIII.[30] When he was twenty-nine he was named Cardinal Deacon by Clement III[31] and given as his title church SS Sergio e Bacco on the Forum.[32] Whilst Cardinal he wrote three books, *On*

---

[25] *Gesta* [*Innocentii P.P.III,*] *PL* 214 (1855) xvii–ccxxviii. F. Ehrle, *Die Gesta Innocentii III im Verhältnis zu den Regesten desselben Papstes* (Heidelberg 1876) for a highly critical account of this work. For its revaluation and reappraisal, see Y. Lefevre, 'Innocent III et son temps vus de Rome. Étude sur la biographie anonyme de ce pape', *Mélanges d'Archéologie et d'Histoire de l'École Française de Rome*, 61 (Paris 1949) pp. 242–5.

[26] *Ibid* pp. 242–3; [M.] Maccarrone, ['Innocenzo III,] prima del pontificato', *ASP* 66 (1943) pp. 59–134 especially p. 60.

[27] *Gesta* col xvii, I. His biographer remarks that he was well-grounded in liturgical chant and psalmody. 'Exercitatus in cantilena et psalmodia'. Imkamp, *Kirchenbild Innocenz' III* pp. 20–3; Maccarrone, 'Prima del pontificato' pp. 68–81.

[28] *Gesta* col xvii, II. 'Hic primum in Urbe, deinde Parisius, tandem Bononiae, scholasticis insudavit et super coaetaneos suos tam in philosophica quam theologica disciplina profecit'. Imkamp, *Kirchenbild Innocenz' III* pp. 23–46; K. Pennington, 'The legal education of Pope Innocent III', *Bulletin of Medieval Canon Law* NS 4 (1974) pp. 70–7.

[29] Lucius III (1181–1185). Maccarrone, 'Prima del pontificato' pp. 81–3.

[30] *Gesta* col xviii, III. 'Hunc sanctae memoriae Gregorius octavus papa, in subdiaconum ordinavit'. Gregory VIII (21 November–17 December 1187); P. Kehr, 'Papst Gregor VIII als Ordensgründer', *Miscellanea F. Ehrle*, Studi e Testi 38, vol 2 (Rome 1924) pp. 248–76; Maccarrone, 'Prima del pontificato' p. 83.

[31] Clement III (1187–1191). 'Et Clemens III papa promovit in diaconum cardinalem, vicesimum nonum aetatis annum agentem', *Gesta* col xviii, III; Maccarrone, 'Prima del pontificato' p. 84.

[32] *Gesta* cols xviii–iv, III, IV; Maccarrone, 'Prima del pontificato' pp. 81–91; *Die Register Innocenz' III*, Bd II: *2. Pontifikatsjahr 1199/1200*, edd O. Hageneder, W.

the Misery of the Human Condition,[33] *On the Mystery of the Mass*[34] and
On the Four Sorts of Marriage.[35] During his pontificate he produced a
Commentary on the Seven Psalms[36] and many Sermons, Letters,
Registers and Decretals.[37] Both during his time as Cardinal and as
Pope, by precept and example, he insisted upon an honest, strict
and sparse code of behaviour.[38] The Lateran Palace became a
changed place.[39] In all these actions Innocent seems to have been
seeking to organise his own life along more ascetic lines and that of
his household on the model of a canonical community.[40] The one
exception was his private chapel where nothing was too good for
the glory of God.[41] Another contemporary view of Innocent comes

Maleczek and A. Strnad (Rome-Vienna 1979), 94, pp. 198–201. For the repairs to
this Church see R. Krautheimer, *Rome: Profile of a City 312–1308* (Princeton 1980)
p. 203 and M. Bonfioli, 'La Diaconia dei SS Sergio e Bacco nel Foro Romano.
Fonti e Problemi', *Rivista di Archeologia Cristiana* 50 (Rome 1974) pp. 55–85.

[33] *PL* 217 (1855) cols 702–46. [*Lotharii Cardinalis (Innocentii III).*] *De Miseria* [*Humane
Conditionis*] ed M. Maccarrone (Lucca 1955).

[34] *PL* 217 cols 773–916; Imkamp, *Kirchenbild Innocenz' III* pp. 46–53; Maccarrone,
'Innocenzo III, teologo della eucarestia', *Studi* pp. 341–65.

[35] *PL* 217 cols 922–68; Imkamp, *Kirchenbild Innocenz' III* pp. 53–63. For a discussion
of Innocent's significant literary and administrative activity during his cardinalate,
see Maccarrone, 'Prima del pontificato' pp. 86–9.

[36] *PL* 217 cols 968–1130: Maccarrone, 'Prima del pontificato' pp. 67–71.

[37] *Sermons: PL* 217 cols 309–690; *Letters:* C.R. Cheney, 'The Letters of Pope Innocent
III' in *Medieval Texts and Studies* (Oxford 1973) pp. 16–38 with a particularly
significant bibliography pp. 37–8; *Register* I and II; *Decretals: Corpus Iuris Canonici*
ed A. Friedberg 2 vols (Leipzig 1879) 2.

[38] *Gesta* XLI: he inveighed against all forms of avarice and cupidity; refused all forms
of gift and bribery; reformed the Chancery and decreed that no official had any
claim to fees except scribes and *bullators* who were to keep to a fixed scale of
charges.

[39] On his election as Pope, he had removed all the precious furnishings of the papal
chambers, substituting simple wooden or glass vessels for gold and silver, *ibid*
CXLVIII and having the money changers' tables taken from the kitchen entrance,
ibid XLI.

[40] His own meals were limited to three courses, those of his chaplains to two and lay
servants were replaced by clerics, *ibid* CXLVIII. Under Innocent, there were
about fifty *capellani* or chaplains who also belonged to the Pope's *familia* and were
fed from the papal kitchens, *ibid* CXLVI. See R. Elze, 'Die päpstliche Kapelle',
Zeitschrift der Savigny Stiftung für Rechtsgeschichte Kanonistische Abteilung 38 (1950)
pp. 145–204; W. Ullmann, *The Growth of Papal Government in the Middle Ages* (2 ed
London 1965) p. 331 n 4.

[41] The Chapel of St Laurence at the Lateran, known as the *Sancta Sanctorum* for its
wealth of relics, was so rich *tam in materia quam in forma* that its like had never
before been seen, *Gesta* CXLV; [S.J.P.] Van Dijk and [J. Hazelden] Walker, [*The*]
Origins of the Modern Roman Liturgy (London 1960) pp. 91–5; G. Marangoni, *Istoria
della Sancta Sanctorum* (Rome 1747); P. Lauer, *Le Palais de Latran. Étude historique et
archéologique* (Paris 1911).

from an anonymous monk away from Rome at the Cistercian house of Santa Maria di Ferraria near Teano in Campania.[42] In addition to describing how Innocent replaced the rich papal vestments with a religious habit consisting of simple white wool and lambskins,[43] he describes how the Pope instituted a universal convent for a better development of the spiritual life of the nuns of Rome.[44]

Two further fragments of evidence survive. One shows us a glimpse of Innocent at Subiaco where he suffered from heat, mosquitos and cicadas without complaint and without disturbing his prayer and contemplation.[45] The other shows his concern for those who might not have been so stalwart in facing such difficulties. While staying 'at that arid Segni' he ordered his chaplains to shorten the Daily Office.[46]

Above all, we have those works written by Innocent himself, though Cheney has warned us about the authorship of the letters and sermons.[47] Nevertheless, an interior consistency in these letters can be discerned to indicate that the overall view was Innocent's.[48] In his theological works, his taste for parallels between words of similar sound and for the transposition of epithets are further indications of his style of writing.[49]

His ascetical work *On the Misery of the Human Condition*, written sometime after the age of twenty-five, is highly relevant here.[50] While it has been described as 'sound, not deep; genuine, not

[42] [*Chronica Romanorum pontificum et imperatorum ac de rebus in Apulia gestis (781–1228) auctore*] *ignoto monacho Cistercensi* ed A. Gaudenzi in *Società Napoletana di Sancta Patria*, 1, Cronache (Naples 1888) p. 34.

[43] *Ibid* p. 34. 'Assumpsit sibi vestos religiosas, id est de lana alba et pelles agniculas'.

[44] *Ibid*, 'instituit etiam universale cenobium monalium Rome, in quo omnes moniales conveniant, nec eis progredi liceat'.

[45] [K.] Hampe, ['Eine Schilderung des Sommeraufenthaltes der Römischen Kurie unter] Innocenz' III in Subiaco 1202', *Historische Vierteljahrsschrift* 8 (Leipzig 1905) pp. 509–35.

[46] Van Dijk and Walker, *Origins of the Modern Roman Liturgy* pp. 97, 267–8 and Appendix 14b pp. 462–4.

[47] Cheney, 'Letters of Pope Innocent III' pp. 22–9.

[48] *Ibid* p. 29.

[49] *Ibid* pp. 31–4; Brentano, *Rome before Avignon* pp. 150–3.

[50] For the suggestion that this work was completed at the beginning of 1195, Maccarrone, *De Miseria*, Praefatio XXXVII. 'Ergo licet assere opus *De Miseria*, a Lothario completum esse initio anni 1195, nempe inter calendas Ianuarias vel diem Decembris anni 1194 ... atque diem 13 Aprilis 1195'.

original',[51] it was a popular and widely read set-piece on the vanity of earthly pretensions and the span of Man's life 'from the heat of love to the meat of worms'.[52] His analytical powers are brought to bear successively on various human conditions, poor and rich; servant and master; celibate and married; good and wicked; each suffering his own particular misery and prevented from being happy.[53] He expounds the consequences which the desire for riches, especially the temptation of money, brings to justice and the outcome of law-suits, of which he had first-hand knowledge.[54] Successive chapters describe examples of pomp and pride resulting in rich clothing and domestic furnishing.[55] The work closes with the traditional scenario of the Last Judgment, the final act of Man.[56]

The material of much of this short work may not have been new, but it contained motifs which are common to all ascetical and moralistic tracts and has the ring of truth and real life about it.[57] His use of language, described variously as 'fantastic, lyrical, funny and crude',[58] his borrowings from Ovid and Horace, as well as his Scriptural allusions, lead us to believe that Innocent enjoyed this playing with words and with the outrageous mocking at the decline of Man into senility.[59] Although there were many jokes at the expense of his readers, the serious nature of this treatise which at first appears to be a transitory academic exercise, remained in Innocent's meditations and its arguments were often repeated in the many letters and sermons of his pontificate.[60] They played a part too in his practical duties, as the examples of the *via ascetica* which he met, ranging from a reflection of the youthful enthusiasm of the

---

[51] Van Dijk and Walker, *Origins of the Modern Roman Liturgy* p. 91.

[52] Brentano, *Rome before Avignon* p. 151.

[53] Maccarrone, *De Miseria* pp. 7–36 especially pp. 20–7.

[54] *Ibid* pp. 39–72, especially pp. 39–43, 59–62. For law suits and payment for justice, compare *Gesta* XLI and CXLVII. His biographer witnesses that the pope 'inter omnes pestes, habuit venalitatem exosam', *ibid* XLI.

[55] Maccarrone, *De Miseria* pp. 69–72.

[56] *Ibid* pp. 75–98.

[57] Maccarrone, 'Prima del pontificato' pp. 102–4, for a discussion of possible sources and influences.

[58] Brentano, *Rome before Avignon* p. 151.

[59] *Ibid* pp. 150–4.

[60] Maccarrone, 'Prima del pontificato' pp. 103–10 and especially 107–8. 'Si vede questo dall'influenza, veramente notevole, che il *De Miseria* ebbe sugli altri suoi scritti'.

treatise to that of its more depressive aspects. Although his reactions may often have been too immediate,[61] Innocent was careful enough to look for ways of change which, in the result, brought some acceptance from those he was either over-chastising or over-praising. The affair of Grandmont and the meeting with Francis are two examples.

His own practical experience of what he considered to be extreme asceticism, the *via ascetica* which had lost its way, came from Grandmont in the Limousin.[62] Indeed, the earliest reference we have to Innocent before he was pope comes from an eye-witness account of the Chapter at Grandmont by Bernard Ithier, chronicler of Saint-Martial at Limoges.[63] He notes the presence there, in May or June 1187, of the young Lothair de Segni.[64] This was precisely the moment of the first great crisis in the Order: the revolt of the laybrothers or *conversi*[65] which was regarded by

---

[61] Brentano, *Rome before Avignon* p. 150.

[62] Among numerous articles on Grandmont, the most useful are [A.]Lecler, 'Histoire de l'Abbaye de Grandmont', B]*ulletin de la* S]*ociété* A[*rchéologique et* H]*istorique du* L[*imousin*] 58 (1908) pp. 44–94; and the following, all by J. Becquet, 'Les institutions de l'ordre de Grandmont au moyen âge', R[*evue*] M[*abillon*] 42 (1952) pp. 31–42; 'Les premiers écrivains de l'ordre de Grandmont', RM 43 (1956) pp. 127–37; 'L'"Institution": premier coutumier de l'ordre de Grandmont', RM 46 (1956) pp. 15–32; 'La règle de Grandmont', BSAHL 87 (1958–60) pp. 9–36; 'La première crise de l'ordre de Grandmont', *Ibid* pp. 283–324; *Scriptores Ordinis Grandmontensis*, ed J. Becquet, CC, *Continuatio Medievalis* 8 (Turnholt 1968); 'Etienne de Muret', *Dictionnaire de Spiritualité* 4 (Paris 1961) cols 1504–14; 'Gerard Ithier', *ibid* 6 (1967) cols 275–6; 'Le Bullaire de l'ordre de Grandmont', RM 46 (1956) 1–75 pp. 82–93, 156–68; *ibid* 47 (1957) 76–93d pp. 33–43, 245–7; Addenda et Corrigenda, *ibid* 53 (1963) pp. 111–33, 137–160. Abbreviated as BUL.

[63] *Chronicon B. Iterii Armarii Monasterii S. Marcialis* ed H. Duplès-Agier, *Société de l'histoire de France* (Paris 1874) pp. 30–129 especially p. 62. Bernard Ithier (1163–1225), novice at Saint-Martial in 1177, ordained deacon in 1185 and priest in 1189, held the offices of treasurer, sacristan and librarian (1204). As he only left the Abbey of Saint-Martial at rare intervals and even then on almost exclusively religious journeys, his presence at Grandmont in 1187 seems of particular significance.

[64] *Ibid* p. 62. 'Ego presens in capitulo cum hoc fieret, et Octavianus, episcopus Ostiensis et Hugo *de Nonans* et Lotharius, qui postea Innocentius papa 111[us] meruit nuncupari, et Poncius, Clarmontensis episcopus'.

[65] Becquet, 'La première crise' p. 298. On the general institution of laybrothers or *conversi* see K. Hallinger, 'Woher kommen die Laienbrüder, ASOC 12 (1956) pp. 1–104; J.O. Ducourneau, 'De l'institution et des us des convers dans l'ordre de Cîteaux (xiie et xiiie siècles)', in *Saint Bernard et son temps*, 2 vols (Dijon 1928–9) II pp. 139–201; J.S. Donnelly, *The Decline of the Medieval Cistercian Laybrotherhood*, Fordham University Studies, Series 3 (New York 1949). For a contemporary comparative view, see M.D. Knowles, 'The revolt of the lay brothers of

Stephen of Tournai as the severest reproach of all; that within 'this extraordinary Order of Grandmont'[66] clerics were subjugated to laymen. Innocent must have been present at the forced resignation of the sixth prior, William de Treignac.[67] He may have witnessed William's departure with two hundred clerics and thirteen *conversi* for Cîteaux and ultimately for Rome to register a complaint at the Curia.[68] This experience, both dramatic and scandalous in his eyes, together with the fact that, later as Cardinal, he was to be personally involved in their suits at the Curia,[69] made a deep impression on Innocent's mind. In 1202 he reminded the abbots of La Ferté, Pontigny, Morimond and Clairvaux, the four daughter houses in dispute with their mother at Cîteaux, of the great dangers of ascetic over-simplification, instancing the scandal of Grandmont, lest through discord they, like it, might fall into ridicule *in derisum et fabulam* and become the laughing stock and talk of all.[70] Nevertheless, Innocent was characteristically still willing to reconsider the way Grandmont had moved through all its crises and to give a new form of approval to the Order,[71] so much so that much later in 1220, Dominic, who owed much to Innocent, was able to consider looking at the reformed Grandmont as an example that might be followed in his Order's institution of conventual mendicancy.[72]

The clerical congregation of the hermits of Grandmont represented a misguided attempt to institutionalise the solitary life at the

---

Sempringham', *EHR* 1 (1935) pp. 465–87 and R. Foreville, 'La crise de l'ordre de Sempringham au xiie siècle: nouvelle approche du dossier des frères lais', *Anglo-Norman Studies* 6 (Woodbridge 1983) pp. 39–57.

[66] J. Warichez, *Étienne de Tournai et son temps* (Tournai-Paris 1937) p. 54 n 50. Stephen, Bishop of Tournai (1192–1203). Becquet, 'La première crise' p. 297.

[67] *Ibid* pp. 301–2. Prior William de Treignac (1170–1187). For a discussion of his priorate see *ibid* pp. 291–9.

[68] *Chronicon B. Iterii* p. 62. 'Grandimontenses gravi dissentione periclantur, ita quod W. prior cum ducentis clericis et xiii laicis de domo sua prosiliens. Rome obiit peregrinus'.

[69] Becquet, 'La première crise' p. 317.

[70] *PL* 214 (1855) cols 1107–8; Potthast I, 1772 p. 155; *BUL* 46b, 22 November 1202. For another almost contemporary view of this crisis, see *The Historia Occidentalis of Jacques de Vitry*, ed J.F. Hinnebusch, *SpicFr* 17 (1972) pp. 124–7.

[71] Privilege of 27 February 1202. The whole text is edited in Lecler, 'Histoire de l'Abbaye de Grandmont', *BSAHL* 58 (1908) pp. 73–6; abbreviated version, *PL* 214 cols 945–8 and *BUL* 38–53 and 53B–61.

[72] Becquet, 'La première crise' p. 324; [M.H.] Vicaire, *Saint Dominic [and his Times]* trans K. Pond (London 1964) pp. 310–11.

expense of everything else.[73] The original founder, Stephen de Muret (d. 1124), a noble hermit, had quite deliberately left no rule of life for his disciples to follow, explaining that he belonged to the Order of the Gospel and wished to be called neither monk, nor canon nor hermit.[74] This was intended to be a complete return to the *vita apostolica* but there were many aspects which owed their origin to the ideas of the Benedictines, Augustinians, Carthusians and others.[75] The customs of the Order of Grandmont were only consolidated into a Rule during the tenure of the fourth prior Stephen of Liciac (1139–1163)[76] and by that time there had been a considerable expansion in numbers of these mendicant hermits whose modest cells remained faithful to the model of the desert.[77] These hermits had renounced property, buildings and lands, flocks and herds, either for work or consumption, but bees from the forest were allowed.[78] There was a contradiction, however, in that, while they had given up all regular resources, they accepted ownership of the monastery, its chapel and its garden.[79] To allow the clerics to apply themselves solely to the spiritual work of contemplation and prayer, without ever leaving the monastic enclosure, the founder had made provision that the *conversi* should attend to temporal affairs and indeed should have authority over

---

[73] For a general discussion of the criticism of eremitism, see G. Morin, 'Rainaud l'ermite et Ives de Chartres. Un episode de la crise de cénobitisme au xie–xiie siècle', *RB* 40 (1928) oo 99–115 and J. Leclercq, 'Le poème de Payen Bolotin contre les faux ermites', *ibid* 73 (1958) pp. 52–84. For accessible accounts of the lifestyle at Grandmont see [B.] Lackner, [*The*] *Eleventh-Century Background [of Cîteaux]* Cistercian Studies Series 8 (Washington 1972) pp. 196–203 and Little, *Religious Poverty* pp. 79–83.

[74] *Regula Venerabilis Viri Stephani Muretensis*, *CC* 8 p. 66; Little, *Religious Poverty* p. 80; Chenu, *Nature, Man and Society* p. 239.

[75] Becquet, 'La règle de Grandmont' pp. 11–15; *PL* 204 (1855) cols 1136–75.

[76] Becquet, 'La règle de Grandmont' pp. 15–30 and 'L"Institution": premier coutumier de l'ordre de Grandmont' pp. 15–32.

[77] *Ibid* pp. 18–21; 'La règle de Grandmont' pp. 35–6; *PL* 204 (1855) col 1151 cap XLVI 'Quod fratres in cella permaneant'.

[78] [Walter] Map, *De Nugis Curialium* ed and trans M.R. James, revised by C.N.L. Brooke and R.A.B. Mynors, (Oxford 1983) pp. 52–5, 112–5. 'Animals they have none, except bees; these Stephen allowed because they do not deprive neighbours of food; and their produce is collected publicly once a year all together'. *PL* 204 cols 1142–3 cap VI 'De bestiis non habendis'.

[79] Becquet, 'La règle de Grandmont' pp. 16–19; *PL* 204 cols 1136–62; Lackner, *Eleventh-Century Background* pp. 200–1.

the clerics in this sphere.[80] In addition, although the clerics should not, except in times of scarcity, seek alms, the *conversi* were eventually allowed to do so.[81] The *conversi* were thus given *de facto* supreme responsibility in the administration of the economy and the clerics were, to all intents and purposes, held enclosed as their pensioners.[82] Although the *conversi* were exhorted to fraternal charity and were specifically warned not to resort to domination, a severe imbalance in the relative proportion of *conversi* to clerics, perhaps in the ratio of as much as seven or eight to one in some cells, caused great tension and placed a heavy strain on this potentially weak link.[83] At times the *conversi* used their authority to persecute the clerics by half-starving them. Such a minor matter as to who rang the bell for collation, became, in such circumstances, a crucial point of difference. If it was not rung—and often it was not—no food was had by anyone.[84]

Although at first papal attitudes to Grandmont were generally benevolent, seeing in it a dynamic order which could absorb and institutionalise the growing appeal of the eremitic life,[85] the crises between clerics and *conversi* led the Holy See to affirm its authority over this form of religious life which could, when diverted from its true *via ascetica*, move dangerously out of control. This insistence upon control did not please many contemporary followers of the life of the hermit. It was, in one case at least, considered to illustrate

---

[80] *Liber de Doctrina*, CC 8 pp. 3–62 caps XV and LIX; *BUL* 13; *PL* 202 (1855) col 1416; *BUL* 21; *PL* 204 col 1375; Becquet, 'La première crise pp. 287, 300.

[81] *PL* 204 cols 1143, 1145; Map, *De Nugis Curialium* pp. 114–5.

[82] Knowles, *From Pachomius to Ignatius* p. 33; Map, *De Nugis Curialium* pp. 113–4.

[83] Becquet, 'La première crise pp. 295–6 and n 45 p. 295. An obituary fragment from Grandmont *c.*1140–1150 bears witness to a ratio of one priest to every seven or eight *conversi*. Some degree of balance seems to have been restored by the early thirteenth century with a proportion then of one priest to two or three lay brothers being considered as an *optimum*, *ibid*, pp. 295, 323. See also C. Dereine, 'L'obituaire primitif de l'ordre de Grandmont', *BSAHL* 87 (1958–60) pp. 325–31 in which he deduces from an examination of Paris BN Lat MS 1138 a precise figure for the proportion of laymen to clerics of one hundred and thirty to twenty three and dates the manuscript to *c.*1120–1160.

[84] *BUL* 12, 19, 21, 22, 24; Becquet, 'La première crise' p. 316; Martène and Durand, *Thesaurus* I, cols 845–7; *PL* 202 col 1415, Bull of Urban III, 14 July 1186, 'Liceat vobis unius campanae pulsatione competentibus horis fratres vestros de laboribus ad ecclesiam convocare'.

[85] Becquet, 'La première crise' p. 283–5; Knowles, *From Pachomius to Ignatius* pp. 16–21.

the over-enthusiasm of a too-youthful pope who ought properly to be more concerned with the form of religious life rather than its spirit.[86] Allowing the *conversi* to be in command had led to the dissipation of the possessions of the Order, the refusal to render accounts and quarrels on innumerable minor matters.[87] Other Churchmen saw the brothers of Grandmont as the loiterers of eremitism, enmeshed in a set of bizarre institutions and with at least twice as many *conversi* as clerics.[88] Innocent saw the inherent weakness of the so-called Gospel Rule which could not be avoided by a simple re-classification of the Order of Grandmont amongst the emerging mendicant orders.[89] He stressed the legitimate char-acter of certain corporate possessions, such as tithes, lands, mills and revenues, and allowed some collection of alms and the receiving of bequests.[90] He reduced the number of *conversi*, im-proved the economic condition of the cells and ordered that, in each one, a named cleric should be empowered to correct clerics and *conversi* alike.[91] This so improved the nature of the Order that later, a second *conversi* revolt was easily suppressed and an order of clerics, analogous to others, came into being after 1219.[92]

With his first reaction to the situation at Grandmont in mind, and after regulating his own household according to his personal *via ascetica* Innocent turned his attention to what was taking place in the monasteries and in the orders. As Pope he had neither the wish nor the capacity to direct the government of each monastery from Rome, but from the beginning of his pontificate he had announced

---

[86] *Walther von de Vogelweide: Werke* ed J. Schaefer (Darmstadt 1972) p. 226. 'Dâ weinte ein klôsenaere, er klagete gote sîniu leit: Owê der bâbest ist ze junc: hilf, hêrre, dîner kristenheit!' 'Far away in a cell, I heard much lamentation. A hermit was weeping there: he was lamenting his sufferings to God: Alas, the Pope is too young: O Lord, help your Christendom!' The date is probably shortly after 1201. I am grateful to Dr W.J. Jones for this reference and its translation.

[87] Becquet, 'La première crise' p. 316.

[88] *Ibid* p. 322–4.

[89] *Ibid* p. 324.

[90] *BUL* 40, 41, 44, 45; Becquet, 'La première crise' p. 319; Lecler, 'Histoire de l'Abbaye de Grandmont', *BSAHL* 58 pp. 73–6.

[91] *Ibid* p. 74; *BUL* 40, 41, 42, 45, 46, 53 and especially 54 for the Bull of 24 December 1211 in which Innocent III confided the reform of Grandmont to the Archbishop of Bourges and the Cistercian abbots of La Pré and Varennes.

[92] Becquet, 'La première crise' p. 324.

that he would wish to favour and develop existing regular religious institutions.[93] He began with the Benedictines.[94]

These monasteries still followed the Rule of St Benedict and maintained their historic role as instruments of the papacy. They were more effective at some times than at others in this role, and in some monasteries more than others. By the end of the twelfth century greater centralisation ought to have resulted from increasd papal jurisdiction but autonomy, built into the Rule itself, still perpetuated the individual nature of each monastery.[95] It must also be said that not all popes had the necessary vigour to reach those on the periphery.

The Benedictine family was very wide. It included traditional Black monk houses, the monastery of Cluny with all its dependencies and the hundreds of Cistercian foundations which sprang up across Europe. In Italy the congregations of Camaldoli, Vallombrosa and Fonte Avellana made up another great religious reserve with a broader Benedictine tradition.[96] Some monasteries were attached jurisdictionally to a mother house but the greater number were without any links at all, remaining isolated, one from another, and united only in their observance of the same rule.[97] Some were firmly under episcopal jurisdiction, others in receipt of papal privileges and some entirely exempt from their diocesan bishop. The degree of internal discipline varied considerably.

The role of the bishops themselves in monastic reform was considered by Innocent in the first year of his pontificate. He wrote to the bishop of Périgueux that since the Pope, who has general control of all churches, could not be everywhere in person, he wished irregularities to be removed by his brethren the bishops who shared his pastoral care.[98] Mandates to individual bishops thus allowed them to discover the moral and material state of religious houses by canonical visitation with subsequent corrections in head

---

[93] Cheney, *Innocent III* p. 180.
[94] P. Schmitz, *Histoire de l'Ordre de Saint Benoît* 3 (Maredsous 1948) pp. 42–55; Berlière, 'Innocent III et les monastères bénédictins', *RB* 20–22 (1920) pp. 22–42, 145–59; Maccarrone, *Studi* pp. 223–46.
[95] Berlière, 'Innocent III et les monastères bénédictins' p. 22.
[96] *Ibid* pp. 23–6.
[97] Knowles, *From Pachomius to Ignatius* p. 6.
[98] *Register* I, 445, p. 668. Letter of 5 December 1198 to Raymond, bishop of Périgueux 'Et quoniam ubique presentia corporali adesse non possumus'.

and members. While he did not hesitate to grant to monasteries the special protection of the Holy See or to recognise the *libertas* of certain religious houses, he was always watchful in cases of tithe exemption and visitation.[99] He never failed to show respect for acquired rights and particularly exercised this in the promise of obedience made by abbots to their respective bishops.[100] He counted on his legates to supplement the work of diocesan bishops, granting them wide powers of correction and extending their jurisdiction over any exempt houses of Benedictines or even of canons regular which were inaccessible to their bishops and so subject to no other Rule than Rome.[101]

But if Innocent knew how to defend episcopal rights, he wished also to establish a clear distinction, both in principle and in fact, between the discipline of an abbot in his monastery and the jurisdiction of the diocesan bishop.[102] He recognised the right of the abbot to watch over and to maintain discipline, leaving the bishop in full possession of his right to intervene in contentious matters. Once he had established this distinction, Innocent could more vigorously defend the real rights of the monasteries, seeking a balance between those rights and legitimate aspirations. Innocent was most anxious to conserve the distinctive character of monasticism of which solitude and retreat were two essential elements.[103] He regarded journeys and time spent in the world, especially in litigation, as incompatible with the peace of the cloister[104] and was always ready to combat the tendency of the *gyrovagus* or wandering monk to break with the stability of the monastery.[105] Yet he showed himself sympathetic to the concept of *transitus*, the passage from one order to another more severe.[106] Thus a Benedictine

---

[99] Berlière, 'Innocent III et les monastères bénédictins' pp. 27–33.

[100] *Ibid* p. 28.

[101] Schreiber, *Kurie und Kloster* 1 pp. 207–09 for some discussion of the emancipation of monasteries from episcopal authority.

[102] Berlière, 'Innocent III et les monastères bénédictins' pp. 29–31.

[103] *Ibid* pp. 33–5.

[104] *Register* I, 161, pp. 229–30. Letter of 30 April 1198, 'Viris religiosis, et his praecipue qui beati Benedicti regulam sunt professi, non credimus expedire, ut, otio claustrali postposito, contra instituta sui ordinis discurrant per curias seculares aut secularibus negotiis involvantur'.

[105] *Rule of St Benedict* ed J. McCann (London 1952) Cap I, De generibus monachorum, pp. 14–17, *semper vagi et numquam stabiles*.

[106] M.A. Dimier, 'Saint Bernard et le droit en matière de *Transitus*', *RM* 43 (1953) pp. 48–82; G. Picasso, 'San Bernardo e il *transitus* dei monachi', in *Studi su S.*

could pass to the Order of Cîteaux but it was not possible for a Cistercian to transfer to a Benedictine house.[107] His statement, made in 1206, in the case of a Durham monk, became the classic justification for such a transfer *ad arctiorem ordinem*, to a stricter way of life.[108]

Innocent was well-informed on the financial and disciplinary state of the Benedictines through canonical visitation, details from legates, complaints from bishops or even from monks themselves.[109] He was also uniquely informed through personal experience, acquired through sometimes prolonged visits.[110] In particular, these visits showed him that the general indebtedness of a house was nearly always accompanied by a lowering of disciplinary standards, reinforcing his view that the *via ascetica* required adequate material provision.[111] Such visits were local, within the Patrimony, and made in his capacity as bishop of Rome. Here and close to home, he was assured of producing and sustaining a salutary moral effect.[112]

We know that, in the summer of 1202, Innocent, with a few cardinals, stayed at Subiaco.[113] On the steep cliff above the lakes of Nero,[114] he found two monasteries where he stayed for a few days

---

Bernardo di Chiaravalle: Nell'ottavo centenario della Canonizzazione (Rome 1975) pp. 182–200.

[107] Berlière, 'Innocent III et les monastères bénédictins' p. 35; *PL* 215 cols 874–5.

[108] *Ibid*, 'Cum ergo dilectus filius R. monachus vester, ad fratres Cisterciensis ordinis transmigraverit, non ut ordini vestro aliquatenus derogaret, sed ut apud eos vitam duceret arctionem'. For an interesting discussion of the problems of transfer from Grandmont to Cîteaux, see Becquet, 'La première crise' pp. 295–6.

[109] Berlière, 'Innocent III et les monastères bénédictins' pp. 35–8.

[110] *Ibid* p. 39; [L.V.] Delisle, 'Itinéraire d'Innocent III, [dressé d'après les actes de ce pontife',] *BEC* (1857) pp. 500–34 especially p. 509.

[111] Berlière, 'Innocent III et les monastères bénédictins' pp. 37, 149–56.

[112] *Ibid* p. 39. On monasteries in general in the Patrimony see *Monasticon Italiae*, I, Roma e Lazio ed F. Caraffa (Cesena 1981) and for a social and economic background to the region, see the important study by P. Toubert, *Les Structures du Latium Médiéval: Le Latium Méridional et la Sabine du ix à la fin du xii siècle*, 2 vols (Rome 1973).

[113] Hampe, 'Innocenz' III in Subiaco 1202' pp. 509–35; *Monasticon Italiae* I pp. 172–5; [Muratori,] *Chronicon Sublacense* [*593–1369*,] 24, VI, ed R. Morghen (Bologna 1927) pp. 34–7.

[114] Hampe, 'Innocenz' III in Subiaco 1202' pp. 519–21. This was the former *Sublaqueum*, site of the imposing imperial villa and the three artificial lakes created by damming the river Anio and only finally destroyed in 1305.

and preached.[115] The upper one, the Sacro Speco, enclosed the cave where for three years, the young hermit Benedict had been instructed in the practice of asceticism.[116] The sight of the excellent discipline maintained there by its monks gave this pope great pleasure.[117] To demonstrate his deep regard for this community, he made a generous gift of six pounds annually from the Apostolic Camera for the use of the prior and brothers,[118] making a special present of a further twenty pounds for new habits for the monks and a two-coloured chasuble to honour God and St Benedict at the altar.[119]

Things were, however, quite different lower down the mountain. At the sister monastery of Santa Scholastica,[120] more important, more richly endowed and more involved with the secular world of the feudal nobility, grave abuses were revealed by Innocent.[121] While there was neither silence nor abstinence, there was embezzling of revenues and a general laxity which included the abbot.[122] Innocent acted quickly to remedy this deplorable situation, at the root of which lay that possession of personal property,

---

[115] Chronicon Sublacense p. 34. 'In illis diebus venit dominus Innocencius papa tercius ... qui personaliter cum paucis cardinalibus venit ad monasterium, visitavit et pluribus diebus stetit; predicavit ibidem et monasterium reformavit...'.

[116] Monasticon Italiae I pp. 172–3; Grégoire le Grand: Dialogus I, Sources chrétiennes, 251 (Paris 1978); Lawrence, Medieval Monasticism p. 19.

[117] PL 214 col 1062, September 1202. 'Accedentes causa devotionis ad locum quem beatus Benedictus suae conversionis primordio consecravit, et invenientes vos ibi secundum institutionem ipsius laudabiliter Domino famulari ...'. Berlière, 'Innocent III et les monastères bénédictins' p. 40.

[118] Chronicon Sublacense pp. 34–6 for the whole text; Potthast I, 1720, 1 September 1202. 'Priori et fratribus iuxta specum b. Benedicti regularem vitam servantibus sex libras usualis monetae de camera b. Petri singulis annis percipiendas concedit'. Also Potthast I, 1835, 24 February 1203.

[119] Chronicon Sublacense p. 36 '...et pro vestibus monachorum emendis xx libras presenrialiter elargimur, planetam de cocco bis tincto Deo et beato Benedicto ad altaris officium offerentes'. For details of the fresco by ? Magister Conxolus depicting Innocent III with St Benedict and this privilege at the Sacro Speco, see Sibilia, 'L'Iconografia di Innocenzo III' pp. 75–8 and Ladner, Die Papstbildnisse pp. 68–72.

[120] Monasticon Italiae I pp. 174–5; PL 214 cols 1064–6; Berlière, 'Innocent III et les monastères bénédictins' p. 40.

[121] Potthast I, 1734, 'Abbati et conventui Sublacensi scribit de quibusdam vitiis emendandis, quae inter monachos illius coenobii irrepserant'. Dated September 1202.

[122] Chronicon Sublacense p. 35 'quia abbas et prior circa correptionem delinquentium erant nimium negligentes'. Also PL 214 col 1066.

against which St Benedict had so energetically fought in the Rule.[123] In the Decretal *Cum ad monasterium* of February 1203,[124] emanating from his visit to Subiaco, Innocent made the particular declaration that 'since the abdication of all personal property, as with the practice of chastity, is so essential in the monastic rule, even the Pope himself has not the right to abrogate it'.[125] His decree for Subiaco thus became one part of his code of reformed monasticism.[126]

In June and July 1208, Innocent stayed at San Germano[127] in the plain below St Benedict's own monastery of Cassino, midway between Rome and Naples.[128] Several times he went up the mountain to stay at this, the most ancient of monasteries, where he personally examined the accounts, considered the state of the various monastic offices and brought to light certain malpractices.[129] He addressed a severe reprimand to Abbot Roffredo,[130] reminding him of his obligations under the Rule and threatening him with canonical penalties if he did not hasten to revive that discipline lost through his own fault.[131] He also obliged Roffredo to repay the deficit in revenue and to increase the hospitality of the house without recourse to further exactions.[132]

---

[123] *RSB* Cap XXXIII, Siquid debeant monachi proprium habere, pp. 84–7; *Chronicon Sublacense* p. 35.

[124] *Corpus Iuris Canonici* ed A. Friedberg 2 vols (Leipzig 1879) II, Decretal of Gregory IX, III, 35, 6, cols 599–600. De statu monachorum et canonicorum regularium. *PL* 214 cols 1064–66; Potthast I, 1734; *Chronicon Sublacense* pp. 34–6, Cum ad monasterium sublacensem personaliter venissemus ...'.

[125] *Ibid* p. 36. 'Nec extimet abbas quod super habenda proprietate possit cum aliquo monacho dispensare, quoniam abdicatio proprietatis sicut et custodia castitatis adeo est annexa regule monachali *ut contra eam ne summus pontifex possit licenciam indulgere*'.

[126] Maccarrone, *Studi* p. 225.

[127] *Ignoto monacho Cistercensi* p. 34. 'Mccviij idem papa mense Iulii apud Sanctum Germanum in terra sancti Benedicti curiam tenuit'; *PL* cols 1593–4; Delisle, 'Itinéraire d'Innocent III' p. 521.

[128] For a recent general background to Monte Cassino, see L. Fabiani, *La terra di S. Benedetto: studio storico-giuridico sull'abbazia di Montecassino dell'viii al xiii secolo* 3 vols, Miscellanea Cassinese, vols 33–34 (Montecassino 1968) and vol 42 (Montecassino 1980). More specific is the important work by H.E.J. Cowdrey, *The Age of Abbot Desiderius: Montecassino, the Papacy and the Normans in the Eleventh and Early Twelfth Centuries* (Oxford 1983) especially pp. 1–45.

[129] Potthast I, 3470; Berlière, 'Innocent III et les monastères bénédictins' pp. 40–1.

[130] Potthast I, 374; *PL* 215 cols 1593–1600.

[131] *Ibid* cols 1593–4.

[132] *Ibid*; Berlière, 'Innocent III et les monastères bénédictins' p. 41.

Innocent demonstrated the importance he attached to the reform of Cassino by the energetic repression of abuses which he had already identified at Subiaco. In September 1215, he drew up a series of statutes to be observed at Cassino,[133] including the abolition of all personal property and peculation, formal interdiction against the alienation of revenues and goods, the restoration of discipline in the community, strict enclosure and the provision of revenues for the sick and poor in the hospital.[134]

The case of Cassino highlighted one particular problem. The choice of an abbot was crucial since upon him depended not only the state of discipline but also the state of the monastic economy, paradoxically so vital to the *via ascetica*.[135] Innocent himself called particular attention to the necessity of making a good choice.[136] The lack of precision in the Rule on the election of the abbot was a perpetual source of trouble.[137] Nor was Innocent any less concerned to ensure the strictest supervision of monastic recruitment. He acted to safeguard the freedom of vocation by criticising all constraint, forbidding the entry of young children and by making a one-year novitiate obligatory for all recruits.[138] Although such reforms were of temporary benefit, none could be really thorough or long-lasting, since they depended, in the last resort, upon individual interpretation in different houses, a particular weakness of the Rule itself.[139]

One major experiment and institutional innovation did, however, mark a new stage in breaking down the isolationism and particularism of some old Benedictine houses.[140] In February 1203,

[133] *PL* 217 cols 249–53; L. Tosti, *Storia della badia di Monte Cassino*, 3 vols (Naples 1842–3) 2 pp. 289–92.
[134] *Ibid* p. 289; Potthast I, 4996, 'Ad monasterii Casinensis reformationem plura capitula statuit', 20 September 1215.
[135] Berlière, 'Innocent III et les monastères bénédictins' pp. 149–51.
[136] *PL* 214 col 168, '... gaudemus plurimum et electionis canonicae apostolicum libenter impertimur assensum'.
[137] Knowles, *From Pachomius to Ignatius* p. 6.
[138] *PL* 214 cols 255–6 speaks of forcible entry into Reading Abbey; *PL* 215 cols 1175–6 tells of a recruit taken to the monks of Clairvaux while ill and *PL* 214 cols 429–30 from Pisa 'unde multa mala noscuntur saepius provenire, cum infirmi ad monasterium iam translati et emissa professione, postquam de infirmitatibus convaluerint, habitum religionis abjiciant et ad propria revertantur'.
[139] Berlière, 'Innocent III et les monastères bénédictins' p. 156.
[140] See the important study by Maccarrone, *Studi* pp. 226–46; also U. Berlière, 'Les chapitres généraux de l'Ordre de S. Benoît' *RB* 18 (1901) pp. 364–98; 'Innocent III et les monastères bénédictins' pp. 156–9; Cheney, *Innocent III* pp. 231–4.

he took an initiative to summon monastic heads to meet together in six provincial chapters for the improvement of discipline in those monasteries immediately subject *nullo medio* to the Holy See.[141] In each of the six regions, a small group of abbots and bishops was appointed to nominate visitors with papal authority *vice nostra*, to go round the monasteries, consider reform and make the necessary corrections.[142] Innocent was well aware of the novelty of these solemn chapters and promised that if the experiment should succeed, he would transform it into a permanent institution to be celebrated each year in a different place.[143] Had this programme been realised, it would have radically transformed life within exempt monasteries. That this experiment of 1203 does not seem to have materialised and could not therefore be transformed into a permanent canonical norm, did not cause Innocent to abandon his idea of direct intervention.[144] The idea came from his experience in the Patrimony and had it worked, would have brought the exempt monasteries into a kind of regional or national congregation, united by an annual chapter and controlled by visitors mandated by the same chapter.[145] In November 1208 another more limited apostolic visitation was organised throughout Tuscany and as far south as Viterbo and Rieti.[146]

If some of these attempts were the fruits of Innocent's own ideas and reforming activity, others give an interesting insight on local initiatives, which he was able to enlarge and develop. In 1206, the archbishop of Lund informed the pope that he wished to unite all the Benedictine monasteries of Denmark by instituting an annual chapter with the abbot of Lund as *rector*.[147] They were weak for

---

141 *PL* 214 cols 1173–4, 'monasteria per Tusciam, Marchiam et ducatum Spoletanum constituta, *nullo medio* ad Romanam Ecclesiam pertinentia'; Maccarrone, *Studi* pp. 328–30.

142 *Ibid* pp. 228–34; Cheney, *Innocent III* pp. 231–5. These provincial chapters were to be held at Perugia and Piacenza for Northern and Central Italy, at Paris, Limoges and Cluny for the kingdom of France and in London for all English monasteries. Notable omissions were Rome and Upper and Lower Lazio, for which the Pope provided directly, the whole of Southern Italy, Germany, the Iberian peninsula, Ireland, Scotland, Scandinavia including the kingdom of Denmark and Hungary.

143 Maccarrone, *Studi* pp. 234–5.

144 *Ibid* pp. 241–2.

145 Cheney, *Innocent III* p. 233.

146 *PL* 215 col 1490; Potthast I, 3539; Maccarrone, *Studi* p. 242.

147 18 January 1206, *PL* 215 cols 775–6; Potthast I, 2663; Maccarrone, *Studi* pp. 244–6.

lack of common customs and this would produce uniform observance.[148] Innocent showed himself favourable but cautious, asking for a report on the institution at the end of four years.[149] In 1207, the canons regular of the diocese of York proposed annual reunions for the discussion of reform[150] while in 1210 a general chapter of all the abbots of the province of Rouen was established.[151] In 1215, at the Fourth Lateran Council, Innocent transformed provincial practices such as these into the law of the whole Church. Canon 12 of this Council, *In Singulis Regnis*, henceforward obliged those abbots and priors, both exempt and non-exempt, of Benedictine and Augustinian houses, to meet together in triennial General Chapters.[152] A more permanent organ of monastic reform, which would maintain monastic discipline and lead towards Innocent's view of a *via ascetica*, had thus been created by giving one particular General Chapter, that of the Cistercians, the status of an approved model.[153]

The presence in the twelfth century of the new order of Cistercians should have represented for Innocent III the ideal *via ascetica* in operation through the first real order in the Church.[154] The Cistercians had faced the problem of autonomous abbeys implicit in the Rule of St Benedict and had succeeded in reconciling this autonomy with the need to preserve standards and ensure uniformity of observance—the need to keep the original ideal from dilution as new foundations proliferated. Their solution was to create a strong federal framework which ensured strict and uniform observance of the Rule by a system of mutual supervision. In this, the chief agencies were the annual General Chapter[155] and the system of filiation between mother and daughter houses.[156] The

---

[148] Cheney, *Innocent III* p. 233.

[149] *PL* 215 cols 775–6.

[150] *PL* 215 cols 1128–9, 17 March 1207; Potthast I, 3045. Kirkham, Guisborough, Bridlington and Newburgh are all specified by name.

[151] *PL* 216 col 312, 20 August 1210; Potthast I, 4067 'ut semel in anno capitulum celebrent ... ac de quarto in quartum annum apostolorum limina visitent'.

[152] *COD* (3 ed Bologna 1973) Canon 12 pp. 240–1; Maccarrone, *Studi* pp. 246–62.

[153] *Ibid* p. 248.

[154] For a magisterial introduction to the Cistercian Order, see Lawrence, *Medieval Monasticism* pp. 146–66. I am especially indebted to this work. Also Knowles, *From Pachomius to Ignatius* pp. 23–30; Little, *Religious Poverty* pp. 90–6.

[155] J.B. Mahn, *L'Ordre Cistercien et son gouvernement* (Paris 1951).

[156] F. Van der Meer, *Atlas de l'Ordre Cistercien* (Amsterdam-Brussels 1965) and F. Vongrey and F. Hervay, 'Notes critiques sur l'Atlas de l'Ordre Cistercien', *ASOC* 23 (1967) pp. 115–52.

Via Ascetica

General Chapter was the most distinctive and influential innovation
and hence, the most imitated, not only by the Benedictines and
canons but later carried to its logical conclusion by the mendicant
orders.[157] It made the Cistercians into an international order,
whose monks could be used as papal agents, the frontier guards of
faith in all parts of Christendom and even beyond.[158] Furthermore,
their observance claimed to be of the most literal kind, a return to
the primitive usage and exact letter of the Rule of St Benedict.[159]
This combination of simple austerity and dynamic central organisation brought spectacular success—but it did not last. Papal privileges were sought and granted; gifts of lands and churches
brought demands of exemption from tithe payments and attendance at diocesan synods.[160] The irony was that the Order, having
renounced wealth in favour of apostolic poverty, had by the end of
the twelfth century, acquired a well-deserved reputation for avarice
and acquisitiveness.[161] Furthermore, while the monks held tena-
ciously to the belief that their privileges were immutable, popes
from Alexander III onwards fought strenuously for the principle
that such privileges might, in certain circumstances, be revoked.[162]
This problem came to a head during the pontificate of Innocent
III.[163]

Innocent was particularly familiar with the Cistercians of the
Patrimony and, above all, with the two great houses of Fossanova
and Casamari, which he singled out for special favour.[164] His

---

[157] Canivez, I (Louvain 1933); Lawrence, *Medieval Monasticism* p. 160.
[158] B.M. Bolton, 'The Cistercians in Romana', *SCH* 13 pp. 169–81 especially pp. 170–3.
[159] Lawrence, *Medieval Monasticism* p. 147.
[160] Maccarrone, 'Primato Romano e Monasteri' pp. 75–107 for a wide-ranging study of papal privileges to the Cistercian Order.
[161] Severest critic of all was Walter Map, *De Nugis Curialium* pp. 85–113 who calls them the Jews of Europe.
[162] Maccarrone, 'Primato Romano e Monasteri' pp. 80–2 especially n 101.
[163] *Ibid* pp. 106–7.
[164] *I Cistercensi e il Lazio*, Atti delle giornate di studio dell'Istituto di Storia dell'Arte dell'Università di Roma, 17–21 Maggio 1977 (Rome 1978); *Monasticon Italiae* I pp. 104–5. The new altar at Fossanova was consecrated by Innocent III on 19 June 1208, Potthast I, 3465 and he gave one hundred pounds 'pro consummatione aedificii ejusdem ecclesiae', *Gesta* CXLIV; Casamari was given two hundred ounces of gold *pro fabrica ipsius*, *ibid* but the building was only completed in 1217 and consecrated by Honorius III. See P. Pressutti, *Regesta Honorii Papae III* 2 vols (Rome 1888–95) I p. 134; F. Farina e B. Fornari, *L'architettura cistercense e l'abbazia di Casamari* (Frosinone 1978); Maccarrone, *Studi* p. 224; *PL* 216 col 21.

reputation amongst the Cistercians of this area remained high and the monk of Santa Maria di Ferraria reported that, after his death, there were verifiable healing miracles at his tomb.[165] Not so amongst Cistercians elsewhere! Later Cistercian historiography bears witness to the very real aversion of the Order to this pope. Caesarius of Heisterbach[166] and Ralph of Coggeshall[167] both report how Innocent was called to order by the Blessed Virgin Mary herself for failing in his indulgence to the Cistercians. An unknown Cistercian abbot, who happened to find himself in Perugia in July 1216, at the very moment of the Pope's death, saw in a vision that Innocent was in danger of eternal punishment.[168] Even more telling was the widely diffused vision of St Lutgard of Tongeren[169] to whom Innocent had appeared after his death. He told her of his narrow escape from Hell, which he had deserved on account of three unspecified sins, through the intercession of the Virgin.[170]

Innocent had earned this dreadful reputation amongst the Cistercians for having challenged the nature and extent of many of their

---

[165] *Ignoto monacho Cistercensi* p. 36. 'Sepultus est in Urbe Perusii provincie Tuscie: ad cuius tumulum, sicut dicitur, ceci, maniaci et aliis infirmitatibus detenti Deo favente sanati sunt'.

[166] *Caesarii Heisterbacensis Monachi Ordinis Cisterciensis Dialogus Miraculorum*, ed J. Strange 2 vols (Köln 1851) 2 Cap VI pp. 7–8.

[167] *Radulphi de Coggeshall Chronicon Anglicanum*, ed J. Stevenson, RS (London 1875) pp. 130–3.

[168] *Chronica Minor Auctore Minorita Erphordiensi*, ed O. Holder-Egger, MGH, SS, 24, p. 196, 'quidam abbas... Cysterciensis, veniens cum suis ad curiam Romanam, qui cepit sompnum meridie in prato ante Perusium, viditque visionem hunc habens modum. Vidit, inquam, ille abbas in sompno ad orientalem plagam Dominum sedentem in excelso throno, faciem habentem versus occasum, circumstante exercitu angelorum in prato; viditque ab occidentali parte eiusdem prati hominem toto corpore nudum, sed infula pontificali decoratum, currentem velocissime versus sedentem in throno et alta voce clamantem: 'Miserere mihi misero, misericordissime Deus'! Et vidit, quod insequebatur illum currentem magnus draco subito persequens eum, ut devoraret ipsum; et veniens ante sedentem in throno alta voce draco clamavit: 'Iuste iudica, iustissime iudex'. Et cum hoc abbas vidisset et audisset, protinus evigilavit, et visio disparuit, nec illius disceptacionis exitum ullatenus scire potuit. Cumque abbas ascendisset in civitatem Perusii, que in monte sita est, audivit sonitum quasi campanarum et luctum plangencium et voces lamentancium et dicencium: 'Heu dominus papa Innocencius defunctus est'.

[169] Thomas de Cantimpré, *Vita Lutgardis Virgine* ed G. Henschenius, ASB, 3 June (Antwerp 1701) p. 245–7.

[170] *Ibid*, 'Tres causae sunt, quare sic crucior: per has autem eram dignissimus aeterno supplicio tradi: sed per intercessionem piissimae Virginis Mariae cui monasterium aedificavi, in fine poenitu et aeternam mortem evasi'.

privileges.[171] The longest lasting dispute was over tithe exemption, which was not resolved until the Lateran Council.[172] The earliest dispute over the obligation to participate in the General Chapter, broke out in 1198 when he himself excused the abbot of Sambucina whom he had engaged to preach the Crusade.[173] Innocent's differences with the Order were further highlighted by the whole question of crusade taxation. His idea was that the whole Church should participate by means of a subsidy imposed universally and without exception.[174] The open and tenacious opposition demonstrated by the Cistercians in this matter was judged by Innocent to be a scandal for the Church.[175] At the end of 1202, in a letter to the abbot of Cîteaux and the four daughter abbeys, he even issued a veiled threat that he might abolish the Order altogether.[176] He reported that *rumores sinistri* had reached Rome, that the Order was deviating from its distinctive custom of simplicity, *consuetudo simplicitatis*, through endless litigation and assertions of superiority. Furthermore, he feared that in the bitter quarrel between Cîteaux and its daughters, there might be repeated just that discord which had divided the Order of Grandmont.[177]

It was, however, on the matter of preaching, whether in evangelising pagans in Livonia and Prussia, in the struggle against heresy or in announcing the Crusade that Innocent revealed the deepest divergence with the Cistercians in regard to their own conception of their position in the Church.[178] In 1198, he had authorised the Cistercian Fulk de Neuilly to encourage religious of no matter which order *tam de monachis nigris quam albis* to the task of preaching.[179] In April 1200, he launched an appeal to all Cistercian

---

171 Maccarrone, 'Primato Romano e Monasteri' p. 112.

172 *Ibid* pp. 125–31; *COD*, Canon 55 pp. 260 and Canon 57, p. 261; C.R. Cheney, 'A letter of Pope Innocent III and the Lateran decree on Cistercian Tithe-paying', *Cîteaux Commentarii Cistercienses* (1962) pp. 146–51.

173 *Register* I, 302, pp. 430–33, 343, p. 513, 358, pp. 538–40; Potthast I, 335, 'Abbatem de Sambucino Siculis verbum Dei praedicantem eosque ad obsequium crucifixi citantem pro excusato habeant'.

174 *Register* I, 257, pp. 488–90; Potthast I, 913 and 915, 28 and 30 December 1199.

175 Maccarrone, 'Primato Romano e Monasteri' pp. 112–3.

176 Canivez, I p. 243 n55; *PL* 214 cols 1107–08, 'Eligeremus enim potius paucos offendi, quam *totum ordinem aboleri*'.

177 *Ibid*. 'Occasionem scandali et dissensionis materiam praecipue fugientes, ne forte, sicut Grandimontenses, in derisum et fabulum incidatis'.

178 Maccarrone, 'Primato Romano e Monasteri' p. 122.

179 *Register* I, 398, p. 597.

abbots and monks that they should co-operate in the work of evangelisation being conducted jointly by Bishop Albert of Riga and the Cistercian Theodore of Treyden in Livonia.[180] In a Bull of 1201, Innocent proposed to reunite all the religious missionaries of this area, whether monks, canons regular or professed religious of other orders, into one regular observance *unum regulare propositum*, wearing one single monastic habit so as to adapt them in the most perfect way to their preaching of the Gospel.[181] But such a papal preaching programme was inimical to the Cistercian General Chapter which in 1200 had punished its own monks for introducing such novelty.[182] Innocent countered this disapproval by claiming in October 1206 to have conceded *potestas praedicandi* to Cistercians active on the Eastern frontiers and specially to Poles working amongst pagan Prussians in the regions of Lokno and Gniezno.[183] These monks were preaching *de nostra licentia* said the Pope.[184] He was well aware that they were suffering by being classed as wandering monks and *gyrovagi*, two categories stigmatised in the Rule of St Benedict because they lived outside their monastery.[185] Further, they had been induced to abandon their evangelisation. To avoid both danger and accusation, Innocent presented to the General Chapter in 1212 a new form of discipline for these Cistercian missionaries, placing them under the vigilance of the archbishop of Gniezno whose job it would be to choose those qualified for this office and present them to the Chapter for approval.[186] The General Chapter of 1213 reluctantly approved this papal request but revealed the Order's rigidity towards the concept of the preaching monk.[187] The obstacle lay perhaps in the nature of

---

[180] Potthast I, 1026; [M.H.] Vicaire, ['Vie Commune et Apostolat Missionaire. Innocent III et] la Mission de Livonie', in *Mélanges M-D. Chenu*, Bibliothèque Thomiste 37, (Paris 1967) pp. 451–66; Maccarrone, *Studi*, pp. 262–72. Albert of Buxhoven, Bishop of Riga (1199–1229); Theodore of Treyden (d.1219).

[181] Maccarrone, *Studi* pp. 267–70.

[182] Canivez, I p. 251; Maccarrone, 'Primato Romano e Monasteri' p. 123 and n224.

[183] PL 215 cols 1009–11; Potthast I, 2901, 27 October 1206; PL 216 cols 315–6; Potthast I, 4074; Henry, Archbishop of Gniezno and the monks Christian and Philip, 4 September 1210.

[184] PL 216, cols 668–70, 'olim de nostra licentia inceperunt seminare in partibus Prussiae verbum Dei'; Maccarrone, 'Primato Romano e Monasteri' p. 124.

[185] *Ibid; RSB* Cap I.

[186] PL 216 col 669.

[187] Canivez, I p. 414 n52. 'Taliter temperet rem gerendam, ut et summo pontifici satisfiat, nec rigor Ordinis enervetur'.

the Order itself, preventing it from responding to the new dynamic perspective revealed by Innocent. The contemplative vocation and retirement of the Cistercians 'in the embrace of Rachel' seemed to be forced into radical change by a ministry 'in the service of Leah'.[188] The Order's structure, based on the purity, discipline and rigour of the Rule, caused its lack of mobility. Innocent's ideal of monastic preaching would have to be realised elsewhere.

The way had been pointed by those Livonian missionaries as early as 1201 or 1202. Unless they were to cause scandal amongst newly converted Christians, the missionaries needed to display the deepest unity in faith and charity.[189] This outward conformity of Cistercians and canons regular in dress and observance, displayed all the aspects of the apostolic life, a way of life which Innocent himself spoke of as *superior*.[190] They had not turned their backs on the ideal of monk or canon in order to become pure evangelical preachers but they stressed the pre-eminent apostolic value of unanimity, that community of life for which the apostles had given the model in the Church of Jerusalem.[191] Nor was this always easy, especially for the Cistercians amongst them. Yet in their life of unanimity, there was a very conscious imitation of the apostles which might indeed have served as a point of departure for an equally apostolic ministry.[192]

Innocent III saw that the Church of the 'new' thirteenth century needed to reorientate its religious towards the missionary zeal of preaching the *vita apostolica*, and, by clear example, of living the *via ascetica*.[193] This was especially so in regard to the Cathars of Languedoc where the Cistercians had not matched those severe exponents of asceticism.[194] Nor were the Cistercians mistaken in seeing papal requirements as dangerous to their own traditions.

---

[188] Maccarrone, 'Primato Romano e Monasteri' p. 130.

[189] Bull of 19 April, 1201 printed in Maccarrone, *Studi* Appendix 3, pp. 334–7.

[190] Vicaire, 'La Mission de Livonie' p. 459; *Corpus Iuris Canonici*, ed A. Friedberg, II, p. 451.

[191] Maccarrone, *Studi* p. 268; Vicaire, 'La Mission de Livonie' pp. 455–6.

[192] *Ibid* pp. 460–1.

[193] Maccarrone, *Studi* p. 334, 'volens *hec moderna tempora* conformae prioribus et fidem catholicam propagae'.

[194] C. Thouzellier, 'La Pauvreté, arme contre l'Albigéisme en 1206' in *Hérésie et Hérétiques*, Storia e Letteratura 116 (Rome 1969) pp. 189–203; B.M. Bolton, 'Fulk of Toulouse: the Escape that Failed', *SCH* 12 pp. 83–93 and B. Hamilton, *Monastic Reform, Catharism and the Crusades (900–1300)* (London 1979).

The place occupied by the cenobitic life within the Church was to undergo a radical revolution in the face of the two new Mendicant Orders, Franciscans and Dominicans.[195]

From the beginning of his pontificate, Innocent had frequently intervened to judge those cases brought to him by individuals or groups who sought papal approval for their way of life.[196] Some of these he warmly commended for their *vita apostolica*.[197] Others he saw as penitential groups, while still more were directed towards diocesan preaching under the immediate vigilance of the local bishop.[198] He dealt with each case on merit, encouraging the presentation of *proposita* or statements of religious intention with a view to inserting them into existing institutions as appropriate. Two particular individuals needed special attention and so could not be dealt with in the normal way. In dealing with Francis and Dominic, Innocent drew on all the lessons he had learned from his experience of monastic and canonical reform. In their differing ways, both men wished to follow a *via ascetica* which would be difficult to formalise. He was helped in his task by the willingness of these two to obey him utterly—and he used this obedience to assimilate them successfully into the Church.[199]

When Francis came to Rome in 1210 with eleven companions to ask for papal approval of their way of life, Innocent acted in a special way to this direct request for confirmation.[200] They were not clerics but only simple laymen who dressed and acted as a penitential brotherhood.[201] They had not been assigned by their bishop any church in which to house their community and it is

[195] Maccarrone, 'Primato Romano e Monasteri' p. 124.

[196] Maccarrone, *Studi* pp. 278–300.

[197] B.M. Bolton, 'Innocent III's treatment of the *Humiliati*', *SCH* 8 pp. 73–82; Guy of Montpellier, 22 April 1198, *Register* I, 97, pp. 141–44; Potthast I, 96 and 102; Hospital of Santa Maria in Sassia, 18 June 1204, *PL* 215 cols 376–80; Potthast I, 2248; John de Matha and the Order of Trinitarians, *Register* I, 252, pp. 354–5; Potthast I, 483, 21 May 1198.

[198] G.G. Meersseman – E. Adda, 'Una communità di penitenti rurali in S. Agostino dal 1188 al 1236', *RHE* 49 (1954) pp. 343–90; Bernard Prim and his penitential community, *PL* 216 cols 289–93; Potthast I, 4014, 14 June 1210; *PL* 216 cols 648–50; Potthast I, 4567, 23 July 1212, sub magisterio et regimine Domini nostri Jesu Christi ac piisimi vicarii eius papae Innocentii et successorum eius'.

[199] A. Matanić, 'Papa Innocenzo III di fronte a S. Domenico e a S. Francesco' *Antonianum* 35 (1960) pp. 508–27.

[200] Grundmann, pp. 127–56; Maccarrone, *Studi* pp. 300–06.

[201] *Ibid* p. 301.

likely that they had already been advised to take the rule of an existing monastic or eremitic order. Within this, they may have been promised recognition as a penitential group. Francis, however, wanted nothing less than full canonical recognition of his way of life. In other words, to found a religious community similar in status and juridical form to those already existing, yet totally new in its inspiration and form of life—completely without possessions.[202] Innocent was aware of the dangers into which a refusal might lead such a passionate and determined seeker after asceticism. Heresy could easily follow. This was clearly a quite singular case to which Innocent gave unique oral confirmation on the understanding that a Rule, no matter how simple, should be written down.[203] He had this confirmation approved by the Cardinals in Consistory without using the accustomed Chancery formula *Religiosam vitam* and the members of this new community, now raised to the status of a *religio* approved by the Holy See, were tonsured, made clerics and granted the *licentia praedicandi ubique*.[204] Francis promised *obedentia et reverentia* to the Pope in an oath usually made only by the bishops of the region around Rome.[205] This was something quite new and showed the willingness of Innocent III to create a special link between the Holy See and this new Order which had arisen in an area immediately subject to the Papacy.[206] Innocent thus reserved to himself the obligations as diocesan bishop of the new community.[207] Once the issue of obedience was settled, Innocent was quite prepared to wait to see how this small group of mendicant lay preachers would develop.[208] It was worth taking the chance of a successful development being able to take root in such urban surroundings.

In September 1215, on the eve of the Fourth Lateran Council, Dominic appeared before Innocent to ask for approval of his

---

[202] *Ibid* pp. 302–04; Grundmann, pp. 127–35 especially n115 pp. 130–31.

[203] *Opuscula sancti patris Franciscii*, Bibliotheca Franciscana Ascetica Medii Aevii, I (2 ed Quaracchi 1941) p. 79. From St Francis's *Testament*, 'Et ego paucis verbis et simpliciter *feci scribi*; et dominus papa *confirmavit michi*'.

[204] Maccarrone, *Studi* p. 304, 324–6.

[205] *Ibid* p. 304 n2. 'Hic ergo concessis, beatus Franciscus gratias egit Deo et genibus flexis promisit domino papae obedientiam et reverentiam humiliter et devote'.

[206] Maccarrone, *Studi* pp. 304–5.

[207] *Ibid* p. 305.

[208] Grundmann, pp. 133–5.

community of mendicant preachers in Toulouse.[209] In addition to preaching more successfully than the Cistercians against the Cathars, Dominic was already a canon regular and had founded a house for women at Prouille and obtained sustenance from Bishop Fulk through a portion of diocesan tithes.[210] He now requested papal confirmation of the approval already given by his bishop which had already raised the status of the preachers at Toulouse to an *Ordo Praedicatorum*.[211] Innocent warmly supported this way of religious life. Indeed Canon 10 of the Council recommended the formation in each diocese of similar communities of preachers in the service of bishops.[212] He took into papal protection the convent at Prouille,[213] using it as a model for his Roman convent of San Sisto,[214] but was not willing to confirm immediately the *Ordo Praedicatorum*. He asked instead that Dominic and his companions should choose an already approved rule.[215] This agreed literally with the new norm of Canon 13 of the Council. Innocent seems to have made it clear that once Dominic had considered all the possibilities and still wished to have a preaching order, then this would be granted.[216] After Innocent's death, Honorius III confirmed the Bull to the Order of Preachers in December 1216[217] in the traditional Chancery formula *Religiosam vitam* and in 1220, a year before Dominic's death, the Order declared for the principle of corporate poverty.[218]

---

[209] *Ibid* p. 141; Maccarrone, *Studi* p. 305; Jordan of Saxony, *Libellus de principiis ordinis praedicatorum*, ed H-C. Scheeben, in *Monumenta Historica S. Patris Nostri Dominici*, I (Rome 1935) p. 44.

[210] *Monumenta diplomatica S. Dominici*, ed V.J. Koudelka and R.I. Loenertz (Rome 1966) pp. 56–8; Vicaire, *Saint Dominic* pp. 115–36; Grundmann, p. 211.

[211] Maccarrone, *Studi* p. 306; Vicaire, *Saint Dominic* pp. 217–39.

[212] *COD*, Canon 10, p. 239.

[213] Grundmann, p. 211; Little, *Religious Poverty* pp. 152–8.

[214] *Gesta* CXLIX, Ad costruenda aedificia Sancti Sixti, ad opus monialium, quingentas uncias auri regis et mille centum libras proviniensium. The work was begun *c*.1208. V.J. Koudelka, 'Le *monasterium tempuli* et la fondation dominicain de San Sisto', *AFP* 31 (1961) pp. 5–81; Maccarrone, *Studi* pp. 272–8.

[215] M.H. Vicaire, 'Fondation, approbation, confirmation de l'ordre des Prêcheurs', *RHE* 47 (1952) pp. 123–41; Maccarrone, *Studi* p. 306.

[216] *Ibid*; *COD*, Canon 13, p. 242.

[217] *Monumenta diplomatica S. Dominici* pp. 86–7.

[218] Vicaire, *Saint Dominic* pp. 310–11. Dominic had been deeply impressed by the example of Grandmont and had attempted to introduce the institution of *conversi* to take over temporal matters from the preachers. The first Dominican Chapter

In all these tasks, Innocent sought to maintain and hand on the true purpose and function of the Church. In so doing, he was able to resolve the papal quandary which all popes of the twelfth and early thirteenth centuries had to face. The administration of the Church seemed to many of them to be of paramount importance and the fact that there are no saints amongst the popes of this period may be seen as an indication of the immensity of this task. With Innocent III, however, the path to holiness, the *vita apostolica*, the *via ascetica* and the road to ultimate salvation could only be followed by constant reference to the Church's sure foundation. With such guidance, not only Innocent, but others were to succeed. Indeed, Dominic would perhaps have been acceptable to more than one pope, but without Innocent III there would have been no St Francis.

Westfield College,
University of London

---

at Bologna in 1220 rejected his ideal, possibly because of Innocent's earlier strictures, choosing instead corporate poverty. *Processus Canonizationis S. Dominici apud Bononiam*, ed A. Walz, *MOPH* 16 (Rome 1935) 32.

INSTABILITAS LOCI: THE WANDERLUST OF LATE BYZANTINE MONKS

by DONALD M. NICOL

T HE Byzantines took more kindly than the westerners of the middle ages to their eccentrics of the spiritual life. They never lost sight of the true meaning of the word *monachos* – a solitary, a man who lives alone with God. The ultimate and deepest purpose of the monastic life was, as Saint Basil himself had declared, the 'salvation of one's own soul'. The way of the *monachos* was a lonely one. For the many who were called it was perhaps only bearable in the gregarious circumstance of a community, a *koinobion* or coenobitic monastery; and Saint Basil believed that they were right. But in the Byzantine world it was always accepted that there would be a chosen few for whom even the *koinobion* was too gregarious. For them the communal monastery would be the primary school of *askesis* from which they would one day graduate to the harder and more rarefied discipline of an *asketerion*, a small group of monks living in a lavra or a skete under the supervision of a spiritual father.

The highest degrees of all, however, were reserved for the very few who had the strength and experience to live quite literally alone with God as anchorites or hermits in a cell, a cave, or a hut. Elements of the same ideal of monasticism surfaced in the west too from time to time, due not least to the influence of John Cassian, though he had his reservations about solitaries who took their solitude to excess. The Carthusian Order revived a way which was more eremitic than coenobitic. But the well-regulated pattern of a Carthusian monastery bears little resemblance to the unplanned and rather rustic muddle of a skete on Mount Athos; and the Carthusians would surely disapprove of the liberated and idiosyncratic monachism practised by some late Byzantine anchorites. Yet in the east such men commanded the respect of emperors.

Justinian liked to lay down the law about everything. But even he, in his legislation about monasteries, made exception for 'those who have left the communal life for the higher calling of the life of contemplation and perfection'.[1] The example of Saint Antony and the desert fathers was always in their minds; but so also were the dangers of rushing at sanctity. In 963 the founder of the first *koinobion* on Mount Athos, Athanasios, was firm and explicit about setting limits to the numbers of aspiring graduates of the spiritual life. Of the 120 monks in his monastery of the Great Lavra only five were to be allowed to branch out and live in *kellia* beyond the walls, and they were to have no more than one disciple apiece. For, he says, 'by long trial, trouble and experience I have found that the best, most profitable and least dangerous form of the monastic life is that in which the brethren live in common, seeking their goal of salvation together ... in complete obedience to their superior'.[2] Saint Pachomios and Saint Basil would have agreed with him. On the other hand Athanasios directed his successors never to obstruct those who, having been steadfast in obedience in the monastery, were truly strong enough to graduate to the solitary life of prayer and contemplation in a hermitage.[3]

Such solitaries were in theory still bound to their parent monastery, which undertook to feed and support them. They were the trained 'athletes of the spirit' and the nature of their calling drove them to seek their *hesychia* or stillness in the mountain tops, the wildernesses and the desert places, such as the rocks of the Meteora in Thessaly or Mount Athos in Macedonia. There were, however, some for whom even the sedentary life of a skete, with its rigorous discipline and mortification, was not enough. They sought to attain still greater perfection by becoming holy fools, stylites, or solitary vagabonds. Some of them moved from monastery to hermitage and back again with a divine disdain of the principle of *stabilitas loci* which had been recommended by the councils and by Justinian. The Council of Chalcedon specifically forbade monks to roam around the cities. They must stay in their monasteries unless authorised to travel by their bishops.[4] Justinian ruled that conscien-

---

[1] Justinian, Nov 5, cap 3, ed G. Schoell and G. Kroll, *Corpus Iuris Civilis* 3 (Berlin 1928) pp. 31–2.

[2] Typikon of Athanasios, ed Ph. Meyer, *Die Haupturkunden für die Geschichte der Athosklöster* (Leipzig 1894) p. 115.

[3] *Ibid* pp. 116–17.

[4] Can. 4. C.J. Hefele, *Histoire des Conciles*, ed H. Leclercq, II, 2 (Paris 1910) pp. 779–82.

tious abbots should not accept a monk who had moved from another monastery; for such behaviour betrays an inconstancy of mind unbecoming to a resolute monk. Bishops and archimandrites should therefore forbid it.[5]

In the Byzantine world these rules were often bent or ignored. Holy fools, stylites and vagrant monks went their own ways. But the thirteenth and fourteenth centuries, being a time of general instability, produced a particularly rich crop of such specialists, several of whom seem to have wandered around the world without much reference to any parent monastery. There were perhaps two main reasons for this. One was the worldliness, wealth and decadence of some of the great monasteries, which was deplored by the patriarchs of the age.[6] The other was the development of Hesychast doctrine and practice, adumbrated by Gregory of Sinai, formulated by Gregory Palamas, and finally pronounced to be Orthodox in 1351. The spread of Hesychasm created an international movement of spirituality which knew no frontiers, at least in the Orthodox world. Hesychasm was essentially a solitary discipline, and its initiates wandered from place to place, partly to spread the word and partly to find the conditions of peace and quiet necessary for their pursuit of *theosis*, or the deification of man. They went back and forth from Mount Sinai to Mount Athos, to the Holy Land, to Bulgaria, to Serbia, to Rumania and to Russia, crossing political, ethnic and linguistic boundaries apparently without noticing.[7]

---

[5] Justinian, Nov. 5, cap 7: p. 33. See E. Hermann, 'La "stabilitas loci" nel monachismo Bizantino', *OCP* 21 (1955) pp. 125–42.

[6] See, e.g., *The Correspondence of Athanasius I Patriarch of Constantinople*, ed Alice-Mary Maffry Talbot (= *Corpus Fontium Historiae Byzantinae* 7: Dumbarton Oaks, Washington D.C. 1975) nos 36, 83. P. Joannou, 'Vie de S. Germain l'Hagiorite par son contemporain le patriarche Philothée de Constantinople', *An Bol* 70 (1952) cc 15–17, pp. 77–85.

[7] D. Obolensky, *The Byzantine Commonwealth. Eastern Europe, 500–1453* (London 1971) pp. 301–2. Two recent studies have drawn attention to the place of holy men in late Byzantine society: Ruth Macrides, 'Saints and Sainthood in the Early Palaiologan Period', *The Byzantine Saint*, ed S. Hackel (*Studies Supplementary to Sobornost* 5: London 1981) pp. 67–87; Angeliki E. Laiou-Thomadakis, 'Saints and Society in the Late Byzantine Empire', *Charanis Studies. Essays in Honor of Peter Charanis*, ed Angeliki Laiou-Thomadakis (New Brunswick, N.J. 1980) pp. 84–114. See also E.W. McDonnell, 'Monastic Stability: Some Socioeconomic Considerations', *ibid* pp. 115–50.

Yet what might be called the 'wanderlust' seems to have set in even before the hesychasts made it a way of life. Saint Meletios, canonised for his heroic opposition to the union with the Roman Church imposed by his emperor in 1274, provides an early example. He came from a village on the Black Sea coast. As a young man he set out alone and on foot in the depths of winter for Jerusalem, and sought instruction in the 'ascetic life' from some holy fathers in the deserts of Palestine. He joined the monastery at Mount Sinai, where he became so celebrated that he had to flee back to Jerusalem. He visited Alexandria, Syria and Damascus, and spent some time in the then still flourishing monastery on Mount Latros near Miletos. He then joined the monks at Mount Galesion near Ephesos. Later he travelled to Constantinople and on to the community on the mountain of Saint Auxentios in Bithynia, where he settled in a small deserted cave. He also built a monastery on the little island of Saint Andreas below the mountain. His final travels were forced upon him by his determination to be a martyr for the cause of true Orthodoxy. The emperor had him arrested and exiled to the island of Skyros, before sending him to Rome where the pope held him as an anti-unionist prisoner for seven years. He died as a confessor for the faith in Constantinople in 1286, four years after the union of the churches had been denounced by both sides.[8]

A lesser known martyr for the same cause in the thirteenth century was Saint Neilos, called Neilos Erichiotes. He too was exiled for his opposition to the union. When it was all over he returned to Constantinople to be hailed as a martyr for the faith and then went back to the Holy Land where he had been as a young monk. He spent seven years at Mount Sinai, seven on Mount Carmel, three in Jericho and fourteen in a monastery by the Jordan – a total of thirty-one years. Then, compelled by irresistible forces, he sailed west by way of the Greek islands to the Peloponnese and thence to Corfu and over to the mainland of Epiros. He came to a place called Erichos and there built himself a little *kellion*, before moving further inland to a cave in the mountains. But, as so often happened in these cases, the hermit's fame attracted disciples, and a monastery came into being on the hillside opposite his cave. The monastery still stands, close to the Greek–Albanian frontier, and its

[8] *Life* of St Meletios, ed Sp. Lavriotes, *Γρηγόριος ὁ Παλαμᾶς* 5 (1921) pp. 582–4, 609–24, and *Ὁ Ἄθως* 2, 8–9 (1928) pp. 9–11.

Instabilitas loci

monks still revere the memory of their founding father Saint Neilos, who died about 1335, at the ripe old age of 160, if his biographer is to be believed.[9] Longevity seems to have been one of the rewards of monastic instability. Saint Athanasios, who was twice patriarch of Constantinople in the late thirteenth and early fourteenth centuries, lived to be ninety-nine. He had become a novice at Thessalonica at the age of twelve. But as soon as his beard began to grow he made for Mount Athos, where he served for three years as a servant and cook at the monastery of Esphigmenou. He then went to the Holy Land and the Jordan, on to Mount Latros and Mount Auxentios, and finally settled in the monastery on Mount Galesion near Ephesos, where he was rather unwillingly ordained deacon and priest. About 1278 he returned to Athos, then to Mount Galesion, and then to the Holy Mountain of Ganos in Thrace. He was appointed patriarch of Constantinople for the first time in 1289.[10]

The Patriarch Athanasios has rightly been described as one of the forerunners of the hesychast movement.[11] But its real begetters were the saints Gregory of Sinai and Gregory Palamas. Palamas led a comparatively settled existence on Mount Athos, apart from a spell of captivity among the Turks, before he became archbishop of Thessalonica.[12] But Gregory of Sinai had been a vagrant in his time. He managed to escape capture by the Turks in Asia Minor and fled to Cyprus, where he attached himself as a novice to a spiritual father. He took his monastic vows at Mount Sinai. From

[9] *Life* and *Testament* of Neilos Erichiotes, ed in part by P. Aravantinos, *Νέα Πανδώρα* 15 (1865) pp. 470–4; more fully by B. Krapsites, *Θεσπρωτικά* 2 (Athens 1972) pp. 160–78.
[10] There are two *Lives* of Athanasios: one by Theoktistos the Studite, ed A. Papadopoulos-Kerameus, 'Žitija dvuch vselenskich patriarchov XIV v., svv. Afanasija I i Isidora I', *Zapiski [istoriko-filolog. fakulteta Imperatorskago S.-Petersburgskago Universiteta]* 76 (1905) pp. 1–51; the other by Joseph Kalothetos and A. Pantokratorinos, 'Calotheti Vita Athanasii', *Θρακικά* 13 (1940) 56–107, and more recently ed D.C. Tsamis, *Ἰωσὴφ Καλοθέτου Συγγράμματα* (Thessalonian Byzantine Writers 1: Thessaloniki 1980) pp. 453–502. His letters are edited by Alice-Mary M. Talbot (see above n 6).
[11] Gregory Palamas himself so described him. See J. Meyendorff, *Introduction [à l'étude de Grégoire Palamas]* (Patristica Sorbonensia 3 Paris 1959) p. 34.
[12] Encomia of Palamas by the Patriarchs Philotheos and Neilos are published in *PG* 151, cols 551–656, 655–78. Cf. Meyendorff, *Introduction*. Anna Philippides-Braat, 'La captivité de Palamas chez les Turcs: dossier et commentaire', *Travaux et Mémoires* 7 (1979) pp. 109–22.

there he went on pilgrimage to the Holy Land before sailing for Crete. It was there that he met a monk called Arsenios who instructed him in the hesychast technique of prayer. From Crete he moved to Mount Athos where he built himself a hermitage in the skete of Magoula. His twelve disciples came from places as far apart as Euboia, Athens, Asia Minor and Bulgaria. Turkish pirate raids on Athos finally drove them out, first to Thessalonica, then on to the island of Chios, where he met another vagabond monk with whom he set up a *hesychasterion* on Lesbos. He finally found his true wilderness in the mountains of Paroria in south-east Bulgaria; and there, but for a brief return to Athos, he settled and died in 1346, having spread the word of the potential deification of man over a large part of the globe.[13] Gregory Palamas was his most famous disciple. But another, to whom he seems to have imparted his sense of restlessness, was Romil or Romylos of Bulgaria. Romil was born at Vidin of a Greek father and a Bulgarian mother. He became a monk at Zagora near Trnovo in Bulgaria and then one of the pupils of Gregory of Sinai at Paroria. After five years as a solitary, 'devoid of all human company', he made for Mount Athos. From there he trudged on to Valona in Albania, and finally to Ravanica in Serbia, where he died before 1391.[14]

The prize for vagabond monasticism must go to Saint Sabas of Vatopedi. Sabas spent the first seven years of his life as a monk in the coenobitic monastery of Vatopedi on Mount Athos. He was then, as his biographer says, a well-trained athlete of Christ and endowed with the grace and stamina to run the higher Olympic race of the spirit. About 1307 he left Athos, mainly because of pirate raids on the coast, and becoming separated from his spiritual father went off on his own, 'giving himself wholly to God'. He sailed for Jerusalem by way of Lemnos, Lesbos and Chios, staying

---

[13] *Life* of Gregory of Sinai by his pupil and later Patriarch Kallistos, ed I. Pomjalovskij, 'Žitie iže vo svjatych otsa našego Grigorija Sinaita', *Zapiski* 35 (St Petersburg 1894) pp. 1–64. The *Life* is paraphrased with a valuable commentary by D. Balfour, *Saint Gregory the Sinaite, Discourse on the Transfiguration* (Athens 1983) pp. 59–91, reprinted from *Theologia* 52–54 (Athens 1981–83).

[14] The Greek version of the *Life* of St Romylos is edited by F. Halkin, 'Un ermite des Balkans au XIVᵉ siècle: La vie grecque inédite de St Romylos', *B* 31 (1961) pp. 111–47. The Slav version was edited by P.A. Syrku, 'Monacha Grigorija Žitie prepodobnago Romila', *Pamjatniki drevnej pismennosti i iskusstva* 136 (St Petersburg 1900).

for a while in Ephesos, Patmos and Cyprus, where his sanctity caused such a stir that he hurried on to Jerusalem. Having visited the holy places he walked to Mount Sinai, where he stayed for two years. He then spent three years in a cave by the Jordan, another three or four years in 'the most arid deserts of Egypt', three years in another cave near the monastery of Saint Sabas by the Jordan, before reverting for a spell to the coenobitic life in the monastery of Saint John nearby. He was then divinely inspired to return to Constantinople and set out by way of Damascus and Antioch. But from there his ship was blown to Crete, where he disembarked and resumed his ascetical habits, wandering for two more years in the wilder parts of the island. From Crete hs sailed to Euboia, where he spent two years in the mountains living on herbs and grass; then he was for two years in the Peloponnese, after which he travelled around Athens, Patras and the rest of Greece for over a year. Finally he found his way to Constantinople by ship; and after some time there he went off back to Mount Athos where he rejoined his monastery as a simple monk. He had been on his travels for a total of twenty years. Later he was summoned to Constantinople where he died in 1349.[15]

What was it that made these eccentrically holy men so restless? Most of them clearly felt moved to go on lonely pilgrimage to Palestine. This was unusual. The Byzantines were never such devoted pilgrims to the Holy Land as western Christians. They had relics enough in their own city of Constantinople. Part of the attraction must have been to see and to live in the places where the earliest spiritual athletes of Christianity had led their solitary lives, in the deserts of Palestine and Egypt. Not for nothing was the original colony of hermits among the rocks of the Meteora in northern Greece known as the 'Thebaid of Thessaly'.[16] The great monastery at Mount Sinai which many of them visited was still a going concern in the fourteenth century. So was that on Patmos. But times were changing. The monastery on Mount Galesion near Ephesos, where Meletios and the later Patriarch Athanasios were monks, was plundered by the Turks when they captured Ephesos

---

[15] Life of St Sabas by the Patriarch Philotheos, ed A. Papadopoulos-Kerameus, ''Ανάλεκτα Ἱεροσολυμιτικῆς Σταχυολογίας 5 (St Petersburg 1898) pp. 190–359.
[16] [D.M.[Nicol, *Meteora*. [*The Rock Monasteries of Thessaly*, 2 ed (London 1975)] pp. 81–2.

in 1304.[17] Those on Mount Auxentios near Chalcedon suffered likewise at about the same time. Those on Mount Latros near Miletos were deserted soon afterwards.[18]

Some of the travels of these holy men were forced upon them by circumstances. The world was a dangerous place infested by brigands and pirates. The biographer of Saint Sabas reports that, about 1307, the emperor wrote personally to all the monks on Mount Athos who were living as solitaries or in sketes. He advised them to make for the safety of the walled and fortified monasteries or to go elsewhere since he no longer had the means to defend them from marauding bands of Catalans and Turks.[19] Many monks were in fact carried off as slaves. It was to escape these perils on Athos that the founder of the first monastery at the Meteora moved down south to inland Thessaly, to the impregnable security of the great rocks that rise out of the plain – rocks, as his biographer says, 'set up by the Demiurge at the creation of the world' for just such lovers of solitude.[20] Here was a place suitably lacking in material comforts and in temptations to vainglory. Here was a place where small colonies of hermits could be accommodated as troglodytes in the caves or as stylites on the tops of the rocks, secure from attack or interference and wholly in control of their own environment, since visitors or pilgrims had to be hauled up in a net one at a time.

Some of these holy men, however, kept on the move to protect themselves not from brigands but from the attentions and occasionally the envy of their admirers. Vagrancy was a form of humility, a hedge against the temptation to vainglory. Saint Maximos Kavsokalyvites, who died about 1365, seldom in fact left Mount Athos. But he acquired his curious nickname, 'the hut-burner', because every time his solitary life was interrupted by a visitor or an aspiring disciple he would burn down his hut and move on somewhere else.[21] Saint Meletios, we are told, became so

[17] C. Foss, *Ephesus after Antiquity: A late antique, Byzantine and Turkish City* (Cambridge 1979) pp. 128–30.

[18] R. Janin, *Les églises et les monastères des grands centres byzantins* (Paris 1975) pp. 48, 219.

[19] *Life* of Sabas, ed Papadopoulos-Kerameus, p. 211.

[20] *Life* of Athanasios of the Meteoron, ed N.A. Bees, Βυζαντίς I (1909) 237–60, especially 244. Nicol, *Meteora*, pp. 91–2.

[21] F. Halkin, 'Deux Vies de S. Maxime le Kausokalybe ermite au Mont Athos (XIVᵉ S.)', *An Bol* 54 (1936) pp. 38–112.

famous at Mount Sinai that he had to escape by night, 'for fear that his fame among men would cause God to deny him the rewards of his (spiritual) labours'. Again he was forced to flee from Constantinople to escape the following that gathered round him, 'because he longed for stillness and not for the adulation of men'.[22] Saint Romil found disturbing the admiring attentions of his fellow-monks, when what he really wanted was 'to live in stillness and to converse alone with God; and for this reason he kept moving from place to place, avoiding disturbance and rejecting human glory'. Even on Mount Athos he was bothered by crowds of hopeful disciples. He tried to get rid of them by building a refuge on the higher slopes of the Mountain where he could be alone with God. But they nosed him out and made him run away to remote Albania and finally to Serbia.[23]

Saint Sabas was even more on the move than most. 'He could not keep still', says his biographer, 'struck as he was by the sweet dart of the Lord'.[24] But Sabas perfected a technique of protecting his inner solitude by disembarrassing himself of admirers. He pretended to be both mad and dumb, a deaf mute for Christ's sake. 'The saint' we are told, 'did not put on this show of foolishness without care and forethought. He trained himself to it ...; and his dumbness was a part of it. He uttered not a word for a total of twenty years'. When he was in Cyprus the whole island was filled with his fame. 'But he, though kind and gentle to all, rejected the well-meaning attentions of the crowd by suddenly sitting down in a foul-smelling ditch of dung and pretending to be a fool for a whole day'.[25] He then fled from Cyprus. On his last visit to Constantinople the Emperor tried to persuade him to accept the office of patriarch. But in his great humility Sabas refused even to be ordained as a priest. The Emperor tried to have him ordained by stealth. There was a precedent for this remarkable procedure in the case of Daniel the Stylite. Daniel had declined to come down from his pillar, but the patriarch contrived to ordain him from down below, using his voice rather than his hands to anoint him in the Spirit. But Sabas was not tricked. He got away and the emperor

---

[22] *Life* of Meletios, ed Lavriotes, pp. 612, 615.
[23] *Life* of Romil, ed Halkin, pp. 131–2, 142.
[24] Life of Sabas, ed Papadopoulos-Kerameus, p. 258.
[25] *Ibid* pp. 235–6, 242–3.

had to run after him in case he disappeared altogether and to promise him that he was free to be himself.[26]

Sabas is the extreme example of idiosyncratic monasticism in the fourteenth century. It would be wrong to conclude that all the hesychasts and solitaries were equally eccentric or antisocial. Not all of them were such compulsive travellers. Gregory Palamas was comparatively static, although he was devoted to the solitary life. So also was Athanasios, founder of the Great Meteoron, once he had found the rock he was looking for. Not all of them fled from the crowds into wildernesses and desert places. Some were temperamentally unsuited to the vagabond and anchoritic life. Isidore, who was twice patriarch in the mid-fourteenth century, had also been a disciple of Gregory of Sinai on Mount Athos. But his master had advised him that he was not called to retreat to the deserts and mountains. Isidore was instructed to live in the world, as a monk in a *koinobion*, to be a pattern and a living example to Christians of the perfect Christian way of life. He therefore lived and prayed 'in the midst of the world' and not in isolation from his fellow men.[27]

The extreme example set by the wandering hermits, however, contributed to the reform and revival of more ordered, coenobitic monasticism in the Orthodox world. Many felt called to enrol in the schools whose training or *askesis* produced such remarkable graduates of the spiritual life. The 'idiorrythmic' form of monasticism, in which the monks live and eat separately in their own cells within their monasteries, may also owe something of its origin to the influence of the anchorites. Lastly it should be observed that the ideal which they represented was upheld and protected for the future by the leaders of their church. For the greatest of the patriarchs of Constantinople in the later fourteenth century were themselves hesychasts who had trodden the same path – among them Philotheos, the hagiographer of so many of these holy men, Isidore, and Kallistos, who wrote the life of Gregory of Sinai.

King's College,
London

[26] *Ibid* pp. 344–7. The substance of this story is repeated by Philotheos in his *Life* of Isidore, ed A. Papadopoulos-Kerameus, *Zapiski* 76 (St Petersburg 1905) pp. 116–17.
[27] *Life* of Isidore, ed Papadopoulos-Kerameus, pp. 62–3, 76–7.

THE RULE OF SAINT PAUL, THE FIRST HERMIT, IN LATE MEDIEVAL ENGLAND

by VIRGINIA DAVIS

THROUGHOUT Europe in the late middle ages there was a perceptible interest in the way of life and ideals believed to have been followed in the early centuries of Christianity. There was little that was new in this interest; reform movements within the Church from the eleventh century onwards had frequently followed such a path. Accompanying this interest however was a desire by laymen to live in a pious and holy fashion; not to enter the coenobitic life rejecting the world as they might have done in earlier centuries but to live a religious life while remaining attached to the outside world. Perhaps the best known manifestation of this spirit was in the emergence of the Brethren of the Common Life in Northern Europe in the fifteenth century; another manifestation of the same kind can be found in the lower echelons of English society in the fifteenth and early sixteenth centuries with the widespread appearance of men who vowed to adopt the lifestyle of the desert fathers while performing labouring functions useful to society – as hermits, following the rule of Saint Paul the first hermit.

Much attention has been devoted to the literary recluses and mystic hermits of late medieval England; men such as Richard Rolle who are remembered for their spiritual writings. For every notable figure, however, there were numerous lesser hermits[1] who left no such records behind them but who quietly laboured away, performing useful social tasks, in particular the repair of bridges and highways. These were men of little or no education, a far cry

---

[1] [R.M.] Clay, [*The*] *hermits and anchorites* [*of medieval England* (London 1914)] is the only work in English dealing specifically with the subject. E.L. Cutts, 'The hermits and recluses of the middle ages', *Art Journal*[12] (1860) pp. 17–19 is a general article, particularly concerned with illustrating the subject. Information about hermits and the eremetic life can be found in an article by P. Doyere under 'Ermites' in *DDC* v, pp. 412–29. Useful also is L. Gougard, *Ermites et reclus* (Liege 1928).

from the literate and pedagogic Rolle. They belonged to the lowest ranks of the religious; the life of the hermit satisfied purely personal spiritual desires and offered no chance of furthering ambitions within the church. It was a bare life in material terms which can have often meant living just above subsistence level.

A number of eremitical rules have survived in England in manuscript form from the late middle ages. These occur both in Latin and in the vernacular. Of these the best known is the *regula heremitarum*, the authorship of which is often erroneously ascribed to Richard Rolle.[2] Other known rules include those attributed to Pope Celestine V and to Pope Linus.[3] It is more difficult to discover who observed these rules or to see their stipulations translated into action, and it may be in practical terms that these rules had a fairly limited following. Many of the minor hermits for whom evidence survives followed the same rather rudimentary and unsophisticated rule, that known as the rule of Saint Paul the first hermit.

Paul of Thebes, traditionally the first Christian hermit, is known only from Saint Jerome's *Life of Paul*. Historically Paul is a much more shadowy figure than his contemporary in the eremitical life, Saint Antony. Jerome's *Life* is a complex mixture of fact and legend[4] but what concerns us here is how he would have been popularly perceived in the late middle ages. An account of his life, based on Jerome, occurs in the *Golden Legend* of Jacob of Voraigne and this briefly outlines the main features as they would have been known in the fifteenth century.[5] This account gives little biographical information for Paul, merely explaining that he fled to a cave in the desert in order to escape Roman persecution. The central episode is concerned with Saint Antony who, learning from a dream that he was not, as he had thought, the first hermit, set out

---

[2] See [H.E.] Allen, *Writings ascribed to Richard Rolle* (New York 1929) pp. 324–29.

[3] These are discussed briefly in Clay, *Hermits and anchorites* pp. 86–88 and Allen, *Writings ascribed to Richard Rolle*, pp. 329–33.

[4] See the references given in *ODCC* under 'Paul of Thebes'. Jerome's *Life* is most easily available in the translation by H. Waddell, *The desert fathers* (London 1936) pp. 33–54 which is based on Rosweyde's edition of the *Vitae patrum* (Antwerp 1615).

[5] *The golden legend of Jacobus de Voragine*, translated by G. Ryan and H. Ripperger (New York 1969) pp. 88–90. This was a popular work in the fifteenth century. Four printed editions were issued in England between 1483 and 1500 *SIC* nos 24873–6.

to search for his rival. When he found Paul he apparently greeted him warmly and then the two men were fed by a raven who carried bread to them – a whole loaf was brought instead of the half which the raven normally provided daily. Finally Antony while on his journey back to his own cell, was told by two angels of the death of Paul. He returned to him and aided by two lions who dug a grave, Antony buried his fellow-hermit, retaining Paul's distinctive mantle of palm-leaves to wear on high feast days.[6]

In the fourteenth century Langland erroneously attributed to Saint Paul the first hermit the distinction of founding the Order of Augustinian Friars.[7] The order of Augustinian hermits or Austin friars as they were to be better known, was founded by Pope Alexander IV in 1256 when his bull *Licet ecclesiae catholica* brought together several Italian communities in the interests of ecclesiastical discipline and efficiency.[8] These men were not hermits in the true sense of the word but rather were mendicants living in community. The hermits who adopted the rule of Saint Paul the first hermit in the fifteenth century were solitaries who followed a style of life based on their perceptionof the lives of the desert fathers. They did not have formal connections with any religious order. They fell more closely into the category described by Langland when he wrote, 'Like a hermit without an order he forms a sect by himself with no rule and no law of obedience.'[9]

---

[6] These were the episodes frequently portrayed by painters who depicted episodes from the life of St. Paul the first hermit. His popular attributes in art are a raven with a loaf of bread, a palm tree and a lion, see G. Ferguson, *Signs and symbols in christian art* (Oxford 1954) p. 138.

[7] 'Yf frere Austyn be trewe; For he ordeynede that ordre', (*William Langland, The vision of William concerning Piers the Ploughman,*] ed [W.W.] Skeat (London 1924) p. 454 C passus XVIII, lines 281–4.

[8] F. Roth, *The English Austin friars 1249–1538* (2 vols New York 1961–66); A. Gwynn, *The English Austin friars in the time of Wyclif* (London 1940); cf. Clay, *Hermits and anchorites*, p. 86, '...some English hermits belonged to a branch of the Augustinians called 'the order of St. Paul the first hermit''. However she gives no evidence for this statement, merely pointing out that they must not be confused with the Augustinian hermits. There is no apparent evidence for this connection with the Augustinians and I have not discovered evidence for an order rather than merely a rule of St. Paul.

[9] 'Y habited as an hermyte, an ordre by hym-selve; Religioun sanq reule and resonable obedience.', B passus 13 lines 285–6, Skeat, p. 402. The translations in the text are taken from *Piers the Ploughman*, [trans J.F. Goodridge, (2 ed London 1966).] p. 160.

It is clear however that the relatively unregulated life of a hermit was open to abuse by men who merely assumed the outward form of the life without the concomitant personal or spiritual commitment. Langland was scathing in his condemnation of these false hermits, describing them as, '... great long lubbers who hated work and who were got up in clerical gowns to distinguish them from laymen and paraded as hermits for the sake of an easy life.'[10] Such criticism must have been widespread in the late fourteenth century for the problem was attacked by Richard II in parliament in 1389 when an anti-vagrancy statute was passed which made it mandatory for accredited hermits to carry testimonial letters from their ordinaries.[11] Thus these men were subject to some episcopal supervision, a fact which has advantages for the historian in that the need to issue letters testimonial meant that episcopal registers began to record the taking of professions by individual hermits.

These professions occur fairly widely in more or less the same form in episcopal registers of the fifteenth century. One example can be taken as typical of many.[12] The profession of Thomas Cornysse as a hermit on 28 October 1450 was recorded in the register of Edmund Lacy, bishop of Exeter. The ceremony took place in the presence of the bishop in his oratory at Chudleigh manor and there Thomas took an oath which was in English: 'I Thomas Cornysshe, not wedded, promise and avowe to God and to oure Lady Seynt Marie and to all the Seynts of heven, yn the presence of yow reverent fader yn God Edmund Bysshop of Exeter, to leve yn perpetue castite after the rule of Seynt Paule the firste hermyte. In the name of the fader and sone and the holy goste Amen.'[13] The recording of the names of the witnesses and their

[10] Piers the Ploughman, p. 26; 'Grete lobies and longe that loth were to swynke clothede hem in copies to be knowe fro othere and made hem-selve eremytes hure eise to have,' C Passus I lines 53–57. Skeat, p. 6.
[11] 'It is accorded and assented that of every person that goeth begging and is able to serve or labour it shall be done of him as of him that departeth out of the Hundred and other places aforesaid without letters testimonial as afore is said, except people of religion and hermits having letters testimonial of their ordinaries', Statutes of the Realm, II p. 58, 12 Richard II, cap 7.
[12] See for example the entries in The register of Thomas Beckington, bishop of Bath and Wells 1443–65, ed H.C.M. Lyte, (Somerset Record Society 49, 50 1934–35), nos 121, 122, 688. On each occasion the bishop is described as investing the hermit with his own hands with a habit suitable to the estate of the hermit. The names of the witnesses were noted on each occasion.
[13] [The] register of Edmund Lacy, [bishop of Exeter 1420–55: Registrum commune] ed [G.R. Dunstan (Canterbury and York Society 1967)] III pp. 88–89.

number and positions indicate that it was a ceremony of some importance. They included the treasurer of the cathedral and the archdeacon of Totnes in addition to the notary who recorded the ceremony. The following week letters testimonial were issued to Cornysse which confirmed that he had taken the above vow.[14]

These formal professions are one source of evidence for the existence of the hermits of Saint Paul. A second related source for the lifestyle of these simple men is the episcopal pontificals used by bishops in English sees in the later middle ages. These were the liturgical books which contained the prayers and ceremonies for a variety of rites used by bishops. Seven English pontificals, all of which date from the fifteenth or early sixteenth century, contain references to the *ordo* either for the benediction of a hermit or for the blessing of his garments, the putting on of which symbolised the adoption of the eremitical lifestyle.[15] Such a service does not occur in pontificals earlier than those of the very late fourteenth century although references to the services for blessing recluses or the enclosing of anchorites are common before this.[16] In a number

---

[14] *Ibid.* p. 90, 6 November 1450.

[15] Surviving pontificals to be found in English libraries are listed in [J.] Bruckmann, 'Latin manuscript pontificals [and benedictionals in England and Wales', *Traditio* 29] (1973),] pp. 391–458. Those containing references to ceremonies for the benediction of hermits or their garments are (i) Cambridge, Corpus Christi College no 79, a London pontifical of the early fifteenth century which has some later additions including the order for the clothing and blessing of a hermit; (ii) Cambridge University Library Ff.VI.1., a York pontifical written in the thirteenth century and enlarged in the early sixteenth century; edited [W.G. Henderson,] *Liber pontificalis Christopher Bainbridge, [archiepiscopi Eboracensis,]* SS LXI 1873); (iii) Cambridge University Library Mm.III.21, written for John Russell bishop of Lincoln (1480–94); (iv) Exeter cathedral library ms no 3513, a pontifical written in the late fourteenth or early fifteenth century which belonged to Edmund Lacy, bishop of Exeter (1420–55) who left it to his cathedral century; edited [R. Barnes,] *Liber pontificalis of Edmund Lacy,*[bishop of Exeter,] (Exeter 1847); (v) Oxford Bodleian MS Rawl C 549, fifteenth century, diocese unknown; (vi) Oxford Bodleian, MS Tanner 5, fifteenth century, province of Canterbury but diocese unknown. (vii) Pontifical belonging to Thomas Bele, titular bishop of Lydda and suffragan to the bishop of London in the 1520s, discussed in [F.] Eeles, 'Two sixteenth century pontificals [formerly used in England', *Transactions of the St. Paul's ecclesiogical society* 7 (1911–15)] pp. 69–90; the section of this manuscript containing the office for the benediction of a hermit of Saint Paul is reproduced by Clay, *Hermits and anchorites*, pp. 199–202.

[16] The service for the enclosure of a recluse can be found for example in the twelfth century collection of pontifical offices written for the see of Canterbury, BL MS Cotton Vesp.D.XV, discussed in Bruckmann, 'Latin manuscript pontificals' p. 436.

of the earlier pontificals the service for the blessing of a hermit is inserted in a later fifteenth- or sixteenth-century hand,[17] a fact which helps to support the idea that this rule only became widespread towards the end of the middle ages. These services are not always specific as to the rule to be adopted by the hermit, but whenever this is the case they refer exclusively to the rule of Saint Paul the first hermit.[18]

The service of making a hermit is very similar in each of the pontificals in which it appears. The following outline of the ceremony is derived from four pontificals. The earliest is an Exeter pontifical written at the very end of the fourteenth century or in the first decade of the fifteenth.[19] The second is a Lincoln pontifical which was the property of John Russell, bishop of Lincoln in the latter part of the fifteenth century.[20] The third and fourth date from the early sixteenth century. The third, known as the Lydance pontifical, belonged to Thomas Bele, the titular bishop of Lydda who was a suffragan in the diocese of London in the 1520s,[21] while the fourth is the York pontifical of Christopher Bainbridge, archbishop 1508–14.[22] Although these pontificals span a period of more than a century the ceremony changed little and they differ little in the main features of the service.

The aspiring hermit came into the bishop's presence carrying with him the garb of a hermit. He knelt before the bishop who questioned him as to his chastity. The hermit then made the oath of profession described above. Although in the pontificals this is quoted in Latin it would usually have been taken by the hermit in the vernacular, the form in which it appears in the episcopal

---

[17] This was the case for four of the pontificals – Oxford Bodleian, MS Rawl. C.549, Cambridge Corpus Christi College MS no 79, Cambridge University Library Ff.VI.1., *Liber pontificalis Christopher Bainbridge*; see Bruckmann, 'Latin manuscript pontificals'.

[18] References to the rule of Saint Paul the first hermit occur in several of the pontificals – Exeter cathedral library ms no 3513, the Lydance pontifical, *Liber pontificalis Christopher Bainbridge* and Cambridge University Library Mm.III.2 and Ff. VI.1. In addition Bodleian MS. Rawl C.549 contains what is clearly a copy of the rule of Saint Paul the first hermit although Saint Paul himself is not named in the text.

[19] *Liber pontificalis of Edmund Lacy* pp. 129–31.

[20] Cambridge University Library Mm.III.21 fo 192^r–^{v}.

[21] Eccles, 'Two sixteenth century pontificals' pp. 82–5.

[22] *Liber pontificalis Christopher Bainbridge* pp. 140–1.

registers. A written form of the profession was signed by the hermit with a cross.

The remainder of the rite was concerned with the blessing of the hermit's garments. An illustration in the pontifical of bishop Clifford of London depicting a bishop in the act of blessing a hermit gives an idea of what these clothes would have been like. They were very simple, consisting of a brown habit over which a white scapular was worn.[23] The vestments were of prime importance as they signified humility of heart, chastity and contempt for the world and worldly things. After blessing them the bishop handed them back to the hermit who was kneeling before him. The casting off of the old worldly garments and the donning of the new was the crucial part of the ceremony and the symbolism of the act was of great importance in an age in which, despite the effects of growing lay literacy, symbols and symbolic actions remained important. It is clear that many of the men who underwent the ceremony and vowed to follow the rule of Saint Paul were illiterate; which would have increased the impact of the ceremony upon them. As the hermit donned his new garments the bishop said, 'The Lord put on thee the new man, which, after God is created in righteousness and true holiness ...'[24] The prayers which were part of this service were appropriate to the occasion – making reference to the giving of manna to the Israelites in the desert and to the forty days spent by Christ in the wilderness.[25]

---

[23] The illuminated initial depicting the ceremony taken from Corpus Christi College Cambridge Ms 79, the pontifical of bishop Clifford of Worcester 1402–7, and of London 1407–21 is reproduced in W.H. Frere, *Pontifical services illustrated from miniatures of the xvth and xvith centuries* (2 vols London 1901 for Alcuin club), II plate ix fig 28; This initial letter comes in the section added to the pontifical by Philip Morgan, bishop of Worcester 1419–26, and Ely 1426–35.

[24] 'Exuat te dominus veterem hominem cum actibus suis et induat te novum hominem qui qui+ secundum deum creatus est in iusticia et sanctitate veritatis', C.U.L. Mm.III.21. fo 192^r.

[25] 'Deus qui filios Israel in heremi solitudine manna ad pascendum celeste quadraginta annis manare fecisti quique vitam heremiticam tam per filium tuum quadraginta diebus et quadraginta noctibus prophetas et sanctos in heremo degentes tibi in heremo placere monstrasti concede propicious ut famulus tuus N similem pro modulo suo eligens vitam sic in proposito heremitice discipline mores suos mutet aptet et componat quatinus perseueranter proficiens ad huius vite perfeccionem attingere et ad gaudia perfectorum valeat pervenire,' Eeles, 'Two sixteenth century pontificals' p. 84. This prayer followed the taking of the profession.

While the benediction service provides a general idea of the humble nature of the eremitical lifestyle and emphasises that it had to be chaste, it conveys little about what these men actually did and just what sort of a life their vows committed them to. For that we must turn to the third source, the rule of Saint Paul the first hermit itself, a copy of which can be found on the final folio of a late-fifteenth-century episcopal register, that of William Waynflete, bishop of Winchester 1447–86.[26] In a contemporary hand on a single sheet which is bound in at the back of the register is transcribed not only the form of a hermit's profession according to the rule of Saint Paul the first hermit but also a rudimentary outline of the hermit's spiritual and temporal duties. These are given in the vernacular under a Latin heading, *Forma professionis heremite oneris debentis secundum regulam sancti pauli hermite et onera eidem minervenda per recipiente ipsius professione*. A similar rule but in Latin is to be found in the sixteenth-century pontifical of Bishop Lydance already mentioned as a suffragan of the bishop of London in the early sixteenth century.[27] The rule itself as it appears in bishop Waynflete's register is preceded by the oath or profession which is very similar to that taken by Thomas Cornysshe and quoted above.

The rule is rudimentary in the extreme. It is mainly concerned with the liturgical aspects of the hermit's day. Details of the prayers to be said at the canonical hours take up more than half of the short text. The only prayers mentioned were the *pater noster* and the *ave maria*, both of which had to be repeated a stipulated number of times on the canonical hours. In one twenty-four hour period the hermit would say in all a hundred and thirty-four *pater nosters* and the same number of *ave marias*: twenty-one of each at vespers, thirteen of each for compline, thirty of each for matins, sixteen for lauds, sixteen for prime, twenty-three for terce and at sexte fifteen of each. On feast days an extra fifty-six *pater nosters* and *ave marias* were added – one for *placebo*, thirty-two for *dirge* and twenty-three for *commendation*. The rule specifically stated that these particular prayers were chosen because the hermits 'were not lettered', a statement backed up by the evidence from the descriptions of the taking of professions in episcopal registers where the hermits are often described as 'signing' their professions with the mark of a

[26] [Hampshire Record Office,] Register [of William] Waynflete, 2 volumes II fo. 40ᵛ.
[27] Edited by Eeles, 'Two sixteenth century pontificals' pp. 69–90 and reproduced by Clay, *Hermits and anchorites* pp. 199–202.

cross.[28] The Latin text of the Lydance pontifical expands this section slightly, adding that if the hermit be *literatus* he was to say the hours of the Virgin Mary with the seven penitential psalms and the litany, the *placebo* and *dirge*. With each of the hours the literate hermit was to say three *pater nosters* and three *ave marias* and was also to say a half a nocturn of the psalter each day.[29]

The remainder of the rule was concerned with the more mundane though important aspects of every-day life; it outlines regulations about clothing and diet and makes some brief references to the type of physical labour to be carried out. As already noted, symbolically at least the clothes were of prime importance. The rule stipulated that no linen was to be worn except for breeches and neither was any long hose to be worn. Shoes were to be of the sandal type.[30] The diet was simple. A hermit of Saint Paul had to abstain from meat every Wednesday. On Friday only bread and water could be consumed. The same restriction applied during Advent and for ten days preceding Lent while at both these times of the year the hermit was to go to confession and receive the Eucharist.[31]

---

28 The description of Thomas Cornysshe's taking of the profession says that, 'fecit talem crucem + in cedula papiri in qua huiusmodi forma professiones fuit redacta', *Register of Edmund Lacy III*, p. 89; The *ordo* for the benediction of a hermit given in each of the pontificals under discussion directs that this should be done, for example, 'Deinde crucis faciat signum in fine professionis', C.U.L. MM.III.21. fo 192ʳ.

29 Si vero fuerit literatus ita quod sciat dicere horas beate marie virginis cum vii psalmis et letania ac placebo et dirige pro defunctis. Extunc cum qualibet horarum illarum dicat ter pater noster cum ave maria et cum dimidio nocturni psalterii semel in die omnibus aliis pretermissis.' Eeles, 'Two sixteenth century pontificals', p. 89; Oxford Bodleian MS. Rawl C. 549, in addition to a fifteenth century copy of the rule in both Latin and English which is very similar to that being discussed, has in a sixteenth century hand, an insertion between fos 11–12 which reads, 'He that will take upon hym the ordre of a hermyte being a priste or within holye ordres must observe thei [injunctions] followyng …to say dayly besydes the other ours of oure lady, the vii psalms and dirge and litany.' He was also expected to say mass daily.

30 'Also y shal were none lynnen clothes except youre breche. Also ye shal were no long [ho]sene but of sekenes or laboure…', Register Waynflete II fo 40ʳ; '…lineis uti non licebit exceptis femoralibus pedulis eciam cum sotularibus solum uti debet caligis semper omissis', Eeles p. 84; Oxford Bodleian MS Rawl.C.459 states that the hermit is not permitted, '…to weare or lye in any lynnon except hys prevy clothes', fo 11ʳ.

31 'And these two tymes [Lent and Advent] to be confessed and howseled', Register Waynflete II fo 40ʳ; Oxford Bodleian Ms Rawl.C.459 adds Whitsun as a third occasion, fo 11ʳ.

As can be seen from the above, the liturgical element of the lifestyle although important was quite limited. Work in the form of physical labour played perhaps the major part in the life of a hermit of Saint Paul. The rule stated, 'Also to avoyde idelness ye be bounde to laboure youre prayers said as is aforesaid reherced for youre dayly fode and to repaire wayes and brigges to youre power.'[32] References to the actual work done by hermits of Saint Paul are few, though numbers of men are recorded making the profession. While references to bridge hermits are quite numerous in late medieval England, both in episcopal registers and in public records, such references tend not to make any mention of what rule the hermit in question is following. In the Winchester register there are references to a number of hermits living beside bridges and an indulgence was issued in 1472 to help John Thomas, bridge hermit of Farnham in Surrey.[33] We do not know what rule he, or others like him, followed but, in view of the section in the rule where the work referred to is solely that of repairing highways and bridges, it is likely that many if not all of the men doing such tasks were hermits of Saint Paul.

If these men were to busy themselves with the repair of roads and other such tasks how were they to support themselves? Though their standard of living appears from the rule to have been rudimentary they still required some degree of sustenance, particularly if they were to engage themselves in hard manual labour. No references to begging or alms collecting occur in either the Latin or the vernacular form of the rule. The Latin rule in the Lydance pontifical again adds detail to that of the Winchester episcopal register. It states that the hermits were also to labour with their hands to obtain food.[34] This could suggest that some may have had small patches of land on which they could grow food – a number of hermits are known to have done this[35] although again there is no indication of what rule they followed. The bishop as ordinary would have had some responsibility to ensure that the hermits in his diocese, espcially those whom he had licensed himself, were

[32] *Ibid.*
[33] Ibid fo 157ᵛ.
[34] 'Et quia ociositas inimica est anime et ne diabolus eum inveniat ociosum suis labori manibus temporibus inter mediis circa victualia acquirenda aut vias et pontes firmiter construendas.' Eeles, 'Two sixteenth century pontificals' p. 84.
[35] Clay, *Hermits and anchorites* p. 101–2.

adequately supported in the same sort of way that he was responsible for unbeneficed clerks whom he ordained. Many bishops therefore issued indulgences to encourage travellers and others to contribute to the upkeep of hermits by almsgiving. In Winchester in the second half of the fifteenth century for example bishop William Waynflete issued indulgences for the support of a number of hermits, among them Richard Hele, described as 'poor hermit of Wandsworth', and the hermit already mentioned who maintained the bridge at Farnham in Surrey.[36] Since Farnham was the site of an important and much used episcopal manor bishop Waynflete used this route regularly and thus would not only have been personally aware of this man's existence but perhaps felt that this was a hermit who particularly deserved support. The indulgence, for a period of fifteen days, was offered to all who gave alms for the repair of the bridge and the support of 'John Thomas, poor hermit', to enable him to carry out his work.

This then was the life chosen by the men who vowed to adopt the rule of Saint Paul the first hermit. These humble men filled their days with a combination of simple prayers and hard physical labour which was an integral part of their spiritual life; they performed a useful social function easing the way of travellers by repairing highways and bridges. These men in rural England continued the ascetic tradition founded by the desert fathers, a continuity which is reflected in the name attached to their rudimentary rule.

The idea of the desert, the desert fathers and the solitary life in general had a strong hold on late medieval England.[37] Although Langland castigated false hermits he equally praised those who adhered honestly to the lifestyle: 'Every anchorite or hermit, monk or friar, if he follows the way of perfection is on a level with the twelve apostles.'[38] In 1495 Wynkyn de Worde printed an English version of Jerome's *Vitae patrum* which had been translated from the French by Caxton. It began, 'Here foloweth the right devoute moche lowable and recomendable lyff of the olde auncyent holy faders hermytes'; it was a choice which demonstrates a demand for such literature.[39] Saint Paul the first hermit appears to have been

[36] Register Waynflete II fos 157^{r-v}.
[37] W. Pantin, *The English church in the fourteenth century* (Cambridge 1955) p. 235.
[38] *Piers the Ploughman* p. 191; 'Ancres and hermytes and monkes and freres peren to apostles thow her parfit lyvynge.', B Passus 15 lines 409–10 Skeat p. 464.
[39] *SIC* no 14507.

especially popular and the attraction of the solitary life and of his example in particular can also be seen in the art of the period. Surviving manuscripts of the Middle English poem *The desert of religion* written *c*.1400 contain illustrations of Saint Paul. Painted rood screens of the period depict him also, as can be seen from that surviving at Woolborough parish church in Devon. Abroad he seems to have been equally popular with artists, appearing for example on the Isenheim Altarpiece painted in Northern Germany by Grunewald in the early sixteenth century.

The hermits of Saint Paul made up just a tiny part of the lay interest in the early church in late medieval England. Saint Paul the first hermit seems in particular to have undergone a renaissance in the fifteenth century when the rule attributed to him predominated as the choice of ordinary lay folk and he was seen as a man whose example should be followed.

Trinity College, Dublin

MULTUM IEIUNANTES ET SE CASTIGANTES: MEDIEVAL WALDENSIAN ASCETICISM[1]

by PETER BILLER

THE first half of a recently published book describes Waldensianism in the Cottian alps *c.* 1500. The author decides to pass over both the Waldensian preachers, whom I shall call 'Brothers', and their literature. He argues that there is insufficient trial evidence about the Brothers, and that in any case their 'ascetic detachment from society' would have made it unlikely that they would have had much influence among peasant Waldensians. Their books were only uncertainly Waldensian, he says, and there is little evidence of their actual use. In the resulting picture of Waldensianism as a popular, rural, lay movement asceticism plays no special part, though there is some question of a Waldensian sense of moral superiority.[2]

The theme of medieval Waldensian asceticism is approached in this paper through an examination, firstly, of what has been left out in that book, the Brothers and their literature. What does the consideration of these show about the role of asceticism in medieval Waldensianism? The paper begins in the alps *c.* 1500, and from there looks backwards.

The first theme is that of the Brothers, and the first witness a Brother of the early sixteenth century called Georges Morel. He seems to have been born in Fressinières,[3] that is, in one of the

---

[1] Acknowledgement is due here to the British Academy for a grant for purchase of microfilms of A[rchives de l'] I [sère] B 4350 and 4351, to Professor J.A. Bossy for comment, and to Dr C.F. Clark and Dr and Mrs T. Lodge for general help. See also nn 3, 5, 33 and 65 below.
[2] [E.] Cameron, [*The Reformation of the Heretics. The Waldenses of the Alps 1480–1580* (Oxford 1984)] pp. 15–16, 66–67. Opposing views for heresy in fourteenth century Piedmont are given in [G.G.] Merlo, [*Eretici e Inquisitori nella Societa Piemontese del Trecento* (Turin 1977)] pp. 46–47, 57–60.
[3] Cameron, p. 181, uses lack of earlier references to Morels in Fressinières to argue against this. This is dangerous as an argument *e silentio*. There is no special reason to doubt origin in Fressinières, which appears early, in a source probably of 1548,

215

western valleys which had been strongly Waldensian for at least one hundred and fifty years. He was perhaps evoking roots in these high parts when referring to visits to *credentes en lors meysons ... en las montagnas*, in *diversas borcas e villages*, in their houses, in the mountains, in various hamlets and villages.[4]

Morel was quite learned: *bien instruict*, and he had been *aux escholes* according to a historian of 1554.[5] He could write in Latin and dialect, use the *Decretum* (probably) for a patristic quotation, and make a stray classical allusion. These are easily matched among earlier Brothers. A quite broad spectrum among the Brothers, from less to more learned, is discernible back in the twelfth century, when the learned wing was headed by Durand of Huesca, the polemicist, and is still discernible in the early sixteenth century, with an allusion in a trial of 1532, on the one hand, to learned of the

---

A. Fromment, *Les Actes et gestes merveilleux de la cite de Geneve*, ed G. Revilliod (Geneva 1854) p. 2 – see p. IV for date. Highland Morels are not implausible: a Guillermus Morel, accused of Waldensianism, was found on the eastern side, Pinasca, in 1387, G. Amati, 'Processus contra Valdenses in Lombardia superiori anno 1387', *ASI* ser 3 (1865) I pp. 32, 34. An unsurnamed Brother called Georges, from Cabrières-d'Aigues, is mentioned in a trial of 1532, and his learning and date suggest possible identification with Morel. Connections between the two places (e.g. there was massive Waldensian emigration from Fressinières to Cabrières in 1495) suggest a context in which one person might be attributed to both, [G.] Audisio, [*Le barbe et l'inquisiteur* (Aix-en-Provence 1979) pp. 9, 98, 102–103, 131. Since the writing of this note Professor G. Audisio, whose *thèse de doctorat d'Etat* on the Waldensians of Provence between 1460 and 1560 is about to be published, has communicated as follows. He has found no Morel among the alpine communities which emigrated from Waldensian localities into Provence between 1460 and 1560, nor among *c.*2000 accusations of heresy examined in registers of the Parlement of Aix and other trials, nor any Morel among the archives relating to Fressinières and neighbouring Waldensian localities which are preserved in Grenoble. However, he points out that Morel is a name attested in the Waldensian valleys of Piedmont, O. Coisson, *I nomi di famigli delle valli valdesi* (Torre Pellice 1975) p. 113, where the name is attested for Pragelato (1265), Perosa (1317), and Torre Pellice (1478). This makes it not improbable that a Morel family existed at Fressinières, given that relations and exchanges between the area of Fressinières and the Piedmontese valleys were intense. In the absence of positive proof to the contrary the historiographical tradition of Morel's origin in Fressinières, present very early, should prevail.

[4] [J.J.] Herzog, [*Die romanischen Waldenser* (Halle 1853)] p. 347n.
[5] J. Crespin, *Le Livre des Martyrs* (Geneva 1554) p. 658. I am grateful to Antal Lökkös of the Bibliothèque Publique et Universitaire of Geneva (which has the first edition, Ba 4148 Res) for sending me a copy of this.

Orders, *hommes doctes*[6] (plural), and on the other Morel's own description of teaching illiterate novices recruited among agricultural workers.[7]

In origin and culture, then, Georges Morel was in one part of the tradition of the medieval Brothers; he was not untypical.[8] His present interest is that in 1530 he was engaged in conversations and literary exchanges with reformers, and in the course of these he prepared a description of the beliefs of the Brothers and their way of life, a self-critical account explicitly held up to invite further criticism from Oecolampadius.[9] This account is an extraordinary and last opportunity for us to examine unreformed Waldensianism.

It contains two striking elements. The first is a description of the selection, training, and reception into the Order of the Brothers. It is one which is amplified and confirmed by almost exactly contemporary statements, those of a Brother in a trial of 1532,[10] and notable earlier descriptions of the *vita et conversatio* of the Brothers from the thirteenth and fourteenth centuries.[11] Put together, these suggest a system not much changed in its essentials between the early years of the Order and 1530.

Conflating[12] these descriptions, we find this: an *ordo*, whose members are *fratres*. Before a candidate's entry there is considera-

---

[6] Audisio p. 102. A *credens'* view of the Brothers (reported in Stettin 1393) – *aliqui ... sutores et eciam aliqui litterati* – suggests a similar spectrum, [*Quellen zur Ketzergeschichte Brandenburgs und Pommerns*, Veröffentlichungen der historischen Kommission zu Berlin 45, Quellenwerke 6, ed D.] Kurze [(Berlin New York 1975)] p. 164.

[7] [V.] Vinay, [*Le confessioni di fede dei Valdesi riformati* (Turin 1975)] p. 36.

[8] Cameron, pp. 180–182 argues the opposite.

[9] The texts of the exchanges are edited by Vinay pp. 36–137; variations of the dialect version are given by Herzog pp. 341–363.

[10] Audisio pp. 53–54, 69–183 *passim*.

[11] [J.I. von] Döllinger, [*Beiträge zur Sektengeschichte des Mittelalters* 2 vols (Munich 1890)] I pp. 92–97; [E.] Werner, ['Nachrichten über spätmittelalterliche Ketzer aus tschechoslowakischen Archiven und Bibliotheken', *Wissenschaftliche Zeitschrift der Karl-Marx-Universität Leipzig* Ges.-u. sprachwiss. Reihe 12 (1963), Beilage] pp. 265–267 (further mss.: Prague Metropolitan Chapter D 54 fols 51ʳ–53ʳ; O 29 fols 137ᵛ–138ʳ); Schloss Harburg II 1 ° 78; Trier Priesterseminar 81 fols 147ʳ–149ʳ; Trier Stadtbibliothek 680/879 f. 87ᵛ–90ʳ); [T.W.] Röhrich, [*Mitteilungen aus der Geschichte der evangelischen Kirche des Elsasses* 3 vols (Strasbourg 1855) I] pp. 42, 51–52. See also [*De inquisitione hereticorum* ed W.] Preger, [*ABAW* 14 (1879)] pp. 209–210, and [I.] Hlaváček, ['Inkvisice ve Čechách ve 30. letech 14. století,' *Československý časopis historický* 5 (1957)] p. 537.

[12] They are analysed in more detail in [P.P.A.] Biller, [*Aspects of the Waldenses in the fourteenth century* (Oxford D.Phil. thesis 1974)] pp. 47–56.

tion of his suitability by the assembled Brothers; there follows a period of probation and training. The rite of entry includes the profession of the three monastic vows, together with the imposition of hands to confer the authority to preach and hear confessions (this second part of the rite is not discussed in this paper).[13] Profession of vows is followed by a second period of probation while in the company of a *socius*, itinerancy, preaching, hearing confessions, and living off alms. Inside a Waldensian house there is a regular daily timetable of *lectio divina* and prayers at mattins and vespers and mealtimes. There is an organisation of annual general chapters, which in earlier times was inter-provincial, including both Germany and Italy.

The broad parallelism between this and the mendicant Orders at an early stage in their development is striking. In all it is a picture which takes us back to Valdes and his followers in the late twelfth century, their *propositum* to follow the evangelical counsels as precepts, and their position in the range of movements in the late twelfth and early thirteenth centuries which united monastic asceticism and itinerant mendicancy and preaching in a new conception of the *vita apostolica*. What we confront in 1530 is something in its essentials still intact, a mendicant Order, frozen at a fairly early stage in its development by its proscription which led to its going underground. A later-thirteenth-century inquisitor's observation that the Brothers went to those not familiar with the Franciscans and Dominicans makes sense within this context.[14]

Unlike the student of the Franciscans and Dominicans the student of the Waldensian Brothers does not have statutes or lives of the Order's saints. His sparser evidence allows occasional glimpses: Morel's description momentarily illuminates the training of a novice in abnegation of the will, the novice having to ask permission to do anything, even touching something or drinking water.[15] The evidence does however suggest one general emphasis, a greater strictness in this clandestine mendicant Order. There may have been a requirement of virginity, not just celibacy, in a

---

[13] Discussed *ibid* pp. 54–63.
[14] Preger p. 213.
[15] Vinay p. 38; Herzog p. 342n.

candidate;[16] automatic expulsion for a sexual lapse;[17] a longer
period of probation after profession of vows, twelve years in one
case; more than three vows (in one of the German sources) – for
example, a fourth vow which spelled out literally a Matthaean
precept, to have no more trust in one's family;[18] finally, the
(perhaps exaggerated) use in clothing of *vestimentis vilibus*.[19]

A second striking element in Morel's text is his allusions to the
Waldensian Order of Sisters, which evoked from Oecolampadius
and Bucer violent reactions. These references[20] constitute our main
direct evidence for these ascetic Waldensian Sisters, presumably
living in the valleys of the Cottian alps, usually passed over in
silence or relegated to footnotes. Girls postulated for entry when
young, *iuvenes*. They took a vow of perpetual virginity (and the
other monastic vows?). In doing so they entered a *religio*, referred
to in another text of 1532 as *ordine de verginita*. They were called
sorores, *serors* in dialect. They were supported by alms. They
followed their way of life in a certain place, though part of Morel's
text suggests the possibility of their sometimes going round with
Brothers, perhaps for secrecy.[21] No evidence suggests a test of
chastity. Finally, there was the assignment of novice-Brothers to
do manual work for a period at the Sisters' place, something
reminiscent of the role of lay-brothers in a double monastery.

Fleeting earlier references are given in Strasbourg in 1400: young
girls, *dohter*, professing the three monastic vows and then becoming Waldensian *Swester*, subsequently living off alms.[22] These

---

[16] Hlaváček p. 537: 'nec recipitur nisi virgo'; Röhrich p. 42: 'der zu nie keinre fröwen
kam, es were zu der ee oder zu der unee'. See however [Paris Bibliothèque
Nationale Collection] Doat 21 fol 218[r], where a *credens* refers to a Brother as his
father-in-law. The requirement in Werner, p. 266, is that the applicant be *castus*.

[17] Vinay p. 40; see however p. 38 and Herzog's comments on a difficult text which
appears to contradict, p. 343n.

[18] Werner p 266: 'quod nolit habere maiorem confidentiam de parentibus suis et
omnibus consanguineis quam de aliis hominibus qualibuscumque,' after Matthew
10: 37–38, 46–50, 19: 29.

[19] *Ibid* p. 265. Schloss Harburg II 1 2° 78 fol 46[rb] refers to the reception of a habit,
presumably (through the need for secrecy) worn only at profession.

[20] Vinay pp. 36, 38, 46 (compare Herzog p. 364n), 60, 68, 76, 78, 80 (propositions of
Angrogna I532); Herzog pp. 342n, 343n, 351n. *Serors* appear in the alpine
mss.—see, e.g., n[34] below.

[21] Compare Döllinger p. 93.

[22] Röhrich pp. 42, 51.

indicate the plausibility of postulating continuity back to the women so evident among the early followers of Valdes and the Sisters, *mulieres Valdenses*, glimpsed in flight and captivity in the southern French trials of the 1240s,[23] and they underline again parallels between underground Waldensianism and the mendicants, with their Sister Orders. The lesson of early medieval historians about the dangers of deducing paucity from paucity of evidence needs to be remembered: an Order of ascetic women needs to be restored to more solid historical existence.

The second theme is that of the Brothers' books. Although their use and character has attracted arid controversy and much about them is elusive, there are parts which can be tethered by juxtaposing them with data from depositions. For example, there appears in the concreteness of the late fifteenth century alpine depositions a Brother of the Tercian family, while another Brother of the family appears as an author in one of the manuscripts.[24] Again, one of the *credentes* in these depositions said that the Brothers always carried a book,[25] and in other depositions stress is laid on its smallness. Smallness is what struck an early sixteenth century visitor of the valleys, who referred to the books as *libricioli*, and French royal commissioners of 1532, who referred to them as *petitz livres*,[26] and

---

[23] P.P.A. Biller, 'Medieval Waldensian abhorrence of killing pre-*c*.1400', *SCH* 20 (1983) p. 138n.

[24] G. Miolo, *Historia breve e vera* ed E. Balmas (Turin 1971) p. 110n; AI B 4350 fol 104[r].

[25] *Ibid* f. 301[r]: 'Interrogatus quid faciunt dicti barbe. Respondit quod semper defferunt librum.' The Brothers are seen at varied times and places reading from books to *credentes*. Röhrich p. 49: 'wanne die winckeler hettent irr bücher, daruss si bredigetent'. Fribourg [Archives d'Etat] GS 26 fol 13[v]: 'legebat ibi in quodam libro.' [J.] Chevalier, [Mémoire historique sur les hérésies en Dauphiné avant le xvie siècle (Valence 1890)] p. 155: 'legere coepit quosdam parvos libros.' P. Allix, *Some remarks upon the Ecclesiastical History of the Ancient Churches of Piedmont* (London 1690): 'unus ipsorum legere coepit unum parvum librum quem secum deferebat.' There are also references to *credentes* using the Brothers' books: 'aliquando legit in libris Valdensium,' Doat 21 f. 274[r]; see also Fribourg GS 26 fols 2[v], 3[r], 7[r], 35[v], 49[v]. In a text of *c*.1266 which appears to bear in an opposite direction – 'Docent eciam et discunt sine libris,' [Quellen zur Geschichte der Waldenser ed A Patschovsky and K.-V.] Selge, [Texte zur Kirchen- und Theologiegeschichte 18 (Gütersloh 1973)] p. 70 – one should perhaps stress *eciam*, and recall the topos of heretics as *illiterati et idiotae* present in this treatise.

[26] R. Cegna, 'La polemica antivaldese di Samuele di Cassini OFM', B[ollettino della] S[ocietà di] S[tudi] V[aldesi] 115 (1964) p. 7n (the books not further identified); J. Sambuc, '"Le procès de Jean de Roma" inquisiteur, Apt 1532', *BSSV* 139 (1976) p. 54.

---

it also strikes the modern reader of these manuscripts, which go down to 3½ × 2¼ inches. A third example is a Waldensian historical text, the *Liber Electorum*.[27] Supplied with a *terminus* by its quotation in 1368 it affords one chronological peg. Again, through its circulation on the one hand in Latin among German-speaking Brothers of the 1360s and its survival on the other hand among the dialect manuscripts, it amplifies the picture of relations between different provinces of the Order. Further, the reference by one German-speaking Brother to his commission of this text to memory exemplifies the function of these books as both direct and indirect instruments for the transmission of doctrine.[28] Finally, the appearance in German depositions of *credentes'* memories of Brothers' sermons, which themselves reflect the historical ideas of this text, takes us to the final point in this journey, the lodging of ideas written in books in the minds of *credentes*.[29]

If depositions thus make the reality and use of these books clear, it is the editorial and critical scrutiny of scholars in Milan and Turin,[30] bearing on the 20 or so surviving alpine manuscripts, which is helping their precise Waldensian character to emerge. It is a character manifested partly in the bias of selection and translation from the Church's literary tradition, partly in the chosen themes of adaptations,[31] and partly in original compositions by the Brothers. As such it may be compared, broadly, with the character displayed both in selection from tradition and original compositions by members of a religious order seen in the library of a later medieval monastic house.

What, then, is found in the Brothers' little books? The largely but not entirely dialect contents of the alpine manuscripts reflect

---

[27] Edited from Klosterneuburg CC 826 fols 215ᵛ–218ʳ and collated with nine mss. in Biller pp. 264–270.

[28] The Brother John Leser writes: 'vestra regula (= Liber Electorum) narrat, ut ego memorie mee tradidi', Klosterneuburg CC 826 fol 243ʳ.

[29] Biller p. 259. The renegade Brother John Leser refers to the Brothers' use of the *fabule* in this text to reassure the *credentes*, Klosterneuburg CC 826 fol 244ʳ.

[30] Many of the dialect mss. are to appear in the series *A[ntichi] T[esti] V[aldesi]* under the general editorship of E. Balmas; vol I is cited n49 below. Representative critical articles by Balmas, dal Corso, Borghi Cedrini and Degan Checchini in *BSSV* from 145 (1979) onwards. See also the following n.

[31] E. Balmas, 'Note su i lezionari e i sermoni Valdesi', *Protestantesimo* 29 (1974) p. 151.

two sides of the Order, the pastoral and the ascetic. Part bears directly on the first, preaching and hearing confessions:[32] thus sermons, and a tract on the imposition of penance. In this the manuscripts match areas noted by Morel in 1530 as of special moral concern to the Brothers in their *credentes'* behaviour – sex, dances, games, songs, and pretty clothing – though the manuscripts add pubs, not noted by Morel.

The other part of the books is directed, explicitly in some cases, at the *fraires* and *serors*, Brothers and Sisters, some being referred to as *li contemplant*, the contemplatives. One text is an example of the literature of *scala spiritualis: Vertucz*, a tract extant in two copies,[33] which expounds thirty steps, including *desciplina, obediencia, castita, perseverenza*, and *contemplacion* – the systematic following of these thirty *gra*, steps, on the ladder leading to God. Another example is one Brother's exposition of the *Song of Songs*. This exalts the ascetic life. It refers to older Brothers, *li velh*, as given over to contemplation. At one point it mounts an exhortation to Brothers and Sisters who are contemporary to the writer and so gives a glimpse of areas of concern to one reformer of the Waldensian Order: Sisters are reminded to be subject to the Brothers, and a Brother's lapse into homosexual sin is castigated.[34]

At the present early stage of editorial and critical study of these manuscripts one can do no more here than evoke their broad character, recall the saturation of this part of the alpine manuscripts with the themes of *lo despreczi del mont*, contempt of the world, and *castita* and *paureta*, chastity and poverty, and the ubiquity in the writings of the simple and monotonous vocabulary of self-mortification: *mortificant lo carn*, mortifying the flesh; *castigue ben lo cors e lo retorne a servetu*, castigate the body well and bring it into subjection; *la via de desciplina*,[35] the way of discipline. Outside the alpine manuscripts there is a tripartite exchange of letters in Latin between Italian and Austrian Brothers and renegade Austrian

---

[32] Cambridge University Library Dd xv 29 fols 100^r–135^v.

[33] Dublin Trinity College 260 fols I^r–78^v (acknowledgement is due here to the librarian for speed in sending a microfilm); Geneva Public and University Library 206 fols I^r–50^r (incomplete; at time of writing about to be published in *ATV* 2).

[34] J.J. Herzog, 'Cantica', *Zeitschrift für die historische Theologie* 31 (1861) pp. 491, 493, 494.

[35] *Six Vaudois Poems* ed H.J. Chaytor (Cambridge 1930) pp. 43 l.81, 27 l.276, 63 l. 38.

Brothers which gives fleeting glimpses of individual reactions
*c.*1368 to the strict regime implied by the manuscripts. A renegade
Brother, Siegfried, taunts his former confreres for their pride in
their prayers and fasting,[36] while the Waldensian Brothers in turn
bitterly reproach another renegade Brother, John Leser, for leaving
the Waldensian Order through abhorrence of its *virtutes* and
disciplina.[37]

Thus far there appears through accounts of the books and the *vita
et conversatio* of the Brothers a two-dimensional picture of the
asceticism of a strict and clandestine mendicant Order. The picture
crackles into life, colour and movement with the addition of the
third dimension, the theme of the function of this asceticism, its
role in the relations between the Brothers and their *credentes*. In
particular, how should we regard the suggestion that the Brothers,
by reason of their ascetic detachment from society, were unlikely to
have been very influential among their followers? The use of
depositions by *credentes* is essential to answer this. Here heaviest
reliance will be placed on interrogations by a late-fourteenth-
century inquisitor, Peter Zwicker, interrogations outstanding for
their sensitive accuracy.[38]

The concrete and circumstantial world evoked by the depositions
suggests immediately a broad duality in the relations between the
Brothers and their *credentes*, a chasm between on the one hand the
ordinary and familiar, on the other hand the set apart, the other.
Familiarity could arise in the first instance from the origin of some
of the Brothers: thus Brother Nicholas Gotschalk was in one sense
a local boy to his sister[39] and others from villages near Stettin who
were questioned 1392–4. A world of everyday, ordinary and little
actions is conjured up: cooking for the Brothers; giving them flour
and eggs; the doing of occasional jobs.[40] Further it was to one's

---

[36] St Florian XI 152 fol 42ᵛ: '... gloriamini de operibus vestris bonis – vigiliis,
ieiuniis, oracionibus, obsecracionibus, graciarum accionibus.'

[37] Klosterneuburg CC 826 fol 235ᵛ.

[38] Substantial extracts are given in Kurze pp. 77–261, and a question formula he used
is given pp. 73–75.

[39] *Ibid* p. 109. Cameron, p. 16 emphasises localism and only lists local men; he does
not mention the Brother de *Bogogna* (? *Borgogna*, Burgundy) reported B 4350 fol
104ʳ. Most of the Brothers reported in the Stettin area were not local in origin.

[40] Kurze pp. 118, 136, 146, 208 etc. See Doat 21: fol 260ʳ, a Brother teaching a *credens*
to make bread; fol 261ᵛ, a *credens* making shoes for Brothers; fol 214ᵛ, a Sister
washing a *credens*' head – service as an act of humility?

own house that a pair of Brothers would come, or to that of a friend, to preach and hear one's confession. The title *barba*, uncle, recorded in the alpine depositions may be partly rooted in this flitting through households.

On the other hand the Brothers were men utterly cut off and set apart, ritually removed from sex, family, property and stability. They were men *die nit zu frowen gingent*, as one Strasbourg *credens* put it, *die lange in den sachen umbe sint gangen*,[41] men who did not go to women, men who had travelled long about this matter. The harsh labour of the long journeys and the darkness of fear are added to the formula of imitating the *vita* or *forma apostolorum*. The Brothers wandered over the lands of the earth, *ambulantes in terris*,[42] and then they came by night. They were persecuted. Their fasting (three of four times a week) was carried out in order to enable them to appear more holy, *sanctiores*, among their followers, wrote one inquisitor,[43] writing not only to criticise ostentation but with a shaft of the prejudicial *topos* about heresy of the contrast between outer appearance and inner reality. He was accurately connecting the visibility of the Brothers' asceticism and the *credentes'* view of them, a view in which the perfection of the Brothers' imitation of the *vita apostolica* shaded into specific acts of asceticism. They were men *ieiunantes multum et se castigantes*, fasting and disciplining themselves much, said one *credens*.[44] They were seen thus, simply, as holy men: *sancti homines, boni et sancti homines, sanctissimos*[45] are the Stettin formulae, and in the German of the Strasbourg depositions holy blessed, *heilige selige*.[46]

Their asceticism set them apart as holy men, and in this rested their power. This is partly the meaning of the image, one of startling vividness, of a *credens*, who envisaged Brothers going through diverse tribulations, fields and thorns to heaven, thence to

---

[41] Röhrich p. 39.

[42] Kurze pp. 77–261 *passim*.

[43] Werner p. 265.

[44] Kurze p. 237.

[45] *Sanctissimos eriam in mundo, ibid* p. 96. Kurze omits most instances of the precise form *credentes* used. Other forms round in the ms., [Wolfenbüttel Herzog-August Bibliothek] Cod Helmst 403: fol 20ᵛ, *probos rectos et veros*; fol 64ʳ, *veros legales*; fol 91ʳ, *optimis*; fol 49ᵛ *iustis*. A form including *sanctos* is most common. See also Fribourg GS 26 fol IIᵛ: *bonis et sanctis gentibus*.

[46] Röhrich p. 60.

return equipped with power and authority.[47] In the few cases where the rite of imposition of hands was known this did not remove the emphasis on holiness as the source of power.[48]

The Brothers' power was wielded in the first instance through confession; its comparative rarity probably heightened rather than diminished the awe in which it was held; it assured salvation. More prosaically, through confession and instruction the Brothers intervened in the mundane. A letter from the late alpine manuscripts suggests its range in the everyday life of settled rural communities: loans, restoring animals, marriages, inheritances, quarrels, and, as Morel mentions, the appointment of arbitrators.[49] The Brothers also acted as doctors. A large crisis could reveal the importance the *credentes* accorded to the Brothers, as in this vignette from the Cottian alps in 1487. Under the pressure of inquisitorial attack the *credentes* of Pragelato come together for a *deliberatio* on what to do. They look to the Brothers: on two successive days a Brother is sent for, to be brought into Fressinières; the two Brothers are not only to hear confessions and encourage but to give advice, *ad consultandos*.[50] The suggestion that the Brothers, through their ascetic detachment from society, may have exerted no influence needs to be stood on its head.

Spasmodic sharp light is cast by the surviving evidence on two particular areas of the Brothers' penitential system, areas which are worth our attention in part because of the way in which they reflect on the Brothers' own asceticism. First, what the Brothers offered *credentes* was a heavy regime, a counterpart to their own strictness with themselves: *gar swer büssen*, in the words of Strasbourg *credentes*,[51] pressure with very heavy penance, in the words of an inquisitor.[52] Penances might be suspended for illness or the require-

---

[47] Kurze p. 223.
[48] Cod Helmst 403 fols 38^r, 48^v, 66^v, 80^r, 106^v.
[49] *Pistola* ed A.D. Checchini, *ATV* I (Turin 1979) pp. 3–10; Vinay p. 42 and Herzog p. 348n.
[50] Chevalier p. 140.
[51] Röhrich pp. 53, 56, 63.
[52] *Quare premis hominem per graue ieiunium, multam orationem?*, Peter Zwicker, *Cum dormirent homines*, ed J. Gretser, Maxima Bibliotheca Veterum Patrum ed M. de la Bigne 28 vols (Lyons Geneva 1677, 1707) 25 col 287d; authorship is established in Biller pp. 354–362. See, however, Selge p. 77, for the possibility of Waldensian criticism of heavy penance in the church *c.*1266. The words used to describe penance in the *Noble Lesson* are strong: *castiar*, give *deciplina*, *Les Troubadours* ed R. Nelli and R. Lavaud 2 vols (Brussels 1960–6) 2 p. 1072.

PETER BILLER

ments of heavy summer labour,[53] but they were heavy: penances of
fasting on one or two days a week on bread and water for a year or
several years are commonplace in the Stettin depositions, and can
be paralleled in the alps.[54] A widow from a village near Stettin
testifying in 1394 made the comparative point completely clear: the
Brothers' penance, she said, was heavier than that imposed by
priests in the Church.[55]

The Stettin depositions illuminate a second area. Sexual sin
predominates in those cases where both sin and penance are
specified, for example, fasting twice a week for three years for
conceiving in adultery, for two years for an accidental (?)
miscarriage.[56] Now, Morel's description of 1530 indicates a norm
of the Brothers' close surveillance of sexual behaviour, in particular
conjugal intercourse. His themes are motives for the return of the
debt, forbidden times, and avoiding giving scandal to others in the
household, themes which are both matched in the latin tract *De
imposicione penitencie* found in one of the alpine manuscripts and also
located in general within the tradition of the treatment of *coitus
conjugalis* in the treatises for confessors which became so widespread after the early thirteenth century.[57] However, within this
tradition the Brothers took up a particular position. The Brothers
are found in the diocese of Passau, *c.*1266, starkly allocating mortal
sinfulness to every act done *absque spe prolis*, at a time when
manuals were analysing a variety of motives for the act and
according them a relatively subtle range of degrees of merit and
demerit.[58] Over two centuries later a Brother is reported in a
deposition enjoining abstention on Fridays and during menstruation as an obligation,[59] at a time when, according to Tentler, such
prohibitions had become a matter of counsel rather than precept.[60]

---

[53] Kurze pp. 219, 238.
[54] Merlo p. 206 (fol 49ᵛ).
[55] Kurze p. 224.
[56] *Ibid* p. 176; see also p. 89, penance being imposed on a woman when she becomes
a widow; [W.] Wattenbach, ['Über die Inquisition gegen die Waldenser in
Pommern und der Mark Brandenburg', *ADAW 1886* I PhK (1887)] p. 47.
[57] Vinay p. 42 and Herzog p. 348n.
[58] Selge p. 88.
[59] Chevalier p. 156.
[60] T.N. Tentler, *Sin and Confession on the Eve of the Reformation* (Princeton 1977) p.
213 on holy times, pp. 210–212 on menstruation (on the latter, tradition *sometimes*
more conservative).

226

One may not be surprised to see a Waldensian translator of Hus's *De matrimonio* extending the passage on avoiding excessive love of one's wife.[61] As tradition developed the Brothers seem to have kept to one severe wing of it: severe on themselves, they were also severe on their followers.

To conclude, it seems that the themes and evidence of the Brothers, their books, their followers and the depositions illuminate each other and make most sense when studied together. The themes and language of those who study the function of ascetic holy men – Brown, Mayr-Harting, Bossy – are largely the themes and language of interrogated *credentes*, especially in the Stettin depositions, and thus seem appropriate to description of the role played by asceticism in the relations between Brothers and *credentes*. Mental reservations and acts of dissimulation partially withdrew the *credentes* from the web of the parish. Into the resulting gap came the (sometimes only) recurrent fleeting presence of the holiness of the Brothers, holiness seen as based on the perfection of their following of the *vita apostolica*, their apartness, their fasting, prayer and self-mortification: their 'ascetic detachment from society'. Conversely, very influential in the affairs of their *credentes*, the Brothers offered to these a severe regime. 'To these', one says, because of course this regime was not an open opportunity in later medieval religion, since Waldensianism had long been largely confined to secret transmission in families, visited in secret by the Brothers.

It was in this world – a world of peasant farmers, servants, landless workers and small tradesmen in villages south of Stettin, upper and lower Austria, the Cottian alps, Provence, Apulia and Calabria, and in a wider social range which included wealthy merchants in some southern German and Swiss towns – that the asceticism of the Brothers, the holy men, was seen and a way of rigour offered. In this world some were repelled: in the Stettin depositions two men are reported leaving because of the Brothers' penitential severity; another coarsely quipped that he would rather go for a beer than confess to the Brothers.[62] Others were attracted. A way of renunciation was offered for lay people, and could be

---

[61] A. Molnar, 'Hus' *De matrimonio* and its Waldensian version', *Communio Viatorum* I (1958) p. 155.
[62] Wattenbach pp. 40–41, 47.

taken: Mechtyld, a smith's wife, from Gross-Wubiser near Stettin, said in 1393 that for twelve years now she had not slept much with her husband, following the directions of the Brothers.[63]

This marriage is a reminder, finally, of the context of such abstinence, communities of largely intermarrying Waldensian families, and introduces the theme of a postcript: the demographic context of asceticism. Cameron has discerned a pattern of comparatively late marriage among alpine *credentes*.[64] A preliminary survey of Stettin *credentes*, far to the north and a century earlier, does not suggest a repetition of this pattern,[65] but further study of the quantifiable data of the Stettin trials may eventually allow the setting of Brothers' recommendations of sexual abstinence in marriage within a more detailed demographic picture. There is a further demographic question concerning Waldensian religious, a question which can never be more than a speculation. The Cottian alps in the later middle ages were densely populated and suffering from recession. There were both migrations *propter paupertatem* and emigrations. Could these economic and demographic conditions have underpinned in part the location of young girls in the houses of Waldensian Sisters – those Sisters about whom we learn from a meeting in the valleys in 1532, the alpine manuscripts, and Georges Morel?

University of York

---

[63] Kurze p. 202; when testifying she was thirty-four.
[64] Cameron p. 104.
[65] Acknowledgement is due here to Mr J. Goldberg for comment on the Stettin data.

LUTHER AND THE ASCETIC LIFE

by GEORGE YULE

LUTHER'S attack on Medieval ascetic practices in general and on monasticism in particular was not because of asceticism as such, nor even because of the abuses that had come into monastic life, but because much of the theology that lay behind them undercut the evangelical understanding of salvation.

> This is the chief abomination of monasticism: we had to deny the grace of God and put our trust and hope in our holy monkery and not in the pure mercy and grace of Christ, as we had promised and begun to do in Christian baptism. For relying on works in order thereby to be justified and sanctified is in reality denying God's grace, as St Paul clearly says (Gal. 5: 4:) 'Christ is become of no effect unto you, whosoever of you are justified by the works of the law are fallen from grace'.[1]

What Luther saw as the problem confronting the Church was, to use a phrase of Calvin, legal repentance which had been introduced into the Western Church largely through Tertullian, whom Luther described as 'a veritable Carlstadt'.[2] Tertullian was a genius and was one of the few Western theologians who knew Greek. He undertook the gigantic task of formulating a Christian theological language out of Latin and coined at least 950 theological words.[3] But because Latin is such a precise language and because one of its chief strengths is its legal vocabulary, Tertullian's translations frequently adopted terms which had a legalistic flavour missing from the original Greek or from the Hebraic idea which the Greek words tried to recapture. For example, 'repent', in Greek, *metanoia*, to face the other way, came out in Latin as *poenitentiam agitur*, to do a

---

*I have made much use of the *catenae* of Luther quotations from *Luther Speaks* particularly under the headings of *monasticism* and *the sacraments*.

[1] *WA*. 38. 159

[2] *W-T*, 1, No. 683.

[3] See Ian Balfour, 'The relationship of man and God in the writings of Tertullian' (Edinburgh, PhD thesis).

penance, which came straight from the law courts where one performed a penalty to acknowledge one's guilt. Through Jerome's Latin Bible, which made much use of Tertullian's translations the Western Church became permeated by this usage.

More importantly, Tertullian's legalism and moralism made many in the West assume that the 'descriptive ifs' of the Bible, (that is seeing law as God's gracious warning of love spelling out the consequences of our sin), were 'prescriptive ifs' for receiving the forgiveness of God. For despite Augustine's insistence on God's grace alone, and despite his insight that we do not do God's will until we delight to do it, thereby destroying a simple legalistic view of sin, the Western Church emphasised both a legalistic view of sin and the need for conditional repentance. Consequently the question 'how am I to be forgiven' displaced the evangelical centre – 'who is this God who forgives sinners in Jesus Christ'. To be forgiven one had to fulfil certain conditions – to be truly contrite, to confess all one's sins and to make a suitable satisfaction for having sinned. This was the form Pelagianism took in the later Middle Ages in the West and was the basis of the piety in which Luther was nurtured. 'I was always thinking', he wrote, 'when will you do enough that God will be gracious to you. Such thoughts drove me to the monastery'.[4] Looking back he saw his whole monastic life basically as a striving to be truly contrite, for true contrition was what the medieval preachers had urged was the *sine qua non* to receive forgiveness.[5]

'I myself was a monk', he wrote,

> for twenty years I tortured myself with prayers, fasting, vigils, and freezing; the frost alone might have killed me. It caused me pain such as I will never inflict on myself again, even if I could. What else did I seek by doing this but God, who was supposed to note my strict observance of the monastic order and my austere life? I constantly walked in a dream and lived in real idolatry. For I did not believe in Christ; I regarded Him only as a severe and terrible Judge, portrayed as seated on a rainbow. Therefore I cast about for other intercessors, Mary and various

[4] *WA*. 37. 661.
[5] Ian Siggins 'Luther and the Catholic Preachers of his Youth' in George Yule ed, *Luther: Theologian for Catholics and Protestants*, (Edinburgh 1985).

other saints, also my own works and the merits of my order. And I did all this for the sake of God, not for money or goods.[6]

His problem at this stage was how could he be truly contrite and so be forgiven.

> When I was a monk I made a great effort to live according to the monastic rule. I made a practice of confessing and reciting my sins and always with prior contrition ... Nevertheless my conscience could never achieve certainty, but I was always in doubt and said 'You have not done this correctly, you were not contrite enough, you left that out of your confession'.[7]

Like Augustine, he realised that there was no upper limit to the commandment to love God and this implied loving God for His own sake, and not even for the sake of saving one's soul, for that would be self love; hence the impossibility of true contrition to achieve this. In order to be forgiven, Luther believed he had to love God totally; but to do this one had to be forgiven.

His discovery, which ran its course over a number of years, culminated in his coming to see that God's righteousness was not God's demand, but His gift, the gift of 'Christ our righteousness', who as true God showed us the heart and mind of the Father, and as true man alone delighted to do God's will and thus fulfilled the law, and by his death on the cross took on himself the full consequences of man's sin, the worst of which was separation from God, and Luther interpreted Christ's cry of dereliction on the cross as just this.[8] Consequently any idea of man contributing to his salvation was both impossible and unnecessary. Salvation was *sola gratia*. God's forgiveness was prior to our repentance and indeed made true repentance possible as it undercut the ulterior motive of trying to love God in order to be saved. This new attitude was reflected in the first of *The Ninety Five Theses* of 1517, 'the whole Christian life is one of repentance'.[9]

---

[6] *Luthers' Works* (American Edition, henceforth *LW*), 24, 23–4.
[7] *LW*, 27, 25. *WA*. 40: 2. 15 (Gordon Rupp's translation E.G. Rupp & B.D. Drewery, *Martin Luther*, 4 London, 1970)).
[8] George Yule, "Luther's understanding of justification of grace alone in terms of Catholic Christology' in George Yule, editor, *Luther: Theologian for Catholics and Protestants*, pp. 94ff. Edinburgh 1985.
[9] *LW*, 31, 25.

This is the prime cause for Luther's attack on monasticism, that in his day it was almost invariably seen as the great work of contrition which could gain God's forgiveness. But this Luther had come to see was making contrition the cause of salvation rather than its result.

In principle for Luther, once legal repentance was repudiated there would be no reason why one could not develop a type of monastic life based entirely on *sola gratia* and the ethics of gratitude. He developed this thought in regard to a vow of celibacy.

> It could be condoned by faith in order to better serve the Christian Church, the gospel and your ministry. A man would do well who desiring to serve the church would have more leisure to do so by abstaining from marriage for then he would need to support neither wife nor child and could say 'I shall let myself be used for the Gospel and the kingdom of God, not like the monks or nuns who wanted to enter the Kingdom of Heaven by the merit of their chasteness, for Christ alone gives us this.' When it is presented to us, we should accept it with gratitude in order to study, to pray, to read diligently and thus build up the Church.[10]

In regard to monks and nuns who did not leave their order he insisted that since no one must be compelled to faith in the Gospel those who wanted to remain in the cloister because of age, force of habit or conscience were not to be expelled or treated unkindly but were to be granted sufficient sustenance so long as they lived. Funds from monasteries should be put into a common chest and used for Christian charity, for the original donors had given money to the monasteries to the glory of God, 'and there is no greater service to God than Christian charity'.[11]

The second main line of attack on monasticism Luther developed was that Christian spirituality should be lived out in daily life.

> For we are not made for fleeing human company but for living in society and sharing good and evil. On earth we have to live amid thorns and thistles in a situation full of temptations, hostility and misfortune. Hence it does not help you at all to

[10] *WA.* 47. 325.
[11] *WA.* 12. 12.

run away from other people for within you, you are still carrying the same old scoundrel, the lust and evil appetite which clings to your flesh and blood.[12]

This last point illustrates Luther's deep understanding of the nature of sin. 'For man makes himself', he wrote,

> a final and ultimate object, an idol ... This crookedness and depravity is described many times in Scripture under the name of fornication or idolatry ... and is in the hidden depths of our nature, nay rather is nature itself wounded and in ferment throughout the whole, so that it is not only impossible to remedy it without grace, but it is impossible fully to recognise it.[13]

Sin was so deep-seated that only the grace of God could eradicate it.

Then he went on to give a positive reason for Christians to live in the world. 'The shepherds after they had seen the light and come to the right knowledge of Christ did not run into the wilderness like the mad monks, but stayed with their calling and thus helped their people.'[14]

What Luther did in effect by these emphases was to open up the way of spirituality to all Christians in their daily lives, as the Brethren of the Common Life intended, but consciously based on an evangelical understanding of the Gospel. In that age of intense lay piety much of the appeal of Luther's new understanding of the Gospel for the pious townspeople was to give them this very direct and clear-cut instruction, so enabling them see that all Christians are called to a life of complete devotion. Those who did not enter a monastery were not second-class Christians. Luther not only released many from a sense of guilt. He also gave them the positive Christian goal of Christian discipleship. For the evangelical *ordo salutis* meant that the grace of God which comes to us in Christ through word and sacrament with the word of forgiveness and union with Christ in faith, calls forth the responding life of prayer and a life of service through gratitude. To this all, without exception, are called. There is no other superior way. The only

---

[12] *WA*. 32. 371.
[13] *LW*, 25, 350–1 (Gordon Rupp's translation, *The Righteousness of God*, 165).
[14] *WA*. 52. 61.

degrees of Christians are those who respond with lesser or deeper faith to the grace of God in Christ, while the forms that response of gratitude take are a matter of Christian liberty.

'One thing and one thing only is necessary for the Christian life, righteousness and freedom. That thing is the most holy Word of God, the gospel of Christ, as Christ says: John 11 "I am the resurrection and the life ..."; and John 8 "If the Son shall make you free, you shall be free indeed"; and Matthew 4: "Man shall not live by bread alone, but by every word that proceeds from the mouth of God".'[15] Luther never looked on the Bible in a legalistic fashion as a book of legal precedents. It was gospel because it was the witness to the incarnation. 'You may ask "what then is the Word of God seeing that there are so many words of God?" I answer ... the Word is the Gospel of God concerning his Son who was made flesh, rose from the dead and was glorified through the Spirit who sanctifies. To preach Christ means to feed the soul, make it righteous, set it free and save it ... This Word of God cannot be received and cherished by any works whatsoever, but only by faith'.[16] For Luther it was essential to see that Christ was gift before He was example.

Faith must never be separated from its object, Jesus Christ. As he said in his *Galatians Commentary* of 1535 'faith takes hold of Christ in such a way that Christ is the object of faith, or rather not the object but, so to speak, the One who is present in faith itself.'[17] This way of seeing faith links Luther's understanding of forgiveness, *Christus pro nobis*, with the emphasis on union with Christ, *Christus in nobis*. This is how Luther caught up the medieval mystical tradition and brought to it a proper Christological perspective. Thus for Luther the emphasis is not on our faith, as if we were saved by our existential decision, but the function of faith is to rely entirely on the grace of God given to man in Jesus Christ. Indeed, this was, as we have said, the basis of his final solution to this problem of legal repentance. Indeed from now on he discussed justification in terms of the incarnation with greater emphasis. This alone shapes his spirituality. Christ was the grace of God. Faith

[15] *LW*, 31, 345.
[16] *LW*, 31, 346.
[17] *LW*, 26, 129. See also E.G. Rupp *The Righteousness of God*, 170.

means relying on Him entirely. Faith is thus both easy, for it is simply receiving the gift of Christ Himself, and intensely difficult, for the flesh is always intruding itself and demanding that it do some work. True piety is simply living more and more by faith in the finished work of Christ and so being united more closely to Him. This is brought about by the Holy Spirit through Word and Sacraments. There are no special spiritual techniques; it is by attending to the Word of God and receiving the sacraments – 'oh it is a great thing to have the Word and a piece of bread'.[18]

The whole point of the Bible was to direct us to Christ. 'The purpose of the entire Scripture is to commend to us the goodness of God who through his Son effected the restoration of the human nature, fallen into sin and damnation, to righteousness and life'.[19] In his prefaces to the books of the Bible, this emphasis is the constant theme. 'Thus this Gospel of God or New Testament is a good story and report sounded forth into all the world by the apostles telling of a true David, who strove with sin, death and the devil and overcame them, and thereby rescued all those who were captive ...'. From this the true spirituality arises 'For this they sing, and thank and praise God and are glad forever, if only they believe firmly and remain steadfast in the faith'.[20] Thus a Christian should meditate on the central part of the Gospel 'and occupy himself with it every day, as the daily bread of the soul', he wrote in his 1522 preface to *Romans*.[21] For Luther one should read the Old Testament in the light of the incarnation and then it too, becomes Gospel for the wayfaring man. One reads Moses not for the law, helpful as that might be, but for 'promises and pledges of God about Christ ...'. 'I read Moses because such excellent and comforting promises are there recorded by which I can find strength for my weak faith'.[22] The Psalter in particular 'ought to be a precious and beloved book' for 'it promises Christ's death and resurrection so clearly, and pictures his kingdom and the condition and nature of all Christendom, that it might be called a little Bible'. 'The human

[18] *WT*., No. 5456.
[19] *WA*. 40. II. 328. See also WA 51.4. 'He who would correctly and profitably read scripture should see to it that he finds Christ in it'.
[20] *LW*., 35, 358.
[21] *LW*., 35, 365.
[22] *LW*., 35, 168–9.

heart', he continued, 'is like a ship on a wild sea driven by the storms ... What is the greatest thing in the Psalter but this earnest speaking amid these storms'.[23]

The other great aids for deepening faith were the sacraments representing the grace of God in the saving work of Christ to the Christian. Before he understood the nature of evangelical repentance Luther said his baptism had meant little to him: 'when such temptations came I found no help either in my baptism or my monkery'.[24] But when his perspective changed his baptism became a great anchor. 'Whenever I am tempted by sin or death I say "I have been baptised". It is the great promise of God's faithfulness towards us'.[25] He therefore strongly attacked Jerome who had argued that baptism blotted out pre-baptismal sins but not those committed after baptism. 'I want nothing to do with that second plank. The ship does not shatter. Baptism does not fail. The Kingdom of grace does not fall but ... abides for ever over us. If I do fall from the ship I simply climb into it again. If I turn away from my baptism I simply turn back to it. If I stray from the Kingdom of grace I simply enter it again. Baptism, ship and grace remain for ever.'[26] Indeed as early as 1519 he wrote 'there is on earth no greater comfort than baptism'.[27]

In the same way on the Eucharist he wrote 'Thus the sacrament is a ford for us, a bridge, a door, a ship and a litter in which and by which we pass from this world into eternal life. Therefore everything depends on faith. He who does not believe is like one who must cross the sea but is so timid that he does not trust the ship'.[28] 'When I preach the death of Christ', he wrote on another occasion, 'I am delivering a public sermon in a congregation. In it I am not giving to any person in particular; he who grasps the saving truth

---

[23] LW., 35, 254–5.
[24] WA., 38.148 quoted J. Mackinnon Luther and the Reformation, I, 102–3.
[25] LW, 36, 58–60 and LW, 35, 36.
[26] LW, 36, 61. LW., 35, 33.
[27] WA. 2. 731. I have noticed that after 1518 Luther, when discussing justification, does so more and more intently and consistently in terms of the Christology of Nicea, because once he saw that Christ himself was the righteousness of God then as he wrote regarding the 'Tower experience' God's righteousness is gift and not demand. Hence the significance of this date 1519 for this quotation showing his change of stance regarding baptism.
[28] WA. 2.753.

grasps it. But when I administer the sacrament I am applying it to him in particular who personally may have the forgiveness of sins purchased through Christ's death. This is something more than an ordinary sermon.'[29]

So the basis of Christian spirituality for Luther is the same for all Christians – the Gospel of the sheer grace of God proclaimed in Word and Sacrament and grasped by faith in the promise of Christ. This enables one to repent and from henceforth the whole Christian life as he summed it up in his Romans commentary was *semper peccator semper penitens semper iustus*, always a sinner, always penitent, always justified.[30]

The call to Christians from this perspective was then continually to place onself under the promise of God in the Gospel in word and sacrament and then basically the Christian life was one of prayer and concern for one's neighbour and the fulfilment of one's social duties.

Prayer for Luther was an essential part of the life of faith.

> Praying is the work of faith alone and something no one but a Christian can do. For Christians do not base their prayer on themselves but on the name of the Son of God in whose name they have been baptised: and they are certain that praying in this way is pleasing to God because He has told us to pray in the name of Christ. Others who undertake to pray in their own name do not know this. They want to prepare and collect themselves until they become worthy and fit enough to pray and so make nothing but a work of it.[31]

So 'Christ's words "in my name" are the prime factor on which prayer is to stand or rest' for '... this frees us from all ... worthless worry concerning our own worthiness.'[32] In this understanding, prayer is an essential part of the Christian life.

> Whatever good may be done is brought about by prayer which alone is the omnipotent empress. In human affairs we accomplish everything by prayer. What had been properly arranged

[29] *LW.*, 36, 348–9.
[30] *LW.*, 25, 258.
[31] *LW.*, 24, 241, (*WA.* 45. 681).
[32] *LW.*, 24, 292–3., (*WA.*46.84).

we keep in order, what has gone amiss we change and improve, what cannot be changed and improved we bear overcoming all the trouble and sustaining all the good by prayer. Against force there is no help but prayer alone.[33]

Prayer overspills into the concern for society and the neighbour that a life of gratitude for the grace of God entails.

Although I am an unworthy and condemned man, my God has given me in Christ all the riches of righteousness and salvation without any merit on my part, out of pure, free mercy, so that from now on I need nothing except faith which believes that this is true. Why should I not therefore freely, joyfully, with all my heart, and with an eager will do all things which I know are pleasing and acceptable to such a Father who has overwhelmed me with his inestimable riches? I will therefore give myself as a Christ to my neighbour, just as Christ offered himself to me; I will do nothing in this life except what I see is necessary, profitable, and salutary to my neighbour, since through faith I have an abundance of all good things in Christ.[34]

So Luther, by basing Christian spirituality entirely upon the grace of God given to mankind in Christ, made it the norm for all Christians. There was no special class of spiritual elite. All were under grace, therefore all were called to faith in the promises of God. This faith was not mere intellectual assent to propositions about the Gospel, but reliance upon Christ who was the whole heart of the Gospel. As we have said, faith for Luther must never be divorced from its object, Jesus Christ. Faith and love coalesce in Christ. This transformed the usual medieval notion of faith as *assensus*, belief in the truths of the Gospel, into *fiducia*, trusting Christ alone as the great promise of God, and underlies Luther's whole understanding of spirituality, giving it its warmth as well as its *rationale*, so making it akin to the spirituality of St. Bernard.

By removing all Pelagianism from the way of salvation Luther made possible the ideal of much medieval lay Christian life, that the common man really could live a life of deep piety within the confines of his daily life. There was no special spiritual estate, for all

[33] *W-T*.6 No 6753.
[34] *LW*., 31, 367.

Christians shared in the royal priesthood,[35] there were no special techniques, for all were given in the Word and Sacraments. 'Vows should be abolished ... and all men recalled to the vow of baptism' ... for some argued 'that a work done in fulfilment of a vow ranks higher than one done without a vow ... Blind and godless Pharisees, who measure righteousness and holiness by the greatness, number or the quality of their works! But God measures them by faith alone, and with Him there is no difference among works, except insofar as there is a difference in faith'.[36] By recalling one's baptism, one's faith was built up. There was no special religious sphere of life, for 'the sphere of faith's works was this world and this worldly government', and here all were called to a life of prayer and the service of one's neighbour.

University of Aberdeen

[35] *LW.*, 44, 127ff.
[36] *LW.*, 36, 74–5.

'PRAYERS FIT FOR THE TIME': FASTING AND PRAYER IN RESPONSE TO NATIONAL CRISES IN THE REIGN OF ELIZABETH I

by C.J. KITCHING

S PECIAL prayers, and masses and processions with a special intention, were well established in English tradition before the Reformation as weapons against adversity, and appear to have been increasingly encouraged under Cranmer's influence until the Edwardian Articles and Injunctions put paid to processions and sounded a note of caution also about fasting.[1] The English Litany, conceived as a procession in 1544, became a static observance from 1547 but in either mode was (and is) a treasury of supplications against most conceivable adversities. The successive Books of Common Prayer went further than the pre-Reformation service books in furnishing prayers for use in times of dearth and famine, war and tumult, plague and sickness and for a time obviated further special prayers and ceremonies. But scarcely were the 1559 Prayer Book and Act of Uniformity promulgated than the staple ingredients of the former and the minimum requirements of the latter for church attendance on Sundays and feast days came to be seen as inadequate to meet spiritual needs in a crisis. Church and state authorities began regularly to print and distribute special prayers to supplement the Prayer Book, tailored to each emergency: both prayers of supplication while a crisis lasted and prayers of thanksgiving when it was over.[2] With them went exhortations to

---

[1] F. Procter, *A History of the Book of Common Prayer* (Cambridge 1855) pp. 228, 239. [*Liturgies and Occasional Forms of Prayer set forth in the reign of Queen Elizabeth* ed W.K.] Clay (Parker Society Cambridge 1847) p. xxxiiin. Instructions for prayers and processions are widely found in bishops' registers: see, for example, *The registers of Thomas Wolsey... John Clerke... William Knyght... and Gilbert Bourne...* ed Sir H. Maxwell-Lyte (Somerset Record Society vol 55 1940) nos 530, 561, 583, 609. *Visitation Articles and Injunctions*, ed W.H. Frere (Alcuin Club 1903) vol 2 p. 124.

[2] *STC* under 'Liturgies'.

all the faithful to more diligent, and more prolonged, attendances at church, sometimes coupled with calls for fasting and almsgiving. The message enshrined in the prayers was usually also expounded in sermons or, where there were no licensed preachers, in homilies of which a second tome was published in 1563 to cover most eventualities.[3] Special homilies were inspired by crises such as the rising of the northern earls and the earthquake of 1580,[4] and a number of other disasters spawned further sermons and pamphlets.

The fourth homily of the second tome acknowledged the spiritual value of fasting, provided it was entered upon for three right reasons: chastising the flesh, making the spirit more fervent and earnest in prayer, and standing as a testimony before God. But with the outward act should go that 'inward fasting which is a mourning and a lamentation in the heart'. On the other hand, there were times and seasons for fasting. It was unnecessary (at any rate for spiritual reasons) as long as good fortune prevailed, but if adversity struck an individual he should fast privately; if it struck a whole town or country then civic or national fasting was appropriate. The authority of the Scriptures, especially the Old Testament, and of the Church Fathers was cited, leaving the listener in no doubt that, by comparison, modern Christians had slipped up.

The seventh homily, on Prayer, while stressing that daily prayer was necessary for all, again emphasised that it was especially needful in time of trouble. And to complete the picture, the eleventh homily, on Almsgiving, regretted the extent to which this work of mercy was now neglected. From this gloomy assessment of the practical achievements of Christians in their key disciplines another lesson was drawn in countless sermons, homilies and prayers (both public and private) by Christians of every hue in Elizabeth's reign. Sin and backsliding stirred up the wrath of God, justly triggering the very adversities required to bring the errant Christian back to his senses in a right relationship with his creator and his 'creatures' the elements. Disasters were therefore commonly interpreted as reminders from 'our heavenly schoolmaster'[5] of

[3] *The Seconde Tome of Homelyes* (1563). The edition here cited is that bound in with the first volume, British Library shelf-mark C.15 a.16.

[4] *An Homilie against disobedience and wylfull Rebellion* (1571) separately printed, and *A godly admonition for the time present*, issued with the prayers after the earthquake, Clay p. 567.

[5] Clay p. 501.

past sins, and warnings of the need for spiritual proof of repentance, for want of which worse might yet be to come. That the public exhortations to prayer were no mere clerical ploy to bring a sluggish people back to church, but rather a heartfelt conviction, may be testified from private sources such as the letter which Bishop Parkhurst wrote to Bullinger on 6 February 1575 concerning the previous year's continuous rain, poor harvest and consequent dearth: 'Do you ask whence this dearth comes? It is because charity is growing cold amongst us'.[6]

The chance survivals of the special Forms of Prayer no doubt poorly reflect the full story of their printing and dissemination. But examples, which range from a single sheet with one prayer to small books of 40 or more pages, open a valuable window into the nation's soul, for with the homilies they formed the standard Anglican response to local and national crises, which for want of other evidence on churchgoing has tended to be neglected in comparison with the spiritual disciplines of the Puritans and the Catholics.[7] Specimen prayers survive concerning bad weather in 1560 and 1585, plague in 1563 and 1593, the advance of the Turks in Europe in 1565 and 1566, the earthquake in 1580, famine in 1586 and a host of rebellions, conspiracies and international incidents including the massacre of Saint Bartholomew and the defeat of the Spanish Armada. By their very nature they covered considerable common ground, and readily lent themselves to resurrection, plagiarism and adaptation in subsequent crises. An extreme illustration of this is found in a copy in the British Library of the prayers for the relief of Christians from the Turk in 1566 where every mention of 'the Turks' has been carefully noted, with the marginal substitution 'Papists'.[8]

The prayers and their accompanying prefaces, and indeed the episcopal letters which commended their use, contain almost as

---

6 *The Letter Book of John Parkhurst* ed R.A. Houlbrooke (Norfolk Record Society vol 43 1975) p. 84.
7 On Puritan fasts see, most recently, [P.] Collinson, [*The Religion of Protestants*] (Oxford 1982) pp. 48, 167–8, 260–3. On Catholic observances see J. Bossy, *The English Catholic Community 1570–1850* (1975) p. 110. Collinson concedes (p. 192) that the parish church may have 'strengthened its hold on the habits and loyalties of the Elizabethan and Jacobean generations'.
8 *A Fourme to be used in Common Prayer... for the preservation of those Christians and their Countreys that are nowe invaded by the Turke...* (1566) British Library shelf-mark 1026 e. 15 (3).

much distilled theology and church history as the homilies, and could have achieved the same effect even if the homilies were never read, as some visitation returns suggest.

> It is every Christian man's duty (said the prayer against the Turks in 1565) ... to pray at all times, yet for that the corrupt nature of man is so slothful and negligent in this his duty, he hath need by often and sundry means to be stirred up and put in remembrance of his duty.[9]

After the earthquake of 1580 the following lesson was drawn, which may serve here as the type for the Hand of God syndrome so often encountered:

> Thy coming down amongst us, to visit our sins in most terrible manner, can not be far off, seeing thou treadest so hard upon this thy footstool the earth, which we most shamefully have polluted and defiled.[10]

The solution was always the same: as the bishop of London wrote to his archdeacons on 14 May 1586 during a famine, 'For appeasing his wrath (it is) convenient that we fall to earnest repentance, prayers, fasting and other deeds of charity'.[11] The continual failure to thank God for his many blessings was, from very early in the reign, adduced as a prime cause of all disasters, but on the way the opportunity was not neglected to indulge in outright Protestant propaganda, which became more blatant as the Queen became apparently more invincible. Into the plague prayers of 1563, for example, was slipped a recollection that

> Thou hast delivered us from all horrible and execrable Idolatry wherein we were utterly drowned, and hast brought us into the most clear and comfortable light of thy blessed Word.[12]

The initiative in compiling the prayers might come from secular authorities – the queen, Secretary of State or Privy Council[13] – and

[9] Clay p. 519.
[10] *Ibid* p. 564.
[11] Hertfordshire Record Office, papers of the archdeaconry of St Albans, ASA 5/2 no 54.
[12] Clay p. 484.
[13] See, for example, *Cal SPD 1547–80* p. 229 and *APC 1578–80* p. 450.

indeed the queen had a hand in one or two herself.[14] But the archbishop of Canterbury or the bishop of London, who would normally be those called on to devise or commission them, might anticipate the request by compiling prayers and submitting them for royal approval.[15] During the plague of 1563, Grindal wrote to Cecil:

> It is to be considered by you in what form the fast is to be authorised, whether by proclamation, or by way of injunction or otherwise; for it must needs pass from the Queen's majesty.[16]

Many Elizabethan bishops were devoted to the practice of fasting (which, of course, for more secular reasons was developed and extended by the State), and none more so than Grindal, who on the same occasion noted that 'in no one thing the adversary hath more advantage against us than in the matter of fast, which we utterly neglect', a view evidently shared by the queen herself.[17]

For the duration of the plague therefore, Wednesdays were made official days of fasting for all aged between 16 and 60.[18] They were to eat simply, taking only one moderate meal during the day, without wine, and giving in alms any money thereby saved. Only the infirm, and heavy-labourers, were exempted. Those who had the leisure were to spend their fast days in prayer and study of the Scriptures. Morning Prayer on these days was to be followed by a 15 minute silence (at least) before the Litany, which in turn was followed by a sermon or homily and the communion service.[19] Fasting continued to be called for throughout the reign in times of crisis, sometimes indeed as a token of thanksgiving rather than repentance, as in the prayers of 1587 after Drake's success at Cadiz.[20] As for the sermons, it has been amply shown how these legitimate, nationally ordained opportunities were turned to strategic effect by the Puritans. It became necessary in 1593 to limit

[14] Clay pp. 472, 666.
[15] *Cal SPD 1547–80* pp. 276, 280.
[16] Clay p. 503n and reference there cited.
[17] *Ibid* pp. 489, 478.
[18] *Ibid* pp. 489–90.
[19] *Ibid* p. 480.
[20] *Ibid* p. 607.

them on such occasions to an hour![21] It is too little remembered that throughout the Reformation changes the faithful were urged to attend church on Wednesdays and Fridays as well as Sundays and feast days, although statutory penalties were not imposed for non-attendance on weekdays and for practical reasons services were often not available then, nor the congregations to attend them. It was recognised when special prayers were promulgated that country parishes might have difficulty in mounting weekday services, and special attention was therefore directed to the towns.[22] That the efficacy of prayers grew with the number of worshippers attending was quite freely assumed. During the plague of 1563 whole families were urged to attend church, taking care to segregate the sick from the whole,[23] and in London the Lord Mayor instructed churchwardens to see that two persons from each household attended divine service every day at 8 am, remaining 'devoutly by the space of one hour at the least'.[24] This appears to have been a local, and perhaps untypical, initiative. During the famine of 1586 a general instruction was issued with the prayers that one member of every household attend morning and evening prayers on Wednesdays and Fridays but, reading on a little, the somewhat more realistic note is struck that 'if there be a convenient number of hearers' a homily may be read.[25]

Once prayers had been authorised, the Church's long-established lines of communication were used for their dissemination. A formal letter from the queen or Privy Council was sent to the archbishop of Canterbury (and York if appropriate, or to the respective deans and chapters *sede vacante*), calling for the appointed prayers to be said. In the southern province the archbishop deputed the bishop of London to inform each diocesan bishop. The diocesans told their archdeacons, the archdeacons their officials or apparitors, who in turn visited every parish presumably either taking copies of the prayers or explaining where they might be bought. Depending on the nature of the crisis, some prayers were devised for use only in a single diocese; usually they were for national use with, perhaps, local modifications and explanatory

[21] *Ibid* p. 490n.
[22] *Ibid* p. 540.
[23] *Ibid* p. 479.
[24] F.F. Foster, *The Politics of Stability* (1977) p. 39.
[25] Clay p. 594.

prefaces where they concerned an event, such as the earthquake or a conspiracy, unlikely to be common knowledge in all parishes. How many copies were printed and how efficiently they were distributed remains open to speculation, but printed Forms of Prayer of a national character have surfaced for the dioceses of Canterbury, London, Norwich, Salisbury, Winchester and York.[26] More localised crises might be met by less formal remedies, as when the mayor and jurats of Rye in August 1579 called the townsmen to public prayer every Monday both morning and afternoon when the bells rang, and to special fasting to counteract the unseasonable weather.[27]

The most direct evidence I have found for printing and distribution comes in fact from just outside our period, when on Tuesday 9 April 1605 the archdeacon of St Albans received notice that special prayers by the archbishop of Canterbury for Queen Anne's safe delivery of a child were with the king's printer in Aldersgate Street and would be ready for collection by 6 am next day. An apparitor was to visit each parish in the archdeaconry and cause the church-wardens to provide one or two copies per parish to be read at Morning Prayer on that very Wednesday if possible, but if not then on the ensuing Friday and Sunday, and thereafter on the same days for as long as might be necessary.[28] This example from so close to London may be quite untypical of distribution elsewhere, and the crisis itself, immediate and short-term, demanded a swift and perhaps unusual response. But on other occasions too a wide distribution was envisaged.[29] When the special prayers were not designed for use on a single occasion the period for which they were to have currency was sometimes stated. Those in thanksgiving for the relief of Malta in 1565, for example, were to be said for six weeks. In other cases they must have lapsed as it became evident that the crisis – plague, famine or bad weather, for instance – had abated, or when new forms were issued in thanksgiving or the nation's deliverance.

[26] For bibliographical details of all the Forms of Prayer see the list in Clay pp. 458–474.
[27] HMC *Thirteenth Report, Appendix IV* (1892) p. 21.
[28] Hertfordshire RO, ASA 5/4 no. 181.
[29] The same Hertfordshire source contains the episcopal letters asking for many other prayers in the 1580s and 1590s. See *Records of the Old Archdeaconry of St Albans ... 1575–1637*, ed H.R. Wilton Hall (St Albans 1908) pp. 47, 50–1, 65–6, 70, 90, 112.

The further option of keeping a particular day each year in thanksgiving for a particular event was introduced on 17 November 1576[30] for the queen's accession and was to become an increasingly popular expedient in the following century, starting with the Earl of Gowrie's plot (5 August 1603) and the Gunpowder Plot (5 November 1605). Of plots and conspiracies, of course, there was no shortage under Elizabeth. It was sometimes politic to condemn them openly by as many devices of public oratory as could be commandeered for the purpose, and special Forms of Prayer were no exception, especially in the 1580s and 1590s. On such occasions the prayers 'fit for the time' were an odd mixture of 'State of the Nation' address and downright Protestant polemic, culminating in 1594 and 1598 with two enormous dissertations[31] on past rebellions and their proven links with 'the see of Rome and seat of the Beast' through 'priests and Jesuits, the very loathsome locusts that crawl out of the bottomless pit'. Prayers such as these surely had a wider audience than the Paul's Cross sermons and the printed religious tracts. If so, they must have contributed largely to the vision of Elizabeth as the divinely protected protectress of the English nation and the Protestant religion, saved, as was stated in 1585, 'from the jaws of the cruel Tigers that ... sought to suck her blood,' and making England a sanctuary for 'thy poor afflicted Saints in these dangerous days persecuted and troubled in many countries ...'.[32] Two years later came the cry, 'Let thine enemies know, and make them confess, that thou hast received England into thine own protection'.[33] By 1601 Elizabeth had become 'Thy First Born, the most renowned and ancient Prince of all that profess thy Name,'[34] an image annually magnified by the skilful choice of prayers and lessons for the queen's accession.

A Church eager to demonstrate that Elizabeth had overcome each successive crisis, and that the nation had survived fires, floods and famines, was understandably loathe to stress all lingering symptoms of divine wrath, which might have undermined the

[30] Clay p. 463n.
[31] Ibid pp. 654–64, 679–88.
[32] Ibid pp. 585.
[33] Ibid p. 604.
[34] Ibid p. 693.

basic thesis. In the whole of the depressed 1590s only a single set of prayers (those of 1593 in time of plague) were directed to social and economic crises. It might also be impolitic to revile every known conspirator, especially if he were of noble line. The prayers after the 1569 rebellion, for example, did not name the rebels, nor did the special *Homilie against disobedience and wylfull Rebellion* of 1571. And whereas after Squire's plot in 1598 the Earl of Essex who had escaped the design on his life was heralded as 'one of the bright stars of our nobility the Earl of Essex',[35] after Essex's own rebellion no names were named, but the bitter message came stridently through when it was rehearsed that 'like unnatural children [they] have rebelled against the Mother of their own lives that took them up from their cradles and laded them with honours and preferments.'[36] Crisis might be an unsure ally in the interpretation of history, and the Hand of God a weapon claimed by more than one school.

In a sense, Elizabeth's reign was not yet the heyday of these special forms of prayer and national days of fasting. Some of the choicest specimens, like that after the Gunpowder Plot, were still to come. But in this short paper I have tried to show how the Anglican Church organised itself to deal with national crises within the framework of fixed forms of prayer, and how by those prayers, much more than through the Prayer Book itself which deliberately had a timeless quality, up-to-date information could be communicated, God's protection of the regime so far could be set forth by authority, and spiritual lessons appropriate to each such crisis drawn, even if only the prayers were said, and no homily read or sermon preached. It was cruelly suggested by the Church's Puritan critics that the man in the Anglican pew was 'capable only of two prayers, for rain or fair weather',[37] and this may contain a grain of truth. But the Church furnished him with a much wider repertoire of prayers, and according to the view of history which they encapsulated, demonstrated how profitable, on the whole, they had proved! At home, his house sweetened with incense, juniper,

---

[35] *Ibid* p. 681.
[36] *Ibid* p. 690.
[37] Collinson pp. 191–2.

rosemary or rosewater, he could pray less formally, alone or in the midst of his assembled family, and use, if he could read, further prayers set forth by authority for the same purpose.[38] Perhaps he, and they, deserve to be taken more seriously.

Historical Manuscripts Commission

[38] See, for example, Clay 503 and his *Private Prayers* (Parker Society, Cambridge 1851) which includes the *Book of Christian Prayers* reprinted several times during the century.

THE RELIGIOUS LIFE IN THE SPAIN
OF PHILIP II AND PHILIP III

by A.D. WRIGHT

ROM the vividly autobiographic *Life* of St Teresa famous images of conventual life in sixteenth-century Spain have been derived; both the dark impression of unreformed monastic existence and the heroic profile of reformed regulars.[1] Before and after that era the social, not to say political prominence of certain figures, friars and nuns, in Spanish life is notorious, from the reigns of the Catholic Monarchs to that of Philip IV and beyond.[2] Modern historical research has indeed highlighted the contribution to political and ecclesiastical development, to early Catholic reform above all, of key members of the regular clergy under the Catholic Monarchs.[3] For monastics, as opposed to mendicants, in post-medieval Spain, the extensive and meticulous researches of Linage Conde have put all Iberian scholars in his debt.[4] The fascinating origins of the essentially Iberian phenomenon of the Jeronymites have recently received new attention from J.R.L. Highfield,[5] but further insights into the true condition of the religious life in the Iberian peninsula of the supposedly Golden Age are perhaps still possible, when unpublished material is consulted in the Roman archives and in those of Spain, such as Madrid, Simancas, Barcelona and Valencia. Considerations of space necessarily limit what can be suggested here, but the development of monastic life in Counter-Reformation Spain is arguably

---

[1] *The Life of Saint Teresa of Avila by Herself*, transl. J.M. Cohen (Harmondsworth 1957).

[2] J. Deleito y Piñuela, *La vida religiosa española bajo el cuarto Felipe* (2 ed Madrid 1963); Q. Pérez, *Fray Hernando de Santiago. Predicador del Siglo de Oro (1575–1639)* (Madrid 1949).

[3] V. Beltrán de Heredia, 'The Beginnings of Dominican Reform in Castile' in *Spain in the Fifteenth Century* ed J.R.L. Highfield (London 1972), pp. 226 *seq*; Highfield, 'Christians, Jews and Muslims in the same society', *SCH* XV (1978) p. 121 *seq*.

[4] A. Linage Conde, *El Monacato en España e Hispanoamérica* (Salamanca 1977).

[5] J.R.L. Highfield, 'The Jeronimites in Spain, their Patrons and Success, 1373–1516', *JEH* XXXIV, 4 (1983) pp. 513–33.

best considered in its extended not just in its stricter sense: for
parallels and contrasts, as well as direct influences, were not
confined by the normal distinctions between the eremitic and the
monastic, the monastic and the mendicant, the old and the new
orders, or even the male and female communities. Furthermore the
intervention of Spanish royal authority in Portuguese affairs between 1580 and 1640, not least in ecclesiastical and regular life,
provides a useful comparative basis for consideration of truly
Iberian conditions.

Royal control in the Iberian kingdoms by the end of the sixteenth
century was of course particularly prominent in the Military
Orders. The financial importance of these Orders and their prop-
erties to the Spanish monarchy has been underlined in recent
work;[6] while the political and financial importance of the priory of
Crato in Portugal at the time of Dom Antonio's deprivation and
Cardinal Archduke Albert's administration is a reminder of the
presence throughout the Iberian kingdoms of the possessions of the
Knights of Malta, alongside those of the native military Orders.
Portugal of course had her own military Orders, just as the
Valencian kingdom was distinguished by that of Montesa.[7] But the
extent to which such Orders controlled ecclesiastical patronage,
exercising jurisdiction and not simply rights of presentation, over
whole areas of country was arguably even greater in Portugal than
in the Spanish kingdoms: so that even the richest Portuguese see of
Evora, held by such determined national figures as Cardinal Henry
and Archbishop Braganza, embraced numerous parishes over
which archiepiscopal rights of visitation were denied, thus inhibit-
ing all diocesan visitation there in practice. The clash of reforming
Catholic bishops in post-Tridentine Spain with such extensive
authority over unreformed enclaves led to pleas for Roman support
against the obstinate defence of royal supremacy by the Council of
the Orders in the face of pastoral considerations.[8] The appointment
and control of secular clergy to serve the parochial cures in such
enclaves, where clerical members of these Orders did not them-

[6] L.P. Wright, 'The Military Orders in Sixteenth and Seventeenth Century Spanish
Society' *PP*, XLIII (1969) p. 34 *seq.*
[7] Archivo General de Simancas [A.G.S.], Patronato Eclesiastico, Legajo 147.
[8] Archivio Segreto Vaticano [A.S.V.], S. Congregatio Concilii, Relatio Visita Ad
Limina, 311 (Evora).

selves serve, were frankly unsatisfactory by post-Conciliar standards, even where Spanish bishops obtained limited rights to provide sacramental oversight or administer confirmation. The frustration of Tridentine ideals by this expression of royal supremacy in Counter-Reformation Spain was completed by the impossibility, experienced by reforming bishops, of improving the enclosure and regular life of related female houses, often of course defined more by social standing than by ascetic vocation, true though that was of female convents in Spain more generally. In this case, arguably the most discouraging of all the problems faced by Iberian bishops after the Council of Trent, the assertion of royal supremacy had practical implications for pastoral care of whole parishes, of large numbers of laity, and not just for the corporate life of the Military Orders and their female convents.[9] The survival of essentially pre-Tridentine conditions in so many aspects of Iberian Catholic life was here epitomised, as by the whole lack of clear distinction between clerics and laymen, civil and ecclesiastical servants of the crown or members of its councils and judiciary, Inquisitors uncertain of the sources of their own authority. With the caesaro-papist assertions of royal authority at the end of Philip II's reign and the beginning of Philip III's reign, knights of the Military Orders had naturally to be excluded from episcopal attempts to prohibit the presence of laymen in the choirs of cathedrals and parish churches, while a royal painter could subsequently depict his own standing in society by the device of his Habit, adorning his self-portrait.[10]

Conditions detrimental to pastoral care were not the preserve of the Military Orders alone however. The canons regular, in the Iberian kingdoms as more generally in the Counter-Reformation Church, presented one of the least satisfactory examples of clerical life. In Spain the survival of regular chapters at some cathedrals of the crown of Aragon provided problems once again not confined to the life of the cloister. Episcopal relations with cathedral chapters in Spain, before and after Trent, were notoriously disputatious, but the Conciliar decree for the appointment of a canon–theologian and a canon–penitentiary at the first post-Conciliar vacancies at each cathedral was particularly difficult to implement in the Spanish

---

[9] Relatio Vis. Ad Limina, 399A, Illerden. I.
[10] Biblioteca Nacional, Madrid [B.N.M.], MS 13019, fols 13ʳ *seq.*

A. D. WRIGHT

kingdoms. To the problems of patronage and funding experienced elsewhere in the post-Tridentine Church, in such appointments, were added peculiarly Iberian difficulties, such as the royal control of cathedral stalls in the kingdom of Granada, and the regular chapters of some Aragonese cathedrals. Despite the support of Philip II for the gradual secularisation of such Aragonese chapters a contrast still remained at Zaragoza, for example, between the New Foundation of secular canons which replaced the regulars at the Seo, and the independent canons regular who remained in this period at El Pilar, barely tolerating archiepiscopal supervision of the secular clerics who actually provided pastoral service at the latter cathedral.[11] Such essentially pre-Tridentine survivals, reminiscent of the earlier history of Burgo de Osma for example, marked Spain once again as distinct from even those areas of post-Tridentine Italy which were under Spanish rule, where only the Sicilian see of Monreale was a cathedral priory.[12] In the post-Tridentine Church more generally canonesses regular were too often distinguished by fierce resistance to any life which was either canonic or regular, but in the Spanish kingdoms the role of the canons regular was once again complicated by royal intervention. The zeal for monastic reform demonstrated by Philip II was undoubted, and in line with that of the Catholic Monarchs or the Hieronymite affections of the aged Charles V; but this zeal, in Philip's case, was not necessarily either well-informed or well-directed at all times. The reform imposed on the Praemonstratensians in Spain, even when the more ambitious royal schemes to subject them to control by more favoured regulars were abandoned, led not to their recovery of a truly pastoral role, as in the Catholic lands of Counter-Reformation Southern Germany and Austria; but rather to their monasticization in the strict sense, symbolized by their enforced exchange of the white canonic choir dress for monastic black, which even a later reversion to white recalled by the retention of a black biretta.[13]

The singular phenomenon of the Hieronymites in the Iberian peninsula in fact drew attention to many other confusions of

[11] S. Congr. Conc., Vis. Ad Limina 162A (Zaragoza I).
[12] Pedro de Ribadeneyra, *Vida de... Diego Laínez...* [Historias de la Contrarreforma] ed E. Rey (Madrid 1945) p. 471.
[13] Linage Conde, *El Monacato* pp. 468 *seq.*

religious nature and purpose in this period, not that of the Praemonstratensians alone. Whatever the eremitic origins of the order, the distinctly activist nature of the Hieronymites' life, even though enclosed, was a paradox evident by the end of Philip II's reign. The royal specification of liturgical detail for the Escorial choir office certainly drew attention to one strand of Counter-Reformation piety, the return to exact performance of liturgical splendours: manifested elsewhere in the post-Tridentine Church by the Benedictines among the old orders, the Roman Oratory among the new, and, within Spain, by the equally precise ceremonial regulation laid down by Archbishop Juan de Ribera for his seminary chapel of Corpus Christi at Valencia, along lines of truly Borromean exactitude. The Escorial foundation of Philip II perhaps symbolised the undoubted transformation of Hieronymite life from the eremitic to the communal; but the legacy of royal patronage was obviously still very much present in the vexed question of appointment to superior office in the order and the rights of the community of the mother house in the election of any superior who was also head of the whole order, an issue contested in the Spanish Benedictine world too. The scholarly and particularly theological activity of the Escorial community was a reminder of the Augustinian connections of the order: the Austin friars in Spain and elsewhere by this period were equally activist, hardly eremitic, certainly communal. But the search for eremitic renewal in pre-Tridentine Catholic reform had nowhere been unmixed with more properly monastic observance, as the Italian history of the Camaldoli and the reformed Benedictine congregation, later Cassinese, recalls. The distinctly political eminence of the Hieronymites in the Spain of Philip II is more marked, not simply by virtue of the courtly nature of the Escorial, but by the complicated financial arrangements for the support of the Escorial community, involving the wider monarchy of the Spanish empire: not only the printing of liturgical books for the overseas realms, but also some revenues derived from the printing elsewhere, by other convents[14] or even other orders, of the *Cruzada* bulls which extended that indulgence, still sold, despite the Council of Trent and continued post-Conciliar complaints by Spanish bishops, to the foreign as well as

---

[14] *Ibid* pp. 423 *seq*, 627, 651.

the home dominions of the king. The royal financial benefit derived from this indulgence was often at odds with the efforts of reforming bishops in Spain, after the Council, to restore true standards of religious practice, not least in the performance of the liturgy and in public devotional life. But royal priorities were more generally expressed by the concern to subordinate Portuguese Hieronymites to Castilian direction.[15]

The role of the Hieronymites thus revealed supremely the caesaro-papism of the Spanish crown and also the absence of clear boundaries between the eremitic and the monastic, the monastic and the mendicant, as well as the growing preoccupation with Spanish, or more truly Castilian, independent management of religious orders within the Iberian peninsula. The Carthusians on the other hand, in Spain as elsewhere before and after the Council of Trent, maintained their own high standards and distinction of religious life precisely by means of an explicit mixture of the eremitic and the communal within the existence of each Charter-house. The reputation of the Carthusians in the late medieval and Renaissance Church, admired for example by the early Jesuits as well as by Thomas More, was again demonstrated by the Portu-guese creation of a Charterhouse, in the Catholic reform of Archbishop Braganza.[16] The Spanish Charterhouses, like those of Italy, continued to display, after the Council of Trent, a striking magnificence of building and decoration, as a result of the patron-age of the great, alongside the real austerity of the inmates' cells. The Baroque extravagance of the sacristy of the Granada Charter-house thus came to balance the refectory paintings which recalled the Carthusian martyrs of Henrician England. Such a building within the final conquest of the Catholic Monarchs however was a reminder that even the strictly enclosed Carthusians could not escape the implications of royal policy with regard to religious orders. Royal concern, echoed even by Archbishop Ribera of Valencia, with the need to exclude French direction from the affairs of the Cistercians in the Iberian kingdoms eventually extended to similar consideration of the links between the Grande Chartreuse and the Iberian Charterhouses. But this was perhaps occasioned

---

[15] A.G.S. Comisaria de Cruzada, Leg. 516.
[16] Ribadeneyra, *Vida de... Ignacio de Loyola* [Historias] pp. 188, 240; Visita Ad Limina, Evora.

rather by the papal demands that Carthusians elsewhere should contribute to the costly creation of the Roman Charterhouse out of the giant remains of the imperial *Terme*, by the magnificent vision of Michelangelo and the grandiose plans of Cardinal Federico Borromeo for S. Maria degli Angeli.[17]

The earliest form of perfectly monastic life in the Church was claimed by the Basilians. Though in Spain the Benedictine objection to this claim took the form of a characteristic contest over monastic habit, it was equally typical that the Spanish Basilians were not purely monastic in origin, but represented a rough union of monastic and eremitic elements. The centralisation growing in reformed orders before Trent and marked in most new orders after the Council was imposed by papal authority on the Basilians as on other orders in the post-Tridentine Church. The treatment of the Basilians in the Spanish-ruled Southern Italian kingdoms was thus for once in relative harmony with the royal concern to establish unity and centralisation among the Basilians in Spain itself. The results thus linked originally monastic and originally eremitic groups in both Northern and Southern Spain. A potential clash between the claims of the Abbot-General in Italy and the royally-promoted independence of religious orders within Spain was inevitable however. Distinctions of practice clearly did develop between Basilians in the two peninsulas, given the defeat of Philip II's plan to impose Latin uniformity on the Greek-rite Basilians of Spanish-ruled Sicily. Whatever the history of papal treatment of Greek-rite Catholics in Southern Italy more generally, in this period papal defence of the liturgical distinction of the Sicilian Basilians, for all the acknowledged ignorance of their members, was clear.[18]

The diversity of Benedictine development in the Iberian peninsula in this period embraced the concern of the reformed Montserrat community to regulate the associated hermits of the holy mountain more strictly, in line with episcopal concern on that subject in the post-Tridentine Church, not only in Aragon or the Balearics but in Italy as well as in Spain more generally. It was the Catalan rather

---

[17] Linage Conde, *El Monacato* pp. 379 *seq*; Archivo de la Corona de Aragon, Consejo de Aragon, [A.C.A.] Leg. 651 [76/3].
[18] Linage Conde, *El Monacato* pp. 473 *seq*; A.G.S., Secr. Prov., Sicilia, Varios, Libro 776, fols 1ʳ *seq*.

than Castilian tradition of Benedictine reform, begun of course
before the Council of Trent, which was imported by Cardinal
Henry to Portugal and thence exported eventually to Brazil. The
eminence of the Valladolid congregation in the kingdoms of the
Castilian crown meant that problems of authority could, once
again, not be avoided, above all the question of the rights of the
community of the mother house in the election of their superior, if
that superior were also to be the head of the whole congregation.
The Valladolid reform represented of course a movement of return
to observance of the rule, of liturgical as well as scholarly and
contemplative life. At first sight the association of the Valladolid
Benedictines, by the early seventeenth century, with the difficult
birth of what was eventually to be the English congregation, with
its avowedly activist missionary purpose, was a paradox. But
despite the inevitably delicate relations with the Jesuits at the
moment of the seminary secession from the English College in
Valladolid, the Benedictines of the Valladolid tradition were more
generally in sympathy, as the Spanish mendicants distinctly were
not, with such Jesuit spiritual initiatives as relatively frequent lay
communion and lay devotions and instruction in the vernacular.
Such pastoral sensitivity to the needs of the laity and indeed of lay
brothers within the cloister contrasted with the pastoral damage
caused, in the Aragonese kingdoms above all, by the considerable
enclaves remaining under the absolute control of Benedictine
monasteries, especially where such communities were themselves
far from reformed, and indeed were decidedly relaxed. Royal
commitment to the reform of such institutions, even their suppression if necessary, was real, but dangerously combined with the
distinct issue of control of regulars for ultimately political purposes, whether within the Spanish kingdoms or in Portugal. The
question of whether abbots were best elected for limited or
unlimited periods was thus complicated by the issue of royal
patronage, while even within the realms of the crown of Aragon
feeling between Aragonese and Catalans could on occasion become
evident. The usual problems, for conscientious bishops after Trent,
of regulating the life of secular clergy appointed to parochial
charges by monastic institutions, of supervising the laity within
such parishes, or of recovering tithes originally intended for the
support of parish clergy from monastic or subsequently lay hands

were thus as difficult in Spain as anywhere.[19] Whereas even Inquisitorial authority in early seventeenth-century Navarre was eventually concerned with the need for reformed religious houses to help bring true standards of Catholic belief and practice to the ignorant laity afflicted by French-imported witch-mania, royal plans, by the end of Philip II's reign, still concentrated on the possible financial gains to the monarchy from dissolution of incorrigible monastic communities in the crown of Aragon, with at most the diversion of limited funds to impoverished cathedral foundations in those realms or the extension of the Military Orders' defences against the external threat of irreligion. The strains of Catalan independence were of course at no time absent from the Montserrat leadership of the reformed Benedictines outside Castile, from the retreat of the Basque-Navarrese Loyola there and at Manresa to the military struggles of the 1640s, and the revival of questions of French patronage, political or ecclesiastical.[20]

Where the Benedictines displayed some of the best aspects of Iberian monasticism in this period, the Cistercians showed some of the worst. Once again the symptoms were most marked in the kingdoms of the crown of Aragon, including Valencia. Relations between the great abbey of Poblet and episcopal authority in the Aragonese crown were perhaps less strained than might have been expected, but Poblet exercised little formal authority, or uncontested authority at least, over other, more troublesome communities. The royal concern to end French headship of the Spanish Cistercians was thus most marked, and openly avowed. Even Archbishop Ribera of Valencia concurred in regarding such Hispanization of the order within the peninsula as necessary, in the face of papal determination to defend the real independence of the order there from royal interference. The general papal policy, after the Council of Trent, to regulate election and length of office among regular superiors, in male and female orders, was in practice at odds with royal intervention in such questions, via viceroys as well as metropolitans, regarding the Aragonese Cistercians. In the end, the order within the crown of Aragon did not suffer the same degree of Iberian isolation as was enforced in Castile and Portugal, because of

[19] Linage Conde, *El Monacato* pp. 117 *seq*, 527.
[20] Archivo Histórico Nacional, Madrid, Inquisición [A.H.N.], Libro 1231, fols 608ʳ *seq*; cf. A.S.V., Segret. di Stato, Spagna, 322, fol 189ʳ.

royal disinclination, in the face of determined papal opposition, to appear to join in the attack of heretical Huguenots on the position and authority of the French headship of the order. Such essentially political considerations however were a distraction from the real needs of reform within the order's Spanish houses, and of solution to the pastoral problem once again created by inadequate provision to parochial cures in monastic possession.[21]

Such weaknesses within the monastic world in Spain were in dramatic contrast to the obvious continued prominence and indeed dominance of the mendicants. The Spanish kingdoms in fact provided the best proof that the pre-Tridentine importance of the friars in the Western Church had not been ended, despite the fierce episcopal antagonism which had reached its vocal culmination at the Council of Trent. The Dominicans of course represented this mendicant victory most eminently, given their continued influence, with members of other orders, in the Spanish Inquisition, as theological experts, even when canons and canonists from the secular clergy came, by the end of the sixteenth century, to monopolise the formal positions of Inquisitor. The successful attack of Dominicans and others, via the Inquisition, on Carranza was a perfect demonstration that even the primate of Spain, though himself a Dominican, was not exempt from the authority of the Spanish tribunal, any more than other bishops were to be in practice, whatever the theory of the matter. Moreover the influence of the Dominicans, in the person of the royal confessor under Philip II, represented just that type of resistance to Tridentine change, based on the confidence of an order supremely identified with pre-Tridentine reform in Spain, which so appealed to the king, in his conscious imitation of the Catholic Monarchs rather than of the emperor. The Dominican attack on primatial authority and episcopal restoration of pastoral control in Spain was continued in the objections provided by the royal confessor for Philip II's interference with the decrees of Cardinal Quiroga's abortive provincial Council of Toledo, in 1582: the implementation of perfectly Tridentine requirements in Castile was obstructed precisely on the grounds that Spanish traditions would thereby be altered.[22] The

---

[21] Linage Conde, *El Monacato* pp. 251 *seq*, 303; Archivo de la Corona de Aragon, Leg. 651; S. Congr. Conc., Vis. Ad Limina, 785 A, Tarraconen. I; A.S.V., Segret. di Stato, Spagna, 320, fols 154^r *seq*; 322, fols 101^r *seq*.

[22] B.N.M., MS 6148, fol 30^r, cf. fols 24^r *seq*; MS13019, fols 81^r *seq*.

dominance of Spanish intellectual life by the Dominicans was also of course demonstrated by the successful campaigns mounted, at Salamanca and Valladolid particularly, against the emergence of the Jesuits as a force in Spanish universities, or in education and society more generally there. The Dominicans were also used as a counterbalance, by the crown, to the supposed anti-Spanish activity of the Jesuits at the time of the union of Portugal to the Spanish monarchy.[23]

Beneath the surface of this impressive resistance to innovation, however, an ironical defeat for Dominican theological conservatism was beginning in Spain, developed in the end by the authorities of universities as well as by bishops and Jesuits. By the end of Philip III's reign Dominican defeat on the issue of the adoption of the doctrine of the Immaculate Conception within Spain was clear *de facto* though not of course *de jure*, even though the Dominican and wider confrontation with Jesuit teaching had spread from Spain, as from Trent, Rome and Louvain, to France. That popular adoption, by civic authorities and lay crowds as well as by episcopal synods, of a doctrine more Marian than the conspicuous Marian devotion of the Dominicans themselves was a remarkable tribute to the powers of survival of the Jesuits, attacked by the Dominicans in Spain as not truly an order, and suspicious to Philip II as not just a dangerous novelty and impossible hybrid, clerks regular, but as 'Theatines', supposedly identified with the interests of the enemy Caraffa, if not with the pope's own new order itself.[24] The failure of the Spanish Dominicans to influence popular piety on this issue, in addition to influencing royal and Inquisitorial policy and directing university developments, is the more interesting, because in some dioceses, after the Council of Trent, mendicants were still employed, with apparent success, as the traditional supplement in the work of preaching and confession to the deficiencies of the secular clergy. Indeed the failure of the post-Conciliar Church in the Spanish kingdoms to develop Tridentine seminaries in most dioceses, a crucial failure in which the negative intervention of Philip II must not be overlooked, meant that this traditional

---

[23] A.G.S. Estado (Portugal), Leg. 410.
[24] J.I. Tellechea Idígoras, *Tiempos Recios. Inquisición y Heterodoxias* (Salamanca 1977) pp. 33 *seq*; cf. Ribadeneyra, *Vida de... Loyola* p. 113.

assistance in pastoral work was still often essential.[25] In such work, as in university life, Inquisitorial examination and overseas missions, the Dominicans were of course flanked by the Franciscans and the Austin friars. The internal divisions of the Franciscans, still real though hardly new after the Council of Trent, were as painful in Spain as elsewhere in Catholic society, and immediately post-Conciliar papal policy, directed to the rapid imposition of observance on conventuals, in the Franciscan as in other orders, proved as unsuccessful there as elsewhere. From such sorrows nevertheless emerged, however painfully, the impressive reform of the observant Recollects, while in Portugal also the Capuchins arrived, despite the antagonism which that movement still encountered in the Church generally until the early seventeenth century at official as opposed to popular level. The political involvements of Italian Capuchins, not least in Spanish-ruled Italy, of course made their members and leaders potentially suspect at the Spanish court, while even Archbishop Ribera of Valencia had his disagreements with them on occasion.[26] The Augustinians perhaps escaped such public difficulties, but all the mendicant orders within Spain included within their still numerous membership unruly and disorderly elements. At Valencia it was thus necessary to relieve a female convent of its Augustinian male superiors for a while, even though Spanish social traditions and resistance to explicit Tridentine provision for such problems prevented in this case the substitution of archiepiscopal for regular control of the convent, as a terrible fate.[27] In many Iberian dioceses after the Council of Trent conscientious bishops, like Archbishop Pedro de Castro in late sixteenth- and early seventeenth-century Granada, faced persistent and vigorous opposition, from regular preachers and confessors, to the clear Tridentine legislation for episcopal examination and control in such crucial pastoral activity. Spanish bishops were particularly hampered in such struggles by the peculiarly Iberian complication of the

[25] A.G.S. Patronato Real, Leg. 22 [22–4], for Philip II and seminaries; S. Congr. Conc., Vis. Ad Limina 2 (Avila), for e.g. of mendicants' contribution to pastoral work.

[26] S. Congr. Conc., Vis. Ad Limina, Evora; R. Robres Lluch, *San Juan de Ribera* (Barcelona 1960) pp. 433 *seq*; A.G.S. Estado, Sicilia, Leg. 1144, fol 158; Napoles, Leg. 1881, fol 192; Milan, Leg. 1910, fols 69[r] *seq*.

[27] A.C.A. Leg. 651 [60].

Cruzada indulgence, in its implications for confessors and penitents, as well as by the general problem in the post-Tridentine Church of papal maintenance of mendicant privileges alongside restored episcopal authority.[28]

Dominicans, Franciscans and Augustinians were thus of positive use to Iberian bishops after Trent, in pastoral work alongside the internal Jesuit missions in Spanish dioceses directed by zealous bishops or by conscientious but courtly and often absent prelates, and in educational provision, again alongside new Jesuit foundations, in some Portuguese dioceses in this period.[29] But many bishops in the Spanish kingdoms also reported the abusive exploitation by male regulars, friars most commonly, of often impoverished female communities under their jurisdiction and spiritual direction. Pastoral care of the laity was also disrupted, in Spain as elsewhere in the long-term development of the Counter-Reformation Church, by the continued pretensions of the mendicants in the conduct of funerals, the attendance at death-beds and the acquisition of bequests; and the proximity of one mendicant community to another remained a problematic burden on social resources in Spain as elsewhere too, despite post-Tridentine regulation of such distance.[30] The hyper-activism of the mendicants thus provides an additional clue, perhaps, to the explanation of the violent opposition which the Carmelites, male and female, encountered in the discalced return to the contemplative ideal, quite apart from the wider fear of *alumbrado* deviance. Though male Carmelites subsequently entered missionary activity in the overseas Iberian realms, the more immediate problem after the Council of Trent, as experienced by a successor to Archbishop Pedro de Castro at Granada, was the claim to exemption from aspects of pastoral authority made by Carmelite friars on the basis of privileges attached to the strict enclosure of the reformed houses, when such enclosure was not in fact observed. There as elsewhere in Spanish sees the admission of the laity, including females, to male convents on the pretext of devotional processions was inex-

---

[28] S. Congr. Conc., Vis. Ad Limina, 370A, Granaten. I.

[29] Visita Ad Limina, 141 (Braga); 193A (Cartagena I); 246A, Compostellan. I; 805A (Toledo I).

[30] Visita Ad Limina, 364, Gienen.; cf. Ribadeneyra, *Vida de... Loyola* pp. 298 *seq.*

cusable in episcopal eyes.[31] Yet it was, by a paradox, precisely the truly enclosed female foundations of the Carmelites which exerted such an influence on lay piety in Counter-Reformation Spain, by promotion of the cult of St. Joseph, alongside episcopal encouragement of the related cult of the guardian angels.[32] By a further irony the relatively early adoption of Teresa of Avila as not just a belatedly approved figure but a formally canonized saint, after her death, complicated the internal and indeed political struggles within the seventeenth-century Iberian kingdoms over the patronage of Spain, in which the traditional claims of Santiago, already at risk from Roman criticism and Braga competition, were effectively challenged by the proliferation of local 'patriotism' relating to the holy patrons of Spanish cities.[33] As with the parallel battle over the doctrine of the Immaculate Conception, a quasi-political dimension thus entered Spanish relations with Rome over the question, reminiscent of Spanish patronage of San Pietro in Montorio at Rome rather than of the local translations and elevations of local cults in Counter-Reformation Spain, whether in Toledo, after Carranza and under Quiroga, or in Valencia under Ribera, or in the divided clerical establishment of Cordoba.[34] The activism of the Spanish mendicants also highlights the role in the peninsula of what might be called the 'lesser' orders. The Minims themselves seem to have retained their essentially late-medieval ascetic purpose in Spain, without developing the extraordinary intellectual and indeed scientific curiosity of the French Minims and their Roman house in the seventeenth century. The Trinitarians and Mercedarians were obviously well placed to continue their sometimes heroic work of redeeming Christian captives in North Africa, even after the expulsion of the Moriscos from Spain. Their equally obvious abuses were also reformed on occasion, as by the intervention of determined Cardinal Protectors like Federico Borromeo. Such abuses were typified by the similar brothers of St. Antony, in

[31] Visita Ad Limina, 370A, Granaten. I; cf. M. de la Pinta Llorente, *Aspectos Históricos del Sentimiento Religioso en España. Ortodoxia y Heterodoxia* (Madrid 1961) pp. 83 *seq.*

[32] A.H.N., Inquisición, Leg. 4511, fol 56ʳ; cf. Visita Ad Limina, 364, Gienen.

[33] P.B. Gams, *Die Kirchengeschichte von Spanien* III 2 (Regensburg 1879) pp. 266 *seq*; B.N.M., MS 13044, fols 163ʳ *seq*; MS 6148, fols 85ʳ *seq.*

[34] B.N.M. MS 13019, fol IIIᵛ *seq*; MS 13044, fols 110ʳ *seq*; A.C.A., Leg. 651 [55/56]; cf. A.H.N., Inquisición, Libro 1280; cf. Ribadeneyra, *Vida de... Loyola*, p. 163.

The Religious Life in Spain

Aragon, with their misuse of funds and improper claims in devotional and confraternity life, just as the pastoral problem presented by the irregular rites of absolution offered by the Aragonese Trinitarians and Mercedarians exemplified a general post-Tridentine issue, of regulars' use of extravagant indulgences and spiritual benefits.[35]

The Counter-Reformation in the Iberian peninsula saw new initiatives in hospitaller work by regulars which if often heroic was also often problematic, given Tridentine prescriptions for episcopal direction of both pastoral and charitable care. The new hospitallers of Saint John emanated from Granada, but there and elsewhere their lowly social composition, embracing for such unpleasant work those rejected by other orders, led to episcopal concern that such 'idiot' brothers were unfit to manage their own increasing revenues and administration. Papal defence of the relative rights of such 'idiots', even within the Tridentine legislative frame, did not however necessarily imply the absence of some justified concern among bishops. Elsewhere in the Spanish-ruled world, in Sicily and Milan for example, the pastoral ambitions of such helpers of the sick, extended to the ordinary faithful, suggested an alteration of purpose which archbishops understandably resisted. So too in the Spanish kingdoms themselves, where such regulars proved capable of wasting their funds on their own members' well being or on litigation, the curse of Golden-Age ecclesiastical as well as lay society in Spain.[36] Such deviation was the more marked in contrast to the initiatives of reforming bishops in Iberian dioceses, following Tridentine provisions, for the reduction of small and inefficient hospitals, even if lay in management, to allow more intensive care and better use of resources. Royal and Dominican resistance to such innovation however limited episcopal success, as secular defence of lay institutions and funds did elsewhere in the post-Tridentine Church. The bishops of richer and sometimes even of smaller Spanish sees had their own impressive tradition of charitable provision and bequest, even if the Portuguese episcopate in this period displayed the most conspicuous charity. Spanish bishops were also co-opted by popes and Nuncios in the general campaign,

[35] Visita Ad Limina, 785 A, Tarraconen. I; IIIA, Barcinonen. I; cf. A.S.V., Spagna, 320 fol 72ᵛ.
[36] Visita Ad Limina, 370A, Granaten. I; 263 A (Cordoba I); 704A (Salamanca I).

265

in the Iberian peninsula as elsewhere, to 'regularise' male tertiaries and older fraternities with hospitaller and charitable duties, against the usual social resistance to change in the Spanish kingdoms. The aim of the assembled bishops at Trent, to impose a regular habit and proper rule on such communities, was not abandoned however, as part of the post-Tridentine drive to end all ambiguity between the ecclesiastical and the secular. As elsewhere in the post-Conciliar Church however such ambitions created confrontation with secular authority over the control of social provision, because of the laity's involvement financially and personally. Roman ideals were here especially at odds with the Castilian campaign for centralisation and Hispanization of regular life under royal control.[37]

Such intensification in Iberia of universal problems was of course notable in the vexed history of the early Society of Jesus. For the two reigns of Philip II and Philip III the problem of the new orders in the Counter-Reformation Church and the opposition of the older, especially mendicant orders is virtually identical in the Iberian kingdoms with that of the existence and constitution of the Jesuits. The Dominican and Inquisitorial suspicion of Borgia, as a peripheral, non-Castilian Spaniard, like Loyola, and of the sympathy he and his 'Theatine' colleagues displayed for Carranza was matched by Philip II's doubts about a vice-regal grandee who had preached in the vernacular, even if Castilian, in Navarre and been the link between the emperor's final retreat – visited also by Carranza – and the Portuguese throne.[38] Inquisitorial sensitivity about Jesuit claims to papal exemption from the Spanish tribunal's authority was the more acute because of the internal, persistent doubts among the Spanish Inquisitors as to the precise sources of their jurisdiction. While the Inquisitor General undoubtedly acted by apostolic authority, this was not evidently true of the actions of other Inquisitors or even of the existence of the Suprema. Lay membership of that Council, despite the occasional doubts of

---

[37] B.N.M., MS 6148, fols 103ʳ seq; cf. A.G.S., Patronato Real, Leg. 22 [22–1]; cf. B.N.M., MS 13019, fols 49ᵛ seq. Cf. L. Martz, *Poverty and Welfare in Habsburg Spain* (Cambridge 1983) p. 71.

[38] Ribadeneyra, *Vida del P. Francisco de Borja* [Historias] pp. 655 seq, 692, 723 seq, 735, 740 seq, 744 seq; cf. Tellechea Idígoras, *Bartolomé Carranza, Arzobispo. Un prelado evangélico en la Silla de Toledo* (San Sebastián 1958) p. 36.

Philip II himself, and direct royal intervention to appoint but also
to dismiss Inquisitors General, as most notoriously on the accession
and on the death of Philip III, made such worries the more
pressing. Canonists within the Inquisition were positive that royal
as well as apostolic authority was involved in the tribunal's
activities, even if operating distinctly in Castile and in Aragon.[39]
Such complications indeed provided a cover for Inquisitorial
inaction, in the reign of Philip IV, when royal supremacy itself was
held by the king to have been offended, in a renewed attack of the
university of Salamanca and other universities on the educational
initiatives of the Jesuits, as earlier in the Spanish universities, such
as Valencia, where Ribera had encountered opposition from canons
and Inquisitors, when acting by archiepiscopal and royal power in
defence of Jesuit education: an ironic association of the Society with
royal not papal authority.[40] The educational triumph of the Jesuits
in Spanish society, as opposed to Portugal or elsewhere in Catholic
Europe, was clearly not achieved at university level but at school
level. The influence of Jesuit schooling was evident at Cadiz for
example, in the disorganisation of Church life there caused by the
English raid, despite episcopal initiative, and royal support under
both Philip II and Philip III, in the work of recovery.[41] The
universal troubles of the Society of Jesus with secular authority, in
Europe and overseas, by the end of the sixteenth century and the
beginning of the seventeenth, and the consequent as well as causal
internal convulsions of the Society over its constitution and even
purpose, were enhanced in the Iberian kingdoms by the royal aim
of establishing peninsula organisation and Castilian dominance
within each religious order. The early identification of the Jesuits
with independent royal authority in Portugal, in dramatic contrast
to the initial suspicion of the Jesuits and their Parisian formation by
Philip II, intent on preventing Spaniards from studying outside the
peninsula in effect, represented a further complication.[42] Even
though at Evora there were eventually tensions between archiepis-

---

[39] A.G.S. Gracia y Justicia, Leg 621; cf. A.H.N., Inquisición, Libro 1280.
[40] A.G.S., Leg. 621, fols 66ʳ *seq.* Cf. Archivo del Reino de Valencia [A.R.V.] Clero:
jesuitas, Leg. 89.
[41] Visita Ad Limina, 354, Gadinen.; A.G.S., Comisaria de Cruzada, Leg. 516 [22].
[42] Tellechea Idígoras, 'Los jesuitas y la real pragmática de Felipe II de 1559', *Tiempos
Recios* pp. 268 *seq.*

copal and Jesuit policy, as found elsewhere in the Counter-
Reformation Church, from Valencia to Milan or Prague, the Jesuit
presence at the heart of Portuguese Catholic reform, at Evora,
Braga or Coimbra itself, led to the unusual courting of Lisbon piety
by Philip II, on his accession to the Portuguese throne, by means of
the collection at São Roque of what was dearest to the monarch's
heart, relics.[43] The influence of Jesuit internal missions in Southern
Spain, in Granada even more than in Valencia or, only belatedly, at
Orihuela, was also clear, whether in charitable work among the
lowest of Sevillian society, criminal elements neglected by other
orders, or in the recovery of the Alpujarras, with the shameful,
impoverished secular clergy of that area, or in the estates of the
Medina Sidonia, with their proximate associations with Portugal
which by 1640 seemed to justify earlier suspicions.[44] The internal
divisions of the Spanish Jesuits were not just those between Castile
and Andalusia however, for court and 'country' Jesuits were
ultimately as divided in Spain as within Portugal itself or in later
seventeenth-century France. The independence of individual Jesuits
in the Lemos-Lerma circles of the early seventeenth-century, as
much as at Rome, then, before or subsequently, weakened the
Society's resistance to royal desire for national segregation within
the Society's supposed papal unity and for Spanish dominance of
the Society's affairs. The election of the Netherlandish Mercurian
as Jesuit general at the very crisis of Spain's policies in Northern
Europe perpetuated suspicion aroused already by Borgia. The
election of the Neapolitan Acquaviva similarly caused disquiet,
even if at a time when the Oratorian sympathies of Clement VIII
were to lead to another period, neither the first nor at all the last, of
papal disinclination to favour the Jesuits.[45] The success of the
Jesuits in peripheral Iberia, despite a cautious refusal to conform to

---

[43] Visita Ad Limina, 141 (Braga); 311 (Evora); cf. A.G.S., Estado (Portugal), Leg.
410; R. García Cárcel, 'Trayectoria histórica de la Inquisición valenciana', in *La
Inquisición Española. Nueva visión, nuevos horizontes*, ed J. Pérez Villanueva (Madrid
1980) pp. 411 *seq*. Cf. Ribadeneyra, *Vida... de Borja* pp. 707 *seq*, 797 *seq*.

[44] A. Domínguez Ortiz, 'Delitos y Suplicios en la Sevilla Imperial. (La crónica negra
de un misionero jesuita)', in *Crisis y Decadencia de la España de los Austrias*
(Barcelona 1969) pp. 11 *seq*; 'La Conspiración del Duque de Medina Sidonia y el
Marqués de Ayamonte' *ibid.*, pp. 113 *seq*; cf. Visita Ad Limina, 378, Guadicen.;
A.R.V. jesuitas, Leg. 58.

[45] L. v. Pastor, *History of the Popes* XXIV (London 1933) p. 182.

metropolitan requirement of preaching in Catalan in the principality, contrasted with their early difficulties in the conservative north and centre of Spain itself, was underlined by their disruptive success in entering the overseas missionfields of the Iberian crowns, urging, against most of their mendicant rivals, the necessity of a native priesthood to which Philip II at least was not sympathetic.[46] The prolonged resistance of the Society within Spain to the growing campaign for *limpieza* was at odds with the policy of the crown, the mendicant and other orders, and prelates like Archbishop Silíceo, as well as the Portuguese preoccupation of even Archbishop Braganza of Evora with the supposed dangers from New Christians.[47] The good relations of Cardinal Quiroga with the Jesuits at Toledo and, generally, at Madrid represented a more remarkable instance of the Society finding a welcome in the ecclesiastical richness of North-Central Spain;[48] but even so the Society, for all its internal Hispanic conflicts, perpetuated a 'papal' image of itself, by conspicuous absence from the courtly bull-fights which popes and bishops, in Spain and Portugal after the Council of Trent, so evidently failed to prohibit or bar to enthusiastic clerics and mendicants.[49] In the reigns of Philip II and Philip III at least Jesuits in Spain rather suffered with the more zealous bishops from the successful alliance of royal, conciliar, legal and Dominican opposition to any Catholic reform which represented change from pre-Tridentine Spanish conditions. In Portugal the very attraction of the Jesuits to episcopal and royal reformers frustrated by the invested powers of monks and Military Orders led necessarily to a relative eclipse of the Society's fortunes after 1580, until the Jesuit connection with independent royal authority emerged there after 1640, with the troubled figure of Vieira.[50]

[46] Visita Ad Limina, 291 (Tortosa); A.S.V. Spagna, 30 fols 387ʳ *seq* for question of native ordinations.

[47] Visita Ad Limina, 311 (Evora); 805A (Toledo I); cf. Ribadeneyra, *Vida de... Loyola* pp. 271 *seq.*

[48] B.N.M. MS 13019, fols 13ʳ *seq*; MS 13044, fols 102ʳ *seq*, 128ʳ *seq*; cf. A.S.V. Spagna, 322, fols 84ʳ *seq.*

[49] B.N.M. MS 5788, fols 98ʳ *seq*; J. Alenda y Mira, *Relaciones de Solemnidades y Fiestas Públicas de España* (Madrid 1903) [I, nos] 516, 522.

[50] For activity of royal councils, e.g. A.C.A., Leg. 651; A.G.S., Patronato Real, Leg. 22; for continued involvement of legal tribunals in post-Tridentine Spanish ecclesiastical affairs, as at Valladolid and Granada: Visita Ad Limina, 370A, Granaten. I; Archivo de la R. Chancillería de Valladolid, Registro, R. Ejecutorias, Sección antigua, Leg. 1063 (Exp. 71), Leg. 1102 (Exp. 71).

As with the Jesuits, so with female religious orders, the problems encountered in the post-Tridentine Church were hardly peculiar to Spain, but rather complicated by distinctive Hispanic conditions. Many Spanish bishops, after the Council of Trent, were able to report to Rome of their success in imposing strict enclosure, in line with Tridentine and papal decrees, on those convents which were under episcopal supervision anyway. Persistent instances of resistance to enclosure tended to come, of course, as elsewhere, rather from convents under regular control or the jurisdiction of Military Orders. But the Nuncio Ormaneto, with his own bitter experience of recalcitrant nuns in his diocese of Padua, could only be aware, like other Nuncios in Spain, of the greater difficulties there than in Italy of solving such problems. The papal and even royal campaign to limit the tenure of office of heads of female houses met the practical difficulty that Spain apparently lacked the Italian tradition of lay boards of guardians, local administrators of conventual properties and revenues. Both peninsulas, in the immediately post-Tridentine era, saw dramatic episodes where nuns, as at Padua, attempted to demolish new enclosures with their own hands.[51] But in Spain social resistance, aided up to a point by Dominican influence on Philip II, was even greater than in Italy to strict enclosure, the limitation of families' and relations' access to nuns, the stricter regulation of nuns' *exeats* for illness or recreation, the prohibition, however ineffectual in fact, of private property or personal servants retained by nuns, translation of rural or isolated convents to urban sites, unions of impoverished convents, in which Spain was rich, or, above all, substitution of episcopal for regular direction of female convents. Such changes, provided for by Tridentine legislation, were resisted as dangerous innovations, with the usual support of male regulars for lay distate. The perpetuation of society ladies' rights of free access to female convents in Spain and Portugal, for prolonged visits on occasion, was a more distinctly Hispanic demand, in the face of papal and episcopal resistance. The episcopal reaction was natural, as when Archbishop Ribera of Valencia allowed the admired reformed Carmelites a foundation in his diocese only in the form of nuns

---

[51] A.S.V. Spagna, 34, fols 283^r *seq*; fols 129^r *seq* for nuns' destruction of enclosure at Zamora, 1588; cf. Paduan threat, 1575: Archivio di Stato, Venice, Capi del Consiglio dei Dieci, Lettere di Rettori, b. 83, no. 161.

following the Augustinian rule, thus subject to his authority as the discalced Carmelites as such could not be.[52] Italy, again, could boast no phenomenon to match the mitred abbess of Las Huelgas, at Burgos, wielding her truly episcopal, not to say princely, jurisdiction symbolized by crozier and not, like assistant bishops, Irish or otherwise, in Iberian sees under absent courtiers or aged zealots, by ring alone, over a vast estate. For the abbess controlled not only the great establishment at Burgos and its dependent clerics and communities, and the foundations of Las Huelgas elsewhere, but also the parochial life of considerable numbers of clergy and laity, even for example in the issue of matrimonial dispensations.[53] Such social and political power was, in extent if not in nature, unknown to Italian bishops in their struggles with recalcitrant nuns. Royal desire in Spain for conspicuously virtuous life within female convents reflected the same unreality as in lay demands throughout the post-Tridentine Church: the end was willed but not the necessary means. Nuncios and bishops delegated in the Spanish kingdoms to impose reformed standards on female communities after the Council were hampered by royal conviction, again reflecting a wider clash in the Counter-Reformation between clerical and lay concepts of the purpose and nature of female conventual life, that such reform was a matter of social policy, and hence of crown authority. In Spain, as elsewhere after Trent, the policies of the ecclesiastical hierarchy were here able to achieve their least success, in the face of lay disagreement, as also on the related issue of confraternities, which equally involved lay funding and non-clerical membership. The issue which shared characteristics of both those parallel contests was the reduction of female tertiaries to the status of truly enclosed nuns, living under a fixed rule and formal vows. Once again a more general conflict in Counter-Reformation society, typified for example by the varieties of Italian response, papal and episcopal, to the educational ambitions of the originally unenclosed Ursulines, was the sharper in Spain, because of the pervasive tradition of *beatas*. These were perhaps reduced, in the long term, by some Spanish bishops at least, to a semblance of regular organisation, but their new appearances were like the

---

[52] Visita Ad Limina, 848A, Valentin. I; cf. A.S.V., Spagna, 322, fol 165^r.
[53] Linage Conde, *El Monacato* pp. 316 *seq*; cf. pp. 304 *seq*; Visita Ad Limina, 156, Burgen.; cf. 249A (Cuenca I).

hydra, and never ended. Evident scandals, of a sexual nature, in enclosed nunneries, or supposedly regular convents, were also, as generally in the Counter-Reformation, reduced if not entirely prevented. But scandal was also ever present potentially, as with the rare need for preventive Inquisitorial action at Toledo, to forestall the pretensions of a beautiful nun, supported by her complacent superior, to preach in the convent chapel to a lay congregation, to the natural alarm of even the male regulars responsible for the convent: mitred abbesses were clearly one thing, but young nuns in biretta and surplice another.[54] At Toledo as elsewhere in Spanish dioceses, episcopal intervention revealed no less anxiety, attempting to regulate even the more innocent production of confectionery and preserves for others' enjoyment by nuns.[55] The employment of idle time was of course the real problem, as elsewhere, and thus by the seventeenth century, in Madrid just as in France or at Milan, suspicions of diabolic possession and hence of witchcraft emerged at female convents, in societies still characterised, despite papal and episcopal post-Conciliar campaigns, by the enclosed daughters of families limiting the transmission of their property through marriage, rather than by girls convinced of their own vocation to the ascetic life. Examination of girls, especially those educated from an early age within convents, to determine real vocation proved as difficult for zealous bishops in Spain, like Pedro de Castro, archbishop of Granada, as for Catholic reforming bishops elsewhere, even in Borromean Milan for example.[56] The unusual emergence of witch-mania in central and indeed courtly Spain, as opposed to peripheral and rural Spain, was also perhaps evidence of the political turmoil of the mid seventeenth century. The emergence of the politically important nun in Philip IV's reign was nevertheless still accompanied by the necessary caution, always displayed by Teresa of Avila, in expressing any claim, even implicit, to special or immediate illumination, given the continued vigilance of the Spanish Inquisition on such issues, even before the revived concern of the Roman Inquisition about such claims, in the light of the Roman following of the Valencian Molinos.[57]

[54] A.G.S. Gracia y Justicia, Leg. 621, fols 71ʳ seq.
[55] Visita Ad Limina, 364, Gienen.
[56] Visita Ad Limina, 370A, Granaten. I; Linage Conde, *El Monacato* pp. 222 seq.
[57] A.H.N., Inquisición, Libro 1280, fols 641ʳ seq; Libro 1231, fols 608ʳ seq; cf. G. Henningsen, *The Witches' Advocate. Basque Witchcraft and the Spanish Inquisition*

The heroic search for true asceticism by the discalced Carmelite nuns, or by a few other female houses in Spain, of Poor Clares for example, was thus the more remarkable. Most female convents troubled bishops rather because of a failure to adjust numbers admitted to financial resources, in Spain as elsewhere in the post-Tridentine Church. As elsewhere too there was thus conflict over regulation of numbers and of the entry dowries paid by families for the reception of their daughters as choir-nuns, whether by bishops or otherwise. More admirable then were the bequests of some bishops, as well as other pious persons, for providing such entry dowries as well as marriage dowries for poorer girls. The damagingly bi-focal vision in Counter-Reformation Church and society of female convents as either depositories for the unmarried daughters of the respectable classes to live in conspicuous virtue or religious houses of prayer and penance was therefore as present in Spain as anywhere else. But a more positive social contribution was made by some female foundations, at Valladolid for example, which managed not only schooling for girls or care for noble ladies separated by family discord or governmental service from their husbands, but also more Counter-Reformation initiatives in the care of reformed prostitutes, or those deemed due for reform, and of orphan and other girls in danger of being forced into such a way of life. Few of these institutions suffered the problems encountered by those charged at Valencia, as a result of discordant royal and archiepiscopal policies with regard to Morisco children retained at the expulsion, with the education as Catholic servants of unruly and consciously non-Christian girls.[58] Elsewhere the general problem was rather that of episcopal responsibility, by Tridentine standards, for the regularisation and enclosure of all female communities, of whatever origin and purpose, as for the supervision of charitable work and auditing of charitable funds, in the face of royal determination to preserve local independence of lay action and central oversight by the crown and its councils and tribunals. If 'regularisation' was, in different senses, a preoccupation of both the post-Tridentine Church hierarchy and the Castilian monarchy within the Iberian kingdoms, it was the episcopate in post-

---

(1609–1614) (Reno, Nevada 1980); cf. L. Kolakowski, *Chrétiens sans Eglise* (Paris 1969) p. 498.

[58] Visita Ad Limina 848A, Valentin. I; cf. A.C.A., C. Aragon, Leg. 594 [9/2]; B.N.M., MS 6148, fols 24ʳ *seq*; cf. A.G.S., Patronato Real, Leg. 22 [22–1].

Conciliar Spain which attempted, in line with episcopal attempts elsewhere then and later, as in seventeenth- and eighteenth-century Italy for example, to regulate hermits and hermitages. If such attempts had only imperfect success, the campaign in Spain, with regard to female hermits, was a natural extension of the ambitions to supervise the *beatas*. Such an issue was also of course related to the post-Tridentine episcopal campaign in Spain to limit female participation in nocturnal vigils or processions, where these were not wholly prohibited, and to segregate congregations by sex in parish churches, even if fore and aft within the nave, so that males could not see females unless by turning their back to the alter, rather than left and right as by Borromean regimentation.[59] The repetition of Spanish episcopal regulations for hermitages or popular processions and other devotions in the post-Tridentine era is however a reminder of the persistence of popular initiatives in even the Iberian Counter-Reformation, never susceptible to perfect control of religious expression, despite the systematic ordering of the formal religious life by the Church hierarchy and the divergent royal priorities of securing national organisation and Castilian direction among the regulars of the peninsula. The varieties of religious experience escaped the regulatory mechanism of even Philip II, and by the reign of Philip III the combined forces of mendicant conservatism, archiepiscopal authority of an unusual degree within Spain inherited from Archbishop Ribera, royal, conciliar and vice-regal power, and even Inquisitorial intervention were defeated at Valencia by popular determination, among local secular clerics and laity of the diocese and province, to establish and promote the cult of an unofficial and unrecognised saint.[60] Diversity, if not individuality, was still possible.

University of Leeds

---

[59] Linage Conde, *El Monacato* pp. 513 *seq.* Cf. W.A. Christian, *Local Religion in Sixteenth-Century Spain* (Princeton 1981); B.N.M. MS 5788; cf. MS 13019, fols 9ʳ *seq*; cf. A.H.N., Inquisición, Leg. 4511.

[60] Visita Ad Limina, 848A, Valentin. I; cf. A.H.N., Inquisición, Libro 1280, fols 646ʳ *seq.*

THE ASCETIC TRADITION AND THE ENGLISH COLLEGE AT VALLADOLID

by MICHAEL E. WILLIAMS

THE history of English Roman Catholicism from the end of the sixteenth century right through to the nineteenth has as one of its main features the rivalries between seculars and regulars, especially between the seculars and the Jesuits. As this dispute primarily, but not exclusively, concerns the clergy it is most clearly seen in the history of those colleges which provided clergy for the English mission. The early history of the English College in Rome is not only the story of English and Welsh rivalry, but of frequent objections to the Jesuit administration and accusations by the seculars of the enticement of students to join the Society. Similar cases are to be found in the history of Saint Alban's College Valladolid, but in this college there is an added dimension. Not only did the seculars complain about the Jesuits but the Jesuits complained of students being enticed away to the Benedictines. Later, a certain amount of bitterness arose out of the establishment of a college directed by the seculars in Lisbon. The Jesuits considered that they should have been placed in charge. What is more, there were even quarrels among the catholics detained in Wisbech castle. The 'stirs' there bore a remarkable resemblance to those at the college in Rome.[1] As Aveling remarks about English Roman Catholicism 'Historians have been defeated by its immense complexities of ecclesiastical intrigue and embarrassed by its sheer ferocity'.[2] The quarrels not only provoke a feeling of distaste in the modern mind – why couldn't these people resolve their differences and get on with their spiritual mission? They also instil puzzlement – are these disputes to be explained solely as political intrigue and in-fighting within the Catholic party? If so, how could such a cause appear attractive or plausible? How could such a house divided

---

[1] T.G. Law, *A Historical Sketch of conflicts between Jesuits and Seculars in the reign of Queen Elizabeth* (London 1889).

[2] J.H. Aveling, *The Handle and the Axe* (London 1976) p. 68.

against itself, stand? I want to suggest that there is an element often overlooked which, although not explaining fully these intrigues and dissensions, nevertheless might help us to understand better what was going on. This can be called the positive attraction of the ascetic ideal. Bossy has stated in reference to the history of the English Catholic community 'martyrology pointed this subject historiographically speaking up a cul-de-sac'.[3] I want to suggest that cul-de-sac or no, the consideration of martyrdom and of life as a preparation for martyrdom is a path that can lead to a vantage point from which one can view this clerical back biting and contentiousness in a clearer light. Evenett in his Birbeck Lectures in 1951[4] pleaded for a better integration of the history of spirituality into ecclesiastical history and in particular devoted some space to a consideration of the origins of the Catholic revival in Spain. He pointed out the overlap of those who abandoned the world with those who remained in it, reforming its practice. Speaking of the Carthusians of the sixteenth century he said 'A larger interest and practical usefulness in the external affairs of the Church were manifest by them at this period than we are accustomed to associate with modern Parkminster or Miraflores'. Following these lines let us turn to certain aspects of Spanish spirituality and its relationship to England.

In the lower corridor of the English College of Saint Alban, Valladolid, among all the other portraits of former students who were martyrs, of rectors, of other notables, hang two of a different sort. All save these are clerical, male, English. These are two Spanish ladies, Doña Luisa de Carvajal and Doña Marina de Escobar. Both these women were attracted to an ascetical life and both found fulfilment of their vocation by identification with their persecuted co-religionists in England.

Among the devout Spanish catholics of Valladolid shortly after the foundation of the English College there, was Doña Luisa de Carvajal y Mendoza.[5] She was one of the rich and pious ladies who

---

[3] J. Bossy, *The English Catholic Community 1570–1850* (London 1975) p. 3.
[4] H.O. Evenett, *The Spirit of the Counter Reformation* (Cambridge 1968).
[5] There were several contemporary lives of Doña Luisa, the best known being El Licenciado Luiz Muñoz, *Vida y Virtudes de la Venerabile Virgen Doña Luisa de Carvajal y Mendoza, su jornada a Inglaterra, y successos en aquel reyno*. Based on this is a life in English; Lady Georgina Fullerton, *The Life of Luisa de Carvajal* (London 1873). The most modern treatment is Camilo M Abad, *Una Misionera Española en la Inglaterra de Siglo XVII* (Comillas 1966).

undertook to dress the 'Vulnerata', an image of Our Lady mutilated by English sailors in the sack of Cadiz in 1596 and now venerated in the College. Her devotion to the image was associated with a regard for the former English College students who had suffered for their religion in England. She had read of the martyrdom of Edmund Campion in a letter she had received from a relative, the former Spanish ambassador in London. But she was most affected by the account of the life and death of Henry Walpole who had been on the staff at Saint Alban's for a short time. This work had been translated into Spanish. Her confessor was a Jesuit and she was introduced to the English fathers at the College and took up residence in a little house nearby, supporting the work of the seminary by her prayers. Like many of her contemporaries harrowing details of torture and death only inspired her the more and she conceived a great desire for a more active support. She decided to travel to England and offer her services to former students who were now missionaries in their native land. After the signing of the treaty between England and Spain she took what remained of her fortune and in 1605 set out for England. She studiously avoided the Spanish colony in London but she found that English Catholics were suspicious of her and afraid of receiving an unknown Spanish woman into their homes. Eventually at the request of her family in Spain she was traced by the ambassador and persuaded to lodge in the embassy itself from where she would be free to visit English Catholics in prison and in need of help. After the Gunpowder Plot scare had died down she was able to rent a house of her own, where she used to entertain. She was a Spanish subject and so there was no question of her being put to death but on several occasions she was in danger of being deported. She addressed the crowd in Cheapside, defending the Catholic faith and trying to convert the tradespeople from heresy. She was arrested and taken before the justices of the peace. Her long black dress and rather plain features led some to believe that she was a man – a priest in disguise – and she was committed to prison. She was eventually released because Cecil was anxious not to offend the Spaniards at this time. She returned to her house and her good works of assisting needy Catholics, supplying them with spiritual reading and encouraging young men and women who thought they might have a vocation for the religious life, by putting them in touch with religious houses on the continent. At Spitalfields she established a small religious community devoted to prayer and almsdeeds. She was again arrested and imprisoned. Once more she was released by the good offices of the ambassador, but this time she was compelled to reside in the embassy and negotiations began to get her back to Spain. She fell ill and died aged forty-eight in 1614. She had spent nine years in England. Her body was taken back to Spain by sea and she left behind a reputation for sanctity; miracles were claimed as a result of her intercession. The cause of her beatification was opened.

Doña Marina de Escobar[6] the other lady, was a native of Valladolid. She too learnt of the troubles of the Catholics in England through her Jesuit confessor, Luis de la Puente, who was resident at San Ambrosio, the Jesuit College where the English students attended lectures. Unlike Luisa she never went to England but she enjoyed visions and mystical experiences. She wrote these down and they were incorporated in a *Life* written by Luis de la Puente. We read there that she had a special place in her heart for English Catholics and she assisted them by prayer and the collection of alms. Among her visions in the 1620s was one of her visiting England where she saw a house full of Catholics with the doors firmly bolted. They were debating among themselves whether to leave their lands and farms and make their way abroad to a Catholic country. There was a knock on the door which immediately caused them to utter sad cries. They did not realise that it was the angels who were knocking. When they opened the door, the room up to now dark and gloomy was flooded with light. They were filled with joy and wished to be crucified along with Christ by the wicked King and the heretics. The vision expresses the idea that the knock of the pursuivants on the door is really an angelic visitation. Persecution, arrest, suffering and death are akin to a spiritual and mystical enlightenment.

These are more than just two pious stories. I wish to call attention first to the fact that both Luisa and Marina were directed by Jesuits. It has been said recently 'The Jesuits, who consciously rejected the ascetic tradition of medieval monasticism in favour of Erasmian moderation, were even more critical than the secular

[6] Luis de la Puente, *Vida Maravillosa de la Venerable Virgen Doña Marina de Escobar* (Madrid 1665).

priests of pre-reformation practices.'[7] Such a statement is open to misunderstanding since it does not do justice to what was happening in the order from the 1560s onwards. The new clerks regular that arose in the sixteenth century and of whom the Jesuits are the best known today, certainly abandoned some of the practices of the monastic life, the seclusion, the distinctive dress, the daily office in choir. Nevertheless the ascetic ideal was never far away. Ignatius himself was an ascetic and a visionary, he was influenced by the Benedictines at Montserrat. Unless he had appealed to the current christian desire for a more mortified life in the following of Christ he would never have gained such wide support. But the difficulty lay in combining an active apostolate with an intense inner life of contemplation. All the clerks regular were from time to time faced with the problem of restraining their more eager men from joining contemplative orders such as the Carthusians. This was not a hankering for the old corrupt monasticism but rather a feeling that only an institution on monastic lines was able to preserve the ascetic ideal. The clerks regular had to combat a lack of confidence in the new form of religious life that they were now proclaiming. If it had been simply an active life quite distinct from the old monastic ideal there would have been no trouble at all. In the 1560s there manifested itself among the Jesuits in Spain a movement towards an eremitical flight from the world[8] and although this was resisted in its more extreme form, nevertheless the ideal of contemplation was not abandoned. It was seen as a necessary concomitant to apostolic activity. One should note that Baltasar Alvarez, the mentor of Luis de la Puente was closely connected with Teresa of Jesus and her reform of Carmel. It is this aspect of the order that one sees in the spiritual direction given to Luisa and Marina.

As far as England is concerned, Persons in his *Memorial* for the future state of England found no place for a restored monasticism. But this is not to be interpreted as a rejection of the monastic ideal. Rather it is a case of purging out the old leaven and introducing a new, more suitable for the changed conditions: namely, the Jesuit

---

[7] A. Dures, *English Catholicism 1558–1642* (London 1983) p. 62.

[8] I. Iparraguirre, *Historia de la practica de los ejercicios espirituales de San Ignacio* (Roma 1958) pp. 474–494; M. Nicolau 'Espiritualidad de la Compañia de Jesus en la España del siglo XVI' in *Corrientes Espirituales en la España del siglo XVI* (Barcelona 1963) pp. 341–361.

combination of contemplation and action. One sometimes forgets that Persons was a spiritual writer, not just a polemicist and politician. Allen and he worked closely together in a common ideal in the founding of Douai College. We should remember that it was the students in Rome who petitioned for Jesuit superiors.[9] Moreover the ease with which Persons assembled a college in Valladolid from disparate students testifies to an attractive positive ideal not found in any other quarter. Even the 'stirs' in Wisbech jail were due in part to the desire of William Weston to organise and promote a deeper spiritual life among the inmates and make the place of detention into a sort of religious house.[10]

In 1599 and again in 1603 there were several cases of students leaving the Jesuit administered College at Valladolid and seeking admittance to the Benedictines.[11] This was a further example of a trend that had been in existence for many years. When one has taken account of the natural rivalries between religious congregations, the almost inevitable student dissatisfaction with their masters, there remains the positive religious motivation. Some felt that the Jesuits were not demanding enough, that the original ideal that had inspired these young men to leave their country and study for the priesthood was better safeguarded by the Rule of Saint Benedict. These 'defectors' were not renouncing the mission to England.[12] Augustine of Canterbury and Gregory of Rome, apostles of England were men of action, but also monks. They wished to follow in their footsteps. The monastery in Valladolid to which they fled, San Benito, had had an interesting history.[13] Originally a foundation of strict observance it had recently been providing

---

[9] 'We ask not for freedom but for discipline' [M.A.] Tierney [ed, C. Dodd, *Church History of England* 5 vols (London 1839–43)] 2 p. cccxlviii.

[10] At the end of his life Weston became the first English rector of Saint Alban's College Valladolid. For the rules adopted at Wisbech under Weston see Tierney 3 CAP. 4.

[11] D. LUNN *The English Benedictines 1540–1688* (London 1980) pp. 19–23, 57–61.

[12] The missionary oath first prescribed in the English College Rome and later extended to other colleges, originally obliged students to take orders when called to them and return to work in England. In 1624, forty five years later, the oath was altered to include a ban on joining a religious order or becoming a professed religious until five years after leaving the college. But membership of a religious order did not necessarily exclude a return to England.

[13] Luis Rodriguez Martinez *Historia del Monasterio de San Benito El Real de Valladolid* (Valladolid 1981).

missionaries for the Americas. The Spanish prior understood the English students' desire for a 'mixed' life and they were admitted, pending the future establishment of an English house of their own. But Persons also understood the problem. He wrote from Rome to Creswell in Spain in these words:

> My good father *quid mihi est in coelo vel ab hoc quid aliud volo super terram* for all our labours for these youths, but only *ut fiat de eis voluntas Dei*. If God Almighty will have them priests that is our first end: to make them good priests for England. If he will have them religious men of what order soever within his church *hoc etiam deputabimus in lucrum*. That he calleth them to a state of more perfection so they go orderly and godly to so high a vocation.[14]

As the Jesuits later admitted when the trouble had died down, it was their best men that had joined the Benedictines and so they took steps to stop the drain by providing a novitiate of their own.

Luisa and Marina not only provide a link between the Jesuits and the ascetic ideal, they also bring together asceticism and martyrdom. The attitude of these ladies to martyrdom is very similar to that of their English coreligionists. Clancy[15] remarks 'The desire of martyrdom among the English Catholics has puzzled succeeding generations of historians. It is only possible to appreciate the part it played in the mystique of the missionaries if we put it in the context of the Counter Reformation as a whole.' Diego de Yepes, a Hieronimite monk, confessor to the King of Spain and later a bishop, wrote in Spanish a history of the persecution in England.[16] It is generally thought that he gained most of his information from the English Jesuit Father Creswell. But there are parts of the history that are very much Yepes' own where he witnesses to a fairly commonly held view of persecution and martyrdom.[17] In Book Three he sets out to explain some of the reasons why God allows persecutions and he reminds the reader that God promises tribulation to the just, quoting Job 'Blessed is the man whom God

[14] Archives of English College Valladolid Serie II Legajo 1.
[15] T.H. Clancy *Papist Pamphleteers* (Chicago 1964) p. 140.
[16] Diego de Yepes *Historia de la Persecucion de Inglaterra* (Madrid 1599).
[17] Yepes views are shared by Pedro de Ribadeneira *Historia Ecclesiastica del Schisma* (Madrid 1588).

chastises'. One cannot enjoy eternal goods except through the
death of the body, neither can we possess them in the next life
without suffering deprivation of them in this. Martyrdom is seen as
a sort of asceticism. A theology of the cross links the martyrs in the
Church with the hermits and ascetics, both witness to the same
love. '*Este amor en la primitiva iglesia llevó a los desiertos de Siria y de
Egypto los Pablos, los Antonios, los Hilariones*'. In the early church
this love led out into the deserts of Syria and Egypt the Pauls, the
Antonys and the Hilarions. But martyrdom has its degrees and
there are various possible situations that lead to it. There is firstly
the threat of a violent death if one does not renounce the faith.
Secondly there is a threat of death, but this is accompanied by the
promise of reward if one apostasises. This is a greater test than the
first since a free choice has to be made. Pedro de Ribadeneira[18]
judges that for this reason a more perfect form of martyrdom is to
be found in England than in those countries like Holland and
France where people are killed simply for being Catholics. But
there is a still greater test and this occurs where not only promises
of reward are made but also one is exposed to arguments that seem
to suggest that the most reasonable course of action is to renounce
the faith. This element of choice indicates that Yepes and others did
not see martyrdom as simply an unavoidable accident. It demanded
fortitude and patience, virtues to be found in those who follow the
path of asceticism. The preparation of the mind and the will for
martyrdom was one of the tasks of those who were spiritual
directors. The Jesuits had already elaborated a rule of life combining activity in the world with a life of prayer and this was
eminently suitable for preparing those who were to live in conditions of persecution. Meyer alluded to this:

> But the end which these exercises held up to those who were
> going to be priests in England was something far higher than
> that which most men aimed at by this means. For them these
> Spiritual Exercises were not merely an occasion for deepening
> the spiritual life, they were a conscious preparation for
> martyrdom.[19]

[18] *Ibid* Liber III cap XXX.
[19] A.O. Meyer *England and the Catholic Church under Queen Elizabeth*. (London 1916)
pp. 108–109.

Delumeau notes the same motivation in the Jesuit missionaries to the New World.[20] In this period, the end of the sixteenth century and the early years of the seventeenth, English Catholics were distinguished from others, including other Catholics, by their vocation to suffer, to lead a life involving a *contemptus mundi*. This was a truly blessed state. It was this rather than particular religious practices, fasts, prayers and the like that gave them their special status.

Such a high calling, to be persecuted and be killed, like the call to the eremitical life, was not easily responded to by everybody. As time went on the possibility of easier conditions, toleration, compromise weakened its appeal and its necessity. This was not an easy calling for the clergy either. Something of the opposition to it can be seen in the history of the seminaries and the 'stirs' at Wisbech. To a non-Jesuit the way of life and spiritual direction in the colleges administered by the Society would appear to be unduly harsh, especially if one were not absolutely convinced that one's destiny on reaching England was indeed to be persecution and violent death.

Trinity and All Saints' College, Leeds

---

[20] J. Delumeau. *Catholicism between Luther and Voltaire* (London 1977) p. 46. 'The thirst for mortification, this rejection of the world and nature, were essential if the unbelievable tortures to which certain missioners were subjected were to be endured.'

PURITAN ASCETICISM AND THE
TYPE OF SACRIFICE

by SUSAN HARDMAN

T HE sacrificial rites of the Old Testament are 'neither dark nor dumb, but mystical and significant, and fit to stir up the dull mind of man to the remembrance of his duty before God.' So preached a nonconformist, Samuel Mather, in the 1660s, recalling with a deliberate or unconscious twist a phrase used in the Book of Common Prayer to defend contemporary rites of which he disapproved.[1] The Reformation that set aside the ascetic ideal of monasticism also saw a revaluation of the place of sacrifice in the life of the Church. While its role in Protestant activity was diminished by the rejection of the Mass as a propitiatory act, teaching about the priesthood of all believers prepared for a new emphasis on the devotion and duty of Christians as 'spiritual sacrifice'; an emphasis informed in puritanism by lessons from the types of the Old Testament. Much is known about puritan religious practice;[2] and of puritan interest in typology, stimulated by Calvin's conviction of the unity of the Old and New Testaments – the same covenant present in each, accommodated to the capacity of a 'Church under age' in Israel.[3] But familiar themes combined can give fresh perspectives: here their combination illustrates one of the ways in which the ascetic ideal was being reformulated

---

[1] [S.] Mather [The] Figures [or Types of the Old Testament (first published Dublin 1683, 1705 edition repr. New York 1969)]; 'On Ceremonies', Book of Common Prayer. (Punctuation and spelling have been modernised except in book titles; capitalisation modernised throughout.)

[2] See, for example, [P.] Collinson [The] Religion of Protestants[: the Church in English Society 1559–1625] (Oxford 1982); [G.S.] Wakefield Puritan Devotion (London 1957).

[3] Among recent studies are S. Bercovitch ed Typology and Early American Literature (Amherst, Massachusetts 1972) which includes an extensive bibliography of typological literature in all periods; B.K. Lewalski Protestant Poetics and the Seventeenth Century Religious Lyric (Princeton 1979); C.M. Polizzotto 'Types and Typology: A Study in Puritan Hermeneutics' (University of London Ph.D. thesis 1975).

among protestants of the third and fourth generation in seventeenth-century England. Sacrifice was not often a dominant theme in their description of the Christian life, and yet, despite an untidiness of evidence, it is clear that certain allusions to Israelite sacrifice were conventional, part of a common rhetoric, a common and powerful imagery. Some representative examples of the conventions follow, organised around simple questions. What were 'spiritual sacrifices' and what practical exercises of devotion and discipline were associated with them? By what means and in what manner should they be offered?

Before going further it might be helpful to introduce the writers whose views will be cited. All were ministers who have been described in some context as puritan, although they well illustrate the varied outward manifestations of puritanism by, for example, their differing responses to issues of church government. Lake has astutely suggested that puritanism is best defined in terms of an 'internal spiritual dynamic... that forced the believer to externalise his own sense of election through a campaign of works... against Antichrist, the flesh, sin and the world.'[4] These men are brought together here by a willingness to offer encouragement and guidance towards that end, in writings which show both a concern for 'practical divinity' and a belief in the instructive value of the Israelite cult for the Christian. They include such expositors of typology as William Gouge (1578–1653), whose commentary on Hebrews was the fruit of almost a thousand sermons preached over thirty years at the Wednesday lecture at Blackfriars, London; and Samuel Mather (1626–1691), already mentioned, a Dublin Congregationalist raised in New England whose sermon series of the 1660s on typology was influential on both sides of the Atlantic.[5] Many are among the 'Affectionate Practical English writers' Richard Baxter recommended in A Christian Directory for a 'A Poor Mans Library':[6] Gouge and another commentator on types, the London minister Thomas Taylor (1576–1633); Lewis Bayly (d. 1631), Bishop of Bangor; Jeremiah Burroughes (1599–1646), suspended

---

[4] P. Lake Moderate Puritans and the Elizabethan Church (Cambridge 1982) p. 282.
[5] [W.] Gouge [A Learned and Very Useful Commentary on the Whole Epistle to the] Hebrews (London 1655) preface; Mather Figures.
[6] [R.] Baxter [A] Christian Directory (2 ed London 1678) p. 194 (Book 3 question 174).

for nonconformity by Wren and later one of the few Congregationalists in the Westminster Assembly; the Essex ministers Richard Rogers (1550?–1618) of Wethersfield and Jeremiah Dyke (d. 1620) of Epping; Henry Scudder (d. 1659?) of Collingbourne Ducis, Wiltshire, and his brother-in-law William Whately (1583–1639) of Banbury. The sermons of notable puritan preachers Thomas Adams of London (fl. 1612–23) and Samuel Ward of Ipswich (1577–1640) have provided samples of sacrificial rhetoric; as have some parliamentary sermons of the 1640s.[7]

Christian tradition has long identified worship, and particularly prayer, as spiritual sacrifice. William Gouge offered a well-worn argument when he claimed that as sacrifice was divinely instituted as the form of due worship in Israel so 'the general equity of performing due worship to God doth still and ever shall remain in force': 'prayer, singing of psalms, reading, preaching, hearing the Word and celebrating the Sacraments... are as sacrifices of bullocks and calves, goats and kids, sheep and lambs, turtles, pigeons and sparrows; and all manner of meat and drink offerings.'[8] How rigorously was this applied to details of devotional practice?

Sabbath worship was rarely discussed with reference to sacrifice – a Sabbath offering is mentioned only once in the Pentateuch.[9] Daily prayer, shadowed by burnt offerings and incense presented each day in the Temple, received far more attention. Paul Baynes (d. 1617) who preached in William Perkins' place at Cambridge after Perkins' death, interpreted Paul's injunction 'Pray always' in light of cultic practice, deriving the custom of morning and evening prayer from Scriptural typology not tradition: 'That we are said to do continually which we... do at fit times daily, as Numb. 28, that was a continual sacrifice which was daily offered, morning and evening.'[10] The principle of daily sacrifice applied not

---

[7] Biographical sketches of all those mentioned appear in *DNB* or in R.L. Greaves and R. Zaller edd *A Biographical Dictionary of British Radicals in the Seventeenth Century* 3 vols (Brighton 1981–4).

[8] [W.] Gouge [*The*] *Saints Sacrifice* (London 1632) p. 243. Similar references are legion.

[9] Numbers 9:9–10.

[10] P. Baynes *The Spirituall Armour* (London 1620) p. 293; also, for example, [W.] Hinde [*A Faithful Remonstrance of the Holy Life and Happy Death of John*] *Bruen* (London 1641) pp. 73–4; [R.] Rogers *Seven Treatises* (London 1603) p. 321; [T.] Taylor *Christ Revealed*[*: Or the Old Testament Explained* (London 1635)] p. 149. See Exodus 29:38–42, 30:7–8; Numbers 28:1–8.

only to individuals in private but to households, each regarded as a
'little Church'. Thomas Wilson (1563–1622), Rector of Saint
George the Martyr, Canterbury, and associate of William Gouge,
told the puritan patron Sir Robert Harley 'I need not commend
unto you, one approved in Christ yourself, that your house should
be a Church for doctrine and discipline, that there should be
morning and evening sacrifice day by day continually...'.[11] Gouge
himself, using the notion of the threefold office of Christ, described
the householder as in the home a lord to govern, a prophet to teach,
and 'a priest to offer up the sacrifice of prayer'.[12]

Daily worship in Israel was supplemented by 'extraordinary'
recourse to God on special occasions and in times of crisis or
rejoicing. Some feasts required extraordinary sacrifices; and sacrifice might mark a public or private fast or formal thanksgiving,
offered for national or personal causes. All this was taken up as a
model for the common godly practice of holding individual and
communal days of fasting or thanksgiving.[13] Edmund Calamy
(1600–1666), Rector of St. Mary Aldermanbury, London, declared
with pleasure of the Long Parliament's programme of worship, and
the extension of fast-day preaching into the country:

> We have... our New Moon Fasts, in which the Word is
> preached, trading ceaseth, and sacrifices of prayer, praises and
> alms are tendered up to God in the name of Jesus Christ. We
> have our Feast of Trumpets, in which our godly ministers
> throughout the whole kingdom lift up their voices as a
> trumpet, and all the whole day, are either the mouth of the

---

[11] Letter of 19 May 1636, BL MS Loan 29/172 fol 105, cited by kind permission of
Lady Anne Bentinck; also S. Clarke *A Collection of the Lives of Ten Eminent Divines*
(London 1662) pp. 7, 450; [S.] Marshall [A] *Peace Offering [to God]* (London 1641)
pp. 49–50; [T.] Worden [*The] Types Unvailed]or the Gospel pick't out of the Legal
Ceremonies]* (London 1664) p. 310.

[12] W. Gouge *The Whole Armour of God* (London 1619) p. 437; also Rogers *Seven
Treatises* p. 397.

[13] Numbers 28–9, Judges 20:26, 2 Samuel 24:25, 2 Chronicles 15:11, Leviticus 3,
7:11–18, Psalm 116:17, Mather *Figures* pp. 191, 194–5. For sacrifices of thanksgiving as antitypes of Israelite peace offerings and their prominence in New
Testament teaching on spiritual sacrifice, see J. Burroughes *Sions Joy* (London
1641) p. 1; Marshall *Peace Offering* p. 24; [J.] Owen [*Exercitations on the Epistle to
the*] *Hebrews* 4 vols (London 1668–84) 4, on Hebrews 13:15.

people to God, or God's mouth to the people, showing unto England their sins... and calling them unto humiliation, and reformation.

Henry Scudder identified the Day of Atonement, 'the solemn day of the fast' as the shadow of all religious fasts. Thomas Taylor concluded from the High Priest's duties on the Day of Atonement that every Christian as a priest must 'every year set apart a day of expiation, to make an atonement for himself, for his house, for all the people... a day of humiliation in serious fasting and prayer.'[14] Taylor illustrates the case that it was not unusual for writers to refer to Israelite rites of expiation as types of penitential or petitionary prayer, without intending to subvert the crucial significance of the rites as types of Christ's redemptive work.

Such 'extraordinary' occasions could be fired by other devotional exercises. Samuel Ward's Thanksgiving Day sermon 'A Peace Offering' encouraged his hearers to offer sacrifices of thanksgiving. When printed it included as an appendix 'A thankfull Mans Calender'; an autobiography in outline suggesting aspects of readers' lives which might provide cause for prayerful gratitude. In the record of God's providences towards him kept by the Cheshire layman John Bruen (1560–1625), something of Ward's principle was at work: after each mercy or judgement noted, Bruen added a phrase such as *Laus Deo*. John Beadle (d. 1667), an Essex clergyman, devoted a tract to persuading readers of the value of keeping an account of providences. In its preface the book was described as wood, as fuel, for a sacrifice of thanksgiving. Although autobiography and records of providences are often regarded as ways in which individuals charted spiritual progress, looking for evidence of election, it seems they also acted as a spur to this duty.[15] Stephen Marshall (1594?–1655) went further, arguing that the 'soul thankfulness' which was an essential part of a 'whole peace-offering'

---

[14] E. Calamy *Gods Free Mercy to England* (London 1642) p. 140; H. Scudder *The Christians Daily Walke in Holy Securitie and Peace* (6 ed London 1635) pp. 37–8; Taylor *Christ Revealed* pp. 149–50.

[15] [S.] Ward] *A Collection of such] Sermons [and Treatises as have been written and published by Mr. Samuel Ward] (London 1627), '[A] Peace Offering [to God]' pp. 48–53*; Hinde *Bruen* pp. 145–8; J. Beadle *The Journal or Diary of a Thankful Christian* (London 1656); also Baxter *Christian Directory* p. 141 and N. Keeble *Richard Baxter: Man of Letters* (Oxford 1982) pp. 139–43.

could be aided by means of which keeping a record was but one:

> thankful hearts have found so much good in remembering of
> God's mercies that they have been careful to... set up monu-
> ments to help their memory, indited Psalms to bring to
> remembrance, gave names to places where mercies were
> received, new names to times when they were received, write
> the names of their deliverance upon their children, that the
> sight of them might quicken their memories and thoughts.[16]

The connection between vows and sacrifice in Israel led to the
association of Christian vows with extraordinary spiritual sacrifice.
Joseph Caryl (1602–1673), preacher to Parliament and member of
the Westminster Assembly, described the relationship of vows,
petition, and praise thus: 'praise is the payment of vows... praying
days are vowing days and praising days are vow performing days...
vows are the dedication of our mercies to God before we receive
them, and praise is the dedication of our mercies to God after we
have received them.'[17]

'Spiritual sacrifice', of course, was not restricted in puritan
thought to acts in the sphere of worship. The injunction 'to do
good, and to communicate, forget not: for with such sacrifices God
is well pleased' led to the inclusion of almsgiving and 'works of
mercy and love' in enumerations of 'gospel sacrifices'.[18] Most
pervasive, however, and more fundamental, were ideas derived
from Paul's plea (Romans 12: 1) that Christians offer themselves as
a 'living sacrifice'; and from the Old Testament spiritualisation of
sacrifice, the 'sacrifice of a broken and contrite heart' (Psalm 51:
16–17), which drew attention to the importance of sincere devotion
accompanying outward act.

The notion of living sacrifice gave 'every act and duty of faith'
the potential to be sacrificial. Sometimes the phrase was equated
with 'gospel obedience' in imitation of Christ. More commonly it

---

[16] Marshall *Peace Offering* pp. 32–3.
[17] Leviticus 7: 16, 22: 21, 27:2, 9–13; Numbers 15:3, Psalms 56: 12, 66: 13–15, 116:
17–18; J. Caryl *The Saints Thankfull Acclamation* (London 1644) p. 12; see Gouge
Saints Sacrifice pp. 247–50.
[18] Hebrews 13:16 (AV), which appeared in the Book of Common Prayer as part of
the exhortation to give to the poor (see also Philippians 4:18, Ecclesiastes 35:3);
[T.] Adams [*The*] *Workes* [*of Thomas Adams*] (London 1620) pp. 91, 988. A
common reference.

was linked with the Pauline theme of Christians' incorporation in Christ's death (Romans 6: 6), Christian 'mortification'. Thus John Owen (1616–83) referred to living sacrifice as 'self-slaughter, crucifying the old man, killing sin and offering up our souls and bodies... to God.'[19] Typology gave a vivid means of illustrating 'living sacrifice', whether conceived as obedience or mortification. Samuel Ward was graphic and direct in preaching that

> the whole duty of all men is to give themselves wholly to Christ, to sacrifice not a leg or an arm or any other piece but soul spirit and body and all that is within us: the fat, the inwards, the head and hoof, and all as a holocaust to him, dedicating, devoting ourselves to his service all the days and hours of our lives...[20]

At the Lord's Supper, 'living sacrifice', interpreted in accord with Old Testament types, could be used to characterise Christians' renewal of their covenant with Christ in the rite. As the Israelites had renewed the covenant by sacrifice, so must Christians, by 'the covenants of offering themselves a living and acceptable sacrifice, or mortification of their sottish lusts, or an holy and obedient life.'[21]

The sacrifice of the broken heart could also represent mortification: brokenness, repentance and contrition in meditation on the brokenness of Christ in his sacrifice,[22] or in the slaying of 'beastly lusts'.[23] Because of its connotations of repentance it was considered particularly appropriate for a day of humiliation, which should be a

---

[19] J. Owen *The Duty of Pastors and People Distinguished* (London 1644) p. 24. Owen incorporated both emphases in comments on Hebrews 13:15, *Hebrews*.

[20] Ward *Sermons* 'Christ is all in all' p. 35.

[21] [J.] Dyke [A] *Worthy Communicant* (London 1636) p. 542; also [C.] Burges [*The*] *First Sermon* (London 1641) p. 27. This is reminiscent of the Prayer of Oblation after Communion introduced in the Book of Common Prayer, 1552. Examples outside the context of the Lord's Supper: W. Carter *Israels Peace with God* (London 1642) pp. 4–5, 36; Taylor *Christ Revealed* pp. 37–8.

[22] [J.] Burroughes *Gospel Worship* (2 ed London 1653) pp. 67–8, 246–9; [F.] Cornwell [*A Description of the*] *Spirituall Temple* (London 1646) pp. 9–10; F. Roberts *A Broken Spirit Gods Sacrifices* (London 1647) *passim*. Devotion to the passion and 'sacred heart' of Christ should perhaps be noted here: see discussion of its relation to Catholic piety in Wakefield *Puritan Devotion* pp. 94–101, with particular reference to T. Goodwin *The Heart of Christ in Heaven toward Sinners on Earth* (London 1643).

[23] Adams *Workes* p. 90.

'heart-breaking day'.[24] Incense had to be crushed before it could be offered: this was a type of the broken heart. Thomas Wilson urged that prayer should be 'perfumed with a concomitancy of several graces as so many spices and some of it to be broken very small having ever the broken heart, the very sacrifice of God most pleasing to him.'[25] Like living sacrifice this sacrifice informed all particular acts of sacrifice, but bore most closely on purity of intention in offering duties to God. John Preston (1587–1628), for a time chaplain to Prince Charles, alleged that such a sacrifice 'is that which sets a high price upon every sacrifice we offer.'[26] It is not unusual to find on title pages of the period illustrations of the sacrifice of the heart: a heart, sometimes broken, burning on a pile of logs, or a heart-shaped vessel on an altar, issuing incense.[27] These reflect, of course, the much wider Catholic and Protestant emblematic tradition of the *Schola Cordis*.[28] It is worth noting that Henry Burton and William Prynne did not take exception to a sacrificial heart on the title page of John Cosin's *A Collection of Private Devotions*, although they found other parts of the design outrageously popish.[29]

Samuel Mather reverenced the ceremonial law as 'one of the richest cabinets of divinity, full of inestimable jewels.'[30] Mather and other commentators tried to clarify further the nature and proper manner of offering spiritual sacrifice by exploring the minutiae of Israelite ritual. While it will be impossible to do more than hint at the complex identifications put forward, some themes call for comment.

With an intensity that must impress, layer upon layer of typolo-

---

[24] [H.] Wilkinson [*The*] *Gainefull Cost* (London 1644) p. 31.

[25] BL MS Loan 29/172 fol 105; also W. Guild *The New Sacrifice of Christian Incense* (London 1608) p. 11; Mather *Figures* p. 403.

[26] John Preston *The Saints Daily Exercise* (London 1629) p. 124 (a common sentiment).

[27] [L.] Bayly [*The*] *Practice of Pietie* (London 1613); Baxter *Christian Directory*; Ward *Sermons* 'Peace Offering'. Ward sometimes designed his own title pages: *Sermons* 'Christ is all in all' has a complex illustration of types of Christ.

[28] [C.] Harvey *Schola Cordis* (London 1647) pp. 76–9; R. Freeman *English Emblem Books* (London 1948) pp. 134–9, 178–9.

[29] J. Cosin *A Collection of Private Devotions* ed P.G. Stanwood (Oxford 1967) plate 2, p. xxxvi; [H.] Burton *A Tryall [of Private Devotions, Or a Diall for the Houres of Prayer]* (London 1628) sig. C. 1ᵛ; W. Prynne *A Briefe Survay and Censure of Mr. Cozens His Couzening Devotions* (London 1628) p. 4.

[30] Mather *Figures* pp. 197, 61.

gical exegesis showed that Christians and Christian sacrifice were acceptable to God only in and through Christ. Discussion of every aspect of the cult elaborated the theme. Two examples, one familiar, one more obscure, will demonstrate this: the unblemished sacrificial lamb required by ceremonial law represented the perfection of Christ and Christians' purity in him (John Murcot's biographer described him as 'a Copy without blot, and a Lamb without spot');[31] the brazen grate within the altar which allowed ashes to fall through but a 'sweet savour' to ascend prefigured Christ's purging of all imperfection from Christians' sacrifice.[32]

Sacrificial instruments suggested to some writers God-given aids to help Christians offer spiritual sacrifice: again, two illustrations. Psalm 118: 27, 'bind the sacrifice with cords, even unto the horns of the altar', led Edmund Calamy to argue, in recommending the making of spiritual vows at Communion, that 'as the beast was tied to the horns of the altar... so these blessed vows and resolutions are heavenly cords to tie the soul faster to God'.[33] (Here the ideas of renewing the covenant at communion by 'living sacrifice' and the association of vows with spiritual sacrifice are brought together.) Others used the text in a similar way outside the context of communion and with no direct reference to vows as a plea for devotion to Christ, or mortification of 'carnal affections'.[34] Mather, however, usually intent on drawing significance from small detail, interpreted binding with cords as merely 'an action of natural necessity unto such a work as the slaying of a beast.'[35] Sacrificial knives were seen as types of the Word of God, the sword of the Spirit. William Perkins described preaching as 'a sacrificing knife whereby the old Adam must be killed in us... and we made an holy and acceptable sweet smelling oblation...'. This was part of the priestly office a Christian minister should fulfil. Thomas Taylor

[31] [H.] Ainsworth [*Annotations upon*] *Leviticus* (Amsterdam 1618) on Leviticus 1:3 and [*Annotations upon*] *Exodus* (Amsterdam 1617) on Exodus 12:5; J. Murcot *The Several Works of Mr John Murcot* (London 1657) p. 47.

[32] Exodus 27:4. Burroughes *Gospel Worship* pp. 110–11; [W.] Guild *Moses Unvailed* (London 1620) p. 113.

[33] E. Calamy *The Art of Divine Meditation* (London 1680) p. 199.

[34] Adams *Workes* pp. 89, 93–5; Guild *Moses Unvailed* p. 112; [W.] Perkins [*The*] *Works [of... W. Perkins]* 3 vols (London 1612–13), 3 p. 112; Worden *Types Unvailed* pp. 181–7.

[35] Mather *Figures* pp. 104–5.

placed first among a minister's duties that of preparing 'not dead beasts but living Christians' as 'sacrifices to the Lord'.[36]

Precepts and prohibitions hedging the sacrificial rites provided rich sacred analogies to help Christians distinguish true sacrifice from false, and to evaluate their own intent. As Moses was instructed to make the Tabernacle exactly according to God's pattern, so spiritual sacrifice, to be acceptable, must be offered as God required. William Gouge believed 'we were as good to be ignorant of the duty itself, as of the manner of performing it...'.[37]

Spontaneity (within due limits) and sincerity went hand in hand. The offering of sacrifices had been laid down in the Law, 'yet none of them were to be offered against the will, but with a good will: for God loveth a cheerful giver, 2. Cor. 9. 7'.[38] The voluntary nature of sacrifice was a type of Christ, who 'died willingly and offered up himself a sacrifice and a whole burnt offering unto God for us.' Type and antitype were a pattern for the Christian: 'so should we in all our services be a willing people.'[39] Ritually unclean offerings shadowed hypocritical service. A sacrifice of prayer made in empty words without 'further proceeding in obedience' was, according to Richard Rogers, 'all lame and maimed, and as odious to God as the mortlings and untimely first born of the beasts.' Thomas Adams pictured a blemished living sacrifice: 'The drunkard is without a head, the swearer hath a garget in his throat, the covetous hath a lame hand, he cannot give to the poor...'.[40] Sacrifices offered in act alone without inner devotion were condemned as dead and stinking carcasses; as the 'sacrifices of fools' or the wicked; or as a niggardly sacrifice like that of Cain.[41] Such

---

[36] Perkins *Works* 1 p. 221, (see Ephesians 6:17); Taylor *Christ Revealed* p. 147, alluding to Romans 15:16). For more general comment on sacrificial instruments as a type of ministry see Ainsworth *Exodus* on Exodus 27:3.

[37] Gouge *Hebrews* on Hebrews 8:5, section 17; also Wilkinson *Gainefull Cost* p. 31; Mather *Figures* p. 193.

[38] J. Downame *Annotations Upon all the Books of the Old and New Testament* (London 1645) on Leviticus 1:3 (published by order of the Westminster Assembly, compiled by a committee which included Gouge). See also Wilkinson *Gainefull Cost* p. 9; Worden *Types Unvailed* p. 185.

[39] Mather *Figures* p. 197; also Gouge *Saints Sacrifice* p. 245.

[40] Rogers *Seven Treatises* pp. 282–3; Adams *Workes* p. 91 (Malachi 1:14).

[41] Adams *Workes* p. 92; Baxter *Christian Directory* p. 105. Ward *Sermons* 'Peace Offering' p. 7 (Ecclesiastes 5:1–2, Proverbs 15:8). Gouge *Hebrews* on Hebrews 8:5 (section 17); [W.] Whately *Prototypes, or, the Primarie Precedent Presidents out of the Booke of Genesis* (London 1640) pp. 24, 31–2.

hypocrisy might afflict Christians who offered spiritual sacrifice without due preparation of their hearts. Gouge urged his readers: 'Think on duty beforehand, and endeavour to prepare thyself thereto. Sudden, hasty, rash, unprepared enterprising on sacred duty is one occasion of failing in the manner of doing it.' Thomas Adams told his congregation 'all outward works a hypocrite may do, only he fails in the heart... man judgeth the heart by the works; God judgeth the works by the heart.'[42]

The fate of Nadab and Abihu, who offered sacrifice with fire God had not commanded and were consumed by a holy fire of judgement, was a cautionary tale well heeded. Jeremiah Burroughes concluded from it that 'in God's worship there must be nothing rendered up to God but what he hath commanded...'.[43] John Preston thought the incident showed that ordinances must be used with due reverence, instancing God's punishment of contemporary Sabbath breakers; Francis Cornwell, Rector of Marden and a Baptist, found in it an argument against 'set prayer', since 'God is so jealous of his glory that he cannot endure his worship should be corrupted with the least mixture of man.'[44] Samuel Ward discussed many different types of 'false fire' including the 'wild fire' of turbulent enthusiasts, who 'instead of burning bright and shining clear... sparkle and spit at others, or like ill-couched fireworks let fly on all sides.'[45] Yet the necessity of fire to make sacrifice burn with 'a sweet savour unto the Lord'[46] called for comment on the flames with which Christians ought to blaze: heavenly zeal. To William Guild, the cooking of the meat offering demonstrated that 'our worship of God should not be raw or zeal-less'. Cornelius Burges (1589?–1665) identified zeal's opposite as 'that lukewarm temper in distempered Laodicea'; claiming of the true 'holy fire of zeal' 'no acceptable sacrifice can be offered without it, no oblation itself so pleasing to God... yet no one grace so much in disgrace.'[47]

[42] Gouge *Hebrews* on Hebrews 8:5; Adams *Workes* p. 947.
[43] Burroughes *Gospel Worship* pp. 8–9 (Leviticus 10:1–3); also Ainsworth *Leviticus* on Leviticus 10:2.
[44] J. Preston *Remaines* (London 1634) p. 271; Cornwell *Spirituall Temple* p. 50.
[45] Ward *Sermons* 'A Coale [from the Altar to Kindle the Holy Fire of Zeal]' pp. 14, 23, extended discussion pp. 10–26; also Adams *Workes* pp. 91–2; Bayly *Practice of Pietie* pp. 316–17.
[46] As in Genesis 8:21; Leviticus 1:9.
[47] Guild *Moses Unvailed* p. 130; [C.] Burges [The] *Fire of the Sanctuarie* [Newly Uncovered, or a Compleat Tract of Zeal] (London 1625) pp. 10, 1–2.

True zeal was of divine origin, like the fire which ignited Elijah's sacrifice to the confusion of the prophets of Baal.[48]

This interpretation of holy fiery zeal leads to consideration of one last matter: the part played by the typology of sacrifice in discussion of the quest for assurance of God's favour, even of election. According to Jeremiah Dyke, 'when a man in prayer... feels his heart set on fire with fervency of holy affections, this is the fire of the Spirit... that comes down from heaven: a sensible testimony of God's acceptance, thus God turns our sacrifices into ashes ...'. If people found themselves cold in wanting to praise God, William Gouge believed, 'the fire that descends from heaven hath not fallen upon the altar of their heart'.[49] Evidence from fire was evidence from fervent feeling, but the principle of gaining assurance from offering sacrifice was also applied to Christians' practice. William Whately, discussing Isaac's worship as a 'prototype', challenged his readers: 'Would you confirm to your own consciences that you be true Isaacs? Ask yourselves then, do you offer these burnt offerings? If not, you be not as Isaac, children of the promise; if yea, you may assure your souls that you be.'[50]

The material surveyed has proved to be of an exhortatory nature. It wields the sacrificial knife, drawing its audience to sacrifice. The selection of sources reflects the bias of the evidence: allusions occur above all in commentaries, sermons and practical guides to the Christian life; each concerned to press home the 'use' of a text. Surprisingly, sacrificial typology plays little part in the conventions of surviving conversion narratives, funeral sermons and godly biography. Later it found communal expression in the sphere of aspiration through hymnody, in the compositions replacing or supplementing metrical psalms which became acceptable to non-conformists early in the eighteenth century.[51]

The number of characteristic themes of puritan piety which

---

[48] Burton *A Tryall* sig. C. (1 Kings 18:38); also Harvey *Schola Cordis* p. 79; Ward *Sermons* 'A Coale' p. 6 (Leviticus 9:24).

[49] Dyke *Worthy Communicant* p. 133; Gouge *Saints Sacrifice* p. 234; also Burges *Fire of the Sanctuarie* pp. 23–4; Ward *Sermons* 'A Coale' pp. 9–10.

[50] Whately *Prototypes* p. 246; also *ibid* p. 97, 2nd pag. 54; T. Cooper *The Christians Daily Sacrifice* (3 ed London 1615) p. 131.

[51] Early examples can be found in J. Stennett *Hymns in Commemmoration of the Sufferings of ... Jesus Christ* (London 1697). It is not uncommon in the hymns of Watts and Wesley.

derived justification or added conviction from the type of sacrifice is striking. They had vigour, certainly, apart from this type: most often discussed without reference to sacrifice, they could be attached to other types (as mortification was to circumcision). But no other Old Testament type provided such a coherent paradigm for Christian devotion and duty; naturally enough, given its place in Israelite religion. Even though the prophetic critique of sacrifice found favour (like the Israelite prophets, these writers knew 'formal religion' and feared God's judgement for it) the 'mystical significance' of the cult as a shadow of life under the new covenant was not to be surrendered. Perhaps this was for reasons beside the demands of Calvinist exegesis. Conventional applications of the type defined and reinforced the well-channelled, orderly, 'freedom' characteristic of much voluntary religion in the period; described elsewhere as 'secondary voluntarism'.[52] Prescribed duties were to be performed in a prescribed manner, yet with a willing, zealous, spirit.

It is ironic that those most disinclined to 'dig Moses out of his grave' – rejecting, for example, the surplice as not only popish but properly belonging to superceded type of the sacrificing priest – could be accused of a 'judaizing puritanism'.[53] Yet through the curiosity and particularity of their interest in the Old Testament is expressed something of the nature of 'voluntary religion', that desire to be 'more than a statute protestant'[54] which lay at the heart of the puritan ascetic ideal.[55]

University of Durham

---

[52] Collinson *Religion of Protestants* pp. 250–2.
[53] Mather *Figures* p. 277; Burges *First Sermon* p. 75.
[54] H. Smith *Jacobs Ladder, Or the High Way to Heaven* (London 1595) sig. C. 3.
[55] I am grateful to Professor P. Collinson and Dr G.F. Nuttall for their comments on an earlier version of this paper.

JOSEPH BINGHAM AND ASCETICISM

by L.W. BARNARD

J OSEPH Bingham (1668–1723) was one of the greatest patristic scholars to have adorned the English Church in its long and chequered history. Born in 1668 at Wakefield he was educated at Queen Elizabeth Grammar School, then at the height of its influence.[1] On 26 May 1684 Bingham entered University College, Oxford where his zeal for persevering study found ample fulfilment in the study of the Church Fathers in their original languages. Bingham was a born student and his ability was soon recognised by his election to a fellowship of his College on 1 July 1689. In June 1691 he became a tutor and one of his first pupils was John Potter who later became archbishop of Canterbury.[2] Bingham's Oxford career now seemed set fair. However the University was, at this period, agitated by the Trinitarian controversy[3] and it was Bingham's fate to become embroiled in this. It cost him his fellowship and brought about his departure, at an early age, from the city and the University which he loved.

Bingham became involved in the Trinitarian controversy through being asked to preach in his turn before the university. He had apparently recently heard what he believed was an erroneous

---

[1] M.H. Peacock, *History of the Free Grammar School of Queen Elizabeth at Wakefield* (Wakefield 1892). University College Oxford's judgement of the School is seen in the testimony of its Master, Dr Arthur Charlett, who in 1718 presented books inscribed *Bibliothecae Publicae Scholae celeberrimae de Wakefield* and others in 1719 with the inscription *Scholae eximiae de Wakefield. ibid* p. 129.

[2] W. Carr, *University College* (London 1902) is a mine of information on the College in the late-seventeenth and early-eighteenth centuries. Bingham was made deacon by the bishop of Oxford, John Hough, on 20 December 1691 and priest on 12 March 1692/3, both in Magdalen College chapel. MS. Oxf. dioc. papers d. 106 fols 137^v, 144^v.

[3] From *c.*1675 the doctrine of the Trinity had become a subject of open discussion in England chiming in with the emphasis on reason which itself was a reaction against the social consequences of 'enthusiasm' among the seventeenth century sectaries. R.N. Stromberg, *Religious Liberalism in Eighteenth Century England* (Oxford 1954) pp. 13–14.

statement of the doctrine of the Trinity from the pulpit of St.
Mary's and he thought it his duty to establish what the Fathers of
the Church, rather than what the Schoolmen, had said on the
subject. The sermon was given in St. Peter-le-East on 28 October
1695 and contained a masterly exposition of the patristic notions of
ousia, persona and *substantia*. The result of the sermon was, for
Bingham, unexpected. He was immediately delated to the vice-
chancellor by J. Beuchamp, a fellow of Trinity, commonly known
as 'the heretick-hunter', as having asserted doctrines false, impious
and heretical, contrary and dissonant to those of the Catholic
Church. The Hebdomadal Board subsequently condemned two
propositions in the sermon as 'false, impious and heretical', and Dr.
South, the author of a *Short History of Valentinus Gentilis*, denounced Bingham as a follower of Dr. Sherlock, dean of St. Paul's,
who was widely held to be a tritheist. The upshot was that
Bingham was forced to resign his fellowship and withdraw from
the university.[4]

Bingham, later in his life, composed a preface to his sermon[5]
which throws an interesting light on his character and his method
in controversy. His appeal was first and foremost to the witness of
Christian antiquity which, he held, supported his view of *ousia,
persona* and *substantia*. He refutes the idea that he was trying to
ingratiate himself with Sherlock – in fact 'he found the Fathers
wounded through Dr. Sherlock's sides' while he was condemned
for saying many things which the Fathers had said before him. Yet
Bingham bore no grudge against his accusers although

I could have wished for their own sakes indeed and the sake of

---

[4] The sermon is printed by R. Bingham in his edition of *The Works of The Rev.
Joseph Bingham M.A.* vol 10 (Oxford 1855) pp. 361–383 subsequently cited as
Works. On Bingham's expulsion from Oxford *Works* vol. 1 pp. xviii–xix.
Bingham resigned his Fellowship on 23 November 1695. No trace of a formal
decision against Bingham has survived in the University records apart from this
note in the Life of Anthony à Wood prefixed to *Athenae Oxonienses* (ed Bliss p.
123): 'the meeting about Mr. Bingham is tomorrow morning at nine of the clock'.
This note is dated All Souls Coll. Oxon 24 Nov. 1695. It is possible that no formal
public censure by Convocation was ever passed and that Bingham withdrew
voluntarily. See however Archbishop Tenison to the Vice-Chancellor Adams 24
December 1695; BL, Add. mss. 799 fol 149 on the complaint that Bingham's
sermon was contrary to the doctrines of the Catholic Church and the Church of
England.
[5] *Works* 10, pp. 353–360.

the public, that they had done it a little more deliberately, and given me that month's time I desired; that I might have rendered my sermon to them, and given them a sight of my reasons, before they had censured me without hearing all that I had to say. And I could have wished also, they had told the world, that I asserted an indivisible unity of the Godhead, as well as three individual substances.[6]

Bingham pleads for a calm manner in Christian disputation and retained a decent respect for the characters of his accusers 'examining reasons without the least unbecoming reflections on their persons'. Such was the dignified character of this great student of Christian antiquity.

Bingham nowhere complained of the loss of his fellowship although this must have been a considerable blow to him, for it cut him off from easy access to original manuscripts of the Fathers. However the renowned Dr. Radcliffe apparently heard of his plight and presented him to the rectory of Headbourne Worthy, a mile from Winchester, and a living valued at one hundred pounds. This was to be the scene of Bingham's most celebrated literary labours.

In 1702 Bingham married Dorothea, daughter of Richard Pococke, and she bore him two sons and eight daughters before he received any further preferment. However the accession of a large family and his consequent straitened financial circumstances do not seem to have depressed his spirits. Modest, gentle and unworldly Bingham pursued his studies with unwearied perseverance. In his great work on the antiquities of the Christian Church, *Origines Ecclesiasticae*,[7] begun in 1702, he tells us that he had to struggle with an infirm and sickly constitution and lacked many of the books he needed, although he was grateful for the use of the valuable Patristic library bequeathed to the dean and chapter of Winchester by Bishop Morley.[8] A striking proof of his circumstances is provided by his copy of Pearson's *Exposition of the Creed* which was

---

[6] *Ibid* p. 358.

[7] *Works* vols 1–8. vol 9 contained his *The Scholastic History of Baptism by laymen* and a *Dissertation on the Eighth Nicene Canon.* vol 10 has Bingham's *The French Church's Apology for the Church of England* and *Sermons on the Trinity, the Divinity of Christ* and other matters.

[8] For Bingham's eloquent tribute to Morley *Works* 1 pp. xlv–xlvi and the further tribute in 1 p. lxxxv.

torn and in an imperfect state. Bingham laboriously transcribed eight missing pages in his own neat hand, although a complete copy could have been purchased for a few shillings. For some seventeen years Bingham's sole income was the endowment of the small benefice of Headbourne Worthy, and this when his domestic expenses were heaviest. However, in 1712 Sir Jonathan Trelawney, the then bishop of Winchester, collated him to the rectory of Havant, outside Portsmouth, and then in the diocese of Winchester.[9] The possession of this living, with the small sums he received from his books, removed in some degree his immediate poverty although in 1720 Bingham lost almost all the profits he had reaped from his incessant toil in the bursting of the 'South Sea Bubble'. However such was his tranquillity that it was said this heavy loss made little impression on him and not for a single day was his study interrupted. He began to prepare a second edition of the *Origines* and had in view a popular abridgement and supplement.[10] However death, not unexpected, came on 17 August 1723 in his fifty-fifth year and he was buried in the churchyard of S. Swithun's, Headbourne Worthy, with a plain stone over his grave recording simply his name, age and year of death. Bingham had frequently expressed a dislike for pompous monuments and an inscription prepared by his first schoolmaster, Edward Clarke, was never erected in deference to his wishes. If the term asceticism refers to a strict and austere life then Bingham's has a good claim to be dignified by that designation.

II

I pass now from this short consideration of Bingham's life to the account of asceticism and monasticism in his work *Origines Ecclesiasticae*. The *Origines* is characterized by immense erudition, a

[9] The record of the grant of a dispensation to hold Havant in plurality with Headbourne Worthy, November 1712, is in Lambeth Palace Library.

[10] The *Origines Ecclesiasticae* was begun in 1702 and the first three volumes were published in 1708–11. Bingham was then diverted into the controversy over lay-baptism and other matters. He resumed the publication of the *Origines* in 1715 and the remaining volumes appeared at intervals up to 1722. The work was translated into Latin and published by J.H. Grischovius of Halle in 1724–9. An abridgement in German was issued anonymously at Augsburg in 1788–96.

Joseph Bingham and Asceticism

reasonableness of approach and a sureness of judgement which is largely free from a narrow controversial spirit. The late Professor A.H.M. Jones described it as 'the most useful and comprehensive work which I know on the organization and discipline of the Church'[11] – a remarkable tribute to a work two-and-a-half centuries old.

Bingham's account of the ascetics in the Early Church is found in Book 7 of the *Origines*. He remarks that while there were always ascetics in the Church there were not always monks. Every Christian who made profession of a strict and austere life was dignified with the name of ascetic – a name which was borrowed from the ancient philosophers. So Origen refers to those who abstain from flesh in order to discipline the body; such abstinence the Apostolic Canons call ἄσκησις, the exercise of an ascetic life. Those, too, who spent their time largely in prayer were thought to deserve the name of ascetics – so Cyril of Jerusalem styles Anna, the prophetess, who departed not from the Temple, as ἀσκήτρια εὐλαβεστάτη, the religious ascetic. The exercise of charity to an extraordinary degree, as when men gave up their estates to the service of God and the poor, also was termed asceticism. So Jerome calls Pierius a wonderful ascetic because he embraced voluntary poverty and lived an austere, philosophic life. Widows and virgins, according to Bingham, were also reckoned among the ascetics, as can be seen from Origen who alludes to the name when he says that the numbers of those who exercised themselves in perpetual virginity among the Christians was great in comparison to the few who did it among the Gentiles.[12] So in the time of Justinian the civil law word *ascetriae* signified the widows and virgins of the Church. Lastly all who underwent extreme forms of hardship for the promotion of piety and religion were called ascetics. So the *Synopsis Scripturae* styles Lucian the Martyr as μέγαν ἀσκητὴν, the great ascetic, because of the hardships he endured in prison, being forced to lie on sharp potsherds for twelve days, with his feet and hands bound in stocks so that he could not move, and denied food. Rather than pollute himself with food sacrificed to idols he chose to die of famine, according to his *Acta Martyrium*. Sometimes the

[11] Bibliography of *The Later Roman Empire* (Oxford 1964).
[12] *Works* vol 2 p. 321.

primitive ascetics were called by other names; so Eusebius and Epiphanius call them σπουδαῖοι, persons eminent for their sanctity and diligence in fasting, prayer and almsgiving. Clement of Alexandria styles them ἐκλεκτῶν ἐκλεκτότεροι, the elect of the elect – while all Christians were called the elect the ascetics were the more eminent of these.

Having established the difference between ascetics and monks (a distinction which, while obvious to us, was not widely understood in his day) Bingham proceeds to discuss the rise of monasticism in some detail.[13] Until *c.*250 there were no monks, only ascetics in the Church; from that time until the reign of Constantine monachism was largely confined to anchorites living in cells in the desert. However when Pachomius erected monasteries in Egypt other countries followed his example and so the monastic life came to full maturity in the Church.

We have no space here to summarize Bingham's account of the rise of monasticism and I will confine myself to some of the more curious items of information which he provides in the *Origines*. Some of this is hard to come by elsewhere. Not all monks lived up to their calling: Bingham instances the case of the *Remboth*,[14] noted by Jerome, who were monks who lived in small groups of two or three, under no rule or government. They lived, not in the desert, but in cities and castles, turning religion to commercial gain. Whatever they sold of their own handiwork, was at a higher price than any others. They were turbulent and contentious, making even fasting a matter of strife. Everything about them was affected – loose sleeves, wide stockings, coarse clothes, often sighing, making frequent visits to virgins and always bitterly hostile to the clergy. At Feast days they indulged in riot and excess. Jerome brands them as the pests of the Church, while Cassian, who also knew about them, designates them *Sarabaitae*.

One of Bingham's more interesting sections is on the *Stylitae* or *Pillarists*,[15] monks who lived perpetually on a pillar or column. The case of St. Simeon Stylites who lived in the mid-fifth century is well known. Even the Egyptian monks, who had sent anathematizing letters against him, came to understand and communicate with

[13] *Ibid* pp. 323–397.
[14] *Ibid* p. 330.
[15] *Ibid* pp. 331–333.

the Syrian saint. Bingham points out that the severity of this way of life made few converts. Evagrius mentions another Simeon who lived sixty-eight years on a pillar and who is commonly called Simeon Stylites Junior. Surius, in his Catalogue of Saints, has the life of Alipius, a certain bishop of Adrianopolis, who renounced his see to live on a stone pillar for seventy years. Alipius had two choirs of virgins and one of monks attending him, with whom he sang psalms and hymns alternately day and night. Bingham clearly regards this as a legend and notes, with acerbity, that 'we scarce meet with any other of this way in ancient history'.

Bingham had a keen eye for the more unusual manifestations of monasticism. In the regions of Syria and Mesopotamia Sozomen, he notes, refers to monks called Βοσκοὶ or *Grazers*. These men lived in the same way as flocks and herds upon the mountains, never dwelling in houses or eating bread or flesh or drinking. They spent their time in the worship of God until feeding time when each went out with knife in hand to get food from the herbs of the field – their only diet.[16] Then there were the long-haired brethren, the *criniti fratres* known to Jerome and Augustine.[17] Certain of these walked in chains, had long hair and goats' beards, wore black coats and went barefoot in winter. Such affectations in habit and dress were frowned on, and monks were to wear simple clothes and short hair as is prescribed by certain *Canons* of Councils.

Voluntary poverty was a *sine qua non* of the monastic life but not all monks could live up to this. Bingham gives the remarkable story of one of the monks of Nitria in Egypt who was punished for hoarding up a hundred shillings as his own property which he had saved out of his daily labour. At his death, when this was discovered, a council of monks had to decide what to do with the money – incredible as it may seem five thousand monks met for this consultation. Some said it should be given to the poor, others to the Church, yet others that it should be given to the monk's parents. Macarius, Pambo and Isidore and others of those called Fathers among them decreed that the money should be buried with the dead monk in his grave with the words 'Thy money perish with thee'.[18]

[16] *Ibid* p. 344.
[17] *Ibid* p. 359.
[18] *Ibid* pp. 365–366.

Bingham largely confines his *Origines* to the patristic period of
the Church. However his profound knowledge extended to English Church History as may be seen from his remarkable account
of the Council of Becanfeld. Bingham refers to the presence of
abbots or fathers at Councils of the Church where they were often
allowed to sit and vote as presbyters – so at the Council of
Constantinople in 448 twenty three archimandrites subscribed with
thirty bishops to the condemnation of Eutyches. However England
seems to have led the way in women's liberation for at the Council
of Becanfeld in Kent held in A.D. 694 abbesses, as well as abbots,
subscribed to the decrees and did so before both presbyters and
temporal lords, according to the Saxon Chronicle. According to
Bingham this is the first time that this had happened in the records
of the ancient Church.[19]

III

It should not be imagined that Bingham was a mere compiler of
curious and out-of-the-way information. He was the foremost
student of Christian antiquity of his day. His appeal was always to
the evidence of ancient writers, not to the opinions of later authors
as to what those writers said or meant. His concern was solely to
recover what the early Church believed and did and to free the
study of Christian antiquity, once and for all, from the shackles of
the scholastic method. Here I have only been able to provide a taste
of the good things which his work, *Origines Ecclesiasticae*, contains
by concentrating on a few extracts from one section of it. Bingham
was a born student. No outward misfortune could shake his faith
or turn him from his life's work. Though he received scant
recognition from the Church of his day his work is a supreme
expression of the spirit of *Ecclesia Anglicana* and to none is the proud
compliment *clerus Anglicanus stupor mundi* more applicable. His
strict, austere, persevering, scholarly life is rightly termed ascetic.

University of Leeds

[19] *Ibid* pp. 373–374.

PLAINNESS OF SPEECH, BEHAVIOUR AND APPAREL IN EIGHTEENTH-CENTURY ENGLISH QUAKERISM[1]

by DAVID J. HALL

T
HE aim of this communication is to illustrate and examine the official attitude of the Quakers to their testimony on plainness in the eighteenth century, with a few examples, limited by available space, of the opinions of individuals.[2] It is also limited to England since official attitudes in America and Ireland were somewhat different;[3] it attempts no comparison with other contemporary English traditions;[4] it cannot do more than touch on such gaps as may have existed between individual practice and official attitude; nor can it make use of the ample surviving local records. To understand what lay behind the testimony on plainness it is necessary to go back briefly to the rise of Quakerism in the mid-seventeenth century.

Owen Watkins, in his classic *The Puritan Experience*, wrote:

> The Quakers testified to a common experience in that what happened to them all was explained as the work of the Spirit of God within, but their doctrine was far less complicated than the Calvinists' and group influence was expressed most prominently in the code of conduct which the Spirit moved them to conform to. The striking unanimity of Friends' witness against

[1] I am deeply indebted to Edward H. Milligan, Librarian of the Society of Friends, for his suggestions about an earlier version of this paper.

[2] I believe that it is reasonable to write of a testimony on plainness despite the argument by Rufus M. Jones that the customs constituting plainness 'do not rise to quite the same level of interior significance as do the "testimonies"' in *The Later Periods of Quakerism* 2 vols (London 1921) 1 p. 147.

[3] There is useful material about the American experience in J. William Frost *The Quaker Family in Colonial America* (New York 1973) chapter 10 and John M. Moore ed *Friends in the Delaware Valley* (Haverford, Pennsylvania 1981).

[4] An obvious comparison is with William Law *A Serious Call to a Devout and Holy Life* (London 1728) especially chapters IV–IX.

war, tithes, oaths, and any form of ceremonious behaviour both established every member's identity with the group and was the most noticeable expression of it. It also represented a measurement of the self against the demands of the world. Like all Puritans, the Friends found in their supernatural allegiance the standards by which to judge the world, and in doing so they found it wanting.[5]

A simple illustration will serve. The standards of the world, and its forms of ceremonious behaviour, were found wanting when in 1659 the twenty-year-old Thomas Ellwood responded to a group of his old acquaintances in Oxford. They 'saluted me after the usual manner, putting off their hats and bowing, and saying "Your humble servant, sir"', expecting, no doubt, the like from me'. Their amazement at seeing him, not moving his cap or bowing his knee 'in way of congee to them' is more than understandable. When at last one of them 'clapping his hand, in a familiar way, upon my shoulder, and smiling on me, said, "What, Tom, a Quaker"' Ellwood found that he 'readily, and cheerfully answered, "Yes, a Quaker"', adding, in later recollection, 'And as the words passed out of my mouth I felt joy spring in my heart'.[6]

Plainness was a levelling testimony in a body stressing equality and protesting against human pride and the spirit of lordship. Thus plainness of speech was a testimony against vain salutations, against the pride which demanded 'You' to social superiors and 'Thou' to inferiors. Plainness of behaviour was a testimony, inter alia, against hat honour, bowing and scraping before social superiors. Plainness of dress was a testimony against men's pride in their status expressed by their clothes. With other radical puritans Quakers testified against the names of the days and months that stemmed from pagan gods. And underlying the testimony on plainness of dress, particularly, was a direct protest against the crushing of the poor.[7]

So much for the genesis of the testimony on plainness. In day to day living Friends up and down the country faced problems as to

[5] Owen C. Watkins *The Puritan Experience* (London 1972) p. 232.
[6] Thomas Ellwood *The History of the Life of Thomas Ellwood...* (London 1714) pp. 33–4.
[7] The standard account of Quaker dress is Amelia Mott Gummere *The Quaker, a study in costume* (Philadelphia 1901).

what was and what was not plain. Disagreements among the area monthly meetings for church affairs were referred to the county quarterly meetings and, in the last resort, to the yearly meeting held in London. From this body minutes of advice were given, or appropriate paragraphs included in its annual epistle which from time to time reminded Friends of the basis of the testimony, as in 1761:

> And here we find it our concern, to revive a truth which is worthy of general remembrance; that no affectation of singularity was the cause of a demeanour, both civil and religious, in our forefathers (or in the faithful of this day,) different in many respects from the conduct of those among whom we dwell. They beholding the vanity, unprofitableness, and insincerity of the salutations, customs and fashions of the world; observing the examples of our blessed Saviour and his followers, with the frequent testimonies recorded in Holy Writ, to the necessity of a self-denying life and conversation, together with the law, and the testimony revealed in their hearts, retained in view the injunction of the apostle, not to be conformed to this world, but to be transformed, by the renewing of the mind, that we 'may prove what is that good, and acceptable, and perfect will of God.' (Rom. xii. 2) May an uprightness of heart, as in the sight of God, ever attend this simplicity of appearance; that none, by a conduct inconsistent therewith, may furnish occasion for the testimony to be evil spoken of or despised.[8]

For the last two decades of the seventeenth century the yearly meeting had asked factual questions on various matters of the county quarterly meetings, which in turn asked them of the area monthly meetings. The eighteenth century for our purpose may be said to start in 1701 when, to the existing questions, the yearly meeting added:

> How have the former advices of this Meeting relating to their Godly Care for the good Education of their Children in the

---

[8] *Epistles [from the Yearly Meeting of Friends held in London to the Quarterly and Monthly Meetings... from 1681 to 1857...*] 2 vols (London 1858) I pp. 321–2.

Way of Truth and Plainness of Speech and Habit, been practised?[9]

This was replaced in 1742 by a new seventh question:

Is it your Care by Example and Precept to Train up your Children in all Godly Conversation, and in the frequent reading the Holy Scriptures, as also in Plainness of Speech, Behaviour and Apparell.[10]

In 1757 this was altered by the addition after 'Children' of the words 'Servants and those under their care' and at the end by 'and are Friends faithful in Admonishing such as are remiss therein?'[11] The set of questions approved in 1755 included another that extended the definition of the testimony:

Are friends careful to avoid all vain sports, places of diversion, gaming and all unnecessary frequenting of alehouses or taverns, excess in drinking, and intemperance of every kind?[12]

The answers to the questions, recorded in the minutes of the yearly meeting, are seldom as useful as we might hope and often fall into a somewhat stereotyped form of words. A sample of answers received from the Warwickshire quarterly meeting to the 1757 version of the seventh question illustrates this point:

(1758) There is a care among Friends to train up their Children & those under their care in a Godly Conversation & in frequent Reading the holy Scriptures, and in plainness of speech, behaviour & apparel, and to advise such as are remiss in these respects.

(1759) There is a Care on the minds of Friends to come up in the discharge of our Christian duty in these Respects, and a care remains upon our minds to deal with such as may walk disorderly.

[9] *Christian and Brotherly Advices* [*Given forth from time to time by the Yearly Meeting in London*] (manuscript, 1738). A number of copies of this manuscript exist and given possible variations in pagination it seems best not to refer to pages but simply to use the subject heading and the year of any extract. The extract above is from the heading 'Questions'.
[10] *Ibid.*
[11] *Ibid.*
[12] *Ibid.*

(1760) A care remains upon the minds of divers Friends to come up in our Christian Duty in these respects and could wish it was more generally so & some care taken to deal with the remiss.[13]

The questions themselves were incorporated in the book of church discipline, first of all in a manuscript form issued in 1738 to quarterly meetings, and then in a more readily available printed form issued in 1783.[14] The epistles of the yearly meeting were drawn on extensively in the compilation and updating of the book of discipline.[15] Of fifty-two headings in the 1738 book of discipline the following, as well of course as the obvious 'Plainness', are relevant: 'Children', 'Conversation', 'Covetousness', 'Days', 'Mourning', 'Scriptures', 'Christian Testimonies' and 'Tomb-stones'.[16]

There were thirteen entries under the heading 'Plainness' in the 1738 book (two of them added later) from 1691 to 1743, with cross-references to entries under 'Conversation' in 1675, 1688 and 1736 and under 'Families' in 1737.[17] Only two were drawn from before 1700, in 1691 the text contained the basic essentials:

> Advised, That Friends take care to keep to Truth & Plainness in Language, Habit, Deportment and Behaviour, that the Simplicity of Truth in these things may not wear out nor be Lost in Our days nor in our Posterity's: To Avoid Pride and immodesty in Apparel, and Extravagant Wiggs, and all other vain and Superfluous Fashions of the World.

In 1700 and 1701 Friends were reminded to bring up their children on the same principles. The effort had to be maintained, parents were exhorted in 1708 and 1709 to be an example to their children.

---

[13] I owe these examples to Edward H. Milligan.

[14] *Christian and Brotherly Advices* and *Extracts from the Minutes and Advices of the Yearly Meeting of Friends held in London* (London 1783).

[15] The epistles were issued in printed form and various collections appeared later such as *Epistles* but there were also for some years in the eighteenth century quite separate written epistles from the yearly meeting.

[16] *Christian and Brotherly Advices* and its successor are referred to in the text as the book of discipline. Six further headings were added before the printed version appeared.

[17] See note 9.

In the meantime 'Excess of Apparel and Furniture' caused regret in 1703 and advice was given to 'avoid...all Extravagancy in Colour and Fashion.' Hair and women's fashion were the source of concern in 1715:

> ...But to our great Grief We find too many of our Young Men, instead of Observing that Gospel Exhortation, To be Sober Minded, have given Way to Lightness and Vanity, and the pernicious effects thereof have led them into Pride, so that some have cut off good heads of Hair, and put on long Extravagant and Gay Wiggs, which they that are not of Profession with us See as a mark of Declension from our Primitive Plainness.
>
> And likewise that your Young Women would Cease from that unseemly and Immodest Appearance of their high heads, and wearing their Gowns Set up like the proud fashion mongers of the World: Certainly both Males and Females who take such undue Measures, Flee the Cross of Christ...

That extract continues at length in the same vein, listing other prevalent exceptions to plainness including bowing and giving flattering titles to men, saying 'Ye' or 'You' to a single person and using the heathen names for the days of the week and the months. A similar passage in 1718 attacked the use of jewellery observing:

> ...too many Women decking themselves with Gaudy and Costly Apparel, as Gold Chains, Lockets, Necklaces and Gold Watches exposed to open view, which Shews more of Pride and Ostentation than for use and Service, besides their vain Imitation of that Immodest Fashion of going with Naked Necks and Breasts, and Wearing hooped Petticoats...

More general complaints about conformity to the world were included in 1732, 1735 and 1739, the last turning to biblical passages for reinforcement.[18] The 1783 book of discipline began the heading with the same passage from 1691 and in all used nine passages that were close to those used in 1738 while some duplication of text was eliminated.

[18] Isaiah 3, 1 Timothy 2:9–10, 1 Peter 3:3–5.

The heading 'Children' emphasised training, in part by example, to avoid the deficiencies observed in some adult Friends. Some departures from plainness may have been revolts against severe upbringings. 'Conversation' as a heading was concerned both with the behaviour of Friends in their own community and the impression given outside, as in 1731:

> It is the Care and Concern of this Meeting to Recommend unto all Friends resorting to any of our Annual Assemblys either in this City or Elsewhere to be very careful at their Inns, or other Places where they may Lodge or Converse, to be prudent in all manner of Behaviour, both in Publick and Private, avoiding all Intemperance in Eating and Drinking, and likewise any foolish Jesting, or undue Liberty whatsoever...

Advice given in 1738 was to 'Avoid Sports, Plays and all such Diversions, as tending to alienate the mind from God...' The heading 'Days' included a letter from the Meeting for Sufferings dated 6th.7th. month 1751 setting out changes in the calendar enacted by government and reiterating in detail the objections to the use of heathen names in the calendar. The testimony against 'Mourning' was again concerned with extravagance in dress as well as conformity to the world. Consistency over 'Tombstones' was not easy to establish and it was suggested in 1717 and 1766 that they should be removed where they existed.

Most of the passages above from the book of discipline were derived from the yearly meeting epistles. There was some reference to plainness, broadly interpreted, in the majority of years in the eighteenth century. Many of the phrases, themes and examples quoted appear again and again. The point most often encountered is the care of children, sheltering them from bad company and frivolous books and with a constant need to 'restrain them from the world's corruption and extravagances, both in habit and language, behaviour and conversation.[19] Often interconnected, plainness in behaviour, speech and apparel was also a regular theme. The worry about involvement in worldly affairs, overreaching in business, covetousness and 'hastening to be rich in the world',[20] and the

---

[19] *Epistles* I p. 108, (1704), see also 1706, 1710, 1717, 1719 etc. to 1791, 1798.
[20] *Ibid* I p. 157 (1720).

313

'leprosy of the great sin of pride' appeared from time to time.[21] Particular risks and distractions were pointed out; sports and plays, excess in eating and drinking were otherwise 'vain diversions' and 'carnal indulgences'.[22] 'Vile and corrupt books' were obviously dangerous and many forms of literature were seen as at best an unworthy alternative to scripture and time-wasting if not evil in content. It was:

> ...seriously advised, that no Friends suffer romances, play-books, or other vain and idle pamphlets, in their houses or families, which tend to corrupt the minds of youth, but, instead thereof that they excite them to the reading of the Holy Scriptures and religious books.[23]

The Friends were constantly anxious to 'disappoint those who are watching for our halting or drawing back again into worldly or fleshly liberty.'[24] Lapses from plainness were also lapses from the standards by which those outside the Society expected to recognise Friends and from 'the plainness of habit, and simplicity of speech and behaviour, which were so conspicuous in our early Friends, and many of their offspring.'[25] A half-hearted attitude to plainness might be the symptom of a serious spiritual malaise. In 1770 the epistle went back to the roots:

> If we suffer our minds to wander from the pure and holy witness of truth, that is placed in every heart, we slide insensibly into the spirit of the world, and the corrupt manners and practices thereof: hence proceed those light and airy appearances, fantastic dresses, unsound language, unprofitable converse, and inconsistent conduct, which too plainly denote a lamentable declension.[26]

The consequences of lapsing were expressed strongly: 'And let not any lust after the vain fashion and glittering gaiety of this fading world; for it will suddenly wither, as the mown grass before the

---

[21] *Ibid* I p. 123 (1709).
[22] *Ibid* I pp. 221 (1738), 338 (1765).
[23] *Ibid* I pp. 157–8 (1720).
[24] *Ibid* I p. 109 (1704).
[25] *Ibid* I p. 212 (1736).
[26] *Ibid* 2 p. 3 (1770).

sun.'[27] Friends were expected, as their ancestors had done, to pass 'the time of their sojourning here, in fear, and in great simplicity of heart as well as of outward demeanour'.[28] There was no room for compromise though that complicated establishing the standards:

> It is not for man to say to his Maker Hitherto I will follow thee, and no further: I must allow myself this and the other liberty, in speech, in dress, in behaviour, in converse, in commerce, or in any kind of self-gratification.[29]

Throughout the century Friends, at least at the national level, seem to have felt that they were increasing in worldliness. This was one factor in a movement begining in the early seventeen-sixties to revive the discipline of the Society. The tendency, and the apparent inconsistency between public claims and individual practice was observed by outsiders. Voltaire connected the situation with the growing prosperity of Friends and wrote that children 'made wealthy by their fathers' industry want to enjoy things, have honours, buttons and cuffs…'.[30] John Wesley felt that Friends were subtle and inconsistent over plainness, overlooking the exceptions among them to their professed standards:

> You say you do 'testify against it in the congregation.' Against what' 'Against gay and gaudy apparel' I grant it. But this is not the thing I speak of. You quite mistake my mark. Do you testify against the *costliness* of their apparel, however plain and grave it may be? Against the *price* of the velvet, the linen, the silk, or raiment of whatever kind? If you do this frequently and explicitly, you are clear.[31]

Though the experience of individuals would usefully comple- ment the corporate views of the Society on plainness expressed so far our experience with contemporary journals and biographies is a little similar to that with the answers to the questions or the

---

[27] *Ibid* 1 p. 109 (1704).
[28] *Ibid* 1 p. 347 (1767).
[29] *Ibid* 2 p. 22 (1774).
[30] Voltaire *Letters on England*, trans by Leonard Tancock (Harmondsworth 1980) p. 36, Letter 4.
[31] Contained in a footnote in editions from the third onwards of Wesley's *Farther Appeal to Men of Reason and Religion* in *The Works of John Wesley* ed Gerald R. Cragg (Oxford 1975) pp. 254–7.

minutes of meetings for church affairs, the bones are there but have little flesh upon them. In his study of Quaker journals Howard H. Brinton points out that there were two public stands adopted following inward change (conversion) in an individual to establish him as a convinced and serious Friend, entrance into the vocal ministry and the adoption of plain speech, dress and behaviour.[32]

Joseph Pike, who lived most of his life in Ireland, wrote a journal in the 1720s which went into some detail about furniture and dress:

> Now...I have mentioned the wearing of plain silks...which are still worn in England by some honest-minded women Friends...I do not, then esteem it an evil in itself to wear plain modest-coloured silk clothes, provided the mind be not affected with a delight in them, and especially worn in a climate where the heat requires it...[33]

Pike observed a general declension in plainness and, writing in 1726 to the national meeting in Dublin, he asked 'are there not those, who have nearly lost or been ashamed of the plain language, both in speaking and writing.'[34] 'Ashamed' is a key word here, being marked as a people apart was clearly a source of embarrassment to some Friends. In 1716 it was alleged that young women Friends in London and Bristol went about in 'the finest of silks and laced shoes, and when they went to Bath made as fine a show as any.'[35] Pike wrote to the well-known English Friend Thomas Story in 1723 about the bad example he thought Story set: '...in some things thou goest a little too fine and modish, and particularly as to thy hat and long hair, &c.'[36]

David Hall of Skipton echoed the yearly meeting epistles in his 1747 *Epistle of Love and Caution*.[37] He tells his readers, assumed to be Friends, that:

> *Ye were once a plain People, distinguishable in divers Respects, particularly in* Plainness *of* Habit, *and* Speech, *from all others; but*

[32] Howard H. Brinton, *Quaker Journals, Varieties of Religious Experience amongst Friends* (Wallingford, Pennsylvania 1972) p. 35.
[33] Joseph Pike, *Some Account of the Life of Joseph Pike of Cork* (London 1837) pp. 60–2.
[34] *Ibid* p. 140.
[35] *Ibid* p. 147–8.
[36] *Ibid* p. 189.
[37] in David Hall, *Some Memoirs of the Life of David Hall* (London 1758) pp. 58–94.

we now can scarce know you to be of the Community of the Quakers,...*but now what Conformity to the* Fashions, Customs, Grandeur, *and* Vanities *of the World are you run and running into*...[38]

Later he goes into some detail of the vanities and while we may wonder how many Friends really were adorned with diamond buckles he is convincing on one fashion:

> But of all the giddy Modes, antick and fantastick Inventions, that ever old Satan or his Agents, with respect to external Dress, have hitherto vampt up, since the Fall of *Adam*; was there ever any Thing contriv'd so much for the Ruin of Female Modesty, and the Incitement to Sensuality and Corruption, as these immodest, indecent, odious, extravagant Hoops, calculated not for the strait, but for the wide Gate and broad Way, leading to Destruction?...'Tis mightily surprising, and really shocking...to think, that any modest Matron, or any chaste young Woman, who is not lunatick or delirious, should ever dare to appear in such an awkward and unseemly Dress...[39]

Hall returns to the theme in his tract *A Mite into the Treasury* and deems the 'modern fashionable Quakers' who *'profess the* Spirit, *yet...live after the* Flesh...*but* Nominal Quakers.'[40]

John Woolman's visit to England in 1772 provided a challenge to the thinking of English Friends on plainness, his example was more extreme than most they encountered.[41] His appearance was described thus by Sarah Hall:

> He wore a coarse cloth like flannel, no cuffs to his coat, a drab hat [more usually described as white] a coarse unbleached shirt, no stock or neckcloth, white woolen stockings, shoes uncurried, the native color, tied with the same. He drank no foreign liquors or tea. He did not choose to drink out of silver or to make use of silver spoons. Herb tea sometimes he drank

[38] *Ibid* pp. 76–7.
[39] *Ibid* pp. 87–8.
[40] *Ibid* p. 166.
[41] Woolman's visit and the nature of the evidence for the narrative accounts of it are fully discussed by Henry J. Cadbury *John Woolman in England* (London 1971).

sweetened with honey. Sugar he never chose. He was indeed a striking pattern of temperance and humility.[42]

Space does not permit proper consideration here of Thomas Clarkson's *A Portraiture of Quakerism* which appeared early in the next century. A good deal of the sympathetic and well-known account of Friends is devoted to the 'Peculiar Customs of the Quakers' and to their justification and validity.[43] Clarkson explains that uniformity in dress applied in principle rather than great detail when he was writing and that there had been gradual development from the seventeenth-century models.[44] He discusses most usefully other contemporary views of Friends.

There is a measure of unity in the observation of, and the attempts to enforce, the testimony on plainness in the eighteenth century, and in the observations of individuals on declining standards in practice. What has not been brought out above is the part played by those Friends unhappy about the application of the testimony as a hedge from the world or as a possibly deceptive surface and outward indication of the spiritual states of individuals. Such Friends must surely have existed. In the nineteenth century the position changed gradually, Friends came more to terms with the world as they came more into contact with it through business, philanthropy and eventually politics and education, and they came individually to see some value in music, secular literature and the visual arts.[45]

University of Cambridge.

---

[42] *Ibid* p. 102.
[43] 3 vols (London 1806).
[44] *Ibid* 1 pp. 271–2.
[45] for some account of this see Elizabeth Isichei, *Victorian Quakers* (London 1970) pp. 145–6, 161–2.

VOLTAIRE AND THE MONKS

by J. McMANNERS

'**Y**OU can never cross the Pont Neuf without seeing a monk, a white horse and a whore', ran the proverb – which was hard luck on the two ladies who stood there and saw the first two but could not find the third: 'Pour la catin, vous et moi nous n'en sommes pas en peines'.[1] Members of the religious Orders in their costumes of black, white, brown and grey were a feature of the scene in the streets of every town, and everyone had a monk or nun among their relatives. Voltaire's sardonic examples of the characteristic features of the civilisation of his day included them: 'man will always be what he is now; this does not mean to say, however, that there will always be fine cities, cannons firing a shot of 24 lbs weight, comic operas and convents of nuns'.[2] Routine gossip slipped naturally into analogies drawn from the cloister – she is as fat as a monk; they were like children at a window crying out when they first see a Capucin friar; you are like a novice who climbs the walls looking for a lover, while the nuns in the chapel pray for her.[3] Voltaire uses monastic titles in jocular descriptions of himself and his friends. He is the 'old hermit', the 'lay brother', the 'solitary', 'brother Voltaire, dead to the world and in love with his cell and his convent',[4] and once, when his play *Octave et le jeune Pompée* was a flop, he decided to be,

---

[1] S-R-N. Chamfort, *Maximes et anecdotes* (Pref. A. Camus, 1963), 63.
In what follows, quotations are from the *Oeuvres complètes de Voltaire*, ed L. Moland (51 vols, 1883–5), abbreviated as M. Also from the *Mélanges* (Gallimard 1961), abbreviated as *Mél*; the *Romans et Contes* (ed H. Bénac, Garnier, n.d.), abbrev. as R; the *Oeuvres historiques* (Pléiade 1957), abbrev. as O.*hist*; the *Notebooks* (ed Th. Besterman, 2 vols 1968), abbrev. as *Note*; and the *Oeuvres inédites* (ed F. Caussy, 1914), abbrev. as Caussy. Letters of Voltaire are cited by reference to the number (e.g. D6697) given to them by Th. Besterman in his revised complete edition (51 vols 1968–77).
[2] *Moeurs*, M 11 p. 21.
[3] D6697, D12073, D4880.
[4] D5045. Other references, D8634, D10664, D16978, D7836, D7858, D8673, D7529.

for a while, 'the little ex-Jesuit', '*le petit défroqué*'.[5] He hopes 'brother' Helvétius will be elected to the Academy: 'these are the most ardent prayers of the monk Voltairius, who from his lonely cell unites himself in spirit with his brethren'.[6] The badinage of monastic seclusion hinted at protest at his long exile from Paris; it also served to mask the social distinctions, which, in spite of familiarity and, even, friendship, were never forgotten between the court grandees and the intellectuals. It was easier for Choiseul to write to him as '*mon cher solitaire*',[7] just as Voltaire avoided routine sycophancy by writing, with exaggerated deference, to Richelieu as '*mon héros*'.

Voltaire was a pupil of the Jesuits, and all his life remained in a love-hate relationship with them. Or, perhaps, it was his old schoolmasters that he loved, and the Jesuits generally that he hated. To Père Porée and Père Tournemine he protested that he owed his talent for writing to their teaching, and whenever he published anything, he was striving to please them.[8] In 1731, he sent to Porée the new edition of his *Oedipe*; he had removed the love affair, which he had put in, against his better judgement, to please the actresses, and he hoped his revision would find favour.[9] (Assuredly it would; Porée's own tragedies, written for his pupils to perform, had no feminine love interest – all was ambition, suspicion and malice, with cruel fathers destroying virtuous sons, claustrophobic dramas which one imagines were psychologically more harmful to schoolboys than the erotic comedies available to their elder brothers in the bohemian underworld of Paris.[10]) At the end of 1738 Voltaire wrote to Tournemine about *Mérope*, which expressed 'some of the generous sentiments that you inspired in me in my young days'.[11] In 1746, he wrote solemnly to the Principal of Louis-le-Grand describing how he owed all his love of letters and

---

[5] D1177, D11982, D12037, D12050, D12063, D12084, D12977.
[6] D9600 (2 Feb. 1761).
[7] D9040 (letters to him as a 'hermit', D8321, D8588).
[8] D1729 (31 Dec. 1738).
[9] D392 (7 Jan. 1731), Cf. D1942 (17 March 1739).
[10] For Porée, J. de la Servière, *Un Professeur d'ancien régime: le Père Charles Porée, S.J., 1676–1741* (1899). For dubious comedies, G. Capon and R. Yve-Pessis, *Les Thèâtres clandestins* (1905) pp. 13–15, 96, 158; Jean-Hervé Donnard, *Le Théâtre de Carmontelle* (1967) pp. 22–5. Cf. Mercier *Tableau de paris* (1778) 6 pp. 128–131.
[11] D1729 (31 Dec. 1738).

of virtue to his old school.[12] There, for seven years he had seen his Jesuit tutors living a 'most laborious, frugal and well-regulated existence', as they toiled to train the minds and morals of youth, scorning to ask for reward. As for dangerous sentiments in his publications, unscrupulous editors had falsified them; 'if there is a single page that would scandalize your parish sacristan, I'll gladly tear it up'. It was, said the good Père Simon de la Tour, 'a judicious, beautiful and touching letter.'[13] A man is not upon oath when writing to the headmaster of his old school, yet it is reasonable to assume that Voltaire, behind the sardonic grin, was sincere.

By contrast, the Voltaire whose writings abound in vituperation of the Society of Jesus is more easily recognisable in the feud which he waged against the Jesuits of Ornex, near to his château of Ferney.[14] In 1760, he was boasting how he had defeated their scheme to buy a property owned by six hard-up brothers, all army officers. The reverend fathers, 'these stinking animals', he says, will never forgive me.[15] To ensure that they did not do so, in the following year he engineered a further discomforture for them, in a shady manoeuvre devised to kill two birds with one anticlerical stone. He was organising legal proceedings against the *curé* of Moens[16] for assault on a young man called Croze.[17] Croze's elder sister waylaid the Jesuit Père Joseph Fessy on his weekly journey from Ornex to take a service in the chapel of the French resident at Geneva, made her confession to him, then alleged that he had refused her absolution until her family dropped its lawsuit against the *curé*. Fessy, who was unable to defend himself because of the secrecy of the confessional, felt he had been 'framed'.[18] Yet, at the very time he was making trouble for poor Fessy (insisting on calling him *Jean* Fessy to make him especially ridiculous), Voltaire

---

[12] D3348 (1 April 1746).

[13] D53350.

[14] D9447, D9499, D9513, D9966, D19635.

[15] D9513 (2 Jan. 1761).

[16] Voltaire had had a tithe dispute against this *curé* (D7996, 12 Dec. 1758; D8011, 29 Oct. 1758), also F. Caussy, *Voltaire, seigneur de village* (1912) pp. 53–6.

[17] The young man went to call on a widow of dubious reputation; the *curé* collected a posse in the local tavern to evict him in the name of morality.

[18] D9631 (Voltaire's account). A lawyer friend wrote to Voltaire to warn him that he was sailing near to the wind (D9623).

was taking an exiled Portuguese Jesuit as a lackey,[19] while his daily companion was another ex-Jesuit, Père Adam, who lived with him at Ferney for thirteen years after the suppression of his Order. No doubt, there was a malicious satisfaction in having a Jesuit priest as a 'butt'[20] – *'ce n'est pas le premier homme du monde'*[21] – but Antoine Adam played chess well and acted as research assistant. He was also an exhibit in Voltaire's campaign for respectability; he said mass in the château, taught the village children and went round soberly in a cassock – exactly as the chaplain of a village seigneur ought to do – and, together with the *curé* of Ferney, he connived at his 'benefactor's' political communions of Easter 1768 and 1769. But it would be unfair to belittle Voltaire's generosity. In his will of 1769[22] he left Adam 3,000 livres (which would have provided an extra income half as much as the exiguous pension he received as an ex-Jesuit). By 1776, however, the two old men had parted coldly. Gossip had it that Voltaire found he now lacked the concentration necessary for chess and scholarly enquiries, so 'having squeezed the orange dry, he threw away the rind'; or perhaps it was all the doing of his dragon of a housekeeper.[23]

Another peculiar member of Voltaire's household was signed on in 1765, when he took a renegade Capucin as a lackey – a short-lived employment, as two years later brother 'Bastian' fled from Ferney as he had fled from his convent in Savoy, taking with him his red livery coat, money, jewelry and manuscripts which he sold to publishers in Lyon.[24] No doubt, Voltaire had been glad to spite the Provincial of Chambéry by concealing his runaway friar.[25] And at the time, he was in a zealous anti-Capucin phase; when in 1766 he heard of a murder in one of their convents in Paris, he relished the story and hoped that the whole lot of them would be

[19] D10098, D10093.

[20] As Thomas Pennant said (Th. Besterman, *Voltaire* (1969) p. 453).

[21] D8057. For Adam generally see D10922 (Jan. 1763), D14984 (April 1768), and Adam to the bishop of Geneva justifying his conduct (D12387, Feb. 1765). Voltaire asked Cardinal Bernis at Rome to get permission for Adam to wear a wig when celebrating (D15764, D15794, D15925); he was glad to draw attention to the fact that he had a chaplain.

[22] Besterman, *Corresp.* 35 p. 453, App D315.

[23] D20376, D2047 – letters of Paul Claude Moulton.

[24] D12920, D14316.

[25] Voltaire liked to cock a snook at authority – cf. his defence of a hermit against his Superior, 'a sort of General of hermits at Toul' in D2580 (Jan. 1742).

thrown out of their friaries and sent back to the plough.[26] Yet he was always on excellent terms with his local Capucins of the convent of Gex. His reward came in 1769 (after his intervention with the duchesse de Choiseul had saved them a considerable sum of money), for Amatus de Lamballe, General of the Capucins at Rome, sent to him a splendid scroll declaring him a member of the Third Order of Saint Francis and temporal patron of the friary at Gex. With glee he now put 'unworthy Capucin' after his signature on his letters,[27] he offered to get deceased mistresses of the maréchal de Richelieu out of Purgatory,[28] and he unrolled his parchment with its portrait of Saint Francis before the astonished eyes of the new *curé* of Ferney.[29]

It was incongruous to have Voltaire as an honorary Capucin, entitled to die in the cowl and hood of the Order, just as it was to have an ex-Jesuit and an ex-Capucin opening the door of his carriage (his niece, Mme Denis, would not allow the Portuguese Jesuit to serve the drinks – she had heard too much about ecclesiastical poisoners[30]). It was even more incongruous to have Père Adam digging out learned references, for much of his patron's research consisted in searching the Scriptures, the Fathers and Church history generally for cruelties, obscenities and absurdities.[31] But he was Europe's greatest writer, and the clergy who denounced him also recognized his genius. A convent of nuns put on his *Mort de César* as their theatrical performance, congratulating themselves on having discovered a drama in which there was no mingling of the sexes (that the girls had to take mens' parts did not worry them).[32] In 1754, Dom Calmet, abbot of Senones, of the

---

[26] D13327 (30 May 1766), D13336, D13337.
[27] D16029 (8 Dec. 1769), D16068, D16207, D16330, D16339, D16340, D16141, D16159, D16160, D16161, D16162, D16173, D16178. Cf. the verses in M.8 p. 535. The General of the Capucins tried to defend himself by saying that he had not actually *signed* the document (D16357).
[28] D16142 (Feb. 1770).
[29] D16249 (March 1770).
[30] My own explanation.
[31] This is not to deny that Voltaire had serious arguments and a serious religious purpose in his gleeful comments (see R. Pomeau, *La Religion de Voltaire* (1969) and B. Schwarzback, *Voltaire's Old-Testament Criticism* (Geneva, 1971).
[32] The nuns of the Visitation at Beaune; see G. Desnoiresterres, *Voltaire et la société française au 18ᵉ siècle* (8 vols 1867–76) 3 pp. 191–4. Voltaire took 20 minutes off to write a prologue specially for them.

Benedictine congregation of Saint-Vanne, invited Voltaire to stay at his abbey and use their library; so, for nearly a month, the great *philosophe* became a Benedictine. 'The monks look for the page and line references and quotations that I ask for', he wrote to Mme Denis, 'Dom Calmet, at the age of 83, climbs up a high and shaky ladder – it makes me tremble to see him – to pull out old books for me'.[33] In return for this hospitality, he sent the three volumes of the *Siècle de Louis XIV*. 'The monks will remember all their lives the honour that you did to our house by the all-too-short stay you made here', Calmet replied.[34] Poor Dom Calmet, so out of touch with the world that he had never heard of Mme de Pompadour;[35] he was the author of vast Biblical commentaries from which Voltaire lifted all the contradictions and embarrassments in the sacred text, substituting his own explanations for the respectable ones, and by way of acknowledgement pouring ridicule on the learned author whose works he pillaged. 'This naïve compiler of so many fantasies and imbecilities', said Voltaire, 'whose simplicity has made him invaluable to whoever wishes to laugh at ancient follies'.[36] It would be unreasonable to expect a professional jester to refrain from comment on Calmet's monumental history of Vampires,[37] or to resist a guffaw at his learned discussion of whether Job's afflictions included the pox,[38] but he might at least have abstained from hinting that the engravings of tortures used by the Jews had been put in to titillate the sadism of the readers.[39] Voltaire got on fine with naïve and friendly religious who showed him proper respect, though in one way or another they were sure to be imposed upon or outwitted. When he was craftily organising for himself a respectable death bed, with no concessions to Christian belief but Christian burial all arranged, it was the abbé

---

[33] D5843, D5845, D5860.

[34] D5874 (July 1754).

[35] *Note*, 2 p. 351, 23 June 1754.

[36] *Dictionnaire philosophique*, M. 19 p. 507.

[37] *Dict. Phil.* 'Vampires', M. 20 p. 547. See Dom A. Calmet, *Traité sur les apparitions des esprits et sur les vampires* (new ed 2 vols 1751).

[38] *Dict. Phil.*, 'Lépre et vérole', M. 19 p. 572. Voltaire had also a serious interest, as the disease raised, in an acute form, the problem of evil (R. Galliani, 'Voltaire, Astruc et la maladie vénérienne', *Studies in Voltaire and the 18th Century* CCXIX (1983) pp. 19–36.

[39] *Prix de la justice et de l'humanité*, M. 30 p. 584.

Gaultier, an ex-Jesuit, who heard his confession and let him get away without having to disown his writings – to the rage of the archbishop of Paris.[40] Another old member of the Society of Jesus had served Voltaire's turn in the role, as it were, of lackey and confidant.

'No one can deny that there are great virtues in the cloisters: there are still monasteries within whose enclosures admirable souls are found, an honour to human nature'.[41] This was once a favourite citation of Catholic apologists, saving up as their punch line the ascription of the quotation to Voltaire. The admission was, in fact, limited by its context. The good and useful monks had flourished chiefly in the past when their numbers were small: '*le grand nombre les avilit.*' On the average, there are bound to be a greater number of vicious characters in secular life, but the trouble with the religious life is, that whatever good men it includes are useless to society: 'we must lament a thousand buried talents and sterile virtues which would have been useful to the world'. This is from the *Essai sur les moeurs*. Wherever elsewhere a dole of praise is accorded to the monks, similar formulae of diminution are employed. They gave great services, but caused great evils, and anyway all this was long ago.[42] The virtuous are few, 'and these are persecuted by the others'.[43] Of course there are those who live austerely: 'I could say it with greater reason of dervishes, marabouts, fakirs and bonzes'.[44]

To Voltaire, there were few useful monastic congregations. At the top of his brief list would come '*les religieux de la rédemption des captifs*', who ransomed Christian slaves from the prisons and galleys of Algiers and Tunis.[45] It would not have been difficult to make fun of those adventurous souls, with their picturesque fund-raising processions, parading their rescued captives in their

[40] See my *Reflexions at the Death-Bed of Voltaire* (Lecture Oxford 1975).
[41] *Essai sur les moeurs*, M. 12 p. 330.
[42] 'Biens d'église', *Dict. Phil.*, M. 17 p. 591.
[43] *Le Diner du comte de Boulainvilliers, Mél.* 13045. *Avis au public sur les parricides, Mél.* 825.
[44] *Le Diner, Mél.* 13045.
[45] 'Alger', *Dict. Phil.*, M. 17 p. 117.

fetters through the provincial towns of France,[46] but Voltaire speaks of them only to praise them. He adds, however, that their very existence 'is shameful to us', as with all our mighty navies we fail to destroy the Barbary pirates. The 'only other useful monks' were the Frères de la Charité who were expert surgeons and ran a model hospital in Paris. The other congregations, says Voltaire, will not recognize them; 'Why? because they work cures, not miracles ... they restore poor women to health, rather than directing their consciences or seducing them'.[47] Then, there were the nuns who nurse the sick. 'Maybe there is no greater sacrifice on earth than that which the weaker sex makes of its youth and beauty – and often enough, high birth also – to care for the mass of misery in the hospitals, the very sight of which is humiliating to our pride as human beings and revolting to our feelings. The peoples separated from the Roman communion have only imperfectly imitated such generous charity'.[48] Then comes the qualification: 'but this exceedingly useful congregation is the least numerous of all.' The criterion for praise is practical utility, narrowly interpreted. The fathers of the Oratory, who did not take permanent vows, receive a passing accolade: 'on y jouit de la liberté qui convient à des hommes'.[49] And, for some reason, Voltaire is not willing to

[46] There were two such Orders. See P. Delandres, L'Ordre des Trinitaires pour le rachat des captifs (2 vols 1903) and, for Notre-Dame-de-la-Mercy, G. Lambert, L'Oeuvre de la rédemption des captifs à Toulon (Toulon 1882). There were also Franciscans working in this field (C. Serpas, 'Les esclaves chrétiens au Maroc', Bull. de l'hist. du Protestantisme français (1930) p. 243.) For their picturesque processions, see S. Moreau-Rendu, Les Captifs libérés: les Trinitaires et Saint-Mathurin de Paris (1974); 'Notes et souvenirs d'Antoine Sabatier; Bull. Hist. du diocèse de Lyon (1923) pp. 161-2 and La Semaine religieuse de Rouen (1876) p. 630. For scandals in processions see L.P. de Bachaumont, Mémoires secrets pour servir à l'histoire de la République des lettres en France (36 vols 1779-89) 30 p. 24 (24 Oct 1785) – some monks and captives drunk; also, 'Mémoires de Moreau de Jonnes', La Révolution française XIX p. 363 - 'Captives' hired from the suburbs of Paris.
[47] Médecins, Dict. Phil. M 20 pp. 57-8. See E. Lequay, Études historiques de l'Ordre de la Charité de Saint-Jean-de-Dieu et ses établissements en France (1854) p. 34 (They had 36 houses, with 355 religious and 3,181 hospital beds). For their model hospital in Paris, page 54.
[48] Moeurs M. 12 p. 324. Voltaire seems to have been unaware of the fact that there were many different Orders of nuns caring for the sick in a multiplicity of foundations (see a listing of some in C. Bloch, L'Assistance et l'État en France à la veille de la Révolution (1908) p. 699. In some institutions, there were numerous sisters – at least 140 in one (See A. Chevalier, L'Hôtel-Dieu de Paris et les Soeurs Augustines, 1650-1810 (1901) p. 449.
[49] He adds: 'Superstitious practices do not dishonour virtue in their houses', Moeurs, M. 20 p. 324.

damn the Minims; they 'do neither good nor harm', he says darkly.[50]

In his surveys of European history, a few individual monks are praised. Roger Bacon was 'a great man', adding however, 'for his time ... how many centuries it has taken to acquire a little rationality'. Furthermore, he discovered gunpowder, an ambiguous contribution to progress.[51] A monk who was martyred by a fourteenth-century Emperor because he refused to break the seal of the confessional, and another who limited the King of Sweden to one meal a day on Wednesdays (for poisoning his brother, a ridiculous penance but notable for its symbolism[52]) are approved as opponents of naked force in barbarous times.[53] Passing approval might fall to a learned religious – for his learning, or to a Jesuit missionary. It was something to have argued against cannibalism among the Red Indians,[54] or spent long years compiling a dictionary of Huron,[55] or reading the Chinese books on astronomy[56] (though in each case, a nice anticlerical point follows – the savages thought the code of Leviticus worse than man-eating, the dictionary is useless now we have lost Canada, the Chinese annals show the story of the Flood is ridiculous). Who would not be moved by the spectacle of the duchesse de la Vallière, deserted by Louis XIV, and becoming a barefooted Carmelite nun? Even so, Voltaire does not approve of her austerities and offers a psychological explanation: 'she believed that God alone could succeed her lover in her heart'.[57] Since the Church is no longer entitled to stand for peoples against kings, and few monasteries do work that is practically useful, the religious can only win approval today if they show kindness. The nun who wrote in favour of old Calas against the

---

[50] M. 12 p. 339. Voltaire is less severe on an Order if it has few members and is not rich. In 1768 the Minims had 975 friars in France and their income was about 400l a head. (P.J. Whitmore, *The Order of Minims in Seventeenth-Century France* (The Hague 1967) p. 454.

[51] *Dict. Phil.*, M. 17 pp. 527, 379.

[52] *Annals de l'Empire*, M. 12 p. 424, *Moeurs*, M. 13 p. 123.

[53] Voltaire thought Alexander III the finest character of the grim Middle Ages because he 'revived the rights of peoples and repressed the crimes of kings' (M. 13 p. 177).

[54] *Dict. Phil.*, M. 19 p. 618.

[55] M. 19 p. 533.

[56] Caussy p. 210.

[57] *Moeurs*, M. 13 p. 123.

cruel magistrates of Toulouse (even though she thought that as a
Protestant he was damned[58]) and the Dominican who confessed the
Chevalier de la Barre before his execution and wept so miserably
that the condemned man had to console him,[59] are accepted as
acolytes of the humanitarian confraternity of the Enlightenment.

As for monks in general, there was only one epoch when they
had been useful to society. In the Dark Ages, they had copied
books, cultivated the soil, and by their example mitigated the
ferocity of barbarous peoples.[60] Thus, they did something to atone
for the role they had played in undermining civilization. Rome had
been brought down 'by two scourges: the barbarians and disputes
over religion' and it had been the monks who wandered in hordes
over the Empire stirring up riots over theological trivia.[61] Gibbon
was not the only one to regret the advent of the barefooted Friars
singing vespers amid the ruins. 'Je frémissais en voyant des récollets
au Capitole', said Voltaire,[62] and he depicts the ghost of Marcus
Aurelius, the philosopher who had ruled the world, astonished to
meet brother Fulgence, swelling with pride because he confesses
the duchesse de Popoli and 'speaks sometimes to the Pope as if he
spoke to a man'.[63] A monastic Order should have no history, says
Voltaire: it should pass unnoticed while the real world goes its
way.[64] But by hoodwinking superstitious princes, the monks
became rich, and their numbers proliferated. The desire to achieve
salvation by founding a new Order,[65] the ambitions of Popes,[66] the
climate of ignorance, the way in which the inspirations of fanatics
are taken over by practical administrators,[67] helped to multiply the
monastic population beyond all reason by the eve of the Reformation.

The peculiar contribution of this multitude to Christendom has
been a series of ludicrous disputes: can the food of mendicants be

[58] D10927 (20 Jan. 1763).
[59] *Relation de la mort du Chevalier de la Barre, Mél.*, 764.
[60] *Moeurs*, M. 12 p. 334–5.
[61] M. 11 p. 241.
[62] *L'A.B.C.*, M. 27 p. 360.
[63] *Dialogue entre Marc-Aurèle et un Récollet*, M. 23 p. 479.
[64] *La Bible enfin expliquée*, M. 30 p. 98.
[65] *Moeurs*, M. 11 p. 282.
[66] *Ibid* 433.
[67] 'La prudence achève souvent les édifices fondés par le fanatisme', *Hist. Parlement de Paris*, M. 15 p. 519. Cf. 'Loyola', *Dict. Phil.*, M. 19 pp. 416–7.

described as their personal property? What form should their cowls and sleeves take? Which order of women could produce the champion in a peculiar kind of egg race?[68] The worst feud was that between Cordeliers and Dominicans over the Immaculate Conception of Our Lady; in so far as it produced explicit speculations in the worst taste, fights in processions and fraudulent visions, Voltaire was glad to chronicle the controversy.[69] The Reformation began with a quarrel of monks. The Augustinians, deprived of their trade in indulgences to the benefit of the Dominicans, put up Luther 'to preach against the merchandize that they were no longer allowed to sell'.[70] Monastic disputes had damaged the decencies of civilization more than monastic corruption: 'the monks who sing the *Pervigilium Veneris* at mattins are not dangerous; those who argue, preach and cabal have done more harm'.[71] And of this sort, the most sinister are those who have been the agents of Catholicism in the persecution of heretics. The Inquisition was 'a Christian invention to render the Pope and monks more powerful'.[72] Dominic was its true founder, and his order carried on his work.[73] The cruel tradition is still with us; within living memory Louis XIV sent Protestant girls to nunneries where the nuns had them flogged, calling in soldiers to do it;[74] the Jesuits have stirred up massacres of heretics in Poland and Lithuania,[75] in Spain you can still see an *auto da fé*, with the multicoloured rabble of friars preceding the executioner in the procession.[76]

As the Catholic armies had lumbered through history with persecuting monks as their vanguard, they had been followed by a baggage train of monastic writers laden with superstitious tales and imbecilic propaganda. There were invented miracles, from Saint

---

[68] M. 22 p. 65; *Lettres philosophiques*, *Mél.*, 42; *Annales*, M. 13 p. 393.

[69] *Traité sur la tolérance*, *Mél.*, 626–7; *Moeurs*, M. 12 pp. 292–3; *Note*, 2 pp. 84, 246. One example of the sort of suspect source used in G. Gargett, *Voltaire and Protestantism* (1980) p. 36.

[70] *Moeurs*, M. 12 p. 283; *Pensées sur le gouvernement*, M. 33 p. 534.

[71] *Dict. Phil.*, M. 17 p. 591.

[72] 'Inquisition', *Dict. Phil.*, M. 19 pp. 485–7.

[73] *Moeurs*, M. 12 pp. 348–50.

[74] *Tolérance*, M. 25 p. 24.

[75] *Discours au confédérés* (1768), M. 16 p. 136; *Essai sur les … Eglises de Pologne* (1767), M. 26 p. 463.

[76] *Candide* cap. 6; *Hist. des voyages de Scarmentado*, R p. 91. Monks lead in the condemnation of the Templars, of Galileo and of Fénelon.

Denis carrying his head, to the 'snow woman' of Saint Francis and the crab which rescued Saint Francis Xavier's crucifix from the ocean.[77] Monastic commentators twisted the Scriptural texts to find references to glorify their Order;[78] their chroniclers used their monopoly of literacy to praise the assassins who gave them land and to denigrate the worthy rulers who tried to make them pay taxation.[79] The Jesuits, coming late on the scene and learned, might be expected to form an exception. Perhaps Voltaire had once thought so, but progressively he turned against his old schoolmasters, collecting absurdities from their publications.[80] His growing hostility is seen in the change of mind about Père Daniel's history of France. In 1751 it was 'well informed, exact, wise and truthful',[81] later on it was 'dry', credulous, sycophantic to power and propagandist – 'enough to make you vomit'.[82] For the ex-Jesuits who dabbled on the fringes of literature, Voltaire's hatred was vitriolic,[83] especially for Nonotte, the compiler of Voltairean 'errors'.[84] The 'ultima ratio jesuitarum' is to blacken the decent deistical Sage of Ferney as an atheist, making him suspect to authority.[85] 'Ils persecutent partout les gens de lettres et les philosophes'.[86] The Society of Jesus aroused his special detestation because it furnished his most effective opponents.

It was, too, the most efficient instrument which the Church could wield to win power over the world. In missionary zeal, the Jesuits outdid all others; they had insinuated themselves at Peking, and ruled, despotically but justly, over their Indian subjects in

[77] 'Voyage de Saint-Pierre, *Dict. Phil.*, M. 20 p. 592; *Moeurs*, M. 11 pp. 243, 153; *Prix de la Justice*, M. 30 p. 567; Caussy p. 247; 'François Xavier' *Dict. Phil.*, M. 19 pp. 200–4.
[78] 'Figure', *Dict. Phil.*, M. 19 p. 141 (The Cordeliers).
[79] *Note*, I p. 282.
[80] *De la Chine*, M. 18 p. 157; *La Gazette littéraire*, M. 15 p. 216; *Fragment*, M. 29 p. 1; *Dict. Phil.*, M. 19 p. 221, M. 18 p. 548.
[81] See J.H. Brumfitt, *Voltaire Historian* (1970) p. 28.
[82] *Moeurs*, M. 12 pp. 510, 538, 547; *Comm. Esprit des Lois*, M. 30 p. 447. Marginal notes M. 29 pp. 413–4. Innuendoes, M. 29 pp. 470, 432. 'Vomit' in D9910 (July 1761).
[83] Desfontaines, M. 8 p. 422, M. 22 pp. 386–7, M. 30 p. 570; Patouillet, M. 20 p. 323, M. 17 p. 408, M. 26 p. 19, M. 19 pp. 546–7.
[84] M. 19 pp. 100–1; M. 20 p. 323; M. 17 pp. 407–8; M. 19 pp. 239, 467.
[85] *Les Honnêtes litteraires*, M. 26 pp. 1501–1. This a general Jesuit policy, *Note* 2 p. 399 and M. 28 p. 136.
[86] *Caussy*, p. 219.

Paraguay. But where they insinuate, they bring civil war,[87] where they rule, they are contemptuous of human freedom[88] – this is because they preach the uniqueness of Christianity, an inevitably intolerant doctrine.[89] In Europe, they manoeuvre for power by acting as confessors to the great, more especially to kings. From Père Tout-à-tous who justifies a courtier in sexual blackmail[90] to Père Daubenton who revealed the secrets of Philip V of Spain to the Regent of France,[91] all these Jesuit confessors are part of an underground organization aiming 'to become masters of the State without appearing to be so'.[92] If all else fails, they resort to assassination. Voltaire complacently lists the Jesuits who have justified regicide, and those who have given their encouragement to actual assassins, including the contemporary plotters against the king of Portugal.[93] The Dominicans are as bad; their murder of the Emperor Henry VII with a poisoned Host[94] and Jacques Clément killing Henry III of France[95] are two of Voltaire's favourite anecdotes. But he is careful not to let the reader think that the blame for these outrages goes no further than the lunatics who committed them or the monks who connived. Christianity, by its very nature, evokes such fanaticism. The assassins picture themselves as Judith, or Samuel hacking Agag to pieces; they are inspired by the hope of heaven.[96] There is no need to look for political ramifications – their only accomplices are 'the sermons of preachers and the discourses of monks'.[97]

[87] 'Japon', Dict. Phil., M. 19 p. 496; 'De la Chine', Dict. Phil., M. 18 p. 150; Lettres chinoises, M. 29 p. 479; D20459.
[88] Comm. Esprit des Lois, M. 30 p. 419. But a more favourable picture of this 'Sparta' in Moeurs. M. 12 pp. 424–5.
[89] M. 19 p. 495; M. 18 p. 150.
[90] L'Ingenu, R. pp. 260, 282. cf. Moeurs, M. 13 p. 26 and La Pucelle, M. 9 pp. 193–6.
[91] 'Confession', Dict.Phil., M. 18 p. 225; Journal de politique, M. 30 p. 399.
[92] As a Chinese statesman says, Relation du banissement des Jésuites, M. 27 p. 4. True, other monks would do the same (Ibid p. 52) and the Order should not be blamed for the crimes of individuals (M. 13 p. 343).
[93] Moeurs, M. 12 pp. 557–9. For Portugal, Siècle Louis XIV, M. 15 p. 396; Hist. Parlement, M. 15 pp. 556, 560–1. See also M. 19 p. 362.
[94] 'Jésuites, ou orgueil', Dict. Phil., M. 19 p. 500; Les Honnêtetés, M. 27 p. 125; Annales, M. 13 p. 387.
[95] Moeurs, M. 12 p. 536; L'Homme aux Quarante Écus, R. p. 331.
[96] Dict. Phil., M. 17 p. 200; L'Henriade, M. 8 p. 134; Hist. Parlement, M. 16 p. 92; also, M. 27 p. 288.
[97] Moeurs, M. 12 p. 560.

Obscurantism, intolerance and political scheming; to Voltaire, the monks provide the extreme examples of the dark doings of *L'Infâme*. Their contributions to progress he limits to the distant past. A balanced account of the monasteries of eighteenth century France would have to notice how they were essential institutions for the richer classes to maintain their life-style and inheritance patterns, how Jesuits, Oratorians and Doctrinaires taught the sons of the élite and the Frères des Écoles Chrétiennes gave technical instruction to the children of the lower bourgeoisie, and the nuns in graded hierarchies taught girls of every social class; how the only resort for the mass of the population in sickness was the ministration of the nuns amidst the squalor of the hospitals; how from the cloister came some of the finest sermons and most refined spiritual writings of the age.[98] In spite of the odd mention – or even, as in the case of the nursing nuns, note of approval,[99] very little of this could be deduced from a reading limited to the works of Voltaire. In the end, even his old schoolmasters, once praised, were dismissed as purveyors of useless information and lacking in interest in their own country.[100] The attempt by the Commission des Réguliers[101] to reform the monasteries did not arouse his interest, perhaps because he thought that, better organized and more austere, the monks would become more of a menace than they already were. Voltaire's picture of Church history has an implacable logic; monks are always engaged in some sort of promotional, propagandist or conspiratorial activity. There is no place in their story for prosaic and genial collaboration with the ordinary life of society.

---

[98] In 1760, in France there were 152 Jesuit *collèges*, 85 of the Lazarists, 71 of the Oratorians and 52 of the Doctrinaires (J. de Viguerie, *Une Oeuvre d'éducation sous l'ancien régime: les Pères de la Doctrine Chrétienne en France et en Italie* (1976) p. 75). The Maurists also had 30 (Schmitz, *Histoire de l'Ordre de Saint-Benoît* (7 vols 1956) 4 pp. 115–9). For the Frères des Écoles Chrétiennes see G. Rigault's huge history (7 vols 1938).

[99] See note 48 above. Cf. at least education is often given free of charge (M. 26 p. 568).

[100] 'Éducation', *Dict. Phil.*, M. 18 pp. 470–3.

[101] The Commission was set up in 1766, the lead being taken by Loméniè de Brienne, archbishop of Toulouse, an ally of the philosophes. (P. Chevalier, *Loménie de Brienne et l'Ordre monastique, 1766–1789* (2 vols 1959–61) I pp. 268, 273–4.

Why do postulants offer themselves to take the vows of religion? Voltaire's explanation does not entirely fit with his view of the monastic institution as an active nuisance. For him, the basic reason is that most religious commit themselves before they know what they are doing; they sacrifice their liberty at an age when the laws do not allow them to dispose of the smallest item of property.[102] They have not yet discovered the attractions of the world and they do not foresee the disillusionments of the cloister.[103] They are 'seduced' by monks and nuns 'who strive to augment the number of people of their kind'.[104] Poverty[105] may be the spur or lack of an assured place in society (as with the daughters of poor nobles who have no dowry).[106] There are a few genuine enthusiasts, but they tend to be simple minded.[107] And once inside the walls, the machinery of the law is deployed to prevent escape, and fugitives brought back face imprisonment, chains and flogging.[108] Voltaire's explanations are pedestrian. As might be expected, he belittles religious fervour, but he also fails to glimpse the psychological promptings that haunt adolescence – which were so obvious to Diderot. 'There comes a moment when practically all boys and girls fall into melancholy,' says the 'maître' in Diderot's *Jacques le Fataliste*.

> They are tormented by a vague unease ... they seek solitude, they weep; the silence of the cloister moves them and the image of the seeming peace in religious houses is seductive to their minds. They mistake the first stirrings of desire as the voice of God calling them to himself, and it is precisely when nature is evoking their longings that they embrace a life-style entirely contrary to nature's demands. The mirage vanishes and the

[102] *L'Homme aux Quarante écus*, R p. 317.
[103] D 5 (23 July 1711).
[104] *Conversation de Lucien, Érasme et Rabelais, Mél.* 721.
[105] *Avis, Mél.* 825; 'Fêtes, *Dict. Phil.* M. 19 p. 116. Monks do not desert like soldiers, because animated by three motives unknown to the troops, 'enthusiasm, hope, and love of good cooking' (D 18720, date 1773–4). *Quarante écus*, R p. 317.
[106] M. 27 p. 4.
[107] *Ibid.*
[108] 'Arrêtes notables', *Dict. Phil.*, M. 17 p. 390. This case of Bernard Castille which Voltaire refers to was a standard example for the lawyers (P-J Guyot, *Répertoire universel ... de jurisprudence* (66 vols 1777–83 + 14 vols in 1786) 49 pp. 79–86. See also *Moeurs*, M. 12 p. 345; *Mél.* 825, *Dict. Phil.*, M. 20 p. 590.

333

voice of nature is heard more clearly and is recognized;
sequestered from life they fall into regret, ... madness or
despair.[109]

The nearest Voltaire came to this insight is a quotation noted in his
common-place books: 'the desire to become a monk is a mental
small-pox usually caught about the age of fifteen.'[110]
The Voltairean analysis presupposed that the monastic vocation
was unnatural, leading inevitably to unhappiness. It was 'slavery', a
'living death', a lifetime of hopeless regret whose only outlet was
the lunatic desire to take revenge on the rest of humanity.[111] There
is no true companionship in the cloister. 'It is a well-known maxim
that monks are people who meet together without knowing each
other, live without affection, and die without regret'.[112] The mind
is ground down into stupidity,[113] the conscience into compromise
– 'the fervent novice of twenty years of age often enough has
become a crafy knave by forty'.[114] The dehumanizing process is
intensified by the separation of men from women[115] and the
unnatural obligation of celibacy. Voltaire claims there is medical
evidence to show how continence causes illness or, even, death.[116]
A necessary feature of monastic life is, therefore, masturbation, and
the temptation to fornication is overwhelming.[117] The Note Books
contain various bawdy stories in which sexual prowess is more
particularly ascribed to the Carmelites and the Cordeliers.[118] These
anecdotes are not found in the published works, but the allegedly
true tales and the inventions of Candide and La Pucelle do, in fact,
accept the predominance of these two Orders of Friars in sexual

---

[109] Jacques le Fataliste (Droz 1976) pp. 238–9.

[110] Note, 2 p. 261.

[111] 'Voeux', Dict. Phil., M. 20 p. 588; Mél., 824.

[112] Quarante écus, R p. 317. Voltaire tends to regard the monastic life as a thwarted
gloomy affair. Some more perceptive critics (of the nuns, at least) saw their
society as petty, silly and gossipy (F.C. Green, La Peinture des moeurs de la bonne
société dans le roman français de 1715 à 1761 (1924) p. 103.

[113] Lettres d'Amabed, R. p. 450.

[114] 'Cromwell', Dict. Phil., M. 18 p. 294. Cf. Moeurs, M. 16 p. 451.

[115] Mél. 824.

[116] 'Onan', Dict. Phil., M. 20 p. 135.

[117] Lettres d'Amabed, R. p. 449.

[118] Note. 1 pp. 86, 157, 164, 181, 238; 2 p. 313.

athleticism.[119] The Jesuits escape with dark hints of pederasty –
when a sodomist was burned in Paris a 'sympathetic spark' caused a
fire in the Jesuit *collège*, and so on. Specific accusations are made
only against ex-Jesuits, the *litterateur* Desfontaines with the chim-
ney sweep boys, and Marsay with his pupil the prince de
Guémée.[120]

The view that monastic life is dangerous to physical and mental
health was common. Montesquieu has medical technicalities about
the 'liquor in the seminal vessels',[121] the madness deriving from
fasting, the degrading effects of solitude and, indeed, of too much
chanting.[122] Four of the nuns in Diderot's *La Religieuse* lose their
reason, but more sophisticated in medical knowledge and psychological awareness than the other writers of the Enlightenment, and
regarding sexuality as at the heart of personality, he also detected
the linkages between inhibitions and sadism.[123] Voltaire's references to the sexual prowess of mendicants or Jesuit sodomy are the
tired flippancies of anti-clericals the world over; Diderot on the
lesbianism of the cloister has an haunting intensity and insight poles
removed from *La Religieuse en chemise* and *Le Portier des
Chartreux*.[124] Diderot's *La Religieuse* is the masterpiece which
emerged from the rash of popular literature on forced vocations. It
was a theme giving scope to pornographers and sentimentalists,
which Baculard d'Arnaud was to diversify with the trappings of
Gothic horror, and above all it was welcome to anticlericals, who
had a field day with their melodramas once the Revolution released

[119] *La Pucelle*, M. 9 p. 812 (the Cordelier Grisbourdon), *Candide*, R. p. 202 (Paquette
seduced by Cordelier); *Les Colimacons du ... père l'Escarbotier* M. 23 p. 508
(Cordelies); *La Fête de Bélébat*, M. 1 p. 287 (Carmes); *Seconde Anecdote sur
Bélisaire, Mél.* 926–7 (Cordelier); *Dict. Phil.*, M. 20 p. 399 (a Mendicant) for
others, *Quarante écus* R. p. 340 (Capucin); *Dict. Phil.*, M. 18 pp. 389–90
(Cistercian).
[120] D 20010 (March 1776); 'Amour socratique', *Dict. Phil.*, M. 17 p. 183; Cf. M. 19
p. 500; M. 17 p. 182 and D 20906.
[121] Montesquieu, *Essai sur les causes qui peuvent affecter les esprits et les caractères,
Oeuvres* (Pléiade 1966) p. 49.
[122] *Ibid* p. 151. For the evil effects of solitude as debated between Diderot and
Rousseau, see *Rousseau juge de Jean-Jacques*, 2e Disc., *Oeuvres* (Pléiade 1964) 1 p.
789.
[123] [G.] May, [*Diderot et 'La Religieuse'* (1954)] p. 191.
[124] *Ibid* p. 126. See also V. Mylner, 'What Suzanne knew', *Studies on Voltaire and the
18th Century* CCVIII (1982) pp. 167–173.

the inhibitions of the theatre.[125] In this spirit Voltaire welcomed La Harpe's *Mélanie* in 1770.[126] Diderot's novel is different. Rome and the secular clergy are depicted as generous and, something Voltaire could hardly understand, Christian consolation in suffering is movingly described. Suzanne in her cell, hands bound, an iron crucifix on her knees, deserted by all, sees the pierced hands and feet, the wounded side, the crown of thorns – '*Voilà mon Dieu, et j'ose me plaindre*'.[127]

Voltaire was a man of feeling, expressed in tearful stage plays, in the preaching of *bienfaisance*, and vibrating in his onslaughts on judicial cruelties and crimes of intolerance.[128] But the cult of pre-romantic melancholy and loneliness was alien to him; he wanted to be read amidst the bustle of a developing civilization,[129] and to live socially and actively, improving the world and extracting recognition from it. That other sentimental resort of the century, more pathetic even than forced vocations, the star-crossed lovers who hide their grief in the shadows of the cloister,[130] did not move him. The despairing passion of Héloise and Abelard, as reflected in inventive translations and endowed by Pope with a background of wild scenery, had become a vogue in France by the mid-century. '*Jamais histoire amoureuse n'a fait tant de bruit*' said a journalist in 1758; Diderot reflected on the story with admiration: '*Comme cet homme fut aimé!*'[131] To Voltaire, Héloise wrote in 'too theological a style' and Abelard was an intelligent man using a 'barbarous jargon'. As for their love affair, it was a subject for a dubious jest – my 71 years have had the same effect on me as the rasor of 'M. le Chanoine' had on Abelard.[132] The pilgrims who

---

[125] E. Estève, *Études de littérature préromantique* (1923) pp. 91–7.
[126] D 16115, D 14044, D 16237. For the real life instances behind La Harpe's play, see C. Todd, *Voltaire's Disciple: Jean-François de la Harpe* (1972) p. 129.
[127] May p. 167. Diderot is too fond of portraying characters in the round to resort to anticlerical caricature – e.g. P. Hudson is witty, agreeable and a good administrator as well as a cynic and a womanizer (*Jacques le Fataliste* pp. 241–8).
[128] See [R.S.] Ridgway, [*Voltaire and Sensibility* (1973)].
[129] Cf. Fontanes in 1783, cit Ridgway p. 252.
[130] [J.] McManners, [*Death and the Enlightenment* (1981)] pp. 421–2.
[131] Charlotte Charrier, *Héloise dans l'histoire et dans la légende* (1933) pp. 407–14, 446, 468, 473. See also for general background, R. Shackleton, 'The Cloister Theme in French Preromanticism', *The French Mind: Studies in Honour of Gustave Rudler* (1952) pp. 173–7.
[132] Cf. D 8484 and D 12583 (Marin to Voltaire).

went to the abbey of the Paraclet to weep before the tomb of the twelfth-century lovers had been reading Rousseau rather than Voltaire.

The Enlightenment had a solid substratum of conventional thought which was not the monopoly of the *philosophes*, had nothing to do with anticlericalism, and only incidental connexions with abstractions like nature and reason, or emotional fashions like *sensibilité*. This was the commonsense determination to increase national wealth and prosperity by getting rid of inefficiency and parasitism, and increasing the labouring population. On every score, the monasteries were censured. Voltaire's *L'homme aux 40 écus* was just the man to do the calculation; 90,000 monks and nuns in France at his own subsistence rate would need 10,800,000 livres to live on, and they have 50,000,000 (and living in common ought to be cheaper).[133] Not surprisingly then, there are abbeys where they drink the best vintages and dine on partridge and pheasant and sleep on feather beds, not unaccompanied.[134] Voltaire was not good on the accountancy details; he could have said more about how the *commende* siphons off so much monastic wealth to the aristocracy,[135] and Nonotte caught him out on his illustration of abbeys with 200,000 livres of income.[136] His speciality was, rather, to denounce the way in which the monks had acquired their property in the first place, by frightening superstitious warriors with fears of Hell and by forging charters.[137] And monasteries always are tight-fisted. So many of them hold tithes, and pay their parish priests a mere pittance,[138] while the indigent rarely find succour at their gates. 'What seek you, my son?' asks the barefooted Carmelite friar. 'Bread, reverend father'. 'My son, we ask

---

[133] *Quarante écus*, R. pp. 316–7. In *Le Siècle de Louis XIV*, Voltaire had said that the wealth of the French Church was not excessive to maintain the numbers of monks and clergy, only it was ill-distributed (*O. hist.* p. 1031).

[134] Curé de campagne', *Dict. Phil.*, M. 17 p. 303.

[135] 'Biens d'église', *Dict. Phil.*, M. 17 p. 591. In M. 19 p. 109 he says that if the commendatory abbot resides locally, this is good for the countryside, if not, not.

[136] Voltaire was driven to inferences from the architect who told him that the plans for the rebuilding of Cîteaux would cost 1,700,000 fr to complete (M. 27 p. 145; D10285).

[137] 'Abbaye', *Dict. Phil.*, M. 18 p. 49; *Diatribe*, M. 29 pp. 361 etc.

[138] *Dict. Phil.*, M. 18 p. 303.

alms ourselves, we do not give any'.[139] And Voltaire tells the grisly tale of how, during the siege of Paris by Henry IV, when the people were eating human flesh and digging up graves for bones to gnaw, the convent cellars were stacked with provisions.[140]

The art in denouncing abuses is to show, in convincing detail, how individuals suffer from them. Voltaire's way of doing this was to use historical anecdotes, to invent naïve complainants telling their story, or to intervene himself with irony and ruthless logic in an actual law suit.

Just such a complaint at law came his way in 1770, when he allied with a local *avocat* who was pleading the cause of the 'serfs' on the lands of the abbey of Saint-Claude in Franche-Comté before the Parlement of Besançon (they were not serfs in the medieval sense, but by the tenure of *mainmorte* their property at death fell to the seigneur unless there were direct heirs living at home to inherit it). For seven years Voltaire pursued this ancient injustice, publishing petitions to the King and forging unreasonable replies of the monks.[141] Best of all, he produced a pamphlet purporting to be the reflections of the *curé* of the abbey, newly come to his parish and astonished by the oppressions he found.[142] He sees a vision of Christ appearing to the cellarer of Saint-Claude, who summarily dismisses the dominical plea for generosity. 'You were the suffering Church, we are the Church triumphant. We gave them the hope of heaven, so we took their land from them'. There were something like a million peasants holding by this servile tenure in the Eastern provinces, but Voltaire is careful not to mention the laymen or secular clergy who are their seigneurs, except to cite a few examples of those who are willing to give up their rights. The Benedictines of Saint-Claude, he argues, are an illustration of 'that hardness of heart, that greed, that hatred of the human race' which the monastic life engenders.[143]

[139] *Aventure avec un Carme*, R. pp. 301–2. (A minor example of tight-fistedness – the Jesuits undercutting the apothecaries of Paris (D15212; M. 25 pp. 261–2).
[140] *Henriade* chant IX, M. 8 p. 250; *Essai sur les guerres civiles*, M. 8 p. 281.
[141] M. 28 pp. 333, 339, 353–60, 368–79. The case eventually is lost (D20704).
[142] *La Voix du curé* (1772), M. 18 pp. 567–76.
[143] *Ibid* p. 573. Generally see Demante, *Étude sur les gens de condition mainmortable en France au 18ᵉ siècle* (1894); G-L. Chassin, *L'Église et les derniers serfs* (1886) and L. Barbedette, 'La terre de Luxeuil à la veille de la Révolution; *Ann. hist. de la Révolution française* (1927) pp. 157–9.

'The riches of a State consist in the number of inhabitants and in their labour'. So says the *philosophe* in a dialogue Voltaire published in 1751, the conclusion being that women should be forbidden to take vows of religion.[144] The year before, he had proposed to finance bourgeois marriages from the revenues of great abbeys: 'a woman who feeds two children and spins renders more service to her country than all the convents'.[145] The theorists of the 'Political Economy' of the eighteenth century, more especially the Physiocrats, were convinced that the population had declined since ancient times – an additional reason for alarm at recruitment to the monastic life. Voltaire went along with this hypothesis of decline until 1763 when he announced his scepticism,[146] and he was aware that, while rulers want increases in population, the general interest of mankind is more concerned with happiness.[147] But he had more than the fashionable populationist doctrine to inspire his condemnation of monasticism. His view of the whole duty of man was utilitarian. He did not disbelieve in prayer, but could not see why it ought to become a profession, and austerities were virtually useless. A few chosen souls, lovers of study, might set themselves apart to adore God and live frugally, and the Chartreux, in their eternal silence, arouse his admiration – yet how much better if these virtues could be useful to the world![148] Omri, a good citizen and family man, given to charity, is worried about his eternal destiny. 'Do you pierce your backside with nails?' asks the fakir. 'Never, reverend father'. 'I'm sorry, you'll never get as far as the nineteenth heaven, it's a pity'.[149]

Voltaire's gospel was one of benevolence, and work. Indefatigable himself, he wanted to reduce the number of holidays, discourage the multitude from resorting to taverns,[150] and set monks and nuns to useful labour. After all, what is the trade of a monk? 'It is to

[144] *Dialogue entre un philosophe et un Controlleur Général*, M. 33 p. 502.
[145] *La Voix sage du peuple*, M. 33 p. 496.
[146] McManners, cap. 4.
[147] D12144 (Oct. 1764). Other writers put the populationist case more severely than Voltaire, e.g. Montesquieu, *Lettres Persanes*, *Oeuvres* (2 vols 1964) 1 p. 305 – 'gulfs in which future races are swallowed up'.
[148] *Moeurs*, M. 12 p. 337. Cf. 'Austérités', *Dict. Phil.*, M. 17 pp. 491–4; *Alzire*, Disc. prélim, M. 2 p. 379; *Sottisier*, M. 32 p. 578; *Discours en vers sur l'homme*, *Mél.* 211.
[149] *Lettre d'un Turc sur les Fakirs*, R. p. 477.
[150] H.C. Payne, *The Philosophes and the People* (1976) pp. 116–123.

have none at all, to engage himself by an inviolable oath to be useless to the human race, to be a laughing stock and a slave, and to live at the expense of other people'.[151] C'est n'être bon à rien de n'être bon qu'a soi'[152] – we have to serve others. The country needs retreats for the aged and infirm and for wounded soldiers; what we have are communities of drones which, paradoxically, demand a test of physical fitness to enter.[153] An Indian philosopher in Paris is astonished to see strapping youths in cowls and rope girdles, 'too great saints to work', while there is a shortage of building labour (no one tells him, of course, about the Capucins turning out with buckets and axes as the municipal fire brigade).[154] Why is France less rich than it used to be, and less rich than the Protestant countries? Because men are going into luxury trades, or becoming lawyers or theologians, or going into monasteries.[155] They are forgetting the rule (put by Voltaire in the mouth of a weaver of Lyon who refused a comfortable monastic vocation): 'chaque homme doit son tribut à la société.'[156] This is why the Mendicants are the especial objects of Voltaire's scorn. Begging is deplorable, and the worst kind of beggar is not the one in rags who solicits your money to get drunk, but the one in uniform who demands tribute in the name of God.[157] Of the 98 monastic Orders, 34 live on alms;[158] we ought to form a band of lay missioners to go round Paris house by house, 'advising fathers and mothers to be virtuous, to keep their money for their families and to support their old age,

---

[151] *Conversation de Lucien, Érasme et Rabelais, Mél.* 70.

[152] *Disc. en vers, Mél.* 436; Cf. *Dict. Phil.*, M. 20 p. 590.

[153] *Lettre d'un ecclésiastique*, M. 29 p. 287.

[154] *Les Embellisements de la ville* ..., M. 30 p. 478. For Capucins as fire brigade see Collas, *Saint-Louis d'Antin et sa territoire* (1932) pp. 64–5; Barbier, *Chronique* ... *1718–63* (8 vols 1857–8) 3 p. 103; Baston, *Mémoires*, edd J. Loth and Ch. Verger (3 vols 1897–9) 1 pp. 104–9, 141; Mme de Genlis, *Mémoires* (1825) 1 p. 38; Restif de la Bretonne, 'Récit d'un incendie; *Les Nuits de Paris* (ed Bachelin, n.d.) 1 p. 67. For the town of Troyes, A. Babeau, *La Ville sous l'ancien régime* (2 vols 1884) 2 pp. 141–4. In Autun, it was the Cordeliers, T.J. Schmitt, *L'Assistance dans l'archidiaconé d'Autun au xviie et xviiie siècles* (1952) pp. 74, xliii.

[155] *Quarante écus*, R. p. 284; *L'A.B.C.*, M. 27 p. 385; 'Population; *Dict. Phil.*, M. 20 p. 252.

[156] 'Fêtes', *Dict. Phil.*, M. 20 p. 116.

[157] *Dialogues entre un philosophe* ..., M. 23, 504.

[158] 'Quête'; *Dict. Phil.*, M. 20 pp. 314–18.

to love God with all their heart and never give anything to the Friars'.[159]

The monasteries are a drag on economic progress, and the remedies, to Voltaire, are straightforward: a massive confiscation of superfluous wealth, and severe restrictions upon the taking of vows. Since by definition the religious have no descendants, confiscation is only a temporary injustice: 'Une injustice d'un jour ... elle en produit un bien pour les siècles'.[160] Monastic vows are a purely human institution unknown to the New Testament,[161] and the State can restrict, prohibit or, even, nullify such vows if they are harmful to society. 'The first of all vows is to be a citizen; this is the primordial and tacit oath, authorized by God, a vow in the order of Providence, an unchangeable, imprescriptible vow'; no one is entitled to override this natural engagement to society without the permission of the magistrates.[162] In Russia, Peter the Great has banned the taking of vows before the age of 30, and has ordered the monks to till the soil and the nuns to serve in hospitals or work with their hands – an edict you'd have thought had been devised in collaboration with one of the early Fathers of the Church.[163] France ought to follow suit, say, by prohibiting all monastic professions before the age of 25.[164]

The French Revolution, without patristic collaboration, went further than the Russian autocrat. The decree of February 1790 opened the gates of monasteries to those of the inmates who chose freedom. Educational and charitable institutions were to stay 'for the present'; others would be suppressed, and in future, the taking of vows was forbidden.

---

[159] 'Scandal', *Dict. Phil.*, M. 20 p. 400. Cf. *Avis ... Calas, Mél.* 824; 'Mendicant'. *Dict. Phil.*, M. 19 p. 324; *Diatribe*, M. 29 p. 370.

[160] *Moeurs*, M. 12 p. 310 (concerning the Reformation in England); *Éloge hist. de la Raison*, R. p. 490.

[161] *Dict. Phil.*, M. 18 p. 194. Papal charges for dispensation show how little vows really matter (*ibid* p. 445).

[162] 'Droit Canonique', *Dict. Phil.*, M. 18 p. 445.

[163] *La Russie sous Pierre le Grand*, O. hist. pp. 429, 576. An attempt to reform in Spain fails (*Note*, 2 p. 379). The laws of China (*Moeurs*, M. 12 p. 431).

[164] *La Voix sage du peuple*, M. 33 p. 496.

This legislation ran far ahead of opinion in the country. The *cahiers* had been full of complaints about monastic wealth and idleness, but scarce one in fifty had proposed getting rid of the religious altogether. It is not often that the historian is presented with such an – apparently – clear example of ideology influencing policy. But there are distinctions to be made, though it would take a great deal of enquiry to be able to make them with assurance. Hazarding a guess, however: the cruder aspects of Voltaire's censures – the polemical and sardonic reflexions on monastic history, on superstition, ignorance, intolerance and political intrigue were probably the least important influence. More significant was the utilitarian idealism which called on every citizen to work for his living, to bring up a family, and generally to contribute to the progress of society; allied to this was the *sensibilité* which was haunted by the nuances of sexual desire, sought to free children from parental tyranny, and regretted useless austerities; reinforcing these sentiments, there was the cult of Nature which endowed family life with an almost mystical significance. If this guess at the comparative force of the influences behind the decree of 1790 is correct, the monks were not so much victims of anticlerical fanaticism, as of the utilitarian, humanitarian and sentimental aspirations of the generation of 1789. Perhaps similar distinctions ought to be made within the mass of arguments indefatigably put out by Voltaire. He hated the Jesuits, but when they were persecuted, he came to pity them.[165] Had he lived to see the Revolution, he would have been moved by the sufferings of monks and nuns, and as for the buffoons who ridiculed the monastic life in melodramas and masquerades – not without support from his writings – he would have turned from them with fastidious contempt.

All Souls' College
Oxford

---

[165] D1078, D14161. He was sad also to lose the Jesuit men of letters (D13337) and he regretted that they had not been kept on to fight the Jansenists (D8965, D11987, D14330).

'A STANDING MIRACLE': LA TRAPPE AT LULWORTH, 1794–1817

by DOMINIC AIDAN BELLENGER

ENGLISH monasticism survived the Reformation only in exile. In the course of the seventeenth and eighteenth centuries many monks came to England as pastors to the Catholic community (indeed all members of the English Benedictine Congregation, revived at the beginning of the seventeenth century, took an oath promising to work in England after ordination), but they lived alone or in small groups and except during the early Stuart period there were no organised religious communities in England which could properly be called monastic.[1] This state of affairs was to change dramatically in the years of the French Revolution when the English communities on the continent were repatriated and a number of French religious made their way to England as *émigrés*. The English communities (including those now represented by the abbeys of Ampleforth in Yorkshire and Downside in Somerset, formerly at Dieulouard in Lorraine and Douai in Flanders respectively) managed to settle in England without too much opposition. These monks had been trained for circumspect behaviour on the mission and were not noticeably 'monastic' in either appearance or behaviour; the complete Benedictine habit was not used at Downside, for example, until the late 1840s[2] and working in parishes away from their monasteries remained the normal expectation of most English Benedictine monks until well into the present century.[3] The same could not be said of the community of Saint Susan at Lulworth in Dorset which provided between the years 1794 and 1817 the setting for the first experiment in fully observant monastic life in England for two hundred and fifty years.

[1] For the Stuart communities see D. Lunn, *The English Benedictines, 1540–1688* (London 1980) pp. 121–45.
[2] H.N. Birt, *Downside* (London 1902) p. 193.
[3] B. Green, *The English Benedictine Congregation* (London 1980) pp. 67–86.

The Lulworth monks followed the Cistercian way of life in its full rigour. The nucleus of the community were monks of La Trappe in Northern France, a house whose observance, some would say fanaticism, was second to none. Not content with the reforms of Armand de Rancé (1626–1700), whose name sent a shiver down the spine of every 'enlightened' man, the monks of La Trappe braced themselves for the dispersal following the French Revolution with still further asceticisms. Under the leadership of Augustin de Lestrange (1754–1827) the remnant of the Trappist community, resident at Val Sainte in the canton of Friborg in Switzerland, developed a life of singular austerity and piety which culminated in 1794 with an attempt to introduce the *laus perennis*, the uninterrupted performance of the divine office.[4] 1794 was the year, too, in which Lestrange (Novice Master of La Trappe) was elected abbot of La Trappe at Val Sainte, and also the year in which the Lulworth monastery was established.

The small group of five or six monks who founded Lulworth Abbey were sent to England by Lestrange not to settle here but as the first stage of a journey to Canada where it was hoped they would be able to make a foundation free from the distractions of politically disturbed Europe. Their passage was booked, but they seem to have missed their boat.[5] Help was at hand in the person of Mr Thomas Weld (1750–1810) of Lulworth Castle in Dorset. Weld, one of the richest and most influential of English Catholic landowners and the father of a future cardinal, was prodigal in his benefactions to the Catholic Church.[6] He also had a special interest in monasticism. On his estates, some three miles from his house, near the village of Wool, stood the ruins of Bindon Abbey, a medieval Cistercian foundation. At the time the Trappists were arriving in England he was supervising the building among the ruins of a small Gothick pavilion which still stands there.[7] He was glad to be able to give refuge to some living monks and perhaps

[4] L.J. Lekai, *The Cistercians: Ideals and Realities* (Kent State 1977) p. 181.
[5] D. Bellenger, 'The French Revolution and the Religious Orders. Three Communities 1789–1815', *D Rev* 98 (1980) p. 26.
[6] J. Berkeley, *Lulworth and the Welds* (Gillingham 1971) pp. 143–208.
[7] *Royal Commission on Historical Monuments: County of Dorset* Vol 2 South-East, Part 2 (London 1970) pp. 402–8.

when the Trappists first made his acquaintance through the good offices of Dr (afterwards Bishop) John Milner (1752–1826), the Catholic antiquary and controversialist, he saw them as fitting into his improvements at Bindon.

In the event, Weld's final scheme for the monks was to be more ambitious. He built the monks a full-scale monastery on a new site. It was situated in a valley between the castle and the sea not too far from the original site of Bindon Abbey. The building, the fragments of which are now known as Monastery Farm (OS 861810), was perhaps designed by John Carter (1748–1817), Milner's architect for the Catholic chapel at Winchester, whose idiom was 'Commissioners' Gothic' with frills.[8] At Lulworth there was less emphasis on the frills. Nevertheless it was no toy-town monastery. The cob-stone construction with its thatched roof provided a complete conventual building which included cloister, refectory, dormitory, workshops, and church (divided into areas for choir-monks, lay-brothers and laity). It would not have appealed to Pugin as a building, but it was not too far distant in atmosphere from the first Cistercian homes. At the time it caused a sensation and the monastery became a tourist attraction for visitors from the local watering places and from far further afield.

Some of the visitors were so impressed by what they saw that they decided to stay and the monastic family grew to such a large size that it was given the status and dignity of an abbey; about one hundred and thirty men were to follow the monastic life at Lulworth.[9] Many of the recruits were from suppressed French monasteries and many others from Ireland, but there were some English aspirants: the first to come, Stephen Hawkins, arrived in 1795.[10] Most visitors were not, however, potential postulants and they included a number of journalists who gave the place the full Grub Street treatment. The contributor to *The Monthly Magazine* was typical of one approach, not uninfluenced I suspect by the

[8] For John Carter see B. Little, *Catholic Churches since 1623* (London 1966) pp. 49–50. His involvement at Lulworth is indicated in a letter of October 1794 from J. Wilmot to T. Weld in the Weld Papers at Dorchester (Dorset Record Office, Weld Papers, R 17).

[9] Stapehill Abbey Archives Dorset, MS History of Lulworth Abbey by Sr M Alberic Vol 4 p. 37.

[10] J. Gell, 'The Return of the Cistercians to England', *Hallel* 10 (1982) p. 82.

picture of monasticism presented in the contemporary best-seller *The Monk* by Matthew Lewis (1775–1818), in finding the whole place revolting, 'a gloomy abode of ignorance and nastiness, which I quitted with a sigh, breathed in compassion of the loss of those whom vice or folly drove for the expiation of real or fancied iniquities into the community of La Trappe'.[11] This attitude was mirrored in the various anti-monastic and anti-Lulworth tracts which were circulated at the time[12] and in the credence given to the wild accusations of one of the monks who left the community, Joseph Power, whose 'revelations' rocked the community and led eventually to its dismissal from England.[13]

Not all printed accounts of the place were hostile. *Catholicon* a short-lived journal intended for an educated Roman Catholic readership, published a highly complimentary description of the place by a Downside monk, probably Dom Luke Bernard Barber (1790–1850), whose brother had transferred his stability from Downside to Lulworth.[14] John Milner, in *The Gentleman's Magazine*, defended the establishment against its detractors, although with a reserve which probably indicated his own misgivings.[15]

Friendly and hostile accounts alike agreed in their description of the life of the monastery while coming to quite contrary conclusions about their observations.[16] At the centre of life at Lulworth was the liturgy. There was a sung conventual high mass each morning. The round of monastic offices included Matins during the night although there seems to have been no attempt to perform *laus perennis*. The services were open to the public but special permission, not readily given, was needed for attendance at the night office. There were also devotions of various kinds. *Catholicon* describes a procession of the Blessed Sacrament around the cloister

---

[11] *The Monthly Magazine* 10 (1803) p. 232.

[12] See notably *The Canonization of Thomas ———Esq., who has lately erected at East L———h a Monastery ...* (London 1801).

[13] [*Woodforde Papers and Diaries*, ed D.H.] Woodforde (London 1932) pp. 105–242.

[14] Catholicon [5 (1817)] pp. 1–10. For Dom Bernard Barber see H.N. Birt, *Obit Book of the English Benedictines from 1600–1912* (Edinburgh 1913) p. 149. For John Baptist Barber see Downside Abbey Archives (Birt Papers C 236 Letters from and about J. Barber).

[15] *The Gentleman's Magazine* Vol 66 part 1 (1796) p. 471. Milner expanded his ideas in *The Inquisition. A letter addressed to Sir John Hippisley, Bart.* (London 1816).

[16] (T.D.) Fosbrooke, [*British Monachism* (London 1817)] pp. 400–10 provides an interesting general account of the community.

on a suitable floral carpet.[17] The variety of religious functions, both liturgical and devotional, was on a scale and openness which the English communities would never have contemplated. The novelty of the rites as far as the English public was concerned is reflected in the illustrations of monastic life at Lulworth in the second edition of Fosbrooke's work on British monachism where every bow and gesture is looked upon as something worth recording and reproducing.[18]

The Cistercian tradition of hard manual labour was rigidly followed at Lulworth. 'I found some of the monks', wrote Father Barber, 'exercising the trades of carpenters, wheelwrights, blacksmiths; others of shoemakers, tailors, weavers and several other professions ... I likewise saw their dairy'.[19] The agricultural work of the monks was one of the chief causes of disagreement between the community and the locality and was gradually curtailed by the Welds during the monks' stay.[20]

The physical comforts allowed to the monks were few. They slept in their habits (which seem to have been worn all the time) in a dormitory 'a long room, with beds on both sides, and a window at each end' on beds which were little better than hard boards.[21] Food was basic.

> Their dinner consisted of a good sized tin dish of meagre soup, seasoned with nothing else but salt, a dish of thickened milk, likewise seasoned with salt, and a good appetite. There were also four or five roasted potatoes, and a good slice of their coarse bread. Water was their drink. ... To remind them not to eat with too much avidity, the Abbot rings a little bell, which he has near him, three different times during dinner. As soon as this signal is given, every monk instantly stops eating, without even swallowing the morsel he may happen to have in his mouth at the time. Not a lip or a finger is moved, until the bell signifies that they may proceed with their meal.[22]

[17] *Catholicon* p. 3.
[18] Fosbrooke facing p. 410.
[19] *Catholicon* p. 4.
[20] Dorset Record Office, Weld Papers R 17. Documents relating to the Trappist Monastery at Lulworth.
[21] *Catholicon*, p. 4.
[22] *Ibid* p. 3.

Father Barber, used to Benedictine fare, looked on every day at La Trappe as a fast day, but was generally impressed by the contentment of the monks. Other visitors were more struck by the somewhat neurotic tone of the establishment. Although the apostate Power is a suspect witness there is a ring of truth about his suggestion that many of the inmates were unbalanced, and there was an alarming turnover rate of novices.[23] The surviving letters of the first prior (1794–1802) of the Lulworth Cistercians, Jean-Baptiste Des Noyers (c.1769–1849), have about them a hysterical character given particular force by the recurrent phrase 'the holy will of God' (the motto of Lestrange's reform) which was used by Jean-Baptiste in justifying all his actions both great and small.[24] The letters, too, from the prior to the guardian of a child who died while in the care of the school attached to the monastery reveal a cloying sentimentality which does not appeal to modern readers.[25]

The monastic school – and it was it would seem a *monastic* school rather than an ordinary school in which monks took a part – attracted even more notice than other parts of the establishment. The boys in the school were few in number but drew attention to themselves by their semi-monastic attire and shaven heads. Even the Catholic authorities felt uncertain. Dr John Douglass (1743–1812), the Vicar Apostolic of London, looked askance at such a public parade of monastic education,[26] as did Mr Weld who had not sanctioned the school's existence. It was closed in 1799.[27]

The reactions of the outside world to the school, and to the monastery which sustained it, can be summarised under three headings: curiosity, reserve and hostility. Lulworth, in common perhaps with all monasteries, became a talking-point in its neighbourhood and a focus of local gossip and suspicion. People were as eager to peep over the monastery wall as they imagined the monks

---

[23] Woodforde pp. 112–13.

[24] Archives de la Grande Trappe Soligny, France, 217. Lettres relatives à la fondation de Lulworth en Angleterre.

[25] G. Carron, *Pious Biography for Young Men: or, The Virtuous Scholars* (Dublin 1840) pp. 315–324. According to Fosbrooke p. 402 the Lulworth monks 'maintained eighty orphan children of the murdered French noblesse'.

[26] Archives of the Archbishop of Westminster, London, Bishop John Douglass's Diary 27 October 1798.

[27] *Ibid* 31 March 1799.

were eager to leap over it. Out of this curiosity – which led one woman at least, Julia Woodforde, to disguise herself as a man to visit the monastic enclosure[28] – came some sort of understanding of what monasticism was about. It was, no doubt, a distorted understanding, but it did reveal to many people for the first time that a monk was not a figure of the fantastic imagination of the Gothick novelist but a real man. The humanity of the monks, however, did not persuade many people that they were a good thing. Reserve towards the monks and their ideals was a position favoured not only by Protestants but also by their English co-religionists. Not only were the English Catholics alarmed by the unfavourable impact of the place on public opinion towards Catholics – an explicit ban on monastic profession, proposed in the Mildmay Bill of 1800, a bill partly prompted by the Lulworth Trappists,[29] would have threatened the future of the many missions manned by monks and friars – but they were also, in general, unsympathetic to the type of monasticism represented by Lulworth. It was, to their minds, excessive in its outward manifestations and in its exaltation of God's fools. The English monks of the time were urbane, solid men who had little time for foreign extremism. There were some, like Br John Baptist Barber, who moved away from the recusant traditions of the English Benedictine Congregation to the Trappists, but these were exceptional. The English Catholics (including most of the English monks) shared, I would suggest, the deep-rooted hostility of the English temperament to the most ostentatious displays of piety.

In conclusion it could be suggested that the importance of the Lulworth Cistercians in the study of monastic history is fourfold. Firstly, the abbey of Saint Susan at Lulworth showed that it was possible for a large religious community, albeit not predominantly a native one, to exist in Georgian England. Its successes as well as its setbacks provided many useful lessons for its Victorian successors. Secondly, the nature of the monastic life lived at Lulworth – the rigour of its asceticism, the dreary routine of its *horarium*, its close following of the Benedictine Rule – showed its affinity with

---

[28] Woodforde p. 108.
[29] D. Bellenger, 'The Emigré Clergy and the English Church, 1789–1815', *JEH* 34 (1983) pp. 407–9.

many other monastic reform movements throughout the ages. It was an attempt to turn the clock back, to search for roots, to expiate sins, to cleanse society. La Trappe at Lulworth was a positive affirmation of values which the French Revolution and eighteenth-century rationalism had attempted to extirpate. Thirdly, in its extreme answer for extreme times, it showed to a chosen few the monastic alternative. The ascetic way can never be the way of the majority. Lulworth provided a setting for the life of that elite who made 'the standing miracle'[30] of Lulworth a reality. The need for an ascetic alternative was as apparent in late eighteenth-century England as anywhere else. Fourthly, the Lulworth community showed the strength and the roots of anti-monastic feelings. The monk, especially the French monk, was an outsider and an outsider by choice. His very marginality made him a threat to all that a still largely community and family-based society held dearest. The monks of La Trappe at Lulworth, in common with all monks, were signs of contradiction.

Downside Abbey

[30] Bristol City Record Office, Western Vicariate Archives 1794–5 p. 76.

CHANGING IMAGES OF ROMAN CATHOLIC RELIGIOUS ORDERS IN THE NINETEENTH CENTURY

by BERNARD ASPINWALL

"" "C AMELOT-Camelot:" said I to myself "I don't seem to remember hearing of it before. Name of the asylum, likely."' so said Mark Twain's Connecticut Yankee at King Arthur's Court.[1] But the irony is that the joke is now on Twain. In examining *The Discovery of the Asylum*, David J. Rothman has persuasively argued that the American asylum which developed in the 1820s and 1830s served a dual purpose.[2] It would create the correct desirable attitudes within its inmates and by virtue of its success, set an example of right action to the larger society. The well-ordered asylum would exemplify the proper principles of social organisation and thus insure the safety of the republic and promote its glory. My purpose is to suggest that the monastery in Europe served a similar purpose. Europeans faced similar social and political problems to Americans and the re-discovery of monasticism paralleled the growth of American institutions and served a similar purpose in the public arena. In the process a more tolerant and sympathetic attitude towards religious orders emerged.

In the first half of the nineteenth century several paintings of Roman Catholic religious orders attracted public attention. The two paintings of St. Francis of Assisi by the seventeenth-century Spanish artist, Francisco Zurbarán (1598–1664) and Charles A. Collins' *Convent Thoughts* are indicative of the changing image of religious communities.[3] In the wake of the French occupation and

---

[1] Quoted in heading to chapter I, John Fraser, *America and the Patterns of Chivalry* (Cambridge 1982).

[2] *The Discovery of the Asylum: Social Order and Disorder in the New Republic* (Boston 1971) and his later *Conscience and Convenience: the Asylum and Alternatives in Progressive America* (Boston 1980).

[3] See Ilse (Hempel) Lipschutz, *Spanish Painting [and the French Romantics]* (Cambridge, Mass. 1972) esp pp. 205–12 and Allen Staley, *The Pre-Raphaelite Landscape*

351

the secularisation of Spanish monasteries, Zurbarán was 'disco-vered' and the knowledge of his work disseminated throughout Europe with considerable influence upon artistic developments. With Murillo's *The Vision of St. Bernard*, his work gave a deeper appreciation and understanding of the religious life so sensationally portrayed in Matthew G. Lewis's *The Monk* (1795). That fascina-tion with the ideal of self-sacrifice, celibacy and religious devotion was to be imported into Britain through the various artists associated with the Pre-Raphaelites. Dante Gabriel Rosetti's *Ecce Ancilla Domini* (1850) shows the influence of the German Nazarene monastic ideas. When *Convent Thoughts* was exhibited the follow-ing year it was attacked as Tractarian and Catholic propaganda, but the intensity of the reaction indicated the changing attitudes. What had been previously dismissed as alien superstitution was becoming rooted in British soil: Oxford and Cambridge men had turned Catholic and entered religious orders. Frederick Faber, the Orato-rian Oxford convert could feel he swept aside invincible ignorance as he walked down the street in his religious habit. What had been bizarre in Matthew G. Lewis or Walter Scott, or in the salacious revelations of Maria Monk and her kind, was becoming more understandable, if not acceptable.[4] It was a process which was to culminate in Thomas Merton, a Trappist monk becoming a best-selling author in twentieth-century America.

The reasons for this transformation were many and varied. The traditional view would emphasise romanticism: the influence of Scott, the dismantling of penal legislation and the general Catholic revival in the wake of the French Revolution. My concern however is the uses of religious orders in a wider world. By 1851 when *Convent Thoughts* was first publicly exhibited, the grounds of religious controversy were shifting decisively to the social implica-tions of Catholicism and Protestantism. In that debate the two main Catholic apologists, Donoso Cortes and Jaime L. Balmes,

---

(Oxford 1973) p. 14: Keith Andrews, *The Nazarenes: A Brotherhood of German Painters in Rome* (Oxford 1964): Maria Monk, *Awful Disclosures of the Hotel Dieu Nunnery of Montreal* (New York 1836); Rebecca T. Reed, *Six Months in a Convent* (Boston 1835). See R.A. Billington, *The Protestant Crusade, 1800–60; A Study of the Origins of American Nativism* (Chicago 1964 ed).

[4] See Bernard Ward, *The Sequel to Catholic Emancipation, 1830–50*, 2 vols (London 1915).

significantly were Spaniards.[5] Against a background of general European social and political unrest they emphasised the stability and order induced by Catholicism. Their conservative apologetic clashed with the dynamic liberal commercial outlook; their static, hierarchical rural order with the fluid entrepreneurial society; their cohesive harmonious people with the undisciplined chaos of urban society. The strength of that point was apparent from the 1820s in the flourishing schemes for new model communities in Britain and America. Owenism was the most obvious but there were numerous other utopian communities proposed and established on both sides of the Atlantic. Mormonism emerged and developed with astonishing rapidity in this period by offering a stable cohesive community here and in the hereafter.[6] Revivalism was another symptom, I would suggest, in this search for order and stability: the mind and soul had to be captured for God. A new community of common outlook had to be created, a community free, as de Tocqueville observed, to conform. There was considerable apprehension for the future. The bloody excesses of the French Revolution and the subsequent revolutions of 1830 and 1848, and the frequency of mob violence in Britain and America gave substance to such fears. To those of a paranoid, conspiratorial outlook, such events were but a continuation of the French Revolution. To some, popular disturbances such as that at Newport, Monmouthshire in 1839 were the work of Russian agents.[7] Demagoguery and despotism were but aspects of the same dangerous tendency. The respectable naturally wanted some organic social ideal to contain and to discipline the newly awakened political and social aspirations of the masses. Removed from traditional social and religious restraints as well as from their native

---

[5] J.L. Balmes, *Protestantism and Catholicism compared in their Effects upon Civilisation of Europe* (London 1849); John T. Graham, *Donoso Cortes: Utopian Romanticist and Political Realist* (Columbia, Mo., 1974). The tradition continued in Cardinal Gibbons' popular *Faith of Our Fathers* which went through many editions.

[6] An excellent summary will be found in W.H.G. Armytage, *Heavens Below: [Utopian Experiments in England 1560–1960* (London 1961)] pp. 77–288.

[7] See for example my 'Robert Urquhart, Robert Monteith and the Catholic Church' *Innes Review* v. (1980) pp. 57–80: [C. de Montalembert,] *The Monks [of the West, 6 vols (London 1906)] 1 p. 127 makes the same point. Also see for example L.L. Richards, 'Gentlemen of Property and Standing': Anti-abolition Mobs in Jacksonian America* (New York 1970).

areas, urban industrial workers presented a serious challenge to stability.

There were several forms of response in the transatlantic world. As already suggested the main American response was to develop the asylum with institutions to correct the poor, the criminal, the orphan, the insane and so forth. In a new nation concerned with regulating a mass democracy with few traditions, such initiatives were understandable. In Britain, the factory village was another response. Owen's New Lanark experiment had paralleled many similar villages in Scotland, like Deanston or Blantyre. Just as the squire had planned model moral villages so factory owners built ideal environments with well-maintained houses and schools, well-regulated public houses and hygienic oversight. Somewhat isolated on free running streams, these villages provided an interim solution until new technology freed industry from the necessity of locating on such sites. In a large urban centre with many alternative forms of employment available, such controls were impossible. As cities became segregated with residential areas for various social groups so the sense of fragmentation followed. By the mid nineteenth century most British cities had lost their sense of compact cohesion as almost 40 per cent of the total population were crammed into them. If revivalism was to respond to that condition, educational initiative was an even more comprehensive attempt to recreate an ideal moral community. For educational innovators like David Stow of Glasgow, the classroom was a microcosm of the larger world. The essential aim of education was to stimulate the Christian curiosity within a close knit community: the inherent moral sense of the children would ensure the effective disciplining of deviants within the group. Stow himself was to train Presbyterian, Catholic and Methodist teachers but, by the mid nineteenth century, differences between secularists and Christians, between rival Christian denominations and between advocates of voluntary and state aided education made that solution less feasible.[8]

Monasticism began to appear in a more sympathetic light. By 1850 various attempts to deal with the social problem seemed discredited or of a dangerous socialist tendency. Chartism had

---

[8] See William Fraser, *Memoir of the Life of David Stow* (London 1868) and James Murphy, *The Religious Problem in English Education* (Liverpool 1959).

shocked churchmen into an awareness of the need for social reform: north of the border it paralleled Christian initiatives with its own church. In 1848 the French *Ere Nouvelle* with the Dominican Lacordaire seems to have had some influence upon British Christian social thought.[9] This ferment was further encouraged by the wave of social romanticism which surged through Britain in the Young England and the Oxford movements to create a somewhat more sympathetic climate of opinion for the religious orders. Under the inspiration of the convert, Ambrose Phillips de Lisle, a close associate of the Young England group, Pugin had built the first monastery in Britain since the Reformation at Coalville, Leicestershire.[10] The Gothic Revival with its idealised notions of the middle ages naturally saw monasteries as the highest expression of Christian life: prayer, education, and immense charitable works among the poor and unfortunates were ample justification. The end of legal restrictions upon religious orders appearing in public in their habits followed in 1848. Ironically enough the first person to appear in a religious habit in public in Scotland seems to have been the radical republican ex-priest, Alessandro Gavazzi in 1851, but by then Walter Scott and the Eglinton tournament had won a hearing for medievalism. The receptivity of the audience to these ideas may be gauged by the convent investigations in Britain and the hilarious antics of the Massachusetts convent investigation in 1855.[11] Suspicion might persist among apprehensive Protestants but religious houses were here to stay.

The respectable Protestant world was beginning to appreciate the positive aspects of medieval life, through the new romantic histories, literature, and art, and through their continental travels. Even travellers in North America returned deeply impressed by Cana-

---

[9] Cf. Leslie C. Wright, *Scottish Chartism*, Edinburgh 1953. Alice Mary Hadfield, *The Chartist Land Company*, Newton Abbot, 1970 is relevant to the general discussion. J.B. Duroselle, *Les Débuts du Catholicisme Social en France 1822–1870* (Paris 1951). The *Rambler* closely followed *Ere Nouvelle* in 1848–49.

[10] See E.S. Purcell, *Ambrose Phillips de Lisle*, 2 vols (London 1900); Phoebe Stanton, *Pugin* (London 1971) pp. 113–17; also see the illustrations showing the central importance of monasteries in A.W.N. Pugin, *Contrasts* (London 1841 ed).

[11] *Scottish Protestant*, 6 September 1851. Also see Basil Hall 'Alessandro Gavazzi' in *SCH* 12, pp. 303–56; R. Sylvain, *Clerc Garibaldien, Prêcheur des Deux Mondes: Alessandro Gavazzi 1809–89* 2 vols (Quebec 1962) 2 pp. 287–441. R.A. Billington, *The Protestant Crusade* pp. 413–15 gives details of the tipsy tour and association with ladies of easy virtue at state expense.

dian religious institutions and their influence upon the masses.[12]
These engines of the Catholic revival could have Protestant and
secular uses. Those usages were to contribute massively to a more
sympathetic and tolerant view of monasticism.

The Oxford Movement was concerned with property, authority
and tradition: in seeking to give intellectual respectability to their
position, the Oxford apostles posed questions about the nature of
the Church, its relationship to the state and its mission to the poor.
Like politicians and others they were apprehensive about the
location of moral authority amid a fluctuating social order, the
proper appreciation of natural talent and ability and the due
recognition of local character: significantly J.B. Dalgairns wrote
several lives of monastic saints which had considerable impact on
both sides of the Atlantic.[13] Others sought a means of criticising the
existing social order as hedonistic, materialistic and indifferent to
the poor. Opposed to the growing centralisation and bureaucratisa-
tion of government in Britain, the old fashioned conservatives felt
their role was being eroded. In short, several groups demanded
clarification of their social status, their sexual identity and the
Christian community's response to the poor. Monasticism, the
'chivalry of God', filled that need.[14]

Within the Catholic Church, considerable tension was developing between liberals and extreme ultramontanes. Amid this bitter
battle the liberal Catholic, Charles de Montalembert published his
The Monks of the West.[15] Reprinted many times in France, Britain
and America over the next fifty years, it remained a classic account

[12] See for example Emily Faithfull, *Three Visits to America* (Edinburgh 1884) p. 371;
Charles Lyell, *Travels in North America*, 2 vols (London 1845) I p. 312: J.R.
Godley, *Letters from America*, 2 vols (London 1844) 1 pp. 70–1, 2 pp. 229–37
among others.

[13] J.B. Dalgairns wrote a series of lives *St. Stephen Harding* (London 1844); *St. Gilbert*
(London 1844) and *St. Aelred* (London 1845). They were very influential in
stimulating the foundation of an American Episcopalian monastery in Wisconsin.
Clarence Walworth, *The Oxford Movement in America* (New York 1974 ed) pp.
106–18.

[14] *The Monks* 1 p. 22.

[15] I have used the London 1906 edition. There were at least two French, two British
and two American editions. See his development through *Du Vandalisme et Du
Catholicisme dans l'Art* (Paris, 1839); *Catholic Interests in the Nineteenth Century*
(London 1852); *The Political Future of England* (London 1856) and *A Debate on India
in the English Parliament* (London 1858). R.P. Lecanuet's *Life* 3 vols (Paris
1899–1902) remains standard.

until superseded by the work of Gasquet and David Knowles. It was the culmination of Montalembert's development. A comprehensive statement by a talented aristocrat, thwarted in his legitimate political ambitions and assailed by his reactionary co-religionists, *The Monks of the West* is a very thinly veiled onslaught on the new ultramontanism and the new despotism in church and state. One of the first original researchers, Montalembert's work was deeply influenced by his political and religious views. Born in England of a French father and a Scottish mother, Montalembert made his work an unrepentant eulogy of British parliamentary institutions. Although initially slow to appreciate the reactionary character of Napoleon III he soon became a most outspoken critic of the regime. An inveterate admirer of British institutions, he produced a series of pamphlets and articles in *Le Correspondant* extolling the virtues of toleration and democracy. Aided by his close friends, Lacordaire, de Falloux, de Broglie and Bishop Dupanloup he vigorously opposed the wild intolerant ultramontane pretensions of Louis Veuillot and his friends. It was a posture which led to him receiving an honorary degree from Oxford and being prosecuted by the French government. *The Monks of the West* was a tract not merely for liberal Catholics but also for the times.

The work was an attempt to reconcile the Church and liberal democratic institutions, to persuade Protestants of Catholic good faith and to create a healthy respect for tradition. The monastery according to Pius IX was 'the bulwark and ornament of the Christian republic as well as of civil society'.[16] Stability characterised the institution as it remained fixed and steadfast in the face of all changes. Deeply imbued with the life of Christ, the community was compassionate, caring and democratic. The abbot was elected on merit by his fellows for a limited period: an authoritative figure he never became authoritarian. The strength of the religious orders lay in their inner spiritual resources rather than 'external strength, the dangerous help of which is invoked too often by blind and cowardly Christians.'[17] These 'paladins of the Round Table' were both a sign and a potent expression of order and security in maintaining the balance between prayer and action.[18] They were,

[16] Encyclical letter 17 June 1847 quoted in *The Monks* I, dedication.
[17] *Ibid* I p. 20.
[18] *Ibid* I p. 22.

as Newman observed, 'rich, diverse, complex and irregular and variously diversified, rich rather than symmetrical with many origins and centres and new beginnings and the action of local influences.'[19] With their spontaneous and responsive spiritual life, they were, for Montalembert the essence of English greatness for they expressed that independent landed interest, that liberty of the subject 'which seems as natural to the muscular and active genius of the ancient Teutonic races as they are alien to modern civilisation.'[20] They were the authentic voice of Christian liberty.

Historically, religious bodies had been the bastions of liberty against the encroachments of the Crown upon the liberties of the subject: flourishing monasteries meant a flourishing sense of freedom. When they were repressed freedom faded, as in recent times when they were attacked by European demagogues and by Russian autocrats.[21] Such a coded message made them the guarantors of bourgeois democracy in Europe and the English-speaking world. They were the finest expression of the English gentleman.

Now John Henry Newman in the *Idea of a University* believed the ideal of the English gentleman was never to jar or jolt.[22] It was a retreat from the ideal of the man of action to a more passive asexual character. Religious orders highlighted this Victorian difficulty. Woman's virginal purity 'assures man's continual striving for a higher morality as well as a conviction of his lack of it.'[23] The endorsement of the moral superiority of woman and the heroic male ideal of sexual self-control were reflections of contemporary cultural tensions. The male was under pressure to achieve, to be aggressive and to succeed within an entrepreneurial society. At the same time he denigrated the idea of success. The nun in the convent was the ultimate realisation of the chivalric ideal: beautiful, challenging and unattainable. She was a perpetual reproach to man and

---

[19] *Ibid* 1 p. 1.
[20] *Ibid* 4 pp. 338–39.
[21] *Ibid* 5 pp. 86–101 esp. Also 1 pp. 104–27.
[22] Quoted in Carol Christ, 'Victorian Masculinity [and the Angel in the House' pp. 146–62, at 160 in *A Widening Sphere: Changing Roles of Victorian Women*, ed Martha Vicinus (London 1977)]. On the ideal see Mark Girouard, *The Return to Camelot Chivalry and the English Gentleman* (New Haven 1981) esp pp. 198–218.
[23] Carol Christ, Victorian Masculinity p. 152. See also D. Hilliard 'UnEnglish and Unmanly: Anglo-Catholicism and Homosexuality' *Victorian Studies* 25 (1982) pp. 181–210.

a perpetual temptation. Through Coventry Patmore and Lord Tennyson these notions became commonplace. The religious order was swept into prominence as being in the mainstream of Victorian life: it was the epitome of social obligation and disinterested public service.

If that was Montalembert's ideal, Charles Kingsley had another. Both wrote about St. Elizabeth of Hungary.[24] A cult figure in the nineteenth century, following her popularisation in Paris through Murillo's painting, James Collinson's Pre-Raphaelite study of 1851 (after which he significantly entered the Jesuit novitiate) and Franz Liszt's oratorio (1865), she highlighted that Victorian fascination with high-minded self-sacrifice of the high born. She was an appropriate choice for, following the death of her husband on the crusades in 1227, she had been driven from the Thuringian court on the pretext that her charities were ruining the state: a suitable motif for a Catholic church confronted with the utilitarian state. Ambrose Phillips de Lisle had translated Montalembert's massively researched work into English in 1840.[25] To Kingsley, however, she was anything but admirable. In his tedious poem he scathingly attacked her celibacy, her irresponsible abandonment of her own children and her dependence on servants to awaken her to perform publicised acts of penance. Her life seem little more than a theatrical performance for the poor. She lacked an integrated humanity: 'your simpering philanthropists becomes as ruthless as a Dominican.'[26]

To the *Scottish Protestant* it was Kingsley's view which rang true. The editor, Rev. A.M. Gibson of Glasgow invariably portrayed Dominicans in full religious robes though in 1851–54 no member of the order was seen in Scotland. Even more significant in the light of the above discussion is the succession of rather pornographic frontispieces in the weekly paper, invariably atrocities perpetrated upon hapless women. Predictably one issue features 'immorality of

[24] Charles Kingsley, *Poems* (London 1884) carries the full text: Ilse H. Lipschutz, *Spanish Painting, passim.* Collinson subsequently spent four years as a Jesuit novice. Robin Ironside, *Pre-Raphaelite Painters* (London 1948) p. 26.
[25] London 1840. Montalembert had researched and written the original work in the midst of his personal search for an ideal wife.
[26] C. Kingsley, *Poems* p. 115, also p. 179.

the Church of Rome – The Monasteries'.[27] Such writings were in the tradition of the revelations of Maria Monk and Rebecca Reed about American nunneries. Although these works demonstrate a high-minded form of pornography, they also cast light upon the problem of poverty. Sex was allegedly what kept the poor in poverty. The ideal presented by religious communities was an acceptable form of sublimation which found a ready response among the respectable. To Archbishop Affre of Paris they were a reproach to those who advocated contraception. To Montalembert they were bulwarks of civilisation. By reinforcing loyalty and chastity within marriage, the religious orders condemned contemporary society which prevented the poor from enjoying that modest comfort essential to family life.[28]

In a more direct way, the monasteries acted as a conscience on behalf of the poor. The romanticised view of the middle ages saw the monasteries as havens of the poor, providing food, shelter and medical care. Christian hospitality prevailed. To radicals like Cobbett, the Reformation by destroying the monasteries had robbed the people of their property: a narrowing of sympathies, absentee landlordism and general exploitation followed. Later radicals picked up the theme. Patrick Dove, the precursor of Henry George, the single tax advocate, attributed the loss of self-respect among the poor to the capitalist legal and economic system. The even more radical H.M. Hyndman could look sympathetically upon monastic enterprise, whilst the Scottish radical, J.M. Davidson, considered the Church of Rome 'truly *Christian* in theory and Socialistic in practice.'[29] That recurring theme in his writings may have had a basis in his economic ideas, but it also had a practical

[27] *The Scottish Protestant*, 1 Nov, 1851. The penny weekly seems to have been distributed through Saturday night street preachers who invariably precipitated a disturbance in the process.

[28] Archbishop Affre 1843 pastoral quoted in *The Monks* 1 pp. 77–8. Paul Thompson, *William Butterfield* (London 1971) pp. 29, 36–9: A.M. Allchin, *The Silent Rebellion: Anglican Religious Communities, 1845–1900* (London 1958) and P.F. Anson, *The Call of the Cloister: Religious Communities and Kindred Bodies in the Anglican Communion* (London 1964) suggest the growing wide appeal of monastic life.

[29] J.M. Davidson, *The Old Order and the New*, (London n.d.) p. 7. Also see W. Cobbett, *History of the Protestant Reformation*, 2 vols (London 1829 ed) I Letters I, 5, 6 and 7 unpaginated: P.E. Dove, *The Elements of Political Science* (Edinburgh 1854) p. 117 and his *The Theory of Human Happiness* (London 1850) pp. 41–4.

propaganda purpose in trying to unite British radicals, Irish Catholics and Land Leaguers into a cohesive force.

Davidson's brother Thomas found even more attractions in monasticism. Renowned for the foundation of the Brotherhood of the New Life, which was to develop into the Fabian Society, Davidson derived considerable encouragement from Antonio Rosmini and his order.[30] Impressed by the extremely tolerant views of Princess Carolyn of Sayn-Wittgenstein, the close friend of Liszt, he was introduced to Rosminian philosophy. He found much of it acceptable. The positive potential of man for good through education and inspiration was peculiarly attractive for its optimistic evolutionary outlook: 'The most truly practical education is that which imparts the most numerous and practical motives for noble action, which creates the most splendid world of thought, love and beneficience in the human soul. Men are weak, sinful and poor because they lack motives to be otherwise. Let education give them those motives and weakness, sin and poverty will vanish from the earth.'[31] Rosmini's ideal society was 'a complex of dependent graded organisms, united and animated by a single supreme independent principle',[32] God. The members of Rosmini's order, the Institute of Charity, although retaining the title to their individual property made a continual sacrifice of it in accordance with the instructions of their religious superior. That model society which he studied closely in the monastery near Domodossola in Italy inspired him: 'our work must result in *our doing*. We must not only know the truth we must live it. And we can only live it by establishing noble and wise social relations'.[33] By fully following the example of Christ, particularly in concern for the poor, men could establish the kingdom of God on earth.

---

[30] See William Knight, *Some Nineteenth Century Scotsmen* (Edinburgh 1903) pp. 221–45 and Norman and Jeanne MacKenzie, *The First Fabians* (London 1972) esp p. 180; Thomas Davidson, *The Philosophical System of Antonio Rosmini-Serbati* (London 1882); Claude Leetham, *Rosmini* (London 1957).

[31] T. Davidson, *History of Education* (London 1900) p. 260.

[32] T. Davidson, 'Antonio Rosmini' *Fortnightly Review* N.S. 30 (1881) pp. 553–84.

[33] quoted in W.H.G. Armytage, *Heavens Below* p. 329. A somewhat overpowering character he held similar critical social views to his brother although he remained hostile to socialism. Cf. Ernest Rhys, *Everyman Remembers* (London 1931) p. 133; J.M. Davidson, *The Gospel of the Poor* (London 1896) and his vigorous nationalist tract *Leaves from the Book of Scots* (Glasgow 1914) and *The Annals of Toil* (London 1899).

Such views were becoming increasingly fashionable in the late nineteenth century. Davidson's close friend, William James, author of *The Varieties of Religious Experience*, his brother J.M. Davidson, and American Progressive reformers found inspiration in the ideals of the religious life.[34] The popularity of Paul Sabatier's *Life of St. Francis* (1894) suggested a new inspirational image for monasticism. As the arts and crafts book-binder and printer, T.J. Cobden-Sanderson, observed after reading the book, 'what is needed now is again the perception of the miracle in the common'.[35] Christianity was a work of art in progress, not a matter of belief but of imagination. To unite the active and passive, the mind and hand, rich and poor was the ideal. Monasticism ennobled the prosaic and humdrum in making freedom of hand and mind subordinate to the co-operative harmony.[36] In the late Victorian crisis of belief that monastic sentiment helped the individual sustain a faith, an Ideal, through a sense of solidarity with like-minded souls and with Humanity at large. On both sides of the Atlantic that chivalric ideal flourished in progressive reform and in the development of a revitalised Christian socialism: 'They knew such exaltation as St. Francis must have known when he threw his garments in the face of his astonished father and faced in triumphant nakedness a World of Clothes.'[37] The monastic sense of heroic service and self-sacrifice found its fullest expression in the settlement-house movement. In Britain and America well-educated individuals gathered together to bring culture and idealism to the masses. Toynbee House, London and Hull House, Chicago were comparable to the monastic ideal. At Hull House, Jane Addams and several single women friends lived a life dedicated to the education, and the provision of medical and social service to the poor: the parallel with a nunnery is remarkable. Freed from familial and sexual demands, such women could realise themselves as nuns might within a community of like-minded characters. In protest against the prevailing social

34 See the considerable correspondence between T. Davidson, and W. James 1881–1900 in the W. James collection Houghton Library, Harvard University.

35 8 Nov 1902, in *The Journals of Thomas James Cobden-Sanderson, 1879–1922*, 2 vols ed R. Cobden-Sanderson (London 1926) 2 p. 39.

36 *Ibid.* 1 p. 277; 2 pp. 39–40, 52, 66, 80–83. Also see Lionel Lambourne, *Utopian Craftsmen: The Arts and Crafts Movement from the Cotswolds to Chicago* (London 1980).

37 Vida Scudder, *Socialism and Character* (London 1912) p. 67. She was active in the settlement house movement as well as Professor of English at Wellesey. Also see Jane Addams, *Twenty Years at Hull House* (New York 1910).

ethos, they found moral consistency and purity of purpose. Where religious orders believed God was with them, these groups had the evolutionary democratic forces which must inevitably prevail.

Numerous other communities in imitation of their religious counterparts came into existence around that time. Not only were they escaping from the unacceptable face of capitalism, from urban industrial society, but they were finding health and harmony with nature in the country. John Ruskin, Elizabeth Blackwell, the woman medical pioneer, and Rider Haggard among many others found a small beginning of utopia in such enterprises. Others, like T.H. Green and his disciples, saw their role in the city promoting citizenship as a religious vocation.[38] Later in the twentieth century Eric Gill and his friends would promote model communities of art and intellect on the land. The ideal remained monastic.

The image of monasteries had changed considerably in the period under discussion. From being the preserve of those in flight from society, they became the ideal moral society. To some extent the change is attributable to the assimilation of Catholicism into the mainstream of transatlantic life, but also to the increasing democratic and secular nature of society. It must be also recognised that monasteries in this period had a function as images of stability, economic and social justice, sexual peace and integrated life uniting mental and physical exertions. That usage as much as any religious motive promoted greater tolerance of and sympathy towards monasteries in the transatlantic world. Their ideal might be achieved by genteel endeavour, compassion and love. It is a worthy ideal to cherish. As yet it has not been generally adopted.

University of Glasgow

[38] See John Ruskin, 'Valle Crucis', in his *Works*, ed E.T. Cook and A. Wedderburn, 40 vols (London 1903–12) 33 pp. 205–254; E. Blackwell, *Essays on Medical Sociology*, 2 vols (London 1902) 1 p. 166; Melvin Richter, *The Politics of Conscience: T.H. Green and his Age* (London 1964) p. 30; W.H.G. Armytage, *Heavens below* pp. 289–384. It is worth noting that monasticism's new image paralleled the development of modern planned communities from the 1840s. See W.L. Creese, *The Search for Environment: The Garden City Before and After* (New Haven 1966) and Gilliam Dorley, *Villages of Vision* (London 1975). Monasteries also illustrate the development of Catholic economic thinking in Le Play and others. See the survey in Alfred Diamant, *Austrian Catholics and the First Republic: Democracy Capitalism and the Social Order, 1918–1934* (Princeton 1960) pp. 3–69.

WILLIAM JOHN BUTLER AND THE REVIVAL OF THE ASCETIC TRADITION

by SISTER ANN FRANCES C.S.M.V.

WILLIAM John Butler, sometime vicar of Wantage in Berkshire and founder of the Community of St Mary the Virgin, gave a concrete and contemporary expression to an aspect of the ascetic idea current among followers of the Oxford Movement, which was revealed in their desire to restore monastic life in the Church in England. The Community founded by Butler was one of the earliest of the indigenous Anglican communities for women. In no way could the desert ideal or the later pre-Reformation models of religious life be reconstructed, nor would they have been appropriate in the climate of the time. However Butler believed, as had Newman, Pusey and others, that the basic principles of monastic life remained valid and they could and should find their place in the contemporary Church of England. It was believed that the Church had the grace and the resources of devotion within itself to give birth to the religious life anew, to continue its nurture and promote its development. Certainly the enhanced spirituality resulting from the example of deep devotion of the Tractarians themselves and that of their followers engendered a religious atmosphere in which new spiritual adventures were made possible.

In the climate of the mid-1840s there needed to be overt charitable aims for the establishment of institutions which would, in many ways, be likely to resemble religious houses which had been thankfully abolished at the Reformation, when the yoke of popery was thrown off. Such aims were provided by the terrible social, moral and economic plight of much of the working population, as the agrarian economy became inexorably metamorphosed into an industrial economy, a process well beyond the point of no return at this time. The conditions of life of the industrial workers in particular were matter for deep concern for philanthropists and churchmen. So the earliest Anglican communities achieved their opportunity to live the religious life while engaging in works of mercy according to the Gospel, dressed in various forms of response to contemporary need.

A brief look at the establishment of the Community of St. Mary the Virgin and at the life envisaged by Butler for the Sisters will demonstrate, it is hoped, continuity with a spiritual ascetic tradition founded in the New Testament, then shaped by St Augustine, but given a new expression according to the views of the Church of England of the 19th century. It will also be necessary to look at a little of Butler's teaching, for example about the vows of religion, in passing comparison with one or two of the more prominent of his contemporary founders, in order to illustrate the theme.

Butler himself was born in 1818, and he was educated at Westminster and at Trinity College, Cambridge. Entering Cambridge in 1836 he was contemporary with Benjamin Webb, and with John Mason Neale who was later to found the Society of St Margaret at East Grinstead. Butler was an early member of the Cambridge Camden Society, in which Webb was the moving spirit, which was founded for the study of ecclesiastical art. He was ordained deacon in 1841 and priest in 1842, serving his title for Orders as assistant curate to Charles Dyson, rector of Dogmersfield in Hampshire, the next parish to Hursley, where John Keble was vicar. Butler had had a little contact with men influenced by the Oxford Movement while at Cambridge, but it was at Dogmersfield that he became acquainted with Keble, Henry Edward Manning, Henry Wilberforce (brother of Samuel whom Butler was later to meet as Bishop of Oxford) and with Charles Marriott and others. Dyson, his rector, was not at Oxford during the Tractarian years, but he had been Professor of Anglo-Saxon in the university, and was among those who supported the principles of the Oxford Movement from a distance.

It is likely that it was at this time that Butler became aware of the desire of the Oxford men for the restoration of monastic life, and it is interesting to note that in 1846 he made a short retreat with Newman's little society at Littlemore in preparation for his work at Wantage. Newman, of course had already gone, having made his submission to the Roman obedience in 1845. Butler was profoundly affected by the deep spirituality of the followers of the Oxford Movement and he adopted a strongly prayerful and ascetic discipline for his own life, adapting it afresh on his marriage which took place in 1843. His marriage was happy and his wife was deeply interested and sharing in his work. In 1846 Butler was offered the living of the parish of Wantage, which he accepted.

The potential value of a praying sisterhood as an agency for assistance in parish work and in training teachers for village school work probably occurred to Butler, or may even have been suggested to him during his first cures. It was certainly in his mind when he came to Wantage. But he made no overt moves in the matter during his first year or so. In 1847, however, Manning, then archdeacon of Chichester, and rector of Lavington in Sussex, introduced to Butler a Miss Elizabeth Crawford Lockhart who was wishing to find a means of living the religious life. Miss Lockhart was one of Manning's penitents and she had been exercised in mind whether she should follow her brother William and her mother into the Church of Rome. At this time Manning had evidently restrained her from this step. It can be said, therefore, that Miss Lockhart's advent and her desire for the religious life provided the occasion and the immediate stimulus for the formation of a sisterhood, as she also brought one or two companions of like mind with her. Years later, though, Butler referred to himself as having been 'consulted' about the formation of a sisterhood to work amongst the poor.

By late 1850 both Manning, who had been acting as 'Father Director' of the Sisterhood and Miss Lockhart, who had been the Superior, had seceded to the Church of Rome. Butler had therefore to set to work on his own, though with steady reference to Bishop Wilberforce, to build the society anew with fresh rules and with much less direct imitation of contemporary Roman Catholic societies than had been the case under Manning and Miss Lockhart.

Butler believed that rules should not be imposed but should largely shape themselves, particularly in the situation in the which the new Sisterhood found itself, its context that of a late post-Reformation Church of England which had no experience whatever of the religious life in its technical sense. As Butler said,

> We have to battle with inexperience, to feel our way cautiously where our forefathers walked with confidence.[1]

---

[1] C.S.M.V. Archives, Wantage, Address at reception of Novices, Feast of the Visitation 1875.

It is significant therefore, that there was no formulation of a comprehensive 'spiritual' Rule of Life before 1860. Up to that time, although there were apparently some spiritual guidelines for the Sisters, there is virtually no information about them. There were however some definitions of the ideals and objects of the Wantage Sisterhood, the first manuscript document being dated 1854. It is interesting to note that Charles Marriott was one of the signatories of this first document, and one of the early trustees for property belonging to the Sisterhood. By 1857 a code of statutes governing the life of the Sisterhood and combining both spiritual and practical elements had evolved, and most of the clauses of this document remained in force, with occasional modifications, until after the Founder's death forty years on, eventually running alongside the Rule he produced in 1860, which was based on that of St Augustine.

Ascetic discipline was present in the life of the Sisterhood from the first. For example, recitation of the Divine Office in addition to participation in Matins and Evensong in church, two-and-a-half hours of private prayer a day, work in parish or school and in the house, frugal meals and very early rising, were all established at the beginning of the Community's life. This full time-table became normative, notwithstanding the Sisterhood's tiny size, which was to remain one of its main features for over twenty years.

From the time when he first conceived the idea of forming a sisterhood to assist him in works of mercy and evangelisation, Butler seems to have had a vision of the kind of society for which he thought there was a need. He envisaged an active life for the Sisters founded upon a base of contemplative prayer, for the development of which he insisted that time be allowed. Such a sisterhood should bear a 'Church of England character'. He had in his mind the way in which St Vincent de Paul's Daughters of Charity went out two by two, hoping that the Wantage Sisters might go out in this way 'into the villages'. Further, Butler thought that elements of the spirituality inculcated by St Francis de Sales and St Jane Frances de Chantal in the Order of the Visitation, might be fruitful in the kind of life he had in mind for his Sisterhood.

Butler taught the Sisters to combine both Mary's and Martha's rôles in their lives, thus establishing the pattern for what came to be called the 'mixed' religious life, as distinct from either the wholly enclosed contemplative or the wholly active 'apostolic' modes. The Sisters' life of service was to grow out of their life of contemplative prayer, in order that a service so nourished should assume the quality of prayer. A considerable part of each day was therefore devoted to purely spiritual purposes. The practical work was strenuous and demanding, testing the Sisters to the uttermost. Butler saw this as part of God's ascetic plan for the Sisterhood, and as following the pattern of Jesus' life in his public ministry with its myriad material demands, yet maintaining a constant communion with God. In 1877 Butler said that it had been felt

> to be the greatest possible blessing to us, that our Sisters were ever worked to their fullest extent, that they were never sufficient to carry on comfortably all we had to do ..., because ... all this brings us more to a sense of our weakness and forces us into the presence of God.[2]

In addition to the work outside the house, the Sisters had the care of 'penitents' or 'fallen women' in the house from very early days. Manning and Miss Lockhart had virtually forced this change of work and thus a change of direction upon Butler, and so he had it to maintain when they left for Rome.

Practical activities notwithstanding, Butler desired that the life of prayer should grow and develop in whatever way God willed. Even though social concerns played so large a part in the early days of Anglican communities, it was essentially the spiritual quality of the religious life that was desired, with its concepts of steadfast dedication and strong ascetic discipline, rather than the actual work that was done.

It is possible that at first, during the thirteen years or so that elapsed between the Community's foundation and Butler's production of his Rule of Life in 1860, the Sisters may have used portions of the Rule drawn up for the Holy Cross Sisterhood chiefly by Dr Pusey. The whole Rule would not have been suitable, even though works of mercy and the inculcation of a deep spiritual life were aims common to both societies, for Butler's cast of mind differed from Pusey's. But Butler evidently had some admiration for

---

[2] C.S.M.V. Archives, Wantage, Preached on the Feast of the Purification, 1877, to Sisters and Associates.

Pusey's Rule as he used it as a source later when compiling the Wantage Sisterhood's first Rule. Also, when Neale consulted Butler about the rules he was framing for the East Grinstead Sisterhood in 1855, Butler sent him the Wantage code of rules mentioned above and added,

> My impression is that you have too many, especially for a beginning. Rules should shape themselves as the work goes on and need occurs. With good people, such as Sisters of Mercy are likely to be, one can risk a little and wait to buy experience. Have you seen the Rules of Saint Saviour's, Regent's Park? They are short sermons, expansions of Saint Augustine's, which of course you know. The advantage of the sermonic rule is that the reading of it gives a devotional atmosphere to the house.[3]

This passage is important because it reveals the trend of Butler's thought during the period when the first guiding documents of the Wantage Sisterhood appeared. Clear expression is given to Butler's idea that the Community pattern should shape itself and teach the way forward. How far Neale himself actually took Butler's advice is not wholly apparent from the first edition of the East Grinstead rules which appeared in 1858. But in any case the nature of the life and work of the two societies differed.

The Reverend Thomas Thellusson Carter, who founded the Sisterhood of St John the Baptist at Clewer in 1851, and Neale himself, both produced more sophisticated first formulations of rules than Butler's, perhaps because they were working a little later, and were therefore in a position to draw upon the experience of the first few communities. Further, Carter and Neale were both men of learning familiar with traditional material upon which to draw, who made names for themselves in various fields of scholarship as well as being deeply spiritual in their outlook. Butler was in no way an academic theologian or a particularly systematic thinker; as Cruttwell wrote in 1899, Butler was 'not a learned man, nor exactly eminent in intellect, but yet original in the truest sense...'.[4] Butler was an intensely practical parish priest with

---

[3] Eleanor A. Towle, *John Mason Neale, D.D.: A Memoir* p. 237.
[4] [C.T.] Cruttwell, *Six Lectures on the Oxford Movement and its results on the Church of England* (London 1899) p. 139.

enormous parochial and educational responsibilities, besides being a deeply spiritual director and pastor to the Sisters. Neale certainly looked to Butler for practical guidance on contemporary interpretations of traditional ascetic principles of religious life.

The fullest and most comprehensive of these sets of early rules for the new communities was probably that of the Holy Cross Sisterhood mentioned above. On the one hand Pusey's document bore the character of a traditional 'spiritual' Rule of Life and it was very fully expressed. Butler, Carter and Neale on the other hand inserted, as it were, a preliminary stage before embarking upon a fully-fledged formulation of a Rule of Life for their respective communities. Their initial documents were comprised of elements of spiritual rule together with elements of a more legalistic and practical nature condensed into short paragraphs. Pusey seems to have used his Rule to shape the life of the Sisters, rather than laying down guidelines and waiting for a pattern to emerge from the experience of the Community which would influence the creation of a rule.

The concept of the traditional three-fold vow of poverty, chastity and obedience, the ancient ascetic discipline characteristic of the religious state, was faintly discernible in the first code of rules at Wantage, and the principle of a common life within which the vows would be lived out, was enunciated. But no explicit shape was given to the vows until a new edition of the Rule was produced in 1897, three years after Butler's death. In the first rules obedience was simply to the rules of the house, though the clause delineating the limits of the authority of the Superior by their very nature assumed the giving of obedience by the Sisters. Poverty consisted in the relinquishment of money or other possessions while actually in the Community; but even then a Sister might administer any property she might hold away from the house. Indeed, at first a Sister was expected to contribute a fixed sum towards her maintenance, though this was waived if necessary. This rather strange notion of poverty had to do with the newness of the experiment of religious life in community in the Church of England, and the as yet unstable situation with regard to life-long commitment. The idea of chastity with its life-long celibate connotations did not appear at all in the first Wantage rules. The notion of a celibate state of life was anathema to those of very protestant mind, though in view of the demographic imbalance of the sexes at the time, it was perfectly plain that many women would never find a marriage partner.

Butler was convinced not only of the need for slow development for the religious life of the Sisterhood, but also for prudence for the sake of the safety and well-being of the Sisters. Although they did obvious things like nursing for highly infectious and sometimes dangerous diseases, Butler saw no reason to jeopardise the experiment by thrusting more of the strange new ideas of the religious life down the throats of his parishioners than they could easily swallow; as it was, there was opposition to the Sisters in the town. At the same time in his teaching of the Sisters themselves, Butler would not countenance any spiritual compromise or accommodation to materialistic standards on their part.

Over the years Butler's teaching changed and developed, but the whole body of it maintained a strong Biblical, Christ-centred, Godward-looking unity. He never held an advanced doctrine about the Virgin Mary, his thinking about her remaining simple but reverent and meditative. He had placed the Sisters under the patronage of Mary in order that they should strive to emulate her pattern of obedience to God. But his devotion to her was not exaggerated, and the Trinity and the love of Jesus were central to his personal spirituality as it was revealed in his teaching of the Sisters. He was not sentimental and would not countenance the use of popular sentimental devotions to Mary. He said, 'You do not come into religion to indulge sentiment. All God's calls involve the reality of self-sacrifice'.[5] Butler spoke often to the Sisters on the subject of vocation, and he had a high view of the call to the religious life. While seeing the Sisters' life in the context of a special call, he believed that the vocation to close union with Christ involved a particular call to sacrifice. He said, 'the world is not called upon to accept poverty, chastity and obedience'[6] and he went on to speak of the Sisters' life as a death, not in hopeless finality, but in Paul's sense of death with Christ in order to rise to new life with him. The call to religious life was a call to 'self-annihilation', in the sense of a denial of the self in its selfishness in order to lead to its

[5] C.S.M.V. Archives, Wantage, Address to the Sisters 1875.
[6] *Ibid*, Notes on Vocation nd.

death, not in any sense of damage to the body. The Sister must die to herself in order that the love of Jesus might be all in all. Truly there was implicit a call to an interior asceticism of a high order.

The sacrificial life was not to be demonstrated by much outward austerity in the Wantage Community, but by the quality of the spiritual life of the Sisters. In this Butler resembled Saint Francis de Sales. It was ever Butler's desire to receive in the Community all who felt themselves called to the life and who proved the reality and validity of their call by their generous response. They had also to be able to sustain the daily round of dedicated prayer and extremely hard work. Butler believed that living conditions should be reasonable without being luxurious – and indeed they were pretty bleak – and that the manner of living and the Rule of Life were sufficiently demanding in themselves to make the endeavour towards the perfect keeping of the Rule a way of holiness in itself, without the addition of extra disciplines beyond the fasts and abstinences of the Prayer Book. In the early days there was in any case considerable hardship and food was sometimes insufficient. Butler would have seen the use of artificial means to bring the body into subjection as extravagant and alien to the character of the Church of England. He used to refer to the 'martyrdom' of obedience to the Rule. Healthy respect for the body given by God for the carrying out of his work for the Kingdom was important. Nothing was permitted which would hinder the Sisters from the performance of their normal duties.

Butler thought that the words 'the love of Christ constraineth me' should 'be written on every Sister's heart'.[7] He believed that such a vocation indicated that God had a special love for the one thus called. It did not mean that she was any more fit for God's service than those around her, nor indeed would he have postulated diminished portions of Christ's love for those not thus called. Here was a paradox: the reason for the choice of those who were called remained a mystery.

In spite of his awareness of Christ's love, Butler was anything but universalist in his outlook. He took the scriptural warnings seriously and for him the possibility of everlasting torment was a reality. The Devil was ever ready with deadly snares and all must

---

[7] *Ibid*, Meditation on vocation. nd.

be constantly on the watch. Because they were called to a privileged walk with Christ which gave them a heightened perception of spiritual reality, the Sisters were therefore the more culpable if they fell short of their best endeavour, and they bore a greater responsibility. He said ' ...in your case a slight fall *is* actually more dangerous, more culpable than in the case of others'. Following Christ the Sisters were to learn obedience by the things that they suffered.

Butler took the view that the vows of religion sprang directly from the life of Jesus as revealed in the Gospel, and demanded imitation of that life. The call to respond and live the life of the evangelical counsels was made by the voice of Jesus. He referred often to the free gift of herself made by the Sister, who pledged herself for life. Before profession she belonged, as it were, to herself and she was free, like Ananias and Sapphira, to retain what she had. But once having made the gift, she was no longer her own but irrevocably Jesus Christ's. Therefore the gift could never be withdrawn.

In common with many clergy Butler believed that once the character of priesthood had been bestowed upon the soul in ordination, it was thereafter indelible. It was impossible to abandon the special character once it had been formally assumed. Similarly he regarded the pledge given in profession and sealed by the Church as irrevocable and indelibly marked upon the soul of the Sister.

As its religious founder Butler drew upon many sources to help him in the establishment of the Sisterhood at Wantage. But all his gleanings passed through the sieve of his uncompromising 'Church of Englandism', emerging as a meld which would not have been wholly unrecognisable to those who walked a moderate path along the 'via media'. Like Pusey Butler visited religious houses on the continent on his frequent trips abroad, and he may have owed quite a lot to Pusey's lead in the matter of sources, although he was unlike him in the manner in which he guided his Community. Butler has been seen as the true 'founder of our religious sisterhoods'[8] even more than Pusey, just because he was original in his interpretation of what a sisterhood should be in the Church of

[8] Cruttwell.

England. He read widely and was familiar with the great spiritual writers and with the lives of men who had, as he put it, 'nobly served our Lord'. This reading included familiarity with the Anglican divines and with the contribution they made to the understanding and practice of the spiritual life. In this he was very much a son of the Oxford Movement.

As the Community of Saint Mary the Virgin became established, Butler seems to have moved closer to Keble and further away from Pusey. Though he still revered Pusey for his holiness and sought his direction from time to time, Keble's uncompromising belief in the Church of England called forth an eager response from Butler. Butler remained on good terms with Pusey, but it seems fairly clear that after the dissolution of a second sisterhood, which had been founded for the running of schools[9] in Wantage (a matter in which Pusey had had a hand), he became disinclined to lean much upon Pusey's judgement in the matter of the conduct of sisterhoods. Butler's hand had been forced by Pusey to form the School Sisterhood before he was ready or thought it right, and after the quick collapse of the Sisterhood there is some indication that he came to resent Pusey's interference in affairs at Wantage. There was a correspondence between them which brought forth a surprising acerbity from Butler.

From Butler's establishment and guidance of the Sisterhood and from his teaching, he emerges as one who attained great mastery in the spiritual life and in the understanding of traditional asceticism. Although his early ideas of slow development and his refusal to impose a formal structured rule upon the Community until many years had passed made him seem more nebulous in outlook than Pusey for example, he does, however, gradually come to stand out as a great founder in his day and one in the true tradition of great founders. His approach was not intellectual but spiritual and pragmatic, strongly seasoned with a common sense which yet left room for the development of the mystical life of love for God. He set himself the task of finding a viable method of living the religious life within the practical and devotional framework of the Church of England of his day. Following the lead of the Oxford

---

[9] See my M.A. thesis 'History of the Community of St. Mary the Virgin, Wantage: Foundation and Early Development' (University of Durham 1974).

Movement he looked back to the New Testament and to the Early Church in order to find guidance for the establishment of ascetic disciplines which might be interpreted afresh for his Community. The result was a surprisingly stable Community with an ethos which has been described as typically English; he would not have asked for more.

King's College, London.

ARCHBISHOP DAVIDSON, BISHOP GORE AND ABBOT CARLYLE: BENEDICTINE MONKS IN THE ANGLICAN CHURCH

by RENE M. KOLLAR

ELRED Carlyle (1874–1955) believed that his vocation was to re-establish Benedictine monasticism in the Anglican Church. His early attempts in London and Gloucestershire failed, but in 1902 the future suddenly looked promising. During that year, he attracted the attention of Lord Halifax, who invited the small group of Anglican monks to settle at his estate in Yorkshire. Here, Carlyle's foundation thrived: the membership grew; he enjoyed the support of influential Anglo-Catholics throughout Britain; and after he obtained the approval of the archbishop of Canterbury, Frederick Temple, for his revival of Benedictine life, Carlyle was ordained a priest in America. In 1906, the Anglican Benedictines moved to Caldey Island, where Carlyle planned to orchestrate the growth and spread of a grand congregation of Anglican monks.

This paper will explore the attitudes of members of the Anglican hierarchy to Carlyle's Benedictine dream from 1902 to 1913. The archbishop of York and the bishop of St. David's had ignored or tolerated Abbot Carlyle's ritualism. Archbishop Randall Davidson and Bishop Charles Gore, however, were forced to evaluate Carlyle's monastery and to investigate allegations of Roman Catholic devotions, practices, and beliefs. However, their respective approach to this problem differed. Archbishop Davidson's policy was conservative and cautious. He laboured to avoid any rash action which might result in a schism. Even when stories of liturgical impropriety reached him, he pursued a timid and indecisive course. Bishop Gore, on the other hand, demanded that the Anglican monks abandon their Roman practices; he would tolerate no compromise, and action must be firm and resolute. Abbot Carlyle refused to yield to the reforming zeal of the bishop of

Oxford. In February 1913, therefore, Carlyle and a majority of his Anglican monks converted to Roman Catholicism.

While the Anglican community was enjoying the hospitality of Lord Halifax, some began to voice their reservations and suspicions to the archbishop of Canterbury. Early in 1904, Archbishop Davidson was asked to comment on the relationship of the Yorkshire monks to the Anglican Church. 'Since the community ... is asserting itself as having received the approbation of the English Church,' an interested churchman enquired of Davidson, is 'the community of monks ... officially recognized by you?'[1] The Primate did not respond, but asked the archbishop of York, William Maclagan, to clarify the status of this questionable Benedictine brotherhood. Maclagan informed Archbishop Davidson that Carlyle's monks worked as laymen in a parish, but 'I have given ... no special sanction ... I have postponed any decision as to my relation with the community until I shall be able to visit the parish.'[2] When another individual asked Davidson to comment on the Anglican monks, he replied that he 'certainly had no connection with any such body.'[3] Again, Davidson demanded an explanation and clarification from Archbishop Maclagan. 'Vague rumours have reached me of the existence of some such brotherhood which claims to have the support of both Archbishops,' Archbishop Davidson informed Maclagan, and 'I have always regarded it as nonsense, but this seems rather definite.'[4]

The archbishop informed Davidson that Archbishop Frederick Temple had authorized the community,[5] but he himself had never

---

[1] L[ambeth] P[alace] L[ibrary], Davidson Papers, Richards to Davidson, 26 January 1862. Randall Davidson succeeded Frederick Temple as Archbishop of Canterbury in 1902. The standard biography of Davidson is G.K.A. Bell, *Randall Davidson* (Oxford 1952).

[2] LPL, Maclagan to Davidson, 6 February 1904. For Archbishop Maclagan's life, see *DNB* and F.D. How, *Archbishop Maclagan* (London 1911).

[3] LPL, Davidson to Finneran, 8 August 1905.

[4] LPL, Davidson to Maclagan, 7 August 1905.

[5] In 1897, Aelred Carlyle asked Archbishop Frederick Temple to authorize his solemn profession as a Benedictine monk. With Temple's blessing, Carlyle pronounced solemn vows in February 1898. In 1902, Carlyle wrote Temple and urged him 'to consider the accompanying petition and to sign and seal in a token of your sanction, and so establish our little community.' LPL, Carlyle to Temple, 28 May 1902. Temple signed and returned the document, and Carlyle interpreted this action as episcopal approval of his Anglican Benedictine revival.

extended approval to the Benedictine brotherhood. 'I have never given authority to the community nor have I entered into any official relations with the Abbot.'[6] Maclagan acknowledged that Bishop Charles Grafton had ordained Carlyle in America,[7] and afterwards he applied for permission to minister in the province of York as a colonial clergyman. Even though 'it is a difficult thing to refuse under the provisions of the act,' Maclagan confessed, 'I have for the present declined and have no wish to give him this authority,'[8] Davidson's reply did not indicate a sense of urgency or alarm. He expressed surprise to see Archbishop Temple's signature appended to the 'so-called Charter,' but he informed Maclagan that 'there appears to be no trace of anything ... called illegal.'[9] Davidson also advised Archbishop Maclagan not to license Carlyle as a clergyman in colonial orders: '...to me it would seem that a man who, with a view to working in England, has to go to America and be ordained by the most eccentric of Bishops there ... cannot appropriately claim that we should recognize him for work as a Priest in England.' Davidson viewed Carlyle's monks as a harmless 'little body of laymen who fashioned themselves as Benedictine monks.' Toward the end of their stay in Yorkshire, Davidson was again asked if he approved of 'the revival of the monastic life in the Church of England as represented by the [Yorkshire] Benedictines,'[10] and he responded that he 'has not himself been invited to give, nor has he given any sanction to the community.'[11] The archbishop maintained that the actions of Archbishop Temple might have been misinterpreted, and more-over, he could not comprehend 'how a community conforming to the Benedictine Rule can conform also to the Doctrine and Discipline of the Church of England.'

On 19 October 1906, Abbot Aelred Carlyle and nineteen Angli-can monks left Yorkshire to take possession of Caldey Island, South Wales, which they had recently purchased through the help

[6] LPL, Maclagan to Davidson, 7 August 1905.
[7] With the approbation of Archbishop Maclagan, Charles Grafton, the Bishop of Fond-du-lac, Wisconsin, ordained Carlyle a priest on 15 November 1904 in America.
[8] LPL, Maclagan to Davidson, 7 August 1905.
[9] LPL, Davidson to Maclagan, 8 August 1905.
[10] LPL, Harding to Davidson, 27 August 1906.
[11] LPL, Davidson to Harding, 8 October 1906.

of generous benefactors. The bishop of St. David's, John Owen, ignored Carlyle's brotherhood; the freedom from episcopal control continued. Archbishop Maclagan had informed Bishop Owen that Carlyle possessed no permission or licence to officiate outside his own community, but for the most part, the abbot had disregarded this limitation. Although 'they have received no definite recognition from me,' the archbishop noted, 'they gave me no trouble, and have been engaged in various good works in their own neighbourhood.'[12] Bishop Owen's supervision of Abbot Carlyle's Anglican monastery was admittedly passive,[13] and with this freedom, the Caldey monastery evolved into a brotherhood which was Roman Catholic in letter and spirit. Carlyle, an extreme ritualist, insisted that the Roman rite replace the Book of Common Prayer, and certain devotions such as Benediction and Reservation of the Blessed Sacrament became an essential part of the Anglican monks' lives. Roman Catholic feasts, such as the Immaculate Conception, were celebrated with pomp and grandeur. Critics of the Benedictine revival on Caldey continued to complain and question its loyalty to the Established Church, and their suspicions were fed by rumours that Abbot Carlyle enjoyed no licence to minister within the Anglican Church. They gleefully pointed to the fact that Carlyle was not registered in *Crockford's*.

On 13 December 1911, therefore, Abbot Aelred Carlyle petitioned Archbishop Davidson for an interview. Carlyle was anxious to discuss the relationship of Caldey to the Church of England, and the abbot also stated that he wanted a licence to minister in the province of Canterbury as priest in colonial orders. 'Seeing that our Community has now become firmly established and is growing rapidly,' Carlyle argued, 'it is necessary for my own ecclesiastical standing to be duly authorized.'[14] Abbot Carlyle claimed that after

[12] LPL, Maclagan to Owen, 6 December 1906. The Owen Papers are deposited at the National Library of Wales, Aberystwyth, Dyfed. They are not currently available for public research. For a biography of Bishop Owen, see the following: *DNB* and E. Owen, *The Later Life of Bishop Owen* (Llandysul 1961).
[13] LPL, Owen to Davidson, 28 December 1911.
[14] LPL, Carlyle to Davidson, 13 December 1911. The majority of the letters between Abbot Carlyle, Davidson, and Bishop Gore dealing with the status of Carlyle and the Caldey monks were published after the 1913 conversion in a pamphlet, *A Correspondence*. The booklet was privately printed and distributed to the friends of Aelred Carlyle. The standard biography of Abbot Carlyle is P. Anson *Abbot Extraordinary* (New York 1958). See also R.M. Kollar, 'Abbot Aelred Carlyle and the Monks of Caldey: Anglo-Catholicism in the Church of England, 1895–1913.' (unpublished Ph.D. dissertation, University of Maryland 1981).

ordination in America Archbishop Maclagan promised to 'receive me back to his Diocese as one of his Clergy in Colonial Orders.' Carlyle later asserted that the licence was never granted because of Maclagan's delicate health. He confessed, therefore, that for the past several years he had been functioning without the required licence, but it was now time to rectify this situation. 'I felt it rather premature to write to you for any permission till I knew more exactly what was needed ... I should have asked you for this permission when we first came to Caldey, but I was strongly advised to wait until our work had passed the experimental stage.' The abbot's petition concluded with a plea for the primate's recognition and sanction: 'if Your Grace will send me the Permission to minister that is usually granted to Priests in Colonial Orders, it will give me the necessary relation to the Episcopate that will ensure the stability of a work which has been built up during the last thirteen years.'

Archbishop Davidson thanked abbot Carlyle for his letter and ensured him that full consideration would be given to his petition. Davidson also requested additional clarification on some points raised by the abbot's letter, and asked to see the correspondence of Archbishops Temple and Maclagan dealing with Carlyle's ordination and evidence of Temple's approval of the Anglican Benedictines.[15] Carlyle immediately forwarded these documents to Lambeth Palace,[16] and was later informed that 'His Grace is making further enquiry and giving consideration to the subject.'[17] Archbishop Davidson did not reply until 14 February 1912, but during the interval he investigated Abbot Carlyle's claims, studied the petition, and sought the advice and counsel of others.

Archbishop Davidson sent Abbot Carlyle's petition to Bishop John Owen and asked him 'to read it and return it ... with your comments.'[18] Owen responded and praised Carlyle: 'I think highly of the Abbot personally. He is a man of distinct ability and force of character and I have found him straightforward and trustworthy.'[19] The status of the monastery, however, remained a difficult prob-

---

[15] P[rinknash] A[bbey] A[rchives], Carlyle Papers, Shepphard to Carlyle, 18 December 1911.
[16] LPL, Carlyle to Davidson, 20 December 1911.
[17] PAA, Macmillan to Carlyle, 23 December 1911.
[18] LPL, Shepphard to Owen, 18 December 1911.
[19] LPL, Davidson to Owen, 20 December 1911.

lem. 'I have always felt that the question of the community,' he told Davidson, 'was very different and I have been reluctant to draw Your Grace's attention to it.' He also recommended that Archbishop Davidson grant Carlyle the licence the abbot desired: Carlyle 'is worthy of Your Grace's permission to officiate in the province under the Colonial Clergy Act.' On the basis of Bishop Owen's recommendation, Archbishop Davidson wrote to Abbot Carlyle and agreed to discuss the question of the abbot's licence and ecclesiastical accreditation. 'You have offered me strong assurance of your loyalty to the Church of England,' Davidson wrote, and the archbishop pointed out his eagerness to support and encourage 'those who are working in loyalty to our Church, even where the usage of their work and worship aren't those which I should personally adopt.'[20] Archbishop Davidson ended on an optimistic note: '... it is my earnest endeavour to give sympathy and support to honest work of whatever kind which is done to the glory of God within the large and reasonable limits of the Church of England.' After an exchange of letters, 6 March 1912 was agreed upon as an acceptable date for the interview at Lambeth Palace.

By January 1912, however, Abbot Carlyle's popularity and prestige within the High Church party began to wane. Tales of extravagance and lavish spending on the part of Carlyle outraged many of his supporters who had struggled to contribute to the revival on Caldey.[21] Moreover, rumours that the abbot was seriously contemplating conversion to Roman Catholicism also reached the ears of his patrons,[22] and his Anglo-Catholic friends believed that a scandal of this magnitude must be checked. Darwell Stone, the librarian of Pusey House, had consulted with other

[20] PAA, Davidson to Carlyle, 14 February 1912.
[21] Caldey Abbey became famous as the most sumptuous and extravagant abbey in England. Numerous towers and turrets, luxurious abbot's quarters, an expensive chapel, and a kitchen constructed on the plans of medieval Glastonbury Abbey comprised Abbot Carlyle's monastery. The Abbey possessed a wide selection of expensive pectoral crosses and rings; and one of his croziers was ivory gilded with silver. Carlyle enjoyed the services of a yacht, and on the mainland Abbot Carlyle travelled in his chauffeur driven Daimler. The abbot's frequent holidays to Italy also shocked and alienated many of his supporters.
[22] In 1907, early 1912, and several times during 1911 rumours and stories circulated among Carlyle's supporters and members of the High Church party that he was on the brink of conversion. Carlyle made no secret that he was flirting with Roman Catholicism.

supporters of Caldey, and concluded that the only way to salvage the Benedictine monastery was to arrange a meeting between Abbot Carlyle and the bishop of Oxford, Charles Gore, whom they believed would be sympathetic to Carlyle. In a letter to Gore, Stone stated that 'we feel that there is a possibility that, if the Abbot could talk with you ... there would be more probability of good resulting. ...'[23] Secession to Rome was a real danger, and Stone emphasised that 'it will give a great shock to many people ... it would be regretted.' H. F. B. Mackay, another patron of the Anglican Benedictines, wrote to Lord Halifax and explained that 'it is just possible Gore might get hold of him and that they might be kept if Gore could be Episcopal Godfather to them.'[24] Consequently, Mackay approached Bishop Gore who consented to meet Abbot Carlyle.[25] The Bishop replied that he 'would very gladly ask the Abbot to Cuddesdon at once if he would write and say he would like to come.'[26]

By the end of February, Abbot Carlyle had accepted Bishop Gore's invitation. Carlyle wrote: 'you have very kindly offered to give me the benefit of your help and advice in some of the matters that are perplexing us as a community at the present time.'[27] Gore answered and agreed to meet Abbot Carlyle on 4 March, two days before the abbot's interview at Lambeth Palace. At this meeting, according to Bishop Gore, the abbot was open and frank about the possibility of conversion to Roman Catholicism.[28] Gore seriously questioned the actions and policies of previous ecclesiastical authorities towards Abbot Carlyle,[29] but found the abbot charming and believed conversion to Rome could be prevented. 'The Abbot of Caldey is here,' Gore informed Archbishop Davidson, 'I like him very much ... he is quite unlike most people going over to

[23] LPL, Stone to Gore, 8 February 1912.
[24] B[orthwick] I[nstitute of] H[istorical] R[esearch], Halifax Papers, Mackay to Halifax, 19 February 1912.
[25] Ibid.
[26] BIHR, Gore to Mackay, 16 February 1912. Recent studies of Bishop Gore include J. Carpenter, *Gore: A Study in Liberal Catholic Thought* (London 1960); A.M. Ramsey, *From Gore to Temple* (London 1962); and B. Reardon, *From Coleridge to Gore* (London 1971).
[27] PAA, Carlyle to Gore, 19 February 1912.
[28] LPL, Gore to Davidson, 28 February 1913.
[29] BIHR, Gore to Halifax, 5 March 1912.

Rome.'[30] Nonetheless, Bishop Gore did not pamper the abbot, but he emphasized the gravity of Carlyle's present 'untenable position' as an Anglican clergyman.[31] Gore pointed out the incongruity between some of Caldey's devotional practices and the traditions of the Anglican Church. According to Bishop Gore, to 'say Mass in Latin seems to me to be morally disastrous for him and everyone connected with him.'[32] The bishop of Oxford believed that Abbot Carlyle honestly wished to remain in the Anglican Church, but Gore also recognized that the *status quo* on Caldey was unacceptable.

Immediately after the interview, Gore wrote to Archbishop Davidson and proposed a plan. His report on Abbot Carlyle was positive, and he recommended 'that we should resolve that he cannot go over to Rome,' but on the other hand, the abbot cannot 'abide where his is.'[33] Consequently, Gore insisted on 'the appointment of a sympathetic commission to enquire and report upon their practices and life,' and as possible members, he nominated two prominent Anglo-Catholics, Darwell Stone and Rev. W. H. B. Trevelyan. The suggestions of this commission, Gore argued, should be handled on the diocesan level, and only afterwards, should the case be submitted to the primate. Quick solutions must be avoided. The irregularities must be rectified gradually because 'in the situation which exists, with 20 years history behind it, abrupt action of ... authority would mean a catastrophe.' Gore also told Lord Halifax that any recklessness on the part of the episcopate would 'make any issue without disaster after all these years very hard to believe possible.'[34]

On 6 March 1912, Abbot Aelred Carlyle met Archbishop Davidson at Lambeth Palace. The abbot immediately addressed himself to the 'granting of a Provincial Licence ... and the doubt that had risen ... about their [the Caldey Benedictines] position in the Anglican Church ...'.[35] Carlyle noted that certain individuals questioned his status as a clergyman because of his exclusion from *Crockford's*, and consequently he felt that 'the time had come for

[30] LPL, Gore to Davidson, 4 March 1912.
[31] LPL, Gore to Davidson, 28 February 1913.
[32] BIHR, Gore to Halifax, 5 March 1912.
[33] LPL, Gore to Davidson, 4 March 1912.
[34] BIHR, Gore to Halifax, 5 March 1912.
[35] PAA, A. Carlyle, 'Original Interview Notes.'

him to seek to obtain such a reasonable and moderate authorization from the Episcopate as the granting of a licence would carry.' The abbot admitted that for nearly a decade he had been functioning as a priest with no licence or permission to preach or conduct services outside of his monastery. 'Will you give me now a licence under the Colonial Clergy Act for officiating in the province of Canterbury,' Carlyle asked Davidson, 'although I neither hold nor ask for Diocesan accrediting, or licence or office?'[36] Abbot Carlyle also sought permission to have a number of his monks ordained, but stressed that they would not pledge allegiance to the Established Church, submit to the control of supervision of a bishop, or be bound to conduct services according to the Book of Common Prayer. These clerics would exercise no 'outside ministrations' and their work would be confined 'wholly within the Order and on the island.' Caldey's priests 'would be ordained not to use ordinarily the Prayer Book except when ministering in the Village Church, but to use ... the Benedictine breviary.'

Archbishop Davidson's reaction to Carlyle's demands was cautious. Instead of pointing out the inconsistencies of the abbot's requests or demanding that he abandon his Roman practices and conform to the teachings of the Anglican Church, Archbishop Davidson listened passively. Carlyle was aware that the archbishop hoped to neutralize a conflict. He maintained that Davidson 'was careful all the way through to avoid expressing any personal opinion, but many times showed himself kindly and well disposed.'[37] 'The Archbishop was very kind but perfectly noncommittal,' Carlyle later wrote Bishop Gore, and 'his Grace has

---

[36] LPL, R. Davidson, 'Interview at Lambeth, March 6, 1912 with the Abbot of Caldey.' As Bishop of Winchester, Davidson praised the growth of religious life, but also pointed out the need for the 'guidance and direction of the episcopal.' 'There is undoubtedly a peril at least,' he maintained, in 'the growing independence ...on the part of some of the religious communities.' LPL, 'Proceedings on the Religious Communities,' 1897 Lambeth Conference. But on the other hand he always cherished the vision of a peaceful, harmonious and unified Church of England; public scandal and discord must give way to compromise. S. Dark, *Archbishop Davidson and the Anglican Church* (London 1929) p. vi. According to Davidson, imprudent or precipitous action on the part of bishops could end in failure and discord. E. Stock, *The Church of England in the Nineteenth Century* (London 1910) p. 80.

[37] PAA, A. Carlyle, 'Original Interview Notes.'

promised to consider the various circumstances of the case, and hopes to let me have his decision before next May.'[38]

Carlyle greatly impressed the archbishop, who believed that the Anglican abbot would not convert. But Davidson also admitted to Bishop Gore that he did 'not see ... [his] way very clearly yet.'[39] Carlyle also confided to Gore that the meeting with Archbishop Davidson had strengthened his courage and desire to remain in the Church of England. 'In all these matters I do not in the least desire to hurry,' Carlyle informed Bishop Gore, 'nor do I wish to press for any sort of authorisation that might not be considered legitimate.'[40] 'The indication that God means for us to stay where we are,' he continued 'is becoming increasingly clear.'

Bishop Gore responded to Carlyle's enthusiasm and reminded him that it was duty of bishops to restore 'the faith and order in the church on a sufficient basis.'[41] Gore had previously written to Archbishop Davidson and demanded that the primate restrain Abbot Carlyle and bring a halt to the episcopal neglect the Anglican Benedictines had always enjoyed. 'You should do something which shows that the Church or you are not satisfied but at the same time would not pull them up too short,' Gore urged the archbishop.[42] Davidson responded and informed the bishop of Oxford he had not yet decided what steps to take.[43] Gore, however, did not waver in his demand for order, and cautioned the archbishop against granting the abbot a licence or sanctioning the Benedictine lifestyle at Caldey. Moreover, Bishop Gore pleaded with Davidson to appoint him as an official visitor to study and reform Caldey: 'Meanwhile, if I can be of any use as a visitor, with the ordinary power of an episcopal visitor, for one year to report to you at the end of the year, I would ... act.'[44] Davidson continued to remain uncommitted. 'I am most grateful to you for your offer to be Visitorially helpful should that seem to be our best way of acting,' the archbishop informed Gore, but 'the subject is delicate

[38] PAA, Carlyle to Gore, 9 March 1912.
[39] LPL, Davidson to Gore, 7 March 1912.
[40] PAA, Carlyle to Gore, 9 March 1912.
[41] PAA, Gore to Carlyle, 14 March 1912.
[42] LPL, Gore to Davidson, 7 March 1912.
[43] LPL, Davidson to Gore, 7 March 1912.
[44] LPL, Gore to Davidson, 19 March 1912.

and anxious ... I am considering it carefully.'[45] By the beginning of April 1912, Archbishop Davidson still had not yet reached any decision concerning Carlyle's petition for a licence or his approbation of the Anglican Benedictines, but he told Bishop Gore that 'the suggestion you have made about you possibly becoming Visitor is a most important one.'[46]

Gore welcomed this opening. He informed the primate that 'the idea of having to do with them is exceedingly repugnant to me for various reasons.'[47] But Bishop Gore agreed that 'the best thing would be for you ask me to consider the question of becoming their visitor and propose this to the Abbot.' Archbishop Davidson finally yielded to Bishop Gore's demands for reform and discipline. At the end of May, the archbishop informed Abbot Carlyle that he would take no action in respect of his licence or the status of the monastery until the Anglican monks elect an Episcopal Visitor. 'The more consideration I give to the subject the more certain do I feel that if your community is to hold a recognized place within the Church of England, it must conform to the general principles laid down by the Committee of the Lambeth Conference of 1897....'[48] 'From what you told me at our interview,' Davidson continued, 'I do not think that you will be unwilling to conform to the general principles there laid down.'[49] The archbishop suggested that 'if your community were to elect as Visitor the Bishop of Oxford, he would not decline to accept the position.'[50]

---

[45] LPL, Davidson to Gore, 19 March 1912.
[46] LPL, Davidson to Gore, 9 April 1912.
[47] LPL, Gore to Davidson, 10 April 1912.
[48] PAA, Davidson to Carlyle, 20 May 1912.
[49] The 1897 Lambeth Conference expressed its views on religious brotherhoods and their relation to bishops. The Conference wanted to prevent the formation of any community which was free from the authority and scrutiny of the local bishop. It therefore suggested that the local bishop become the *ex officio* visitor of the brotherhood, and 'the brotherhood...must not be allowed to work in any diocese without the consent of the bishop.' Each foundation must have an Episcopal Visitor. If the Church of England should choose to recognize a brotherhood, then it certainly has 'a right to require submission to order, and submission to order depends on its relation to the Bishops...' In devotion and liturgical matters, the communities must remain loyal to the Book of Common Prayer, and to safeguard this, a 'constitution...should be submitted to the Bishop's approval.' LPL, 'Proceedings on the Religious Communities,' Lambeth Conference, 1897.
[50] PAA, Davidson to Carlyle, 2 May 1912.

After some hesitation, Carlyle accepted the archbishop's suggestion. He informed Davidson that 'I hope and believe we shall be glad to welcome the opportunity of electing a Visitor in the person of Bishop Gore ... and meanwhile I will write a preliminary letter to tell him what we are doing, and invite him to come and see us at Caldey....'[51] By this action, Carlyle maintained, Caldey could boast 'a distinct recognition of the authority of the Episcopate.'

> ... it is essential to the canonical existence of the Community, the exercise of proper authority by Superiors, and the validity of Religious Profession, that the living Authority of the Church should be sought and obtained. No spiritual jurisdiction can be exercised unless Episcopal authority is duly imposed, not arbitrarily or capriciously, but according to the well-known and generally accepted rules of the Catholic Church.

Carlyle also pointed out that 'the knowledge of these facts has been a strong influence all through our Community Life in helping us to make sure of our ground and to avoid mistakes.'

Archbishop Davidson responded to the abbot's letter and expressed his joy that the Anglican Benedictines had accepted his proposal to nominate Bishop Gore to become its official visitor. 'It is a great satisfaction to me to learn that your community accepts the suggestion that an Episcopal Visitor should be elected with a view to the exercise of responsibilities in connection with the Society and its life.'[52] The primate urged Carlyle to contact Gore immediately, and, with characteristic caution, suggested a procedure: 'I am very sure that in the whole matter we must act quietly, deliberately and with a due regard to the importance of precedents that we may be establishing.' The archbishop was confident and optimistic that a peaceful solution could be forged; the office of visitor and the expertise of Bishop Gore were the key. Confident of success, Archbishop Davidson contacted Bishop Gore and remarked that 'it is to me a source of very real relief to think that you consent to bring to bear ... the knowledge and personal experience which are yours.'[53]

[51] LPL, Carlyle to Davidson, 29 August 1912.
[52] PAA, Davidson to Carlyle, 5 September 1912.
[53] LPL, Davidson to Gore, 5 September 1912.

Abbot Carlyle's delay in inviting Bishop Gore to accept the office of visitor caused him some anxiety. Gore complained to Archbishop Davidson that 'no communication such as I was led to expect giving me a preliminary invitation to consider the question of becoming their Visitor has come from the Community or the Abbot of Caldey.'[54] On 3 October, however, Abbot Carlyle formally approached Bishop Gore:

> With regard to my great hope that at our next Annual Chapter ... we may be privileged – in accordance with the wishes of the Archbishop – to elect you as our Episcopal Visitor, it would now be of great use to me in conferring with my Brethren on the subject if you would allow me to tell them definitely that you might be willing to accept such election.[55]

Carlyle emphasized that Archbishop Davidson had made it clear that 'the best method of further regularizing the status of our Community will be in the appointment of an Episcopal Visitor. ...' Abbot Carlyle also strongly encouraged Gore to visit Caldey and 'become personally acquainted with the Brethren, and at the same time have an unfettered opportunity to judge of our particular needs and aim.' Carlyle concluded with a statement of his expectations: 'We gladly welcome the opportunity that is coming to us of receiving the proper recognition and sanction of Episcopal Authority for the Doctrine and Practice in which the life of the Community has grown up.'

Gore's response indicated how he would approach the sensitive question of the Anglican Benedictines; it was official, straightforward, and firm. He told Carlyle that he was deeply interested in the growth of religious communities in the Church of England, but there were certain preliminaries he must demand before he could become Caldey's Visitor. The bishop informed Abbot Carlyle that the 'office of a Visitor ... is to maintain a certain constitution and rule of devotion, and the consent of the Visitor would be necessary to any alteration to it.'[56] A Visitor must carefully consider the

---

[54] LPL, Gore to Davidson, 30 October 1912. Davidson recognized Gore's anxiety and replied that 'they take weeks to answer letters, and I do not know that any great harm arises from their delay in making application to you...' LPL, Davidson to Gore, 5 March 1912.
[55] PAA, Carlyle to Gore, 3 October 1912.
[56] PAA, Gore to Carlyle, 7 October 1912.

liturgy and common worship of the community. Consequently, Gore requested Caldey's 'constitution, rules and rites, other than those contained in the Prayer Book,' for study. He apologized for the trouble this would cause, and also informed Abbot Carlyle that he could not personally visit Caldey. 'I cannot manage this year, and probably the first stages of our negotiation can be conducted in writing.'[57]

In response, Abbot Carlyle promised to send Bishop Gore the documents he required and expressed his sorrow that the bishop could not visit Caldey. Carlyle, therefore, referred to Gore's previous suggestion that a delegation of priests visit Caldey and report on the community's devotions, and he suggested that Rev. W. H. B. Trevelyan and Darwell Stone observe the brotherhood 'to prepare such a statement as might be laid before you.'[58] Gore's reply was straightforward. He asked the abbot to supply him with information about his ordination, its circumstances, and his present position or status in the Church of England. Bishop Gore also agreed that a 'commission of priests to report would still be useful,' and he informed Abbot Carlyle that he would enquire if Stone and Trevelyan would agree to this proposal.[59] By the end of October, therefore, Abbot Carlyle was committed to the selection of Bishop Gore as Caldey's Visitor. To renege or back out now would compromise his boast of loyalty to the Established Church. The omens, however, were unpromising: Caldey's future growth and his own position in the Anglican Church depended on the recommendation of a Visitor; and Bishop Gore's preliminary queries and demands indicated that he would be exact and demanding.

Carlyle forwarded to Bishop Gore the required documentation in November 1912.[60] He admitted that he possessed no clerical

---

[57] *Ibid.* Carlyle later used Gore's refusal to visit Caldey as an example of the Bishop's uncompromising attitude, but the reason for not visiting Caldey was the Bishop's full schedule. In October, Bishop Gore had scheduled 35 public functions, in November, 38, and in December he was occupied daily up to 17 December, and the next four days were devoted to diocesan ordinations. See *Oxford Diocesan Magazine*, September–December, 1912.

[58] PAA, Carlyle to Gore, 21 October 1912.

[59] PAA, Gore to Carlyle, 24 October 1912.

[60] Carlyle enclosed a copy of Archbishop Maclagan's Letter Dimissory and stated that he did not make the usual Oath and Declaration of Assent at his ordination in America. Material on the history of Caldey and its monastic principles, *The Benedictines of Caldey Island* and *Our Purpose and Method*, were also forwarded to

licence: 'On coming here, we decided to wait till it was seen that
the Community could remain permanently on the island, before
approaching the Archbishop of Canterbury about my licence.'[61]
'My most earnest endeavour from the inception of this Community,' the abbot concluded, 'has been never to take any step without
Episcopal guidance.' But Gore had already recognized problems. In
his invitation to Darwell Stone to visit Caldey, Gore revealed that
he was anxious and felt 'the profound difficulty of the situation.'[62]
In November, Gore informed Archbishop Davidson of the serious
difficulties which Stone and Trevelyan would face: ' ... they are
conscious that there are certain things a bishop could not possibly
sanction. ...'[63] 'Certainly they are conscious at Caldey that they are
in a false position,' Gore told the archbishop, 'but fundamental
changes are difficult to make rapidly.'

Stone and Trevelyan arrived on Caldey Island on 3 January 1913.
After talking with the abbot, reviewing the rules and constitutions
of the brotherhood, and enquiring about the liturgy and devotions
of the monastery, they drew up a report for Bishop Gore, which
Abbot Carlyle endorsed. The Stone-Trevelyan Report[64] singled
out the following questionable practices: use of the Roman missal
instead of the Prayer Book, celebration of the Immaculate Conception and Assumption, Exposition of the Blessed Sacrament, ven-
eration of relics, eucharistic processions, Benediction, and perpetual Reservation of the Blessed Sacrament. In general, however,
Stone and Trevelyan painted a positive view of the Anglican monks
and emphasized 'that the Community as a whole is wishful to be in
due relationship to the Episcopate, and that you [Bishop Gore]
should become the Episcopal Visitor.' Stone also sent his personal
recommendation to Bishop Gore. 'Rather than risk the loss to
English Benedictinism of so high a favour,' he urged Gore to adopt
a conciliatory approach.[65] Serious study and consideration should

Gore. Finally, Carlyle sent facsimilies of Archbishop Temple's authorization for
his profession and election as an Anglican abbot.
[61] PAA, Carlyle to Gore, 4 November 1912.
[62] P[usey] H[ouse] L[ibrary], Stone Papers, Gore to Stone, 24 October 1912. Bishop
Gore sent the same invitation to Rev. W.H.B. Trevelyan.
[63] LPL, Gore to Davidson, 28 November 1912.
[64] PHL, Stone and Trevelyan to Gore, 21 January 1913.
[65] PAA, D. Stone, 'The Benedictines of Caldey Island.'

be given to Caldey's unusual position; compromise should prevail over rash action.

With typical bluntness and dispatch, Bishop Gore informed Abbot Carlyle that before he could become Caldey's Visitor, the abbot must accept four conditions. Moreover, he wrote, these 'preliminaries seem to me to be obvious and to be outside all possibilities of bargaining and concession, and I do not think it is worth going on until these preliminary points are taken for granted.'[66] Gore demanded the following: the property of Caldey to be legally secured to the Anglican Church;[67] the Book of Common Prayer must be used exclusively; the doctrines of the Immaculate Conception and Assumption must be abandoned; and Benediction, Reservation of the Blessed Sacrament, and the exposition of relics must be curtailed. 'I cannot promise that this list is inclusive,' he also informed Abbot Carlyle, 'I should have very carefully to attend to a number of details and bear in mind on the one hand the general principle of policy and on the other hand the exceptional position of your Community.'[68] Shocked by this policy, Carlyle urged Bishop Gore to reconsider his position: 'it seems to me hardly fair to the Community to put before them at once what is merely a series of negotiations that "lie outside all possibilities of bargaining and concession."'[69] But Gore refused to compromise: 'I think I had rather hold to the method suggested in my letter.'[70] He assured the abbot that 'my point was and remains that there are certain matters with regard to which I feel sure to start with, and I think we had better arrive at an understanding about them before going further.'

[66] PAA, Gore to Carlyle, 8 February 1912.
[67] The ownership of the property was vested in Abbot Carlyle alone. The three established Anglican brotherhoods, the Cowley Fathers, the Society of the Resurrection, and the Society of the Sacred Mission, had legislated that their property would be vested in a trust under the supervision of the Anglican Church. The Established Church always tried to regulate and oversee the property owned by religious brotherhoods. The 1908 Lambeth Conference report on brotherhoods stressed that 'provision for due rules as to the possession and disposition of property' should be stipulated in the community's bylaws. 'Report of the Committee Appointed in 1897 to Consider the Relations of Religious Communities With the Church to the Episcopate,' Lambeth Conference, 1908.
[68] PAA, Gore to Carlyle, 8 February 1913.
[69] PAA, Carlyle to Gore, 11 February 1913.
[70] PAA, Gore to Carlyle, 14 February 1913.

If Carlyle's monks approved of Bishop Gore's demands, the existence of Benedictine life as lived on Caldey would be destroyed. Conversion to Rome, therefore, became an appealing alternative.[71] Gore, therefore, urged Abbot Carlyle to re-examine his position and remain in the Anglican Church. As for the ownership of the island, the bishop argued that he wanted 'only ... a reasonable assurance that the property was held properly in trust for a community in Communion with the See of Canterbury.'[72] In respect to the curtailment of certain liturgies, Gore stated 'that the authority for some of your devotional practices is so specifically a later Roman authority as to be inconsistent with the appeal' to primitive catholic traditions. He also pointed out the chief inconsistency in the abbot's position: 'It seems to me that you are accepting and rejecting the same authority at different points, and that cannot be a satisfactory basis on which to stand.' But the bishop's desire to have Abbot Carlyle modify the lifestyle of Anglican monks ended in failure.

Abbot Carlyle informed Bishop Gore on 22 February that he and a majority of his followers were converting to Roman Catholicism. After recounting the circumstances behind his invitation to the bishop to become Caldey's Visitor, he attacked Gore and denounced his 'cold formal demand' for the 'unconditional submission' of the community and his rejection of 'our special spiritual needs [which] do not seem to have deserved any consideration.'[73] The abbot also ridiculed the 'anomalies of the Church of England' and its 'boasted comprehensiveness.' Abbot Carlyle sent this letter before he received Bishop Gore's request of 22 February pleading with him to reconsider. Later, however, the abbot even dismissed this call for restraint: 'Very gladly would I have consulted other people ... had you held out the slightest hope ... that you were prepared to modify your first requirements.'[74] On the same day that Carlyle informed Bishop Gore of the monks' decision to convert, Archbishop Davidson was also notified:

> I am writing to tell your Grace that the negotiations between
> Bishop Gore and our Community about the office of Visitor

[71] PAA, Community of Caldey to Gore, 19 February 1913.
[72] PAA, Gore to Carlyle, 22 February 1913.
[73] PAA, Carlyle to Gore, 22 February 1913.
[74] PAA, Carlyle to Gore, 25 February 1913.

have broken off, and that as the result of his Lordship's preliminary requirements, which he has placed outside 'all possibilities of bargaining and concession,' we find ourselves, as a Community, obliged to ask admission to the Roman Catholic Church.[75]

Bishop Gore subsequently believed that the plan for an Episcopal Visitor was a ploy, and maintained that 'the application for me to become Visitor ... [was] used as affording an excuse for saying they were driven out of the Church of England.'[76] When Carlyle finally decided to leave the Anglican Church, Gore declared that the abbot 'has used me to provide him with the useful excuse.'[77] Archbishop Davidson appreciated Gore's insight, but remained characteristically uncommitted. 'I am still puzzled to decide to my own satisfaction whether he is a crafty man who has been trying by guile to get what he could not get straightforwardly, or simply a fairly honest enthusiast without balance of judgment.'[78] But even Lord Halifax believed that Carlyle staged the confrontation with the Anglican authorities. The viscount told Darwell Stone that 'the Bishop of Oxford's letter ... has given the Abbot just the excuse he was perhaps looking for...'.[79]

The role of Archbishop Davidson during the February crisis was essentially passive. He delegated and relinquished all authority and power to Bishop Gore, whose methods and procedure he sanctioned. After the decision to convert was taken, Davidson informed Gore that he did not 'demur to what you have done and written ... [and] what I have seen strikes me as eminently reasonable and considerate on your part...'.[80] Davidson's chief consideration, moreover, was not theological propriety or the possibility of a scandal, but he wanted to retain ownership of Caldey Island for the Established Church. 'It is a wretched business', he told Gore, 'and seems to betoken a real trickiness....' The archbishop contended that Carlyle '... could not possibly transfer to Rome money which had been given ... because his order was remaining in the Church

[75] LPL, Carlyle to Davidson, 22 February 1913.
[76] LPL, Gore to Davidson, 25 February 1913.
[77] LPL, Gore to Davidson, 28 February 1913.
[78] LPL, Davidson to Gore, 26 February 1913.
[79] PHL, Halifax to Stone, 24 February 1913.
[80] LPL, Davidson to Gore, 24 February 1913.

of England.'[81] Prompted by Bishop Gore, however, the archbishop did not pursue this issue.[82]

Nonetheless, many of the faithful had appealed to Archbishop Davidson to retrieve Caldey and to stop the conversion of its abbot and monks. One individual claimed that 'the loss will be great'.[83] Since the abbot was 'a man of highest ability,' it will be 'a spiritual loss to us.' The archbishop responded that Abbot Carlyle 'has insisted upon the retention of usages so absolutely alien to and repudiated by the Church of England that formal recognition ... would be impossible without a breach of the promises made by Bishops at their consecration.'[84] Another layman begged him 'as head of the Church of England to prevent them going to Rome ... [because] this will be serious to the Church.'[85] Davidson simply replied that he was sad about the decision of the Anglican Benedictines to convert.[86] On the other hand, a father of one of the monks congratulated the archbishop on his policy towards Caldey and argued that 'it is more honest that they should call themselves Roman, which they have been all alone except in name....'[87] Davidson acknowledged 'the anxious and unsatisfactory matter of Caldey' and thanked Admiral Anson for his support. 'It is genuine satisfaction to me to find that there are those who ... have had the opportunity of judging the matter in another way are in agreement with what I have tried to do.'[88]

Unlike Randall Davidson, Charles Gore remained resolute during the controversy with the Anglican Benedictines. He refused to

---

[81] LPL, Davidson to Gore, 26 February 1913.

[82] The ownership of Caldey Island and whether the monks should return funds became an emotional issue after they had converted. Some argued that everything must be returned to the Anglican Church. On the suggestion of Lord Halifax, a commission was formed to study and solve the problem. Its membership included: Halifax, Carlyle, Lord Balfour of Burleigh, Athelstan Riley, the Duke of Norfolk, and the Roman Catholic Bishop of Menevia, Francis Mostyn. One piece of property, Pershore, was returned to the Anglican Church. But Caldey and gifts given to Carlyle while an Anglican remained in his possession. Carlyle agreed, however, to repay a flat sum of £3,000.

[83] LPL, Brook to Davidson, 26 February 1913.

[84] LPL, Davidson to Brook, 1 March 1913.

[85] LPL, Felling to Davidson, 3 March 1913.

[86] LPL, Davidson to Felling, 7 March 1913.

[87] LPL, Anson to Davidson, 13 March 1913. Admiral Anson was the father of Peter Anson, one of the monks and future biographer of Abbot Carlyle.

[88] LPL, Davidson to Anson, 13 March 1913.

4000# RENE M. KOLLAR

sanction the life and liturgy of Caldey. If the monks would not change, they were free to depart. The bishop did not object to the publication of his correspondence by Abbot Carlyle, and he anticipated a hostile reaction from the abbot's friends. Gore, therefore, published his explanation of the events on Caldey to counteract some 'very untrue account of what I have done.'[89] He criticized those who accused him of being 'too peremptory in insisting on the use of the Prayer Book.' Gore argued that 'no single bishop has the right to sanction any other rite or to allow the clergy to omit the recitation of the divine office which are enjoined upon them all.' When Carlyle invited him to become Caldey's Visitor, the abbot was aware 'that the Benedictine Community … was in an unsatisfactory position.' Consequently, Gore pleaded with his detractors to judge the case on the merit of the negotiations between himself and Abbot Carlyle. 'Meanwhile,' Gore suggested, I wish those of my friends who are anxious about the matter to read my letters.'[90] Even Abbot Carlyle recognized the difficulties of his Anglican Benedictines remaining within the Church. During the months following the conversion, Carlyle expressed sympathy towards Bishop Gore's principles, 'I am sure you were rightly guided so far as the Church of England was concerned,' Carlyle wrote Gore, and 'personally I would have let the matter rest.'[91]

It was Bishop Gore, the reformer, and not Archbishop Davidson who forced Abbot Carlyle to recognize the inconsistencies of his Anglican Benedictines. If the abbot and his monks accepted certain standards, only then would their status be regularized and episcopal approval granted. Three conflicting ideals and standards influenced the history of Benedictine life in the Church of England: Abbot Carlyle's Roman practices and desire for autonomy, Archbishop Randall Davidson's urgency to avoid scandal and schism, and Charles Gore's dedication to reform and uniformity. These irreconcilable forces drove the Caldey monks to Roman Catholicism.

Saint Vincent College and Seminary

[89] 'Caldey,' The Oxford Diocesan Magazine, April 1913, p. 51.
[90] Ibid, Gore was annoyed that Carlyle did not publish the entire correspondence: 'I hoped, as I have said, that the correspondence would be — not alluded to in fragments in the press, but published entirely.'
[91] PAA, Carlyle to Gore, 20 November 1913.

396

SELF-DENIAL AND THE FREE CHURCHES: SOME LITERARY RESPONSES

by DAVID KEEP

THE ascetic ideal found in wandering holy men in the east and in the self- and world-denying vows of regular clergy and laity in the middle ages came down to English nonconformity through puritanism. Bunyan's pilgrim, like Benedict and Francis was passing through a temporary and evil world. Their attitude to life was that of the Sermon on the Mount, on the lips of the shepherd lad:

> 'I am content with what I have,
> Little be it, or much.'

Wesley blended the high Anglican discipline of Jeremy Taylor and the Oxford Holy Club with his field evangelism and exhorted his Methodists to 'Gain all you can; save all you can; then give all all you can.' The gain was to be without doing harm to anyone. The Methodist was 'to despise delicacy and variety, and be content with what plain nature requires.' He was to 'waste no part of it ... in costly pictures, painting, gilding, books; in elegant rather than useful gardens.'[1] The Methodist was to avoid sensuality, curiosity and vanity. Wesley's sermon on 'The use of money' is regularly quoted and is required reading for every Methodist preacher.

This scrupulous modesty was followed by strict evangelicals like the banker Henry Thornton, and by the early Brethren. Lord Congleton with an income of £1200 rented a house in Teignmouth for £12 per annum and furnished it in deal and pewter. He allowed the table to be stained to help his maid. Anthony Norris Grovens gave away his flourishing dental practice in Exeter. He attempted to become an Anglican missionary living by faith before he became independent. He reiterated Wesley's principle: 'The Christian motto should be – labour hard, consume little, give much, and all to

---

[1] John Wesley, *Sermons on Several Occasions* (London 1754) pp. 579–86.

Christ'.[2] His brother-in-law George Muller followed the same pattern. A profligate Prussian theological student, he saw the error of his ways in Exmouth and was appointed pastor of Ebenezer Chapel, Teignmouth on £55 a year. After his marriage in 1830, the couple decided to give up the stipend and trust in God. In the first year their income was £131 18s. 8d. They developed the great orphan houses in Bristol on the same principle, and though they often got down to the last crust, money always came.[3] Robert Chapman of Barnstaple gave up a promising legal career to live by faith alone in a terraced cottage.[4] I know evangelists and missionaries who do the same today, and may indeed represent the major part of protestant missionary work.

The only established denomination which has preserved its ethos of mission alongside the poor is The Salvation Army. The Methodist Conference of 1984 and certain bishops in northern sees have proclaimed the need to identify, but even the modest stipends and parsonages of ministers in the eighties, to say nothing of their education and lifestyle keep them separate. The followers of William Booth accept a lower standard of living and a stricter discipline in where they serve. The purpose of this paper is to look at the nineteenth century through the eyes of novelists and essayists in order to establish whether nonconformists lived up to their puritan and ascetic standard. William Booth saw by 1890 what was happening to their ideals. His judgement on 'The Vicious' indicates clearly what happened to Wesley's injunctions on money:

> There are many vices and seven deadly sins. But of late years many of the seven have contrived to pass themselves off as virtues, Avarice, for instance; and Pride, when re-baptised thrift and self-respect have become the guardian angels of Christian civilisation; and as for Envy, it is the corner-stone on which much of our competitive spirit is founded.[5]

William Booth realised that the reality of nonconformist life was very different from the disciplined piety they professed. Wesley had criticised 'Quaker linen', but the pursuit of quality and quantity

---

[2] Roy Coad *A History of the Brethren Movement* (Exeter 1976) pp. 17, 67.
[3] Nancy Garton *George Muller and his Orphans* (London 1963) pp. 32–39.
[4] W.H. Bennett, *Robert Cleaver Chapman of Barnstaple* (Glasgow 1902).
[5] William Booth in *Darkest England and the Way Out* (London 1970) p. 46.

in all things which could be regarded as morally acceptable was taken up with enthusiasm by the emergent lower middle class in the nineteenth century. The particular sin attributed to nonconformists in literature was gluttony. While it is not possible to include the fat boy in *Pickwick Papers*, Mark Rutherford's minister John Broad in *The Revolution in Tanner's Lane* was 'a gross, heavy-feeding man' and the main pleasure of that congregation was lavish picnics.

Mrs Oliphant in her often overlooked novel *Salem Chapel* described the delight of the deacon when overcrowding forced him to drink from a sugar basin.[6] The most vigorous example is J.B. Priestley's description of the tea meeting of an extreme protestant sect supported by the East Anglian equivalent of 'rice Christians':

> The forms were a solid mass of eaters and drinkers and the tables were a solid mass of food. There were hams, and tongues and rounds of cold beef and raised pies and egg salads; plates heaped high with white bread, brown bread, currant teacakes, scones, dishes of jelly and custard and blancmange and fruit salad; piles of jam tarts and maids of honour and cream puffs; then walnut cake, plum cake, chocolate cake, coconut cake; mounds of sugar, quarts of cream and a steady flow of tea. ... The appetite was not tickled, not even met fairly; it was overwhelmed. The Second Resurrectionists were worthy of the colossal meal spread before them. The highest of high teas had met its match.[7]

Now this is fiction and almost parody in its echoes of the Messianic banquet. It does however, in literary form, reflect not only constant chapel feasts, but also the peasant folk-knowledge that fat is fit, and vital if man and beast were to survive the hungry months from midwinter to firstfruits in that rural calendar when Lent was always longer than forty days. It is not very different from V. S. Pritchett's account of a tea for Sunday-school teachers at his grandfather's Congregational manse:

> We got back to my grandmother's parlour where the sun shone through the little square lights of her windows, to see one of

---

[6] Margaret Oliphant *Salem Chapel* (London 1862); Mark Rutherford *The Revolution in Tanner's Lane* (London 1887) pp. 252, 235–7.
[7] J.B. Priestley *The Good Companions* (London 1929) p. 219.

my grandmother's masterpieces, a state tea laid out on the table. The scones, the tea-cakes, Eccles cakes, jam tarts, iced tarts, her three or four different kinds of cake, sultana, Madeira, seed and jammed sponge, her puffs and her turnovers were set out in all their yellows, browns, pinks and, as usual, in her triumph, my grandmother was making a pettish little mouth, "Laying" that "nowt like it" would be seen on any table in the town.

Pritchett commented about his Yorkshire forbears: 'they were also frugal, close and calculating about money ... home life was laborious and thrifty'.[8] The minister smoked secretly in the privy and only drank the odd glass of home-brewed ale on a distant farm. The puritan creed as practised in nonconformity was 'waste not, want not!' It was by no means ascetic so far as food was concerned, and even when discipline was applied there, as with Ephraim Tellwright in Arnold Bennett's *Anna of the Five Towns*, the saving was invested to build up capital. Fasting was the judgement of God on improvidence, not a discipline to be pursued for spiritual benefit, and certainly not for health and beauty.

If gluttony was the most conspicuous vice in dissent, it was accompanied by an increasing commitment to pleasure, so long as this was cultural and supported by the burgeoning education industry. While sensuality in the form of the pleasures of sex and alcohol remained taboo, the pleasures of the table came to be accompanied by the more subtle delights of romance and beauty. Wesley's puritan rejection of the arts weakened in the latter half of the nineteenth century. The Sutton family in *Anna* used their wealth to give their daughter the benefits of culture and travel while still expecting her to serve in chapel and community. Anna gained her knowledge of the world from the free library. Wesley had always allowed 'useful' knowledge and in Methodism even the strictest 'reading' schools were not limited to the Bible. Doreen Rosman has demonstrated how the attitude to fiction changed, led by the moral and informative romances of Sir Walter Scott.[9] Music followed reading, with choral singing being advocated as morally

[8] V.S. Pritchett *A Cab at the Door* (London 1969) pp. 37–40.
[9] Doreen Rosman 'Evangelicals and the Novel' *SCH* 14 p. 301 and *Evangelicals and Culture* (London 1984).

uplifting as well as often devotional: the practice of some brass bands of including a hymn at every concert indicates the blending of the religious and the aesthetic which was to modify the rigour of the evangelical service and led to the Pleasant Sunday Afternoon and the Sacred Concert by the end of the century. Tolerance of painting was more cautious though much affected by the biblical illustrations of the Pre-Raphaelites. Edmund Gosse describes how his father paid a shilling each for them to see Holman Hunt's *Finding of Christ in the Temple*. This was the first work of art he had ever seen, apart from paintings of botanical specimens. Hunt was acceptable because of the subject matter and the accuracy of his detail.[10]

The nineteenth-century puritan followed Kant's famous analysis that men are driven by the pursuit of goodness and the pursuit of happiness; while the search for the former may lead to the latter, the reverse is never true. With confidence they sang with John Newton:

> Fading is the worldling's pleasure,
> All his boasted pomp and show;
> Solid joys and lasting treasure
> None but Zion's children know.

Within half a century of Newton's death in 1807 this was no longer strictly true. Rising living standards and rising expectations, mass produced formal clothing and consumer goods, above all the parlour piano made nonconformists all too readily the slaves of pomp and show as the sign of progress. Success was seen as natural and divine reward for hard work. The more secret pleasures were still taboo – but only brought judgement when they led to the divorce courts. Hugh Price Hughes's 'nonconformist conscience' proved to be a very specific, and in the tragic case of Parnell, potentially harmful weapon.

There are many other examples of parodies of puritanism in literature from Ben Jonson's *Alchemist*, through Dickens' *Bleak House* to Dylan Thomas and his liberated peers in the twentieth century. Why did writers pillory the piety of the lower middle classes so vigorously? Hypocrisy is almost by definition the stuff of

[10] Edmund Gosse *Father and Son* (London 1970) p. 164.

literature and the fictitious gluttons are in the direct tradition of the anti-clerical tales of Chaucer and Rabelais. Most of the criticisms of greed and miserliness were drawn from life. The gospel does call the rich man to renounce all and become a beggar, but paradoxically it promises that all are bidden to the King's feast with appropriate garments and starry crowns. It was this element of the good news assisted by Samuel Smiles' restatement of the work-ethic in *Self-help* which was applied by the children of Methodists and Independents alike to this life. Their models remained the busy-bee and the ant, their fears the hunger of the 1790s and the 1840s. Food is the preoccupation of the poor, the fuel of the heavy manual worker, and as standards of living rose the great Quaker chocolate families were at the peak of a huge pyramid of grocers and provision merchants. The repeal of the Corn Laws in 1846 and the rapid development of steam refrigeration transformed the diet of the urban population of Britain and was accepted thankfully as a right by the majority.

There is a second theological deduction to be drawn from the fictitious and actual Free Church attitude to eating. Jesus had taught that there was no need to fast while the bridegroom was present.[11] For the evangelical follower of Wesley who had experienced the 'warmed heart', and was in contemporary terms a charismatic, Jesus was present and the Christian fast limited to Good Friday. The Christian was called upon to share, not to abstain from food, hence the reintroduction of the love-feast and those almost forgotten Sunday School treats and Whit-walks with provision for all. The soul-searching of Hurrell Froude over indulgence in an egg provoked laughter more than respect, though as has been indicated, there was an ascetic tradition in the Brethren movement. Methodism has always been more known for cheerfulness and good fellowship than for renunciation, as is seen still in the injunction to preachers and congregations to 'have a good time.' The modern generalised use follows naturally from the movement of the service into the concert and of the treat into the package holiday. The enjoyment of reading has become a virtue almost for its own sake acceptable on the twentieth-century Sabbath because it was quiet, and irrespective of the content of the book.

---

[11] Mark 2: 20.

Only in the pleasures of sex and drink did the free churches have to wait for the new morality of the 1960s. During the nineteenth century the nonconformist conscience was firmly conditioned to defend total abstinence from pleasure in the specific form of alcohol. Teetotalism was meant to be a step to raising the standard of living of the poor and part of the growth in personal holiness. It became a new circumcision for evangelicals and some catholics. John Kent sees it as a weapon in the class-war of the religious middle-class:

> Teetotalism symbolised for such people their repudiation of the social values of those whom they were expected to regard as their social superiors, as well as their social contempt for the social values of the working-classes; it offered a new and simple way of criticising both the aristocracy and the proletariat.[12]

There is a strand of asceticism which might have impinged on the Free Churches and which was closely tied to theosophy and the rediscovery of Indian religions. I thought I had found a link between nonconformity and vegetarianism in an article by the food reformer Eustace Miles entitled 'How to live on threepence a day'.[13] In its advocacy of scrupulous economy by the rejection of meat and proprietary foods in favour of pulses, bran and vegetables bought in bulk it linked the monastic cellarer with the modern health food shop. It has recurred as a theme in the literature of the churches, albeit a minor theme. More recently Margaret Harwood used her column in the *Methodist Recorder* to advocate a simple vegetarian diet, but the mainstream tradition must be sought in ethical free-thinkers and secular publishers like George Newnes, who launched *Tit-bits* on the proceeds of a vegetarian restaurant.[14] One thing shared by food and health reformers was the Calvinist desire to force their will on others. It is seen today in the advocates

---

[12] John Kent, *Holding the Fort* (London 1978) p. 88.
[13] Eustace Miles 'How to live on threepence a day' *Messenger of the Free Churches* (1907) pp. 94–5. Survey of poverty indicated that some families had only this amont *per capita*, for example Lady Bell found families spending 7*s*.5*d*. per week. Dr Edward Smith published a diet at 4½*d*. per day in 1864. The poor preferred white bread and tea to slow work-house-like messes of rice and barley recommended in *The Family Economist* (1848) in John Burnett *Plenty and Want* (London 1968) pp. 208, 187, 54.
[14] Susan Budd, *Varieties of Unbelief* (London 1977) p. 67.

of dietary reform and in the booming sport and leisure industry. Personally, I am not sure that taking part in sport should be classed with leisure: it seems to carry a good deal of the ethos of the stylites and the flaggellants and should perhaps be seen as a resurgence of the ascetic ideal. Fitness is replacing abstinence as the shibboleth of our society and has the same legalistic virtue that it isolates one possibly moral activity in contrast to the whole.

I have argued in this paper that asceticism as such played little part in nonconformist religion in the nineteenth century. The rising classes were frugal, but they rose for that very reason, prodigal only in their insurance policies. They fought for respectability. Only those who have lived in the back streets of towns can appreciate the significance to the poor of three feet of front 'garden' or a tiny, airless vestibule called with gross distortion a 'hall'. For most of the new lower middle classes there was no possibility of the grand renunciation of St Francis. They knew the life of rural rigour: I knew the son of a prosperous farm who was allowed either cream or jam on his bread, but never both as they were cash products. In defence of nonconformity, it must be reiterated that there is a total distinction between self-denial and deprivation. The former may well be good for the soul: the latter is certainly not for the body and gives little energy for spiritual development. That is why 'mission alongside the poor' is difficult and patronising. The poor know that clergymen and ministers of organised denominations have total security and respectability in this life – and the world to come. They fear they have neither, and perhaps like Alfred Doolittle, do not want them.

Rolle College, Exmouth

FREEDOM THROUGH DISCIPLINE:
THE CONCEPT OF LITTLE CHURCH

by CLYDE BINFIELD

M ETHODISM ... left a stigma on the mind of the eighteenth-century poor whilst helping at the same time to smother the growth of a working-class consciousness. Its doctrines perverted all that was healthy in men's emotions, its creed was cruel and grim, its view of life bleak and joyless. Its place in society closely resembled that of a malignant tumour.

Thus a Sheffield undergraduate essayist, year of 1983. The essayist was Methodist bred. For him liberation lay in bondage to E. P. Thompson, year of 1963. His student vigour is as much to be applauded as his interpretation is to be deplored. For him as for so many much older historians the bold stroke or the broad view has become in fact a sweeping into tunnel vision and the emancipation has become in fact a confirmation of old folk wisdom: Methodism is puritanism is repressive is reprehensible. We come very close to the heart of the present volume's matter: asceticism, or the attainment of spiritual perfection by means of self-discipline. Or at least we come very close to the heart of the matter as it is vulgarly seen, for although asceticism is not a word which is too frequently applied to English protestant Dissent, its associations with discipline, abstinence and repression are far too frequently so applied.

Asceticism in the Anglo-Saxon protestant context means puritanism. It is English protestantism's great negative affirmation. For historians of English protestant Dissent it is an embarrassment. The reason for this lies less in Dissent's tendency to explosion and sectarian extreme than in its much stronger tendency to the religious mainstream. For puritanism is a fact of daily life. It is a disciplined perspective which follows naturally from Dissenting church order, from Dissenting polity. It is literally a political fact. That church order follows naturally from scripture, so the political fact is also a fact of faith. It is also an economic fact, for self-discipline and abstinence were seldom optional extras where dissenters from a national church were concerned. Nonetheless

Dissenting church order naturally depended upon established church order. So from the Dissenting historian's point of view it is more instructive to turn the Dissenting ascetic tradition on its head. It is more interesting to realise that we are dealing less with self-discipline than with communal discipline and less with explosions of the ascetic *ideal* than with the accommodation of an ascetic *tradition* to a national culture.

At this point one of Patrick Joyce's stimulating themes from *Work, Society and Politics* becomes relevant.[1] It concerns the way in which the northern employer class of the 1830s and 1840s left its iron days behind it for a period of power and prestige. But within that class there was a cultural tension, a disunity indeed, whose key was religious. It was Nonconformity which provided the chief source of this cultural disunity and which distinguished the attitudes of many northern employers from those in comparable sections of the growing political nation: it was the dissent of Dissent which was the soul of what was most distinctive in the mental universe of industrial capitalism.[2] Nonetheless in the tension between the cultural, political and religious enticements of the establishment and the constant repulsion of the establishment's pretensions it was the enticement which overcame the repulsion. The distinctiveness mellowed and faded. There developed a dominant, unitary cultural style and a common politics.[3]

It is important to note that this dominant style was still a fusion of styles, even if it was a fusion of unequal quantities. Where it concerns the ascetic tradition, that is to say the puritan self-discipline consequent upon particular ecclesiastical polities, the observer is faced with two possible explorations. One is to follow puritan values into the establishment. The other is to see how established values might be accommodated within the puritan discipline. In each case the puritan tradition has become an option rather than a necessity, for it is the political nation with which we are dealing. In either case where better to start than with youth, especially the youth of a gathered church?

---

[1] P. Joyce, *Work, Society and Politics. The Culture of the Factory in Later Victorian England* (1980; paperback ed 1982).
[2] *Ibid* p. 5.
[3] *Ibid* p. 5.

Freedom Through Discipline

When it came to the nurture and Christian formation of children and young people a gathered church was faced with a dual challenge: that of the world's children, and that of its own. This paper's immediate concern is the response within the puritan tradition of certain English Congregational churches, and one church in particular, to the challenge of their own children, from the last quarter of the nineteenth century to the outbreak of the Second World War, with a special emphasis upon the 1920s and 1930s. The aim, unlike the length, is modest. It is to examine the response of local churches rather than of increasingly influential national headquarters. Inevitably this is selective history, since an examination of *independent* congregations, even when in union with each other, cannot easily be otherwise. It is saved from the extremities of selection by the pervasiveness, from congregation to congregation, of certain attitudes formed and then spread by ministers who were their churches' *representative* figures in a way that Methodist ministers or Episcopalian clergymen could not be. It is an essay in the spread of ideas and practice; but it is more than that, for it is an essay, using the churches' children as a focal point, in the development of churchmanship, particularly puritan churchmanship, and the exploration of community, particularly puritan community, often along contradictory paths; it touches upon aspects of social class and current fashion and it draws into the picture an architectural dimension which should not be divorced from the complex that makes for a gathered church in the English puritan tradition.

Evangelism among the world's children, among whom their own grandchildren might be found if the ways of providence proved hard, was a natural extension of a gathered church's obedience to the gospel imperative. From the late eighteenth century it issued in the Sunday school movement, a teeming sub-culture with its own ramifications to allow for ragged schools at one end or for young men's movements at the other. The churches' concern at the effectiveness of it all was perennial, proclaimed at annual assemblies, agonised over in specially convened conferences, explored in the religious press. As to their efficiency, the Sunday schools, at least those before 1850, have been persuasively championed by T. W. Laqueur and Jeffrey Cox has, *en passant*, produced figures which testify to a relative effectiveness even in decline.[4] As to their complexity, there remain sufficient buildings, usually for the years after 1850, whose monstrous size and ingenuity of plan, frequently after American models, demonstrate the sophistication as well as the care with which the matter was addressed. In 1903 the Sunday School Union, a national and largely Nonconformist body, introduced the graded Sunday school, a carefully structured system, again after an American model, which in the next twenty years became normal for the larger school. The combination of rigour and flair which this demanded of its operators justified the establishment of a college at Birmingham, Westhill, for the training of Sunday school teachers. Nonconformists felt that they knew about education, especially at its chalkface.

It might be argued that evangelism among the world's children was the least of the problems faced by a gathered church. The real problems began once the evangelism took effect. The great Sunday schools were white dominions, hot, strong and embarrassing on sovereignty. It was easy enough for the small town or village church whose schools were down in the chapel basement or back vestry. It was relatively easy for the larger church in a county town or a sensible suburb whose schools were housed in an ambitious but adjacent complex in a socially strategic area. The difficulties began when an urban church operated a confederacy of schools in widely spaced, if uniformly deprived areas; and the difficulties were most apparent when the mother church was in a socially pretentious suburb, for then the Sunday school accommodation would be minimal, even non-existent, and the church's activity would be concentrated outside the suburb. This was sometimes because of restrictions placed by the suburb's developer, or it was because some comfortably placed gathered churches generated no demand for Sunday schools of their own. For generally speaking, and the force of this varied socially as well as geographically, the Sunday school with its inevitable misfits and poor and dirty lame ducks, was not a place to which caring church members sent their own children. Herein lay the churches' chief failure. They reached the

[4] T.W. Laqueur, *Religion and Respectability. Sunday Schools and Working Class Culture 1780–1850* (Yale 1976); J. Cox, *The English Churches in a Secular Society. Lambeth, 1870–1930,* (Oxford 1982) pp. 225–9, 307–8.

world's children, poor and dirty misfits some of them, they influenced those children and even kept their loyalty, for many Sunday schools developed into highly successful adult schools; but the last chasm, that between church *membership* and Sunday school *attendance*, was too often unbridgeable, spiritually and socially so, as well as generationally and physically.

There was a further problem, to which gathered churches were particularly vulnerable. A Sunday school's strength depended on the mother church's missionary vigour. Current cliché gives the suburban church a ninety-year life: thirty years growing, thirty years consolidating, thirty years declining. The Victorian urban church, more off-centre than town-centre, had a riskier life and a brisker life expectancy. Its school and missions battled on, many of them beyond their parent's lifetime. But their vigour was permanently impaired. Neither were matters made easier by the fact that in another sense it was a declining problem. There were fewer of the world's children to reach anyway. This strengthened the churches' need to retain their own children and it made them redouble their efforts to fuse their own children and their Sunday school children. In the twentieth century a rapidly changing social climate made this fusion desirable as well as necessary.

Evangelism among the church's own children was a cumulative problem. Even where bridges, some of them erected with considerable skill, crossed to and from the Sunday school, it was still seldom the natural thing for the church's children to cross them, except perhaps as helpers or teachers in embryo. Vital religion might be more easily hoped for among the church's children, but it could never be taken for granted, and if the pressures of the world were less brutal for them, the pressures of society were more pressing. In every sector of public life normal standards were still Anglican standards; national standards were still defined morally and spiritually by the national church. How then should a gathered church, socially and often physically on the move, gather its own children and ensure their formation within its own polity and faithful to its discipline, as Christians? Was it enough to deal with the problem by Boys and Girls Brigades, from the 1880s, or Scouts and Guides, thirty years on and socially more assured? Such a solution was more indirect than any Sunday school.

There is evidence that the churches' concern for maximum Sunday school effectiveness intensified in the 1860s and that their concern for the ingathering of their own young intensified from the 1870s. This was not just with elementary weekday education becoming universal and compulsory, but with secondary education too becoming a matter of practical moment for increasing numbers of chapel families, some of them with children at boarding schools. Neither concern was new. The novelty lay in the methods that were considered, the changes in theological perception which made possible the consideration of those methods, and a secular context which waited for no Christian. Could a puritan integrity be maintained within such changes? What price an ascetic tradition here?

Thus, emphasis on the Incarnation, the manly Jesus, led naturally to family considerations: to God as father; to manly Jesus, Christ yet not yet Christ, as elder brother. The appeal of this to gathered Christian communities of large Victorian households is understandable, and the place of the children in such family churches becomes a matter not just for conversion (since a gathered church, however familial, is nothing if not the expression of a felt religion) but for social convenience too. The concern for the place of the church's children within the church's life might lead, therefore, not just to innovation but to a weakening of churchmanship and thence to a relaxation of the puritan disciplines, or perhaps a reappraisal. This is not a problem which a gathered church is competent to solve (that is a matter for grace) but it is a problem to which a gathered church must address itself if it is to survive, let alone grow for more than a generation or two. Life is in living with the problem, not in the solving of it.

Those whom the problem most exercised were the ministers. All hope of solution lay with them. This was not because gathered churches were minister-dominated churches (indeed, in popular estimation they were quite the reverse; outsiders criticized them as deacon-dominated), susceptible to the power of public oratory and the cult of personality, but because the minister was the gathered church's *representative figure*. His influence depended on his credibility. He was a *Christian* minister in response to a call, a mixture of compulsion and vision for which there was no necessarily rational or accessible explanation. He was a *Congregational* minister because a particular gathered church had recognised his call. There was a mutuality not just between one man and God, but between God, that person, and the whole people of God. That threefold mutuality was the constant, regulating factor in a Congregational minister's life. Therein lay his discipline, the source of that asceticism which was second nature.

The particular sensitivity of Congregational churches to the place of children within the fellowship was defined, then directed, by a series of ministers from a variety of areas and theological shadings, although they tended to be advanced and they were fascinated by *worship*. They were influential because they were representative, credible men whose call, once recognised, was shared by their people and thus diffused across the entire Congregational confederacy. They were representative in another way, for frequently they were set in a denominational cousinhood, often several generations deep as well as several marriage connexions across, at once a Jacob's ladder to past saints and a railway across society.

Among such mid-Victorian Congregationalists, representative here as in other ways, a key figure is James Baldwin Brown, to whose theology, ministry and personality the concept of brotherhood was easily applied, the more so for Brown's being his church's *enfant terrible* but never its black sheep. Brown's ministry in South London, first in Lambeth from 1846 to 1870 and then in Brixton until 1884, was one of the most seminal of Victorian Congregational ministries. Brown was a young man's minister, indeed a young minister's minister, self-consciously so. He was also a very London-suburban minister. His only provincial pastorate, which was also his first, was short, marked by the memorable clash at a Derby Sunday School Union meeting when Brown, speaking on training methods, urged teachers to stress God's fatherly love rather than the sinfulness of his children.[5]

Brown was a new man to the end of his life. He had all the radical missionary's moral inflexibility. His exact contemporary, Eustace Rogers Conder, represented to the end of his life the flexibility of the older school.[6] Conder ministered at weighty but contrasting

---

[5] For Brown (1820–1884) see C. Binfield, *So Down to Prayers* [*Studies in English Nonconformity 1780–1920*] (London 1977) pp. 190–9. The Derby Sunday School Union meeting is described pp. 193–4.

[6] For Conder (1820–1892) see C[*ongregational*] Y[*ear*] B[*ook*] (1893) pp. 214–6.

churches – Poole from 1844 to 1861; East Parade Leeds from 1861 to 1892. His familial Dissent, like Brown's, was generations deep and marriage connexions wide. Brown was chairman of the national Congregational Union in 1878, Conder of the Yorkshire Congregational Union in 1879, and Conder's chairman's address was a criticism of all that Brown represented. 'What is freedom of thought? You have no more right to think as you please than to act as you please'.[7] But when Conder called a church 'a free brotherhood', he was not so far from Brown, nor was he so when he stressed repeatedly to his people the importance of the worshipful spirit, nor when he gave 'five minutes sermons for little people' at morning service.[8] Conder was also surprisingly close to Brown in his public admission, whether as chairman of the Union in 1873 or as a senior statesman of the International Congregational Council in 1891, that the 'old Theology, known inaccurately, but intelligently enough, as Calvinism' had gone for good.

> The old theology did not perish under the assault of a rival system. It did not quail before a logic more rigorous than its own. Scarcely have the rudiments of any such system yet appeared. It expired because an atmosphere had been created in which it could not breathe.[9]

For Conder, who was at once and inextricably denominational leader and congregational pastor, and who was never an *enfant terrible*, the implications for his denominational churchmanship had to be carefully worked out. The man who described a local church as a 'free brotherhood' was also conscious of it as an organised society, its *members* marked off from its *adherents*. It was the nature of the demarcation that concerned him – the requirements for membership, the limits of communion, and especially the place of children in a church where communion worship was communal worship and where there might be no grounds for barring twelve

---

[7] He continued: 'Truth has the same imperial claim over the intellect as duty over the conscience. There are laws of thought as well as of conduct, and true liberty lies in intelligent and willing obedience.' F. Wrigley, [*The History of the Yorkshire Congregational Union* (1923)] p. 110.

[8] C. Binfield, *So Down to Prayers* p. 96.

[9] D. Macfadyen, *Alexander Mackennal B.A., D.D., His Life and Letters* (1905) pp. 165–6.

or thirteen-year olds from the privileges of membership.[10] Conder posed questions about this, unusually pertinent ones in the context of his own church in Leeds, a family church whose most intelligent younger generation, not least in his own family circle, were finding more liberation in the parish church than any Congregational one.

In 1873, replying publicly to Dr. Curteis's notorious Bampton lectures, with all the dignified extravagance of the older school of pulpit rhetoric, Conder compared episcopacy (like the cedar), Methodism (like the palm) and Independency in whose corn-fields he spied 'innumerable stalks in close phalanx ... [covering] the hills and valleys with a green mantle of promise and a golden robe of plenty; while from amid their host of bristling spears the low-nesting lark soars, and sings the song which of all earthly songs mounts nearest Heaven.' Conder's was a carefully worded extravagance for the lark-sheltering corn of Independency, 'bolt upright, heads on a level', too easily made for 'minds like needles, sharp, narrow, one-eyed, which might be useful enough if they could but be threaded and kept stitching, but when loose are always running into somebody's feet or fingers', wedges 'to split unity in pieces'.[11] And he came to accept, perhaps to hope, that 'the unification and solidification of all the Independent Churches would probably result in something very like Episcopacy.[12]

Conder's concerns fuelled by his experiences in off-centre Leeds, may be picked out elsewhere. In the late 1880s, for example, at Cheetham Hill Congregational Church in north suburban Manchester, P. T. Forsyth replaced one morning service each month with a children's service; and his first full published work, *Pulpit Parables*, was a sermon for young people.[13] In the 1880s Forsyth was still a young Turk, a Baldwin Brown man, writing radical pieces for the *Manchester Examiner*, but he ministered to a church whose radicalism took a special form. In 1869 *A Form of Morning and Evening Service*, which ran to creed, chants, sung amens, sung

---

[10] This is the concern of his chairman's address to the Congregational Union in May 1873, the theme "Discipleship". *CYB* 1874 pp. 28–31.

[11] *Ibid* pp. 19–20.

[12] F. Wrigley p. 136.

[13] Jessie Forsyth Andrews, 'Memoir', in P.T. Forsyth, *The Work of Christ* (1938) p. XIV. For Forsyth (1848–1921) see W.L. Bradley, *P.T. Forsyth, The Man and His Work* (1952).

sentences, and so on, had been carefully compiled for its use from the *Book of Common Prayer*, that liturgy, as the preface put it, 'which is rendered venerable by its use for three centuries by the Protestant Episcopalian Church, and portions of which are hallowed on the channels of the devotion of the Church Catholic during many ages of its history.'[14]

Cheetham Hill was a Congregational sport no doubt. Its *Prayer Book* services may not have lasted for very long, and P. T. Forsyth's ministry there was short; but it was not a unique church, and Forsyth's stature as a major theologian was formed by his twenty-five years in the pastoral ministry at the service of distinctive churches, as well as by his twenty years at the head of a theological college. He was, genius notwithstanding, as pastor and tutor a representative Congregationalist, and although he reacted against his earlier radicalism his development was not inconsonant with it: Cheetham Hill fed the reservoir from which Forsyth drew his churchmanship.

More obviously and immediately representative of his denomination from the late 1880s, a puritan after the manner of Sir Philip Sydney rather than of Praise-God Barebones, was the young minister of Kensington Chapel, C.S. Horne. There he established a Children's Guild, whose first secretary was his future wife, Katharine Cozens-Hardy:

> From the first he made a practice of giving a short children's address in the morning service. Of these addresses the older children were encouraged to take notes, and once a quarter the minister met all the children of the congregation, talked over their notes with them, and then joined them in tea and games. The children were also taught to work for the poorer children of the church missions.[15]

Baldwin Brown's Brixton Hill, P. T. Forsyth's Cheetham Hill, Eustace Conder's East Parade, Silvester Horne's Kensington, large south London suburban, smallish North Manchester suburban, powerful northern city off-centre, capital city west end, differed significantly from each other. Hest Bank, near Morecambe, dif-

---

[14] *Form of Morning and Evening Service, For the Use of Free Churches* (1869) p. iii.
[15] W.B. Selbie, *The Life of Charles Silvester Horne* (1920) p. 70.

fered again. Its atmosphere in the years between 1906 and 1911 is best described by its leading layman, T. H. Mawson, the fashionable landscape architect:

> On Sunday morning we all met at the little Free Church, one of the smallest in the country, holding, when packed, just one hundred worshippers, including the choir, which was largely confined to members of my own family and their friends. This church was presided over by the Rev. Herbert Gamble, M.A. … a preacher … with a rare genius for understanding young people … and fully alive to the claims of beauty as an element in worship … developing a form and order which were unique for a small village church.
>
> From this service the children and their friends and the pastor would troop down to the Bungalow for lunch, where we usually sat down to the number of eighteen. The afternoon was spent at tennis … After tea there was the early evening service, … the sermons … perfect cameos … always finishing to the second – twelve minutes in the morning and eight minutes in the evening. The entire service was full of beauty and helpfulness, though lasting less than an hour.
>
> At Mr. Gamble's request I gave the children's address, limited to five minutes. This in a large number of Free Churches is a feature of morning worship, but I always think ours was somehow different. There was no attempt at theology, but a frank recognition of the mental capacity of young folk, whose powers of observation and love for all created things we endeavoured to cultivate, so that I made practically the whole of my children's addresses short, simple studies of nature.[16]

Mawson was regarded, and regarded himself, as a high church Nonconformist, although if his memory of the long Edwardian garden party, Free Church style, is to be accepted, his high churchmanship lay more in form than in content. Nonetheless Hest Bank's undemanding happy family Sundays are a recognisable distillation, twenty-five years on, of the combined atmosphere of

---

[16] T.H. Mawson, *The Life and Work of An English Landscape Architect. An Autobiography* (ndc 1927) pp. 111–12. For Gamble (1873–1938) see *CYB* (1939) p. 698.

Cheetham Hill, Brixton Hill and East Parade, made credible by a young minister whose first pastorate this was, a young Oxford-educated minister too. Herbert Gamble belonged to what was already an influential group of Free Church ministers, Oxford men, trained at Mansfield College and thus in the general estimation high-fliers, with a flair for life and learning, few enough to know each other well. In 1911, the year that Gamble left Hest Bank, another Mansfield man, who was Wadham as well, Vivian Pomeroy, became minister at Greenfield, Bradford, the largest of Bradford's thirty Congregational churches, and theologically (and politically) the most notorious (or advanced) of them all.[17]

Pomeroy was at Greenfield from 1911 to 1923. In that period the church secretary was Percy Lund, the printer, publisher and private theosophist, who was also superintendent of the chapel's Educational Institute, and it was the development of this institute (its motto 'The Institution of the Dear Love of Comrades', its aim, with Walt Whitman freely quoted, 'the culture of the human soul, in order that the latent divine nature of man may be more fully experienced') that marked the most distinctive aspect of Pomeroy's ministry.[18]

The core of the Institute was its afternoon Sunday school, each week save in August. It was not large as city schools went (three hundred children, twenty-five to forty teachers, four departments) but in its arrangements it combined the efficiency of the graded school with a family softness which would have been fey anywhere but in Bradford, and with a startling eclecticism which would have been unthinkable thirty years earlier. Here puritanism vanished into faery and derringdo.

The Greenfield afternoon child began as a Bud or Blossom. At the age of eight he became a Voyager. He was a Crusader when he

---

[17] There are brief accounts of Vivian T. Pomeroy (1883–1961) in *Mansfield College Reports* (1963/4) p. 8; *Mansfield College Magazine*, 165 (July 1964) p. 212. Greenfield's notoriety was the doing of Pomeroy's predecessor Thomas Rhondda Williams (1860–1945), minister at Greenfield 1888–1909.

[18] The following account is based on *The Educational Institute of Greenfield Church, Carlisle Road and Lumb Lane, Bradford* (Bradford nd) pp. 3–12; *Greenfield Congregational Church, Bradford: Church Manual 1915*, and much information provided by Mr. and Mrs. D. Steele. For Percy Lund (1863–1943), founder of Lund, Humphries and Co. see 'Mr. Percy Lund: Death of a Well-Known Bradford Man', *Bradford Telegraph and Argus*, 15 February 1943.

was twelve and an Experimender at the age of sixteen. He could, if he wished, experiment and mend (for that is what Experimenders did) for the rest of his life. Otherwise it was morning church, though for the young in years that could still mean the League of Chums, or, as it was in 1915, the League of Splendid Children.

Buds and Blossoms were children 'in the early morning of life' who modelled, cut paper and drew, not just to gain but to express 'some idea of beauty and love'. They heard stories, or acted them out, about happy homes and fairy lore and nature: 'all of which feed the place of wonder and furnish the house of the mind with pleasant pictures'. The object of this was to enable them to see in what they did 'the figure of the "Dearest One"'. It was at Bud and Blossom time (or a Children's Festival) that the minister 'christened' or 'dedicated' a child.

Voyagers were hardier souls, 'like little ships ... just venturing from port and setting sail on the stormy ocean of the world ...' They must learn 'the art of life-navigation; how to steer their vessels wisely, and to avoid rocks and shoals'. They too learned through the telling of stories, but this time of adventure and discovery, of heroes and heroines, and, at the last, of the 'Great Pilot'.

The stories told to the Crusaders (who 'zealously strive to overcome evil') now verged on the lecture. They were about old myths or new scientific discoveries. Thus the Crusaders would perceive the laws of nature and respond to the challenge of the Kingdom – and be ready for the lifelong challenge offered to each Experimender.

Experimenders were the Senior Department. They were Percy Lund's special concern, and separate from the rest. They experimented with Sunday afternoon lectures and discussion; and there was ritual. An Experimender was enrolled at 'a short ceremony designed to express the brotherhood and unity of all taking part'. He (or, of course, she) could then intensify this membership by joining a Study Circle, which might be reading Henry George's *Progress and Poverty*, or be turning to poetry or be visiting a museum or a hospital or a factory. Or there was the Girls' Guild, which had for an aim 'practical support to movements towards feminine welfare'. Or there was the Pilgrim's Path, for the Inner Circle of the Experimenders, whose procedure may be best explained as a series of semi-dramatic ceremonies, or mystery plays, wherein the Experimender may travel like a pilgrim from grade to grade, each simple, but beautiful and impressive ritual representing a step in the evolution and emancipation of the soul expressed and implied in metaphor, symbol and sacrament. The various stages of the journey involve also a distinctive form of worship by pictorial and dramatic action. Co-operation and mutual help, brotherhood and friendship are fundamental principles of this symbolic Pilgrim's Path.

Here began a more structured encounter with the Greenfield Church itself, in the shape of seasonal festivals in the chapel, each one 'a processional and recessional, with banners and flowers or evergreens, a pictorial episode embodying symbolically some myth, tradition, or truth of deep significance'. These were some myths indeed – Demeter and Persephone, Narcissus and Echo, Hyacinthus and Apollo, the Divine Flame of the Sacred Hearth, Love's Harvest, the Transformation of Winter into Spring, the Adoration of the Mother; the whole 'a successful attempt to make worship no longer dull and colourless, but captivating to the child's rich imagination'.

Alas, the pilgrim's path led back to earth with the League of Chums, those young people who attended morning service. Vivian Pomeroy had a special story for them each week.[19] Greenfield's chums, each vowing 'to act fairly, to stand up for the littlest, and to look for a chum in everyone', were leagued with the universal League of Chums organised by a religious weekly, *The Christian Commonwealth*. It was the world of Arthur Rackham bumping against that of Arthur Ransome on a Bradford Sunday, with a Delius (in fact three, Rudolph Delius, his wife, and their daughter Daisy) in the congregation, assimilated to the old style Sunday School, passing by the world of the Boys' Brigade for that of the Scouts (Greenfield's was the 80th Bradford troop).

The point of Pomeroy's work is that of this paper: it was eccentric, and yet characteristic of the denomination. Thus, at the

---

[19] Pomeroy had a genius for stories, many of which (including several Greenfield children's addresses) were published in *The Merry Monopedes and Other Stories for Children* (ndc 1916) and *Legends of Lumb Lane* (1923).

same time there were similar, if less picturesque, developments at Penge, a new Congregational Church on London suburbia's Kentish fringes. The Penge church was English gothic, massive and free. Its minister, Ernest Barson, whose ministry from 1909 to 1947 turned him into 'Barson of Penge', acknowledged three dramatically disparate fathers in God: C. H. Spurgeon, in whose orphanage he had been reared; P. T. Forsyth, in whose college he had been trained and who preached at Penge's opening; and Bernard Snell, who had succeeded Baldwin Brown at Brixton Hill.[20] If Barson was their spiritual child (and Spurgeon's paternity was surely one of piety alone), his church was Brixton Hill's spiritual grandchild, its architecture encouraging a responsive liturgy and a gowned choir, its atmosphere encapsulated in the gift in 1919 of an oak memorial lectern

> to give an opportunity for the laymen further to assist the Minister in public worship by reading the Scripture lesson. Both men and women were chosen ... the young people also serving in this manner on the last Sunday in each month: thus, with the responsive orders of service and laymen reading the lesson, was the congregation fully integrated in all public worship.[21]

In 1919, too, a young woman, Kathleen Denham, was appointed as minister's assistant at Penge, with special responsibility for developing a fully graded Sunday school and ensuring its integration at the appropriate stage, with adult church: for this she devised Promotion Services. In the eyes of many Congregationalists Penge perfected the graded school, and went beyond it indeed, as perhaps is symbolised by the Chapel of Youth which was created in the church's north transept in 1934.[22]

Neither Greenfield Bradford, nor East Parade, Leeds, had been either city centre or suburban. They were off-centre, although in their prime, which had been brief, there had been a touch of the west end about them both. Cheetham Hill and Brixton Hill were

[20] For E.J. Barson (1877–1956) see *CYB* (1957) p. 510.
[21] (A.D. Banfield) *Penge Congregational Church 1908–1958 Golden Jubilee Celebrations* (Penge 1958) p. 12.
[22] *Ibid* pp. 11–12; C. Binfield, 'English Free Churchmen and a National Style' [*SCH* 18] p. 521.

truly suburban, planted in the nick of time, and inner suburban before three generations were out. Penge was a younger variant. Ealing Green, older than any of these, was by contrast the most fortunately place of suburban causes.[23]

Here the puritan classes fused with their established equivalents into the nation-forming class. Here was a world of work which had leisure in its grasp. Here was true responsibility. It was Ealing's oldest Free Church, starting with the nineteenth century and always more of a suburban village church (its first meeting place called Wisteria Cottage) than a true village church (even Ealing's squires were Rothschilds, down at Gunnersbury Park, regularly contributing to the chapel's good causes, which made it unique among Congregational churches). Its stated church life began in the 1830s and from the first it attracted retired people of substance without fashion, or the widowed and single of respectability without too much means. There was the rich tradesman, like Oxford Street's William Cutting who in the 1840s had been one of the major backroom influences on the founders of the YMCA and who in the 1860s started at Ealing Green a Tract and Visiting Society such as had worked so well for him at Craven Chapel. There were mercantile families, the Amhersts of Castle Bar House and the Mirrielies of Elm Trees, Russia merchants who had moved in from Slough.[24] There were ministers in retirement, some of them pulpit grandees. Kensington Chapel's John Stoughton, of Cromwell House, was of this sort; Mayo Gunn from Sevenoaks and Warminster, whose wife was a tobacco Wills, and Alfred Holborn, resting from Bradford, with a son at Oxford, were of the other sort. To such as these were added with the arrival of a sensible railway service a fivefold mixture of intermarrying respectables: commuting businessmen such as Robertson of Woodside, on the Common, the Amhersts' son-in-law, variously described as a rich pawnbroker and a jeweller-cum-property dealer,

[23] In addition to its reliance upon the records of Ealing Green United Reformed Church, the following account owes much to correspondence and conversation with G. Ronald Howe, P. Knight, Lady Mott, Revd. Dr. G.F. Nuttall, the late M.M. Rix, Mrs Barbara Horder West (whose typescript, The Horder Saga, dated October 1969, was of particular value), the late Mrs. Phyllis Taunton Wood and the Revd. Mary I Wyatt. Information from these sources is subsequently marked p[ersonal] i[nformation].
[24] A Mirrielies daughter was the first wife of Augustine Birrell.

and certainly rich; or the Callards of Conifer Crest, who made sweets, the Congregational counterweight to the Baptist Bowsers of Ferme Park; or the Plaistowes, who also made sweets, but of a cheaper sort; or J. C. Fuller and Howell Jones who worked in the City. There were businessmen who serviced this and other suburbs – the Batemans, with their string of opticians' shops; the Stowells 'of Chelsea' who were wine merchants. Inevitably there were the professional men, bank managers, solicitors and doctors, civil servants: the Shepheards of Beaumont House; the Horder brothers, Leslie in the Bank of England, Gerald a quantity surveyor; W. H. Whiting, the naval architect who was at the Admiralty; Sydney Herbert Wood, at the Ministry of Education. Above and beyond all these were the women and the teachers. In the twentieth century it was markedly their church. To the inevitable widows, wives and spinsters were added the career girls. But whether widow, wife or spinster, puritan Ealing woman cut a fine figure: Irene Benn, Sir John Benn's daughter; Edna Wills, from a non-tobacco branch of the tobacco family; Grace MacDonald, who married an ex-Lord Mayor of Manchester, and became Lady Davy; Maud Russell Beasley, 'always very ecstatic and very holy'; Lucy Robertson, seventy-two years a member, with her uniformed maids and large garden; Phyllis Taunton Wood, from a Baptist family, who had been one of Tissington Tatlow's S.C.M. secretaries, a 'ravishingly beautiful' woman, with a good voice and definite choice of phrase, who published her own poems on her own press and was attracted to the church by its 'intelligent atmosphere'. It was for such as these in 1916 that the church replaced its deacons, whom it felt must be male, with church councillors, who might be female. Beyond all these there was a male scattering of radical intelligentsia: 'John Oxenham', the author, whose unveiling in novel form of Jesus's *Hidden Years* entranced the new career-girl and S.C.M. generation; Cuthbert Plaistowe, secretary of the Industrial Co-partnership Association; McIntosh, the local Labour party agent. And there was civic pride, for once Ealing became a borough, Ealing Green provided its councillors. Major Stowell, Howell Jones and J. C. Fuller were mayors, and councillor Fuller became chairman of the Middlesex Education Committee, and a figure at the county's Guildhall. It was, in sum, a thoroughly solid church, not distinctly class-conscious, although the better-off tended to be Sunday morning worshippers, but leisured and leisurely, its people chatting in the church garden after service on summer Sunday evenings. 'I don't think a tramp would ever have come into that church'.[25]

Its buildings reflected this: lancet-windowed, twin-spireleted gothic of 1860, its pretentiousness emphasising its inescapably pinched respectability, yet excellently placed at the heart of Ealing Green, next to a trio of Italianate houses called Victoria Terrace, and directly across from Pitzhanger, Sir John Soane's Roman stage set of a suburban villa. It was all chapel and no church from the outside, successively enlarged and significantly gentrified from within, and with its stern battlemented manse to one side, more solidly assured than the chapel was able to be.

So eligibly strategic a cause was bound to succeed. Indeed, the surprise is that its membership was not larger. In 1910, amidst the heat of the Edwardian afternoon, Ealing Green *chapel* seated seven hundred and its *church* stood at two hundred and ninety-seven; Haven Green, the Baptist church across the Broadway to the north, visually more ambitious, sat eight hundred and eighty and had a membership of four hundred and fifty-nine.[26] The reason both for Ealing Green's stability and for its growth within limits lies with its representative figures: the ministers.

Ealing Green's ministry was a distinctive progression, marked by upsets but never by schism, each pastorate leading naturally to the next, each pastor a man of substance and increasing education. For present purposes the first to be noted is William Isaac, minister from 1856 to 1874 and a retired tradesman who, since he was the travelling partner of the Piccadilly firm still trading as Swaine, Adeney and Briggs, was financially secure.[27] Thus the village suburb on the eve of its rapid transformation into a commuter suburb (with gas laid on from 1857) had a credible Congregational

[25] *pi*; E[aling] C[ongregational] C[hurch]: Register of Members of the Church from *c.*1834. For 'John Oxenham' (his real name was Dunkerley, 1852–1941) see K.L. Parry, *Companion [to Congregational Praise* (1953)] p. 480.

[26] But the Congregationalists had the larger Sunday School: two hundred and sixty nine children to the Baptists' two hundred and thirty six. *CYB* 1910 p. 275, *Baptist Handbook* 1910 p. 100.

[27] For William Isaac (died 1877) see *CYB* 1878 pp. 323–4. Edward Swaine, the firm's principal, was a leading London Congregational layman. Adeney too was a Congregational name. Indeed Isaac's predecessor at Ealing Green was the Revd. G.J. Adeney.

focus, his salary £120 with house provided (£300 by 1873), sufficiently credible indeed for his obituary to describe at length a deliciously suggestive royal moment in his business life.[28]

Isaac's successor was a young and beautiful Cambridge man, who had come down with a first class degree and mind. Henry Arnold Thomas was a manse son trying out his paces before a grander call. He was at Ealing Green only from 1874 to 1876, but he succeeded his father at Highbury, Bristol, and remained there for the rest of his ministerial career. Arnold Thomas was to his generation, only with a more catholic spirituality, something of what Eustace Conder had been to his. Ealing Green was the least part of his ministerial life, but just as Eustace Conder is remembered, if at all, by a children's hymn, Arnold Thomas is best recalled by a hymn of brotherhood, 'Brother, who on thy heart didst bear/The burden of our shame and sin'.[29]

John Byles, who was minister from 1876 to 1896, was a contrast in personality. The Byleses began, ran, and owned the *Bradford Observer*, a many-branched family of radicals, ministers, politicians, publicists, brewers, educational high-achievers, whose Congregationalism was fringed with Quakerism and Unitarianism. Ealing Green was his third church, and he came to it for a rest. Almost at once there were changes. Byles was recalled, thirty years on, for his 'genius in addressing children'. In July 1878, echoes of Eustace Conder's musings aloud earlier in the decade, a Junior

---

[28] 'On the occasion of his late Royal Highness Prince Albert visiting England just preceding the time when his engagement to Her Majesty was made public', Mr. Isaac, in returning from Germany happened to be a passenger in the same vessel. An accident on board detained them for a night, which was spent on deck by the Prince and Mr. Isaac in familiar conversation. Many questions were put by the Prince with respect to political and other matters concerning the people with whom he was to be soon closely connected. Sound sterling advice was given to the young Prince with reference to his non-interference with political parties, and the policy of throwing himself into the home life and customs of the people', and Isaac was subsequently called to Windsor to meet the prince's father and brother.

He was not always so honestly circumspect. In Italy his determination always to be the Christian traveller led him to put tracts 'in the Italian language in ... the out-of-the-way places in St. Peter's at Rome, when an English gentleman came up to him, and in a few quiet words gave him a caution that if he valued his safety he would find his way to his hotel by a circuitous route and as speedily as possible'. *Ibid* pp. 323–4.

[29] For Henry Arnold Thomas (1848–1924) see N. Micklem ed *Arnold Thomas of Bristol* (1925). The hymn is 556 in *Congregational Praise*.

Membership was instituted at the church: people under eighteen, who were admitted to communion and to church meetings, but who had not yet a right to vote in church decisions; and the Lord's table was opened to 'all who love and follow the Lord Jesus', a significant difference from the welcome offered in Isaac's time to *accredited* members of other churches. Byles left Ealing in 1896, became a Unitarian in 1898 and died in 1901. His was the first of three solid ministries, eccentric yet representative, and definitive for Ealing Green.[30]

The second of these ministries was that of William Garrett Horder, 'strong, handsome and bad-tempered', with a 'fine brain, a bad liver and a frightening large grey handlebar moustache', and a look of permanent disapproval. By virtue of his wife he joined a comfortably circumstanced Dissenting cousinhood, as widely spreading as the Byles' but with a larger reach. Mrs. Garrett Horder was an East Parader, from Leeds. Her father and grandfather were Leeds textile manufacturers. Samuel Morley, the millionaire hosier, was a first cousin once removed; so, by marriage, was J. H. Whitley, the future Speaker. Horder's training for the ministry had been at Cheshunt College under the superfine Henry Robert Reynolds, who had preceded Eustace Conder at East Parade, Leeds, and was probably more responsible than any other college principal for spreading a quality of sweetness across the Congregational ministry. Sweetness was not Garrett Horder's line, but refinement was.[31]

Ealing (he disliked the tendency, confirmed by his successor, to call it Ealing Green) was Horder's fifth, last, and longest ministry. He came from College Chapel, Bradford, a smaller cause than Greenfield, self-consciously select in its ministers and in its atmosphere, but one of four or five influential Congregational churches, three of them within a quarter mile of the city centre, which set the tone for Bradford Nonconformity. Greenfield was the advanced

---

[30] Byles (1839–1901) was also the first of a trio of literary ministers. His stories included *The Legend of St Mark* and *Spring Blossoms and Summer Fruit*. Information about his ministry comes from ECC *Year Books* 1876–1896 and R.C. Davis, Notebook [Giving History of Ealing Green up to 1946], an ms abstracted from church minute books. For the Byles circle see (F.G. Byles) *William Byles by His Youngest Son*, (Weymouth, privately printed, 1932).
[31] For W. Garrett Horder (1841–1922) see *CYB* 1924 p. 98; *pi*.

church, socially, politically and theologically so; Horton Lane had been the millionaires' church; Salem, the Byles family church, fitted between them. College Chapel stood for a thoughtful intellectualism.

Horder's reputation fitted naturally into this. He was one of Baldwin Brown's younger admirers, attending his funeral, preaching a memorial sermon, and articulating a similar Independency. In 1881 he had resisted pressure to become minister of George St. Oxford, which was casting about with some desperation for a man to meet the opportunity now open to Free Churchmen in that university town.[32] When he came to Ealing he was already widely known as an author (*The Sunlit Road, The Silent Voice, The Poet's Bible, The Other World*) and hymnologist, the friend and correspondent of George Matheson and George MacDonald. His claim to a larger fame already rested on *Worship Song*, a compilation described by his official obituary as the 'model of what a good hymn book should be', and by a leading layman of the next generation as the 'perfect product of the Hampstead mind ... a literary Keating's powder ... a sort of spiritual insect killer fatal to worms'.[33]

Worship Song was not in fact the product of a Hampstead mind but of a Wood Green and an Ealing Green mind. Horder ministered at Wood Green from 1873 to 1893. There, in 1884, he collected 841 *Congregational Hymns* (chants and anthems extra) which developed into *Hymns Supplemental to Existing Collections* ('noteworthy for its many importations from America') and so to *Worship Song* in 1898, expanded in 1905.[34] *Worship Song* was widely popular, a compre-

---

[32] I am indebted to Dr. D.A. Johnson 'Pastoral Vacancy and Rising Expectations: The George Street Church, Oxford, 1879–86'. *Journal of the United Reformed Church History Society* 3, no. 4, Oct. 1984, p. 136.

[33] CYB (1924) p. 98; B. Manning, 'Some Hymns and Hymnbooks', *Transactions of the Congregational Historical Society IX* (1925) p. 140.

[34] K.L. Parry, *Companion* pp. XXXV–VI, 381. In 1922 the *Yorkshire Observer* recalled that *Worship Song* began with Horder's need for a hymnbook for the children of his bible classes. 'He could find nothing suitable, and a friend suggested that he should compile one himself ... the book ... made a new departure in childrens hymnody, and has affected every hymnal published since. Mr. Horder kept in the background the foolish aspirations after the other world which hymns used to put into the mouths of children". Undated obituary cutting attached to College Chapel Bradford Minute Book 1856–1896, now with the archives of Congregational College, Manchester, held at John Rylands Library, Manchester.

hensive expression of Victorian hymnology at its most catholic, although not its most Catholic, and therefore acceptable to 'advanced' Free Church congregations. Ealing turned to Horder's hymns in 1890, and College Chapel Bradford in 1884; Penge and Greenfield had adopted *Worship Song* by 1912.

The Wood Green mind was ripe for retrospective celebration. Horder's predecessor there sent in from Freiburg an appreciation of what he believed Horder's exemplification of it to be: It belonged

> emphatically to the nineteenth century, which is itself a protest against mere authority – whether of a class, of a church, of a book, or of priests; and which reserves its supreme homage for the one thing alone that is called Truth ... In large part [Nonconformity] means such a man as Mr. Horder ...[35]

The Wood Green minds met at the chapel's Guild of St. John, a sort of literary society, with Horder as Warden, a manuscript magazine and social evenings at members' homes, there to learn, for example, of the American poets, the lecturer (who was not Horder) 'speaking of most of them in terms of the highest praise', the audience, who were not so sure (and 'a fair proportion of whom were ladies'), reading some of them aloud.[36]

Transferred to Ealing Green by way of Bradford, the Wood Green mind developed autocratic tendencies and not just at the family dinner table. There was an attempt to unseat the pastor in 1900, and further disturbance in 1909. Ealing Green was a middle class church, more assuredly so than Wood Green, made progressively comfortable, its worship becoming progressively smooth, with printed service sheets (an American idea) full of thoughtful mottoes. But one of its near neighbourhoods was working class, with unemployment a problem and at this constituency was aimed a battery of communal self-helpery – the Sunday school; the Lancaster Road British Schools, founded in Isaac's time with Rothschild patronage; the Lend a Hand Society, the Clothing Society, the Coal Club and Nursing and Medical Society, all run in Byles's day; the temperance work, the Slate Club and Boys' Club

---

[35] *Wood Green Congregational Church*, undated (March 1893), unpaginated leaflet in the possession of Horder's granddaughter Lady Mott.
[36] *Ibid.*

and Girls' Club, and Christian Endeavour and Young Men's Gymnasium Class, all added by Horder. In Horder's time there was a 'want of sociability' at Ealing Green, a need for 'mutual kindness and affability', which exercised Horder, evidence of those chasms in Christian living, most obvious between Church and Sunday school, from which no Congregational church, however comfortably circumstanced, was immune.[37] It was Horder's successor, Wilton Rix, at once Horder's continuation and his contradiction, who addressed himself with most care to the problem.

Like the Byleses and Horders, the Rixes were well placed denominationally. Wilton Rix's traditionary puritanism, captured in the title of one of his books, *Denton Ancestors*, went back, a preacher a generation, to the Great Ejectment of 1662 and beyond that, supposedly to Dutch protestant refugees. It was a web of Wiltons, Parkers and Rixes, East Anglian parsons, farmers, physicians and attorneys. Rix's immediate background was craft-artistic. His father, Parker Rix, was art director for Doulton's pottery in the great days of the Lambeth Art Pottery, and he had some connexions with Harold Rathbone's Della Robbia pottery in the Wirral. An extension of this atmosphere was provided by Mrs. Wilton Rix, passionate, unconventional, strong-willed, 'gypsy mentality – looked like one: no dress sense'.[38]

Like Vivian Pomeroy and Herbert Gamble, Wilton Rix belonged to the first Oxford generations of Congregational ministers. He was a Mansfield man with a threefold passion for the quality of worship, the idea of the Church, and the engagement of youth in its service. He was an Independent in that his religious practices were not in the general Congregational run of things, but his fascination was with the disciplined side of church life: the *order* of worship, the *ordered* development into membership. He was a literary man who did not find it easy to write, a young people's minister who did not always relate naturally to the young. Order, therefore, properly understood as a means of liberating development, was a matter of concern to him. He had to work hard at the

---

[37] This information is again derived from ECC *Year Books*, especially from 1896; R.C. Davis, Notebook; and from a Book of Statements about Horder's ministry up to 1910.
[38] For Rix (1881–1958) see CYB (1960) p. 435, *pi*.

natural qualifications of ministry: his sermons were careful, and on the long side, his pastoral visits were equally careful, their care concealed by a personal charm and his ability to give all his attention to those who sought him out. His chief memorial, Little Church, was both architecturally and institutionally a liberation of puritan church order to permit the Christian formation of the church's children.

The chapel to which Rix came in 1922, was, despite his predecessor's improvements, a very dated building:

> a Victorian Gothic barn of a church with cavernous galleries, a green beige, and mahogany colour scheme where the congregation worshipped a great central organ in a service led by the minister confined to a dominating beaten copper pulpit. Behind was an institutional church hall, a vestry and a kitchen. At the bottom of the adjoining manse garden was a disused "laundry", a brick box that would accommodate about thirty adults or forty children. Here WER was able to organise his pioneer children's church.

This description is by Rix's son.[39] It is a Sunday morning memory. Sunday afternoon was the Sunday school's preserve and to this Rix turned his first attention. He copied Ernest Barson of Penge with the appointment in 1923, at £400 a year for two years (Rix's stipend was £600), of a Minister's Assistant, Marguerite Sapp: the Sunday school was to be her particular preserve.[40] But the Ealing Green Sunday school was a separate world and likely to remain so, largely working class in composition. Between its afternoon children and the morning children there was the usual gap, a social one, in education and expectation.

Ealing was a family suburb, especially so between the wars, and it was to family needs that Rix turned his best attention. Rix was not an original man, or rather, his originality lay in his diversity of temperament, at once catholic and reformed, mystic and aesthetic. His mind was derivative but it was not a magpie's mind: 'All that he derived', recalled his successor, whom he often astounded,

---

[39] pi.
[40] Unless otherwise indicated information about church decisions at Ealing Green is taken from R.C. Davis, Notebook.

'passed through his own mind and spirit and became peculiarly his own'.[41]

Little Church began in 1924, and took physical shape in 1925–6; the idea, according to one source, came from a church member, councillor Howell Jones. The encouragement certainly came from another member, Lucy Robertson, recently widowed in the prime of middle age, rich in her own and her late husband's right, passionately, intelligently (words applicable to many of the Ealing Green women) musical, with two sons (one a Guards officer, who danced with the queen, the other a priest, soon to join the Society of the Servants of Christ, in Poona) but no grandchildren. Mrs. Robertson's money, her organisational skills and her culture (it was she who introduced the Rixes to the music of Ravel and Debussy and Delius, who backed Rix in tampering with *Worship Song*, and who urged him into publishing his first book of sermons), were determining forces, which the Rixes perhaps took too easily for granted.[42]

In retrospect, however, or so he told his friends, Rix had his own view of Little Church's inception and of how

> one spring evening ... when walking in the orchard behind the Manse garden he thought of the boys and girls who played there and gathered walnuts in the autumn – and of the solitary child he had sometimes seen sitting in the gloomy gallery of the Church during a Sunday morning service. He determined that Ealing Green should have a children's church where boys and girls could learn to worship and to love Jesus Christ.[43]

By the end of 1925 Rix was explaining his scheme to the *Daily News*.[44] By 1936 it was sufficiently institutionalized, and of such wide interest, that Rix described it at length in a booklet whose very appearance celebrated the artistry and order of the conception: an illustration, 'Animals All', from an Eric Gill woodcut, and another, of Langford Jones' bas-relief in concrete set over the door

---

[41] D. Harris, in [*The Reverend Wilton Edwin*] *Rix* [*December 10th 1881 – December 15th 1958*] : *A Memorial* (1959) pp. 8–9.
[42] pi.
[43] D. Harris, in *Rix: A Memorial* p. 7.
[44] *Daily News*, 15 December 1925.

to Little Church, of a child kneeling at one of Little Church's rush seated chairs, 'A Throne Set in Heaven'.[45]

Rix set the scene. A church, such as Ealing Green, with an adult membership of around two hundred and fifty and a Sunday school whose attendance averaged at a hundred, might expect to have a Children's Church of seventy to eighty. Children's church (Little Church was the name he used) and Sunday school were at once separate from each other and necessary for each other. The afternoon school was for that 'constant stream ... who came from unattached homes' whose parents 'we conveniently call pagan'.[46] It was Rix's development for children of the concept of morning church that was so arresting. He meant not 'a promiscuous gathering of boys and girls into a children's service where they "do everything but preach"' but a disciplined means of drawing the children of members steadily into their own membership beginning with the full worship of the gathered church. 'Worship in the fellowship of the Church means contact with a society of people from all ages from six years to seventy ... [C]hildren need even more visible and concrete evidences of the fellowship of the Church than adult members demand ... We have aimed at creating an unforced fellowship between children and adult members of the Church from earliest years'. This meant, in Ealing Green practice, a rota of four Little Church leaders to give addresses, a further dozen to give occasional addresses, and another dozen helpers. 'By these means girls and boys from the age of six are in immediate and natural contact with the adult fellowship of the Church'.[47]

In the inter-war years fellowship in a church like Ealing Green which agonized over the unemployed in distant counties brought into relief that other problem 'usually crouching at the door' – class distinction. Rix was a realist: 'When parents pay for their children to go to a certain kind of school in order to ensure a good accent, and when they place them under a certain kind of social discipline, they do not see the point of breaking down that environment on a

[45] W. Rix, *Little Church* (nd *c*.1936).
[46] 'By pagans we mean that large part of the community who are indifferent to the Church and who read their Sunday newspapers with the close attention their fathers gave to the Bible, and who attend the cinema as regularly as their parents did their chapel, and whose attitude is that they are as decent as the man next door and perhaps better', *Ibid* pp. 2–3.
[47] *Ibid* pp. 1–4.

Sunday while they try to build it up during the week'. But for his own church he was sanguine: Ealing Green was so placed 'that we must hold out our hands in two directions towards very different types of families, and we are glad to join people of various outlook in one fellowship'.[48]

To this end the Little Church fellowship was for all aged six to thirteen, whether in Sunday school or morning congregation, who had attended four times in succession and whose parents were agreeable. They were then considered by Little Church, but also by the deacons of Big Church too, who thus shared with the leaders of Little Church the responsibility of admitting new members. The result of this care was that almost all the children of the morning congregation and half of those in the afternoon Sunday school became Little Church members.[49]

The starting point was morning worship. Those who came with their families were urged to sit with them, the rest were welcomed by the leaders and their helpers.

> We have a rule that 'The way into Little Church is through Big Church door'. Every child ... must have been present at adult worship so far as the reading of the Gospel and the children's hymn ... They leave the church in a little procession during a short voluntary, and they will finish their own service in time for returning home with their parents. They thus learn instinctively that they are grafted on to Big Church.[50]

Thus Rix began to address himself to the matters of liturgy, of ritual and movement:

> a set service is used, and they have not to compose their own order Sunday by Sunday. We use three forms within which the

---

[48] *Ibid* pp. 4–6. Rix told this horror story (*ibid* p. 5): 'A certain London church had two Sunday Schools, one under the church roof for children of members, and the other in a mission-hall. Certain teachers, feeling that such a distinction was contrary to the spirit of Christ, succeeded in merging the two Sunday Schools on the church premises. Within six months, however, the number of children of church members left in the Sunday School had dwindled almost to nothing, and the rest had been sent to Crusader classes'.

[49] The Sunday school proportion of Little Church people was 'limited by the fact that many parents will not take the trouble to prepare their children for morning worship, as the activities of their Sunday do not seem to begin in earnest until the midday meal'. *Ibid* p. 7.

[50] *Ibid* pp. 9–10.

hymns, prayers, readings, and responsive psalms can be changed ... [C]hildren like the order of a set service, though they know how to exploit and enjoy disorder if they are allowed to fall into it. None the less, a place must be found within the framework both for movement and for variety [since] ... children ... do their thinking, as it were, at the end of their fingers and toes ... For the sake of movement we reverse the usual procedure when taking the offering, and the children march round the church to a stirring tune and place their pennies in a plate which is held by two children at the top of the centre aisle. Then the prayer for the blessing of the offering is made when all have returned to their seats.[51]

And with this ritual inspiration the children had let off steam before the address.

We secure variety in the service in many ways. 'Little Chapter' is read by a small child. These are short and well-known passages from the Bible which follow the season of the year, and thus children learn to connect certain Sundays with great events in the life of Jesus Christ. All these 'Little Chapters' are contained in the service book which each child possesses, so that there are no delays and muddles over finding places in the Bible ... The Bible lesson for the Sunday is read by an older boy or girl who is chosen beforehand. This reading follows a lectionary which covers two years.[52]

At this point church order, indeed church structure, come to the fore. Each child who joined Little Church was given *My Little Church Book*, for 'a child likes something to handle and possess'. The idea for this was Rixian: it was derivatively original. The idea came from one of Rix's earlier pastorates but the *Sunday School Chronicle* noted a striking similarity in this to the League of Young Worshippers which was strong in many Baptist churches.[53] *Little Church Book* was a manual of church order. It contained a letter from the minister, a record page (for children like writing down

[51] *Ibid* pp. 10–11.
[52] *Ibid* pp. 11–12.
[53] *Ibid* p. 13; 'A "Little Church" for Little People', [*The Sunday School Chronicle and Times* 7 July 1927], p. 427.

important dates: so here they might inscribe the date of their joining Little Church); a certificate of membership, alternative forms of worship, Little Chapters, twenty five psalms for responsive use, prayers, and a lectionary which took the child through the prophets, epistles and gospels in two years. The certificate of membership contained these words:

> He is affectionately urged by the members of the Church to be present at the Lord's Supper, which is the sign of Church membership among Christian people. They hope for the time when he will of his own desire confess his faith in Jesus Christ as his Teacher, Redeemer, and Lord, and become a full member of the Church.[54]

Little Church was not full church, but it had a full church order. It had eight deacons (boys and girls, although in 1927 the *Sunday School Chronicle* had criticised the maleness of Little Diaconate)[55] retiring by a six-monthly rota; their duties were 'very simple and develop a sense of order and habit'. These deacons, supervised by an adult (who for much of Little Church's existence was Mrs. Robertson), chose the hymn (from a list provided), and the readers of Little Chapter and the collectors of the offering, and they formed a committee which, like the Big Church diaconate, met monthly with the minister as chairman. Thus Rix came to know each leading Little Churchman personally, for by now they were approaching school leaving age and the stage after Little Churchmembership: Junior Church membership. To prepare for this they attended the minister's quartet of classes, held every other year, on church, bible, sacraments and Christianity. Rix took care to explain his thinking here: every Christian community that practices baptism

> has accepted the view that the child is in some sense a member of the Christian community and has come into relation with Jesus Christ. It also becomes more and more clear that the Free Churches need some grade of membership for the child at the adolescent period corresponding to confirmation in the Anglican Church.

[54] W. Rix, *Little Church*, pp. 13–16.
[55] 'A "Little Church" For Little People', p. 427.

Junior membership supplied this need at Ealing Green, reviving, but on a different basis, one of John Byles's innovations fifty years earlier. Full membership was still reached 'by profession of faith in maturer years' (the church was still a gathered church) but now junior members had their names brought to full church meetings, were asked to promise to attend worship at least once each Sunday, and to be of good report, and in return for accepting these responsibilities they were accorded the privilege of communion 'the world wide sign between all Churches and Christians'.[56]

There remains another element which was inseparable from the genius of Little Church: the creation of buildings to house the conception, to link it with Big Church and to express all that was new and not just updated in Little Church. Buildings and church proceeded together. The church visible began in 1924 when (a double suitability) Mr. Malet's adjacent carpenter's yard, became available.[57] At once a fund was launched for Little Church, Church Parlour, Small Hall and the necessary kitchens and lavatories. An outlay of £3500 to £4000 was envisaged, made possible by proceeds from the sale of the old British Schools and by the encouragement of Lucy Robertson. What set the scheme apart was the combination of conception, site, and architect.

The conception has been described. The site was difficult, approached from the outside world by a narrow passage, at the mercy of blind walls, squeezed into the carpenter's yard and out of the manse garden. The architect was Percy Morley Horder, Garrett Horder's son, a man of wayward, frustrated genius who was now at the peak of a career that was as yet fashionable and successful.[58] Ecclesiastically Percy Morley Horder was a Chesterbelloc man well on the way to Rome, but this commission was held in spiritual and financial check by his association with Ealing Green (where a brother, two sisters and two sisters-in-law were still members or attenders) and by the professional abilities of Gerald, his quantity surveyor brother.

[56] W. Rix, *Little Church*, pp. 17–23.
[57] The chief source for the following account, unless otherwise indicated, is the church's Building [Extension Committee] Minute Book 1925–1931.
[58] For Percy Morley Horder (1870–1944) see *DNB* and C. Binfield, 'English Free Churchmen and a National Style', pp. 521–3. Horder was the architect of Penge Congregational Church.

The building scheme was the sort of communal exercise that such churches as Ealing Green had long ago brought to a fine art. Strategic people were formed into committees – Mrs. Robertson to lay the foundation stone, councillor Fuller to chair the building committee, councillor Howell Jones to be its treasurer, McIntosh the Labour agent to deal with publicity, and as many Horders and Horder connexions as might be. Sanctified ingenuity was exploited to the utmost to raise money – concerts of course, and a grand period bazaar, and Melting Snowball Teas. The children too were brought into the swim of things. They examined the architect's model of Little Church; their mothers subscribed to the foundation stone, with each mother's initials carved on it, and the words 'Out of the mouths of babes and sucklings Thou has perfected praise'; they bought a brick each for the Church. Inevitably, and as was increasingly the case with Morley Horder, there were delays and changes of plan and mounting costs. The initial £3500 rapidly became £4500. In the event £6364 was required (£2000 of it from Lucy Robertson) and even that excess had been desperately held within bounds by a Gerald Horder driven to distraction by his brother's ways. The world too contributed its tensions: would the General Strike affect the opening in June 1926? And one building scheme bred another, here as elsewhere, an interlocking of building, Little Church, daily church, liturgy and drama, a tide flowing into Big Church itself.

Where Garrett Horder would have been autocratic, Wilton Rix took care at every step to share his unfolding plans. The opening of Little Church was just such an unfolding, a four day exercise in fellowship and worship: a day of prayer ('First the Spirit, then the ceremony'), a day of opening ('for our own people only'), a day of services and dedication, a day of public meeting, each day a settling in to new buildings. Rix described them:

> The architect ... has done wonders in making a beautiful thing of the blank wall of Little Church which is to be seen from the manse garden. The roof is Italian tiles of a rich red colour, and he [Morley Horder] has broken the monotony of the wall half-way down by a line of the same tiles. A small piece of the ground has been left unoccupied, and that is converted into a paved garden, bounded upon one side by a yew hedge. When

435

the beds are full of flowers there will be a beautiful outlook from the large windows of the Church Parlour.

That parlour, 'specially dedicated to work undertaken by the Women's Council' was Morley Horder at his best. It was a puritan room, freely seventeenth-century, after the manner of similar rooms which Horder had contrived for Congregationalists at Penge, at Muswell Hill, and at the rebuilt Cheshunt College. It was

> a room which does not need elaborate furnishing, for the simple panels of the walls and ceiling are in themselves beautiful and restful. Three tables for needlework, two chairs at the fireplace and a row of chairs down either side of the room will fitly furnish it.

By contrast, and like too much of the executed scheme, with its yellow brick, flat roofs, pokey kitchen and superabundance of corridor, the Small Hall was Horder at his cheapest. This was a club room for Scouts and Guides and the Girls' Club and the Young Men's Club. It was low-walled, with unplastered surfaces of yellow brick. For it was Little Church itself, properly called 'one of Congregationalism's loveliest buildings',[59] which held the eye outside and captured the heart within.

Outside, in the 'Garth' with its walnut tree and beds of antirrhinums, 'when the sun shines upon the red-tiled roofs and the yellow walls, hints of a small court in some town of Italy are awakened in the memories of those who have been there': which was Rix's intention, for the *style* of the church followed a holiday in Assisi.[60] Inside, it was a miniature essay in Byzantine puritanism, an experiment of restraint in tone and texture and symbol: walls of white plaster, woodwork in stippled blue, blue curtains in the chancel to set off a small wooden cross painted gold, rush-bottomed chairs in the nave, and a barrel roof between whose supporting pillars and the walls ran two white aisles framed in black tiles.

> The Golden Cross set in blue of an Eastern night, the white purity of the walls, the soft light of a summer eve, the quiet

[59] *CYB* (1960) p. 435.

[60] *Programme* [for the Ealing Green Puritan Market, 18–20 November 1926]; *p.i.*

strains of music create an exalted sense of worship in the presence of the Infinite and Eternal.[61]

Such an atmosphere was Catholic, but its symbolism was all Reformed:

> Though Little Church is built with a chancel in the traditional way, which allows the end of the Church to be empty, and to avoid any distraction for the eye, nevertheless it should be noted that it is furnished with an old refectory table and not with an altar. The three chairs signify that the Minister who presides is no more important than the layman or laywoman in the fellowship of the Church, and at the Communion Service it is our custom that the Minister first gives the bread and the wine to those who are aiding him at the service, and then he receives from one of them. We are, therefore, standing by the traditional Puritan view of the Communion Service and trying to give it expression. The Communion Service means to us the common meal of Christ's people, and He is the unseen Presence who binds them together. The Table in use in Little Church dates from 1625, somewhere about the time when John Bunyan was born, when Nonconformists were beginning to impress themselves upon English life. The three leather chairs are of Flemish origin of the same period, and Holland, be it remembered, was one of the strongest seats of the movement on the Continent.[62]

This gloss on the appearance of Little Church at its opening in July 1926, a month late, is valuable because it emphasises its integration, as it were in reverse, with the Ealing Green community. Little Church was a cathedral for the children of the church but it was also a puritan lady chapel for their parents, the church itself. It was a place for communion services on sparsely attended Sunday evenings or for special acts of worship and devotion.

So the full scheme developed: parlour, hall, and church, that was both lady chapel and cathedral; table and rush chairs, tables and rows of chairs, bread and wine and offering, needlework and teamwork, worship, and drama, and celebration.

[61] 'Church Member' in *Ealing Green Magazine*, cutting in church records.
[62] Cutting in church records.

437

The worship was there from the first Thursday, with Little Church open from mid afternoon to early evening for silent prayer, and A. G. Matthews, one of Rix's Mansfield College friends, to speak on 'Moods for Prayer', five talks in an evening of preparation. With the opening Friday came the dedication, the congregation moving from Garth to Parlour to Small Hall to Little Church, each opened by a different person, at each a verse sung of the hymn 'Christ is made the sure Foundation', and at each a prayer offered: a nature prayer in the Garth, a fellowship prayer in the Parlour, in the Hall a prayer for health and activity. In Little Church came the placing of cloth and cups and plates on the table, Bible on the reading desk, Little Church Book on the prayer desk, with three hymns, and readings and further prayer. On opening Sunday there was early communion in Little Church, then mid-morning service, with another of Rix's Mansfield friends, Malcolm Spencer, preaching in Big Church while Rix took the service in Little Church; and in the afternoon there was a change of key with a Sunday school festival addressed by one of the denominational extroverts, Charter Piggott of Streatham. So to the Monday public meeting, when a B.S.A. motor combination was presented to Arthur Stowell ('of Chelsea'), now a missionary at Bellary in South India, with two hymns sung from *Worship Song*, and a third, 'O son of Man, Our hero strong and tender', sung to the Londonderry Air.[63]

Thereafter Big and Little Church became the not easily distinguishable focal points of drama, worship and celebration. The bazaar, for example, spread over three November days in 1926, was a Puritan Market, with teas and table d'hôte suppers, Mrs. Leslie Horder at Fancy Needlework and Mrs. Gerald Horder at Crackers and Stationery. Its puritanism comprehended life-size models of Charles I and Queen Elizabeth, Saint John, Longfellow, Minnehaha and Hiawatha, Raleigh, Livingstone and Shakespeare, Portia and Peter Pan; but each day's programme was prefaced by a motto from Milton, with a motif of a puritan. The Ealing Green Players acted each day; the vicar of Ealing led in prayer on the second day; and on the third and children's day, the children recited from A. A. Milne's *When we were very young*.[64]

[63] *Brochure* for Church Dedication Services, 1–5 July 1926, in church records.
[64] *Programme*.

The November Puritan Market led to a December Festival in the shape of Christina Rossetti's *Pageant of the Months*. In 1927 the Little Church Christmas Festival took the form of Rix's adaptation of *Pilgrim's Progress*. Here, consciously or not, was recaptured a past moment of Ealing Green's history, for in April 1839 church meeting had resolved that 'when there was no business before the Church, a portion of the Pilgrim's Progress should be read to the members – with a view to the edification of the Church'.[65]

Rix's was a meticulous *Progress*. In an admirably printed and excellently annotated programme, he described it as 'a corporate act of service to God'. It was also a very family *Progress*, with Rix as Bunyan, his wife as Christiana, his daughters Marigold and Rosemary as Patience and Passion. One of Gerald Horder's daughters was a Shepherd of the Delectable Mountains and her aunt Eleanor Plaistowe, 'a very warm and ample woman', helped with the costumes. Lucy Robertson provided the incidental music.[66] Mrs. Robertson was in her element at such times. For the Chester Medieval mystery play, or for André Obey's *Noah* she made her own arrangements, in the latter case of Tchaikowsky marches. For *Job*, to costumes based on William Blake's illustrations, she adapted Vaughan Williams's ballet music, without permission, in the year of its composition.[67] Rix too was in his element, for such productions, increasingly held now in Big Church, were largely his creation, built around his people.

> Indeed he needed to have us there before he could create them. They grew during rehearsal. He designed the costumes, which were expertly made by an army of needlewomen under the direction of someone who was herself 'creative'. Then programmes were designed, lighting erected, music chosen. There were singers and dancers as well as actors. Almost all the week-night work of the church was suspended while a pageant was being rehearsed. It was all very exciting and worthwhile.[68]

Occasionally, and with less success, Rix ventured into more formal work. Henri Ghéon's *Marvellous History of St Bernard* was

[65] R.C. Davis, Notebook.
[66] *Programme*, 20–22 December 1927; *pi*.
[67] *pi*.
[68] *pi*.

the most ambitious production, performed in Big Church in 1933, nine years after its debut at Menthon. Rix took great care over this. The costumes were specially made, with wigs by Nathan. St Bernard's *Marvellous History* was too Roman a play for many, so Rix prefaced the venture with a sermon in Big Church. Like *Pilgrim's Progress*, the *Marvellous History* was a 'corporate act of service to God.' No actors were named in the programme and applause was discouraged. Instead there was a careful description of the subject, the setting, and the scenery: this was designed by a niece of Rix who became a professional artist. The whole was 'a reflection of the tenth century'. At various times the stage represented 'the top of the Pass, the courtyard of the Castle of Menthon, and the entrance to the Monastery at Aosta; and perched above all, is a window out of heaven which is quite as real to the mediaeval mind as the local castle...' Through this mediaeval setting the subject 'clearly sets forth a great gospel truth, namely, that he who accepts his divine call must accept also his cross, but through his cross human life will be cleaned and raised.'[69]

Thus Little Church became a crucible for puritan innovation in art and leisure and ritual where the puritan ascetic emerged as the puritan aesthetic. It was here that Rix, who 'never ventured rashly in Big Church', could adventure out at 6.30 in the morning with his May Day Litany and Breakfast, and his evening Michaelmas Litany.

> Great arrangements of wild flowers, foliage, berries ... according to the season, were carried in procession. The litanies were partly verses from scripture and partly extracts from poems, some written by members of the congregation. These were joyous occasions.[70]

Now it remained to exploit what was left of the site's potential. In 1934 it was decided to complete the Garth's enclosure with craft rooms fitted with art tables and a loom to teach the right use of creative leisure. But this scheme remained a dream, largely because Morley Horder's plans were 'quite useless [he] obviously had not grasped the idea of use to which the buildings were to be put'[71], but perhaps because the real potential lay now in Big Church.

[69] *Programme* 1933.
[70] *pi.*
[71] R.C. Davis, Notebook.

Rix, as has been suggested, trod circumspectly in Big Church. There he wore cassock and gown, with his Oxford hood for red letter days. For the rest he was a collar-and-tie man, never a dog-collar man. His own tendencies were for stricter liturgical forms but his wife checked some of these. Rix liked to kneel for prayer rather than sit for it or crouch for it, and many in the congregation knelt, but not Mary Rix; and in Big Church, anthem and preliminaries apart, and printed service-sheet smoothness apart, the usual Nonconformist form prevailed.[72] Nonetheless order crept visibly into Big Church. The lead-lighted windows which in Garrett Horder's day had replaced the panes of warehouse glass in their turn gave way to stained glass insets. The stained glass was good, but it was not entirely in harmony with its setting. Then, in the summer of 1929, provoked by the total collapse of the organ, a full transformation of Big Church was set in train, with Percy Morley Horder once more as architect, giving his services free. The green and mahogany became white and light blue; the side galleries went; concealed lighting was introduced; the open timbered roof was plastered to become a barrel vault, not very happily, since it had to be a slightly pointed barrel, to allow for the west windows. In the nave the pews were tilted back to allow for comfort and prayer rests or hassocks. At the pulpit end, the organ pipes were moved to each side and there camouflaged in a light blue wooden case, designed by Horder. The walls too were panelled in blue painted wood, and doors let into them to allow for more flexible pageants rather than necessary access. Thus the pulpit end became a chancel, with choir-stalls in limed oak on each side, parish church fashion, robed choir to fill them and Rix to lead worship from one of them. To one side of the stalls was the pulpit, to the other the lectern, each in limed oak, each with wood carvings from the studio of Eric Gill, each with a plaque in memory of Garrett Horder and his wife, of gospel oak from Boston Manor in the pulpit, and of bronze in the lectern. Stalls, lectern and pulpit were the gifts of Gerald and Percy Morley Horder. At the rear of this new chancel, in the recess vacated by the organ, stood the table, a Cromwellian table, like that of Little Church. This too was given by the Horder brothers: and at the entrance to the chancel, over the arch, and after considerable thought, was placed not a cross itself,

[72] pi.

but the pattern of a cross. The floor was carpeted by Mrs. Robertson who, inevitably and anonymously, had guaranteed the whole scheme. The cross appeared in 1936; the Horder gift came in 1931, shortly before the Gerald Horders retired to the Sussex countryside; but the bulk of the transformation was effected within a year, by 1930.[73]

In 1939, when he had retired from active pastoral ministry, Wilton Rix summed up his views on worship in a paper given to the Free Church Fellowship, a group of 'catholic' Free Churchmen. He began provocatively:

> ... there is no certainty that on any particular Sunday the central facts about Jesus Christ will be proclaimed ... The sermon may be on some topical theme, the hymns may be chosen to support it, and a dozen verses of Scripture may be read which are edifying only because they confirm the subject running in the minister's mind. On the other hand, in every Roman Church the Mass bears witness day by day to the central fact of the Gospel, namely the death and sacrifice of the Son of God for man's sins.[74]

But some of what he wrote was an echo of Eustace Conder sixty years earlier:

> ... we see our fathers coming out from the Roman Church not to be free to introduce any new mode of worship that might suit the moment, but to clear the old one of superstition, and to restore to it the evangelical standards of the New Testament ...

The framework of worship was clear: hymn, bible, sermon, the elements in communion, prayer.

> [I]n our hymns we proclaim our belief by praising God for the blessings we know in Jesus Christ incarnate in our human life, crucified for us, victorious over death, and reigning at God's

---

[73] Building Minute Book 1925–1931, R.C. Davis, Notebook; *pi.*

[74] W.E. Rix, *On the Improvement of Public Worship* (1939) unpaginated pamphlet reprinted from *Transactions of the Free Church Fellowship Summer Conference*, September 1939. The following quotations are taken from the pamphlet. The author has in his possession Rix's privately printed *The Ealing Book* (1936) of litanies and intercessions (including May Day and Michaelmas Litanies), prayers and collects.

right hand. It is natural for Protestants to be lyrical ... Hymns are the credal framework of our service ... [I]t is in hymn singing that a congregation can in a militant way shout back the victory of Christ.

As for scripture; 'The saving Word concerning Christ is to be "broken", as the Bread is "broken" and distributed at the Lord's Table, for the congregation is indeed at the same feast.'

Thus emerged 'a rough framework in our typical form which united us with the Christian Church worshipping through the ages, and we should do well to recognise it and respect it. Then let us use it with a pliancy natural to churches which claim to be free. In words which were spoken concerning Calvin's service: "It can and ought to be bettered; it ought not to be transformed".'

Rix never quite resolved the tensions in his churchmanship between the Independent and the Congregationalist, each Reformed yet Catholic. Paradoxically the 'catholic' element of his churchly composition most set him apart from the general run of Congregationalists, only holding him to them (and them to him) because of the strong Independency, so characteristic of the dominant values of their formative years, which marked many of their leading men, and to which they had a temperamental and sentimental affinity. But it was his communal sense of the fellowship of the church from cradle to grave, far stronger than mere brotherhood, and his genius for turning other men's visions into his own, and then for communicating his visions to those best able to actualise them, that brought Rix very close to the ideal of a Congregational minister and made him, the more so for his uniqueness, not just the representative figure for his smallish congregation but a representative figure for Congregationalism itself. Rix advocated what would have been incredible for Congregationalists of a previous generation in a way that was entirely credible to Congregationalists of his own generation, and in a way that was entirely consonant with a whole clutch of disparate tendencies among them. Most important, he communicated this to the rising generation, especially of Little Churchgoers on the verge of joining the first large generation of college students and undergraduates, for these were the first great days of the Student Christian Movement.

One dimension remains to be described: that of social conscience, which was so large a part of the appeal of S.C.M. In differing circumstances this dimension had also marked out the Greenfield Church in Bradford, and the Brixton Hill Independents. It was more an *on*-working than an *out*-working of the Nonconformist Conscience.

At Ealing Green it was the dimension most likely to unite Little Church and afternoon Sunday school, the 'working class chaps in their early twenties ... who were cast for appropriate parts in ... religious dramas and would be the carpenters who built the scenery and would help with the lighting',[75] and the middle class young who were given the major acting parts. This dimension showed in the church's concern in 1924 about 'the uses of wireless from a religious standpoint'; about disarmament and the League of Nations; about Locarno in 1925, and the Kellogg Pact in 1928; about the unemployed or about the spring week in 1927 devoted to 'Work, Play and the Church Militant'. The concern for the unemployed ranged from councillor Fuller's mayoral fund of 1922 to the inquiries of 1928–9 when a special church meeting sent Rix and Gerald Horder to the Durham coalfields to see how the church could best provide 'personal and corporate Christian service' for three mining churches served by an evangelist, Mabel Snowball, who in her turn came to Ealing Green. The spring week on work and play was opened by councillor Fuller, with speeches to follow, on health, world peace, Scouting, Guiding, youth, and children's books. There was Percy Dearmer to talk on Arts and Pictures, and there was the inevitable pageant, this time about 'Humanity Delivered'.

In the 1930s these burgeoned into Church weekend conferences held away from Ealing. In 1934, for example, there were two such conferences, one held at Jordans, the Quaker shrine, when forty-six to fifty people considered the useful crafts; the other was on Peace, with Norman Angell and Leyton Richards of Carr's Lane to address it. This led to a Peace Study Circle and it was in this atmosphere that Albert Schweitzer spoke at an evening service in 1935 or that in June 1939, two months after Rix had left Ealing and

[75] *pi*. Information in this paragraph and the next is drawn from R.C. Davis, Notebook.

on the eve of war, the church resolved to appoint a committee 'to advise young men who were conscientiously opposed to compulsory military service or who werè uncertain'.

The impact of Rix's Ealing Green in the 1930s is best described by one of the career girls, on her way to becoming a technical librarian, whom Rix attracted to the church.[76] She was a nineteen-year-old, with a low church mother and a lapsed Congregational father, who was dissatisfied with the Anglicanism which had formed her and who, at this crucial moment, was urged to come to Ealing Green by a friend in her office.

> If Ealing Green had been a typical Congregational Chapel I don't know whether I should have been attracted. But I found a building of some beauty, a robed chair, the type of church to which I was accustomed with a minister's stall, lectern and pulpit, a minister wearing a cassock and gown (though not a clerical collar). Provision was made for members of the congregation to kneel for prayer and many of them did. One chant was sung during the service which began with sung responses. Therefore I found some familiar things, and at the same time I found a freedom in the worship, particularly of the prayers, which was liberating. In December 1931 I became a member of the church, which later both my parents joined.

This led to Little Church, as one of the rota of helpers, sitting every so often with the children.

> There was no systematic teaching – that was left to the afternoon Sunday School where I taught – but there was a great deal of training in churchmanship, and of the most comprehensive kind. Ealing Green opened many windows for me. It was there I discovered that being a Christian involved more than the salvation of my own little soul, and that the gospel could be preached through action and caring. Also that the gospel sheds light on every aspect of life. Through guest speakers and discussion, sometimes on a week-night evening at the Ealing Green Society, and sometimes an evening service, we were encouraged to form an opinion on such matters. It was also the

[76] *pi.*

period of slump and unemployment, and again we were not only invited to examine the causes but also to take part in relief work through occupational clubs for the unemployed. We had speakers such as Albert Schweitzer, a very young Hugh Gaitskell, and a famous woman Labour M.P. from Tyneside, a small woman with flaming red hair who enjoyed a verbal battle with W. R.... All this made a great impression on me. But so also did the realisation that in a church community one could have parties and all kinds of fun.

"Community", that was the word. W.R. saw the church as a community in which people with many different gifts could serve. He would often speak of those who taught, those who prayed, those who engaged in creative art, made music and so on. And it was in the pageant that the whole church community became involved.

After Rix had left Ealing this young woman became church secretary, and eventually she entered the ministry, a course which in retrospect might be dated to the advice which Rix had given her, when nothing had been further from her mind: 'I don't think I should advise you to enter the ministry'. That advice notwithstanding, her call to ministry in the 1960s was attributable to the impact of one church and its minister in the 1930s on a young woman in her twenties.

> He motivated a social conscience in us without switching us over to the 'social gospel'. We had Bible Study in house groups. We were encouraged to apply the teaching of Jesus to the whole of life ... He was constantly reaching out to new aspects of the faith, and new ways of experiencing it. He taught us how to worship. How to see beauty and to look for it. How to use all our powers in the service of God. I still hanker after the kind of dignified and semi-liturgical worship we had at Ealing Green, and in my present ministry I have to restrain myself from what I find is unwelcome here ...

Thus it was for one of Rix's young people nearly forty years on.

Little Church closed with the outbreak of war, and was barely rescued thereafter. The need for it had gone in the 1950s. The initial liberation into *worship* had itself become institutionalised, at the expense of that liberation into *faith* which remains the gathered church's prime source; and the disciplines of the 1920s and 1930s were applied less easily to young people, 'children' no longer in the 1950s.

The *concept* of Little Church, however, had become part of Congregationalism's established thinking about the place of children, the church's children, in the church. Sunday schools were steadily disappearing into junior churches and morning worship was becoming family worship for Family Church. The direct influence of Ealing Green in this is not to be doubted. For example, Charter Piggott spoke at Little Church opening in July 1926, and in February 1927 a 'Children's Church' was started for his own flourishing church (four hundred and seventy-eight members strong) in Streatham.[77] The Streatham Children's Church had its deacons (two boys, two girls), elected for two to three months of service; it had its choir and its church meeting. 'We want to train the children in Worship and Reverence. We have talks on Prayer and the children join in the prayers and sing the responses ...' There was, too, a New Year's Day Promotion Service from Children's Church to adult church, and an unveiling of a copy of Margaret Tarrant's 'All Things Bright and Beautiful' with room for its companion picture, 'The Dayspring From on High'. In the United States Dr. Boynton Merrill's Second Parish Congregational Church, Newton, Massachusetts, had a Children's Church which was part of a very conscious and comprehensive 'high Congregational churchmanship'.[78] And in Massachusetts Vivian Pomeroy returns to view.

When Pomeroy left Bradford Congregationalism it had been for New England Unitarianism. From 1924 to 1954 he ministered at First Parish Church (Unitarian), Milton, Massachusetts, 'charming, talkative and witty', knowing the value 'of being very English with those people'.[79] Milton too had Little Church next to Big

---

[77] *Streatham Congregational Church Manual* (1928) p. 9.

[78] A.L. Drummond [*The Church Architecture of Protestantism*, Edinburgh 1934] p. 219, Dr. Merrill was a "high" Congregationalist as his installation address made clear: 'The appeal of the altar, rising white in the dim light of a lovely chancel, is perfectly legitimate'. *Ibid* p. 228–9.

[79] *pi.* He continued to write children's stories: *The Enchanted Children*, 1938; *Another Story Please* (Boston, Mass.) 1947.

Church, white steepled on its Green, and an English visitor who spent Christmas with the Pomeroys in 1941 referred to it in a letter home. The visitor, who knew Matthews and Rix and Malcolm Spencer as well as Vivian Pomeroy, for he too had been a Congregational minister, was now a Roman Catholic priest. He was W. E. Orchard. He found Pomeroy's Unitarianism 'nearer to us than when he was a congregationalist in Bradford', and as for Mrs. Pomeroy, 'she is just Catholic in most things; her children's chapel has an altar with the Virgin and Child on it'.[80]

In the 1930s such schemes (Virgin and Child and altar apart) became more frequent, especially in large suburban churches. Sometimes the innovatory impulse was restricted to an S. C. M. flavoured youth activity as perhaps at Chingford where H. J. Gamble, minister from 1918 to 1935, created a Guild of the Round Table for his young people,[81] or at Otley, where John Marsh was minister from 1934 to 1938. Marsh was an S. C. M. inspired Mansfield man who later became Mansfield's principal, in which capacity he preached a memorial address for Wilton Rix. At Otley he formed a 'Felawschipe', a company of young men and women, purified Chaucerians sharing Christian adventure in their pilgrimage. They had their Felawschipe room, their choir and dramatics, their rambles and their hiking holidays, and their May morning and Wayfarer's services.[82] Elsewhere, full children's church was increasingly the aim. In 1933 Eric Hodgson, fresh at the very prosperous Woodford Congregational church, was determined to secure the fusion of church and Sunday school. So a Little Church, consciously on Ealing lines, was formed, its members leaving adult worship each Sunday morning a quarter of an hour after the service began for worship of their own in a specially oak-panelled hall. In the course of the decade, as numbers grew from fifteen to fifty and as the age range widened, Little Church fused with the Sunday school to form a graded junior church for children up to the age of thirteen. This began, as Family Church, in September 1939.[83] At

[80] W.E. Orchard, letter of 1 January 1942. I am indebted to Miss Elaine Kaye for this reference. For Orchard (1877–1955) see *From Faith to Faith: An Autobiography of Religious Development* (1933).

[81] For Gamble (1888–1978) see *United Reformed Church Year Book* (1980) p. 254.

[82] Patricia Hunt, *A Century and a Half. The Story of the Congregational Church in Otley 1821–1971* (Otley nd [1971]) pp. 15–16.

[83] R.L. Galey, *The History of the Woodford Green United Free Church*, (Woodford 1968) pp. 42–4.

Freedom Through Discipline

the same time Avenue Church, Southampton, under Stanley Herbert (minister 1930–38) introduced its junior church 'as soon as we had the delightful Little Chapel for such use'. In the 1950s its members had reached a hundred, its attendance averaged sixty and in 1958 they too fused with Avenue Sunday school to form a 'Graded Morning Junior Church'.[84] Along the coast, in Bournemouth, John Short's Richmond Hill, one of the largest of English Congregational churches, founded a 'Little Church' in 1937. This one too survived to the 1950s when a properly constructed Little Church, 'a most beautiful sanctuary, seating about 150, and specially designed to capture the imagination and inspire the mind and heart of a child' was built in memory of Short's predecessor, J. D. Jones. It was opened in 1954.[85]

Those are Congregational instances, Milton apart, but the idea spread beyond Congregationalism, and one Methodist example might be adduced here. 'Little Church', Alverstoke, was built in 1937 as part of the Methodist National Children's Homes Jubilee.

> In the planning of the building there have been incorporated provision for a type of worship which it is hoped will be co-operation by responses in Orders of Worship, simple and direct, which make full use of the words of Scripture, of prayer, and of devotional music. In this way there will be opportunities for sharing such parts of the service as can be used to help young people to realize that the service is their own, and not merely for them ...[86]

The context for this was 'a beautiful Franciscan Chapel ... which, without extravagance either in effect or cost, completes artistically its surroundings of natural charm. All those who feel that the good, the true, and the beautiful share common ground, will recognise at

---

[84] Dora Caton, *A Short History of The Avenue Congregational Church Southampton* (nd *c.*1968) pp. 32, 42, 47.
[85] J.T. Davies, *Richmond Hill Story* (1956) pp. 60, 68–9.
[86] The *Opening of 'Little Church', Alverstoke, Wednesday June 23rd 1937, Order of Proceedings*. F.W. Lawrence, the architect, had designed Church of the Peace of God, Oxted, where A.G. Matthews and Wilton Rix had ministered and where Matthews still lived. John Litten, the principal of the Homes, had previously lived in Ealing. "'See these Books?" said Uncle Jack to his sister, "look, Nan, how beautifully each service is arranged – one for each Sunday in the month, and look ... all arranged telling them what to do.'" Alice Campling, *The Little Church*, (Alverstoke nd) p. 6.

once, and with great gratitude to its product, the appropriateness of the present building ...'. Inside, stained glass windows gave 'in a distinctive way a pictured representation of the life of our Lord, from His nativity to His Ascension', and they had a special bearing on the place of youth and childhood in Jesus's teaching.[87] Here was puritan art disciplined into puritan freedom, for here were to be children disciplined into the freedom of the saints, puritan style and suburban style. Was it asceticism or its counter, which is perhaps for puritans the true asceticism? Was it merely aesthetics for the once ascetic, a cultural conscience for the semi-detached, or was it indeed puritanism's authentic contribution to the national culture, a determination to reach out for the ideal which was all the more fiercely contrived because the real was known to be of passing account?

Little Church Alverstoke of 1937 and Little Church Ealing of 1926, one Methodist, one Congregationalist, Franciscan both, had this in common: they united the ideal and the real in the service of youth. 'To come into Little Church', Wilton Rix told a group of Cambridgeshire Congregationalists in 1926, 'is like coming into light and peace and harmony.' The fullness of Rix's vision, the spiritual perfection attainable through the discipline of worship, order and art, is missed unless the rest of what he told those Congregationalists is recovered: 'That is because the architect made Little Church right. Through the tinted windows the sun makes rosy patterns on the white walls, and a golden cross hanging on blue curtains catches the eyes as you enter, with stone pillars for the aisles. ...'[88]

University of Sheffield

[87] *Ibid.*
[88] A.L. Drummond, pp. 218–9.

ABBREVIATIONS

AASRP	*Associated Archaeological Societies Reports and Papers*
AAWG	*Abhandlungen der Akademie [Gesellschaft to 1942] der Wissenchaften zu Göttingen* (Göttingen 1843–)
AAWL	*Abhandlungen der Akademie der Wissenschaften und der Literatur* (Mainz 1950–)
ABAW	*Abhandlungen der Bayerischen Akademie der Wissenschaften* (Munich 1835–)
Abh	Abhundlung
Abt	Abteilung
ACO	*Acta Conciliorum Oecumenicorum,* ed E. Schwartz (Berlin/Leipzig 1914–40)
ACW	*Ancient Christian Writers,* ed J. Quasten and J. C. Plumpe (Westminster, Maryland/London 1946–)
ADAW	*Abhandlungen der Deutschen [till 1944 Preussischen] Akademie der Wissenschaften zu Berlin* (Berlin 1815–)
AF	*Analecta Franciscana,* 10 vols (Quaracchi 1885–1941)
AFH	*Archivum Franciscanum Historicum* (Quaracchi/Rome 1908–)
AFP	*Archivum Fratrum Praedicatorum* (Rome 1931–)
AHP	*Archivum historiae pontificae* (Rome 1963–)
AHR	*American Historical Review* (New York 1895–)
AKG	*Archiv für Kulturgeschichte* (Leipzig/Münster/Cologne 1903–)
AKZ	*Arbeiten zur Kirchlichen Zeitgeschichte*
ALKG	H. Denifle and F. Ehrle, *Archiv für Literatur–und Kirchengeschichte des Mittelalters,* 7 vols (Berlin/Freibug 1885–1900)
Altaner	B. Altaner, *Patrologie: Leben, Schriften und Lehre der Kirchenväter* (5 ed Freiburg 1958)
AM	L. Wadding, *Annales Minorum* 8 vols (Rome 1625–54); 2 ed, 25 vols (Rome 1731–1886); 3 ed, vol 1–, (Quaracchi 1931–)
An Bol	*Analecta Bollandiana* (Brussels 1882–)
Annales	*Annales: Economies, Sociétés, Civilisations* (Paris 1946–)
Ant	*Antonianum* (Rome 1926–)
APC	*Proceedings and Ordinances of the Privy Council 1386–1542,* ed Sir Harris Nicholas, 7 vols (London 1834–7)
—	*Acts of the Privy Council of England 1542–1629,* 44 vols (London 1890–1958)
—	*Acts of the Privy Council of England, Colonial Series (1613–1785)* 5 vols (London 1908–12)
AR	*Archivum Romanicum* (Geneva/Florence 1971–41)
ARG	*Archiv für Reformationsgeschichte* (Berlin/Leipzig/Gütersloh 1903–)
ASAW	*Abhandungen der Sächsischen Akademie [Gesellschaft to 1920] der Wissenschaften zu Leipzig* (Leipzig 1850–)
ASB	*Acta Sanctorum Bollandiana* (Brussels etc 1643–)
ASC	*Anglo Saxon Chronicle*
ASI	*Archivio storico Italiano* (Florence 1842–)
ASL	*Archivio storico Lombardo,* 1–62 (Milan 1874–1935); ns 1–10 (Milan 1936–47)
ASOC	*Analecta Sacri Ordinis Cisterciensis [Analecta Cisterciensia since 1965]* (Rome 1945–)

ABBREVIATIONS

ASOSB	*Acta Sanctorum Ordinis Sancti Benedicti*, ed. L. D'Achery and J. Mabillon (Paris 1668–1701)
ASP	*Archivio della Società* [*Deputazione* from 1935] *Romana di Storia Patria* (Rome 1878–1934, 1935–)
ASR	*Archives de Sociologie des Religions* (Paris 1956–)
AV	Authorised Version
AV	*Archivio Veneto* (Venice 1871——); [1891–1921, *Nuovo Archivio Veneto*; 1922–6, *Archivio Veneto-Tridentino*]
B	*Byzantion* (Paris/Boston/Brussels 1924–)
Bale *Catalogus*	John Bale, *Scriptorum Illustrium Maioris Brytanniae Catalogus*, 2 parts (Basel 1557, 1559)
Bale, *Index*	John Bale, *Index Britanniae Scriptorum*, ed R. L. Poole and M. Bateson (Oxford 1902) *Anecdota Oxoniensia*, medieval and modern series 9.
Bale, *Summarium*	John Bale, *Illustrium Maioris Britanniae Scriptorum Summarium*, (Ipswich 1548, reissued Wesel 1549)
BEC	*Bibliothèque de l'Ecole des Chartres* (Paris 1839–)
Beck	H–G Beck, *Kirche und theologische Literatur im byzantinischen Reich* (Munich 1959)
BEFAR	*Bibliothèque des écoles françaises d'Athènes et Rome* (Paris 1876–)
BEHE	*Bibliothèque de l'Ecole des Hautes Etudes: Sciences Philologiques et Historiques* (Paris 1869–)
Bernard	E. Bernard, *Catalogi Librorum Manuscriptorum Angliae et Hiberniae* (Oxford 1697)
BF	*Byzantinische Forschungen* (Amsterdam 1966–)
BHG	*Bibliotheca Hagiographica Graeca*, ed F. Halkin, 3 vols + 1 (3 ed Brussels 1957, 1969)
BHI	*Bibliotheca historica Italica*, ed A. Ceruti, 4 vols (Milan 1876–85) 2 series, 3 vols (Milan 1901–33)
BHL	*Bibliotheca Hagiographica Latina*, 2 vols + 1 (Brussels 1898–1901, 1911)
BHR	*Bibliothèque d'Humanisme et Renaissance* (Paris/Geneva 1941–)
Bibl Ref	*Bibliography of the Reform 1450–1648, relating to the United Kingdom and Ireland*, ed Derek Baker for 1955–70 (Oxford 1975)
BIHR	*Bulletin of the Institute of Historical Research* (London 1923–)
BISIMEAM	*Bulletino dell'istituto storico italiano per il medio evo e archivio muratoriano* (Rome 1886–)
BJRL	*Bulletin of the John Rylands Library* (Manchester 1903–)
BL	British Library, London
BM	British Museum, London
BN	Bibliothèque Nationale, Paris
Bouquet	M. Bouquet, *Recueil des historiens des Gaules et de la France, Rerum gallicarum et francicarum scriptores*, 24 vols (Paris 1738–1904); new ed L. Delisle, 1–19 (Paris 1868–80)
BQR	*British Quarterly Review* (London 1845–86)
Broadmead Records	*The Records of a Church of Christ, meeting in Broadmead, Bristol 1640–87*, HKS (London 1848)
BS	*Byzantinoslavica* (Prague 1929–)
Bucer, *Deutsche Schriften*	*Martin Bucers Deutsche Schriften*, ed R. Stupperich and others (Gütersloh/Paris 1960–)
Bucer, *Opera Latina*	*Martini Buceri Opera Latina*, ed F. Wendel and others (Paris/Gütersloh 1955–)
Bull Franc	*Bullarium Franciscanum*, vols 1–4 ed J. H. Sbaralea (Rome 1759–68)

ABBREVIATIONS

	vols 5–7 ed C. Eubel (Rome 1898–1904), new series vols 1–3 ed U. Höntemann and J. M. Pou y Marti (Quaracchi 1929–49)
BZ	*Byzantinische Zeitschrift* (Leipzig 1892–)
CA	*Cahiers Archéologiques. Fin de L'Antiquité et Moyen-âge* (Paris 1945–)
CaF	*Cahiers de Fanjeaux* (Toulouse 1966–)
CAH	*Cambridge Ancient History* (Cambridge 1923–39)
CalRev	*Calamy Revised*, ed A. G. Mathews (Oxford 1934)
CalLP	*Calendar of the Letters and Papers (Foreign and Domestic) of the Reign of Henry VIII*, 21 vols in 35 parts (London 1864–1932)
CalSPD	*Calendar of State Papers: Domestic* (London 1856–)
CalSPF	*Calendar of State Papers: Foreign*, 28 vols (London 1861–1950)
Calvin, Opera	*Ioannis Calvini Opera Quae Supersunt Omnia*, ed G. Baum and others *Corpus Reformatorum*, 59 vols (Brunswick/Berlin 1863–1900)
Canivez	J. M. Canîvez, *Statuta capitulorum generalium ordinis cisterciensis ab anno 1116 ad annum 1786*, 8 vols (Louvain 1933–41)
Cardwell, Documentary Annals	*Documentary Annals of the Reformed Church of England*, ed E. Cardwell, 2 vols (Oxford 1839)
Cardwell Synodalia	*Synodalia*, ed. E. Cardwell, 2 vols (Oxford 1842)
CC	*Corpus Christianorum* (Turnholt 1952–)
CF	*Classical Folia, [Folis 1946–59]* (New York 1960–)
CGOH	*Cartulaire Générale de l'Ordre des Hospitaliers de St.-Jean de Jerusalem (1100–1310)*, ed J. Delaville Le Roulx, 4 vols (Paris 1894–1906)
CH	*Church History* (New York/Chicago 1932–)
CHB	*Cambridge History of the Bible*
CHistS	*Church History Society* (London 1886–92)
CHJ	*Cambridge Historical Journal* (Cambridge 1925–57)
CIG	*Corpus Inscriptionum Graecarum*, ed A. Boeckh, J. Franz, E. Curtius, A. Kirchhoff, 4 vols (Berlin 1825–77)
CIL	*Corpus Inscriptionum Latinarum* (Berlin 1863–)
Cîteaux	*Cîteaux: Commentarii Cisterciensis* (Westmalle 1950–)
CMH	*Cambridge Medieval History*
CModH	*Cambridge Modern History*
COCR	*Collectanea Ordinis Cisterciensium Reformatorum* (Rome/Westmalle 1934–)
COD	*Conciliorum oecumenicorum decreta* (3 ed Bologna 1973)
Coll Franc	*Collectanea Franciscana* (Assisi/Rome 1931–)
CR	*Corpus Reformatorum*, ed C. G. Bretschneider and others (Halle, etc. 1834–)
CS	*Cartularium Saxonicum*, ed W. de G. Birch, 3 vols (London 1885–93)
CSCO	*Corpus Scriptorum Christianorum Orientalium* (Paris 1903–)
CSEL	*Corpus Scriptorum Ecclesiasticorum Latinorum* (Vienna 1866–)
CSer	*Camden Series* (London 1838–)
CSHByz	*Corpus Scriptorum Historiae Byzantinae* (Bonn 1828–97)
CYS	*Canterbury and York Society* (London 1907–)
DA	*Deutsches Archiv für [Geschichte,-Weimar 1937–43] die Erforschung des Mittelalters* (Cologne/Graz 1950–)
DACL	*Dictionnaire d'Archéologie chrétienne et de Liturgie*, ed F. Cabrol and H. Leclercq (Paris 1924–)

453

ABBREVIATIONS

DDC	*Dictionnaire de Droit Canonique,* ed R. Naz (Paris 1935–)
DHGE	*Dictionnaire d'Histoire et de Géographie ecclésiastiques,* ed A. Baudrillart and others (Paris 1912–)
DNB	*Dictionary of National Biography* (London 1885–)
DOP	*Dumbarton Oaks Papers* (Cambridge, Mass., 1941–)
DR	F. Dölger, *Regesten der Kaiserurkunden des oströmischen Reiches (Corpus der griechischen Urkunden des Mittelalters und der neuern Zeit,* Reihe A, Abt I), 5 vols: 1 (565–1025); 2 (1025–1204); 3 (1204–1282); 4 (1282–1341); 5 (1341–1543) (Munich/Berlin 1924–65)
DRev	*Downside Review* (London 1880–)
DSAM	*Dictionnaire de Spiritualité, Ascétique et Mystique,* ed M. Viller (Paris 1932–)
DTC	*Dictionnaire de Théologie Catholique,* ed A. Vacant, E. Mangenot, E. Amann, 15 vols (Paris 1903–50)
EcHR	*Economic History Review* (London 1927–)
EEBS	Ἐπετηρισ Ἑταιρειας Βυξαντινων Σπονδων (Athens 1924–)
EETS	*Early English Text Society*
EF	*Etudes Franciscaines* (Paris 1899–1938, ns 1950–)
EHD	*English Historical Documents* (London 1953–)
EHR	*English Historical Review* (London 1886–)
Ehrhard	A. Ehrhard, *Uberlieferung und Bestand der hagiographischen und homiletischen Liberatur der griechischen Kirche von den Anfangen bis zum Ende des 16. Jh,* 3 vols in 4, *TU*50–2(=4 series 5–7) 11 parts (Leipzig 1936–52)
Emden (O)	A. B. Emden, *A Biographical Register of the University of Oxford To 1500,* 3 vols (London 1957–9); *1500–40* (1974)
Emden (C)	A. B. Emden, *A Biographical Register of the University of Cambridge to 1500* (London 1963)
EO	*Echos d'Orient* (Constantinople/Paris 1897–1942)
ET	English translation
EYC	*Early Yorkshire Charters,* ed W. Farrer and C. T. Clay, 12 vols (Edinburgh/Wakefield 1914–65)
FGH	*Die Fragmente der griechischen Historiker,* ed F. Jacoby (Berlin 1926–30)
FM	*Histoire de l'église depuis les origines jusqu'à nos jours,* ed A. Fliche and V. Martin (Paris 1935–)
Foedera	*Foedera, conventiones, litterae et cuiuscunmque generis acta publica inter regis Angliae et alios quosvis imperatores, reges, pontifices, principes vel communitates,* ed T. Rymer and R. Sanderson, 20 vols (London 1704–35), 3 ed G. Holmes, 10 vols (The Hague 1739–45), re-ed 7 vols (London 1816–69)
Franc Stud	*Franciscan Studies* (St Bonaventure, New York 1924–, ns 1941–)
Fredericq	P. Fredericq, *Corpus documentorum inquisitionis haereticae pravitatis Neerlandicae,* 3 vols (Ghent 1889–93)
FStn	*Franzikanische Studien* (Münster/WErl 1914–)
GalC	*Callia Christiana,* 16 vols (Paris 1715–1865)
Gangraena	T. Edwards, *Gangraena,* 3 parts (London 1646)
GCS	*Die griechischen christlichen Schriftsteller der erste drei Jahrhunderte* (Leipzig 1897–)
Gee and Hardy	*Documents illustrative of English Church History* ed H. Gee and W. J. Hardy (London 1896)

ABBREVIATIONS

GEEB	R. Janin, *La géographie ecclésiastique de l'empire byzantin;*
CEM	*1, Le siège de Constnatinople et le patriarcat oecumenique,* pt 3 *Les églises et les monastères* (Paris 1953);
EMGCB	*2, Les églises et les monastéres des grands centres byzantins* (Paris 1975) (series discontinued)
Golubovich	Girolamo Golubovich, *Biblioteca bio-bibliografica della Terra Santa e dell'oriente francescano:*
	series *1, Annali,* 5 vols (Quaracchie 1906–23)
	series 2, *Documenti* 14 vols (Quaracchi 1921–33)
	series 3, *Documenti,* (Quaracchi 1928–)
	series 4, *Studi,* ed M. Roncaglia (Cairo 1954–)
Grumel	V. Grumel, *Les Regestes des Actes du Patriarcat de Constantinople,*
Regestes	1: *Les Actes des Patriarches,* 1: 381–715; II: 715–1043; III: 1043–1206 (Socii Assumptionistae Chalcedonenses, 1931, 1936, 1947)
Grundmann	H. Grundmann, *Religiöse Bewegungen im Mittelalter* (Berlin 1935, 2 ed Darmstadt 1970)
Guignard	P. Guignard, *Les monuments primitifs de la règle cistercienne* (Dijon 1878)
HBS	*Henry Bradshaw Society* (London/Canterbury 1891–)
HE	*Historia Ecclesiastica*
HistSt	*Historical Studies* (Melbourne 1940–)
HJ	*Historical Journal* (Cambridge 1958–)
HJch	*Historisches Jarhbuch der Görres Gesellschaft* (Cologne 1880–, Munich 1950–)
HKS	*Hanserd Knollys Society* (London 1847–)
HL	C. J. Hefele and H. Leclercq, *Histore des Conciles,* 10 vols (Paris 1907–35)
HMC	*Historical Manuscripts Commission*
Holzapfel	H. Holzapfel, *Handbuch der Geschichte des Franziskanerordens*
Handbuch	(Freiburg 1908)
Hooker, *Works*	*The works of . . . Mr. Richard Hooker,* ed J. Keble, 7 ed rev R. W. Church and F. Paget,. 3 vols (Oxford 1888)
Houedene	*Chronica Magistri Rogeri de Houedene,* ed W. Stubbs, 4 vols *RS* 51 (London 1868–71)
HRH	*The Heads of Religious Houses, England and Wales, 940–1216,* ed D. Knowles, C. N. L. Brooke, V. C. M. London (Cambridge 1972)
HS	*Hispania sacra* (Madrid 1948–)
HTR	*Harvard Theological Review* (New York/Cambridge, Mass., 1908–)
HZ	*Historische Zeitschrift* (Munich 1859–)
IER	*Irish Ecclesiastical Record* (Dublin 1864–)
IGLS	*Inscriptions greques et latines de la Syrie,* ed L. Jalabert, R. Mouterde and others, 7 vols (Paris 1929–70) in progress
IR	*Innes Review* (Glasgow 1950–)
JAC	*Jahrbuch für Antike und Christentum* (Münster-im-Westfalen 1958–)
Jaffé	*Regesta Pontificum Romanorum ab condita ecclesia ad a. 1198,* 2 ed S. Lowenfeld, F. Kaltenbrunner, P. Ewald, 2 vols (Berlin 1885–8, repr Graz 1958)
JBS	*Journal of British Studies* (Hartford, Conn., 1961–)
JEH	*Journal of Ecclesiastical History* (London 1950–)

ABBREVIATIONS

JFHS	*Journal of the Friends Historical Society* (London/Philadelphia 1903–)
JHI	*Journal of the History of Ideas* (London 1940–)
JHSChW	*Jounral of the Historical Society of the Church in Wales* (Cardiff 1947–)
JIntH	*Journal of Interdisciplinary History* (Cambridge, Mas., 1970–)
JLW	*Jahrbuch für Liturgiewissenschaft* (Münster-im-Westfalen 1921–44)
JMH	*Journal of Modern History* (Chicago 1929–)
JMedH	*Journal of Medieval Hisotry* (Amsterdam 1975–)
JRA	*Journal of Religion in Africa* (Leiden 1967–)
JRH	*Journal of Religious History* (Sydney 1960–)
JRS	*Journal of Roman Studies* (London 1910–)
JSRAI	*Journal of the Royal Society of Antiquaries of Ireland* (Dublin 1871–)
JSArch	*Journal of the Society of Archivists* (London 1955–)
JTS	*Journal of Theological Studies* (London 1899–)
Kemble	*Codex Diplomaticus Aevi Saxonici*, ed J. M. Kemble (London 1839–48)
Knowles, *MO*	David Knowles, *The Monastic Order in England, 943*–1216 (2 ed Cambridge 1963)
Knowles, *RO*	, *The Religious Orders in England*, 3 vols (Cambridge 1948–59)
Knox, *Works*	*The Works of John Knox*, ed D. Laing, Bannatyne Club/Wodrow Society, 6 vols (Edinburgh 1846–64)
Laurent, Regestes	V. Laurent, *Les Regestes des Actes du Patriarcat de Constantinople,* 1: *Les Actes des Patriarches*, IV: *Les Regestes de 1208 à 1309* (Paris 1971)
Le Neve	John Le Neve, *Fasti Ecclesiae Anglicanae 1066–1300*, rev and exp Diana E. Greenway, 1, St Pauls (London 1968); 2, Monastic Cathedrals (1971) *Fasti Ecclesiae Anglicanae 1300–1541* rev and exp H. P. F. King, J. M. Horn, B. Jones, 12 vols (London 1962–7) *Fasti Ecclesiae Anglicanae 1541–1857* rev and exp J. M. Horn, D. M. Smith, 1, St Pauls (1969); 2, Chichester (1971); 3, Canterbury, Rochester, Winchester (1974); 4, York (1975)
Lloyd, Formularies of Faith	*Formularies of Faith by Authority during the Reign of Henry VIII*, ed C. Lloyd (Oxford 1825)
LRS	*Lincoln Record Society*
LQR	*Law Quarterly Review* (London 1885–)
LThK	*Lexicon für Theologie und Kirche*, ed J. Höfer and K. Rahnes (2 ed Freiburg-im-Breisgau 1957–)
LW	*Luther's Works*, ed J. Pelikan and H. T. Lehman, American edition (St Louis/Philadelphia, 1955–)
MA	*Monasticon Anglicanum*, ed R. Dodsworth and W. Dugdale, 3 vols (London 1655–73; new ed J. Caley, H. Ellis, B. Bandinel, 6 vols in 8 (London 1817–30)
Mansi	J. D. Mansi, *Sacrorum conciliorum nova et amplissima collectio*, 31 vols (Florence/Venice 1757–98); new impression and continuation, ed L. Petit and J. B. Martin, 60 vols (Paris 1899–1927)
Martène and Durand Collectio	E. Martène and U. Durand, *Veterum Scriptorum et Monumentorum Historicorum, dogmaticorum, Moralium Amplissima Collectio,* 9 vols (Paris 1729)
Thesaurus	*Thesaurus Novus Anedotorum*, 5 vols (Paris 1717)

ABBREVIATIONS

Voyage	*Voyage Litteraire de Deux Religieux Benedictins de la Congregation de Saint Maur*, 2 vols (Paris 1717, 1724)
MedA	*Medium Aevum* (Oxford 1932–)
Mendola	*Atti della Settimana di Studio*, 1959– (Milan 1962–)
MF	*Miscellanea Francescana* (Foligno/Rome 1886–)
MGH	*Monumenta Germaniae Historica inde ab a.c. 500 usque ad a. 1500*, ed G. H. Pertz and others (Berlin, Hanover 1826–)
AA	*Auctores Antiquissimi*
Ant	*Antiquitates*
Briefe	**Epistolae 2: Die Briefe der Deutschen Kaiserzeit**
Cap	**Leges 2: Leges in Quart 2: Capitularia regum Francorum**
CM	*Chronica Minora* 1–3 (= *AA* 9, 11, 13) ed Th. Mommsen (1892, 1894, 1898 repr 1961)
Conc	*Leges 2: Leges in Quart 3: Concilia 4: Constiutiones et acta publica imperatorum et regum*
DC	*Deutsche Chroniken*
Dip	*Diplomata in folio*
EPP	*Epistolae 1 in Quart*
Epp Sel	*4: Epistolae Selectae*
FIG	*Leges 3: Fontes Iuris Germanici Antique, new series*
FIGUS	*4: , in usum scholarum*
Form	*2: Leges in Quart 5: Formulae Merovingici et Karolini Aevi*
GPR	*Gesta Pontificum Romanorum*
Leges	*Leges in folio*
Lib	*Libelli de lite*
LM	*Ant 3: Libri Memoriales*
LNG	*Leges 2: Leges in Quart 1: Legs nationum Germanicarum*
Necr	*Ant 2: Necrologia Germaniae*
Poet	*1: Poetae Latini Medii Aevi*
Quellen	*Quellen zur Geistesgeschichte des Mittelalters*
Schriften	**Schriften der Monumenta Germaniae Historica**
SRG	*Scriptores rerum germanicarum in usum scholarum*
SRG ns	* , new series*
SRL	*Scriptores rerum langobardicarum et italicarum*
SRM	*Scriptores rerum merovingicarum*
SS	*Scriptores*
SSM	*Staatschriften des späteren Mittelalters*
MIOG	*Mitteilungen des Instituts für österreichische Geschichtsforschung* (Graz/ Cologne 1880–)
MM	F. Miklosich and J. Müller, *Acta et Diplomata Graeca medii aevi sacra et profana*, 6 vols (Vienna 1860–90)
Moorman, *History*	J. R. H. Moorman, *A History of the Franciscan Order from its origins to the year 1517* (Oxford 1968)
More, *Works*	*The Complete Works of St Thomas More*, ed R. S. Sylvester and others Yale edition (New Haven/London 1963–)
Moyen Age	*Le moyen âge. Revue d'Histoire et de philologie* (Paris 1888–)
MRHEW	David Knowles and R. N. Hadcock, *Medieval Religious Houses, England and Wales* (2 ed London 1971)
MHRI	A. Gwynn and R. N. Hadcock, *Medieval Religious Houses, Ireland* (London 1970)
MHRS	Ian B. Cowan and David E. Easson, *Medieval Religious Houses, Scotland* (2 ed London 1976)

MS	Manuscript
MStn	*Mittelalterliche Studien* (Stuttgart 1966–)
Muratori	L. A. Muratori, *Rerum italicarum scriptores,* 25 vols (Milan 1723–51); new ed G. Carducci and V. Fiorine, 35 vols in 109 fasc (Città di Castello/Bologna 1900–)
NCE	*New Catholic Encyclopedia,* 15 vols (New York 1967)
NCModH	*New Cambridge Modern History,* 14 vols (Cambridge 1957–70)
nd	no date
NEB	*New English Bible*
NF	*Neue Folge*
NH	*Northern History* (Leeds 1966–)
ns	new series
NS	New Style
Numen	*Numen: International Review for the History of Religions* (Leiden 1954–)
OCP	*Orientalia Christiana Periodica* (Rome 1935–)
ODCC	*Oxford Dictionary of the Christian Church,* ed F. L. Cross, (Oxford 1957), 2 ed with E. A. Livingstone (1974)
OED	*Oxford English Dictionary*
OMT	*Oxford Medieval Texts*
OS	Old Style
OHS	*Oxford Historical Society*
PBA	*Proceedings of the British Academy*
PG	*Patrologia Graeca,* ed J. P. Migne, 161 vols (Paris 1857–66)
PhK	Philosophisch-historische Klasse
PL	*Patrologia Latina,* ed J. P. Migne, 217 + 4 index vols (Paris 1841–64)
Plummer, *Bede*	*Venerabilis Baedae Opera Historica,* ed C. Plummer (Oxford 1896)
PO	*Patrologia Orientalis,* ed J. Graffin and F. Nau (Paris 1903–)
Potthast	*Regesta Pontificum Romanorum inde ab a. post Christum natum 1198 ad a. 1304,* ed A. Potthast, 2 vols (1874–5 repr Graz 1957)
PP	*Past and Present* (London 1952–)
PPTS	*Palestine Pilgrims' Text Society,* 13 vols and index (London 1896–1907)
PRIA	*Proceedings of the Royal Irish Academy* (Dublin 1936–)
PRO	Public Record Office
PS	Parker Society (Cambridge 1841–55)
PW	*Paulys Realencyklopädie der klassischen Altertumswissenschaft,* new ed G. Wissowa and W. Kroll (Stuttgart 1893–)
QFIAB	*Quellen und Forschungen aus italienischen Archiven und Bibliotheken* (Rome 1897–)
RAC	*Reallexikon für Antike und Christentum,* ed T. Klauser (Stuttgart 1941)
RB	*Revue Bénédictine* (Maredsous 1884–)
RE	*Realencyclopädie für protestantische Theologie,* ed A. Hauck, 24 vols (3 ed Leipzig, 1896–1913)
REB	*Revue des Etudes Byzantines* (Bucharest/Paris 1946–)
RecS	Record Series
RGG	*Die Religion in Geschichte und Gegenwart,* 6 vols (Tübingen 1927–32)
RH	*Revue historique* (Paris 1876–)

ABBREVIATIONS

RHC	*Recueil des Historiens de Croisades,* ed Académie des Inscriptions et Belles-Lettres (Paris 1841–1906)
Arm	*Historiens Arméniens,* 2 vols (1869–1906)
Grecs	*Historiens Grecs,* 2 vols (1875–81)
Lois	*Lois. Les Assises de Jérusalem,* 2 vols (1841–3)
Occ	*Historiens Occidentaux,* 5 vols (1844–95)
Or	*Historiens Orientaux,* 5 vols (1872–1906)
RHD	*Revue d'histoire du droit* (Haarlem, Gronigen 1923–)
RHDFE	*Revue historique de droit français et étranger* (Paris 1922–)
RHE	*Revue d'Histoire Ecclésiastique* (Louvain 1900–)
RHEF	*Revue d'Histoire de l'Eglise de France* (Paris 1910–)
RHR	*Revue de l'Histoire des Religions* (Paris 1880–)
RR	*Regesta Regum Anglo-Normannorum,* ed H. W. C. Davis, H. A. Cronne, Charles Johnson, R. H. C. Davis, 4 vols (Oxford 1913–69)
RS	*Rerum Brittanicarum Medii Aevi Scriptores,* 99 vols (London 1858–1911). *Rolls Series*
RSCI	*Rivista di storia della chiesa in Italia* (Rome 1947–)
RSR	*Revue des sciences religieuses* (Strasbourg 1921–)
RStI	*Rivista storica italiana* (Naples 1884–)
RTAM	*Recherches de théologie ancienne et médiévale* (Louvain 1929–)
RV	Revised Version
Sitz	*Sitzungsberichte*
SA	*Studia Anselmiana* (Roma 1933–)
sa	*sub anno*
SBAW	*Sitzungsberichte der bayerischen Akademie der Wissenschaften,* PhK (Munich 1971–)
SCH	*Studies in Church History* (London 1964–)
ScHR	*Scottish Historical Review* (Edinburgh/Glasgow 1904–)
SCR	*Sources chrétiennes,* ed H. de Lubac and J. Daniélou (Paris 1941)
SF	*Studi Francescani* (Florence 1914–)
SGra	*Studia Gratiana,* ed J. Forchielli and A. M. Stickler (Bologna 1953–)
SGre	*Studi Gregoriani,* ed G. Borino, 7 vols (Rome 1947–61)
SMon	*Studia Monastica* (Montserrat, Barcelona 1959–)
Speculum	*Speculum, A Journal of Medieval Studies* (Cambridge, Mass., 1926–)
SpicFr	*Spicilegium Friburgense* (Freiburg 1957–)
SS	*Surtees Society* (Durham 1835–)
SSSpoleto	*Settimane di Studio sull'alto medioevo,* 1952– , Centro Italiano di studi sull'alto medioevo, Spoleto 1954–)
STC	*A Short-Title Catalogue of Books Printed in England, Scotland and Ireland and of English Books Printed Abroad 1475–1640,* ed A. W. Pollard and G. R. Redgrave (London 1926, repr 1946, 1950)
Strype, *Annals*	John Strype, *Annals of the Reformation and Establishment of Religion . . . during Queen Elizabeth's Happy Reign,* 4 vols in 7 (Oxford 1840)
Strype, *Cranmer*	John Strype, *Memorials of . . . Thomas Cranmer,* 2 vols (Oxford 1824)
Strype, *Grindal*	John Strype, *The History of the Life and Acts of . . . Edumund Grindal* (Oxford 1821)
Strype, *Memorials*	John Strype, *Ecclesiastical Memorials, Relating Chiefly to Religion, and the Reformation of it . . . under King Henry VIII, King Edward VI and Queen Mary I,* 3 vols in 6 (Oxford 1822)

ABBREVIATIONS

Strype, *Parker*	John Strype, *The Life and Acts of Matthew Parker*, 3 vols (Oxford 1821)
Strype, *Whitgift*	John Strype, *The Life and Acts of John Whitgift*, 3 vols (Oxford 1822)
sub hag	*subsidia hagiographica*
sv	*sub voce*
SVRG	*Schriften des Vereins für Reformationsgeschichte* (Halle/Leipzig) Gütersloh 1883–)
TCBiblS	*Transactions of the Cambridge Bibliographical Society* (Cambridge 1949–)
Tchalenko	G. Tchalenko, *Villages antiques de la Syrie du Nord*, 3 vols (Paris 1953–8)
THSCym	*Transactions of the Historical Society of Cymmrodoriou* (London 1822–)
TRHS	*Transactions of the Royal Historical Society* (London 1871–)
TU	*Texte and Untersuchungen zur Geschichte der altchristlichen Literatur* (Leipzig/Berlin 1882–)
VCH	*Victoria County History* (London 1900–)
VHM	G. Tiraboschi, *Vetera Humiliatorum Monumenta* 3 vols (Milan 1766–8)
Vivarium	*Vivarium: An International Journal for the Philosophy and Intellectual Life of the Middle Ages and Renaissance* (Assen 1963–)
VV	*Vizantijskij Vremennick* 1–25 (St Petersburg 1894–1927), ns 1 (26) (Leningrad 1947–)
WA	*D. Martin Luthers Werke*, ed J. C. F. Knaake (Weimar 1883–) [*Weimarer Ausgabe*]
WA Br	*Briefwechsel*
WA DB	*Deutsche Bibel*
WA TR	*Tischreden*
WelHR	*Welsh History Review* (Cardiff 1960–)
Wharton	H. Wharton, *Anglia Sacra*, 2 parts (London 1691)
Whitelock, *Wills*	*Anglo-Saxon wills*, ed D. Whitelock (Cambridge 1930)
Wilkins	*Concilia Magnae Britanniae et Hiberniae A. D. 446–1717*, 4 vols, ed D. Wilkins (London 1737)
YAJ	*Yorkshire Archaeological Journal* (London/Leeds 1870–)
Zanoni	L. Zanoni, *Gli Umiliati nei loro rapporti con l'eresia, l'industria della lana ed i communi nei secoli xii e xiii, Biblioteca Historica Italica*, 2 series, 2 (Milan 1911)
ZKG	*Zeitschrift für Kirchengeschichte* (Gotha/Stuttgart 1878–)
ZOG	*Zeitschrift für osteuropäische Geschichte* (Berlin 1911–35) = *Kyrios* (Berlin 1936–)
ZRG	*Zeitschrift der Savigny-Stiftung für Rechtsgeschichte* (Weimar)
GAbt	*Germanistische Abteilung* (1863–)
KAbt	*Kanonistische Abteilung* (1911–)
RAbt	*Romanstische Abteilung* (1880–)
ZRGG	*Zeitschrift Religions- und Geistegeschichte* (Marburg 1948–)
Zwingli, *Werke*	*Huldreich Zwinglis Sämmtliche Werke*, ed E. Egli and others, CR (Berlin/Leipzig/Zurich 1905–)